ALBERT E. HARTUNG
GENERAL EDITOR

A Manual of the Writings in Middle English

1050–1500

ALBERT E. HARTUNG
GENERAL EDITOR

A Manual of the Writings in Middle English

1050–1500

By Members of the Middle English Division of the
Modern Language Association
of America

Based upon
A Manual of the Writings in Middle English 1050–1400
by John Edwin Wells, New Haven, 1916
and Supplements 1–9, 1919–1951

THE CONNECTICUT ACADEMY OF ARTS AND SCIENCES, NEW HAVEN, CONNECTICUT
MCMLXXXVI

ua

© 1986 by The Connecticut Academy of Arts and Sciences

Published for The Connecticut Academy of Arts and Sciences by Archon Books, The Shoe String Press, Inc., Hamden, Connecticut 06514.

Printed in the United States of America

The paper in this book meets the guidelines for permanence and durability of the Committee on Production Guidelines for Book Longevity of the Council on Library Resources.

Publication of this book was assisted by a grant from the publications program of the National Endowment for the Humanities, an independent federal agency.

Library of Congress Cataloging-in-Publication Data (Revised)

Main entry under title:

A Manual of the writings in Middle English, 1050–1500.

"Based upon A manual of the writings in Middle English. 1050–1400, by John Edwin Wells, New Haven 1916, and supplements 1–9, 1919–1951."
    Vols. 1–2: general editor, J. B. Severs; V. 3– A. E. Hartung.
    1. English literature—Middle English, 1100–1500—History and criticism.   2. English literature—Middle English, 1100–1500—Bibliography.   I. Wells, John Edwin, 1875–1943. A manual of the writings in Middle English, 1050–1400.   II. Severs, Jonathan Burke, ed.   III. Hartung, Albert E., 1923– ed.   IV. Modern Language Association of America. Middle English Group.
    PR255.M3   016.820′9′001   67–7687
    ISBN 0–208–01220–6 (v. 3)
    ISBN 0–208–02107–8 (v. 7)

10/21/86

Volume 7

XVII. JOHN GOWER

by

John H. Fisher, R. Wayne Hamm,
Peter G. Beidler, and Robert F. Yeager

XVIII. PIERS PLOWMAN

by

Anne Middleton

XIX. TRAVEL AND
GEOGRAPHICAL WRITINGS

by

Christian K. Zacher

XX. WORKS OF RELIGIOUS AND
PHILOSOPHICAL INSTRUCTION

by

Robert R. Raymo

PREFACE

A collaborative project of the Middle English Division of the Modern Language Association of America, and published by the Connecticut Academy of Arts and Sciences (as was its predecessor, the Wells *Manual*), this Manual of Middle English Literature has now reached its seventh volume with the present publication. The chapters comprising the present volume with the cut-off dates for complete coverage of all serious studies for each are as follows: XVII (John Gower—through 1984); XVIII (Piers Plowman—through 1984); XIX (Geography and Travel Writings—through 1983); XX (Works of Religious and Philosophical Instruction—through 1983). For each chapter also an attempt is made to list later studies with some fulness up to the time of going to press (November 1985), although no claim is made for completeness of coverage. A full account of the principles followed by the editors of the work will be found in the preface to volume (formerly fascicule) 1.

On behalf of the Middle English Division and on his own behalf, the General Editor would like to express his profound and admiring gratitude to the editors who have contributed to this volume. Although Middle English studies could at no time in their history ever have been considered a phlegmatic area of scholarly endeavor, the chapters in the present volume are particularly expressive of the wide range of new discovery and the energetic and vigorous reassessment of traditional areas that characterize our field at present. It is also extremely gratifying to recognize those scholars, specifically mentioned at the beginning of the separate chapters of the present volume, who have given freely of their own knowledge and of the results of their own research so that the usefulness and currency of these chapters may be the best that is possible. Their unselfish contribution to Middle English studies in this respect gives a particularly satisfying and heart-warming definition to the term "scholarly community."

Finally, the General Editor wishes to thank the National Endowment for the Humanities for its financial support (now continued over several years) of the contribution made to the project by his editorial assistant, Mrs. Marilyn C. Dunlap, who has been with the *Manual* since its third volume. Her capable and unflagging industry, her devotion and loyalty to the purposes of the project are in large part responsible for the existence of the present volume, which is now made available to its users.

Albert E. Hartung
General Editor

CONTENTS

XVII. JOHN GOWER

by

John H. Fisher, R. Wayne Hamm,
Peter G. Beidler, and Robert F. Yeager

The editors acknowledge with gratitude the generous assistance given by Jeremy Griffiths, Kate Harris, and Derek Pearsall in helping them to bring the lists of Gower manuscripts up to date. These three scholars are currently bringing to completion *A Descriptive Catalogue of Manuscripts of the Works of John Gower,* forthcoming from Garland Press. This book will describe the contents, provenance, location, foliation, date, and condition of the Gower manuscripts, and will include an analysis of Gower's language by Jeremy Smith. The editors are fortunate to have been granted access to the contents of parts of this catalogue in advance of publication.

The documentary record of John Gower's life is sparse and often confusing. The most recent treatment is John H. Fisher's *John Gower* (1964), which has been used as a general source for this commentary.

Several branches of Gowers flourished in the fourteenth century, and within each branch John was a common name. J. Leland identified the poet with the Gowers of Stittenham (Yorkshire), an identification accepted as late as H. Todd (1810). On the other hand, J. Weever had early identified Gower with Kent, and in 1828 H. Nicolas adduced documentary evidence of the Kentish affiliation, which has been widely accepted. Yet the followers of Nicolas have missed a second Yorkshire branch of Gowers, seated at Langbargh, a family more prominent in the fourteenth century than that of Stittenham; furthermore, the arms of the Langbargh Gowers resemble those of the Kentish Gowers as well as the arms on the poet's tomb. Apparently Leland was half right, for it seems probable that the poet may have been born in Yorkshire and brought to Kent as a child in the family of Gowers who were in the service of the Countess of Athol. Moreover, recent work by M. Samuels and J. Smith on dialectal clues in Gower's language has confirmed that Gower's formative years were spent in Kent and West Suffolk.

The traditional birth date is 1330; Gower would have been old enough to enter the Inns of Court in the 1350s and to earn enough money to begin investing in real estate in the 1360s. In 1365 the poet bought a manor called Aldington Septvauns in a transaction of questionable legality, even though after litigation Gower's claim to the property was adjudged just. Enough of the unsavory lingered to cause G. C. Macaulay to identify this transaction not with the poet, but with some other John Gower, a "villainous misleader of youth." But there is no reason to shield Gower, who clearly was the purchaser; the affair was a mess, but probably not a fraud. Gower's was the same social station as his friend Chaucer's, the upper middle class of franklins, merchants, and lawyers, with some connections with the court, although we have no record of Gower's employment by the king or in government. Where he obtained his capital is not clear. He seems to imply (in *Mirour de l'Omme,* line 21,772) that he is not a clerk, but he seems to have had some sort of professional involvement with the law. His outrage at abuses among lawyers would not be inconsistent coming from a self-righteous insider, but his allusions to both common and canon law are so general that they could have come to him through popular sources. Gower evidently retired, at least partially, in the mid-1370s. Leland says that at this time he helped rebuild the church of St. Mary Overeys Priory in Southwark, where we find him living at the end of his life. The Priory provided the ingredients necessary for his literary work: a library, possibly a scriptorium, and a serene atmosphere. After 1375 the poet was associated with a stimulating and productive circle of friends who shared his social and intellectual interests: John Hende, mayor of London; Ralph Strode, the "philosophical" lawyer, mathematician, and astronomer; Thomas Usk; Thomas Hoccleve; and, of course, Geoffrey Chaucer. This circle flourished until Chaucer left London in 1386, and Strode died in 1387.

Gower's friendship with Chaucer is attested to by the power of attorney Chaucer gave him when he went to Italy in 1378, and, after 1382, by Chaucer's mentioning him and Strode in the dedication of *Troilus and Criseyde.*

In 1832 Gower purchased two manors, Feltwell in Norfolk and Multon in Suffolk, in the same year leasing them for life to an investment group. On 23 January 1398 he was licensed to marry Agnes Groundolf. This was evidently his first marriage—there is no record of any other, and references in his poems that have been adduced to demonstrate a possible earlier liaison are unconvincing. His will, dated 15 August 1408, was proved 24 October 1408, so his death must have occurred within this period. Unaware of the will, all writers from Leland to Todd wrongly dated the death as 1402. The poet left effects to various religious establishments, and to his wife he bequeathed £100, certain furnishings, and the rent from his two manors.

Gower's tomb, which still stands in Southwark Cathedral, is our only positive identification of the poet with the Southwark businessman, but its evidence must be approached with caution. The monument has twice been moved since 1800. The chapel of St. John, its original site, is no longer extant. The monument has been heavily restored since 1958, mainly on the basis of older descriptions. The tomb is surmounted by a polychromed stone effigy of the poet, with long auburn hair and a small forked beard, wearing a chaplet of roses, a habit of purple, and the collar of golden "SS." On the adjacent wall are a painting of three virgins and Gower's arms: "a field argent, on a chevron azure, three leopards' heads gold, their tongues gules; two angels supporters, on the crest of a talbot." Gower's three books form a pillow under his head. The languages of these three books reflect the three subdivisions of this commentary.

1. FRENCH WORKS

CINKANTE BALADES [1]. Anglo-French; survives in a single manuscript, which also contains the *Traitié, In Praise of Peace,* and Latin verses adapted from *Vox Clamantis.* The manuscript itself was evidently occasioned by Henry's coronation in 1399, but the contents represent earlier stages of the poet's career. Only Macaulay dated the balades as late as the manuscript; T. Warton and G. L. Kittredge dated them before 1380. The sequence may represent the order in which the lyrics were composed: the first 40 are idealistic and emotional; the last twelve sound moralistic and disillusioned. In form they are curiously symmetrical: 27 are in seven-line rime royal; 27 are in eight-line "Monk's Tale" stanzas; all but one have envoys. The poems show no great influence of the French balade tradition of Machaut, Deschamps, and Froissart, and, in fact, if written before 1380, would as a sequence actually antedate the French sequences. The poems are in the tradition of the troubadours and their successors, and it has been suggested that they were originally composed for recitation at the London "Pui," a bourgeois religious, charitable, convivial, and musical organization with roots in southern France. The poems present a courtly treatment of love, yet they are impersonal and abstract. Voicing Gower's life-long obsession, they firmly advocate lawful, married love.

TRAITIÉ POUR ESSAMPLER LES AMANTZ MARIETZ [2]. This work comprises eighteen Anglo-French balades in rime royal, none with envoy, but each with a sidenote explaining moral implications. There are thirteen manuscripts. The collection belongs to the period of the *Confessio Amantis* or later. Perhaps it is so late as to have been occasioned by Gower's marriage. The poet clearly thought of the *Traitié* as an addendum to the *Confessio* because in seven of the ten manuscripts it is joined to the *Confessio* by a transitional note. These balades sum up the major themes of the *Confessio*: the superiority of reason over sensuality, the transience of the flesh versus permanence of the spirit, the superiority of divine over human love, the lawlessness of adulterous sexual love versus the lawfulness of marriage. An English translation by John Quixley about 1400 makes the *Traitié* one of the earliest English balade sequences.

MIROUR DE L'OMME [3]. The original title of this Anglo-French poem was apparently *Mirour de l'Omme*; subsequently, Gower changed the title to *Speculum Meditantis*, probably to echo the titles of the other works, *Vox Clamantis* and *Confessio Amantis*. The poem was lost until Macaulay guessed that it would be found under the title *Speculum Hominis* rather than *Speculum Meditantis*. In 1895, in the Cambridge University Library, he found the manuscript under the French title. This unique text, MS Cambridge University Library Additional 3035, has a table of contents, but after this four leaves are missing, and others are missing at the end. The poem thus survives in 28,603 of its original 31,000 octosyllabic lines, in stanzas riming aabaabb-babba. Because there is no dedication, prologue, epilogue, or colophon, we know little of the history or provenance of the manuscript. The lack of other copies suggests that the poem was not intended for wide circulation, although it is possible that the legal references were intended for a small audience of the poet's London circle. Because it does not mention the king's youth, the *Mirour* must have been substantially complete before Richard's accession in 1377. Its reference to the Great Schism of 1378 gives a useful terminus ad quem. The evidence, in sum, suggests a compositional span of 1376–1378.

For its material and treatment, the *Mirour* is indebted to penitential and confessional manuals of a sort that would have been available to Gower in the library of St. Mary Overeys Priory. It has been argued that it is associated with the *Somme le roi* tradition (see XX [4–6]). The *Mirour* falls into three sections: an allegory on the origin of sin and death and a description of the birth of the vices and virtues (lines 37–18,420); a complaint against the estates (lines 18,421–27,360); and a life of the Virgin Mary (lines 27,361–29,945). Gower's method was to move from an allegory on the origin of sin and death to a generalized description of the vices and virtues, and then, gathering strength and color, to a very specific criticism of the London scene of the 1370s. In the brilliant opening allegory (which, as was pointed out by J. S. P. Tatlock, resembles Milton's allegory of the birth of sin and death in *Paradise Lost,* Books I and II), lawless sex is depicted as the typical sin which brings about human discord. In order for perpetual warfare to be ended, man must learn to control all depraved instincts through reason, law, and Empedoclean love. The *Mirour* thus works out the implications of reason and personal virtue in preparation for the discussion of national virtue which follows. In anticipation of the ideas most succinctly expressed in the *Traitié,* the poet begins the *Mirour* by stressing the degradation and transience of temporal love, which leads to bestiality. From this abstract allegory, the poet moves to a generalized discussion of the vices and virtues, and finally to concrete contemporary criticism. At first he takes a benign attitude toward the peasants, giving a conventional view of natural equality. But finally he comes to criticize both the tyranny of the rich and the rebelliousness of the poor. With startling clarity he foresees the Peasants' Revolt: the nobility "do not guard against / the folly of the common people, / but permit that nettle to grow / which is so violent in its nature. / He who observes the present time / may soon fear that, / if God does not give help, / this impatient nettle / will very suddenly sting us, / before it can be brought to justice" (lines 26,487 ff.). In abandoning reason and a rational hierarchy and sinking into bestiality, the peasants reflect the failures of their leaders, especially the king. In the beginning the poem defends the king's role in the war with France; but when Gower gets to kingship in his catalogue of the estates, he criticizes the crown's taxation of the clergy in order to prosecute the war. G. Stillwell sees also a veiled criticism of the Alice Perrers relationship and a warning against the dangers of petticoat rule (lines 22,807 ff.). The section ends with a treatise on the responsibilities of the king. If the *Mirour* shows a prejudice, it is for wealth, trade, and business—the rising bourgeoisie of which the poet was a part. Gower defends capital investment, but, not understanding the principles of interest, lashes out at the usury of the Lombard bankers. An attack on bad lawyers and judges and the poor organization of ecclesiastical courts provides a transition to the discussion of natural and human laws as instruments of order and peace. The responsibility of the populace is to support the social hierarchy under the king; rebellion against aristocracy is rebellion against reason, law, and divine order. This poem is a vigorous opening statement of Gower's life-long theme: beginning in a withdrawn, devotional mood, it ends with national issues which are taken up in greater detail in *Vox Clamantis*.

2. Latin Works

VOX CLAMANTIS [4]. This work comprises 10,265 Latin elegiac verses in seven books, each with a prologue. There are eleven manuscripts in three versions. The earliest hypothetical version, apparently completed before 1381, was composed of Books II–V of the present text. To the second version, evidently completed between 1381 and 1386, Gower added Book I with its Visio of the Peasants' Revolt, and the Epistle to the King in Book VI. In this version the king is absolved of responsibility for England's troubles, which are blamed on his council. The structure suggests that Book I is an addition; Book II has only 620 lines, a length more appropriate as a prologue than as a book. Also, after Book I the Peasants' Revolt is not mentioned again in the poem. In the third version, begun in the 1390s and completed after 1399, Gower's view of Richard is thoroughly disillusioned.

Dating the *Vox* raises several questions. The first version of the poem does not mention the Great Schism of 1378, and M. Wickert argued that Gower could hardly have neglected this signal example of the decadence of the papacy if it had already occurred when he was writing. This omission indicates a date before 1378 for the early version. If so, Gower must have been writing this version of the *Vox* at the same time as he was writing the *Mirour*. Indeed, the two poems show a close resemblance of treatment of all the estates except the king's. Why would Gower write two works on the same subject in two languages at nearly the same time? The *Mirour* had been the poet's private meditation, but in the *Vox* Gower says, "Quod scripsi plebis vox est" (What I have written is the voice of the people, VII.1468). In this poem Gower's complaint is a public one against the king. Latin was, of course, the language of serious political discussion. So the poem's audience must have been the "Caesarian clergy" who administered the kingdom in Chancery, the Exchequer, and the Royal Secretariat.

The *Vox* draws upon Peter Riga, Nigel Wireker, Godfrey of Viterbo, and, most heavily, Ovid. The sources are not followed slavishly, but are adapted to express Gower's own complaint against the king and society. The poem opens with a prologue set on a warm summer day. Book I is a dream allegory vividly describing the fearful effects of the Peasants' Revolt of 1381. The rebels, having lost their reason, have been transformed into raging animals in rebellion against the natural order. The city is a symbol of order; the peasants, of rapine. From this dramatic dream, Gower turns to a criticism of the different classes: the corruption of the clergy (Bks II–IV); the debasement of knighthood and discontent among the peasants, merchants, and artisans (Bk V); the dishonesty of lawyers and the foolishness of the king (Bk VI). Book VI presents a synthesis of law, the common good, and kingship. The role of the king is defined judicially—i.e., the king is grouped with lawyers, judges, and bureaucrats, not with warriors. The king's task is to keep the legal machinery operational, and he himself must submit to law and reasonable self-control. Book VII, like the *Mirour*, presents a view of man as a microcosm which, because of the taint of the Seven Deadly Sins, has steadily declined in virtue. This microcosm is symbolized by Nebuchadnezzar's vision of a great statue with head of gold, legs of iron, and feet of iron and clay, which appears both at the end of the *Vox* and at the beginning of the *Confessio Amantis*. Near the end of the *Vox* is a memento mori, a view of the terrible consequences of sin and death, likewise closely related to the allegory at the beginning of the *Mirour*. Thus the three poems reinforce and play upon one another. The *Vox* ends with a diatribe against unlawful lovers which gives a clue as to how we are to read the *Confessio*: carnal love is divisive, fleeting, and painful; it should be replaced by divine love, which leads to unity and salvation.

Wickert and Dwyer see *Vox Clamantis* as a penitential sermon, complete with scolding, exhortation, and warning. But the poem more directly embodies the features of the moralistic complaint, a literary genre expressing concern for the decline of the human condition because of sin and an analysis of the Seven Deadly Sins. It also embodies a criticism of the estates. The poem's chief accomplishment is that, although these themes have no organic relationship, Gower contrived to combine them with political theory to produce a synthesis of the estates peaceably united under the king's justice.

CRONICA TRIPERTITA [5]. Written in 1399–1400, shortly after Richard's deposition, this work concludes Gower's commentary, begun in *Vox Clamantis*, on the king's tragic career. In four of the five surviving manuscripts it follows the *Vox*, so it seems likely that in 1400 Gower viewed the *Vox* and the *Cronica* as a continuous whole. The poem is Lancastrian propaganda under the guise of history: after a disquisition on the evils of divisiveness, the poet blames the king's hard heart for the rebellion of the Apellants, who are characterized as model Englishmen, and for the king's treacherous revenge in 1397. Gower deplores the committee rule of Richard's last year, praises Henry's triumphant restoration of order, and concludes with an account of Richard's death from "melancholy." Gower here echoes Bracton's view of the king as responsible to Parliament as well as to God.

In addition to these two important works in Latin, Gower also wrote some twenty-odd MINOR LATIN POEMS [6]. These have been little noticed, though Macaulay reproduces most of them (4.343). They are listed in the bibliography below under a single number. Because of their relative unimportance and their having been composed in Latin rather than in Middle English, they are not singled out for individual commentary here.

3. ENGLISH WORKS

CONFESSIO AMANTIS [7]. The many manuscripts diverge enough to present a complex textual picture. Three versions, or recensions, have been identified. The first recension, probably completed by 1390, survives in 31 manuscripts. It attributes the poem to an encounter on the river with King Richard, to whom the book is dedicated. It also contains a eulogistic passage on Chaucer. The second recension, apparently dating between June 1390 and June 1391, is mainly distinguished from the first by its rewritten conclusion, which omits praise of Richard—perhaps after the king's great quarrel with the citizens of London, with whom Gower emphatically identified. In addition, some of the seven manuscripts of this recension have a new preface and dedication to Henry of Lancaster. Gower is here announcing a new allegiance, but quietly; hence there are only seven manuscripts of the second recension as compared with 31 of the first. There is evidence that this recension was private, and that the first recension remained the official version throughout Richard's reign. The chronology is important in refuting the charge of political opportunism that has been leveled at the poet because of this shift in allegiance. In 1391 Gower had as yet no indication that Richard would fall or that Henry would ever be king. The change was probably based on political and moral ideology rather than on any desire to escape a sinking Ricardian ship—an evidence of courage rather than sycophancy. The second recension substitutes a passage on the responsible state for the praise of Richard. Curiously enough, in this recension the Chaucer allusion is absent, and by some this has been seen as sinister evidence of a quarrel between the poets, for which further evidence has often been found in the Man of Law's Headlink. But we need not take this suggestion too seriously; Lydgate mentions no such falling out, and we may suppose that the friendship evidenced by the Gower attorneyship and by Chaucer's dedication of the *Troilus* to Gower and Strode continued. Of lesser importance in establishing the identity of the second recension are certain textual changes: the second adds to Book V (Chastity, lines 6395 ff., Tale of Lucius, lines 7086 ff.), to Book VII (Jew and Pagan, lines 3207 ff.), and cuts from Book V (Largesse, lines 7701 ff.). It also rearranges passages of Book VI (lines 665–964 are moved to follow line 1146). The so-called third recension manuscripts— eleven in all—derive from MS Bodley Fairfax 3, evidently compiled at the time of Henry's accession by conflating the texts of recensions one and two.

Macauley had thought that some of the corrections in some of the manuscripts were made under Gower's direction. This matter is by no means settled, however, and requires further study.

Confessio Amantis is written in the courtly London English of the end of the fourteenth century. Macaulay's edition includes a substantial essay on the poem's orthography, phonology, and dialect (2.xcii, cxx), and Lewis's *Allegory of Love* (p. 198) incorporates a celebrated appreciation of the poem's language. Beyond these little has been written about Gower's English until quite recently, when work on the Middle English Dialect Atlas has focused the attention of M. Samuels, M. Laing, J. Smith and others on the features of Gower's language. The poem consists of 34,000 octosyllabic couplets remarkable for smoothness and regularity and for Gower's consistent respect

for the natural stress of the words. Latin verses are used to introduce the
various books and at other divisions of the text, and there are copious Latin
marginal glosses in prose; R. F. Yeager has suggested that these Latin lines
are more significantly functional than has been recognized. The work is
divided into a prologue and eight books, each of which except Book VII
deals with one of the Seven Deadly Sins. Book VII has been seen as digres-
sive, but it is actually a pivotal treatise on the education of the ruler. Recent
criticism, especially by D. G. Schueler, has shown that the poem's structural
principle is conversational—not so dramatic as the *Canterbury Tales,* but more
so than the *Legend of Good Women.* The bulk of the conversation takes place
between the penitent, Amans, and his confessor, Genius, whose instruction
provides occasion for the tales and exempla which constitute half the poem.

In the Prologue the poet determines to balance "sentence" and "solas," but his first concern is
moral: he begins with criticism of the times, for which he uses the symbol of Nebuchadnezzar's
statue. Book I turns from overt moralization, the poet resolving to write of love, which is irresistible
and irremediable, as he knows from his own sufferings. He narrates a waking vision: on a morning
in May, sick for love, he finds himself in a green meadow, where he prays to Venus and Cupid for
mercy. In answer, the two gods appear to him. Cupid passes him by after thrusting a fiery dart into
his heart; Venus, however, tarries to question him, and he laments that he has served her and
received no reward. She says that she must test his sincerity, and bids him confess to her priest,
Genius. The confessor, an ambivalent figure, structures his inquisition and instructions around the
Seven Deadly Sins of love. Book I, from line 575 to the end, treats of pride and its opposite, humility.
Book II takes up envy and its remedy, charity. Book III deals with the branches of wrath and its
contrary, mercy. Included in this section is an excursus on the legality of war, which has been seen
as gratuitous, but which actually supports Gower's theme of divisiveness as the opposite of love.
Book IV takes up sloth, but this section dwells more fully on the enemies of sloth, knightly prowess,
gentilesse, and labor. Book V covers avarice and its remedy, largesse. An interesting side issue here
is jealousy, which Gower sees as avarice in love. Another digression is on the religions of the world.
In Book VI Gower takes up gluttony and sorcery. Book VII is the heart of the *regimine principum*
theme of the poem: a lecture to the king on responsible government, based on Aristotle's advice to
Alexander. Book VIII climactically takes up the sin which Gower sees as typical of all the others,
lechery, and its lawful contrary, marriage. From VIII.2029 to the end, the poem concludes its
allegorical framework: Genius counsels Amans to abandon love, an activity unsuited to his old age
and feebleness. He should instead turn to reason. But Genius does agree to petition the gods of love
on the Lover's behalf. Venus is not impressed. She mocks the poet's age and counsels him to abandon
his absurd suit. Cupid, seemingly softened since his first appearance, approaches with a train of the
world's great lovers and begs Venus to help Amans, who now asks to be excused from the court of
love, and proposes to submit to reason. Cupid withdraws the fiery dart, Genius grants him absolution, and Venus heals him and sends him away with the gift of a black rosary to where "vertu moral
dwelleth, / Wher ben solas, as men telleth" (VIII.2925). In the first version Venus then sends a
message to her servant Chaucer, urging him to finish his testament of love (presumably the *Legend
of Good Women*), as Gower has finished his. The author concludes with a final commendation of the
king. In the second version all of this is replaced by a prayer for the state of England and a disquisition on the duty of a king.

The first edition of *Confessio Amantis* was Caxton's, in 1483, a composite text drawn from three manuscripts. Caxton's intentions were shrewdly practical. He wanted the poem to be dedicated to a "good" king, Henry IV, rather than a "bad" one, Richard II, but he also wanted to restore the lines referring to Chaucer. In the next edition, 1532 (and reprinted in 1554, with corrections), Thomas Berthelette commented directly on Gower's relation with Chaucer, and included the dedication to Richard II as well as that to Henry IV. Berthelette also discussed the language, and took up the problem of variant manuscripts. Apart from a reprint of Berthelette's 1554 version by Chalmers in 1810, there was no further edition until that of Reinhold Pauli in 1857; soon afterwards came G. C. Macaulay's four-volume edition of the complete works, 1899–1902, which still stands unsuperseded. The *Confessio Amantis* was the first English literary work to be translated into a foreign language. Apparently before 1400 the poem was translated into Portuguese, a version which has not survived, although P. E. Russell has recently discovered references to its title. Perhaps before 1425 the poem was translated out of the Portuguese into Castilian prose: the *Confisyon del amante,* now preserved in the Escorial (MS g.II.19).

Gower's artistry has always been apparent in his versification. Macaulay calls him a master of the octosyllabic couplet, and finds his verses smooth, easy, and fluent, with a more even meter than that achieved by Chaucer. His verse is flexible, with skillful employment of caesura, enjambment, and use of sentences and paragraphs, rather than the line, as rhetorical units. C. S. Lewis called Gower "our first considerable master of the plain style in poetry." R. Daniels has argued for his familiarity with the rhetoric of Geoffrey of Vinsauf, but J. Murphy emphatically disagrees, arguing that both Chaucer and Gower were unacquainted with formal rhetorics, their knowledge of which was no more than could be learned from grammar-school texts.

It has commonly been felt that much of Gower's accomplishment lies in his skill in relating the 133 stories in the *Confessio Amantis.* Z. Leonhard finds that Gower does not usually change facts or even emphases found in his sources, but merely discards unsuitable material. Gower's original insertions include speeches, prayers, and laments. He generally humanizes his sources, substituting romantic pathos for grimness. The details are specific and visual. For example, Gower describes the loathsomeness of the hag in Florent more vividly than does the "realistic" Chaucer. Surprisingly, Gower seldom interrupts his tales by undue digression or moralization. Fison has seen in them a well-developed architectonic sense, with slow movement toward a tragedy which itself flashes by in a moment. Pearsall's conclusion damns with the usual qualification: "Gower is an uncommonly fine narrative poet, by any but the highest standards." Yet some of our reservations about Gower's poetic control may result from ignorance of his contexts. R. F. Yeager has illustrated this possibility recently by showing that Gower's audience thought sorcery to be a branch of gluttony; hence the "confusing" digression of Book VI would not have seemed so to a contemporary audience; C. A. J. Runacres, P. Miller, E. Porter, and especially A. J. Minnis, in several recent studies, have found Gower's structure to be clarified by deeper comprehension of medieval literary theory.

Gower's complex relation to his sources has been frequently explored. J. A. W. Bennett has found in Gower an "unmedieval" love of classical tales, many of which he was the first to relate in English. He came to them mainly through French and Latin; of Greek he had no knowledge. Among his classical sources are Horace, Livy, Hyginus, Valerius Maximus, Josephus Flavius, Statius, the *Historia Alexandri,* and Servius' commentary on Virgil. Gower's favorite source, as always, is Ovid. The most detailed treatments of the poet's mining of Latin literature are by C. Mainzer and D. Speed, and, more recently, P. Beidler has discussed the changes Gower made in the tales he derived from the *Metamorphoses.* M. Neville has demonstrated that while fifteen of the tales derive from the Vulgate, the Bible is seldom quoted literally; Gower preferred paraphrase to direct translation. For example, Gower's use of Nebuchadnezzar's image does not come directly from the Vulgate, but through Boccaccio. As R. F. Yeager has shown, Gower had also mastered a complex style of allusion to a multiplicity of texts. Other Christian sources include Methodius, Isidore of Seville, Gregory, Peter Comestor, Giles of Rome, and Augustine. Important new work by A. J. Minnis has demonstrated Gower's extensive reliance on the *auctores.* The principal French sources are the *Roman des sept sages,* Godfrey of Viterbo, Benoît de Sainte Maure, and the *Roman de la rose,* which may have provided the frame for the Lover's confession to Genius. Bennett has observed that both the *Roman de la rose* and the *Confessio* are a type of *ars amatoria* which relates courtly love to Christian thought. C. Dédéyan has shown that Gower made no use of Dante; the references, like those in the *Legend of Good Women,* could have come through Boccaccio, in addition to whom Gower also used Guido delle Colonne and Brunetto Latini. The *Secretum Secretorum* was also mined extensively by Gower, as has been shown by M. Manzalaoui. Among English writers, Gower is clearly indebted to Nicholas Trivet, and less plainly to Langland and Brunne. One would expect Chaucer to be the English author most likely to have influenced Gower's matter and manner, but, curiously, this influence is nowhere clearly demonstrable. Indeed, Fisher has argued just the opposite, that Chaucer, although the superior artist, was throughout his career influenced by the moralistic matter of his friend Gower.

It is in the criticism of the *Confessio*'s thematic structure that Gower scholarship has advanced most conspicuously during the past twenty years. C. S. Lewis enunciated the traditional view of the poem as a treatment of courtly love. But if it is read in the context of *Mirour de l'Omme* and *Vox Clamantis*, as scholars are increasingly asking us to read it, a different theme emerges— Empedoclean love functioning as a social cement. The strong suggestion of the earlier poems is that the "moralitas" which Lewis saw as peripheral is central, and that courtly love is a subordinate concern. What then is the *Confessio*'s genre? P. Clogan has argued that the poem is a satire—a parody of the manuals of penitential instruction—in which the Seven Deadly Sins are used as a criticism of man's nature; and P. Miller has also urged a satirical reading, while proposing a carefully medieval definition of satire. Dwyer sees the poem as a piece of Augustinian asceticism, with an ascent through seven stages from fear to wisdom. R. Peck sees it as a Boethian consolation and— like G. Coffman and E. Porter—as a political treatise, a "speculum regis." D. Schueler views the list of sins in the poem as an outgrowth of the confessional tradition, but the tenor of the earlier poems and the Prologue's lament over the decline of society suggest a stronger influence of the genre of the complaint, as detailed by J. Peter but staunchly contested by P. Miller. The decline is caused by the Seven Deadly Sins, which Gower always treated in their social context, as the cause of social discord. Gower consistently argued that just as individual sin leads to social chaos, individual virtue leads to social order. Thus, for Gower, love is not just a glamorous and amoral passion, but a requirement of individual salvation and social stability. In society, each estate is responsible for doing its own duty, for binding itself to the others through love, which is institutionalized as law. The estates are coordinated by the king, which explains the *Confessio*'s concern with the theme of *speculum regale*. Thus, though Book VII has often been seen as a digression, it is actually the focal center of the whole work, a plan for the practical implementation of the more abstract doctrines expressed in the other books. What emerges is a treatise on the education of the prince in his socially binding role. The lesson is composed of three parts, "theoretique," "rhetorique," and "practique." The last consists of truth, liberality, justice, pity, and chastity. Justice receives the fullest treatment, bringing to a climax Gower's obsessive concern with the common good as dependent upon royal enforcement of the laws. The king, the legal system, and a peaceful nation are interdependent; the king is the maintainer of justice which sustains the love which binds society together.

Much of the recent criticism has sought to explicate the mythography of the *Confessio*. Increasingly it is felt that our interpretation of the work depends upon our understanding of the roles of Venus, Cupid, and Genius. This allegory provides the thematic tie between the beginning of the *Mirour* and the end of the *Confessio*: the procreative urge is the emanation of the creative energy of divine love. Schueler sees the dynamics of the poem as Amans' quest for knowledge of man's use and misuse of his creative energies. Amans rediscovers his own neglected creativity, not, as he had hoped, on the sexual plane, but on the spiritual plane. In the end he can turn from selfish concern for his own gratification to concern for the common good. The part that Venus, Cupid, and Genius play in this re-education of the Senex Amans is ambivalent and complex. The gods of love traditionally represent amoral or even immoral love, and are antagonistic to reason and divine order. Yet here we find them advocating reason and law. Their priest, Genius, gives advice not only on courtly love, but on lawful married love, and on ascetic love. Thus he is no mere representative of the carnal, but of the divine forces of unity. The provenance of this peculiar characterization has been much argued. G. Economou sees the *Confessio* as part of a continuing debate on love beginning with Alain de Lille's *De Planctu Naturae,* Jean de Meun's part of the *Roman de la rose,* and Chaucer's *Parliament of Fowls.* In Alain, Genius is the priest of Natura, and with her represents fertility within lawful bounds. In Jean, however, Natura and Genius stand for the blind, irrational procreative urge, whose relation to morality is neutral. Further, Jean's Genius confuses matters by also becoming priest of Venus, with whom

Natura is at odds. Gower has solved this difficulty by restoring a close relationship between Venus and her superior, Natura. Thus, according to this view, because Gower's Venus insists on rational procreation, she is clearly not the goddess of immoral courtly love, and Gower can be excused from the charge that Courthope, Macaulay, Dodd, and Lewis have brought against him: that the *Confessio* fails because the character of Genius fails. The view of Genius, then, as a priest of courtly love, hopelessly contradicting himself by acting as a Christian priest, must be abandoned. In this view, if Genius is seen as an agent of God, the Prime Mover, the heretofore perceived tension between Gower's morality and his courtly material disappears, because the priest in fact mediates between man's self and the divine will, inducing Amans through reason to renounce his unsuitable biological urge so that his spiritual nature can be fulfilled. The problem of Gower's placing Genius under Venus does not exist, according to this view, for the goddess of love is herself an agent of Natura, who is, in turn, an agent of God's providence, and Genius sees his ultimate allegiance more clearly than does his mistress. Thus, the allegory tells us that, unlike the earlier critical responses to it, the restlessness and amoral urges of love can be subordinated to social and divine ends through the legal and moral institutions of marriage and justice, which are designed to maintain social stability. Yet another important recent study, by P. Gallacher, interprets Gower's use of the figure of Mercury, using mythographic approaches.

In summary, recent criticism of the *Confessio Amantis* has shown that the theme of the *Confessio*, rich, subtle, and humane, converges with the master argument of Gower's whole life work, from the praise of married love in the early *Cinkante Balades* to the final instructions to "les amantz marietz" in the *Traitié*.

IN PRAISE OF PEACE [8]. Written in 1399, this work survives in only one manuscript and in Thynne's edition of Chaucer. It contains 385 pentameter verses riming ababbcc. Probably Gower's last English poem, it praises Henry's succession and carefully details the new king's claim to the throne: fortune, God's grace, lineage, and popular election. But the old poet shows no sign of sycophancy; he warns the new ruler against presuming on the right of conquest, and reminds him that the crown is responsible for the peace and protection of the church during the schismatic crisis.

BALADE MORAL [9]. This short poem in English pentameter verses is not now thought to be by Gower.

XVIII. PIERS PLOWMAN

by

Anne Middleton

In addition to my warmest appreciation for the kind assistance and consideration over the years of many *Piers Plowman* scholars, I should like to express a special debt of gratitude to A. I. Doyle and Toshiyuki Takamiya for information about particular manuscripts, and, especially, to the Athlone editors: E. Talbot Donaldson, who as the original editor of this chapter is largely responsible for its organization and for the bibliography through 1957; George Kane, who with characteristic vigilance read in detail, and more than once, both bibliography and commentary; and George Russell, who generously took the time to make available both textual and manuscript information from his forthcoming Athlone C-text. Their kindness has been particularly helpful at this fruitful juncture in *Piers Plowman* studies.

Anne Middleton

The long alliterative poem generally called *Piers Plowman,* or *The Vision . . . Concerning Piers the Plowman,* was composed during the last 40 years of the fourteenth century, and has survived in three distinct versions, represented in a total of over 50 manuscripts and some fragments. Though its earliest printer (1550) knew the poem in more than one version, the differences between the three were not fully identified until Skeat, the first modern editor of the poem, who designated them the A, B, and C texts, denoting his view of their order as three successive stages of composition. All three versions, however, were copied and circulated from the first decades following their creation, without distinction except as more or less complete versions of what was evidently considered one work.

The large number of manuscripts of a poem in three versions, and their textual relations—to say nothing of the literary and historical interpretation of these texts and the differences between them—makes the critical history of *Piers Plowman* one of the most complex and controverted in Middle English studies. Many of the issues it has raised are still debated, though the terms and evidence in the debate usually differ from those in which they were first posed. Nearly all matters of historical and aesthetic interest concerning the poem—not only those of date, authorship, and the circumstances and milieu of production, but problems of poetic form, style, and genre—remain to some degree involved in the assessment of its peculiar textual fortunes. (On the distinctness of the three versions, see Bibliography: MAN-

USCRIPTS [1], CLASSIFICATION OF MSS AND PROBLEMS OF ED-
ITING [4], and Kane, A-Text, "Manuscripts and Versions.")

The A Version and the Form of the Text

A is a poem of about 2500 unrimed alliterative lines, consisting of a prologue and eleven passus, the term used to designate those divisions of the
long poem which other writers might have called books, fittes, or cantos.
The A version has survived in seventeen manuscripts and a binding fragment. It is also represented by a portion of just over 200 lines in the second
passus of three closely related manuscripts (MSS 19, 28, 29) of the B version.
In some A manuscripts, the C version of the poem continues from the point
where the A version ends (see Bibliography: [1], INFORMATION ABOUT
MSS [3], and [4]). It has recently been suggested (Rigg and Brewer edn) that
one of these manuscripts (MS 38, Z: Bodley 851) represents in its Prologue-
Passus 8 a very early form or draft of the A version rather than, as all
previous editors have believed, an extremely corrupt and conflated text.
Skeat considered this portion of the manuscript "mere rubbish, written out
from imperfect recollection"; Kane describes it as a "conflated and sophis-
ticated text, worthless for editorial use." It has been interpreted as a version
anterior to the A text (the Z version) by its editors, who date this portion of
the manuscript between 1376 and 1388. Whether or not this interpretation
is accepted, the editors argue, the "scribal version" presented by the A-
portion of the Z manuscript has sufficient intrinsic interest to justify its
publication, since its readings are not represented in the critical apparatus
of any edition. The meaning and standing of "scribal versions" have been
central to all textual discussion and editorial debate on the poem. The Z
version seems unlikely to alter fundamentally the issues in that debate.

Some manuscripts suggest a form of the A text defined by rubrics at the
heads of passus, and by a colophon between Passus 8 and 9, in which the
Prologue and Passus 1 through 8 are the "*visio . . . de petro plowman,*" and
the "*vita de dowel, dobet et dobest*" comprises Passus 9 through 11. In these
manuscripts, Passus 10 is headed "*passus primus de dowel,*" and so forth. (This
sort of rubrication is also found in some B and C manuscripts, indicating
the beginning of "dobet" and "dobest" sections in later passus. See below.)
The status and interpretation of this division of the poem have been debated.

Some have viewed the colophon as indicating that the A text was regarded as two distinct poems, or separately conceived parts, a "Visio" and a "Vita." This view came to be expressed chiefly in connection with the argument that the composition represents the work of more than one author (see Bibliography: AUTHORSHIP CONTROVERSY [12], especially Moore, MP 11.177). The final *explicits* of all three versions, however, refer to the entire text as the "*liber*" or "*dialogus de petri plowman*," the "*tractus*" or "*tractatus piers plowman nominatus*," and the like, suggesting that the colophons marked the parts of what was considered a single work or "book" (see Bibliography: [4], Chambers, MLR 6.302; and AUTHORSHIP [11], Kane, *Evidence*).

The contents of the poem in any of its versions defy simple paraphrase. A very brief summary of the parts of A will, however, enable subsequent discussion.

The A text comprises three successive dream visions, separated (at the beginnings of Passus 5 and 9) by brief waking intervals in which the speaker reflects upon his encounters and his further search. The narrator is not at once identified by name, but is called "Will" by one of his allegorical instructors in the third dream (see below).

The Vision encompasses two of these dreams. The first (Prologue and Passus 1 through 4) befalls the speaker "on a may morwenynge on maluerne hilles," and discloses a landscape—a tower, a dungeon, and a field "ful of folk" between them—and an explicator of it, Holy Chirche. After answering some questions put by the dreamer, she reveals the operations of Lady Meed in the world; these, and the attempt to resolve the question of who shall marry Meed, occupy the remainder of the first dream. The second, contained in Passus 5 through 8, presents first a call to repentance and general confession, then, for his first and longest appearance in the poem, the figure of Piers Plowman. He volunteers to lead the folk on their pilgrimage to Truth, if they will first assist him in finishing his work on the field. This dream ends in what has become one of the poem's major *cruces* of interpretation. A pardon sent from Truth to Piers is challenged by a priest, whereupon Piers in anger tears it apart. The dreamer wakes from the second dream musing on the meaning of these events.

At the beginning of Passus 9, the speaker, "robed in russet," sets out "for to seke dowel," and again falls asleep. In this third dream he encounters a succession of instructors: Thought, Wit, Study, Clergy, and Scripture. The A text ends with the dreamer claiming that he still lacks secure knowledge of "what is dowel," and observing that book-learned clerks are particularly easily swayed from "riȝte beleue," while the simple faith of "plouȝmen and pastours of bestis" can pierce "with a paternoster the paleis of heuene."

It is this three-dream narrative of A that will be both expanded internally (by over 700 lines), and greatly extended (by over 4000 more), to become the B version.

In three A manuscripts, this conclusion is followed by a short and fragmentary twelfth passus of partly doubtful authenticity. One of these (U; see Bibliography: [1], MS 6) is mutilated at the end of nineteen lines; the second

(J; MS 17) stops after 88 lines; the third (R; MS 4) offers a conclusion to the poem and a report of its maker's death. These lines (89–117) report that "wille," who "wrouȝthe þat here is wryten and oþer werkes boþe," has died, and that the present composer, one "Iohan but," has "made þis ende." (See Bibliography: [4] and [12]; Chambers, MLR 6.302.) If John But is to be identified with the King's Messenger of that name whose death is recorded in 1387 (see Rickert, MP 11.107), and his remarks about the author of this version are taken as accurate testimony, then they may provide a *terminus ad quem* for the composition of all versions of the poem—if, that is, the "oþer werkes" But mentions are those portions of the B or C continuation which were known to him, but not available to him for copying (Chambers, MLR 6.302). The contents of this short passus encourage some such interpretation; after the first few lines, they seem to offer a confused precis of later narrative developments. Early in this century, however, But's remarks were among the evidence adduced in support of the argument that the B and C revision and continuation were by a different composer or composers than A.

But's conclusion offers important contemporary testimony about the poem, and its historical and literary aspects may be considered separately. His naming of the author, though it may have been based on inference from the signature passages (see below), agrees with a fuller ascription in another early piece of external evidence, the rubric in Trinity College Dublin MS D.4.1 (V; MS 51). Kane (*Evidence*, pp. 26–35; see Bibliography [11]), considers the entire testimony likelier to be truthful report than a fabrication, but the accuracy of But's knowledge of the circumstances of the author's life and death is not fully determinable. But's perception of what constituted the form of the poem itself, the book or "werkes" of "peres plowman and mechel puple also," has significance as literary testimony apart from the historical accuracy of his report. His conclusion shows, Kane argues, that But regarded the A version as in want of an ending, and knew that more had been written on the same subject by the time he himself "made þis ende." Moreover, it implies that But considered all these "werkes" to have a single integrity which he ascribes to a single maker: he refers to "þat here is wryten and oþer werkes boþe" as "þis werk" and attributes it to "wille."

It is uncertain where But's work begins, and the authenticity of the earlier portions of Passus 12 is variously regarded. Donaldson (C-Text Poet) considers it genuine, the work of the A author, to perhaps line 98; Manly ascribed it to the author of the A Vita through line 54; Chambers saw John But's work as beginning at line 89, while admitting the possibility that the entire passus might be his. As Chambers noted, "the matter does not admit of proof" in any direction.

Internal references to events of the 1360s, among them Edward III's Norman wars (Skeat A-Text, 3.182–201; Kane A-Text, 3.174–95), and a "southwestryne wynd on satirday at eue" (Skeat A-Text, 5.16; Kane A-Text, 5.14)— a storm which is recorded by a chronicler as having occurred on Saturday, January 15, 1362—have led to the view, now generally accepted, that the A version was largely composed in that decade, though perhaps completed near its end (see Bibliography: DATE [10], A-Text, especially Bennett, PMLA 58.566).

The B Version and the Form of the Text

The B version revises and expands A's approximately 2500 lines to about 3200, inserting blocks of new material into A's narration and exposition, and continues it with about 4000 more lines, bringing the number of passus from eleven to twenty. It has survived in sixteen manuscripts and a fragment, and is represented in part of one manuscript of the A class (H³; MS 9), from the beginning of the poem to a point about 100 lines into the fifth passus, from which the poem continues as an A text. The B version is also represented by Robert Crowley's 1550 printed edition of the poem, which went through three impressions in that year. The first was made from a lost B manuscript; the second was reset with corrections from another B manuscript, also lost. The third may have similarly used another manuscript (see Bibliography [3]: Illston 1953, Crawford 1957, and Kane-Donaldson B-Text); it was this third impression that was reprinted in 1561 by Owen Rogers. One of the B manuscripts (MS 25a) is a sixteenth-century transcription of Rogers' edition.

Some B text manuscripts maintain the general division laid down in A between Visio and Vita, and subdivide the extended Vita by rubrics defining Dowel, Dobet, and Dobest; these divisions are probably scribal (see Bibliography [3], Adams 1985). The B revision adds new material to the two dreams constituting the A Visio, but leaves their boundaries essentially intact, redividing the passus in the second vision so that it, and the Visio, close at the end of B Passus 7 (corresponding to A Passus 8). Among B's new materials in this part of the poem is a parliament of rats and mice who deliberate the belling of the cat (Skeat B-Text, Prologue 87–209; Kane-Donaldson B-Text, Prologue 87–210). This episode has been considered an allusion to the Good Parliament of 1376, and has figured in the dating of the B text. In the second dream, B has expanded the confessions of the folk before Repentance, developing the scene toward a fuller presentation of the deadly sins.

The dream which contained the A Vita is continued by the B reviser, and five more are added, nearly tripling the total length of the poem, which in the B version encompasses eight dreams in all. Two of the six which constitute B's Vita themselves contain a vision-within-a-dream. The first of these begins a few lines into the B addition; the other, a swoon or spiritual ecstasy, occurs in the first dream of Dowel. In general, the boundaries between the visions receive less emphasis as distinct parts of a narrative progression in the B and C continuation than in the earlier portion of the poem, and they do not always coincide with passus divisions. Though the rubrics dividing the B continuation into Dowel, Dobet, and Dobest probably are not authorial, it will be convenient in describing the contents of this version to note where they occur. Dowel in B comprises two dreams, presented in Passus 11 through 14, Dobet two dreams (Passus 15 through 18), and Dobest two (Passus 19 and 20). These are joined by brief waking intervals, in which the speaker reports his own increasing dissociation from the ordinary concerns of the world, his "folly," and his growing absorption in his visions. Though narrative summary of the B continuation is unsatisfactory as an account of poetic meaning or method, it provides a reference point for subsequent discussion.

Dowel, largely following the A version, starts with the third dream at the beginning of B Passus 8 (corresponding to A Passus 9), opening B Passus 11 with a new development in the intellectual quest and initiating a new dream-within-a-dream. The dreamer, who has not waked from his visionary encounter with Scripture, is "scorned" by her, and in his "wo and wraþe" he falls into a "merueillous metels," in which Fortune leads him into a "lond of longyng." He meets a succession of new figures, among them the virtuous pagan emperor Trajan and a creature called Recklessness, who present further problematic aspects of the relations between works, faith, learning, and reason which had occupied the conclusion of the A Vita. As he wakes troubled from this subordinate vision, he is met by one more new figure, who invites him to say "what Dowel is." This figure, who in the first line of Passus 12 introduces himself as Ymaginatif, attempts to resolve the apparent conflict between "clergy" and "kynde wit" as sources of knowledge. His disappearance at the end of the twelfth passus ends the first dream of Dowel.

The fourth dream of the poem, the second of Dowel, occupies Passus 13 and 14, and presents two main encounters, a banquet with a "doctour" of divinity, and a meeting with Hawkyn "the actyf man." In the first of these, the dreamer attends a banquet at which Clergy and Conscience engage a learned and gluttonous "maistre" of the friars in an effort to define Dowel. Dining with Patience at a side-table meal of penitential bread and water, the dreamer challenges the Doctor for a definition. The episode ends when Conscience decides to set out with Patience on pilgrimage to learn more. Their encounter with the minstrel Hawkyn begins the second episode of the dream.

Hawkyn bewails the sins that stain his one garment, because of his way of life in the world. In introducing himself as a wafer-seller, Hawkyn refers (Skeat B-Text, 13.268–71; Kane-Donaldson B-Text, 13.267–70) to the dearth of bread in 1370 "whan (John) Chichester was Maire" (of London), another of the allusions used to assign the composition of the B text to the 1370s. Though Conscience urges Hawkyn to penance, and Patience recommends patient poverty as a remedy, the passus, and the fourth dream, end with Hawkyn's plaintive wail that sinfulness seems inevitable, and he is shamefully unworthy even of his one cloak.

Passus 15, headed in some manuscripts "finit Dowel et incipit Dobet," acts as a prologue to a new poetic development. The visionary notes that in his search for Dowel "my witte weex and wanyed til I a fool weere." Rocked asleep by Reason, he dreams again, this time of a creature whose many names reflect his several aspects in the functions of the soul. (This creature, usually referred to in discussions of the B text as Anima, will be called Liberum Arbitrium in the C revision.) His presentation of the works of charity in the Christian community occupies the entire passus. The dreamer opens Passus 16, labelled the first of Dobet, by asking for a further explanation of charity. The reply, that charity is a "ful trie tree" tended by Piers the Plowman, introduces the dominant figure of a new visionary display. At the mention of Piers' name, the dreamer falls into a spiritual ecstasy, and in this state imagines that Piers himself shows him the tree and its meaning. Piers explains that the tree is endangered by the foul weather of the world, by the flesh, and by the devil, who seizes its fruit as fast as it falls, carrying it off to darkness. As Piers strikes out after the fiend to recover his fruit, the holy spirit "in Gabrieles mouþe" announces that Jesus will joust for it and determine its rightful possession by judgment of arms. Piers is said to teach Jesus "lechecrafte his lif for to saue," making him a "parfit practisoure" to heal the sick and sinful. A brief narration of Christ's ministry and betrayal ends the dream-within-a-dream.

The remainder of Passus 16 and all of 17 return us to the main dream, the fifth of the B version. Recovered from his swoon, and looking for the vanished Piers, he meets a man on a "mydlenten sonday." This figure, a herald of arms, says he is Faith "of Abrahames hous." He, too, seeks someone he has seen before, who commanded of him a sacrifice of bread and wine. Asked about the burden he carries "in his bosom," he opens his cloak to reveal a "precïouse present" of souls, now "attached" by the devil but awaiting deliverance by Christ. This revelation coincides with the appearance of a second figure, ending the sixteenth passus.

The new figure introduces himself as "Spes," a spy (or scout), in the person of Moses. The letters patent he bears are stone tablets inscribed with the New Law, "love God and thy neighbor," and "gloriously" glossed; "Spes" seeks him who keeps the seal. As the three travel together they meet a Samaritan riding on a mule, on his way to a joust in Jerusalem. At the same moment they encounter a man who has fallen among thieves and lies wounded in the road. The herald and the "spy" both flee rather than assist the victim. The Samaritan binds the man's wounds and leaves him at a grange to be cared for until he can return with the "salue for alle sike" that will heal him. After a long discourse with the dreamer, in which he explains the Trinity by means of two extended analogies— the fist, fingers and palm of a hand; and the wax, wick, and flame of a candle—the Samaritan departs in haste for Jerusalem, and the dreamer wakes from the vision that began with Anima in Passus 15.

Passus 18 comprises a single dream, the second of Dobet and the sixth of the B text. The dreamer experiences the events of salvation history, from Palm Sunday to the Resurrection, in a series of vividly realized actions. The vision opens with the triumphal ride into Jerusalem of a champion who resembles both the Samaritan and Piers Plowman. Soon after the dreamer learns that this knight will joust to win what the fiend has claimed, the scene shifts: first to a debate among the four daughters of God—Mercy, Peace, Truth and "Rightwisnesse"—about the justice of the coming Redemption, and testimony by Book of Christ's fulfillment of the prophecies; then to a vividly and extensively dramatized Harrowing of Hell. Just returned from the field of trial and spent with his struggle "for mannes soule sake," Christ claims by law what he has won by joust. The four daughters of God dance for joy as the dreamer wakes to the sound of Easter morning church bells, and urges his wife and daughter to reverence the cross as a jewel.

The two visions of Dobest form the last two passus, and remain unrevised in C. The seventh dream of the B text begins a few lines into Passus 19, as the dreamer falls asleep at Mass, and sees a figure like Piers the Plowman "peynted al blody" carrying a cross. Conscience explains that this is Christ as conqueror, and interprets Christ's life as establishing the church on earth, and ordaining the form of the Christian community and the crafts that sustain it. Grace puts Piers to the plow and to planting the cardinal virtues, ordering him to build the barn of unity to house the harvest when it ripens. As in the second dream of the Visio, Piers' work for the community and his banquet for true laborers are disrupted by figures who assert their singular wills under the color of cardinal virtues: guile claims to be prudence, and main force is called fortitude. At this reemergence of conflict within the community, the dreamer wakes, ending the passus.

As the last passus begins, the dreamer wanders, heavy-hearted and hungry at noonday, and meets Need, who urges him to follow the example of those who have invoked the cardinal virtues. Since "nede haþ no lawe," he explains, the dreamer may take what life requires, as long as he observes the spirit of temperance: God himself chose to come into the world as a needy man. Following this speech, Will dreams that Antichrist in human form ravages the world; only fools defy him. Conscience attempts to gather the folk into Unity Holichurche and calls upon Kynde to defend them. Though Kynde sends fevers and pestilence, they fail to persuade the folk to leave sin. Conscience then calls upon Elde. His ministrations leave the dreamer bald, toothless, lame, and impotent, and bring him into Unity, but many remain without as the general siege continues. Calling finally upon Clergy, Conscience enlists the friars to heal those wounded by sin, and admonishes them to live by their rule. The sick still prefer the pleasing medicine of the flatterers to the effective but painful remedy of penance. As Sloth and Pride prepare an assault upon the weak and suffering, Conscience, in search of true healing, vows to set out on pilgrimage once more to seek Piers Plowman, and the dream and the poem end.

The B text is usually assigned to the 1370s on the evidence of allusions to contemporary events such as we have noted. Most of these are concentrated in the period 1376–79; the next-to-last passus has been thought to allude to the Great Schism of 1378 (see Bibliography [10], *B-Text*, especially Bennett, MÆ 12.55), and most scholars believe that the B version was completed soon after that. Fowler, who considers the position and interests expressed by B strikingly more conservative than those of A, believes on these grounds that the B text is likely to postdate the uprising of 1381 (see Bibliography [12], *Style and Thought*: Fowler, *Literary Relations,* p. 184). This dating of B, and this view of the differences between A and B—which suggest to Fowler that B was composed by a different poet than A—are not widely supported (see Bibliography [12], and below).

The C Version and the Form of the Text

The C version is a thorough revision of the B text. It is less than 100 lines longer than B, but shifts large blocks of material to other places in the poem, omits segments of B material, and adds several new long passages. It also closely reworks several sections throughout the poem, with the exception of the last two passus. Though minute in places, the revision does not appear to have been systematic.

The C version is represented in unmixed form by eighteen manuscripts, one of which (K; MS 37) lacks a good deal of the beginning and last third of the poem, and a fragment containing parts of less than two passus; it also appears in seven manuscripts which begin as A texts (one very corrupt) and continue as C, and in three B manuscripts which read C Prologue through 2.131 (3.131 by Skeat's numbering) at the beginning.

The passus are redivided in C to number 22 instead of B's twenty. The C manuscript used by Skeat numbered its Prologue as Passus I, and Skeat adopted its numbering for his C text, so that the last passus in his edition is the twenty-third. (Pearsall's edition [see Bibliography: EDITIONS [2], *C-Text*] and the forthcoming Athlone C text [see Bibliographical Note] return to the form of a Prologue and 22 passus found in most manuscripts.) For these reasons comparative description of the C revision is particularly cumbersome, and the thoroughgoing character of the reworking in many places makes it difficult to guess convincingly at its aims in each particular case. Donaldson's account (C-Text Poet) remains the fullest. In the effort to ascertain the purposes and motives of the C revision, attention has been mainly on a few striking and substantial additions and excisions.

The Visio portion of the C text is much expanded, in large part by the moving of a good deal of Hawkyn's speech into the confession of the folk in the second dream. There is also a new and notoriously difficult grammatical analogy of about 100 lines added to Conscience's speech to the king in the first vision, explaining the difference between legitimate and illegitimate reward, *mercede* and *mede*. Two substantial new passages, however, both loosely concerned with true labor and fraudulent claiming of charity, also increase the length of C's Visio. The first of these passages, sometimes referred to as the "autobiographical" episode, adds a waking interlude, about 100 lines long, between the first and second dream (Skeat C-Text, 6.1–108). In it the speaker is accosted by Reason and Conscience "in a hote heruest" and asked to account for his way of life. The second is a long addition of about 200 lines concerning the truly needy and false beggars, included in the application of Truth's pardon in the second vision. In the C revision Piers does not tear the pardon; instead the priest and Piers continue quarreling about it as the dreamer wakes.

The alterations in the C Vita are on the whole more pervasive and varied, and the most intensive revision is in the Dowel passus and the first vision of Dobet. Large parts of Study's and Clergy's speeches in the first dream of Dowel are omitted or moved elsewhere, and the boundaries of visions are shifted. The beginning of the first dream-within-a-dream, of the land of longing and Recklessness, is moved forward, so that much of the dreamer's perplexity about the role of "clergy" and good works in salvation is contained within it. The quandaries which ended the A text are thereby made part of the dreamer's experience of worldly fortune in the land of longing, and much of the dreamer's speech, including a newly inserted praise of patient poverty (Skeat C-Text, 14.1–100), becomes that of Recklessness, now apparently a sort of alter ego for the dreamer.

C also omits the break in B between the dream containing the encounter with Hawkyn, the last of B's Dowel, and B's new dream introducing Anima, which forms a prologue to Dobet; these together now constitute the fourth dream. The latter figure, now called Liberum Arbitrium, also becomes the expositor of the Tree of Charity; he assumes in this scene all the functions of Piers, who had expounded its significance in B, and the dream-within-a-dream which had presented him in B is eliminated. The encounter with Abraham and Moses and the Samaritan which follows Liberum Arbitrium's departure is of uncertain status. At its beginning it seems to be a waking encounter, but after the Samaritan departs, the dreamer "wakes" as he did at this point in B.

The vision of the Crucifixion and Resurrection, the second of Dobet, is less drastically revised than earlier portions of the Vita, and the two final dreams remain unrevised, either because the composer was satisfied with them, or because death or other circumstances prevented his finishing his task.

The dating of the C text is more doubtful than that of A or B. Skeat assigned it to 1393, on the basis of a passage added to the first vision (C-Text, 4.203–10), which he took to allude to Richard II's quarrel with London in 1392, and what he saw as other references to Richard's efforts to raise money from a recalcitrant citizenry early in that decade. Jusserand (see Bibliography [10], *C-Text*), seeing in these passages a reflection of conditions following the Parliament of Shrewsbury in 1398, favored 1398–99. More recently, a thesis by Sister Mary Aquinas Devlin recommended a date over a decade earlier, 1387 at the latest. Her chief evidence is the appropriation of C passages by Thomas Usk, in his *Testament of Love*. These are at most echoes rather than exact quotations, but if they do allude to the C-text, Usk's execution in 1387 marks a *terminus ad quem* for this version of the poem. If John But has been correctly identified, his death, also recorded in 1387, corroborates this dating. For want of further decisive evidence one way or another, this terminus has been accepted by most scholars. (For discussion of the dating of all three versions, see Bibliography [10]).

Language and Versification

Before attempting to describe the LANGUAGE [8] and VERSIFICATION [9] of composition, one must recognize that all extant manuscripts of the poem in all its versions are at a considerable remove from an authorial original. While certain relationships among surviving copies can be shown, their genetic history is not to any useful degree recoverable. (See Bibliography [2–4].) An editorial consequence of this state of affairs for the Athlone editors has been their decision to "correct and restore" the text of each version without recension—that is, to decide upon particular readings lection by lection, without positing the greater authority of the readings of any single manuscript or group of manuscripts designated more authoritative as a whole (see Bibliographical Note). The widespread occurrence of convergent variation, and the indeterminably great number of intermediaries between the writer's text and extant copies also mean that while it is possible to locate, from the language of individual manuscripts, their place of copying, it is not possible to make a direct inference from stemmatic evidence about the poet's native dialect or the place of composition.

From a survey of the dialect evidence of 36 manuscripts of all three versions, Samuels (ESts 44.81) concluded that in extant C texts the language of the area around the Malvern Hills predominates; that the B text circulated chiefly in the London and Worcester areas; while the A texts that survive are mostly from various "peripheral" areas. This broad picture has subsequently been refined by codicological study as well as by further dialect mapping (see Bibliography [3], particularly Doyle 1982 and 1983). But it provides no basis for conjecture about where any version of the poem was composed, though the distribution of the C version may corroborate other evidence that the poet was known in the Malvern area.

The evidence of Langland's alliterative practice has long been held inconclusive, for a combination of reasons. Both the vocabulary and the alliterative pattern of lines have been extensively affected by the normalizing activity of scribes, and until recently it has not been possible to discern consistent patterns through these corruptions. When such patterns are studied systematically, moreover, the lexical evidence is not decisive. The poet used more than one dialectal form of some words in alliterative position within the line, much as other alliterative poets used variational synonyms, for poetic convenience; for instance, both Northern *kirke* and Midlands and Southern *chirche* are used to alliterate. More telling evidence lies in his grammatical rather than lexical usage, and its patterns are revealed in his least obtrusive— and most distinctive—alliterative verse practice. Much more frequently than other poets, he assigns alliterative function to small and often lightly-stressed grammatical words in the line, such as pronouns and auxiliary verbs. His use of *ar(e)n* as well as the b-forms of the present tense of the verb "to be"— *beþ, buþ, beoþ, ben*—in alliterative position implies a Midland rather than Southern region; the third-person feminine pronoun *heo* or *he*, required by alliteration far more frequently than *scheo* or *sche,* confines the poet's dialect to the West and South and excludes London. Two other usages delimit the area further: The alliteration of *f-* with *v-* restricts the possible area within the West Midlands to Herefordshire and southwest Worcestershire, and the alliteration of *h* with vowels rules out Herefordshire. These are the four criteria used by Samuels (MÆ 54.232) to define the poet's dialect as belonging to southwestern Worcestershire, an area including Malvern.

Considered in the broadest terms, the versification of *Piers Plowman* falls within the norms of most late fourteenth-century alliterative verse: approximately 70 percent of its lines appear to be of the commonest type *aaax,* for example (see Bibliography [9]: Oakden, Sapora). Yet in several details the poet's practice is distinctive: both freer and more complex in its handling of variations of the norm, and in its use of secondary patterning within the line. Most commentary has dwelt, even to excess, on its differences from much of the rest of the contemporary alliterative corpus, while it has rarely specified with precision the nature and locus of the differences.

One reason for the absence of effectively detailed comparative study has been the corruption of texts, not only of *Piers,* but of several other poems lacking modern editions adequate to the purpose, which might provide a base for close comparative analysis. The faulty alliteration in several manuscript lines, preserved by Skeat's edition, has given rise to a widespread impression that the poet was sublimely impatient of mere niceties of craft. Skeat's remark, that he "frequently neglects to observe strict rules, and evidently considered metre of much less importance than the sense," implicitly conflates the effects of textual corruption with the poet's characteristic verse techniques, and attributes both to a poetic temperament laudable for its aversion to formality of language or regularity of meter—a tendency some others have associated with the writer's express castigation of sterile formalism in spiritual life. This conflation of prosodic and ideational effects is common in general descriptions of the craft of *Piers.* Yet while much modern scholarship has emphasized the traditional patterns of thought informing the poem, the care with which these are combined, and its richness and resonance of intellectual effect, there has not as yet been a similarly thorough revaluation of its verbal and prosodic techniques.

A second limitation in many accounts of the poet's verse craft has been the blurring of several aspects of his practice in describing and analyzing his characteristic effects. Its differences in vocabulary from other poems in the later medieval alliterative corpus are in part due to the poet's themes and general decorum. Some alliterative poems contain subdued expository or homiletic passages which more closely approximate the formal and rhetorical effects of *Piers* than do the heightened battle set-pieces often cited from these poems to emphasize *Piers'* distinctive traits. Its syntax is generally perceived as more informal and varied, less mannered and marked by phrasal addition, than that of other alliterative poems, but this contrast may in part be one of quality rather than a matter of particular styles within the alliterative verse system of later Middle English. More distinctive than either the poet's vocabulary or syntax in themselves, yet much more elusive to systematic demonstration, is the great variety of rhythmic and intellectual interest within the line, created by interplay between alliterative patterning and the metrical accent sustained by lexical, phrasal, and semantic stress. The general technique has more often been remarked than understood. The fullest account to date is that of Kane (see Bibliography [9], Kane 1981), who describes the poet's several ways of achieving this "modulation." Lines frequently contain a secondary or extrageneric alliterative pattern rather than a single one. Vocalic alliteration, and alliteration on grammatical or otherwise unstressed words, and the use of alliteration to confer surprising semantic emphasis, are all frequent, and contribute to the "subdued" rather than formal and ceremonious effect so often remarked in the verse. While debate continues over details of the poet's verse practice, and there are particular disagreements with some of the Athlone editors' emendations *causa metri,* the discussion enabled by the Athlone edition, and further accounts of syntax and versification to appear in Volume IV of this edition, should make possible a fuller understanding of these matters than Skeat's text permitted.

The models or antecedents of the poet's verse technique have so far proved as elusive as his particular sources. In its variety and informality of effect, it has sometimes been compared to good idiomatic prose. This, and frequent local resemblances in subject matter and hortatory manner to homiletic writing, have prompted broad comparisons of style (see below, and Bibliography: SOURCES [13], Owst). More recently, a cadenced prose which appears to emulate in English the clausal rhythms and alliterative ornament of Latin dictaminal style has been considered as a possible influence (see Bibliography [9]: Salter, Blake, Lawton). Cadenced composition, in both Latin and English, is nourished by a number of tributary streams, and it is likely to prove difficult to locate the poem precisely among them. The entire terrain in which prose and verse technique meet in Middle English is in need of more detailed mapping. It appears that the poet's choice of the alliterative verse form was a venturesome and complex gesture, influenced by a number of cultural factors, and his use of it at once eclectic and independent.

Authorship

For most of its history, *Piers Plowman* has been assumed to be the work of a single author, usually called William Langland. He is so named in both near-contemporary ascriptions of various forms in manuscripts—the fullest being that of V (MS 51), a C manuscript in Trinity College Dublin—and in several occurrences in all three versions of word-play on all parts of this name. "Will" is an actor in all three texts, and in all three this name is given to the dreamer; in the B and C versions the words "long" and "land" also figure together with the name "Will" in more than one instance of what has usually been considered a form of punning signature. Near the beginning of his encounter with Anima, the dreamer says of himself "I haue lyued in londe . . . my name is longe wille" (Skeat B-Text 15.148; Kane-Donaldson B-Text 15.152), and the "lond of longyng" at the beginning of the B addition might be another such usage. Another early tradition, traceable to the circle of John Bale in the sixteenth century, names the author as Robert Longland. This ascription seems to have originated in a manuscript corruption of the opening line of the Vita, in which "yrobed in russet" has become "I Roberd" or "Robert": manuscripts M of the A-class (MS 14) and F of the B-class (MS 21) both have this reading of the line.

R. W. Chambers' essay "Robert or William Langland" compares the signatures to those in other medieval vernacular poetry, and Kane examines the broader uses of this poetic "I" in *The Autobiographical Fallacy in Chaucer and Langland Studies*, as does Donaldson in the final chapter of *C-Text Poet*. The most comprehensive survey of both the problem of authorship and the author's name, and the early attributions and the convention of signatures, is Kane's *Piers Plowman: The Evidence for Authorship*.

Early in the poem's literary life, this general assumption of single authorship was not examined, in part because recognition of its versions as distinct from its manuscript variants came slowly and gradually. There were some demurrers before Skeat. Wright (see Bibliography: [2], *B-Text*; [4], *ABC-Texts*), who first recognized B as an earlier version than C and considered it superior, thought B and C were by two different authors. The hypothesis of multiple authorship was raised to sustained critical attention in an article in 1906 by J. M. Manly, and developed in 1908 in his essay on the poem in the *Cambridge History of English Literature* (see Bibliography [12]). In his view as many as five authors, including John But, were involved in producing the three versions of the poem. Though the "authorship controversy" has now virtually vanished from serious critical consideration, it occupied a large share of the space and energy devoted to the poem early in this century. Both the appearance and disappearance of the issue are instructive for understanding the subsequent emphases in *Piers Plowman* studies. While Manly's conception of the poem, and his kind of argument, were largely rendered obsolete in the process, responses to his claims formed a watershed in scholarship on the poem, and forced modern study of it into being.

The prominent place in which Manly chose to state his case at length in part explains the vigorous and detailed debates it engendered (see Bibliography [11–12] for the main documents and a chronology of the dispute), but only in part. His interpretative strategy resembled that of several nineteenth-century accounts of long, complex, and usually anonymous works from early or traditional societies. His hypothesis followed a generation of scholarship which had analyzed the Homeric poems, the *chansons de geste*, and *Beowulf* as aggregates of separate works, accretions representing stages of construction by several composers. Manly proposed it to account for what appeared to him major gaps in literary structure: incoherences within versions, and discrepancies of sense between versions, so pronounced that they implied to him a succession of revisers, each misunderstanding and patching a predecessor's work. His argument included a specific textual hypothesis, a "lost leaf" in the second vision of the A text, to explain the absence of Wrath and a section on restitution in the Sloth episode, and the continued incoherence of these passages in the B revision. It is important, however, to recall that Manly's views neither began in, nor referred to, close study of the textual evidence. No manuscript suggesting such an arrangement of leaves appeared—as Manly's opponents, such as Chambers, and even those partially persuaded of the merits of his hypothesis, such as Bradley, were quick to observe. Though Manly promised more detailed studies of dialect, meter, and style to support the differences he saw between versions, these did not appear. Chambers ackowledged Manly's role in bringing about more detailed collation of the A manuscripts, a project undertaken by Manly's student, Knott.

More fundamental to Manly's hypothesis were some formal and generic assumptions, which determined his sense of what constituted flaws in the poem. In his view, the first two visions of the A text defined the nature and merits of the poem, and the failures of its continuators. All subsequent adherents to Manly's views have likewise assigned to A a privileged position in interpreting the form and development of the work. Manly saw the A Visio as satire, and its author as a man of "unerring hand," who "never himself forgets for a moment the relation of any incident to his whole plan." Because he is writing satire, Manly argued, the author of A disguises his identity with the fictive name Will, which has no necessary reference to the author's name. From this perspective, Dowel and its further development in B and C represent a failure to sustain the genre and techniques of the first two visions, rather than an expansion of a poetic plan. His arguments made very little reference either to contemporary writings, or to other documented instances of literary works which circulated in multiple versions during the lifetime of the author, and presented similar problems to contemporary and later interpretation. On both grounds, but particularly the latter, he was criticized at length by Jusserand, who had published a decade earlier the first modern book-length critical study of the poem. On the former, as well as on textual matters, he was challenged by Chambers. At stake were not only the literary structure, techniques, and genre of the poem, but the status of its persona, Will. Manly's somewhat ahistorical and rationalistic views of these matters were disputed, as scholars explored the literary traditions contributing to the poetic idiom of the work.

In retrospect, the "authorship controversy" appears to have forced into focus some fundamental textual and critical issues. At about the same time that Manly's claims drew renewed attention to the quality of available texts, modern methods of textual criticism were beginning to be applied to the poem, and to medieval vernacular poems generally. Metrical and dialectal tests of authorship receded in importance as scholars came to recognize the highly mediated form of their evidence for authorial practice in the surviving manuscripts. The likelihood of settling the authorship question by establishing better texts, as Bradley had hoped, gave way to a perception of the necessary circularity of this project. Since textual decisions involved distinguishing authorial from scribal readings, notions about authorship figure in the establishing of texts, and do not simply derive from them, as Manly and his successors seem to have expected.

A second major consequence of the debate, though it was slower to develop, was an important shift in the historical and critical vocabulary brought to the interpretation of the poem. Defining this author's *usus scribendi* in several broader senses required comparative literary-historical study. Scholars saw the need to consider the author's style in a historical context, to distinguish idiosyncratic opinions from commonplace ideas, to understand the structural principles of medieval long poems, and to interpret allusions and influences. From debate about "unity of authorship" followed consideration of the very nature of authorship and unity in medieval works. As scholars took up the larger questions of form, convention, and tradition which still concern medieval literary study generally, *Piers Plowman* scholarship became more broadly comparative and critical, and found its object to be not simply the great English historical monument it had been to the nineteenth century, but a great European vernacular poem.

Sources and Literary Relationships

If poetic originality is measured by the difficulty with which one may discern clear sources of literary imitation, or generic similarities to other poems, *Piers* must be counted among the most original literary productions of any period. Its specific literary models, either in Latin or the vernaculars, have eluded identification, though several general traditions are apparent. There is little evidence of familiarity with specific ancient or medieval Latin poems, though there is much piecemeal citation of verse. The few quotations from medieval Latin satirists and epigrammatists may have been drawn from compilations rather than from first-hand acquaintance. Similarly, although French tags occur in the poem from time to time (e.g. the song in the opening scene, *dieu saue dame emme*, Skeat A-Text, Prologue.103, and Kane A-Text, Prologue.103), they appear, like the bits of English tales and proverbial lore, as snatches of verbal and ideational melody rather than as sustained or meaningful formal influences. Resemblances to earlier French allegories (De-guileville's *Pelerinages*, Rutebeuf's *Voie de Paradis*, the *Roman de Fauvel*) have been discussed (see Bibliography: [13], Owen 1912 and Cornelius 1932, and COMPARISONS AND LATER RELATIONSHIPS [14], Isaacson 1976), but no certain borrowings have been established. There is no demonstrable ac-quaintance with French court lyric or narrative, or with Italian literature. The poem draws upon the same general fund of "estates satire" used by Jean de Meun, Chaucer, and Gower, as well as by vernacular homiletic mor-alists (see Bibliography [13] and [14], especially Mann 1973), but its debts to specific sources have been harder to identify than those of Chaucer.

The relation of the poem to other English alliterative poems of the four-teenth century is obscure, partly because of the difficulty of dating or local-izing many of them, but also because the subject and manner of treatment of *Piers* is quite unlike that of any other single alliterative poem. Claims of particular verbal borrowing, as distinct from dictional similarity, have not been convincingly sustained. Recent scholars have rather emphasized the possible indebtedness to *Piers* of other alliterative poems, such as *The Parlia-ment of the Three Ages, Death and Life,* and *St. Erkenwald,* as well as those long seen as pervasively influenced by *Piers*: *Richard the Redeless* and *Mum and the Sothsegger.* (See XIII [244–246] in *Manual,* vol. 5.) In general narrative pro-cedure and style it more closely resembles alliterative Biblical paraphrase and didactic verse than historical romance. It declares no definite relation-ship to any other single kind of English poem, except by way of contrast: it contains the first mention of "rymes of Robyn hood and Randolf Erl of Chestre" (Skeat B-Text, 5.402; Kane-Donaldson B-Text, 5.395). This and other references to popular song and story are disparaging, however, rele-gating such amusements to the haunts of idleness.

The question of sources has long been involved with discussion of the nature and extent of learning exhibited in the poem. One of its immediately striking features is the use of interspersed Latin quotations, only a few of which still remain unidentified. Many are scriptural, drawn most frequently from the psalms, gospels, and epistles. They also show the likely influence of various kinds of collections and compendia: patristic, homiletic, and en-cyclopedic material, legal maxims, *sententiae,* and proverbs (see Bibliography: TEXTUAL NOTES [7]: Hort 1938, Fuller 1961, Alford 1974 and 1984, Lindemann 1977; [13]: Sullivan 1932, Quick 1982). The poem also shows

occasional evidence of familiarity with contemporary university-level grammatical and theological learning and controversy, and considerable acquaintance with legal procedures, verbal formulae, and statute law (Birnes 1974,
Alford 1977, and, in CONTEMPORARY RELATIONSHIPS, MAINLY
NON-LITERARY [17], Baldwin 1981) which is stronger in the later than
the earlier versions of the poem. It is difficult to ascertain what sort of
education or career might have produced this unique assembly of lore. A
university education for clerical office is possible; some have suggested that
it might have been fragmentary or incomplete. Donaldson (C-Text Poet)
proposed, on the evidence of statements "Will" makes about himself in the
poem, that the author might have been a cleric in lower orders, earning a
living praying for those who paid for his services. His knowledge of legal
formulas might indicate employment as a legal scribe. No single explanation,
however, has accounted satisfactorily for both the uneven character and combination of literate references in the poem.

The manner in which the poem expresses the poet's learning, and assim-
ilates its verbal and cultural influences, has for this reason attracted more
attention than the search for sources *per se*. The chief antecedents of its
expository method and form have been found in clerical compendia, aids to
scriptural study, and verbal tools of homiletic composition. Owst and Salter
(see Bibliography [13] and [14]) have described its similarities to medieval
sermons, both in construction and themes. Dunning recognized its pervasive
use of canonical methods of scriptural interpretation. Robertson and Huppé
(see Bibliography, GENERAL INTERPRETATION [15]) saw it as informed
by detailed and deeply worked out exegetical schemes, radiating from the
scriptural quotations and constructed to be readable on four levels of meaning. Alford has described the method of the poem as that of "verbal concordance," the linking of verbally and doctrinally related texts as an aid to
composition and memory as well as to interpretation, in the manner can-
onically recommended for commentaries and sermons. All these studies
point to the nearest approximation to structural principles thus far generally
evident in the poem: they are those of the great volume of doctrinal and
ethical works, of no common form, which were given impetus by the Fourth
Lateran Council and propagated in both Latin and the vernaculars from the
thirteenth through the fifteenth centuries. Both in intellectual content and
in techniques of invention and disposition, the poem is now seen as deriving

from this body of writing. Though its debts to particular works in this tradition have not been fully traced, there have been a number of illuminating
local analyses (see Bibliography: [7] and [13], and DISCUSSION OF PAR-
TICULAR PROBLEMS [16]).

Later Relationships and Interpretations

Frequent and impassioned commentary in the poem on the ills of contemporary society, particularly on ecclesiastical and economic abuses, have led
to consideration of its relation to Wyclif's doctrines, to Lollardy generally,
and to the uprising of 1381. A number of works clearly Lollard in sentiment
allude to the poem, or were broadly influenced by it. The "letter" of the
dissident priest John Ball to the peasants of Essex in 1381 refers to Piers
Plowman and to "dowel" and "dobettere." (For this and other works, in the
"plowman" tradition, see Chapter XIII, Poems Dealing with Contemporary
Conditions, in vol. 5 of this *Manual.*) Other works use the plowman as an
ideal figure in a varied program, both broad and topical, of social and moral
complaint, anti-clerical or anti-fraternal satire, and criticism of courtiers,
lawyers, and public venality generally (see Bibliography [17])—themes
treated sporadically in *Piers* with great detail and feeling, though usually in
a more complex poetic framework than is found in its imitators. Among
these imitations are *Richard the Redeless* (thought by Skeat to be by the same
author, and published along with *Piers* in Skeat Oxford), *Mum and the Sothsegger,* XIII [246] (once thought to be part of the former), the *Plowman's Tale,*
XIII [110] and *Piers the Plowman's Creed,* XIII [109]. The extent to which
such complaints, either in *Piers* or in the several poems postdating it and
influenced by it, are specifically Lollard in tenor, has been debated. The date,
situation, and disposition of each of them is crucial to interpretation. As
McFarlane (*Lancastrian Kings and Lollard Knights*) has pointed out, in the later
fourteenth century it is hard to tell the difference between orthodox and
Lollard moral teaching and private devotion, and criticism of ecclesiastical
abuses need not imply theological heterodoxy. It was only in the early fifteenth century that their social significance shifted markedly. Questions concerning the poet's orthodoxy, and his attitudes toward social disaffection and
religious dissent, were raised frequently in early scholarship on the poem,

and have recently been raised again, in the light of work on the Wycliffite movement and its texts.

Recent interest in the relation of the poem to contemporary controversy, following two generations of critical and scholarly work on its resemblances to dogmatic writing and teaching, in one sense brings its critical history full circle, for it was chiefly as a reforming treatise that the poem attracted the widest attention from its own time to at least the end of the seventeenth century (see Bibliography [17], especially Gradon 1980). For some, whose marginal comments and references to the poem reveal their reading of it, it was a sober and practical compendium of moral and spiritual truth; for some (e.g. Puttenham), it was a satire. But for virtually all its early readers, it concerned not only general truths, but particular ecclesiastical and moral issues exploited by successive generations of reformers. Though the poet's own manifest social and theological views, to the extent that they can be ascertained with any confidence, seem orthodox and traditional, even conservative, his manner of proceeding made the poem strike both early and modern readers as heterodox, even inflammatory. An impassioned poetic address and fresh effect in using traditional materials is apparent to some degree in all three versions, though according to some critics there is less reformist zeal and indignation in the last version. Since revision generally in the poem less frequently alters the substance of thought than its manner of expression, it may be that fuller formal study of its techniques, and comparison of them to the favored literary procedures as well as doctrines of the reformers, will help to clarify its relations to contemporary religious and social movements.

Controversial aspects of the poem have always figured in its critical history. If some of its Tudor audience found it proto-Protestant, some of its Victorian and even later readers took it as a document in a broad and optimistic account of English history as a gradual progression of constitutional and ecclesiastical rectification. Its specifically literary character, and the poetics and poetic intentions that inform its production, were largely neglected until the present century. As Anthony Colaianne has noted, in a valuable introduction to his recent annotated bibliography of the poem (see Bibliography [19]), assessments of the poet's artistic capabilities and designs have often been based on "a more general misunderstanding of the overall literary climate of the later Middle Ages," contained in the division by earlier literary historians of later fourteenth-century poetry into the two categories "courtly" and "popular." In this oversimple scheme, Chaucer generally represented the one tradition, *Piers Plowman* the other, with considerable distortion of the social situation and literary milieu of both.

This dichotomy, each half of which both misrepresented and undervalued the variety of forms of religious expression, has now been altered in two ways. On the one hand, historical study—social, intellectual, and textual—has given fuller, and different, accounts of medieval life. Studies of courts, schools, regal and ecclesiastical administration, and other institutions as loci of literate activity have produced new understanding of "courtly" and "popular" culture, and permitted more concrete notions of a particular writer's situation. On the other hand, literary scholars have examined more closely the traditions, techniques, and rationales of allegorical writing and reading. This mode, often in the nineteenth century considered reductive, tiresome, and antithetical to the poetic imagination—in some sense subliterary—has in mid-twentieth-century criticism come into its own as a system of serious theoretical and literary-historical analysis. The change may in part be due to the mediating critical influence of literary modernism, which can countenance "inconsistencies" and abrupt fissures in narration, and non-naturalistic representation, as purposeful and expressive artistic procedures.

It is in such critical circumstances that the individual talent as well as the traditions evident in *Piers Plowman* have received a new kind of study and appreciation since the 1930s. In his influential introduction to allegorical literature, published early in this period (see Bibliography, GENERAL REFERENCES [18]), C. S. Lewis directed attention both to the conventional materials and technique of the poem, and to the power of its "intellectual imagination": "Its only oddity is its excellence: in *Piers Plowman* we see an exceptional poet adorning a species of poetry which is hardly exceptional at all." Valuable general interpretations of the poem from that decade to the present have emerged from the broad critical rehabilitation of allegorical and figurative literature signalled by Lewis' book: the books of Frank, Bloomfield, Ames, Kirk, Carruthers, and Aers, among others, and a host of substantial articles (see Bibliography [15], [16], and [18]). These have interpreted the poem as an artistically coherent allegorical composition, rather than a compendium of complaint and opinion. Recent writers have also discussed the views of art and language implicit in such literature, and in the interpretative practices that accompanied its production.

Though Lewis and others authorized the serious study of a body of medieval poetry not previously widely favored, the particular "species of poetry" to which *Piers* belongs—its most basic poetic form and genre—is still debated. Bloomfield, in *Piers Plowman as a Fourteenth Century Apocalypse,* presents what may be the fullest systematic discussion of several possible literary models: the allegorical dream narrative, the dialogue or debate, encyclopedic satire, and quest narration. He also examines the complaint, the commentary, and the sermon as other modes of discourse which have influenced the poem. The apocalyptic mode which figures most centrally in his own account is, however, treated less as a literary form or genre than as a dominant perspective or system of thought, enabling the poet to combine historical and spiritual themes in a work which has both the tonal urgency and instability of reference of prophecy. Formal and generic discussion of the poem has generally been subordinated to thematic concerns, and overshadowed by the continuing effort to find the intellectual lineage and the specific historical situation of the work.

Scholarship of the past 30 years has shed much light on particular cruces of interpretation. Among the problems which have received fruitful attention are some of the key terms and abstract entities of the poem, such as Ymaginatif, Kynde Wit, and Liberum Arbitrium, and the intellectual context of some of its more perplexing passages in the arguments of theology, speculative grammar, sign theory, and contemporary legal thought. Taken together, these detailed elucidations portray a very different kind of poem from the "popular," mystical, or reformist work described by earlier scholarship. The *Piers Plowman* they present is in principle rather than by default or defect "difficult poetry." It engages complex theological and epistemological questions, in a genuinely speculative rather than simply didactic fashion. The aesthetic values implied in a work of such a kind, and the question of the audience for such themes and procedures, have only recently begun to be seriously explored.

Surveys of Scholarship

The volume and quality of scholarly and critical work on the poem in the past 50 years are impressive. Bloomfield's survey of the subject in 1939 (see Bibliography [19]) identified two desiderata, besides basic textual studies, for future work: close verbal study of the poet's meaning, his "words and lines," and accounts of the intellectual and social backgrounds of the poem rather than sources and "influences" to establish its frame of reference and cultural significance. Several admirable examples of both, as well as the fruits of long textual labors, appeared. Over 30 years later David Fowler (1971) assessed many of them, commending a general increase in respect for the intellectual and aesthetic qualities of the poem. He called, however, for further work on its immediate historical context. Some has since appeared, and will continue to emerge from historians as well as literary scholars. Among the projects likely to illuminate the poem are those dealing with aspects of late fourteenth-century English society: the court and patronage, legal training and administration, manuscript production, specific religious institutions, and the forms of lay piety and of religious and social dissent—as well as studies of the character and uses of literacy in particular social groups, and the "archaeology of reading." These inquiries may be expected to elucidate the poetics as well as the meaning of the work.

The current climate of scholarship suggests that many of the descriptive categories within which the poem was studied 60 years ago have largely collapsed or changed form, and a few new ones have appeared to succeed them. The recently published editions may be expected to have a strong shaping effect on the course of further study. New texts, along with continued exploration of medieval literary history and theory, will permit more detailed disclosure of the rich late fourteenth-century literary landscape, and the situation within it of this culturally important and imaginatively brilliant poem.

For SELECTIONS [5] and TRANSLATIONS AND MODERNIZATIONS [6], see Bibliography. For MISCELLANEOUS [20], see Bibliography and Bibliographical Note.

XIX. TRAVEL AND GEOGRAPHICAL WRITINGS

by

Christian K. Zacher

The writings gathered here are arranged in chronological order rather than in categories. Distinctions between the geographical pieces and the travel accounts would disguise the natural interdependence of the two kinds of writings. So, too, any discrimination among these works on the basis of their being more or less religious or secular (pilgrimage accounts as opposed to other travel itineraries, for instance) would suggest a configuration that denied the frequent mixture and overlap of those large categories. A chronological survey reveals the obvious increase in vernacular geographical and travel writing during the fifteenth century (only one quarter of the surviving material antedates 1400), nearly all of it in practical prose. Virtually none of it reflects the enlarging horizons of contemporary continental geographers and travellers; as is evident from John Rastell's complaints in *The Four Elements* and from the early English book trade, this general English indifference to the new geographical knowledge and discoveries continues through the first part of the sixteenth century.

While all of this material seems best approached chronologically, it can be instructive to sort the travel writings separately according to the three-part classification Howard has suggested for pilgrimage writings. Some are mere logs—either itineraries marking places and distances or lists of pilgrimage sites and indulgences—which served as mnemonic and memorializing devices. Guides are elaborated logs, glosses meant (like *The Stations of Rome*) to assist visitors at a particular place or (like *A Rutter of the English Coast*) to direct travellers along a particular route. Narratives are more developed guidebooks, based on actual (or imagined) travels, intended (like *The Itineraries of William Wey, The Stations of Jerusalem, Information for Pilgrims unto the Holy Land,* and *Mandeville's Travels*) to commemorate individual journeys and chart the way for others. As illuminating as such a generic classification can be, chronology still underlines best one of the most typical literary features of medieval travel writing—its cumulative indebtedness. Authors who travelled in fact (or in fiction) commonly honored authority as much as personal experience by borrowing from the accounts of their predecessors. Nowhere is this practice more apparent than in *Mandeville's Travels,* which is the most important and successful late-medieval book about the world in large part because of its complex blending of alleged travel experience with a reliance on written authorities. The Commentary and Bibliography attempt to underscore this habitual dependence of the medieval travel-writer by noticing significant sources and literary relations.

Generalizations about travel and geographical writing from medieval England would on the whole be confirmed by a consideration of writings which for different reasons are not discussed in this chapter: those travel and geographical works accounted for elsewhere in the *Manual,* those not composed in the vernacular, and those which are known to have existed but now are lost.

Several items of geographical value are treated with other emphases in the *Manual. The Description of Durham* (XIII [9] in *Manual,* vol. 5) is a brief twelfth-century encomium on the city; *The Shires* (XIII [173]), in a version copied about 1500, catalogues the typifying qualities of counties and peoples (and should be compared with [2] below). The extent of late fourteenth-century English geographical knowledge is represented in portions of Trevisa's translations of Higden's *Polychronicon* and Bartholomaeus Anglicus's *De proprietatibus rerum* (see the chapters on Chronicles and on Science and Information); Caxton's 1480 edition of the former (IX [54] in *Manual,* vol. 3) and his 1481 publication of *The Mirror of the World* (IX [28]), a prose translation of the thirteenth-century encyclopedic work by Gossouin de Metz, reflect largely traditional geographic information and little of the newer discoveries. The *Pilgrim's Song* (XIII [172]) realistically describes life aboard an English pilgrim ship bound for Compostella; and Caxton's French-English phrase-book (IX [26]) provides a handy companion to the pilgrim guidebooks and travellers' advice manuals. *The Libel of English Policy* (XIII [249]), composed in the 1430's, demonstrates how apparently unconcerned English leaders were about maintaining a strong navy and control of the surrounding seas (and also reveals that trading ships from Bristol and Scarborough in times past had been visiting Iceland). Lastly, there is Rastell's interlude, *The Four Elements* (XII [31] in *Manual,* vol. 5), printed sometime after his failed voyage to the new-found lands in 1517; the play is a product of his wide familiarity with earlier and recent geographical and travel writing (including perhaps *Mandeville's Travels*) as well as a plea for greater public attention to the new lands.

Rastell complained that English contemporaries had only slight geographical learning because of their inability to read Latin, and it is apparent, as might be expected, that much of the geographical and travel writing of medieval England was composed in Latin. Notable among early works are Gerald of Wales's late twelfth-century reports on Ireland and Wales, which are superior in their descriptive geography to later vernacular productions. The extant native Latin pilgrimage narratives, travel diaries, and itineraries from the time are almost as numerous as the vernacular examples and properly belong to the full study of medieval travel writing in England. They include a handful of fourteenth- and fifteenth-century Holy Land pilgrimage logs, narratives, and lists of stations; itineraries for merchants and religious, listing routes within and out of England; the complete narratives of William Wey (see [13] below); documents tracing the travels of various important figures; and the *Itineraries* of William Worcestre, the record of the early antiquarian's several journeys through England between 1477 and 1480.

Also omitted from discussion here are the now lost English writings about travel and geography. Two merit particular notice. William Brewyn's late fifteenth-century Latin guidebook for pilgrims to Rome at one time also contained an English account of the stations of Jerusalem and the Holy Land which is now missing from the manuscript. The more famous *Inventio fortunata,* a Latin narrative allegedly written by Nicholas of Lynn following travels in the North Atlantic during the mid-fourteenth century, was known to geographers and cartographers in England and on the continent up through the sixteenth century. Unknown since then except in an indirect and summary form, the *Inventio* eventually may be shown to have had some relation to *Mandeville's Travels* and late medieval geographical discussion in light of Seymour's announcement in 1974 that he possessed a Middle English fragment of the work.

An understanding of medieval English travel and geographical concerns requires some consideration of both English cartographic contributions during the period and the known late fifteenth-century English investigations in the Atlantic. Several maps of medieval Britain, inasmuch as they in part embody pilgrimage routes and road systems, graphically supplement contemporary written itineraries; a variety of other, local maps are significant for the English inscriptions they bear as well as for their relation to the progress of geographical description (see [23] below). Records of westward voyages by the Cabots and other Bristol sailors furnish proof, not found among English travel and geographical writings, that there were insular connections with wider European exploratory activity (see [16] below).

THE SHIRES AND HUNDREDS OF ENGLAND [1] estimates the length and breadth of England and gives the number and names of bishoprics, archbishoprics, and shires (grouped according to the three laws). Written after 1250, the piece amounts to 58 lines of printed prose.

A LIST OF 108 ENGLISH TOWNS [2] names towns and their chief attributes or products in a mixture of French and English (e.g., "Merueille de Stonhengh," "Archiers de Wals"). There is no overall geographical coherence to the list but parts of the sequence suggest the compiler had some plan of organization in mind. The piece has affinities with a later English-Latin poem on the properties of seven English cities (titled by Rigg *The Stores of the Cities*); in each, for instance, Coventry is remembered for its soap. Both of these should be considered along with an item Wells originally titled *The Characteristics of Counties*; Robbins (XIII [173] in *Manual*, vol. 5) describes it as a "catalogue of the characteristics of the English counties" but retitles it *The Shires*, creating a possible confusion with [1] above. In discussing *The Characteristics of Counties*, Wells remarked without supporting information that it "reminds of the Warwickshire Seven Towns rimes." It now seems very probable that the unidentified seven towns rimes and *The Stores of the Cities* are one and the same.

A GEOGRAPHY IN VERSE [3] survives in one manuscript of the late fourteenth century. Headed "Recapitulacio omnium terrarum ciuitatumque tocius mundi" and composed in irregular lines with some attention to rime, the piece divides the known world into the usual three regions of medieval T-O maps and enumerates the countries of Asia (in 26 lines), Africa (23 lines), and Europe (29 lines). Prester John's legendary kingdom is singled out, and an attempt is made to distinguish African countries according to their distances from Asia and Europe.

THE STATIONS OF ROME [4], in predominantly octosyllabic couplets, describes for prospective pilgrims the relics and indulgences to be found at the churches and shrines of Rome. Probably in circulation by the late thirteenth century, this popular guide emphasizes the sacred city (and some early church history) and depicts little of the marvels of Rome. As much as a spiritual guidebook, it seems to be a brief for the superiority of Rome over Compostella or the Holy Land as a pilgrim destination (see [14] below). "Hit were no neod to mon in cristiante / To passe in to þe holy lond ouer þe see / To Jerusalem ne to kateryne," for the indulgences at Rome are plentiful and sufficient. Surviving in both verse and prose versions, which vary considerably in content, it underlies later guides to Rome like those by the Purchas pilgrim [9], Capgrave [12], Wey [13], William Brewyn, the compilers of *Information for Pilgrims unto the Holy Land* [17] and *Arnold's Chronicle* [18], and other eastward-travelling English pilgrims.

MANDEVILLE'S TRAVELS [5], a first-person narrative of European, Near Eastern, and Asian journeys made during the early fourteenth century, was probably composed in French, on the Continent, around 1357, possibly by an Englishman. According to Seymour, the Mandeville textual authority, the French original of the *Travels* was circulating in England by 1375 and formed the basis for the first English prose translation (extant in 32 manuscripts and known as the Defective Version because it lacks the account of Egypt). Three other English prose translations followed, a now lost version made in the late fourteenth or early fifteenth century and the Cotton and Egerton versions done in the early fifteenth century. Until the publication of the Cotton Version in 1725, the only form of the work available in printed editions was the Defective Version. From the fifteenth and early sixteenth centuries there survive seven other English renditions of the *Travels*: the Bodley Version, a prose abridgment of the lost English translation, which emphasizes the exotic and fabulous elements of the original; the imperfect Metrical Version, a sensationalized retelling in couplets totalling 2949 lines which develops Sir John Mandeville into an English romance hero and, apart from some attention to Rome and the Holy Land, describes mostly marvels; the Stanzaic Fragment, an incomplete account in 313 lines of both Mandeville's and Marco Polo's encounters with the Great Chan and Mandeville's interview with the Sultan; the prose Epitome, a redaction summarizing Holy

Land pilgrimage sites and routes as well as information on Asian regions; prose extracts from the original concerning Biblical matters and information useful to Holy Land pilgrims (Ashmole); further extracts in prose of a religious and devotional nature (Digby); and the short Ripon fragment, two discontinuous pages containing several passages from the *Travels*. (In that these last four partial renderings ultimately derive from the Defective Version, they may not finally warrant designation as discrete versions; a forthcoming critical edition of the Defective Version will help to clarify their relation to that earliest English form of the work.) The English versions of the *Travels* account for only a little more than 40 of the nearly 300 known manuscripts of the work written in all of the major European languages.

Debate about the identity of "Iohn Maundevylle knyght" has never been fully resolved. The evidence no longer supports claims that once linked authorship of the book to Jean de Bourgogne, a Liège physician, and Jean d'Outremeuse, a notary of the same place. Some recent studies have revived the previously rejected possibility that the author was an Englishman and may have been an experienced traveller as well. However much he might have travelled, the author read and skillfully conflated in his narrative a whole library of sources—histories, travel accounts, romances, encyclopedias, and geographical and cosmographical writings among them. The book subsumes virtually all kinds of medieval travel and geographical writing. Much of its originality (more recognizable in the full, prose versions) resides in its combination of two usually distinct medieval literary genres, the pilgrim guidebook and the description of wonders of the more distant East. For medieval and later audiences it had a complex appeal and seems to have been variously prized as a devotional pilgrim manual, a homiletic treatise, a satirical reflection on western Christians, an instructive report on marvels and remote places, a book of romance adventure, and (particularly because of its discussion of the size and circumnavigability of the globe) a handbook for later generations of navigators and intellectual geographers. Modern study of the *Travels* has been concerned less with the older questions of sources and authorial identity and more with this diversity and interplay of genres and with the narrative functions of the Mandeville persona.

In the Prologue Mandeville explains that, since for some time there has been no crusade, he, a knight born in St. Albans and for years a far traveller, will compose a book to meet the need of the many Christians who "desiren for to here speke of the Holy Lond" (Cotton).

The first part of the book (chapters 1–15) portrays the world European pilgrims would encounter in taking one of the several land or sea routes to the Holy Land. Mandeville sketches the possible itineraries; informs readers on distances, local history, customs, marvels, relics, and foreign alphabets; and describes at some length the pilgrimage sites in and around the Holy Land. Throughout he displays a wide experience and tolerant skepticism (warning pilgrims to disbelieve claims of the monks of Cyprus that they possess half of the true cross, mentioning that he himself owns a piece of the crown of thorns, noting doctrinal differences between the Roman and Greek churches, and recalling how he declined an offer to marry one of the Sultan's daughters). Chapter 15 is a digest of Islamic customs and belief and includes a lecture by the Sultan about the sinfulness of western Christians and their consequent crusading failures.

The second part of the book recounts Mandeville's exploration of the wonders of the non-Christian world farther east. He discovers there fantastic animals and humans of surprising shapes, powers, and behaviors (some of which are parodies or reminders of Christian practices). He discourses on the roundness of the earth and argues from personal experience, measurement, and anecdote that the world could be circumnavigated (chapter 20). He describes the home of the Amazons, the Well of Youth (at which he drank), the land of the pygmies (whose laborers are giants), the dominion of the great Chan of Cathay, the region of the Tartars, the realm of the legendary Prester John, the bastion of Gatholonabes and his band of assassins, the Vale Perilous (which Mandeville but not all of his companions survived), the isle of Bragman (where people live in preternatural harmony), and at the easternmost edge of the world the earthly paradise (about which Mandeville says "ne can I not speken propurly, for I was not there"). Near the end he states his conviction that "wee knowe not whom God loueth ne whom God hateth" and that most of these non-Christian peoples seem to know the "God of Nature" through "hire naturelle wytt." He closes by admitting that, in order to allow future travellers something to report, he has not included all that he saw and knows of the world.

ADVICE FOR EASTBOUND TRAVELLERS [6] is a short, anonymous fifteenth-century compilation of practical counsel about the risks and attractions of travel in the Mediterranean and Near East. Its author, an obviously experienced traveller (and perhaps a merchant), describes the route of the trip across Europe to Venice and from there by sea and land to Egypt, Jerusalem, Syria, and Turkey and then by sea back to England. Mixed in with this itinerary is a wealth of useful if sometimes repetitious advice. Travellers are cautioned to avoid displaying money or revealing travel plans, to seek out inexpensive lodgings in certain Italian towns, to choose knowledgeable guides who speak several languages, to purchase shipboard bedding and a cage for chickens before leaving Venice, to obtain the doge's letters of recommendation to his Venetian legates in Egypt and Syria, and to depart from Venice for the East in September rather than in March. In Mandevillian fashion, the author remarks knowingly on various places of interest, danger, and importance in the Levant, recommends numerous cures for the costive and the diarrhetic, notes good and bad wines, reminds travellers that many relics are faked, and warns homeward-bound travellers to beware of the pirates who might enslave them. His more general advice is to be alert and fair, "for englissh men have but litell love in meny parties." He finishes with an observation Columbus would echo: "the further ye go, the more ye shall se and knowe."

THE BOOK OF MARGERY KEMPE [7], extant in one mid-fifteenth-century manuscript, contains the record of pilgrimages made in the early fifteenth century by Margery Kempe of Lynn (born ca. 1373). According to this dictated autobiography, she was moved by her own desire to see the holy places and then by the Lord's specific command that she visit Rome, Jerusalem, and Compostella. Her accounts include scant description of the shrines and relics but do depict the hardships faced by a daring, solitary woman pilgrim given to public exhibition of an extreme piety.

After earlier making short pilgrimages to local English shrines, Margery sets out in 1413 or 1414 on the long journey to Jerusalem. Following a thirteen-week pause at Venice, she sails to the Holy Land where she makes the usual stations and, on Calvary, first experiences the loud crying that will become a prominent feature of her contemplative life. During the three weeks she spends visiting various sites, the Saracens (but not her own countrymen) are always solicitous toward her. On her return home she endures the ostracism of her fellow pilgrims, enlists the protective companionship of one Richard of Ireland, goes to Assisi, and visits the customary stational churches in Rome. Leaving Rome after Easter, she goes north to Middleburgh and sails safely back to England despite "gret tempestys & dyrke wedyr," reaching Norwich in May of 1415.

Two years later she leaves Lynn for Bristol on pilgrimage to Compostella. In Bristol she finds Richard of Ireland and repays him a loan, then waits six weeks for an available pilgrim ship. Her very brief report of this trip mentions that she spent seven days sailing to Spain, fourteen days there, and five days sailing home.

Kempe recounts local pilgrimages made between 1417 and 1433, among them journeys to the shrines of the Holy Blood of Hayles, St. William at York, and Walsingham. In the spring of 1433, at the age of about 60, she begins her third and most arduous overseas pilgrimage (accompanied initially by her daughter-in-law). Departing from Ipswich, her ship is driven off course into Norway by "greuows & hedows" storms. After a few days she sails on to Danzig, staying there five to six weeks, then proceeds to Stralsund and Wilsnak (home of the shrine of the Precious Blood). She venerates the relics of Aachen, falls in and out with different bands of pilgrims as she makes her way back to Calais, and arrives home by ship via Dover.

For a fuller discussion of Kempe's book, see the chapter on Mystical Writers.

THE PILGRIMAGES OF THE HOLY LAND [8] is a prose summary of the holy places and their attendant indulgences. Lacking instructions on itineraries and the details of travel, it seems to have been intended more for the edification of nonpilgrims than for the guidance of actual travellers.

See the Holy Land portions of *The Itineraries of William Wey* [13] and *The Stations of Jerusalem* [14] below.

PURCHAS'S PILGRIM ITINERARY [9], a verse account, in four-stress couplets amounting to 1694 lines, commemorates an unidentified English pilgrim's journey to Compostella, Rome, and Jerusalem in about 1422. Four lines in Latin (533–36) place the author in the company of two English clerics then in Italy on business; one of them was Walter Medford, Dean of Wells Cathedral. It is likely that the description of Rome is drawn in part from *The Stations of Rome* [4]. The only known version is that printed by Samuel Purchas in 1625 from a manuscript found in Robert Cotton's library and dated "c. 1425" by Purchas.

The pilgrim's travels take him from Plymouth through Bordeaux to Compostella, across Portugal and Spain into Provence, and over the Alps at the Mt. Cenis pass; from Venice he sails to the Holy Land where he visits the normal pilgrimage sites. In the last 152 lines he recounts the trip home to England. His account includes information on indulgences and rates of exchange as well as commentary on peoples' dress and eating habits, personal observations of two weddings and a funeral, and notices of several universities. He helpfully translates odd foreign names into English. Several times he insists on the truthfulness of what he records by assuring the reader that he was an eyewitness; for instance, he describes only those Holy Land pilgrimages "that I have gon," and in discussing pilgrimages into Egypt he confesses he did not himself make them. While in general the author writes in the past tense of a returned traveller, at moments of religious intensity during his Holy Land visitations he adopts the present tense of a fervid guide. As Richard says, it is difficult to determine whether the work is more "un guide à l'usage des pèlerins ou un récit de pèlerinage."

THE WAY UNTO ROME AND SO TO VENICE AND TO JERUSALEM [10] is a mid-fifteenth-century log for the pilgrimage route from England to Jerusalem, contained in a collection of the works of Hoccleve and Lydgate. Its list of 71 place names comprises the overland route through Germany (known as the "Duche way") to Rome and Venice with subsequent stops at the "ylondys" between Italy and Jaffa. It can be compared with the itinerary preserved in [19] below.

GUIDE TO THE HOLY LAND [11], a long fifteenth-century prose treatise, preserves the engaging, first-hand experiences of an unknown pilgrim's two visits to the holy places. His personal recollections begin and end at Venice (where prospective travellers are warned to make careful, specific arrangements with the ship patron they select). The account describes the traditional attractions of both the Holy Land and the regions surrounding it, although, as the author confesses, "ne I nor none of my feloshippe ded visyte" the latter. As a guidebook the report provides useful information about itineraries and distances, the routines particular to various sites, available hospital care, the behavior of the Saracens, and the activities of other Christian sects. As a narrative, presented in a mixture of present and past tenses, it captures the piety and danger of the preeminent medieval journey; at one point the author fondly recalls bathing in the Jordan and cutting down "smalle trees" on the banks for souvenirs, and at another he remembers how in the harbor at Crete "Wee hadde a mervelus thundreng and lightnyng and att last an erthequak bi whiche the towne of Candia tremled and also oure gali in the water and caused vs to haue grete fere of goddes poyneshment."

THE SOLACE OF PILGRIMS [12], by John Capgrave (1393–1474), is extant in a single, possibly holographic manuscript (and two brief fragments); it is considered to be the best medieval English description of Rome. This learned, prolific East Anglian, from 1453 to 1457 Prior Provincial of the Order of St. Augustine in England, was the author of Biblical commentaries and other theological writings, saints' lives, biographies, and history. He composed his long (170 printed pages) prose guide to historical and Christian Rome soon after making a pilgrimage there in 1449–50.

In a prologue Capgrave underscores the importance of first-hand travel reports by invoking the examples of Pythagoras, Plato, Livy, Jerome, Marco Polo, and John Mandeville. Capgrave's crediting Mandeville with having "made a book ful solacious on to his nacyoun" acknowledges Mandeville's own remark that Christians find "gret solace" in hearing about revered holy places. (See [5] above.) Declaring that the truth of his account depends on written authorities but also on his own observations and opinions, Capgrave divides the book in two, treating first the monuments and topography of pagan Rome and then the numerous churches (and their accompanying indulgences) in the Christian city. An extension of the second section, incomplete in the manuscript, describes the dozen or more Marian churches that are the object of special pilgrim devotion.

Capgrave's admitted uncertainty about the authenticity of much that he sees and hears, along with his general inquisitiveness, makes the work more a personal narrative and less a reprise of earlier guides to the Roman *mirabilia* and stations. (See [4] above.) Of particular interest are Capgrave's comments on the shape of ancient Roman and contemporary English theaters (part I, chapter 5), his curiosity about the rumored catacombs (I, 7), and his thoughts on why women pilgrims are forbidden entry at crowded shrines (II, 5) and why there are so many surviving pieces of the true cross (II, 52).

THE ITINERARIES OF WILLIAM WEY [13] mirror the experience of late medieval pilgrimage more completely than any other English account. Wey (1406–76), a fellow of Exeter College, a founding member of Eton, and later an Austin canon at Edington, composed this English-Latin book late in life after a journey to Compostella (1456) and two trips to Jerusalem (1458, 1462). A large (seven foot by sixteen and a half inch), colored map of the Holy Land survives, possibly of Wey's making, and it is believed to have been designed as a supplement to his Holy Land memoirs. Intended, as Mitchell says, "for an English public travelling in an orthodox and economical manner," Wey's book is a thorough and reliable manual of travel for other pilgrims as well as a record of his own pilgrimages.

Four parts of the book containing practical information are in English: the opening item, an explanation of changes in currency travellers must make in going from England through Italy to Syria (in prose); the second item, "A preuysyoun," Wey's careful checklist of the equipment to be obtained and arrangements made by pilgrims before departing for Jerusalem (also in prose); the third item, a 352-line verse itinerary in four-stress couplets describing the circuit of the Holy Land pilgrimage sites (see [14] below); and, following Wey's report of his second voyage to Jerusalem, an English-Greek vocabulary list. Wey's narrative of the Compostella journey, in Latin, includes an English couplet about the hazardous southernmost point of England: "Be the chorel neuyr so hard, / He shall quwake by the berde ar he passe Lyzarde."

Wey's checklist for pilgrims embarking at Venice is even more precise than

the one found in *Advice for Eastbound Travellers,* [6] above, specifying as it does
the advantages of arranging a package tour with the ship's patron and the
exact kinds and amounts of food, drink, medicine, bedding, and monies
pilgrims should take with them. Typical of the shrewd advice throughout is
his reminder that pilgrims, when riding on mule-tours in the Holy Land,
"be not to muche byfore, nether to fer byhynde yowre felowys, for drede of
screwys." His verse itinerary summarizes the chief attractions of the established Holy Land pilgrimages; it imitates *The Stations of Jerusalem* [14] in a
few places, although both pieces probably derive from a common verse-
advertisement for the holy places. (Compare also the itineraries in [19] below
and the list of Holy Land stations in [8] above.)

Wey's narrative-guidebook reveals him to be an uncomplaining, eager traveller, observant of more than the pilgrimage shrines. His essay on the ten
reasons that can lead people to make the Holy Land pilgrimage embraces
the range of pious and worldly motivations for travel. Nearing Compostella,
he counts 84 ships in the harbor, 32 of which he notices are English; he
provides an account of the annual ceremonial marriage of the doge to the
sea, which he witnessed in Venice in April 1462. One of Wey's English companions on the 1458 Jerusalem pilgrimage, John Tiptoft, Earl of Worcester,
arranged for Mass to be celebrated on Mount Calvary, and Wey delivered
the sermon at it. (Wey also wrote a book of Latin sermons, a copy of which
he gave to Syon Monastery.) At his death his collection of pilgrimage souvenirs included relics as well as wooden miniatures of the holy places.

The narrative of Wey's first Jerusalem pilgrimage can be usefully examined (as Mitchell has shown) in conjunction with those written by five other,
non-English pilgrims who made the voyage in his company. It should be
compared also with *Information for Pilgrims unto the Holy Land* [17], which
draws heavily on it.

THE STATIONS OF JERUSALEM [14], surviving in two slightly differing
fifteenth-century versions, presents a seeming eyewitness report of a completed pilgrimage to the Holy Land. The itinerary describes a departure
from Venice, stopovers at the pilgrim ports of eastern Mediterranean islands,
and the standard Holy Land pilgrimages to places associated with the lives
of Jesus, Mary, the Apostles, and early Church figures.

As a guidebook for other pilgrims, its value lies in its itemizing of the indulgences attaching to various holy places and especially in its evocation of the Biblical and spiritual significance of those sites. The author frequently dramatizes an important episode in the lives of Jesus or Mary by having them speak (and in the Huntington manuscript version the meeting between Mary and Elizabeth is highlighted by the insertion, after line 724, of 80 lines of the *Magnificat* from Lydgate's *Life of Our Lady*). In response to the emphasis of *The Stations of Rome* [4], this work insists that the preeminent goal of pilgrims should be the Holy Land, since "Fore all þe pardone þat is in Rome / There is þe well, & thens it come."

Suggestions that *The Stations of Jerusalem* is very similar to the English verse itinerary found in William Wey's itineraries [13] are overstated; one couplet (lines 357–58) appears in Wey and there are echoes of a few other lines, but the many dissimilarities (and differences between the sequences of the two itineraries) argue for at most an indirect relation between the two pieces. The poem consists almost entirely of irregular four-stress couplets, although at the beginning and end there are flourishes of riming quatrains, sestets, and octets.

See also the list of venerated sites in [8] above.

A RUTTER OF THE ENGLISH COAST [15] is extant in three late-fifteenth-century manuscripts (one of which belonged to the Pastons, another to John Astley) which suggest an earlier original. It is one of but a half dozen or so European pilot-books that date from before the sixteenth century. Like other rutters, this one provides mariners with coastal place names and their compass bearings from one another, landmarks visible from sea (e.g., the "parissh steple"), information on the direction and flow of tides and the periods of high and low tide at various ports, and a list of soundings and types of sea bottoms (particularly for the island of Ushant and the southern English coast). The sailing directions chart routes along the east and south coasts of England (from Berwick-upon-Tweed to Land's End), the Atlantic coasts of France and Spain (down to Gibraltar), the west side of England up through the Bristol Channel and St. George's Channel, the coasts of Wales and Ireland, and the Bay of Biscay. Burwash has shown that this rutter differs from contemporary continental rutters in arrangement and detail and that it was intended for sailors very familiar with the English coastline. It was a source for the popular *Rutter of the Northe* compiled by Richard Proude in the mid-sixteenth century.

See also under [18] below the sailing directions offered in *Arnold's Chronicle*.

THE CABOT VOYAGES AND BRISTOL DISCOVERIES [16]. There are no known contemporary narratives in English memorializing the Atlantic voyages of John and Sebastian Cabot and the exploratory activities of Bristol merchants and sailors in the late fifteenth and early sixteenth centuries. However, there is an abundance of documentary evidence from the time, much of it in English, which chronicles Atlantic exploration during the reign of Henry VII and confirms particular voyages undertaken by John Cabot in 1497 and 1498. While the evidence, as Williamson says, "is meagre and the reading of some of it uncertain," it deserves study as part of the record of late medieval English travel and geographical writing.

The pertinent documents, assembled by Williamson (1962) and Quinn (1979), include information about the pre-Cabot discoveries of Bristol sailors, the voyages of John Cabot, later Bristol explorations, and the early sixteenth-century voyages of Sebastian Cabot. One important document, not discovered until 1956, is a letter in Spanish written in 1497–98 by a Bristol merchant, John Day, to the Grand Admiral in Spain (apparently Christopher Columbus) concerning John Cabot's voyaging. In it Day (who also lived in London under the alias Hugh Say) makes what is the earliest known reference to the now lost *Inventio fortunata,* a fourteenth-century Latin account allegedly by Nicholas of Lynn about supposed travels in the north Atlantic, a copy of which Day says he had intended to send to his correspondent along with two other items he did enclose, an edition of Marco Polo and "a copy of the land" (possibly a version of Cabot's running chart). Day's letter refers as well to earlier fifteenth-century Atlantic commerce and exploration undertaken by merchant adventurers out of Bristol, a fact known to the early fifteenth-century author of *A Libel of English Policy* (see XIII [249] in *Manual*, vol. 5) and alluded to by William Worcestre in his *Itineraries* around 1480.

The continuing debate by historians, geographers, and cartographers over the meaning of the evidence surrounding English maritime ventures in this period has underscored the major role played by Bristol (especially through its mercantile relations with Portugal and Iceland) in encouraging English interest in westward exploration.

INFORMATION FOR PILGRIMS UNTO THE HOLY LAND [17] is testimony to the continuing English participation in the Jerusalem pilgrimage during the late fifteenth and early sixteenth centuries. The three published de Worde editions of 1498, 1515, and 1524 (only one copy of each of which survives) derive from the original late fifteenth-century version composed presumably in Latin, possibly by an otherwise unknown "mayster Larkes" (see [22] below), chiefly indebted to *The Itineraries of William Wey* (see [13] above), and in large part translated into English prose some time before de Worde's first edition. Like the pilgrimage account in Purchas [9], Wey's book [13], and *Advice for Eastbound Travellers* [6], this work blends advice and instruction with the narrative of a specific Holy Land pilgrimage. Just 57 printed pages in length, it would have been a conveniently portable guidebook for travellers.

The work has eleven sections: an itinerary for the route from Calais to Italy, some of which is in Latin; an itinerary for "the duche waye" (see [19] below), partly in Latin; information on rates of exchange between England and Syria; suggestions about provisions for the voyage from Venice to Jaffa (nearly all of which is copied from Wey); a list of the tolls and admission fees for places along the Holy Land itinerary (Latin); the narrative of one band of pilgrims' journey to and throughout the Holy Land, the conclusion of which is in Latin; a brief report of a return trip as far as Italy (Latin); a short reflection on the brevity and vanity of this world (Latin); lists of numbers and helpful phrases (e.g., "Thou shalt be payed to morow," "Where is the tauerne") in "Moreske" and Greek and a list of numbers in Turkish; an abbreviated stations of Rome (Latin) (see [4] above); and a note on the signification of parts of a church (Latin).

Calendar references in the pilgrimage narrative suggest that the journey occurred in 1481, 1487, or 1492. This third-person account describes a June departure from Venice of 46 pilgrims "in a shippe of a marchauntes of Venyse callyd John Moreson," stops at the eastern islands, perils at sea, the hazards of the labyrinth on Crete, the temperate Mediterranean climate, and the pilgrimages (and accruing indulgences) to be found in the Holy Land and Egypt.

THE COPY OF A CHART COMPASSING THE CIRCUIT OF THE WORLD [18] is a catalogue in prose of the known countries of the world, made by the London merchant Richard Arnold (died 1521?) and included in the miscellany he compiled sometime before 1503. Although known as *Arnold's Chronicle*, the miscellany is actually a derivative collection of varied documents about ancient and contemporary London life, some of which reappear in sixteenth-century chronicles. The volume also preserves the earliest known version of *The Nut-Brown Maid* (see VII [61] in *Manual*, vol. 3). *The Copy of a Chart*, one of several geographical and travel pieces in the collection, was reprinted a number of times in the sixteenth century under the titles *Mappa Mundi* and *The Compost of Ptholomeus*; it is preceded in the volume by a note on the dimensions of England (see [1] above), which gets repeated in two contemporary MSS, Balliol 354 and Lansdowne 762 (ff 2^b–3^a), and it is followed by a description of the stations of Rome (see [4] above), the Sultan's letter to the pope (from *Mandeville's Travels*), a log for the distances between towns from Calais to Naples, and a selection from *Mandeville's Travels* on Saracen customs and belief (see [5] above). This assortment of information reflects the ordinary range of late medieval English travel interests but none of the more recent advances of continental geographers or the activities of Bristol seamen.

Arnold introduces *The Copy of a Chart* (that is, a map) by mentioning his source, a "gret bok" on the parts of the world commissioned by Julius Caesar, and he says the reliability of that work is attested by Bartholomaeus Anglicus, Marco Polo, Ptolemy, and Aristotle. Having "nedur lust ne leysour to copy alle tho book," Arnold merely presents a list of countries according to their locations in the four quarters of the earth (noting also such attractions as the trees of the sun and the moon and the ark of Noah atop Mount Ararat). Following this four-part list are three paragraphs of information on sailing directions and distances, in miles, from Flanders by way of Gibraltar to Syria, from Syria back to Venice, from Syria along the coast to Egypt, and from Turkey back to Ireland and England (see [15] above).

THE WAY TO ITALY [19] is a log of the towns and intervening distances (given in miles) along the two major land routes from England to Italy. One is "The waie fro Ynglonde to Rome by Frawnce" (which lists 82 place names and the distances between them); the other is "The waye fro Ynglonde to

Rome by Flanders and Duchelonde" (81 names). The work also identifies five shorter itineraries for the routes from Rome to Naples (11 names), Rome to Venice (26), another for Rome to Venice (18), Venice north through the Alps (21), and Venice to Milan (9). William Wey's record of his trip from England to Rome duplicates the second of these itineraries (see [13] above).

See also the itineraries described in [10] and [17] above.

THE PILGRIMAGE OF SIR RICHARD GUYLFORDE TO THE HOLY LAND [20] was written by Guylforde's unknown chaplain and travelling companion after the 1506 journey and before Pynson's 1511 publication of the prose narrative (only one copy of which survives). Guylforde (1455?–1506) served Henry VII as engineer and shipbuilder, privy councillor, and controller of the royal household. While on pilgrimage, he and another companion (John Whitby, prior of Gisburn in Yorkshire) grew ill, died in Jerusalem, and were buried in Mount Syon cemetery.

Although he borrows considerably from the narrative of Bernhard von Breydenbach's 1483 pilgrimage, Guylforde's chaplain convincingly reports the particular pilgrimage he and his group made. He describes what any pilgrim might see (Venice's famed relics and the doge's Corpus Christi procession) but also records unique observations (the artillery and bustling naval activity in the harbor of Venice, for instance, something Guylforde would have noticed). He notes the eastern island birthplaces of Helen and Venus and complains vividly about the "bare, stynkynge, stable grounde" of the cave he and others were kept in by the Saracens upon landing at Jaffa. After discussing Guylforde's death and the pilgrimages of the region, the chaplain depicts a part of the pilgrimage journey not commonly found in such narratives, the return-trip home. It takes the chaplain and his group more than four months to sail back to Venice; his narrative here dwells memorably on the unending wintry storms at sea, the frightened pilgrims' vows to go on other pilgrimages if spared, the repair of a lost rudder, the defection of some passengers to other ships, and the fear of enslavement by the Turks, all of it adding a realism rarely encountered in pilgrimage narratives.

See [21] below.

THE PILGRIMAGE OF SIR RICHARD TORKINGTON TO THE HOLY LAND [21] is the journal of a trip made to the Holy Land in 1517–

18 by the parson of Mulberton, Norfolk. Torkington apparently carried with
him as a guidebook a copy of the Guylforde chaplain's recently published
narrative (see [20] above); his observations and itinerary amount to little
more than a wholesale replication of the chaplain's account. Most of the time
he copies the earlier narrative verbatim. At many points, however, in order
to authenticate the fact and dates of his own journey, he omits observations
of the chaplain which he himself could not have made (noting, "As they say,
I saw it not"); and he adds to or sometimes abridges descriptions (retelling
the chaplain's story of the return-trip storms at sea, for instance, but with
less anxiety and detail). He does record events peculiar to his own trip (such
as the Jewish wedding he witnessed on Corfu), and when he borrows he
often rearranges the material to fit the sequence of his own journey (for
instance, reporting a visit to the tomb of Lionel, son of Edward III, in Pavia
as an event occurring on the trip out rather than, as in the chaplain's pilgrimage, during the return voyage). If Torkington's memoir is not an act of
forgery, his conspicuous dependence on an earlier narrative for an account
of what he also personally experienced exemplifies more obviously than most
medieval travel writings the habit of merging authority and experience.

THE PILGRIMAGE OF ROBERT LANGTON [22], which survives in
one copy of Copland's 1522 edition, commemorates the several journeys of
Robert Langton of Appleby, Westmoreland, to shrines in Spain, France, Italy,
and Germany sometime during the 1490's and early 1500's. Langton (died
1524) was one of the founders of Appleby Grammar School; he studied at
Padua and (in 1493) at Bologna and held a variety of ecclesiastical appoint-
ments in England.

His book, the last known medieval English pilgrimage account, is a collection of brief diary entries (in Latin) marking his itineraries, followed by
a series of annotations (in English prose) on 42 of the more important places
he visited. His travels took him to Compostella, Venice (the subject of his
longest note), Rome, and Cologne as well as to numerous smaller shrines;
and the annotations constitute a valuable catalogue of the treasures and relics
known to late medieval pilgrims.

Langton occasionally interrupts his generally pious observations to record
other kinds of information, for instance, noting that nearby Padua is the
tomb of Petrarch, "no saynt / but a grete clerke," and that at Naples is a

grotto where Virgil was buried. Most striking is his notation that in Rome "at Beluidere aboute the hyl be certayne antiquitees / as ye statue or ymage of Lacaon in whyte marble / with his .ii. sones by hym wrapped with serpentes. And therby is Venus cum Cupidine. Also Appollo cum Pharetra." The Laocoon was found and exhibited in 1506, and Langton's apparently firsthand account here may stem from a visit to Rome in that year or after.

In a short preface to his book, Langton recommends that Jerusalem-bound pilgrims consult "mayster Larkes boke," adding that "to me and other englysshe pylgrymes that went this yere it was a grete light guyde and conducte." Larke may have been the pilgrim-author of *Information for Pilgrims unto the Holy Land* [17].

MEDIEVAL MAPS WITH ENGLISH INSCRIPTIONS [23]. A variety of maps produced in medieval England provide a natural complement to English geographical and travel writings of the period in that some of them visualize and draw upon travel itineraries and many of them contain English inscriptions.

There survive from before 1500 no vernacularly inscribed examples of the portolan sailing chart or the traditional T-O world map (neither Gerald of Wales' map of about 1200 nor the map in Hereford Cathedral made by Richard of Haldingham about 1300 carry English nomenclature). However, there are a number of extant English land maps with vernacular inscriptions which represent some or all of the British Isles. Among the mid-thirteenth-century manuscripts of the chronicles of Matthew Paris are preserved four maps of Great Britain which are thought to be constructed around an itinerary between Dover and Newcastle. The famous Bodleian Gough map (ca. 1360) likewise reflects the experiences and needs of travellers in its reliable description of roads, distances, and places; it is the first European road-map of an entire country. Another map of Britain, anonymous and based on the Gough map, dates from about 1400. The Englishman John Hardyng supplemented an account of Scotland and the description of his journey there in 1418–21 with a schematic map (existent in three manuscript versions) which depicts and names towns, castles, and other inhabited places.

A related kind of English cartography, the local map or plan, survives in unexpected abundance. Of the 34 local maps and drawings from before 1500 so far discovered, five contain inscriptions entirely in English, and eighteen

others feature a mixture of English and Latin notations. For the following
list of such maps, arranged chronologically, I am indebted to Professor Paul
D. A. Harvey, the authority on these maps, who generously furnished me
with material from his and R. A. Skelton's forthcoming *Local Maps and Plans
from Medieval England,* which gives full transcriptions of the maps and discusses each one in detail. The list below identifies only maps containing
English writing (labelled E) or a mixture of English and Latin; the numbers
correspond to Harvey's:

3. Wildmore Fen, Lincolnshire (1224–49)
4. Peterborough, Northamptonshire (mid- or late fourteenth century)
5. Isle of Ely, Cambridgeshire, and Holland, Lincolnshire (late four-
    teenth century)
6. Cliffe, Kent (late fourteenth century–1408)
8. Isle of Thanet, Kent (late fourteenth century–1414)
10. Sherwood Forest, Nottinghamshire (E, late fourteenth century–early
    fifteenth century)
12. Inclesmoor, West Riding of Yorkshire (ca. 1407)
13. Exeter, Devonshire (ca. 1420)
14. Tursdale Beck, County Durham (ca. 1430–ca. 1442)
15. Durham (1439–ca. 1442)
16. Shouldham, Norfolk (1440–41)
17. Durham (1440–45)
18. Boarstall, Buckinghamshire (1444–46)
19. Clerkenwell and Islington, Middlesex (E, mid-fifteenth century)
21. Chertsey, Surrey, and Laleham, Middlesex (mid- or late fifteenth cen-
    tury)
22. Staines, Middlesex (1469–ca. 1477)
23. Deptford, Kent and Surrey; Lambeth, Surrey; London (E, 1470–78)
24. Barholm, Greatford, and Stowe, Lincolnshire (late fifteenth century)
25. Deeping Fen, Lincolnshire (E, late fifteenth century)
26. Dartmoor, Devonshire (late fifteenth–early sixteenth century)
27. Denham, Buckinghamshire, and Harefield, Middlesex (ca. 1478)
29. Northwest Warwickshire; Tanworth in Arden, Warwickshire (E,
    1497–1519)
30. Exeter, Devonshire (1499)

XX. WORKS OF RELIGIOUS AND PHILOSOPHICAL INSTRUCTION

by

Robert R. Raymo

In the preparation of this chapter I have incurred many debts, but none greater than to Dr. A. I. Doyle of the University of Durham whose path-making studies on this subject and vast knowledge of Middle-English manuscripts, so generously and patiently shared, have been of inestimable value to me. I offer him my sincere and profound gratitude. Special thanks are also due to Dr. George A. Thompson, Dr. Sally Sanderlin, Ms. Eileen Bentsen, and Dr. Judith Glazer for their help and support. I am also indebted to Dean John Leyerle and Dr. Sarah Ogilvy-Thomson for the loan of unpublished texts, to Ms. Jean F. Preston, Dr. B. S. Benedikz, and Ms. Sara S. Hodson for verifying manuscript material in the Princeton, Worcester Cathedral, and Huntington libraries, and to Dr. V. A. Gillespie and Dr. Stella Brook for permission to read their dissertations.

Robert R. Raymo

1. Works of Religious Instruction

I. Long Compilations of Religious Instruction

1. Versions of *Manuel des péchés*

HANDLYNG SYNNE [1]. A free verse translation by Robert Mannyng of Brunne of the Anglo-Norman *Manuel des péchés* (or *pechiez*). It runs (in Sullens's edition) to 12,638 lines in rough, octosyllabic, riming couplets, and survives in three nearly complete copies and six fragments and extracts. The *Manuel* was composed in Lincolnshire in the third quarter of the thirteenth century and was later expanded to include devotional and ascetical material. 25 known manuscripts testify to its continuing popularity throughout the Middle Ages. The ascription of authorship to William of Waddington in some manuscripts is now considered spurious. *Handlyng Synne* consists of a prologue and commentary embellished with illustrative tales and anecdotes on the Ten Commandments, Seven Deadly Sins, Sacrilege, Seven Sacraments, Twelve Points of Shrift, and Twelve Graces of Shrift, corresponding to Books 2, 3, 4, 5, and 7 of the primitive *Manuel*. Book 1 on the Articles of the Faith was omitted. The later accretions of Books 6, 8, 9, and 10 were (if

Mannyng knew of them) ignored. Although *Handlyng Synne* follows the general form of the *Manuel*, it drops nine of the French tales, substitutes alternative versions of two others, and directly translates only about half of the 8,500 lines that occupy Books 2 to 5 and 7. On the other hand, it expands the commentary by a third or more through the insertion of a considerable number of explanatory passages, extensive social commentary and complaint, and the introduction of twelve new tales—topical stories for the most part—that were designed to appeal to a popular, regional audience. The result is a work perceptively different from its source. The *Manuel* is an exemplary guide for priests on how to instruct their parishioners regarding confession and how to hear their confession. *Handlyng Synne* is addressed to the common people and is meant to assist them in the examination of their consciences prior to confession. It appears from lines 10,807–10,818 and 11,306–11,310 that Mannyng himself read it to a lay congregation probably in connection with a course of Lenten instruction. He began *Handlyng Synne* in 1303 as a Gilbertine canon in Sempringham Priory and completed it in 1317. The prologue, which relates a few details of his life and discusses the scope and purpose of the work, was written sometime after its completion. According to Dr. A. I. Doyle, it may have been still in composition as late as 1332. Mannyng's other work, the metrical *Chronicle of England* based on Wace and Peter of Langtoft, was completed in 1338 at Sixhills Priory where he spent the last years of his life. Both *Handlyng Synne* and the *Chronicle* reveal him to be a man of genuine learning, broad human sympathy, and strong moral conviction. He has little to offer as a poet, but he was a born storyteller, as Pearsall remarks, and his edifying narratives are full of verve and variety.

The manuscripts of *Handlyng Synne* are separated from the time of its composition by nearly a century at least and are at one or more removes from their exemplars. None is complete or free of scribal revision and confusion, and none preserves the author's original dialect which is presumed to be Lincolnshire. A new edition by Sullens replacing Furnivall's is based on the smoothest and most complete of the manuscripts, Bodleian Library Bodley 415. Unfortunately, it lacks explanatory notes and glossary. A parallel text edition of the Bodley, Yale, Cambridge, and Dulwich manuscripts, together with the corresponding portions of the *Manuel des péchés*, is in preparation by Dr. Susan Schulz and Dr. Raymond Biggar for the Early English Text Society.

In the early fifteenth century an anonymous Midlands poet composed a 3000-line commentary with 23 illustrative tales on the Seven Virtues Opposed to the Seven Deadly Sins, the Five Wits, the Seven Deeds of Mercy, the Seven Sacraments, the Seven Principal Virtues, and the Seven Gifts of the Holy Ghost and appended it to the fragment of *Handlyng Synne* in Cambridge University Library MS Ii.4.9. A partial copy of this commentary is also found in British Library MS Harley 3954. Sullivan regards it as a "Continuation" and argues that it represents "an attempt by a new composer confronted with a fragment of the original *Handlyng Synne* to complete it upon what he took to be original lines."

Ker discovered twenty lines of verse about secrecy at confession "*ex libro qui vocatur manuele pecche*" in Westminster Diocesan Archives, London, MS H.38, an early fifteenth-century Carthusian miscellany. The lines are not from *Handlyng Synne,* and may derive from a lost translation of the *Manuel des péchés.*

OF SHRIFTE AND PENANCE [2]. A literal and nearly complete prose translation of the *Manuel des péchés* dating from the late-fourteenth or early-fifteenth century. It lacks Book 6 and four tales. The epilogue is placed between Books 8 and 9 which appears in a shortened form. The English translator was apparently aware of the different styles employed in the expository, homiletic, and devotional portions of his French source, but his slavishness prevented him from reproducing them with any success. The identification by Hope Emily Allen of the Anglo-Norman manuscript from which he worked—British Library MS Harley 4971—makes it possible to study his techniques as a translator closely. The dialect is predominantly Midland with an admixture of Kentish and Southern forms. An edition by Tess S. Singer and Klaus Bitterling is in preparation for the Middle English Texts series.

PETER IDLE'S (or IDLEY'S) INSTRUCTIONS TO HIS SON [3]. A didactic poem in rime royal divided into three books and written between 1445 and 1450. Book 1 is a miscellany of worldly wisdom and practical advice culled from two widely circulated Latin treatises by Albertanus of Brescia entitled *Liber consolationis et consilii* and *Liber de amore et dilectione Dei et proximi*. Books 2 and 3 are an abridgment of *Handlyng Synne* interspersed with passages taken from Lydgate's *Fall of Princes*. The ending of the poem is lost together with several exempla from the Seven Deadly Sins and subsequent sections owing to the mutilated and fragmentary state of the ten extant manuscripts. It is clear from a version of the *Instructions* in an early sixteenth-century manuscript recently acquired by the British Library, Additional MS 57335, a version unknown to its modern editor, Charlotte D'Evelyn, that Idley realized his intention (as expressed in the Prologue to Book 2) of reworking *Handlyng Synne* in its entirety and covering the Ten Commandments, the Seven Deadly Sins, Sacrilege, the Seven Sacraments, the Twelve Points of Shrift, and the Twelve Graces of Shrift. He was not an accomplished poet, and his work, although it enjoyed contemporary popularity as embodying the parochial wisdom of its age often embellished wih aureate diction, makes tedious reading today. His career in public life was more distinguished than his career as a man of letters. A Kentishman, he rose from county bailiff to Controller of the King's Works under Henry VI. The *Instructions* are written in a Midland dialect.

2. Versions of *Somme le roi*

AYENBITE OF INWYT [4]. A close literal translation of the *Somme le roi* extant in British Library Manuscript Arundel 57. According to the preface and colophon which are in the same hand as the text, it was written at Saint Augustine's, Canterbury, and finished on October 27, 1340, by Dan Michel of the Northgate who is presumed to be the translator as well as the scribe. Dan Michel has been identified with a secular clerk who took priestly orders in 1296 and later became a Benedictine monk. He must have been 70 and more when he wrote the text, and this may account both for the somewhat archaic nature of his script and the conservative features of his Kentish dialect, as Dr. Pamela Gradon has noted. Among the 24 works he left to Saint Augustine's library was an unidentified copy of the *Somme le roi*. A second copy of the *Somme le roi* in Saint Augustine's library has been identified as British Library MS Cotton Cleopatra A.v. W. N. Francis advanced the view that either the exemplar or a copy of Cleopatra was the text from which the *Ayenbite* was translated, but he appears to have been mistaken. The work, although of inestimable philological value, has little or no literary interest. There are many inaccuracies in the translation, owing in part perhaps to an imperfect source, and its slavishness often makes comprehension difficult. Certainly there are few if any felicities of expression or style. The author informs us in the epilogue that it was written in Kentish to keep fathers and mothers and other kindred of the neighborhood from sin. After a brief preface and a detailed table of contents, he follows his source, a compilation made by Friar Laurent in 1280 for the use of Phillippe III, and gives expositions of the Ten Commandments, the Articles of the Creed, the Seven Deadly Sins, the Sins of the Tongue, then instructions how to die and how to distinguish good from evil, and finally expositions of virtue in general, the Seven Petitions of the Pater Noster, and the Seven Gifts of the Holy Ghost. It is unlikely that his work was widely read or known.

Appended to the *Ayenbite,* in the same hand and dialect, and presumably by the same author, are a collection of prayers (see [24], MS 30), a translation of the Pseudo-Anselmian *De custodia interioris hominis* (see [134]), and a treatise on the difference between man and beasts [164].

THE BOOK OF VICES AND VIRTUES [5]. An anonymous Southeast Midlands prose translation of the *Somme le roi* executed about 1375. The complete text is extant in three manuscripts. W. N. Francis, its editor, was of the opinion that it was based on the family of *Somme* manuscripts represented by British Library MS Royal 19.C.ii. Carruthers, however, in a recent comparative study of English translations of the *Somme,* argues that it is closer to the tradition stemming from Bibliothèque Mazarine MS 870 and the closely related British Library MS Additional 54180. The translation is not free of inaccuracies, but it is the most graceful and polished of the Middle English versions of the *Somme.* Its style is more elaborate and rhetorical than its source, and it shows a marked preference for words and phrases of French origin. The Simeon copy of *The Book of Vices and Virtues* (British Library Manuscript Additional 22283) substitutes the *Standard Orthodox Exposition of the Ten Commandments* [43] for the *Somme*'s version and, in addition to the *Somme*'s version of the Pater Noster commentary, provides a text of the short version also found independently in University College, Oxford, MS 97. The copy of *The Book of Vices and Virtues* in British Library MS Additional 17013 contains a copy of the *Standard Exposition of the Pater Noster* commentary [33] in addition to the *Somme*'s.

OTHER VERSIONS OF SOMME LE ROI [6]. In addition to *Ayenbite of Inwyt* and *The Book of Vices and Virtues,* there are at least eight other translations, partial or complete, of *Somme le roi.* All are in Midlands prose of the fifteenth century.

(a) A literal translation of the sections on the Seven Deadly Sins and Learning to Die, less than a third of the entire *Somme,* in British Library MS Royal 18.A.x. Dr. A. I. Doyle notes that it corresponds at least in part with Bodleian Library MS Ashmole 1286.

(b) A literal translation of the section on the Seven Deadly Sins, ending imperfectly in the discussion of lying, the fifth of the ten sins of the tongue, in British Library MS Additional 37677.

(c) A translation of the section on the Seven Deadly Sins, preceded by a brief disquisition, not from the *Somme,* on the nature of sin, when and why it occurs, and its harmful effects, in British Library MS Harley 6571.

(d) A faithful translation of the sections on the Seven Gifts of the Holy Ghost and Learning to Die in Bodleian Library MS Ashmole 1286.

(e) A translation, indifferently executed by a priest for his personal use, of the last half of the *Somme,* beginning with the section on Learning to Die, in Corpus Christi College, Cambridge, MS 494.

(f) *Adventure and Grace,* a nearly complete and literal translation of the *Somme,* lacking only the section on the Articles of the Faith, in Bodleian Library MS e.Mus.23. The title is explained in the Colophon: "þeras I was not perfecte of the language of frensch by symple undirstondyng of the langage methought it was Vertues I aventured to draw it into Englisch. And in many places ther I coude not englisch it grace of the Holy Ghost yafe me englisch acordyng to the sentans wich come of grace. So þe ferste bygon with aventure and so folowide grace." It was made in 1451 by a "Knight of King Henry the Sixth" whom Dr. E. Wilson and Dr. A. I. Doyle have identified as Sir Robert Shottesbrook of Faringdon, Berkshire.

(g) A translation of the first chapter of the section on Learning to Die said in the three extant manuscripts (Bodleian Library Douce 322, Cambridge University Library Ff.5.45, and British Library Harley 1706) to have been extracted from a work, otherwise unknown, entitled *Toure of All Toures.*

(h) *Ryal Book,* an accurate and readable version of the *Somme* made by William Caxton at the request of a London mercer, probably William Pratt, and finished 13 September 1484. It may have been printed within a year thereafter, but more probably in 1487 or 1488. Wynkyn de Worde and Richard Pynson reprinted it in 1507. It is complete save for the substitution of a much longer and totally different treatment of the Commandments from that of the *Somme.*

3. Works Derived from *Somme le roi*

SPECULUM VITAE [7]. A translation and rearrangement of material drawn from *Somme le roi,* Rolle's *Form of Living,* and other unidentified sources in over 8,000 short couplets. The dialect of the original is either Northern or Northeast Midland. 40 known manuscripts attest to its considerable popularity. Some of them incorrectly attribute its authorship to Rolle, others, with considerably greater probability, to William of Nassyngton, proctor of the ecclesiastical court of York, who wrote a *Treatise on the Trinity* and possibly a paraphrase of Rolle's *Form of Perfect Living.* It was composed in the third quarter of the fourteenth century and received a searching scrutiny by the Chancellor of Cambridge University and his Council in 1384. In the introduction the author declares that he intends it to be read aloud for the instruction of illiterate men who have no knowledge of either French or Latin. He begins with a discussion of the profit and worth of the Pater Noster, then provides a long initial commentary on its opening words, *Pater Noster qui es in celis,* incorporating an exposition of the Ten Commandments, the Articles of the Faith (not from the *Somme*), Seven Sacraments, Seven Principal Virtues, and Seven Works of Bodily and Spiritual Mercy, and concludes with an exhaustive analysis of the Seven Petitions of the Pater Noster which gain the Seven Gifts of the Holy Ghost. These, in turn, remove from the soul the Seven Deadly Sins and replace them with the Seven Virtues which lead it to the Seven Beatitudes and Seven Rewards. Dr. A. I. Doyle regards the *Speculum* as a "kind of vernacular sermon-book which makes a conscientious effort to give the listeners a balanced and comprehensible picture of life in relation to the Church and to God." Venetia Nelson finds the focus of attention on the Vices and Virtues and properly observes that "of the works that sought to present the episcopally approved catechesis [in the fourteenth and fifteenth centuries] it is at once the most straightforward in content and the most elaborate in structure." A critical edition of the *Speculum* for the Early English Text Society is in preparation.

A MYROUR TO LEWDE MEN AND WYMMEN [8]. An abridged prose version of the *Speculum Vitae* written in the Southwest of England during the late fourteenth or early fifteenth century. The only significant departure from its source (apart from the occasional introduction of exemplary or explanatory material) is the substitution of a new introduction developing its central theme of a mirror whereby "lewde men and wymmen . . . may see God þorgh stedfast byleve and hemself þorgh mekeness." The author was an orthodox secular priest who wrote in a simple, unadorned, occasionally rhythmical style in keeping with his evangelical purpose of instructing "lewed and menliche lettred men and wymmen" in the elements of the faith.

JACOB'S WELL [9]. A collection of 95 sermons elaborately developing the penitential theme that mankind must be cleansed of sin as a "wosy pytt" is cleansed of pollution. The instruments to be used for this purpose are Contrition, Confession, and Satisfaction, together with the elements of the faith, including the Five Inner and Outer Wits, the Virtues opposed to the Deadly Sins, the Creed, the Works of Bodily and Spiritual Mercy, the Ave Maria, the Pater Noster, and the Ladder of Heaven consisting of Charity, Truth, Justice, and Mercy. The author of this ingenious and relentless moralization is unknown, but he was almost certainly a Franciscan preaching in the area of Salisbury (where the unique manuscript of his work survives) in the early fifteenth century. For much of his material, he is heavily indebted to the *Speculum Vitae* [7] and the *Alphabetum Narrationum*. The dialect is London with some Kentish forms.

Caxton's translation of the *Doctrinal of Sapience,* a widely circulated French prose text of the late fourteenth century based largely on the *Somme le roi,* has already been discussed in the *Manual* (see IX [45] in vol. 3). Some passages are drawn directly from the *Ryal Book.* The topics it covers are the Twelve Articles of the Faith, Charity, the Seven Deadly Sins, the Seven Gifts of the Holy Ghost, the Seven Sacraments, the Ten Commandments, the Five Wits, the Pater Noster, the Ave Maria, and Purgatory, Hell, and Heaven.

4. Version of *Miroir du monde*

MIRROURE OF THE WORLD [10]. A graceful and idiomatic translation of a conflated version of the *Miroir du monde,* composed anonymously before 1280, and the *Somme le roi,* composed by Friar Laurent in 1280 for the use of Phillippe III of France. The basic source of both works is Guillaume Perrault's *Summa vitiorum et virtutum.* Although the *Somme* which derives in part from the *Miroir* far outstripped its rival in popularity, scribes in the late fourteenth and fifteenth centuries produced different combinations of the two texts. Dr. E. Brayer distinguishes four such combinations, and it is to one of them, which she designates redaction y, surviving in ten manuscripts, that the Middle English translator had access. The *Mirroure* provides commentary on the Ten Commandments, the Articles of the Faith, the Seven Deadly Sins, Confession, the Petitions of the Pater Noster, the Gifts of the Holy Ghost, and the Seven Virtues. It is uniquely preserved in Bodleian Library MS Bodley 283, owned and perhaps commissioned by Thomas Kippyng, draper and citizen of London, with illustrations by a Utrecht artist working in London during the late fifteenth century. The dialect is London with an admixture of Devonshire forms which are probably of scribal origin.

5. Works Derived from *Miroir du monde*

DISCE MORI [11]. A vast compendium of religious doctrine intended for private reading. It was compiled for a religious, not necessarily a nun, called Dame Alice by a highly educated priest, perhaps her confessor, probably of Syon Abbey, who was 59 at the time of its composition in the early fifteenth century. It consists of five parts, commencing with *Ars Moriendi* and continuing with commentaries on the Seven Deadly Sins, temptations and tribulations, penance, and the Pater Noster and Seven Gifts of the Holy Ghost interspersed with much familiar didactic and devotional material, including a form of confession and a summary of the elements of the faith (Seven Deadly Sins, Seven Virtues, Seven Sacraments, Seven Works of Bodily and Spiritual Mercy, Twelve Articles of the Faith, and Ten Commandments). The treatise concludes with a long Exhortation, apparently appended sometime after the composition of the main body of the text, to contemplation and the love of God. Its main sources are a conflated version of *Miroir du monde* and

Somme le roi, Raymond of Pennaforte's *Summa casuum poenitentiae,* David of Augsburg's *Formula novitiorum,* the *Chastising of God's Children,* an *Honest Bede* [177], a "Lytil tretise aȝenes fleischly affecyoneȝ and alle unthrifti lustis" [Jolliffe, no. K.1], Mechtild of Hackeborn's *Liber spiritualis gratiae,* and various works of Rolle and Hilton. Doubtless many other sources remain to be identified. There are two extant manuscripts, Jesus College, Oxford, 39 and Bodleian Library, Oxford, Laud Miscellaneous 99, which are closely related. The dialect is East Midland. There may be an excerpt in the Hopton Hall manuscript.

IGNORANCIA SACERDOTUM [12]. A compendium of religious doctrine compiled after Lyndwood's *Provinciale* (1433) and derived entirely from *Disce Mori,* the material having been abridged and rearranged specifically for the use of parish priests as a guide to virtuous conduct and an aid to preaching. It discourses on the Creed, the Seven Sacraments, the Works of Bodily and Spiritual Mercy, the Ten Commandments, Penance, and the Seven Virtues, concluding with a form of perfect living. The editor used Jesus College, Oxford, Manuscript 39. In an original prologue he urges his fellow priests to lead virtuous lives, reminding them that they are bound to a counsel of perfection. They are exhorted to occupy their hearts with pure thoughts and their bodies with good deeds and to preserve the highest order on earth—the priesthood—in cleanness. At the end of the prologue is a paraphrase of the ten points "how a man may most profite to himself and plese God" ascribed to Saint Bonaventure.

6. Versions of *Livre des bonnes meurs*

VERSIONS OF LIVRE DES BONNES MEURS [13]. The *Livre* is a condensation and translation into French of the second and third parts of the *Sophilogium* (or *Sophologium*), a handbook of the liberal arts and a guide to Christian life, which circulated widely in Europe during the fifteenth and sixteenth centuries. The *Sophilogium* was composed about 1404 for Michel de Creney, Bishop of Auxerre. The *Livre* was completed in 1410 for Jean, Duke of Berry. Earlier, between 1404 and 1407, a translation into French of a portion of the first part of the *Sophilogium,* dealing with the liberal arts, was made for Louis, Duke of Orléans, under the title of *Archiloge sophie.* The

Latin original and its French translations were the work of Jacques Legrand, a celebrated Augustinian preacher and master of theology in Paris during the late-fourteenth and early-fifteenth centuries. He is known to have made at least two visits to England on diplomatic business for the Duke of Berry. Although the *Archiloge* achieved only limited popularity, the *Livre* was widely read and excerpted. Four independent English translations entitled *Book of Good Manners*, *Book of Good Condicyons*, or *Sophiloge of Wisdom*, were made in the fifteenth century. Caxton's version, executed in 1486 and printed in 1487, has been briefly discussed in the *Manual* (see IX [40] in vol. 3). According to E. G. Duff, it was based on an edition printed by P. le Rouge at Chablis in 1478. He dealt freely with the original, omitting many passages and transposing chapters. An earlier version by John Shirley who ascribed the original to "John of Wiegnay" was completed in 1440; it survives in his holograph manuscript, British Library Additional 5467. Lindström suggests that he may have followed the French version in Cambridge University Library MS Ff.1.33. A third version is in British Library MS Harley 149 and a fourth in Glasgow University MS Hunterian 78 and Henry E. Huntington MS HM.39872 (formerly Beaumont College [Old Windsor]). Professor Denton Fox has recently proposed that the latter version may be the work of Stephen Scrope.

7. Version of *L'Ordinaire des Chrétiens*

THE ORDINARYE OF CRYSTYANYTE (or OF CRYSTEN MEN) [14]. A. Chertsey's translation of *L'Ordinaire des Chrétiens* printed by Wynkyn de Worde in 1502 and 1506. It is divided into five books and deals with the Sacrament of Baptism, the Twelve Articles of the Faith, the Ten Commandments, the Seven Deadly Sins, the Five Commandments of the Church, the Works of Bodily and Spiritual Mercy, the Twelve Manners of Spiritual Almsgiving, Confession, Penance, the Pains of Hell, and the Joys of Paradise. The French source, composed in the third quarter of the fifteenth century, was first printed about 1485 and frequently thereafter.

8. Native Compilations

SPECULUM CHRISTIANI [15]. A translation of a widely circulated Latin-English pastoral manual compiled in the late fourteenth century for

the use of the clergy. It served several different but complementary purposes—as a vehicle for the instruction of the laity in the rudiments of belief
according to the Peckhamite formulae, as a confessional guide, and as a
practical compendium of miscellaneous material to assist the clergy in the
execution of their duties. It is not, as Pfander argued, mainly a preaching
manual, but it almost certainly had a homiletic function, and parts of it may
have been used for public recitation. It is composed of eight quasi-indepen-
dent treatises called "tabulae" whose sparse commentary is supported by
numerous citations from scriptural and patristic authorities interspersed
(both in the Latin and in the vernacular texts) with didactic and devotional
verses in English. The compiler made extensive use of an earlier fourteenth
century Latin manual entitled *Cibus animae* and drew other material from
Peckham's *Constitutions,* Peter Lombard's *Sentences,* Rolle's *Form of Living,*
Grosseteste's *Templum Domini,* the *Speculum Sacerdotis,* an anonymous *Treatise
on the Priesthood,* and Flete's *De Remediis contra temptaciones.* The verse, which
is written in different dialects and meters (mainly quatrains and couplets),
also had an independent life and is found in manuscripts other than of the
Speculum Christiani. The English translation survives in a single manuscript,
British Library Harley 6580, dating from the mid-fifteenth century when
the popularity of the *Speculum* was at its height; its dialect belongs to the East
Midlands in the area of Lincolnshire. There is no evidence to support Holmstedt's assertion that the anonymous author of the *Speculum* was a Franciscan
and its translator a Lollard. In the view of Dr. Vincent Gillespie, who has
closely studied its sources and cultural tradition, it is probably the work of
a Carthusian of Mount Grace and/or secular priests of York Minster.

The Prologue draws a distinction between preaching and teaching and dwells on the need to
dispel ignorance of God's word as well as on the responsibility of the clergy for the cure of souls
and the instruction of the laity in the basic tenets of the faith, as prescribed by the *Lambeth Constitutions.* The first table treats of the Athanasian and Apostles' Creeds; the second of the Ten Commandments with the rewards and punishments of those who observe and those who violate them,
and the Two Precepts of the Gospel; the third of the Seven Works of Bodily and Spiritual Mercy,
the Seven Principal Virtues, the spectacle of righteous and sinful men on their death beds, the
former borne to heaven, the latter to hell, concluding with an account of the General Judgment; the
fourth of the Seven Deadly Sins. The fifth table discusses the three things that defile man (the sins
of heart, mouth, and deed), the three things that cleanse him of sin (contrition, confession, and
satisfaction); the six things that preserve him from sin (fear of the punishments of sin after death,
avoidance of wicked company, temperance in food and drink, honest work, protection of the wits
from evil deeds, hearing and reading God's word), the three things that lead him to virtue (the
example of holy men and women, the great goodness and mercy of God, meditation on the joys of

heaven and the pains of hell). The sixth table relates the popular tale of the king who summoned four philosophers to account for the disasters that had befallen his kingdom. Each gave three replies: the first said, Might is Right, Light is Night, Fight is Flight; the second, Single is Double, Friend is Foe, Weal is Woe; the third, Lust is Law, Thief is Reeve, Pride has Place; and the fourth, Will is Counsellor, Reason is Wrong, God is Dead. The seventh table entitled the *Boke of Wysdom* calls on man to amend his life, recognizing that the wisdom of this world is but folly. The eighth table is a miscellany of familiar devotional and didactic materials mainly on eucharistic and penitential doctrine and practice together with a summary of the contents of the compilation. It includes a Levation prayer, a penitential prayer to the Blessed Virgin (in verse), the duties and dignity of the priesthood, three things needful to curates (light, sight, and salt or wisdom), the four kinds of priests (those that follow gluttony, lechery, or vainglory, and those that follow righteousness), a moralization of priestly vestments, a defense of the claustral life, the sins of idolatry, the three kinds and the two "lettyngs" of prayer, tribulation as heaven's gate, patience in adversity, the ability of men to resist the devil's temptation, a meditation on the vanity of worldly desires, a brief *ars moriendi*, a warning against presumption, the three kinds of apostasy, the seven ways sins are forgiven (baptism, martyrdom, confession and penance, tears, almsdeeds, forgiveness of our malefactors, charitable works), the sins of the Britons, the obligation to pay tithes, the proper bases of marriage, impediments to the payment of the marital debt, the nine tokens of man's love of God, how virtue is turned to vice and vice to virtue, false flattery as opposed to the compassionate and measured correction of vice, and impartial justice.

BOOK TO A MOTHER [16]. A long prose treatise by a country priest to his widowed mother (and by extension to a lay audience generally) who is considering a religious life. He bids her follow the life of Christ in the world, drawing out its lessons for all those who seek salvation and holding up Mary as the model of true and perfect discipleship. The *Book* is heavily scriptural, about a fourth of it consisting of illustrative Biblical material, and it can be regarded as an extended commentary on Matthew 12.50. Other borrowings come from patristic sources, the *Legenda Aurea*, the Pseudo-Bonaventuran *Meditationes Vitae Christi*, and the *Ancrene Riwle*. The central metaphor may have been derived from the *Charter of Christ* [187]. Although the four extant manuscripts belong to the fifteenth century, they are all imperfect copies at one or more removes from the original which is thought to have been composed between 1370 and 1380 in a Southwest Midlands dialect. The author was probably educated at Oxford and was fundamentally orthodox, although he slightly reflects Wycliffite doctrine on predestinarianism and dominion by grace. He often rails against contemporary corruption among both the clergy (especially the religious clergy) and the laity, and he urges a close imitation of Christ as a means of reform.

After stating his purpose, the author provides a summary of the elements of the faith—the Pater Noster, Ave Maria, Creed, Ten Commandments, Seven Works of Bodily Mercy, and Seven Gifts of the Holy Ghost, the last three items being accompanied by brief explanations. Then the Beatitudes are related to the Seven Gifts of the Holy Ghost, and selections from the first three chapters of the Canticles are set forth as the proper "song" for the soul possessed of the Seven Gifts and Beatitudes. Finally, the Seven Sacraments are enumerated. Following this presentation, the author addresses his mother: Since children can pay no greater honor to their parents than to seek their salvation, I have chosen for you a book that teaches all men to be Christ's brother, sister, and mother, a book from which you will learn Christ's lessons of meekness and well-ordained love, of good deeds, and obedience to the Commandments. This book is Christ. Observe His life. Learn of His humility, poverty, and chastity—virtues with which He endowed Mary. Be at one with Christ through Sacred Scripture and imitate Mary whose name signifies the sorrow of penance and the star of good example. From Anna learn to be a good widow. Stay, mother, within the cloister whose four walls are prudence, justice, fortitude, and temperance. Let Christ be your abbot. His Rule is but to be meek and humble of heart. Learn from the Gospel how men shall be Christ's friends and disciples and shall glorify His Father. Here follow selections from the New Testament. The treatise concludes with an appeal to obey the Commandments.

MEMORIALE CREDENCIUM [17]. A long compilation of unknown authorship which originated in Gloucestershire in the early fifteenth century. Despite its Latin title it was composed for "lewed men that konne not understonde latyne ne frenssche." Its main sources are William of Pagula's *Oculus sacerdotis (Dextera pars)*, a Latin treatise on the remedies of the Seven Deadly Sins known as *Postquam*, Raymond of Pennaforte's *Summa Casuum Poenitentiae*, Thomas Chobham's *Summa Confessorum*, Edmund of Abingdon's *Speculum ecclesiae*, and John de Burgo's *Pupilla Oculi*. Nearly two thirds of the work is occupied by an extended commentary on the Ten Commandments (introduced by a version of the *Ten Vengeaunces of God* [48]) and the Seven Deadly Sins and their Remedies. The remainder consists of chapters on Penance, Tribulation, Temptation, and Charity, and brief expositions of the elements of the faith, including the Petitions of the Pater Noster, Three Theological Virtues, Articles of the Faith, Seven Sacraments, and Four Cardinal Virtues. The *Memoriale* is extant in four complete and four partial manuscripts. Its closest affinity is to *Pore Caitiff* (see the chapter on English Mystical Writings in a later volume of the *Manual*) which it resembles in its purpose and its fluent, unadorned prose.

PRICK OF CONSCIENCE (or STIMULUS CONSCIENCIE or KEY OF KNOWING or THE FLOURE OF CONSCIENCE or SPECULUM HUIUS VITE) [18]. A long eschatological poem describing the wretchedness of man's nature and condition and expounding popular doctrine on the four last things—death, judgment, heaven, and hell. It contains a prologue and seven parts and runs (in Morris's edition) to over 9,600 lines in short riming couplets. Judging from the number of known manuscripts as well as from their geographical distribution and dialectical diversity, it was the most popular English poem of the Middle Ages. Its authorship remains a mystery. It has been misattributed to Richard Rolle and Robert Grosseteste. Similarities between the *Prick of Conscience* and the *Speculum Vitae* led Hope Emily Allen to suggest that William of Nassyngton was the author. In Derek Britton's view, the *Prick of Conscience, Speculum Vitae, Band of Loving* (Brown-Robbins, no. 11), and *Stimulus Conscientie Minor* (Brown-Robbins, no. 244) are the work of a single poet. There can be no doubt of his wide learning. The *Prick of Conscience* is based on a large number of Latin and French sources, among them, St. Augustine's *De civitate Dei,* Honorius of Autun's *Elucidarium,* Bartholomaeus Anglicus's *De proprietatibus rerum,* the French version of Robert Grosseteste's *De penis purgatorii,* Hugh Ripelin of Strassburg's *Compendium theologice veritatis,* Innocent III's *De contemptu mundi,* and various works of Anselm and Bernard. It circulated in four versions. The Main (or original) Version was composed in the north of England, probably in Yorkshire, about 1350 and survives, in the form of complete or incomplete copies and extracts, in 104 manuscripts, many of them owned by the secular clergy for whom the poem provided a valuable source of didactic and homiletic material not otherwise accessible in English. The *Prick of Conscience* was also available in a Southern Recension, originating in the Thames valley, which exists in eighteen manuscripts; an abbreviated version entitled *Speculum Huius Vite* which exists in two manuscripts of the early fifteenth century; and a Latin prose translation, probably of the late fourteenth or early fifteenth century, which is extant complete in five manuscripts and partially in a sixth. The English works indebted to the *Prick of Conscience* include *Of the Flode of the World* [180], *þo Whele of Fortune* (Brown-Robbins, no. 230), *Stimulus Conscientie Minor* or *Markys of Meditacion* (Brown-Robbins, no. 244), and, possibly, Chaucer's *Parson's Tale.*

The Prologue notes that God, the beginning and end of all things, made man, His chief work, in His own likeness and endowed him with reason and free will. If he is to take the way of wisdom and attain eternal bliss, he must first acquire self-knowledge, taking care to avoid the obstacles that stand in its way—beauty, popular favor, the fervor of youth, and wealth. This work is divided into seven parts. *Part I* treats of the wretchedness of man's nature. His life is full of misery and corruption until the end death takes him and his foul body becomes food for worms. *Part II* describes the condition of the world. Here man is but a pilgrim whose eternal abode is beyond the visible world. It is perilous for him to love the world which is fickle and deceptive, the devil's servant, God's enemy, like the sea, a wilderness, a forest, a battle field. Dame Fortune helps it to defeat man. Wealth draws him from the right way. The wise man will place no trust in the world where evil is called good and good evil, knowing that eventually God's vengeance will descend on the wicked. *Part III* is on death, the fear of death, and the four special reasons for this fear. It is attended by great pain and anguish. About the dying man gather horribly disfigured devils. He is confronted with the stark realization that he must soon give an account of his life and is uncertain of his future state. Man should prepare himself for death well in advance and think of the last day. *Part IV* describes the location and purpose of Purgatory, its seven pains, the sins that send to Hell, venial sins and their ten remedies, and the means (prayer, almsdeeds, fasting, and the Mass) by which the pains of Purgatory may be shortened and alleviated. Through the power given to Saint Peter, the Church can release Christendom from the debt of pain in Purgatory. *Part V* is on the signs of Doomsday—the destruction of Rome, the coming of Antichrist, the Fifteen Tokens of the Day of Doom, and the Judgment. *Part VI* describes the location and the fourteen pains of Hell—heat, cold, filth and stench, hunger, thirst, darkness, the hideous sight of devils, vermin, beating by devils, gnawing of conscience, scalding tears, shame and disgrace, bands of fire, and despair. *Part VII* is on the joys of Paradise—everlasting life, rest, goods, peace, pleasure, light without darkness, day without night, summer without winter, riches, nobility, honor, power, security, delights, joy and happiness, play, laughter, melody and song, praise, friendship, love and harmony, rewards, reverence, obedience, virtues, wisdom, beauty, and the sight of God—together with the special dowers of the body (brightness, swiftness, strength, freedom, health, perfect joy, and everlasting life) and of the soul (wisdom and knowledge of the Trinity, friendship, unity and concord, power, honor, security, and perfect joy). The heavenly city is described, and a contrast is drawn between the beauty and bliss of the saved and the corresponding misery and pains of the damned. This treatise is called the *Prick of Conscience,* for whoever reads it with understanding will be stirred to dread, love, and meekness and be brought to the right way of life.

Reference should also be made to the commentaries on the Pater Noster, Ten Commandments, and Creed contained in *Pore Caitiff* and to the commentaries on the Seven Deadly Sins, Seven Principal Virtues, Ten Commandments, Seven Sacraments, Twelve Articles of the Faith, Seven Petitions of the Pater Noster, Seven Gifts of the Body and the Soul, Seven Works of Mercy, and the Punishments of Hell found in the *Mirror of Holy Church.* Both works are discussed in the chapter on English Mystical Writings in a later volume of the *Manual.*

Two severely damaged and faded fragments of fifteenth-century instructional religious poems are in Cambridge University Library MS Additional 4407 (Robbins-Cutler, no. *3339.8) and British Library MS Cotton Vitellius F.XIII (Robbins-Cutler, no. 3458.5).

II. Manuals of Instruction in the Elements of the Faith

1. Compilations of Elementary Instruction

THE LAY FOLKS CATECHISM (or JOHN GAYTRYGE'S SERMON)
[19]. A rhythmical prose translation and expansion of Archbishop John Tho-

resby's instructions to the clergy of the Province of York concerning the religious education of the laity. The instructions were modelled on Archbishop Peckham's *Lambeth Constitutions* of 1281 and provided brief expositions of the articles of the Creed, the Ten Commandments, the Seven Sacraments, the Seven Works of Mercy, the Seven Virtues, and the Seven Deadly Sins, concluding with the promise of an indulgence of 40 days to all who learned them. They were issued in 1357 together with the vernacular version made at Archbishop Thoresby's request by John Gaytryge (alias Gaybrige, Gaytring, de Taystek, de Caterick), a monk of St. Mary's Abbey, York. Although the contents of the instructions are rudimentary, confining themselves to the fundamentals of Christian belief and practice, they mark, as Dr. Vincent Gillespie has observed, "a significant stage in the evolution of the vernacular pastoral manual by conferring official approval on and encouraging the circulation of a vernacular version of his [Thoresby's] Latin original." Gaytryge's introduction makes clear that the work was primarily intended for oral transmission by a priest to his parishioners in church. Many of the manuscript colophons refer to it as a "sermo" or "predicacio." The title, *Lay Folks Catechism,* by which it is commonly known, is misleading and without authority. Later in the fourteenth and throughout the fifteenth centuries its use was extended to both private reading and public recitation. No other vernacular compendium of elementary religious instruction matched its popularity. It survives in distinctive Northern and Southern forms, in the Trinity College version ([20] below), in *Quattuor Sermones* ([21] below), and in a Wycliffite redaction which more than doubled its original length. Dr. David Lawton has demonstrated that the Sermon was written in rhythmical prose under the influence of the *ars dictaminis* rather than in unrimed alliterative verse.

TRINITY COLLEGE CAMBRIDGE MS 305 (B.14.19) [20]. An expanded prose version of the *Lay Folks Catechism* dating from the early fifteenth century with the addition of a section on the Pater Noster and Ave Maria. The earlier Lollard prose version of the *Lay Folks Catechism* in Lambeth Palace Library MS 408 (MS 17 in [19] above) also contains an additional, although unrelated, Pater Noster section.

QUATTUOR SERMONES [21]. A prose adaptation by William Caxton of the *Lay Folks Catechism* following the format of the Trinity version (introduction and seven tenets of the Christian faith, including the Pater Noster sections) with the incorporation of materials from *Pore Caitif* and other works of religious instruction, among them, possibly, *Speculum Christiani* [15], *The Book of Vices and Virtues* [5], and Lavynham's *Treatise on the Seven Deadly Sins* [106]. To the exposition of the tenets of belief is added a short, independent treatise on penance possibly related to *The Clensyng of Mannes Soule* [84], concluding with *The General Sentence of Excommunication* [229], identical with that found in Bodleian Library MS Rawlinson A.381, and a *Bidding Prayer* [203]. Caxton printed the first edition of *Quattuor Sermones* between June 30, 1483, and March 26, 1484. A second edition appeared shortly thereafter and a third edition possibly in 1491. It was issued again by Rood in 1486 and by Pynson and Wynkyn de Worde in 1493. A combined edition with Mirk's *Festial* was printed by Wolfgang Hopyl in 1495 and by Martin Morin in 1499. None of the fifteenth-century prints bears a title. Its modern title, clearly a misnomer, was given it by bibliographers who mistakenly regarded it as a collection of four sermons.

SACERDOS PAROCHIALIS [22] and EXORNATORIUM CURATORUM [23]. The *Sacerdos Parochialis* is a prose manual based on Peckham's *Lambeth Constitutions* for the use of parish clergy. It is extant in ten fifteenth-century manuscripts and circulated widely in the south of England as an alternative text to the *Lay Folks Catechism*. It deals with the Pater Noster, Ave Maria, Creed, Ten Commandments, Seven Deadly Sins, Seven Principal Virtues, Two Precepts of the Gospel, Seven Sacraments, the Sentence of Excommunication, and the Bidding Prayer. The last two items are sometimes omitted. The Seven Works of Bodily Mercy, although not a part of the original program of instruction, appear in several manuscripts. British Library MS Burney 356 also has the Five Wits and miscellaneous religious verses, Bodleian Library MS Rawlinson D.913 a form of confession (see [88] below), and Bodleian Library MS Bodley 110 a copy of *De Visitacione Infirmorum* [215].

A later compilation, *Exornatorium Curatorum*, printed by Wynkyn de Worde (ca. 1515) and reprinted by Richard Pynson (ca. 1520) and Henry Pepwell (ca. 1530), bears some similarity to the *Sacerdos Parochialis* and may have originated with it. It is also addressed to the parish clergy and covers much the same material, treating the Creed, Ten Commandments, Seven Works of Bodily Mercy, Seven Deadly Sins, Seven Principal Virtues, Seven Sacraments, and the five troubles or temptations at the hour of death and how to overcome them.

MISCELLANEOUS MANUALS [24]. In addition to the comprehensive works of religious instruction and the compendia derived from Peckham's and Thoresby's constitutions, a vast number of manuals for public and private use were available to the clergy and laity during the Middle Ages. They often combined in whole or in part the basic formulae of belief derived from episcopal legislation with other kinds of religious material to satisfy a multiplicity of needs. Dr. C. A. Martin, who has made an extensive study of this literature in connection with his forthcoming edition of Edinburgh University Library MS 93, suggests that they be studied not as collections of independent texts but within the specific framework of the codices in which they are found. Thus he proposes a classification into: (1) manuals in which the elements of the faith are the sole or predominant texts probably for the use of the clergy in catechizing the faithful; (2) manuals inserting the elements of instruction into predominantly liturgical and homiletic texts such as Horae or Primers; (3) manuals combining the elements of instruction with devotional and moral texts such as Edinburgh University Library MS 93; (4) manuals blending the elements of the faith with meditative texts such as *The Mirror of Sinners* and *The Three Arrows of Doomsday* (see the chapter on English Mystical Writings) in order to direct the readers' thoughts to the Last Day; and (5) miscellaneous extracts of manual material and devotional and moral texts to provide guides to a more perfect way of life. The identification and description of manuals according to these criteria, the complex interrelationship of their texts, their locations and dialects, as well as their associations with contemporary religious movements all remain to be established.

A GOOD AND A PROFITABLE TABLE OF THE FEYTH OF CHRISTIAN PEOPLE [25]. A comprehensive tabular summary of the elements of the faith with the inclusion, perhaps at a later date than the original composition, of several items not usually found in manuals.

The table consists of the following items: Seven Principal Virtues, Seven Deadly Sins and the opposing Virtues, Seven Deeds of Bodily and Spiritual Mercy, Seven Sacraments, Seven Petitions of the Pater Noster, Seven Gifts of the Holy Ghost, Two Principal Commandments of the Law, Ten Commandments, Five Outer Wits, Four Counsels of Christ that belong to a perfect man (sobriety and humility, poverty of spirit, chastity, charity), Eight Beatitudes, Seven Dowers of a Glorified Man (see [243–244] below), Principal Joys of Paradise (see [243–244] below), Principal Pains of Hell (see [245–246] below), Six Ages of the World, Seven Ages of Man, Twelve Articles of the Faith and how they were made, Spiritual Clothes of the Soul (Innocence and Matrimonial Chastity), and Spiritual Nourishing of the Soul (God's Word).

BACULUS VIATORIS [26]. A dialogue entitled *The Traveller's Staff* between Bubulcus (a ploughman) and Clericulus (a youth or young clergyman) on the elements of the faith is conducted mainly in Latin, but the Pater Noster, Ave Maria, and Creed are given in English prose and the Ten Commandments, Seven Deadly Sins, and the Seven Works of Bodily Mercy in English verse. The Baculus, or staff, of instruction will presumably support the ploughman in his pilgrimage through life. Its source is probably *Pupilla oculi.*

A RYGHT PROFYTABLE TREATYSE [27]. A miscellany of the elements of the faith, occasional prayers, and devotional works compiled from French and English sources by Thomas Betson, a late-fifteenth-century monk of Syon Abbey. It was intended for the instruction of both clergy and laity. The elements of the faith include: Form of Confession, Pater Noster, Ave Maria, Creed, Two Commandments of the Law, Seven Virtues opposed to the Seven Deadly Sins, Seven Deeds of Bodily and Spiritual Mercy, Seven Gifts of the Holy Ghost, Four Cardinal Virtues, Seven Sacraments, and Ten Commandments. Among the tracts are *VII Things to Bear in Mind* [103], *A Short Remembrance of Confession* [89], *VII Degrees of Humylyte* [75], *VII Degrees of Obedience* [82], *VII Degrees of Patience* [72], and *XV Degrees of Charity* [59]. Many of the same materials are found in St. John's College, Oxford, MS 173 and Caxton's *Ars Moriendi* [218]. The *Treatyse* was printed by Wynkyn de Worde in 1500.

THE POEMS OF WILLIAM OF SHOREHAM [28]. Seven poems extant in a single manuscript, British Library Additional 17376, dating, it would appear, from the second quarter of the fourteenth century. William, a native of Shoreham near Otford in Kent, was an Austin Canon of the priory of Leeds and became vicar of the neighboring Chart sometime after 1320 when it was appropriated to Leeds by Walter Reynolds, archbishop of Canterbury

(1313–27). His death, probably at an advanced age, if indeed he was the William de Shoreham ordained acolyte by Peckham at Croydon in 1287, occurred during the archiepiscopate of Simon Mepham (1327–36) whose patronage he may have enjoyed. According to a colophon at the end of the fourth poem, Mepham granted a quadragene to those who said the Pater Noster and Ave Maria for the repose of William's soul.

Four of the poems were intended for a lay audience as part of an oral instruction on the elements of the faith. The first poem in 320 intricate seven-line stanzas of varying length riming abcbded begins with a reflection on the shortness of life, the inevitability of death, and the sacraments as a means of salvation. Then follows an exposition of the individual sacraments, concluding with matrimony which occupies over a quarter of the work. The second poem in 43 eight-line stanzas of alternate four and three stresses riming abcbdbeb deals with the Ten Commandments, first divided into two groups of three and seven, the former related to the love of God and the latter to the love of mankind, and then explicated individually in the traditional order with frequent exhortations to mankind to obey them. The third poem in 424 four-stress stanzas riming abab discusses the evils of sin in general, its origin, the differences between original and actual sin, and the seven deadly sins with particular attention to pride. The fourth poem is incomplete. Its purpose may have been to provide a compendium of universal history after the manner of *Cursor Mundi* [31]. It gives an explanation of the Trinity, Creation, origin and purpose of Evil, and the Fall, breaking off after the Redemption at line 894. Of the remaining pieces, two are Marian lyrics and the third is a version of the *Patris sapientia* (see [227]).

William was a learned scholar, a conscientious churchman, and a more competent and inventive poet than is generally recognized. He was ill-served by a careless copyist whose dialect was different from his own. Fundamental work remains to be done on his text, sources, and style which he shaped as a suitable medium for oral instruction and public devotion.

THE POEMS OF JOHN AUDELAY [29]. Preserved in a single manuscript, Bodleian Library MS Douce 302, written in the first half of the fifteenth century.

John Audelay served as a chantry priest to a Shropshire lord, Richard Lestrange, and later lived in the Augustinian abbey at Haughmond near

Shrewsbury until his death not long after 1426. He describes himself as deaf and blind. It is altogether doubtful that he is the author of all the 55 poems in the Douce manuscript which he regarded "as an anthology of spiritual counsel to be entitled Concilium Conciencie or Scala Celi." Many of the poems, particularly among the carols, must have been adapted from earlier compositions; others, however, can be confidently ascribed to Audelay and show considerable technical virtuosity. Several pieces on didactic and devotional themes constitute in the aggregate a course of instruction in the elements of the faith. A sequence of five carols, identical in length and structure (27 lines each; five stanzas riming ababc, plus refrain), deals with the Ten Commandments, Seven Deadly Sins, Seven Works of Mercy, Five Wits, and Seven Gifts of the Holy Ghost. There are also poems on the Petitions of the Pater Noster (seven eleven-line stanzas riming ababababcdd), *De Visitacione Infirmorum et Consolacione Miserorum* [219], *Hours of the Cross* (ten nine-line stanzas riming aaaabcccb) [227], *De Meritis Missae* [197], *Nine Virtues* (102 lines in eight thirteen-line stanzas, imperfect at the beginning, riming ababbcdcdeeed) [157], *Christ's Shedding of Blood against the Seven Deadly Sins* (23 six-line stanzas riming aabccb), a Levation prayer (an introductory six-line stanza followed by eight eight-line stanzas riming aaabcccb and three six-line stanzas) [204], *Sunday Observance* (sixteen thirteen-line stanzas riming ababbabacdddc), and an acephalous treatise on the Seven Deadly Sins (263 lines in twenty thirteen-line stanzas riming ababbcbcdeeed). The dialect is Northwest Staffordshire.

AN ABC OF DEVOCIONE [30]. A versified compendium of instruction and devotion in 36 rime royal stanzas comprising a poem to the Cross, the Petitions of the Pater Noster, Ave Maria, Credo, a Form of Confession, Grace before and after Meals, and prayers for salvation and the souls in purgatory found in the English Register of Godestow Abbey.

CURSOR MUNDI (or THE CURSOR O THE WORLD) [31]. A monumental, versified history of man from the Creation to Doomsday consisting of a prologue and seven parts corresponding to the seven ages of the world together with four concluding poems and in some manuscripts an additional six or seven poems on devotional and instructional themes. There are three different forms of the text. The original, composed by an anonymous parish

priest in the north of England about 1300, contained the complete chronological history and four concluding poems, as described in the Prologue
(lines 131–222); it may survive in the fragmentary Edinburgh manuscript.
This version was later expanded to include the six or seven additional pieces
found in three Northern manuscripts (Cotton, Fairfax, and Göttingen), although not all of them are found in any single manuscript. Finally, a Southern version appeared, containing only the Prologue and chronological
history, probably in the mid-fourteenth century. It is extant in four Southern
manuscripts (Arundel, Trinity, Laud Misc. 416, and British Library Additional 36983).

In its fullest form the *Cursor* runs to almost 30,000 lines generally in short
couplets. Octosyllabics change to septenaries in the account of Christ's passion, and there are occasional passages of mono-riming lines. The appended
poems employ a variety of verse forms. From internal evidence it is clear
that the text was intended for oral recitation.

Its materials are drawn from an exceptionally large number of sources.
In addition to the Vulgate, extensive use was made of Peter Comestor's
Historia scholastica, the Old-French Bible of Herman de Valenciennes, an
anonymous Old-French poetic paraphrase of Genesis and Exodus, *Post Pec-
catum Adae*, *De Imagine Mundi* and *Elucidarium* of Honorius Augustodunensis,
Legenda Aurea, New Testament apocrypha, Grosseteste's *Chateau d'Amour*, Is-
idore of Seville's *Etymologiae*, Wace's *L'Establissement de la Fete de la Conception
Notre Dame*, *De Revelatione* of Pseudo-Methodius, and many others.

A critical edition by Sarah M. Horrall of the Southern version, using the
Arundel manuscript as the base text, is in progress. The Northern versions
are available in Morris' parallel text. Although the transcriptions are generally accurate, the critical apparatus is altogether out-of-date, and a new
edition with a full commentary on the manuscript relations, language,
sources, and style is a prime desideratum of Middle English studies.

Despite its length the *Cursor* is a work of astonishing fluency in a lively,
popular idiom that was designed to appeal to a lay audience. The three
forms of the text, the dates and diversity of the manuscripts and the considerable influence it exercised on the medieval drama attest to its well-deserved
success throughout the fourteenth and fifteenth centuries.

Prologue. Men wish to hear rimes and to read romances relating to the matter of antiquity, Britain, and France, and stories of princes, prelates, and kings. Each man likes to hear what pleases him best. The wise wish to hear wisdom, the fools folly. The tree is known by its fruit. Now none is held in fashion unless he loves "paramours." But such love is illusory. It is here today, gone tomorrow. Soft beginnings have hard endings. The best lover is the Virgin Mary. Poets should write of her beauty, goodness, truth, and pity. She is the lady of ladies, raising sinful men when they fall. In her honor I shall compose an enduring work about the world in English for the love of Englishmen. French rimes are plentiful. What is there for the person who knows no French? I write for the unlearned English. My book is called 'Course of the World' for it "almost over-runs all."

The Seven Ages of the World. The First Age gives an account of the Trinity and the Creation; the nine orders of angels; the fall of Lucifer and his cohorts; the nature of man's soul; the meaning of the name Adam; the life of Adam and Eve in Paradise; the Temptation and Fall; the state of the world after the Fall; Cain's fratricide and God's curse upon him; Seth and the seeds of the Rood-tree; the death of Adam and his genealogy; the worsening corruption of the world; and God's decision to cleanse it. The Second Age treats of Noah's flood, his sons, and their progeny; the building of the Tower of Babel; and the confusion of tongues. The Third Age treats of Abraham, Lot, Ismael, Jacob, Esau, Joseph, Moses, Joshua, Samson, Samuel, and Saul. The Fourth Age treats of the reigns of David, Solomon, and their successors to the Babylonian Captivity. The Fifth Age treats of the family of the Virgin Mary; Isaiah's prophecy of Christ, incorporating the allegories of the Four Daughters of God and the Castle of Love and Grace [182]; the conception, birth, and child-hood of Mary; the Annunciation; and the birth and childhood of Christ. The Sixth Age treats of the Baptism of Christ; the Temptation; the chief events of His ministry; His Passion, Death, and Resurrection; the Harrowing of Hell; His Appearance to the Apostles and Ascension; the ministry of the Apostles; the later life and Assumption of Mary; and the Finding of the True Cross with its virtues and symbols. The Seventh Age treats of Antichrist; the Fifteen Signs before Doomsday (Brown-Robbins, no. 3367, more properly considered a monitory piece); the events of Doomsday; the Pains of Hell; the Joys of Heaven; and the world after Doomsday.

The work ends with the author's exhortation to his fellow men to repent-ance and four concluding poems: A Prayer to Our Lady (seventeen short coup-lets), The Sorrows of Mary (119 six-line stanzas riming aabccb), Apostrophe to Saint John (twelve six-line stanzas riming aabccb), and the Founding of the Feast of the Conception of the Virgin (117 short couplets). Seven additional poems are found in the Cotton Vespasian, Göttingen, Fairfax, and four other man-uscripts: Exposition of the Creed (58 short couplets following a prose version of the Creed), Pater Noster and Its Exposition (134 short couplets), Prayer to the Trinity (fourteen six-line stanzas riming aabccb), Hours of the Cross (nineteen six-line stanzas riming aabccb and two nine-line stanzas riming aabccbddb), Song of the Five Joys of Our Lady (thirteen five-line stanzas riming aaabb in the Göttingen MS only), Book of Penance (Prologue and three parts; nearly 2,000 lines in short couplets), and Cato's Distichs (62 six-line stanzas riming aabccb, beginning imperfectly, in the Fairfax MS; probably an independent poem). A treatise on shrift similar to the Book of Penance in Sion College, London, MS Arc. L.40.2/E.25 appears to have been largely incorporated in Jacob's Well [9].

2. Translations, Paraphrases, and Expositions
of the Individual Elements of the Faith

i. Pater Noster

PATER NOSTER [32]. Translations and paraphrases of the Pater Noster appear independently in verse in National Library of Scotland MS Advocates 18.7.21 (three quatrains), Salisbury Cathedral MS 82 (ten lines), Pavia University MS 69 (five couplets), University of Edinburgh Manuscript 205 (Laing 149) (eight lines), and Cambridge University Library MS Ee.1.12 (Pater Noster and Ave Maria combined in a single poem in three rime royal stanzas) and in prose in British Library MS Cotton Vitellius A.xii and the Fairfax-Blakeborough Fragment. Versifications of the Pater Noster are also incorporated in the Northern Homily Cycle (Brown-Robbins, no. 2715) and in the *Floure of the Commaundementes* [46].

Two verse prayers based on the Pater Noster appear in Corpus Christi, Oxford, MS 59 and Cambridge University Library MS Additional 5943 (Brown-Robbins, nos. 1617, 2738). There are four lines on the significance of the Pater Noster in Trinity Hall, Cambridge, Manuscript 16 and British Library MS Royal 5.A.vi (Brown-Robbins, no. 3648).

Reference should also be made to Lydgate's *Paraphrase of Pater Noster* (XVI [138] in *Manual*, vol. 6).

STANDARD EXPOSITION OF THE PATER NOSTER [33]. A short tract widely distributed as an independent text as well as incorporated in the Wycliffite version of the *Lay Folk's Catechism* [19] and the copy of *The Book of Vices and Virtues* in British Library Additional 17013. Although it has been ascribed to Wycliffe and printed among his works, there is no internal evidence to support the attribution.

The Pater Noster surpasses all other prayers in authority, subtlety, and profit: in authority, for Christ Himself taught it; in subtlety, for its seven petitions contain all that we need to know for salvation; in profit, for Christ Himself shall hear it. The first petition, Our Father That art in heaven, hallowed be Thy name, urges us to be united in charity and meekness with the Trinity and the Church. The second petition, Thy kingdom come, is addressed to the Son Who came down to earth to found a kingdom called Holy Church which at the day of Doom will rise to heaven. The third petition, Thy will be done, is addressed to the Holy Ghost, for He is the love of the Father and the Son. The second part of the Pater Noster contains four petitions. The fourth petition, Give us this day our daily bread, asks for three things: bodily sustenance, the Sacrament of the Eucharist, and God's Word. The fifth petition, Forgive us our debts as we forgive our debtors, asks God to forgive us our sins as we forgive our brethren on earth. The sixth petition, Lead us not into temptation, asks that He lead us not into the mire of sin lest we be trapped in it. The last petition, Deliver us from evil, asks God to preserve us from the worst sin, the sin against the Holy Ghost, death without repentance. May God out of His great mercy keep us from this evil.

TRACT IN HARLEY AND NORWICH CASTLE MUSEUM [34]. A considerably more ambitious commentary on the Pater Noster than the *Standard Exposition* relates the petitions to the Seven Principal Virtues, the Seven Virtues of the Gospel, and the Two Precepts of the Law. It makes use of the same materials as the *Speculum Vitae* [7] and survives in two early fifteenth-century manuscripts also containing copies of Lavynham's treatise [106].

The Pater Noster has the authority of God Who made it. It is short and easy to learn for it contains but seven petitions, and it is sufficient for it contains all that is needed for body and soul both in this life and the life to come. *Our Father That art in Heaven, hallowed be Thy name*: God is our Father and Father of all things, our Creator, Redeemer, and Comforter. We honor His name of Father and ask Him to show us mercy. His name should be worshipped as the name of all names. *Thy kingdom come*: The Kingdom of God is Holy Church on earth and Holy Church in heaven. We pray by this petition that Holy Church on earth become Holy Church in heaven. *Thy will be done on earth as in heaven*: This petition means that we do nothing save in conformity with His will and pleasure and that we love what He loves, hate what He hates. *Give us this day our daily bread*: In this petition we ask five manners of bread—the word of God, the Sacrament of the Altar, grace, blissful life without end, and bodily sustenance. *And forgive us our debts as we forgive our debtors* (i.e., the debts of sin, not temporal debts): Our sins are against God, against our neighbors, against ourselves. We ask forgiveness for all these trespasses. *And lead us not into temptation*: Send us grace to withstand it. Temptation makes a man know himself and his heart. *But deliver us from evil* (i.e., the wickedness of the world, the flesh, and the devil): Say the Pater Noster against the seven deadly sins. Against pride say Hallowed be Thy name, against avarice say Thy kingdom come, against envy say Thy will be done, against sloth say Give us this day our daily bread, against wrath say Forgive us our debts as we forgive our debtors, against gluttony say And lead us not into temptation, and against lechery say Deliver us from evil. By the seven petitions we ask for the seven principal virtues needed by the soul. When we say Hallowed be Thy name, we ask for perfect faith; when we say Thy kingdom come, we ask for perfect hope; when we say Thy will be done, we ask for perfect charity. When we say Give us this day, we ask for justice, our spiritual food; when we say Forgive us our debts, we ask for prudence; when we say Lead us not into temptation, we ask for fortitude; when we say Deliver us from evil, we ask for temperance. By the seven petitions we also ask for the seven gifts of the Holy Ghost, the seven virtues that Christ put forth in the Gospel—humility, benignity, grace to sorrow and mourn for our sins, love and desire for righteousness, mercy, purity, and peace—and the two precepts of Law, love of God and love of neighbors.

THE PATER NOSTER OF RICHARD ERMYTE [35]. A long prose exposition extant in six manuscripts, addressed to a nun. It falls into two parts, the first consisting of a eulogy of the Pater Noster and a discussion of prayer in general and the second of an orthodox exposition of the seven petitions.

Its main sources are *The Mirror of Saint Edmund,* the *Ancrene Riwle,* and the *Holy Boke Gratia Dei.* Use is also made of biblical and ecclesiastical authorities, especially Augustine, Bernard, and Jerome. Hope Emily Allen and F. G. A. M. Aarts, the editor of the treatise, reject its attribution to Richard Rolle in the Westminster manuscript. It is in fact the work of a well-educated priest, perhaps a member of a religious order, of broad human sympathies writing in the southeast Midlands during the early fifteenth century. His style shows few felicities, but it is marked by a simplicity and lucidity that is in keeping, as Aarts notes, with the practical end he has in view.

THE MIRROR OF SAINT EDMUND AND OTHER SHORT VER-SIONS [36]. A short exposition of the Pater Noster extracted from *The Mirror of Saint Edmund,* although attributed in some manuscripts to the early-fifteenth-century Carthusian miscellany, *Speculum Spiritualium,* is found independently in seven manuscripts. A short tract on the Pater Noster interpolated in the Simeon copy (British Library MS Additional 22283) of *The Book of Vices and Virtues* is also found in University College, Oxford, MS 97. Other short expositions of the Pater Noster, all apparently independent, are: (1) British Library MS Burney 30; (2) Bodleian Library MS Bodley 789; (3) Sidney Sussex College, Cambridge, MS 55; (4) Cambridge University Library MS Ff.6.33, following the *Mirror of Saint Edmund* version but unrelated to it; and (5) Magdalene College, Cambridge, MS Pepys 2125. An exposition of the Pater Noster in Lincoln Cathedral MS 91 may be related to the version in *Sacerdos Parochialis* ([22] above). An incomplete version of a Pater Noster commentary appears in a copy of Mirk's *Festial* (British Library MS Harley 2403). Johannes de Irlandia's *The Miroure of Wysdome,* written about 1490, contains a long prose commentary on the petitions of the Pater Noster.

Two prose prayers made of the petitions of the Pater Noster are in Cambridge University Library MS Kk.1.3.

In addition to the *Speculum Vitae* [7], five expositions of the Pater Noster are found in verse: (1) Bodleeian Library MS Douce 141 and Cambridge University Library MS Dd.11.89 (591 lines in short couplets); (2) Bodleian Library MS Additional E.6 (128 lines in couplets); (3) Saint John's College, Cambridge, MS 28 and Trinity College, Cambridge, MS 605 (58 lines);

(4) Lambeth Palace MS 487 (304 lines in couplets); and (5) Bodleian Library MS Douce 302 (seven eleven-line stanzas by John Audelay, [29] above).

Reference should also be made to *Cursor Mundi* [31], *The Paternoster Play* (XII [24] in *Manual*, vol. 5), *How the Plowman Lerned His Pater Noster* (Brown-Robbins, no. 3182), the Pater Noster for St. Bernard's palfrey, an exemplum in the Northern Homily Cycle (Brown-Robbins, no. 3865), and Lydgate's *Exposition of the Pater Noster* (XVI [137] in *Manual*, vol. 6).

ii. Ave Maria

THE AVE MARIA [37]. The Ave Maria exists independently in English verse in seven different versions, all of which are short, ranging from four to nine lines, and devoid of literary merit. A long devotion on each of the Latin words of the salutation is uniquely extant in a late fifteenth-century manuscript, British Library Royal 17.A.xvi, and consists of nine ten-line stanzas, ending imperfectly in what appears to be the next-to-last stanza. A hymn to the Blessed Virgin on the Angelic Salutation (Brown-Robbins, Robbins-Cutler, no. 1024) is similar to it.

A short exposition of the Ave Maria in prose is extant in Lincoln Cathedral MS 66. Two Wycliffite treatises on the Ave Maria have been previously discussed in the *Manual* (see vol. 2, III [15, 58]). An orthodox exposition of the Ave Maria in British Library MS Additional 30897, ff. 66ᵃ–77ᵃ, of the early fifteenth century may derive from a homily.

iii. Creed

CREED [38]. Translations and paraphrases of the Apostles' Creed appear independently in verse in Bodleian Library manuscripts, E Musaeo 160 (one twelve-line stanza), Rawlinson D.913 (eleven eight-line stanzas, imperfect at the beginning), and Rawlinson Poet 175, in Lambeth Palace Library MS 853 (fourteen quatrains), in Cambridge University Library MS Gg.4.32 (twenty couplets), and in British Library Arundel MS 292, and Edinburgh University MS 205. It appears in prose in Bodleian Library MS Douce 246, in Cambridge University MSS Ff.2.38 and Gg.4.12, in Emmanuel College, Cambridge, MS 27, in St. John's College, Cambridge, MS 121, in British Library MSS Arundel 292, Harley 3724, Harley 6580, Additional 60577, and Cotton

Nero A.xiv, in Edinburgh University Library MS 93, in Glasgow University Library MS Hunterian 512, and in the Blickling Hall MS. A prose version of the Nicene Creed appears in Bodleian Library MS Junius 121. There is a verse translation of the Athanasian Creed in Bodleian Library MS Bodley 425 and a prose translation in British Library MS Additional 36683, University College, Oxford, MS 179, and Trinity College, Dublin, MSS 70 and 195. A version of the Apostles' Creed appears in the Rawlinson manuscript of the *Cursor Mundi* [31] (Brown-Robbins, no. 1375).

HOW JUDICARE CAME INTO THE CREED [39]. An acephalous poem—42 lines in five eight-line stanzas riming ababbcbc—against the seven deadly sins, warning transgressors to consider "how Judicare came in the Creed," i.e., to consider the most elementary of all lessons, obedience to God's law, and to prepare for the Judgment.

HOW THE APOSTLES MADE THE CREED [40]. A legend found in the Pseudo-Augustinian sermon, *De Symbolo,* according to which the Apostles composed the Creed, each contributing a clause, is recounted in four fifteenth-century poems, one of which is not without literary merit. It combines the theme of the formulation of the Apostles' Creed with the theme of the Apostles' careers (probably from the *Legenda Aurea*), concluding with an apostrophe to Mary, in thirteen ten-line stanzas, with alliteration and internal assonance, generally riming ababcbcbcc (British Library MS Additional 32578). There are other versions in prose, including a long exposition according to the Apostles. It is also found incorporated in longer works of religious instruction, among them, *Pore Caitiff, Floure of the Commaundementes* [46], *Doctrinal of Sapience, The Book of Vices and Virtues* [5], *Ayenbite of Inwyt* [4], *Speculum Christiani* [15], *Speculum Vitae* [7], *Myrour to Lewde Men and Wymen* [8], *Mirroure of the World* [10], and Stephen Scrope's *Epistle to Othea.*

A CHRISTIAN MANNES BILEEVE [41]. A long, prose commentary on the twelve articles of the faith making extensive use of scriptural and ecclesiastical authorities, chiefly Augustine, Bernard, and Gregory. Its style is highly rhetorical, and in its account of Christ's passion and death (article 4), it resembles the literature of affective piety. It survives in four manuscripts.

Short expositions of the Creed deriving from the *Mirror of Saint Edmund* appear in Cambridge University Library MS Ff.2.38, British Library MS Additional 60577, and Edinburgh University Library MS 93.

iv. Ten Commandments

TEN COMMANDMENTS [42]. Metrical translations and paraphrases of the Ten Commandments appear in Bodleian MSS Rawlinson poet 32 (five couplets), Liturg e.7 (seven quatrains), Hatton 26 (eight couplets), and Ashmole 59 (five couplets; a version of the piece found in *Speculum Christiani*); New College, Oxford, MS 88 and Trinity College, Cambridge, MS 323 (five and eight couplets respectively, two versions of the same poem); Exeter College, Oxford, MS 47 (ten lines); Trinity College, Cambridge, MS 43 (five couplets); University College, Oxford, MS 96 and Cambridge University Library MS Ff.6.15 (five couplets); Lambeth Palace Library MS 853 and British Library MS Harley 665 (twelve quatrains based on the following item); British Library MSS Harley 78 and Additional 22283, Lambeth Palace MS 853 (following the previous item), and St. George's Chapel, Windsor, MS E.1.1 (thirteen eight-line stanzas entitled *Kepe Wel Cristes Comaundement*); and British Library MS Cotton Caligula A.ii (four eight-line stanzas), and elsewhere. Twelve verses on the Commandments from the *Fasciculus Morum* are found independently in Gray's Inn, London, MS 15. There is a metrical homily on the Ten Commandments among the Kildare poems (see XIII [33] in *Manual,* vol. 5, and Brown-Robbins, no. 2344). Ten riming lines on the Ten Commandments were added to the Pierpont Morgan Library copy of Caxton's *Royal Book* (IX [39] in *Manual,* vol. 3) in a sixteenth-century hand (Robbins-Cutler, no. 2695.5). There is also a version in *Cursor Mundi* [31], lines 6471–6477.

STANDARD ORTHODOX EXPOSITION OF THE TEN COMMAND-MENTS [43]. A widely disseminated tract composed in the East Midlands sometime during the last quarter of the fourteenth century. Kellogg and Talbert, following Arnold, call it the Orthodox or "Pre-Existing" Commentary to distinguish it from the various versions attributed to Wyclif and his followers. A detailed study of these treatises by Dr. Anthony Martin has brought to light their exceedingly complex textual relationship, and he has proposed a new classification of them, not according to their literary or cultural background but according to "textual and structural, or architectonic, principles," into rhetorical, discursive, and mixed rhetorical-discursive groups. The *Standard Exposition* is classified as discursive, i.e., dialectical and somewhat less rigidly organized than the compact and repetitive structure characteristic of the generally Wycliffite rhetorical groups. Combinations of the two groups are found in several manuscript versions as well as in the Wycliffite version of the *Lay Folks Catechism* [19]. An edition by Ms. Rachel Pyper of Corpus Christi College, Oxford, is in preparation.

All manner of men must obey God's Commandments. No man can be saved without obeying them. Christ bade man, if he would enter the bliss of heaven, to obey the Commandments. They divide into ten and two. Both relate to charity—to the love of God and neighbors. So it is that Moses gave two tables of the Law. The first table teaches man to love God and contains three Commandments, the second table to love his neighbor and contains seven Commandments. The First Commandment is *Thou Shall Have No False Gods before Me.* The greatest love should be accorded to God Who is the best and most worthy of love. To do otherwise is to love a false God and to break the First Commandment. Three manners of men, in particular, break this Commandment: the lechers and gluttons who follow the flesh; the covetous who follow the world; and the proud who follow the fiend. Against the temptations of the flesh be moderate in eating and drinking and chaste in your bodies. Against the temptations of this world be content with what God sends you in justice. Against the temptations of the fiend be satisfied with your estate. Set your heart and your love upon God above all things. The Second Commandment is *Thou Shall Not Take the Name of Thy Lord God in Vain,* that is, you shall not swear by any name of God without cause, as Christ Himself bids in the Gospel of Matthew (V). If you swear, swear only to the truth when you are called to witness or by constraint of your sovereign, in the interests of justice. The Third Commandment is *Be Mindful to Keep Holy the Sabbath Day.* God courteously allows us to work six days a week to sustain our bodies which in a short time will rot and become food for worms. It is reasonable that one day a week men busy themselves chiefly about acquiring spiritual goods for the benefit of their souls which shall live without end. Today the holy day may properly be called the sorry day, for it is spent in scorn of God and His saints. It should be spent in church-going, prayer, meditation, confession, and, if you are a priest, preaching and teaching God's word, or, if you are a layman, visiting your neighbors and bringing them to a life of virtue and charity and otherwise performing works of mercy. Of the remaining seven Commandments the first is *Honor Your Father and Mother,* for in so doing you will be long-lived upon earth. A man may properly love his father and mother most after God. And this love would consist in helping and comforting them in need and praying for them after death. There are three kinds of parents to be honored: natural parents, Christ and His mother Mary, God and Holy Church. The second Commandment of the second table is *Thou Shall Not Slay* unlawfully or wrongfully. Only God gives life to the body; only He can take the soul from the body. You can never know whether it is good for the soul to abide in the body or be removed from it; only God knows that. There are three kinds of manslaughter—manslaughter by hand which is violent crime; manslaughter by tongue which is defamation of character; and manslaughter by heart which is envy or hatred for their fellow Christians. The third Commandment of the second table is *Thou Shall Not Commit Lechery.* Bad as this sin is between a single man and woman, it is much worse between wedded men and women, and still worse if it involves priests who should be a mirror of purity to their parishioners. This Commandment forbids lechery in will, word, or deed. It was ordained by God in paradise and confirmed by Christ in the Gospel. It betokens the union of Christ and Holy Church by grace. The fourth Commandment of the second table is *Thou Shall Not Steal.* Theft is of many kinds. It may be accomplished by robbery, fraud, or coercion. Merchants may make reasonable profits. The fifth Commandment of the second table is *Thou Shall Not Bear False Witness against Thy Neighbor.* A man may bear false witness against his neighbor in word or deed or in word and deed together. The sixth Commandment of the second table is *Thou Shall Not Covet Thy Neighbor's House Nor Desire Thy Neighbor's Wife*. In these words, says Saint Augustine, is forbidden all manner of covetousness or the desire to commit lechery. Such as a man is in his heart, soul, and will, such is he before God Who knows both body and soul. He wishes all to be pure within and without. In this Commandment God forbids all manner of impure and unlawful coveting and desiring of fleshly deeds and orders you not to covet your neighbor's house, i.e., his household, or daughter, or maid, or especially his wife. The seventh Commandment of the second table is *Thou Shall Not Covet Thy Neighbor's Servant Nor His Maid Nor His Ox Nor His Ass Nor All Things Which Are His*. Hereby God forbids all manner of theft. Men may not wrongfully steal or covet other men's goods, for, as Saint Paul says, covetousness is the root of all evil. Be content with what God has sent you, for if you have little, you shall have little for which to account on the day of reckoning. If you keep these Commandments, heaven's bliss will be your heritage.

Two related versions of the *Standard Exposition* are found in Leeds University MS Brotherton 501 and in British Library MSS Cotton Vespasian A.xxiii and Harley 2250. The latter version is Northern and contains a preface describing man as a pilgrim journeying towards heaven or hell. Whoever keeps the Commandments is said to take the road to everlasting bliss; whoever breaks the Commandments is bound for damnation. The Harley manuscript adds an account of the woes that befall men who break the Commandments. An explicit in the Cotton manuscript ascribes the work to Abbot Phillip of Leicester.

JOHN LACY'S TREATISE ON THE TEN COMMANDMENTS [44]. A short treatise by the Northern anchorite, John Lacy, incorporating *exempla* drawn from Gregory's *Dialogues* and other sources.

God has given us Ten Commandments which every man, be he secular or religious, must observe perfectly for the salvation of his soul. For man was made to obey God, to fear Him, and to keep His Commandments. God has placed His curse on all those who fail to obey His Commandments. Everything they and their family do will be accursed, and they shall all be punished in hell. But, says God, those who keep My Commandments shall have My blessing and eternal reward—they and their family.

Some men claim that they cannot keep God's Commandments because they are too difficult. But that is to ascribe a defect to God Who cannot command us to keep what cannot be kept. If the Commandments are hard, think of the reward.

The Commandments teach us to love God and our neighbor. All refer to charity, for without charity no man may be saved, and the basis of charity is love of God and neighbor. Here the story is told of a woman who was slandered by a neighbor and, becoming ill because of it, refused to forgive him even on her death bed. She was damned and later appeared to her neighbor, urging him to repent and undergo penance for his slander of her.

The First Commandment is against false gods. Three types of men break this Commandment: those who believe and trust in witchcraft or who hold false and evil opinions concerning the faith of Holy Church; those who leave the service of God; and those who for love of the flesh, delight, fear of physical pain or death, or for the favor of men, go against God's bidding. The Second Commandment is against those who take God's name in vain. They are those who swear unnecessarily, falsely, or habitually. Idle swearing is wrong; swearing on legal oath is not. The story is told of a knight devoted to Mary who appeared to him with a dismembered child in her arms and informed him that he, among others, because of his swearing, was responsible for the child's condition. The knight repented and made a good end. Another story is told of a knight who swore by God's spear. When he died, a friend prayed for the repose of his soul. But an angel appeared, informed him that the knight was damned, and led him to hell to observe the burning soul. Suddenly a devil came by and drove a spear through it. The Third Commandment bids man to observe the Sabbath and other feasts. They who break it love earthly gains more than worship. They are covetous. Good men should spend the Sabbath hearing divine service and performing Works of Mercy. But there are those who spend the holy day in gluttony and waste. The tavern is their church. Thither come the deadly sins—Pride boasting of his exploits, Avarice swearing and bargaining, Lechery with ribald stories, Gluttony the steward of the household, Sloth the marshal of the hall urging Idleness to cheer the company, Wrath accompanied by Envy reckoning the accounts as treasurer of the household. The Fourth Commandment is Honor Your Father and Your Mother, and obey them in all lawful matters. When they die, pray and fast for them and have Masses sung for them. Neglect these duties, and many adversities will befall you and your children. Praying for them and performing good deeds in their name will release them of the bonds of purgatory. Also honor Holy Church and its servants, for they are our spiritual father. The Fifth Commandment is Do Not Kill. They break it who slay with hand, word, or will and who withdraw from man his living or sustenance. Holy Writ condemns all three forms of killing. The Sixth Commandment bids us deal with no woman but in true matrimony. This Commandment condemns all manner of lechery. A man may be guilty of lechery with his wife. Love between a single man and a single woman is a deadly sin, adultery is a greater sin, and incest still greater. The worst sin of all is sodomy. The Seventh Commandment forbids sacrilege (stealing from church or misusing its goods), usury, taking a man's goods wrongfully, misrepresenting goods, withholding proper labor for hire, any form of thievery, denying workmen their hire, oppression of tenants or subjects, neglect of duties to Holy Church, and defamation of character. The Eighth Commandment forbids false witness against one's neighbor and other forms of deceit and hypocrisy and misleading interpretations of scripture. The Ninth Commandment forbids man to covet his neighbor's wife, daughter, or servant. The Sixth Commandment forbids lechery and the willful consent thereto. Here is forbidden the will and desire for an occasion to commit lechery. The Tenth Commandment bids man not to desire his neighbor's goods, nor to deprive him of them by devious means, nor to desire any man's death for the sake of his heritage.

DIVES AND PAUPER [45]. A long prose commentary on the Ten Commandments in the form of a dialogue between Dives, a rich man, and Pauper, probably a mendicant preacher, written in the southeast Midlands between 1405 and 1410. It is prefaced by a short, lively discussion entitled "Holy Povert" on worldly and unworldly styles of Christian life. Pauper's defense of poverty and his exposition of the theology of the Commandments occupies the bulk of the treatise which runs to some 200,000 words. Despite its length and prolixity, the treatise can be read with considerable interest. It is generally well written, occasionally even eloquent, and it contains a wealth of incidental information on the social, religious, and political history of the time. Its author was not Henry Parker, a Carmelite monk of Doncaster, as Bale suggested, but an orthodox cleric, perhaps a Franciscan, probably a canonist, of wide learning who made extensive use of the works of Richard of Middleton, Thomas Dockyng, Nicholas de Lyra, and Bartholomaeus Anglicus. An edition by Dr. Priscilla Barnum is in progress.

THE FLOURE OF THE COMMAUNDEMENTES OF GOD [46]. A translation by A. Chertsey of the *Fleur des Commandments de Dieu* printed by Wynkyn de Worde in 1505, 1510, and 1521. It is a commentary on the Ten Commandments profusely illustrated by exempla drawn from the sermon series and *Promptuarium* of Johannes Herolt and interspersed with verses on the Ten Commandments, Seven Deadly Sins, Seven Virtues, Creed, Works of Bodily and Spiritual Mercy, and the Five Commandments of the Church. The verses on the Ten Commandments are also found in Wynkyn de Worde's 1513 edition of the *Matyns of Our Lady* (STC, no. 15194) and the verses on the Five Commandments of the Church in his 1502 and 1506 editions of *The Ordynarye of Crysten Men* (STC, nos. 5198, 5199).

A TRACT ON THE TEN COMMANDMENTS [47]. A spirited commentary on the Ten Commandments extant in three early fifteenth-century manuscripts. It is indebted in part to the standard, orthodox exposition.

What man today knows the Ten Commandments, Pater Noster, or Creed? He should realize that as he was born so will he die and be saved or not by his obedience to the Ten Commandments. (There follows a text of the *Four Tokens of Salvation*; see [146] below.) Hence the Ten Commandments must be preached and taught. Yet the clergy neglect their duty in this regard. And men are slow to learn. If they fear the cursing of popes, bishops, and vicars, should they not also fear the cursing of God? The First Commandment is Do not set false gods above me. Gluttons and lechers, covetous men, and proud men break this Commandment. To keep it, you must believe in the Trinity, fear and love God, and keep his Commandments. The Second Commandment forbids men to take God's name in vain. Swearers give four excuses: (1) By swearing, they keep God in mind; (2) swearing is only an innocent habit; (3) God is merciful and just and will be indulgent to swearers; and (4) men will believe them only if they swear. The excuses are false and easily refuted. The Third Commandment is Keep the Sabbath. Work six days, but reserve the Sabbath for the sustenance of your soul. But what man cares for that? He cares only about how to please his wretched body in all his sinful lusts, to lie abed, to come late to church and behave badly at service, and then to go to the tavern. The Fourth Commandment is Honor your father and mother—not merely in words, but in deeds. There are three kinds of parents—natural parents, the spiritual father who has cure of souls, and best of all, Almighty God. Parents should teach their children God's lore—the Pater Noster, the Ave Maria, the Creed, the Ten Commandments—but they really teach them the devil's lore. The Fifth Commandment is against manslaughter by tongue, heart, or staff. The Sixth Commandment is against lechery between single men and women, between wedded men and women, and, worst of all, between women and priests. Noah's flood and the destruction of Sodom and Gomorrah resulted from lechery. The Seventh Commandment is against theft (including the incorrect use of weights and measures, as when a taverner fills a measure with froth), the Eighth Commandment against bearing false witness against neighbors, the Ninth and Tenth Commandments against coveting a neighbors's wife, household, or goods. Keep the Commandments. Do not think that by giving a penny to a pardoner, or by having Masses sung by friars and priests, or by founding chantries and colleges you need not keep the Commandments.

A closely related version of this text is in British Library MS Harley 211. It concludes with a short treatise, doubtless of independent origin, on the rewards a man shall have who keeps the Commandments.

A man who keeps the Commandments shall be like a tree bearing chastity, sobriety, and other good works of which shall come everlasting joy. Christ promises that the Trinity shall dwell in him, God will love him as a kin and hear his prayers, no evil will grieve or harm him, and he will be led to heaven.

Other independent expositions of the Ten Commandments are found in: (1) British Library MS Harley 4172 and Bodleian Library MS Laud Misc 210; (2) Bodleian Library MS Rawlinson Poet 145, a fragment only; (3) Trinity College, Cambridge, MS 337, possibly Wycliffite, and (4) Henry E. Huntington Library MS HM.744, a fragment only. For William of Shoreham's version see [28] above.

TEN VENGEAUNCES OF GOD [48]. A short tract following the exposition of the Ten Commandments in Pierpont Morgan MS 861 and British Library MS Harley 2343. It is based on Exodus 7.19 to 12.30. A version of this text is incorporated in *Memoriale Credencium* [17].

Here are God's ten acts of vengeance against the Egyptians for breaking the Ten Commandments. For breaking the First Commandment, God turned all the waters of Egypt into blood. For breaking the Second Commandment, God multiplied frogs throughout Egypt save where the children of Israel lived. For breaking the Third Commandment, God brought lice from the dry sands of Egypt. For breaking the Fourth Commandment, God visited Egypt with all manner of flies. For breaking the Fifth Commandment, God afflicted their beasts with a murrain. For breaking the Sixth Commandment, God sent boils, blisters, and blains. For breaking the Seventh Commandment, God sent thunder, hail, and lightning, destroying much of Egypt's crops. For breaking the Eighth Commandment, God sent a great multitude of locusts which destroyed what was left of Egypt's crops. For breaking the Ninth Commandment, God sent such a thick darkness over Egypt that no man could see his brother or move from where he was for three days. For breaking the Tenth Commandment, God slew all the first-begotten, both man and beast.

SUNDAY OBSERVANCE [49]. A treatise defending the shift of religious observance from Saturday to Sunday is in British Library MS Harley 2339 of the first half of the fifteenth century. An apocryphal letter from Christ to "divers places" ordering man to amend his sinful life and especially to desist from work on Sunday is in Durham University Library MS Cosin V.iv.2 (1477). For Audelay's version see [29] above.

v. Works of Mercy

THE SEVEN WORKS OF BODILY MERCY [50] and THE SEVEN WORKS OF SPIRITUAL MERCY [51]. There are four short pieces in prose, one in a mid-fifteenth-century religious miscellany, University of Leeds Library MS Brotherton 501, sternly warning man that he must account for the works of bodily mercy at the Judgment, another, perhaps of Wycliffite origin, in Bodleian Library MS Lyell 29, exhorting man to observe the works of bodily and spiritual mercy after the example of Christ for the sake of his salvation, and two others in Bodleian Library MS Bodley 841 and St. Cuthbert's College, Ushaw, MS 28, a version of the *Speculum Christiani* [15].

Mnemonic verses on the works of bodily and spiritual mercy are found in Salisbury Cathedral Library MS 126 (two stanzas in seven couplets), Henry E. Huntington Library MS 127 (two eight-line stanzas), the *Speculum Christiani* [15] and the *Floure of the Commaundementes* [46], and on the works of bodily mercy alone in Bodleian Library MS Ashmole 1286 (seven lines). A confession for negligence of the works of bodily mercy in four six-line stanzas appears in the late fourteenth-century Vernon and Simeon manuscripts and the early fifteenth-century Worcestershire Miscellany. Three quatrains on almsgiving are found among the Muchelney Memoranda.

vi. Virtues

SEVEN PRINCIPAL VIRTUES [52]. Expositions and summaries of the Seven Principal Virtues are frequently incorporated in *compendia* of the elements of the faith, both in verse and in prose, and in the comprehensive works of religious instruction. A poem on the Seven Principal Virtues in seven eight-line stanzas, imperfect at the beginning and the end, was printed about 1500. Verses for a pageant or mumming spoken by the Seven Principal Virtues survive in a blockbook broadside of the late fifteenth century (Robbins-Cutler, no. 338.5).

THRE GOOD VERTUES [53]. A treatise on the theological virtues concluding with an unnoticed text of *The Sixtene Condiciouns of Charite* [58].

> Faith is the foundation of all other virtues. Some men fail for lack of faith, thinking that God will reward them with heaven for their loyal service. Others lose their faith through worldliness or adversity. Still others have their shields of faith pierced by the spears of their enemies and are often killed. They are believers in many truths. But, as Saint James says, he that is bound to keep the Commandments must keep them all; he that breaks one is guilty of all. God asks all men to cherish the virtue of hope which differs from faith in that it pertains to things to come. Saint Paul was ravished to heaven and saw its secrets and said all is worthless without charity. We should all know what constitutes charity. Saint Paul describes its sixteen properties.

For a longer Wycliffite version of this text see III [22] in *Manual*, vol. 2. It is also found incorporated in Wycliffite versions of the *Lay Folks Catechism* [19].

FAITH HOPE AND CHARITY [54]. A paragraph describing each in a sentence.

FAITH (or A SHORT DECLARATION OF BELIEF) [55]. An independent piece also found incorporated in the Trinity and Ryland manuscripts of the tract on *Charity* [57].

> Be steadfast in the faith, brother, for without it it is impossible to please God. With it the Holy Ghost draws us to assent to the truth. There are three kinds of belief. Some men believe God, others in God, still others to God. He believes God who believes that God is the Lord and Maker of all creatures. He believes to God who believes all His Words are true. He believes in God who loves Him above all things and his neighbor as himself.

A Comfortable Tretys (to strengthyn and comfortyn creaturys in the feyth specially hem that arn symple and disposed to fallyn in desperacyon), a related text in Corpus Christi College, Cambridge, MS 268, begins with the same statement, assuring men that, if they ground their faith upon Christ, they will go safely through life.

ON FAITH AND REASON [56]. 29 four-line stanzas riming aaab urging the claims of faith to reason and citing transubstantiation as one of many miracles inexplicable by reason. It is extant in a late fifteenth- and early sixteenth-century manuscript, Victoria and Albert Museum Dyce 45.

CHARITY I [57]. A tract on the love man owes to God and his neighbor and the eight points of a well-ordained love drawn from portions of the *Fervor Amoris*. It is incorporated in the tract on *Faith* [55] in the Trinity and Rylands manuscripts.

A brief text on charity, ending incompletely, is in St. John's College, Cambridge, MS 95.

THE SIXTENE CONDICIOUNS OF CHARITY [58]. Perhaps the most widely circulated text on charity in Middle English literature, it exists in seven prose and two metrical versions. Other copies are incorporated in the *Thre Good Vertues* [53], the St. John's College, Cambridge, confessional manual ([203], MS 49), and comprehensive works of religious instruction.

> St. Paul (1 Corinthians 13.1, 4–8) says: If I speak with the tongue of men and of angels, and have not charity, I am become as sounding brass or a tinkling cymbal. He that is charitable has these qualities: (1) He suffers wrong patiently; (2) he is benign; (3) he has no envy; (4) he does not respect evil; (5) he does not puff with pride; (6) he does not covet worldly honors; (7) he seeks not goods for himself but profit for Holy Church; (8) he harbors no wrath even though he suffers wrong; (9) he does not think evil; (10) he does not take pleasure in evil; (11) he takes pleasure in God's truth; (12) he humbly accepts whatever befalls him; (13) he believes all that God says as the supreme truth; (14) he hopes all that befalls God's children is good; (15) he resolutely bears all the evils that befall him; and (16) he is no more found wanting than is God's love. If a man possesses these qualities, he will come to bliss.

The metrical versions are eight short couplets in National Library of Scotland MS Advocates 18.7.21 and fourteen eight-line stanzas in Cambridge University Library MS Ii.6.39 and Lambeth Palace Library MS 853.

XV DEGREES OF CHARITE [59]. Four quatrains.

> These are the degrees of perfect charity according to Saint Paul: (1) Be patient regardless of adversity; (2) be generous to the needy and do good for evil; (3) do not envy the prosperity of others; (4) multiply good works; (5) bear no malice to prosperous neighbors; (6) be pleased to be of low degree and loath to be of high degree; (7) toil for others as for yourself; (8) never be provoked to anger or revenge; (9) do not think evil of another whatever the provocation; (10) take no joy in evil; (11) rejoice in truth and righteousness and hate dissimulation; (12) bear adversity or tribulation for the sake of righteousness; (13) believe in the teaching of the Church; (14) place your trust in God's promises; and (15) abide in hope to receive His reward and everlasting glory.

A copy of this work is incorporated in Betson's *Treatyse* [27] and Caxton's *Ars Moriendi* [218].

A TRETIS OF PERFIT LOVE [60]. A tract based on biblical and patristic authorities, particularly Augustine, Jerome, and Gregory.

The Apostles were "fleshly" until the Holy Ghost descended upon them. By this is meant that whatever a man does in this world, however great or noble in human terms, is "fleshly" unless he receives the Holy Ghost. Therefore, a man must make himself worthy to receive the Holy Ghost or his deeds will be worthless. Five things above all enable a man to receive the Holy Ghost: (1) He must make a good confession and do penance for his sins; (2) he must be meek and humble; (3) he must have love and charity; (4) he must be devout in prayer as were the Apostles between Ascension and Pentecost; and (5) he must be prudently abstemious in matters of meat and drink which lure man to the "fleshly" life and lead him to sloth in spiritual works.

SIXTENE TOKENES OF LOVE [61].

If you love your friend, you will be eager to speak of him; you will gladly hear him; you will often think of him; you will serve him graciously; you will not withhold his goods; you will not offend him; you will make it up to him if you do offend him; you will rejoice in his honor and prosperity; you will be sorry for his adversity and displeasure; you will regret his absence; you will approve of his behavior; you will be intent on pleasing him; you will attract others to him; you will not give away what he has given you; you will follow his advice promptly; and you will ask of him only proper favors.

CHARITY II [62].

Charity shall last beyond all other things, for God Himself is charity, and he that dwells in charity dwells in God and God in him. Therefore, He has taught men the meaning of charity and commanded them, if they desire salvation, to hold it in their heart, soul, and mind. Charity is to love God above all things and one's neighbor as oneself. When you are concerned to please God and flee sin more than to win worldly rewards or enjoy sensual pleasures, when you are prepared to suffer adversity and poverty for the love of God and to do penance for your sins, it is a sign that you love God with all your heart. To love your neighbor as yourself means that you do not will, desire, or suffer anything to befall him which you would not also will, desire, or suffer to befall you and that you perform the seven works of mercy for his benefit.

THOU SCHALT LOVE THI LORD [63]. An exposition of Luke 10.27.

You shall love your Lord God with your whole heart, life, mind, and strength, and your neighbor as yourself. These are the two commandments of the law. You love God with your whole heart, i.e., with your whole understanding, when you bend your efforts to know His infinite might and righteousness, wisdom, charity, and mercy. You love God with your whole life when you dispose your life in youth and age, prosperity and adversity, to the worship of God in purity and piety, praising and thanking God for His grace, goodness, and mercy. You love God with your whole mind when you contemplate His goodness and His painful passion and death and the dreadful day of Doom. You love God with your whole strength when you exercise all your power in His service and use your five wits well. You love your neighbor when you wish him well in body and spirit.

FOWRE TOKENS OF LOVE [64].

Four signs indicate whether you love God in charity. The first is if you are determined to hear His word; the second, if you are determined to keep his Commandments; the third, if you ever reflect on your past sins without contrition; and the fourth, if you are strongly resolved never to offend God again.

VERSES ON CHARITY, PURITY, AND HOPE [65]. 59 short couplets ending imperfectly, possibly extracted from a longer treatise.

DEUS CARITAS [66]. Seven eight-line stanzas riming abababab bidding man to observe caritas for his salvation.

PATIENCE I [67]. A text drawn from Saint Gregory's *Homily XVIII*.

Christ says in Luke (21.9): In your patience you shall possess your souls. Patience is the root and keeper of all virtue. It is to suffer meekly and without sorrow the evils that other men perpetrate against us. Charity is patience. It is a virtue before men to suffer adversity, but it is a virtue before God to love them who wrong us.

PATIENCE II [68]. A paragraph of aphorisms on patience promising God's reward.

PATIENCE III [69]. A treatise addressed to men "that wil ben perfit" and drawn from biblical authorities, Augustine, and Ambrose.

Many men suffer the despite of the world. That is hard to bear, but it is meritorious in the sight of God. The favor of the world destroys man. What will the man who cannot bear adversity patiently say at the Judgment when God shows him the torments He suffered for him? Why, O man, can you not suffer the little wind of a venomous tongue? Follow Christ's example and endure the contumely of the world. God will save no man who is not prepared to suffer patiently. Which of the Apostles, martyrs, confessors, virgins, or saints was saved without tribulation? They who want victory without battle or a crown without victory have an inordinate desire for worldly pleasure. We are tempered by suffering and by suffering learn patience and humility.

HOW MEN SHULDE BE MEKE AND PACIENT [70]. A short text based on John 8.

> When Christ hid Himself from those who would cast stones at Him, He cast out pride. If our Lord God fled the wrath of these men, how much more ought men to flee the wrath of neighbors?

THE BOOK OF TRIBULATION [71]. An anonymous late fourteenth- or early fifteenth-century translation of the *Livre de tribulacion* on the twelve profits or "services" of tribulation extant in three manuscripts: Bodleian Library MS Bodley 423, the basis of Alexandra Barrett's recent edition, and British Library MSS Harley 1197 and Arundel 286, the latter an abridgment. The dialect is East Midland. Another version of the *Livre* entitled *The Sermon of Tribulation* is found in St. John's College, Cambridge, MS 188, ff. 112^b–152^b, and Columbia University MS Plimpton 256, ff. 38^a–58^a, both of the fifteenth century (Jolliffe, no. J.3d). There are also two Middle English translations of the shorter version of the Latin source of the *Livre*, *De XII utilitatibus tribulacionis* (Jolliffe, nos. J.3b and c). Full treatment of these works is reserved for the chapter on English Mystical Writings in a later volume of the *Manual*.

VII DEGREES OF PATIENCE [72]. Possibly in roughly riming quatrains.

> Do not resist evil or return evil for evil. Love your enemy and do good for evil. Do not complain against adversity, but account it as sweet as incense. Take it as a medicine and be glad for it. Thank God for adversity and welcome even more of it. When you no longer complain of adversity, then be fain.

A copy of this work is incorporated in Betson's *Treatyse* [27] and Caxton's *Ars Moriendi* [218].

OF PACIENCE IN SICKNESS [73]. A short devotion.

> If a man knew how profitable sickness were to him, he would not wish to live without it, for the sickness of the body is the health of the soul.

VERSES ON PATIENCE [74]. Four lines on patience are found in Durham University Library MS Cosin V.iii.9 and two couplets embedded in a Latin treatise in Bodleian Library MS Lat theol d.1. The first stanza of a poem on the twelve degrees of patience appears in Caxton's *Ars Moriendi* [218]. There are 72 lines in varying metres on patience in adversity in a late fifteenth-century manuscript, Bodleian Additional B.60.

VII DEGREES OF HUMILITY [75].

Cast your glance downward and show humility in mind and body. Beware of high and clamorous speech and see to it that your words are few, well-chosen, and reasonable; do not laugh lightly. Be still and keep silence, obeying the common rule. Regard yourself as the vilest of all creatures and, so pronouncing yourself, acknowledge your unworthiness. Be patient in tribulation, confessing your sins often with great contrition. Be subject to all people, and forsake your own will. Avoid sin for fear of the Lord.

A copy of this work is incorporated in Betson's *Treatyse* [27] and Caxton's *Ars Moriendi* [218].

VII DEGREES OF HUMYLYTE [76]. A text paralleling the *VII Degrees of Pryde* [120]. Its source is Saint Anselm's *De similitudinibus*.

Saint Anselm says in a book of contemplation that there are seven degrees of humility. The first degree is for a man to realize that he is a despicable wretch. The second degree is to feel remorse that he is a despicable wretch. The third degree is to confess and acknowledge his base nature. There are many men who acknowledge their nature to themselves but want others to hold them in high esteem. The fourth degree is to desire other men to despise him and to persuade them to do so. The fifth degree is to suffer patiently the insults of other men and do little or nothing about them. The sixth degree is patience to allow other men to insult him and in consequence to suffer adversity. The seventh degree is to suffer all manner of adversity without complaint.

A version of this text is incorporated in *A Myrour to Lewde Men and Wymmen* [8].

XII DEGREES OF HUMILITY [77]. A translation of the *capitula* appended to Saint Bernard's *De duodecim gradibus humilitatis* with the addition of exempla from the *Vitas Patrum* and Gregory's *Dialogues* and *Commentary on the Penitential Psalms*. The eleven extant manuscripts testify to its widespread popularity among both the clergy and the laity during the fifteenth century. Its dialect is Southeast Midlands, probably London.

Saint Gregory says that no man without humility can trust God to forgive his sins. Another doctor says that the man who acquires virtues without humility is like one who carried dust in his open hand. A great wind came and bore it away. For all his patience, chastity, sobriety, obedience, discretion, and honesty, he goes about openhanded in the wind, ever ready to receive worldly praise and honor which are the devil's wind and blow all virtues away unless they are enclosed in humility. The meek man would prefer to be reproved than praised, rejected than honored. He would be a universal outcast. He deems all men's trespasses small, his own trespasses great. Meekness is the realization of one's own wretchedness. It alone brings man out of the devil's snares. The story is told of an angel who led a holy man to a high mountain and showed him the world full of the devil's snares. The holy man asked how they could be avoided. Only by humility replied the angel. Few strive for salvation. Do not look back, brother, but attend to God's work and determine to love Him ever more fervently. Since you have great need to learn of humility, I shall tell the twelve grades recounted by Saint Bernard. The first grade of humility is to be lowly in heart and deed to the least and most unworthy of men. The second is to be sparing of speech. The third degree is to observe good demeanor and keep good company, avoiding light laughter, plays, wanton behavior. The fourth degree is to remain silent until spoken to. The tongue is the gate of the soul. Open the gate and the devil may enter and get mastery of the soul. The fifth degree is to obey the commandments of the Church in working, eating, drinking, etc. The sixth degree is to hold oneself the least and worst of all men. The seventh degree is to deem oneself unworthy of God's benefactions—riches, health, power. The eighth degree is to confess humbly to the priest. The ninth degree is to obey God's Commandments even though they be harsh. The tenth degree is to accept illness cheerfully. The eleventh degree is to be subject to all men in all lawful matters and not to be hindmost in the love of God. The twelfth degree is to forswear the will to sin.

A version of this text is incorporated in *A Myrour to Lewde Men and Wymmen* [8].

HUMILITY [78]. One paragraph.

A man is meek if he is unmoved by opposition to his will and if he eschews a harsh response and remains without rancor when he is despised, falsely accused, and slandered.

THE VIII TOKENES OF MEKENES [79].

The eight tokens are: (1) that a man takes no offence if he is snubbed or demeaned by an inferior; (2) that he shows no insolence after receiving an honor; (3) that he accepts no flattery; (4) that he does not bestow evil for evil; (5) that among his compeers he is first at work, last in order; (6) that he gives thanks for God's benevolence; (7) that he obeys as readily as he commands; and (8) that, if he is elevated to any estate or office, he regards himself as a subject rather than a sovereign.

A version of this text is found incorporated in the *Book to a Mother* [16].

VERSES ON HUMILITY [80]. A metrical version of the *XII Degrees of Humility* [77] in seven short couplets is found in John of Grimestone's Preach-

ing Book. There are four lines defining humility in British Library Manuscript Harley 7322.

THRE THOUT3 [81]. One paragraph probably extracted from a longer work.

Three attitudes protect us from the devil's subtle deception: humility, mercy, and dread. Humility is like a garment containing every color, for it is suitable on all occasions. Mercy is like a white garment, for it cleanses and washes away sins. Dread is like a red garment, for it induces the greatest fear. Our Lord clothes us in these colors before we go to Him.

VII DEGREES OF OBEDIENCE [82].

Do what your sovereign bids without complaint and without exception. Do it cheerfully, promptly, humbly, and with all your power. Be obedient to the end of your life.

Betson's *Treatyse* [27] and Caxton's *Ars Moriendi* [218] contain copies of this text.

vii. Sacraments

DEFENSES AND EXPOSITIONS OF THE SEVEN SACRAMENTS [83]. A vigorous orthodox defense of the Sacraments based upon scriptural authority, particularly the words of Christ, is extant in University College, Oxford, MS 123. A similar treatise in British Library MS Royal 17.A.xxv founds the authority of the Sacraments on biblical texts and others drawn from Jerome, Chrysostom, Augustine, Ambrose, Bede, Peter Lombard, and Bonaventure. It concludes that God Himself ordained them and placed them in His church for the remission of sin. To think otherwise constitutes heresy. A brief exposition of the Sacraments in Bodleian Library MS Bodley 938 emphasizes that none but the clergy can administer the Sacraments save in time of grave need. The ministering of the Sacraments by the clergy is a sign of the spiritual cleansing by which God absolves the soul of sin. There is a brief exposition of the Sacraments, imperfect at the beginning, in Trinity College, Cambridge, MS 374 which contains a strong defense of the doctrine of transubstantiation in the section on the Eucharist.

A short polemical treatise, citing scriptural authority to prove the existence of purgatory, follows the defense of the Sacraments in the Royal manuscript.

An exposition of the Sacraments from *The Mirror of Saint Edmund* is found incorporated in three manuscripts previously listed—Cambridge University MS Ff.2.38, British Library MS Additional 60577, and Edinburgh University Library MS 93—and in Trinity College, Cambridge, MS 323 (B.14.50) of the fifteenth century.

THE CLENSYNG OF MANNES SOWLE [84]. A long prose treatise composed toward the end of the fourteenth or the beginning of the fifteenth century by a clerical friend or confessor for an East Midland nunnery, perhaps Barking, and later probably extended for use by the laity. It falls into three parts, each of seven chapters, which define, explain, and defend the three actions necessary for penance, namely, Contrition, Confession, and Satisfaction, whose effect on the soul is to wash it free of sin. Part II includes an exposition of the Twelve Articles of the Faith, the Seven Deadly Sins, the Ten Commandments, the Five Wits, the Seven Works of Mercy, and two forms of confession adapted for the religious life. At the close of Part III is a discussion of the reformation of man's soul which, as Jolliffe notes, is closely related to the *Formula noviciorum*. The source for much of the treatise is a late redaction of Raymond de Pennaforte's *Summa casuum poenitentiae*. Additional material has been drawn from the Pseudo-Bernardine *Tractatus de interiori domo,* Bernard's *Sermo XXV de diversis,* Grosseteste's *Templum Domini,* Innocent III's *Libellus de eleemosyna,* and other patristic and scholastic authorities. The central metaphor is based on Isaiah 1.16, Psalms 50.9, and 2 Kings 5.10. It is preserved in its entirety in four manuscripts—Bodleian Library Bodley 923, Cambridge University Library Ii.1.2, British Library Harley 4012, and Throckmorton—and partially in Magdalene College, Cambridge, MS Pepys 2125, British Library MS Sloane 774, and Durham Cathedral MS Hunter 15. The dialect is London.

WEY TO PARADISE [85]. Incomplete at the beginning and end. A translation of the anonymous *Voie de Paradis* based on the revised version of Robert de Sorbon's *De tribus dietis.* The unique manuscript dates from the late fourteenth or early fifteenth century and is profusely if rather crudely illustrated.

The sinner loses the company of God, earns His wrath, and forfeits the benefits of paradise. To be of His company again and to receive the prebends of paradise, he must take three journeys, each of three miles. The first journey is called true contrition. On this journey man must feel wrath that through sin he has deserved hell, lost the goods of grace and glory, and angered God. The second journey is called true confession. By the first journey man leaves the court of justice and by the second enters the court of mercy. Confession is essential to salvation. It shuts the gates of hell, opens the gates of paradise, reconciles the sinner to God, and turns great hatred into great love. Confession is required for all men, for all men are sinners. All are like the rich man on horseback, i.e., in a state of grace, who is waylaid by robbers, i.e., the deadly sins. Sloth throws him off his horse. Wrath steals the bridle of patience and silence in adversity. Envy destroys the clothing of his soul, i.e., charity. Pride removes his sword, boots, and spurs, i.e., the fear of God, the dread of temporal death, hell, and the long penance of purgatory. Avarice steals his purse and the money it contains for alms and deeds of mercy. Gluttony removes the thong and girdle of his sobriety, moderation, and abstinence. Finally, he loses his breeches, i.e., his continence, virginity, and chastity, to lechery. The devil will send four sergeants—evil hope of long life, wicked shame, evil deed, and hypocrisy— as advocates to the court of mercy to discourage him from confession which, if it is to be efficacious, must be complete. All the circumstances of the sins must be revealed in order to determine their degree of seriousness. The entire confession must be made to the same person, and he must review the penitent's guilt with respect to the seven deadly sins and the Ten Commandments which constitute a ladder to heaven. Confession must be made freely, frequently, and without delay, and must not depart from the truth. The third journey is called satisfaction. It is achieved by drawing others to good deeds through prayer and spiritual works of mercy, by feeling sorrow and affliction for sin through reflections on man's wickedness, the hour of death, and the Passion of Christ, and by mutual forgiveness through deeds of mercy.

TELL THI SYNS [86]. One paragraph.

Tell your sins and feel sorrow for them. Without sorrow there can be no forgiveness. Give full details of your sins. Name them, and declare why, when, where, in what manner, and how often they were committed.

EXHORTATIONS TO CONFESSION AND EXAMINATION OF CONSCIENCE [87]. Two brief texts preserved in Trinity Hall, Cambridge, MS 16, and Cambridge University MS Dd.6.26.

CONFESSIONAL MANUALS [88]. Five confessional manuals, all unpublished, are extant in late Middle English. The first, in Saint John's College, Cambridge, MS 257, consists mainly of a long series of interrogations which the confessor in an examination of conscience addresses to the penitent on the seven deadly sins, Ten Commandments, seven deeds of bodily and spiritual mercy, five inner and outer wits, seven principal virtues, the virtues opposed to the seven deadly sins, the beatitudes, and the seven gifts of the Holy Ghost. A second, and considerably shorter, series of interrogations follows to determine whether the sinner is sorry for his sins. Finally, the con-

fessor advises the sinner how to amend his life and to counteract the deadly sins and imposes upon him an appropriate penance. The portions of the text dealing with the virtues and the gifts of the Holy Ghost incorporate explanatory and occasionally devotional matter, including a text of the *Sixteen Conditions of Charity* [58]. A second manual, imperfect at the beginning and end, in British Library MS Harley 4172 is also framed in the form of a long series of interrogations designed to examine the penitent's conscience. The topics deal with the seven sacraments, Ten Commandments, will of God, five wits, and worldly goods. A third manual, in British Library MS Cotton Vespasian A.xxv, was intended for the use of the young, inexperienced priests. It describes the three kinds of penance (solemn, public, and private) and when each is appropriate, and instructs the confessor how to examine the penitent on the seven deadly sins and their branches and to lead him to repentance through reflection on Christ's passion. A fourth manual, in British Library MS Sloane 1584, addresses a series of interrogations specifically for husbandmen, married women, single women, and servants. The Cotton and Sloane manuscripts contain a second manual which may have been intended for the use of both priests and laymen. After a curious speculation on the origins of confession—it is said by some to have come into being after the fall of Adam or Cain, by others in the time of Joshua, and by still others when Christ founded Holy Church—it advises laymen that they may shrive themselves and others when death is imminent, but at other times they must confess to priests, observing the points of true confession (cf. *Wey to Paradise,* [85] above). A priest is instructed to hear confession in a privy place in church and to conceal his face from the penitent. If he is satisfied with the confession, he may impose penance immediately; if he is not satisfied, he is to urge the penitent to disclose all his sins and remind him of the pains of hell and the joys of heaven. A true Christian will then respond with a good confession, but if he fails to do so, the priest should examine his conscience with a series of interrogations on the seven deadly sins, Ten Commandments, fourteen articles of the faith, seven works of bodily and spiritual mercy, seven sacraments, and five wits. Finally, a short manual in Bodleian Library Manuscript Rawlinson D.913, possibly an abridgment of a long work, directs a priest, if the penitent does not confess his sins by the Ten Commandments, seven deadly sins, seven works of mercy, and five wits, to interrogate him according to these points. Once the priest is satisfied that the penitent has made a good confession, he may enjoin penance after his discretion: against pride, works of meekness; against wrath, works of lowliness; against envy, works of charity, etc. No man who cannot say the Pater Noster, Ave, and Creed may be shriven unless he promises to learn them as soon as possible.

A GUIDE TO CONFESSION [89]. An exposition of the Seven Deadly Sins, Ten Commandments, Twelve Articles of the Faith, and Seven Sacraments for the use of penitents. There is a close resemblance in subject matter between this exposition and the examinations of conscience in the Confessional Manuals. A similar treatise entitled *A Short Remembrance for Confession* is found in Betson's *Treatyse* [27] and in St. John's College, Oxford, MS 173. It presents certain topics for review by the penitent preparing for confession.

ON DAYLY OR FREQUENT CONFESSION [90]. A brief text, citing Saint Bernard and "other holy doctors" as authorities, apparently intended for the clergy.

When a man confesses daily or frequently, he should not make a long confession, but briefly declare those sins which weigh most heavily upon his conscience—first, mortal sins and those about which he may be in doubt as to whether they are mortal or venial, and secondly, venial sins collectively which cannot be easily confessed one by one, such as idle words, negligence in reading or praying, loss of time, or distraction.

HOW THOU SCHALT RYSE FRO SYNNE [91]. One page.

Hate sin worse than poison. Sorrow for sin more than for the loss of all your worldly goods. Determine to sin no more. Go to confession and make amends for your sins. Pray to God and fast with moderation from meat and drink. Perform deeds of bodily and spiritual mercy.

HOU MANY MANERS WEYES SYNNE IS FORYEVE [92].

Sin is forgiven by baptism, martyrdom, fervent love and charity, weeping for sins, confession, sadness of heart and travail of body, amendment of life, prayer of saints, good faith, correction of fellow Christians for their wicked deeds, forgiveness of wrongs, and almsdeeds.

There is a similar version in *Speculum Christiani*, table 8 [15].

THE FOUR MANER OF WASSHINGIS [93]. Perhaps the conclusion to, or an excerpt from, a longer work on confession or penance similar to *The Clensyng of Mannes Soule* [84] which also appears in the Harley manuscript.

> The soul is washed by contrition, penance, satisfaction, and charity. A man should weep inwardly and wash his soul with contrition. The spots of sin cannot be removed without penance. No man is sinless, says Saint Augustine. Therefore, be not afraid to disclose your sins to the priest and receive the sacrament of penance. Satisfaction makes the soul shine. Take example of Mary Magdalen. Charity is the foundation of faith. Without it man's works cannot endure or abide. Fasting, prayers, and pilgrimage count for little unless they are grounded in charity. He who purposes to dwell with God must dwell with charity.

SEVEN WASHINGS OF SIN [94]. One paragraph in John Lacy's manuscript, St. John's, Oxford, 94, related to *Hou Many Maners Weyes Synne is Foryeve* [92].

> Sin is absolved by baptism, martyrdom, almsgiving, conversion of neighbors to virtue, forgiveness of wrongs perpetrated against us, reception of the Sacrament of the Altar, satisfaction and weeping for our sins.

SEVEN THINGS NECESSARY FOR PARDON [95].

> All men and women should know the seven things that dispose them to win the pardon of Sion. They must have faith in Holy Church, the desire to receive the pardon, and the disposition to receive it reverently. They must have contrition and sorrow for their sins, go to confession, visit the monastery of Sion, and do good deeds thereafter.

SEVEN THINGS THAT PREVENT MEN FROM READING THE BOOK OF THEIR CONSCIENCE [96]. A brief text possibly related to the *Twelve Lettings of Prayer* [248].

> The seven obstacles are that men continue to sin, excuse their sins, perceive others' sins but not their own, conceal their sins, suppress good intentions, multiply their sins, and are greatly occupied with worldly matters.

VERSES ON THE INDIVIDUAL SACRAMENTS [97]. There are three poems on confession: (1) a treatise by the northern anchorite, John Lacy, entitled *Hou That a Man Sall Knowen the Perelles That Longeth to Schrifte*, in 200 long, irregular lines, occasionally lapsing into prose, and interspersed with Latin, perhaps intended as a guide to confession by the seven deadly sins; (2) a treatise, perhaps by a mendicant preacher, of 164 generally four-stress lines in quatrains on the necessity of Lenten confession and the procedures for a good confession; and (3) an acephalous treatise of 764 lines which, according to Ker, is prosified in *Jacob's Well*. There are ten lines on *Penance* and its reward in paradise in Trinity College, Cambridge, MS 323. *A Book of Penance* is among the miscellaneous poems appended to *Cursor Mundi* [31]. A poem on the indissolubility of marriage is discussed among Service and Service-Related Works [214]. Eucharistic poems include the *Sacrament of the Altere,* sixteen eight-line stanzas, and four fugitive pieces on the Host.

In addition to the metrical versions of the Seven Sacraments listed among the miscellaneous compendia of the formulae of belief, there is an independent version in five couplets in British Library MS Additional 24660. For Shoreham's version see [28].

viii. Sins

THE XII ABUSIONS (or MYSUSES) [98]. A translation of a Latin treatise misattributed to Saint Augustine.

The twelve abuses are: (1) a wise man without good works; (2) an old man without religion; (3) a young man without obedience; (4) a woman without purity of soul; (5) a rich man without alms; (6) a lord without virtue; (7) a contentious Christian; (8) a proud pauper; (9) an unjust king; (10) a negligent bishop; (11) a pupil without discipline; and (12) a pupil without God's law.

HOW THOU SHALT NOT SET LYTLI BY SYNNE [99]. A short instruction noted by Ker in a late fourteenth- or early fifteenth-century Carthusian miscellany.

SIX MANER CONSENTIS TO SYNNE [100]. A short text extant in four Middle English manuscripts.

A man consents to sin if he assists in its performance, defends it, advises it, withdraws his help against it, or fails to reprove it.

THE THREE SPEECHES IN THE HEART [101].

This is how a man may know which speech in his heart is of the flesh, the world, or the devil, and which is of God. Saint Bernard says that if he has an untimely desire for unnecessary meat or drink, he may be sure the speech is of the flesh. It is also of the flesh if he has any thoughts of lechery or other physical self-indulgence. It is the speech of the world if he takes pride in the goods of fortune, nature, or grace and regards himself as better than other men. It is the speech of the devil if he feels malice—envy, hatred, anger, etc.—toward his fellow man. It is God's speech if he feels himself lowly and sinful, if he is stirred to meekness, charity, patience, purity, and good deeds.

FOURE ERROURS [102]. A popular, fifteenth-century treatise based on biblical texts drawn from Matthew, Paul, and John.

If a man finds any part of God's law difficult to comprehend, let him purge himself of these four errors: worldliness, fleshly lust, false avarice, and vainglory. A man who yields to these errors is a servant to vice and a traitor to God, and he shall never have a real understanding of the truth.

VII THINGS TO BEAR IN MIND [103].

Seven things we should ever bear in mind—our daily sins, the brevity of life, the uncertainty of the day of death, our instability and frailty, the Judgment, the pains of hell, and eternal glory.

A copy of this text is incorporated in Betson's *Treatyse* [27].

THE FORM OF LIVING [104]. A poetic version, in 431 short couplets, of the first six chapters of Richard Rolle's treatise (see chapter on English Mystical Writings in a later volume of this *Manual*). Adapted to a general audience, it focuses on sin and how to combat it and omits all mention of the solitary life and matters dealing with mystical devotion and practice.

ON DEADLY AND VENIAL SIN [105]. A short treatise of Northern origin consisting of passages drawn from the works of Saint Augustine, Saint Gregory, and Saint Thomas Aquinas on the distinction between mortal and venial sin.

A LITIL TRETYS ON THE SEVEN DEADLY SINS [106] by Richard Lavynham, the Carmelite friar and Oxford theologian who is credited with drawing up the list of heresies of John Purvey preserved in the *Fasciculi Zizanorum* (see III [52, 56] in *Manual,* vol. 2), achieved a large audience in the later Middle Ages, providing preachers with a useful storehouse of sermon material and parish clergy and lay readers with a concise and lively instrument of religious instruction. Forms of confession (see [211–212] below) often accompany it in the manuscripts. The affiliations of the fifteen extant manuscripts are difficult to establish. Van Zutphen bases his edition on a mid-fifteenth-century manuscript, British Library Harley 211, which belonged to the Carmelites of Ipswich and Norwich in East Anglia and which contains a colophon ascribing the treatise to Lavynham. His learning appears genuine and considerable. For the animal lore and symbolism he was indebted to Hugh Ripelin of Strassburg's *Compendium theologicae veritatis,* which may also have suggested to him the form of the treatise, and Bartholomaeus Anglicus' *De proprietatibus rerum.* Among his other sources are Augustine, Jerome, Bede, Gregory, Isidore of Seville, Peter of Blois, Peter Lombard, Alanus de Insulis, Innocent III, and Ralph Higden. He wrote in his native Suffolk dialect toward the end of the fourteenth century.

The purpose of this treatise is to describe the "common conditions" of the seven deadly sins by figure and example and their branches. Pride is like a lion. It is the worst of vices as is plain from Lucifer. It arises in a man's heart from the gifts of nature, fortune, and grace and has eight branches (Presumption, Vainglory, Rebellion against Authority, Boldness, Hypocrisy, Hauteur, Shamelessness, Sinning openly). Avarice is like a hedgehog and has eight branches (Idolatry of Money, Ambition, Niggardliness, Treason, Usury, Simony, Theft, Sacrilege). Wrath is like a wolf and has three degrees (Hatred of Heart, Mouth, and Deed) and seven branches (Hatred of Heart, Malice of Mouth, Working of Vengeance, Fierceness of Disposition, Manslaughter, Impatience, Blasphemy). Envy is like a hound and has four branches (Rejoicing in Another's Misfortune, Distress over Another's Good Fortune, Backbiting, Sowing of Discord). Sloth is like an ass and has eight branches (Sluggishness, Delight in Soft Clothing, Fine Foods, etc., Idleness, Recklessness, Tardiness, Cowardice, Wanhope, Heaviness). Gluttony is like a bear and has four branches (Greed, Lustiness, Excessive Eating and Drinking, Inordinate Desire for Fine Food). Lechery is like a hog and has eight branches (Simple Fornication, Adultery, Incest, Rape, Violation of Chastity, Abuse, Pollution, Sins against Nature).

A TRACT ON THE DEADLY SINS [107]. Imperfect at the beginning and end. The portion of the text that survives deals with Ire, Sloth, Avarice, Gluttony, and Lechery. Sins of the Tongue are discussed after Lechery, the text breaking off soon after the beginning of the section on Cursing. The tract is not a translation of the *Somme le roi,* but is clearly related to the tradition.

A TRACT ON THE SEVEN DEADLY SINS [108]. A brief tract describing the sins as closely related to each other and taking their origin from pride which is given the most detailed treatment.

An exposition of the seven deadly sins from *The Mirror of Saint Edmund* is found in Bodleian Library MS Bodley 416, British Library MSS Additional 10053 and 60577, and Westminster School Library, London, MS 3.

PRIDE, ENVY, AND WRATH [109]. A brief exposition of the seven deadly sins emphasizing man's pride in the goods of nature, grace, and fortune and the vices that derive from it. It is followed in the Society of Antiquaries manuscript by a list of seven virtues opposed to the deadly sins.

DEVILS AND DEADLY SINS [110].

There are seven devils who bestir men to the deadly sins: Lucifer to pride, Leviathan to wrath, Beelsebub to envy, Mammon to avarice, Belial to gluttony, Behemoth to sloth, Asmodeus to lechery.

NOTES ON THE DEADLY SINS [111]. A collection of notes on the deadly sins follows a copy of *Pupilla oculi* in Salisbury Cathedral MS 126.

FIVE SINS AGAINST THE HOLY GHOST [112].

Presumption or overhope, despair or wanhope, hardness of heart, rejection of the grace of the Holy Ghost, false oaths.

THE TEMPTACIONS OF THE DEVILLE [113].

The devil tempts us by the seven deadly sins and their branches. A good angel, however, warns us against them and shows how they bring us low. To each sin, however, he offers an alternative in the form of an opposing virtue—to pride, meekness; etc.

MAN'S ENEMIES [114].

Since man for fear of death or the loss of his worldly possessions is on guard against his enemies night and day, all the more ought he to be on guard against his far more perilous spiritual enemies— the world, the flesh, and the devil—who would deprive him of his spiritual goods and bring him to everlasting death. They assail him through the covetousness of the eye and the flesh and through pride of life. For pride of life is the sin of the fiend from which also come envy and wrath. Covetousness of the eye is the sin of the world from which come sloth and avarice. From the covetousness of the flesh come gluttony and lechery. [The text concludes with a conventional explanation of the seven deadly sins.]

PRIDE, WRATH, AND ENVIE SYNNES OF THE FEND [115]. A short, popular text taken from Bonaventure and extant in fourteen manuscripts, some of which are clearly Wycliffite. It generally concludes with the treatise, *The World Is Contrary to God* [131]. Other copies are found incorporated in miscellaneous manuals [24] such as Trinity College, Cambridge, MSS 601 and 1099 (nos. 28, 29).

Pride, wrath, and envy are sins of the devil, covetousness and avarice sins of the world, gluttony and lechery sins of the flesh. They are the broad highway to hell, and many men recklessly take it. As man cannot acquire worldly goods without great effort, so he cannot put aside his sins and keep the Commandments without great effort. [There follows a brief exposition of the sins, concluding with *The World Is Contrary to God.*]

A version of this text is incorporated in the *Form of Confession* found in the Vernon manuscript (Bodleian Library Eng poet a.1); see [211], MS 26.

GIVE ME LICENSE TO LIVE IN EASE [116]. Eleven twelve-line stanzas riming ababababbcbc on the seven deadly sins and their remedies.

As I walked out on a May morning, I heard a man say, "O God, how long shall I live in pain?" He fell to his knees and prayed: "Sweet Jesus, give me license to live in ease and keep the Commandments. Grant that I may never come into Lucifer's cabin. None can heal my wounds but a curate who understands them and their remedies. Pride is the gravest of my wounds; the best remedy for it is humility. Envy burns my breast; the remedy for it is charity. Wrath ravishes my body; the only remedy for it is the herb called love-ache. I am swollen with avarice which can only be cured by an herb called almsgiving. For sloth the remedy is an herb called watch-and-pray; for gluttony a plaster called abstinence; for lechery a root called chastity. Other good herbs for my disease are confession, contrition, and satisfaction."

Remedies against the Seven Deadly Sins, a prose treatise based on material drawn from the *Ancrene Riwle,* appears in a late fifteenth-century devotional compilation, *The Tretyse of Love,* printed by Wynkyn de Worde. This work will be treated in the chapter on English Mystical Writings in a later volume of the *Manual.*

AUGUSTINUS DE PECCATIS VENIALIBUS [117]. 27 irregular couplets extracted from the *Prick of Conscience* [18]. The attribution to Saint Augustine is spurious.

When a man or woman drinks more than is fitting or proper, when you are in a position to help but fail to do so, when you turn the poor away from your door, when you eat in time of fasting, when you oversleep and come tardily to divine service, when you say your prayers too late or show too little devotion, when a man has intercourse with his wife from lust rather than from a desire to beget a child, when you are slow to visit the sick, imprisoned, troubled, or sinful and neglectful in assisting the souls in purgatory through prayers or alms, when you fail to act as peacemaker, when you speak to a man too harshly, when you flatter a man excessively, when you chatter idly in church and yield to distraction, it is a venial sin. When you swear, when you banish an innocent man, when you are suspicious without grounds for suspicion, it is a venial sin which Saint Augustine says is the reason why many souls suffer in purgatory. There are many more venial sins than I have mentioned. No man can know them all.

ON THE REMISSION OF VENIAL SINS [118]. An excerpt from Caxton's *Ars Moriendi* [218].

Venial sins may be absolved by: (1) taking holy water; (2) receiving the Eucharist; (3) saying the Pater Noster; (4) beating one's breast out of remorse for our sins; (5) saying the Confiteor at Mass or at other times; (6) receiving the sacraments; (7) hearing Mass; (8) beholding the sacrament of the altar; (9) receiving a priest's or a bishop's blessing at Mass; (10) performing works of mercy; (11) receiving pardons; (12) enduring martyrdom; (13) performing penance; (14) granting forgiveness to trespassers; (15) giving good example; (16) converting others to a life of virtue; (17) showing patience; (18) having contrition for sin; and (19) all good deeds.

DECEM REMEDIA CONTRA PECCATA VENIALIA [119]. Twelve short couplets, extracted from the *Prick of Conscience* [18].

There are ten remedies against venial sins: holy water, almsdeeds, fasting, the Eucharist, prayer, especially the Pater Noster, daily confession, the blessings of a priest and bishop, remorse for sins, and Extreme Unction. Venial sins committed in great number may weigh so heavily on the soul as to constitute a mortal sin.

VII DEGREES OF PRYDE [120]. A short text paralleling the *VII Degrees of Humylyte* [76]. It is found in two fifteenth-century manuscripts.

The seven degrees of pride in a man are: (1) to hold himself better than he is; (2) to defend and excuse his sins; (3) to take pleasure in temporal goods; (4) to desire other men to hold him better or worthier than he is; (5) to take offense if his wishes are opposed or his faults criticized; (6) to vaunt his ability to return ill for ill; and (7) to rejoice that he has so much personal power and is so well maintained by magnates that he can do wrong with impunity.

AYENST THE EXCUSACION OF LECHERY AND OTHIR DEDLY SYNNES [121].

Saint Augustine observes that no man can be taken by the devil unless he assents to it. So the devil flatters and deceives us to leave him the weapons with which he would destroy us—to give our hearts to wicked thoughts, our tongues to evil speech, our hands and other members to sinful deeds. He lures us to concupiscence with wicked thoughts. No man sins against his will.

POLLUCION [122]. A passage adapted from Cassian's *Institutes* (chapter 6).

Pollution generally occurs when a man emits semen other than during lawful intercourse with a woman. It may result from indulgence in food and drink, passionate kissing, or physical contact. According to Saint Bernard and Saint Augustine, it is a mortal sin unless it occurs in sleep. A man who masturbates in his sleep should refrain from receiving the Sacrament the next day. A priest who masturbates in his sleep, however, should not refrain from saying Mass, for that is the devil's strategy. There are worse pollutions than masturbation in the sight of God. One is petting, another is sodomy, a third (and worst of all) is intercourse with an animal. Only a bishop can pardon these sins.

AGAINST SWEARING AND FLATTERY [123]. Two paragraphs warning against swearing and flattery as instruments of the devil. A marginal note indicates that the paragraph on swearing was taken from an exposition of Ire in a discussion of the deadly sins contained in an unidentified Book of Shrift.

LOKE AFTIRWARD THAT THOU BE WEL OCUPIED [124]. A short admonition to avoid sin, particularly sloth, found in a late-fourteenth- or early-fifteenth-century Carthusian miscellany. It is apparently an excerpt from a longer instruction or sermon.

PUNISHMENTS FOR ADULTERY [125]. One paragraph apparently extracted from a longer work.

A man living in adultery will suffer these punishments on earth. He will be poor, or die suddenly, or lose a limb, or be imprisoned because of his ill repute, etc. [thus the manuscript].

MISCELLANEOUS VERSES ON SIN [126]. A general warning to avoid sin and its consequences has been added in a sixteenth-century hand to a copy of *The Book of Vices and Virtues* in British Library MS Additional 17013; it consists of seven quatrains and a concluding six-line stanza. There are eighteen quatrains on the evils of backbiting in British Library MS Royal 18.A.x. Two couplets describe a slothful man in National Library of Scotland MS Advocates 18.7.21. British Library MS Harley 7322 contains four fugitive pieces on the evils of pride, envy, and lechery. Three quatrains against pride, envy, and wrath appear in British Library MS Harley 957, four lines *contra luxuriam* in British Library MS Sloane 2275, and a carol on pride as the source of all sin in Balliol College, Oxford, MS 354 and British Library MS Sloane 2593 (see XIV [358] in *Manual*, vol. 6). There is a poem on the twelve kinds of usury in 89 irregular couplets in British Library MS Egerton 2810. There are thirteen couplets against swearers and seven alliterating mono-riming lines on the seven deadly sins in Lambeth Palace MSS 78 and 180.

An acephalous treatise on the seven deadly sins and their remedies in twenty thirteen-line stanzas is in Bodleian Library MS Douce 302.

A Song of Galaunt, previously discussed in the *Manual* in the chapter on Poems Dealing with Contemporary Conditions (see XIII [160] in vol. 5), includes a series of stanzas describing the seven deadly sins.

There are several versions of a prayer by the *Seven Times Christ Shed His Blood against the Seven Deadly Sins* (Brown-Robbins, nos. 292, 1701, 1707, 1708) in addition to Audelay's *Remedies against the Seven Deadly Sins* (Brown-Robbins, nos. 1702, 4185, 4200) and penitential lyrics incorporating some or all of the deadly sins. For two metrical homilies on the seven deadly sins, see Brown-Robbins, nos. 1776 and 3400, and for Dunbar's *The Dance of the Seven Deidly Synnis*, see X [78] in *Manual*, vol. 4. For William of Shoreham's version, see [28] above.

Discussion of Quixley's *Exhortacio contra vicium adulterii*—a version of Gower's *Traitié pour essampler les amants marietz* (Brown-Robbins, no. 4105; see XVII [2] in this volume)—is reserved for a later section of the *Manual*.

Attention should also be called to a prose homily on the seven deadly sins in British Library MS Harley 2391.

ix. Gifts of the Holy Ghost

THE GIFTS OF THE HOLY GHOST [127]. The gifts alone are briefly described in prose in British Library MS Lansdowne 388, Emmanuel College, Cambridge, MS 246, and Society of Antiquaries, London, MS 300 and in 33 short couplets in Cambridge University MS Ii.4.9. A list of the gifts appears in Bodleian Library MSS Lat. liturg. e.17 and Hatton 26. For Audelay's version, see [29].

x. Beatitudes

BEATITUDES [128]. The Beatitudes in verse are found alone in three versions. Two of them—one a single quatrain, the other (probably incomplete) seven couplets—appear in John of Grimestone's Preaching Book (National Library of Scotland MS Advocates 18.7.21) and were undoubtedly used for public recitation. A third version entitled *A Lerning to Good Levynge* in twenty eight-line stanzas riming abababab also describes the vices opposed to the Beatitudes and concludes with a special address to the preaching clergy. A fourth version which originally may have had an independent life is incorporated in Saint John's College, Cambridge, MS 28 of the *South English Legendary* (Brown-Robbins, no. 2724). A brief explanation of the Beatitudes in prose appears in British Library MS Additional 30897 and seven other manuscripts. *A Sermon for All Saints Day* in British Library MS Cotton Titus D.xix provides an extensive commentary on the Beatitudes. Discussion of this work is reserved for the chapter on Homilies.

III. Guides to the Christian Life

NO MAN MAY SERVE TWO LORDIS [129]. A short text comprising a collection of commonplaces from the Bible, Augustine, Jerome, Chrysostom, and Erigena.

No man may serve two masters, for he will love the one and hate the other, support the one and despise the other. You may not serve God and riches. Hear this, man of avarice; hear this, Christian. A man may not serve riches and Christ. He that serves riches becomes subject to the devil and suffers a harsh and deadly lordship. If man loves God, says St. Augustine, he must hate riches; if he loves riches, he must hate God. Christ did not say that man may not have God and riches. What He said is that no man may serve God and riches. If you are rich and your wealth does not make you a proud or violent thief, you are the master and not the servant of your riches. Chrysostom advises us not to be overzealous to feed and clothe our bodies. Jerome asserts that we should attend to our spiritual food and clothing. The body is temporal, the soul eternal. What does it profit a man, etc? Augustine calls business the daughter of despair. Good works lead to hope, wicked to despair. Man must not be busier than the birds of the air or other beasts. He was made to live in this life, like the beasts, but also, unlike the beasts, to live after death and indeed more after death than before. Be not busy, then, over worldly things—food and clothing—but about God's kingdom and His righteousness. These are the goods which are to be coveted above all other things. We shall be judged by our good works, not whether we were born rich or poor. Avoid superfluity. All you require is each day's necessity.

TWO WEYES CONTRARIOUS [130]. A short treatise extant in two fif- teenth-century manuscripts.

As Holy Writ and holy doctors bear witness, there are two opposing ways leading to two opposing ends. The one is the way of virtues and the observance of God's Commandments which leads to the bliss of heaven. The other is the way of vices and sins which leads to the unending pains of hell. This road is broad and pleasant for a time, and many take it. The other is hard and narrow, and few take it because it is difficult at the start, and many foolishly turn off to the other road which appears easy. In time, however, the narrow road becomes easier to traverse than the broad road, as is demonstrated by the life of the lecher who finds it increasingly difficult to maintain his physical charm, to contend with the gnawings of his conscience, to put aside his lust. Lust is a great torment because it is never fulfilled. The lustful suffer special torment in the hour of death. Sinners shall ever sing in hell: "We have forsaken the hard way for the way of sin which, however pleasurable it may seem, is nonetheless exceedingly harsh and bitter."

THE WORLD IS CONTRARIE TO GOD [131].

God loves meekness and submissiveness, the world pride and rebellion; God loves peace and patience, the world strife and wrath; God loves mercy and charity, the world cruelty and envy; God loves cleanness and chastity, the world harlotry and foul lusts; God loves measure and poverty, the world covetousness and avarice; God loves penance and abstinence, the world gluttony and drunk- enness. So you have before you good and evil, sweet and sour, life and death, virtue and vice, joy and pain, day and night. Pray to Christ and Mary for strength to keep the Commandments and eschew sin.

HOW LORDIS AND HOUSBONDEMEN SCHULDE TECHE GODDIS COMAUNDEMENTIS AND THE GOSPEL TO SUGGETTIS AND AN- SWERE FOR HEM TO GOD ON DOMESDAY [132]. A tract extant in two fifteenth-century manuscripts and partially in a third. It draws extensively upon Old Testament authorities, particularly the Book of Daniel and the Books of Kings, Saint Augustine's *Commentary on John,* and the pseudo-Au- gustinian *Treatise to an Earl* (III [65] in *Manual,* vol. 2).

Almighty God commands every man to tell his sons how He led His people out of the land of

Egypt. Let this be as a token in your hand, He says, and as a remembrance before your eyes. Let the law of God be ever on your lips. "I have commanded you to love the Lord with your whole heart, soul, and strength." Bear these words in your heart at all times both at home and away. Teach them to your sons and grandsons. Saint Augustine advises Christians generally to govern their houses, their sons, and their retinues. God loves discipline; it is a wayward and false innocence to slacken the bridle to sins. Lords and husbandmen should somewhat exercise the office of a bishop in teaching the Commandments and maintaining discipline. They must teach their subjects the love and sweetness of the heavenly kingdom and the bitterness of hell, and to avoid the seven deadly sins, especially blasphemy, following the example of such Biblical kings as Nebuchadnezzar, Jehosaphat, Josias, Ezechias, and David, who preached the law of God to their people.

The work appears orthodox, although not without a degree of Wycliffite sympathy, and dates from the late fourteenth or early fifteenth century.

SIR JOHN CLANVOWE'S THE TWO WAYS [133]. A moral treatise urging Christians to avoid the "broad way" which leads to damnation and to follow the "narrow way" which leads to salvation. Two copies are extant: a complete text in University College, Oxford, MS 97 and a fragment in British Library MS Additional 22283, both of the late fourteenth century. A headnote in the University College copy states that it was composed during the author's last journey to Constantinople where he died in October 1391. Perhaps his exclusive reliance in the text on Biblical authority—notably the Psalms, the Gospels, and the Epistles—suggesting his lack of access to a library provides indirect confirmation of this assertion. The dialect is London. About its author much is known. Clanvowe was a celebrated soldier, administrator, diplomat, and chamber knight at the courts of Edward III and Richard II. A friend of Chaucer, he was a member of a prominent group of well-educated knights—Lewis Clifford, Richard Sturry, Thomas Latimer, William Nevill, John Montague, and John Cheyne—suspected of Lollard sympathies. The tone of *The Two Ways*, however, is cautiously non-controversial, and although some sympathy with Lollardry may be detected, there is clearly no specific espousal of its tenets. Clanvowe's editor, V. J. S. Scattergood, ascribes to him the authorship of *The Boke of Cupide* (VII [47] in *Manual*, vol. 3).

The broad way leads to damnation, the narrow way to salvation. Whoever is found on the broad way at the moment of death will suffer the pains of hell. Whoever is found on the narrow way at the moment of death will enjoy the endless bliss of heaven. Therefore, we should meekly cry out to God for His mercy to show us the narrow way and give us grace to leave the broad way. They are foolish, indeed, who reject Christ's teaching out of fleshly lust or worldly pleasure. The narrow way is to keep the Ten Commandments. We enter it through a narrow gate which is fear of God, leaving behind our wicked desires and evil deeds. The world, the flesh, and the devil will attempt to divert and dissuade us, but we should take example of the saints who took the narrow way to salvation and follow their teaching. They were men and women of all ages and conditions, and we should imitate them. The devil is a liar. His arguments against true belief are specious and false. We must be vigilant, for he is full of wiles and lures us to hell through excess. Virtue is the mean between extremes which are vices. We must rule our flesh and keep it under proper rein. We must despise the world and seek our treasure in Heaven. Worldly riches are false; heavenly riches are true. Nor are worldly honors true honors. Before God all virtue is honor, and all sin is shame. The world, however, bestows its honors upon warriors and fighters, and those that destroy and conquer many lands and lay waste and plunder on behalf of men who already have enough and who squander their wealth on meat, drink, clothing, and building construction, and live in ease, sloth, and many other sins, and who proudly take vengeance for every wrong they suffer. We must avoid evil company and eschew taverns and brothels, although the world calls those in God's way fools and those in the devil's way good fellows. The statement has been made that the narrow way to salvation is to keep the Commandments. It follows that the broad way to hell is to break the Commandments. We should love God above all things and our neighbors as ourselves. For He made us to His own image and likeness out of nothing and ordained us for the bliss of heaven, created the earth for our use and comfort, took flesh and shed His precious blood to redeem us after Adam's fall. The love of God and neighbor is reasonable, delightful, and profitable. The words of Christ, the Apostles, and other authorities of Holy Writ make clear that no man may come to the bliss of heaven who has not in his will to keep the Commandments as does he who loves God above all things and his neighbor as himself.

VOR TO SSEAWY THE LOKINGE OF MAN WYTH INNE [134]. A stilted and occasionally inaccurate rendering of the pseudo-Anselmian *De custodia interioris hominis* appended to the *Ayenbite of Inwyt* (see [4] above).

Our Lord Jesus Christ says: If the master of a house knew a thief were coming, he would keep watch and would not allow himself to be robbed. By the house is signified intellect with its many attendants, thoughts, emotions, sensations, and deeds. The servants will be slothful unless the master firmly controls and regulates them. Were he idle, the thoughts, eyes, ears, tongue, and all other wits would grow wild. The house signifies the conscience in which the master dwells with the virtues. There is not one thief to undermine the house, but many. They are the devil and his catchpoles. Lest he be negligent, the master diligently guards his house against them, appointing Prudence as his door-keeper with the support of Strength. Equity sits in the midst, giving each his due. No one knows when the thief will come. Prudence admits some messengers to alert the household. The messenger of death enters and demands silence. He says: I am Dread, and a reminder of Death who is to come. Prudence asks: Where is Death? When will she come? Dread replies: She will not delay, and is near, but I do not know the precise day or time when she will arrive. Prudence says: Who will come with her? Dread says: A thousand devils will come with her and bring great books, burning hooks, and fiery chains. In the books are written men's sins. The hooks are used to draw the souls from the bodies of those under their jurisdiction. With the chains they are bound and drawn into hell. Prudence asks: Whence do you come? Dread answers: From hell. Prudence asks: What is hell? What do you see in hell? Dread answers: Hell is immeasurably wide and bottomless, full of intolerable fire, incomparable stench, sorrow, darkness, endless groaning, without hope of good and with an abundance of ills. There I see all manner of torments, weeping, and gnashing of teeth. Intolerable cold gives way to intolerable heat. The soul is consumed by worms. No sound is heard but woe! woe! Such is hell, and a thousand times worse. Prudence asks: What shall we do? Brothers and sisters, be prudent and watchful in prayer, giving thought to things that are good. Patience adds: Let us come before God's presence in confession and in psalms. Strength says: Withstand the devil by faith. Clothe yourself in God's armor: the hauberk of justice, the shield of faith, the helm of salvation,

the sword of the Holy Ghost. Equity says: Let us live soberly, righteously, meekly. Prudence announces: There is another messenger waiting without. Equity orders him to be admitted. He identifies himself as Love of Everlasting Life. I have come from heaven, he says, and have seen God as
in a mirror. I saw the ineffable mystery of the Holy Trinity, Christ bearing the wounds of the Passion
on His body, the Virgin Mary enthroned above all the orders of angels and of man, among them,
the prophets and patriarchs, the Apostles, the martyrs, the confessors and doctors of the holy church,
monks, and the fellowship of maidens. Prudence enquires about the life of the blessed. They live,
enjoy, love, rejoice, praise, are swift and secure, explains the messenger; they live their life without
end. Their life is the sight and knowledge of the Holy Trinity. They enjoy God's counsel and judgment, and learn the origin and courses of all things. They love God with an infinite love. They
rejoice in God and their own holiness. Such is their bliss that they praise God without end. They
are swift for their body goes wherever their soul wills. They are secure in this life of wisdom, love,
bliss, praise, and holiness. Strength asks: Who shall part us from Christ's love? Tribulation or sorrow?
Equity says: Get rid of the first messenger, for love of God drives out Dread. Strength and Temperance order Dread to leave. Thus should we cast away fear and turn to the love of the heavenly
country.

A GOOD TRETYS TO GODE LEVYNG TO ALL MANER ASTATES OF THE PEOPLE [135]. A series of moral injunctions on righteous living, after the manner of estates literature, to all classes of society, but with particular reference to "grete men and myghty and their iustices."

Mighty men: Do not oppress your subjects or be oppressed by them. Destroy evil customs and
usages. Make good laws for the common profit. Hear the causes of the poor, widows, and orphans.
Take no gifts. Work for the love and harmony of neighbors. Eschew extortion. *Rich men*: Take
nothing wrongfully. Do not despise neighbors. Support the poor. Have compassion for laborers.
Poor men: Serve rich men cheerfully. Do not envy them, or backbite, or be impatient. Do not steal,
or harbor thieves, or accept their thefts. Abstain from lust in holy times. Eschew all japes, lies, and
evil words. Keep your children home at night. Give them good example. *Children*: Obey your father
and mother. Accompany them to church. Do not steal. Avoid discord. Be polite. Learn not to spend
your wages on proud and gay apparel. *How a man shall behave on hearing Mass*: Do not speak or look
around you. Come to Mass fasting, and think of God and His passion. Listen attentively to the
sermon. Give alms and an offering. Do not leave the church until the Mass is over, and give thanks
to God. *Maidens*: Speak little, and be simple in heart and array, thinking always on Mary's virginity.
Beware of dancing, and be not familiar with young men. Do not allow them to feel or grope. Do
nothing illicit, and reject flattery. Use no foul language. *Widows*: Dress modestly and preserve chastity. Do not entertain men at home. Pray continuously. Take the advice of wise men and reflect on
the lives of Saint Anne and Saint Elizabeth. Keep an upright household, and walk about the streets
but little. *Merchants*: Do not transact business on Sundays or holidays. Pay your debts on time, and
acquit your pledges. Do not lie. Use right balances and true weights, and give even and fair measure.
Hosts and guests: Do not admit evil men. Do not steal from guests or harm them, and submit honest
bills to them. *Taverners*: Do not allow men to play at dice or cards or to blaspheme God, His mother,
or saints, within the tavern. Do not receive common women. Give full measure. Do not brew your
own wines or dilute them. *Women*: Do not dress in an uncomely fashion. Be still in church and
elsewhere. Shun pride, and do not lead other women to pride. Resist dishonest advances. *All men
generally*: Avoid evil men, gluttony, and drunkenness. Honor priests, religious, and holy church, and
hear divines and doctors. Help the poor. Keep holidays. Avoid backbiting and foul language. Avoid
blasphemy, lying, swearing, lecherous words and people. Observe the laws of holy church and fulfill
all penances. Give alms, make restitution. Think on the joys of heaven and the pains of hell.

HOW ECH MAN AND WOMAN MAY LERNE TO LOVE AND SERVE GOD ECH IN HIS DEGREE [136]. A treatise of the three estates extant in British Library MS Harley 2339, a Middle English miscellany of instructions and exhortations in verse and prose, probably meant for the private reading of a secular priest. It is of London origin and dates from the first half or middle of the fifteenth century. No specific source of the moralization has been found. Its figurative illustration of the birds is developed from Matthew 6.26. Dr. A. I. Doyle, its editor, regards it, together with Clanvowe's *Two Ways*, [133 above], and other estates literature delineating the social and spiritual responsibilities of the clergy and laity, as a manifestation of the development of evangelical piety which owed its origin at least in part to the Lollard movement.

There are three classes of men: laborers, nobility, and clergy. All should love God and take example of the birds which clerks call lovebirds—the lark, the nightingale, and the turtledove. The lark rises at dawn, flies as high as she can to heaven, and gives thanks to God in song; then she descends to earth and feeds. She takes cover in a storm. Laborers should learn to serve God thus. When they rise in the morning, let them examine their conscience for sin and make amendment and practice charity throughout the day. If the devil stirs up a storm to tempt them to sin, let them take cover, knowing if they yield to it they shall suffer torment in hell forevermore. Lords and ladies and all others above the station of laborers should serve God like the nightingale who sings in a green grove winter and summer, a thorn in her breast to keep her from sleeping, and brings forth children who learn by nature to sing like her. So should great men worship God night and day, not sleeping in sin, but ever wakeful in good works, a thorn piercing their breasts, that is, with compassion for the poor. Let them teach their children to sing God's praises throughout their lives. The turtledove has but one mate during her life and feeds only on pure wheat. So should the clergy love God all their lives. For we are wedded to Holy Church, and Christ is our husband as head of the church, and our souls are His spouse. He is our pure wheat, and they that make Him their daily food shall have life without end.

IFF THOU HAVE GODIS OF GRACE [137].

If you have goods of grace as virtue, or goods of kind as strength, or goods of fortune as worldly wealth, spend them well and discreetly while you may. Otherwise they will appear as accusers at your judgment. Keep the Commandments.

IX POYNTYS [138].

A man who wishes to advance in the way of perfection and to please God must have these nine points in his heart: (1) Deem yourself wretched, foul, and unworthy of God's favor. Displease yourself, and seek to please God alone. Do not desire to be held good and meek, holy and virtuous, but such as you are. (2) Do not take offense at what befalls you, but at sin only and the things that lead to sin. (3) Take care to love poverty, meekness, and simplicity and to conform your way of life to Christ's. (4) Despise no creature, however evil, sinful, unworthy, or simple he appears, but have pity and compassion for all. (5) Judge no man, for you cannot know the operation of grace in his soul. (6) Love your neighbor as yourself. (7) Love no man or woman or anything else but for the love of God. (8) In all your works be sure to have God in mind. Worship Him and be well disposed toward your neighbor's welfare. (9) If you have these points in your heart, bear in mind that it is through God's goodness that you have been granted so much grace and perfection. Contemplate the other benefits He has bestowed on mankind—the image of Himself in the soul, food in this life, bliss in the next. Contemplate His passion, and feel sorrow for all that He suffered for you, a sinful wretch.

CLENNESSE OF SOWLE [139].

CLENNESSE OF SOWLE [139]. An excerpt from Saint Catherine of Siena's *Dialogo* extant in eight fifteenth-century manuscripts mainly of Northern provenance. It appears as part of a longer extract from the *Dialogo* in British Library MS Harley 2409, ff 71ᵃ–72ᵃ. Jolliffe distinguishes three versions of the passage, but versions A and C, summarized below, are related and offer a more satisfactory text than the B version.

A devout woman (or soul) asked our Lord for cleanness of soul. He appeared to her and said: If you would have your wish, you must be in perfect union with Me and do as follows. First, you must forsake your own will and pay no heed to the will of men but only to My will and Commandments, and deem that I allow nothing to befall you or others but for the best. Secondly, do not judge your neighbors according to your own lights, but leave the judgment of them to God. Judge only yourself. Thirdly, let your soul have Me always in its sight, and set your heart only on Me. Make Me the beginning and end of your works. Thus will you achieve cleanness of soul and everlasting bliss.

GOSTLY RICHESSES AND VERTUS OF SOLE [140].

GOSTLY RICHESSES AND VERTUS OF SOLE [140]. A Northern text extant in three fifteenth-century manuscripts which, according to Jolliffe, is drawn from *Cibus animae*, the source of the *Speculum Christiani* [15].

The riches and virtues of the soul are holy faith without error, steadfast hope without presumption or despair, pure love of God and fellow man, meekness, mildness, weeping for sins, chastity, abstinence, hunger for justice, sobriety, stillness, pity, patience, devout prayer, love of the poor, strength to suffer meekly for Christ's sake any tribulation that may befall, prompt obedience to God's bidding and the ordinances of Holy Church.

VI THYNGES THAT WILLE BRYNG A MANNYS SOULE TO HEVYN [141].

The six things that will bring a man's soul to heaven are confession, devout prayer, sharp penance, almsgiving, avoidance of evil fellowship, and hearing the word of God preached. Above all, and in addition, he must have perfect charity.

GOD'S WORDS TO SAINT MOLL (or MAWDE) [142]. An extract from Mechtild of Hackeborn's *Book of Gostlye Grace*.

Our Lord God (or Jesus) spoke these words to His holy spouse and virgin Saint Moll (or Mawde): In all your works keep three things in mind: (1) Whatever service or favor you receive from another accept modestly and cheerfully, giving thanks to Me; (2) whatever you do do it meekly to honor and please Me; (3) do not complain of any adversity or illness that may befall you through My will and sufferance.

TWELF POYNTES [143]. An excerpt from the *Revelations of Saint Birgitta, Book 2, Chapter 16*, intended for the instruction of women (see the chapter on English Mystical Writings in a later volume of this *Manual*).

God appeared to Saint Birgitta [Bryde] and said: "Daughter, be meek in spirit and humble in all your works. Fear nothing but your sins. Love all manner of people for my sake—even your enemies. I command you to do three things and not to do three things. I command you to love Me above all else, to cast away all manner of pride and haughty bearing, to hate the lusts of the flesh. I command you not to love, hear, or speak idle or dishonest words, not to eat or drink excessively, and to flee and forsake the fellowship of worldly joys and desport. I suffer you to have a reasonable amount of sleep, to eat and drink within reason, to keep vigils temperately for My worship. I counsel you to labor in fasting, waking, praying, and other good works, to use your physical, spiritual, or worldly goods for the worship of God, to contemplate the great benefits I have bestowed on you and the pain and passion I have suffered for you. Remembering the bitter death I suffered and contemplating the dreadful day of doom will draw you towards Me. Above all I command and counsel you to obey My laws.

The text is extant in three slightly different versions. It is also incorporated into *A Moralization on Articles of Clothing* [179].

FOURE THINGIS THAT MAKEN GOD OURE FREEND [144].

(1) Living faith, (2) purity of heart, (3) observance of the Commandments, (4) patient suffering.

HAVE IN MYNDE [145].

Bear in mind that you have but one God Who made you of nothing and gave you your wits, your limbs, and other worldly comforts. Consider also how sinful you are, and that, were it not for God's care, you would fall into all manner of sin. Moreover, if you possess any virtue or enjoy the favor of a good life, realize that it comes from God and not from yourself. Be mindful how long and how often God has allowed you to sin and how patiently He waits for your conversion, having suffered so much for your salvation.

FOUR TOKENS OF SALVATION [146]. A passage erroneously attributed to Saint Augustine, extant in nine late fifteenth-century manuscripts.

A man will be saved if he has (1) a pure and active devotion in prayer to God, (2) true love for
God, (3) genuine contrition for sin, and (4) continual mindfulness of the passion of Christ.

FOURE THINGIS BE NEDEFUL [147]. A two-page tract extant in ten
fifteenth-century manuscripts.

To attain salvation a man must hear the word of God and His law, understand the word of God
and His law, follow the word of God and His law, and finally, continue in good works to the end of
his life.

IX PERFECCIONS [148]. A short text of unidentified origin.

Saint Francis taught his brethren these nine perfections—the perfection of the man who weeps
for his sins and is happy to confess them, the perfection of the man who regards himself as the
lowest of all creatures, the perfection of the man who withdraws his heart from all earthly creatures,
the perfection of the man who strives to love and serve his enemy without bitterness or dissimulation,
the perfection of the man who loves all good men and women and who has great compassion for all
evil men and women, the perfection of the man who loves rebuke and loves him who rebukes him,
the perfection of the man who is glad to serve everyman but accepts no service in return, the
perfection of the man who is mindful of God's favors to him and other creatures and thanks Him
for them, and the perfection of the man who controls his tongue.

V POYNTES [149].

Good Christians who wish to attain salvation must (1) thank God for His goodness and say the
Pater Noster, (2) go to Church, (3) say grace before meals, (4) be honest in their business dealings,
and (5) repent of their daily sins at night.

ON THE SOUL [150]. A translation of a treatise identified in the colophon
as *Reclusorium animae*. It deals with the nature of the soul and its similitude
to the angels as a marvel of creation. The importance of patience and prayer
to the soul is emphasized, and, since it is possessed of a body, it is advised
to be governed carefully by the five wits. The translation is of little merit.

OF WIDOWHOOD [151]. A tract instructing widows to live virtuously
and eschew worldly pleasures. Its main source appears to be Luke 2.36.

Widows should know their calling and live virtuously in holy and devout prayer and abstinence, avoiding not only all enticing and immoderate meat and drink but also all worldly wealth and fleshly dalliance. Saint Paul bids widows not to be light-hearted gadabouts running hither and thither from house to house or town to town, but to be steadfast in good manners, sober of countenance, of few words, and to abide at home employed in virtuous occupations. Anna, the daughter of Phanuel, was widowed after seven years of marriage and lived to 85, ever a widow and never leaving the temple where she spent her time night and day in fasting and prayer. Thus, said Origen, did this lady deserve by long fasting and prayer to receive the gift of prophecy. Bede observes that the highest good a woman may receive is the gift of virginity. If a woman loses her husband, she should remain a widow forever. Even while her husband is alive, she ought to crave a life of widowhood, and, if that should not be her hap, nevertheless the Lord will crown her will and purpose. Widows who live devoutly and serve God without man's company to the end of their lives and impart the same rule of life to their children will be rewarded sixtyfold after death. And men and women who have defiled their virginity but have made amendment with sorrow and penance, persevering in purity to the end of their lives, will be crowned true widows. There are three kinds of widows. The most perfect, and the ones destined for eternal reward, are widows like Anna who serve God in fasting and prayer night and day. Below them are those who must first govern their sons and households. The third are those who luxuriate in food and physical pleasure. Of them it is written: the widow that lives in delight is dead. All widows, then, are not equal, nor do they please God who are perceived as widows only in body and not in deed. She that is truly a widow shall trust in the Lord and be busy in prayer night and day. Saint John distinguishes the true from the false widow by her good works. There are some rich, noble, and powerful widows who do not nurture their sons to God but to the world, and reject good works and seek to please men more than Christ. Be you holy and meek evermore and perform works of mercy and righteousness. Obey the Commandments. Spend your time in prayers and alms.

A MIRROUR FOR MAYDENES [152]. A spirited treatise addressed principally to maidens but also intended for priests urging them to avoid "pride of clothes." It survives in a single manuscript of the early fifteenth century severely mutilated at the beginning and along the outer edges.

This treatise is a mirror for maidens who would be Christ's spouse and forsake marriage to man's flesh which will rot away in a short time, and it speaks mainly about pride of clothes. Priests and maidens should surpass knights, wedded folk, and widows in the holiness of their lives and be a model of behavior to them. They should bring light to the world in charity and poverty. A maiden should not dress in a courtly manner, for thereby she surrenders the outward tokens of Christ's poverty like a proud woman who abandons her poor husband. Follow the poverty of Christ Who at His birth was placed in a cradle naked for lack of clothes before two beasts whose breath preserved Him from the cold. Christ appeared to His disciples not in curious clothes, but as a poor gardener. To Peter He appeared as a servant. Be as the heavenly host of maidens undefiled by sin in the apocalyptic vision. When we adopt fine clothes, we adopt the livery of Lucifer and forsake the livery of Christ. There are numerous examples in the Old Law and the New of devout men wearing sackcloth and the broken skin of goats and camels. Priests, too, should be as virgins seeking the road to salvation.

A NOBLE TRETYS OF MAYDENHODE [153]. A vigorous composition extant in two fifteenth-century manuscripts. The central image is ultimately derived from Canticles 2.2. Its immediate source is St. Bernard's *Sermones in Cantica Canticorum* 48.1–2.

Ecce virgo concipiet et pariet filium. Although Isaiah's words were said of Mary, they apply to all maidens, for every good maiden bears many children who will play before her in the bliss of heaven. These children are good works and fair virtues—meekness, chastity, patience, righteousness, moderation in eating, drinking, and other activities, strength to withstand the temptations of the devil, suffering all the adversity, disease, and tribulation of this life, compassion for the distress of others. But not all who are called maidens bear these children. There are three degrees of maidens. The first are undefiled in deed, but are disposed to foul speaking and evil touching. The second are undefiled in deed or speech, but lack the purpose to live chastely. The third are undefiled in word or will and are fully determined to live chastely. The first, although they do not consent to the deed, are guilty of sin because they lead others to desire them. Solomon denounces them, as does Jerome in *Ad Eustochium.* They are like a dunghill covered with snow or a reed that is fair without but weak and hollow within. Such maidens seem holy, but their heart is rooted in the mire of lust and is totally lacking in good thoughts, holy meditations, and spiritual goodness. They are like the serpent that showed himself to Eve. The second keep their bodies and hearts pure, but they really wish to be wedded. They are not yet one with themselves or steadfast in spirit. Saint Paul speaks of them, and Saint Chrysostom. They are wedded in their souls and earn none of the rewards that come to maidenhood. They are less worthy than the married in the view of Saint Augustine. The third are those who wish to remain chaste always. They keep their hearts pure and holy both in body and in soul and their thoughts in Christ.

Holy Writ recommended maidenhood. It was not commanded but counselled by God. It is hard to keep on earth, for it is akin to the life of angels. Hence, it deserves greater reward in heaven. Maidens are God's angels on earth. Elias was taken up to heaven because he remained pure on earth. Daniel the prophet was preserved from the lions because he resisted the lusts of the flesh. His companions were protected from the fire by the shield of pure maidenhood. Christ himself through his life showed his approval of maidenhood, as did the Virgin Mary, Saint John the Baptist, and Saint John the Evangelist.

Maidens surpass in merit both wives and widows in the view of Saint John Chrysostom. They are the most worthy of all mankind. Being pure, they follow the Lamb of God into the joys and bliss of heaven and are next to God.

It is wrong to counsel maidens to marry. Bernard tells the story of a maiden who, having entered a nunnery of her own volition, was beseeched by her parents to return home. She rejected their plea and rebuked them severely.

The pure maiden is the spouse of Christ. She is like the lily which surpasses other flowers. The lily has six leaves and within the leaves three fair grains. The six leaves are soberness, i.e., moderation in meat and drink, occupation with honest work lest idleness lead to lechery, meekness, silence, love, and fear of the Lord. The three grains are the three crowns that come to maidenhood in heaven: purity without spot or filth or corruption before the throne of God, joy in union with Christ and the company of angels and saints, worship without end for their clean life on earth.

A similar text is in *A Myrour to Lewde Men and Wymmen* [8].

A TRETIS OF MAYDENHOD [154]. A brief text citing Matthew, Paul, and Augustine as authorities.

Sister, we desire your spiritual advancement. Matthew's parable of the sower and the seed was spoken of wedded men and women, virtuous widows, and pure maidens. Chastity has many rewards. To preserve it, avoid the sight and touch of men. Rejoice in God without complaint, and desire to serve Him always. By doing so, you preserve and foster clean maidenhood. Avoid foul language. Do not chatter or gad about or be vain about your beauty. Avoid swearing, chiding, and fine array (the alestake of lechery). Take Christ as your spouse, and follow the example of Saints Margaret, Cecilia, Catherine, Agas, Agnes, and many other holy virgins.

THE COUNSELS OF SAINT ISIDORE [155]. A collection of moral admonitions to good conduct arranged in brief paragraphs under such rubrics as "Of evil thoughts," "Of Chastity," "Of Continual Prayer," "Of Fasting," "Of Drink," "Of Patience," "Honest Conversation," "Sin of Backbiting," "Of Conscience," "Confession," etc. Its source is the spurious *Monita* or *Consilia Isidori*. Originally intended for a religious audience, it apparently reached a wide range of lay and clerical readers in the fifteenth century.

THE FIVE WITS [156]. Comprising Parts II and III of the *Ancrene Riwle* (IV [1] in *Manual*, vol. 2), the former consisting of an extensive commentary on the outer wits, it was, in the opinion of the editor, A. C. Baugh, freely adapted to a lay audience in the mid-fifteenth century, probably by the London preacher and poet William Lichfield (see VII [3] in *Manual*, vol. 3); it is preserved uniquely in British Library MS Royal 8.C.i. R. E. Lewis, however, regards it as a new work in two parts, independent of its original. The matter requires further investigation.

Another extensive prose commentary on the outer wits, containing a short Wycliffite interpolation, bears some similarity to the exposition in the *Ancrene Riwle*. It exists in British Library MS Harley 2398 of the early fifteenth century and may originally have been part of a longer treatise addressed to a lay and clerical audience. R. H. Brenner of the University of Nijmegen has an edition in hand.

To stir and excite man to love Him, God made him a royal palace in which to dwell, i.e., this wide world, which He filled with pleasures to disport him. He also made him a private dwelling in his palace, i.e., his body, with a small private room to rest in, i.e., his heart, and five small windows through which to look out and determine what to receive with profit and reject as harmful. If these windows are not wisely governed, foul airs of deadly pestilence enter the closet of the heart and infect the soul. Then follows a detailed explanation of the proper custody of the senses—sight, hearing, smell, taste, and touch.

There are also two brief commentaries in prose on the outer wits, the first in two fifteenth-century manuscripts, Glasgow University Library MS Hunter 520 and Princeton University Library MS Garrett 143, and the second in Bodleian Library MS Lyell 29 of the early fifteenth century.

Five lines of verse on the outer wits occur in Bodleian Library MS Bodley 549.

Mention has already been made of Audelay's carol on the outer wits (see [29] above).

The inner and outer wits are described in twelve four-stress couplets in six manuscripts: Cambridge University Library Ff.2.38, Magdalene College, Cambridge, Pepys 1584, British Library Harley 1706 and 2339, Lambeth Palace Library 491, and St. Cuthbert's College Ushaw 28. A list of the outer and inner wits appears in Trinity College, Cambridge, MS 337 and in Bodleian Library MS Lyell 29 preceding the aforementioned commentary on the outer wits.

A meditation of the five outer wits concludes a version of *The Contemplations of the Dread and Love of God* in University of Pennsylvania MS 8 of the early fifteenth century.

NINE VIRTUES [157]. An instruction urging practical devotion and simple charity over formal penance and public observance. It originated on the Continent perhaps as early as the thirteenth century and achieved an immense popularity throughout Europe in the fourteenth and fifteenth centuries, circulating both in Latin and in the vernacular under the name of Albert, Archbishop of Cologne, often identified with Albertus Magnus who, however, was never Archbishop of Cologne. Miss Allen (Allen WAR, p. 317), who studied the piece among the spurious works of Rolle, suggested a possible identification of Albert with Albert Suerbeer of Cologne. The versions vary considerably in the arrangement and exposition of the articles. Some, moreover, represent them as the invention of the author in the person of Jesus Christ, others as a revelation (specifically dated 1345 in some manuscripts) by Christ to the author or a good man. There are thirteen versions in Middle English prose, and three in verse. The latter include: "A Good lesson of IX Vertewis," 202 lines in couplets; "Neghen Pyntes of Gret Vertu," 114 lines in couplets; and an acephalous version by John Audelay, 102 lines in thirteen-line stanzas riming ababbabacddac.

Here begins an instruction containing nine articles by Master Albert, Archbishop of Cologne. He spoke these words in the person of Jesus Christ (or Jesus Christ spoke these words to Albert or a good man in a revelation): Give a penny to the poor for love of Me during your life, and it shall please Me and profit you more than if men offered a heap of silver in your behalf after your death. Shed a tear for My suffering and passion on your behalf, and it shall please Me and profit you more than if you shed as many tears as there is water in the sea for vain and changeable things. Break your sleep to worship and praise Me, and it shall please Me and profit you more than if men commission twelve knights in your name after your death. Do not speak ill of your neighbor, and do no harm, and it shall please Me and profit you more than if you went barefoot so long that men could follow you by the tracks of your blood. Cheerfully suffer abuse for love of Me, and it shall please Me and profit you more than if you suffered as many rods to be broken on your body as may lie in a great field. Harbor the poor and do good to the needy, and it shall please Me and profit you more than if you fasted 40 years on bread and water. Do all the good you can and bring peace and love to your neighbors, and it shall please Me and profit you more than if you were ravished to heaven daily. Pray directly to Me, and it shall please Me and profit you more than if My mother and all the saints in heaven prayed Me in your behalf. Love Me above all other creatures, and it shall please Me and profit you more than if you were to die in an attempt to climb up and down a pillar reaching from earth to heaven and sharp as razors.

THE POWERS OF MAN'S SOUL [158]. A short prose treatise extant in two manuscripts, Bodleian Library Bodley 938 and Cambridge University Library Kk.6.26, with strongly Wycliffite associations. It is of Northern origin.

The powers of man's soul are five. Three—Mind, Reason, and Will—are called primary; two—Imagination and Sensuality—are called secondary. All but Mind are working powers. Mind contains and comprehends the rest. I do not mean to suggest that the soul is divisible, but merely that the things on which the powers of the soul operate are divisible, the primary matters being spiritual, the secondary physical. Reason and Will work with the aid of Imagination and Sensuality in all spiritual matters. Imagination and Sensuality work without the aid of Reason and Will in all physical matters, but without Reason and Will they cannot know the virtues and conditions of physical creatures or the cause of their being. All of them work in conjunction with the five wits. Reason is the power by which we distinguish good from evil, good from better, evil from worse, worse from worst, better from best. Before original sin Reason could do this naturally, but now it is blinded and must be illuminated by grace. Will is the power by which we choose good after it has been determined by Reason and through which we love God. Once it worked perfectly, but since original sin it must be anointed with grace. Imagination is the power by which we procure the images of all things present and absent. Once it served Reason with perfect obedience, but now, unless it is restrained by the sight of grace, it continually conjures up disordered images as fantasies. Sensuality is the power by which we know physical creatures. Since original sin it must be kept under control to prevent us from falling into sin.

HOW MAN IS MADE TO THE IMAGE OF GOD [159]. A text based on Saint Augustine's *De Trinitate,* Books 10 and 14. Although the manuscripts in which it appears are strongly Wycliffite, its content appears perfectly orthodox. It is of Northern origin.

Man was not made like the rest of creation by the word of God alone but by the counsel of the Holy Trinity and the work of God's majesty. All the more, then, ought he to love God by virtue of the special honor he received in being made to His image and likeness. The image is to be seen in the nobility of the soul suffusing his entire body, no more in one place than another, an image of the unity of Almighty God. The soul, like the Trinity, has three qualities—mind, will, and understanding—and is neither perfect nor complete without them. Man is commanded to love God by these three qualities. The more virtuous he is the nearer he is to God and the stronger is his likeness to his Maker. God made man wonderfully to His likeness in the first Adam and still more wonderfully remade him to His likeness in the second Adam, Who is Christ.

A similar treatise is extant in Cambridge University Library MS Kk.6.26. A brief extract from *Cibus Animae* entitled *De Anima Pulchra* states that every clean Christian soul is fair and in the image of God.

If you would know how it stands with your soul, ransack your conscience and consider the state of your will. If you are firmly rooted in the faith of Holy Church, if you turn from all deadly sin, if you do not willfully break the Commandments, if you made your confession, performed your penance, and determined never to sin again, then your soul is in God's likeness.

The piece is of Northern origin and is extant in two manuscripts, Cambridge University Dd.14.26(3) and Trinity Hall, Cambridge, 16.

CHARITE ALLE THING LEEVETH [160]. A short prose treatise addressed to a nun.

Dear sister in Christ, if we dispose ourselves to charity, we shall understand the nature of the soul. For whoever is in charity cleaves to God and dwells in God, as Saint John says, and whoever cleaves to God is one spirit with Him and deems all things. The knowledge of the spirit is in contrast to the knowledge of the flesh. The flesh knows other things, itself least, as the eye sees other things but not itself. The spirit, in knowing itself, principally knows all things when it is one with the spirit of God. Therefore, the person who does not know himself knows nothing—neither his own nor another's soul. Sister, if you would acquire knowledge of the soul, you must rule your five wits and mortify your flesh, love God and keep the Commandments, and be good and merciful to your neighbor.

ICHE CRYSTEN SOWLE HATH THRE MYGHTES [161]. Jolliffe (no. H.2) notes that this piece is related to the *Formula noviciorum* and to the conclusion of *The Clensyng of Mannes Sowle* [84].

Every Christian has three powers: reason, will, and mind—reason to know God, will to love God, mind to rest in God. Sin blinds the reason, cripples the will, and renders the mind unstable. The beginning of the reformation of the reason is to believe in the common faith of holy church. The perfection of reason is to understand the basis of his belief through the illumination of God and to see God in contemplation. The beginning of the reformation of the will is to withstand sin and to perform good works diligently. The perfection of the will is to will nothing that is not in accordance with the will of God and to be inspired by love of God. The beginning of the reformation of mind is to put aside vain thoughts and place his thoughts in God. The perfection of mind is to engage in meditation and prayer without distraction, and, oblivious of self and earthly things, to rest in God.

THE NATURE OF MAN [162]. An incomplete prose treatise in British Library MS Harley 2398 and two related manuscripts, Glasgow University Library MS Hunter 520 and Princeton University Library MS Garrett 143, both of the fifteenth century.

Whoever desires to love Christ must have knowledge of his nature, his origin, his Creator, the purpose of his creation, and how he can fulfill that purpose. Man has a twofold nature—bodily and ghostly, earthly and heavenly, bestial and spiritual. His bodily nature is first in the order of time, his ghostly nature is the soul which distinguishes man from beast and which ought to have the flesh under its governance. The soul has two aspects, one called sensuality which deals with the flesh through the outer wits and the other called spirit which distinguishes between good and evil, truth and falsehood, profit and loss, and has three powers—mind, will, and understanding. Through the experiences of the five wits, sensuality gives to spirit a clearer understanding of the invisible Godhead and moves it to love of its Creator. Man must consider his origin. He was not made because God required his service, but to occupy the place left vacant by the angels. He was formed of the unworthiest element, earth, and to earth he will return. He was conceived in sin and in sin born to this world. His soul, albeit in the image of the Trinity, was made of nought. Let him, therefore, take no pride in his origin, but be aware of his wretchedness and worship his Maker, acknowledging His excellence and moved by His goodness. God is mirrored in man's soul and seen in His creation. He may be known through faith and love. One is insufficient without the other; both are necessary. Faith without love is of no value. Love cannot exist without faith. Here the treatise breaks off.

HOW RESON SCHAL BE KEPER OF THE SOULE [163]. A translation of the *Revelations of Saint Birgitta*, Book 7, Chapter 7, probably intended for a clerical audience (see the chapter on English Mystical Writings in a later volume of this *Manual*).

A mighty king built a house where he lodged his daughter whom he dearly loved. To her he assigned a warden and gave him this charge: My daughter has deadly enemies. Therefore, be wary and guard her wisely. Take careful heed to four things: (1) that no enemy undermine the house; (2) that no enemy climb over the high outer walls; (3) that no enemy break down the four inner walls; (4) that no enemy enter by the gates of the house. By this house is understood man's body which our Lord God, the King of heaven, made of earth. By the king's daughter is understood man's soul formed by the power of Almighty God and placed in man's body. By the warden is understood man's reason which is ordained to keep and govern the soul after the will of God. By the foundation is understood a good and firm will upon which are placed good works which strengthen the soul and defend it from enemies. Reason must protect the will from being undermined by perilous engines and subtle suggestions to the detriment of the soul. Reason must also protect against an enemy climbing over the high outer walls, i.e., charity which surpasses all other virtues. The devil desires nothing more than to leap and skip upon these walls. By the inner walls is understood the four delights a man should fervently desire in his soul: (1) to see God in His everlasting glory; (2) to hear the sweet voices of angels praising and worshipping God without end; (3) to praise and worship God with the angels; (4) to have enduring comfort and consolation in heaven. By the gates of the house is understood such necessities as food, drink and sleep, which are indispensable to man but which must come under the rule of reason lest the soul become sluggish in the service of God.

NAMMORE NE IS BE TUENE ANE MANNE AND ANE BESTE BOTE INE ONDERSTONDYNGE [164]. A treatise on the difference between men and beasts following the *Ayenbite of Inwyt* [4] in BL Arundel MS 57. It is in the hand of, and probably by, the *Ayenbite*'s scribe and author, Dan Michel. Its source is unknown.

Understanding distinguishes a man from a beast. Boast of no other virtues. Flies surpass you in swiftness. A peacock's plumage is fairer than you. How are you worthier?—In respect of God's image. Where is God's image?—In thought and understanding. By virtue of man's ability to think and understand, he is superior to a beast. Man's light consists in the light of thought. Do not, O men, live in darkness; do not be untrue, unjust, evil, thievish, vengeful, worldly. For this, indeed, is to live in darkness. The light does not leave you; rather do you leave the light. The blind cannot see even in the midst of sunshine. Do not live in darkness. The world is dark, for the lovers of this world live in darkness, and the world is evil, for those who dwell in the world are evil. Christ died although He had no reason to die. You disdain death although you have every reason to die. Suffer with good will according to your merit as He Who delivered you from everlasting death suffered with good will. God made angels as well as small worms, but the angels are worthy of heaven, the worms of earth. If He placed the worms in heaven, you would reproach Him. If He made angels of foul, stinking flesh, you would blame Him. But God is not to be reproved. For all men are made of flesh. What are they but worms? And of worms He makes angels. Everyone perceives which heart is raised to God; everyone bears the weight of his flesh. Be resolute through abstinence that the heart may be cleansed and raised to God.

HOW A MAN SHULDE KNOWE HIMSELF [165]. A short treatise attributed to Saint Bernard in the single extant manuscript.

Saint Bernard says: Man, it is better for you to know yourself than the virtue of herbs, the course of the stars, the nature of beasts, the complexion of men, and all things in heaven and on earth. Many men know many things but not themselves. Therefore, man, take care what you were before your birth and what you are from birth to death. You know not what you will be after death. You were made of vile matter and clothed in a foul bloody skin in your mother's womb. Then you were brought forth in sin to the wretchedness of this life. After death you will be food for worms and ashes. Why do you make yourself fair with precious ornaments and fat which worms will devour in the grave after a few days? Why do you not make your soul fair with good works which are to be presented to God and His angels in heaven? Why do you have so little value for your soul? Why do you place your flesh before you as a lady and your soul behind as a handmaiden? Why do you permit the handmaiden, your flesh, to have "ladyship" over the lady, your soul? That is a great disgrace.

VERSE TRACTS ON SELF-KNOWLEDGE [166].

(a) *Love God and Drede.* 21 eight-line stanzas riming ababbcbc addressed mainly to heads of state.

Every head of state should beware of deceitful advice, oppression, and injustice. Uphold the law;

take good counsel. Love and fear God, and know yourself. Do not abuse a commoner to please a few. Compose quarrels; apply the law evenhandedly; avoid favor and vengeance. Govern according to God's Commandments. He will call every man to a reckoning. Turn your heart from worldly pleasures and give it to God. Banish mischief from the realm and punish rebellion. Do not be revered out of fear. The sinner makes God his enemy. He should stop before his soul goes to hell. Choose heaven or hell. The man without charity will never be saved. Observe the golden rule. You will have to account for all that you have acquired amiss. Do not trust too much or too little to God's mercy. Conscience will tell you whether you are worthy of salvation or damnation. Despoiling the poor will be condemned. Works of mercy will be rewarded. Judges should hear both sides, take no bribes, and decide on the facts. Neighbors should reconcile quarrels. Enmities should not be allowed to smolder. Flee folly, and follow wisdom. Man, know yourself; love and dread God.

(b) *Each Man ought Himself to know.* Nine twelve-line stanzas riming aba-bababcaca in the Vernon and Simeon manuscripts.

Every Christian should know himself and be aware of his mortality. He will die as his parents did. Let him confess while he can and strive to save his soul by amending his sins. Consider what God has done for you. He has made you in His own image and died for you. All passes—worldly honors, goods, strength, etc. Only conscience can save you.

(c) *Man, know thy self and lerne to dye.* Fifteen eight-line stanzas riming ababbcbc.

Man's soul is immortal, his body mortal. Learn to die wisely. Let not your works prove you a fool. All men must die and be judged. Wealth will be of no avail after death. Practice virtue, confess, and repent of your sins. Give alms to the poor. God will demand a full accounting. Do not be guilty of too much or too little hope in God's mercy. Do not rely on the almsgiving or prayers of other people. Heaven or hell is in God's hands. Repentance buys mercy. Be a friend to yourself while you may.

(d) *Know thyself.* The concluding 36 lines of an acephalous poem in eight-line stanzas riming ababbcbc.

. . . Therefore, be your own friend. Think what you are. Do not be destroyed by pride. Know yourself. If you are a churchman, consider that Jesus is your salvation. In order that you may destroy temptation and perform your office all the better, live in virtuous contemplation, and know yourself. Do well, and think upon your end. All should reflect on the peril of sin and cry God's mercy.

(e) *The Conflict of Wit and Will* has been previously discussed under Dialogues, Debates, and Catechisms (VII [29] in *Manual,* vol. 3).

TROUTHE HOPE LOVE [167]. A collection of injunctions on truth, hope, love, honor, reverence, compassion, mercy, mildness, purity, holiness, and steadfastness.

THE ABSEY OF SEYNT BONAVENTURE (or THE LYFE OF A RE-LIGIOUS PERSONE) [168]. A fifteenth-century Franciscan instruction uniquely extant in British Library MS Cotton Faustina D.iv.

As a religious person you must learn to be meek and humble, to fear God and your superiors, to keep the company of virtuous men, to show sympathy for men in adversity or distress, to observe poverty and love simplicity, to follow the common customs of the house and avoid singularity, to give audience and credence to the Word of God and them that teach it, to desire not to fulfill your own will but God's, to do all that you do only to please God, to keep your tongue from evil, to go from strength to strength in virtue and good deeds, to refrain from meddling in matters that do not concern you, to eschew idleness and spend your time in virtuous occupations, to disclose your tribulations and temptations to your confessor, to avoid a presumption of your own holiness and virtue, but to thank God for His great gifts and benefits, to perform your obligations promptly and cheerfully, to observe moderation in meat and drink, to suffer wrongs and rebukes patiently, to thank God for small gifts of grace, to ascribe your virtue to the Lord, to direct your life and meditation to Christ, to join in the hymns and psalms which the clergy sing in Holy Church, to love God with your whole heart and mind, and to edify your brother and your neighbor with good example.

THE SEVEN COMMANDMENTS OF THE NEW TESTAMENT [169]. One paragraph.

(1) Love God above all things and your neighbor as yourself; (2) Cultivate meekness and forswear lordship; (3) Be steadfast in your devotion to truth and in your rejection of all manner of falsehood; (4) Suffer distress and wrong in this world without resistance; (5) Forgive your brethren's trespasses against you; (6) Be poor in spirit but not beggarly; and (7) Be chaste.

FIVE POINTS ON GOOD LIVING [170].

Thank God and say the Pater Noster on rising. Go to church and hear Mass devoutly, meditating on Christ's passion and especially on His five wounds. Say Grace before meals. Conduct your business honestly. Examine your conscience before retiring, and repent of your sins, purposing not to repeat them the following day. Live as you would die!

SEVEN TOKENS OF CHRIST'S LOVE [171].

A man may deem that he has Christ's love when his desire for earthly goods and his lust slacken, when he is possessed of a burning desire for heaven, when his tongue speaks of heaven rather than of earth, when he is devoted to spiritual exercises and finds them sweet, when things once hard seem easy because of love, when he has the strength to endure all anguish and adversity, hating nothing but sin, loving nothing but God, and when he takes joy in tribulation. The suffering that comes from illness brings three benefits with it—it strengthens the soul, purges it of sin, and leads to greater glory.

THE FIVE COMMANDMENTS OF THE CHURCH [172]. Five lines accompanying an illustration in Book 2, Chapter 16, of *The Ordynarye of Crystyanyte* (or *of Crysten Men*) [14].

Hear Mass on Sundays and holy days of obligation. Confess your sins at least once a year. Receive the Eucharist at Easter. Observe all feast days. Fast on the vigils of Ember Days and during Lent.

For *The Lyfe of Soule,* a dialogue on the life of Christian perfection intended for both a lay and a religious audience, and *The Holy Boke Gratia Dei,* a compilation on the three degrees of grace and man's dependence upon and proper use of it, see the chapter on English Mystical Writings in a later volume of this *Manual.*

IV. Allegorical Works

1. Works Based on Allegorical Devices

A TRETYSE OF GOSTLY BATAYLE [173]. Extant in seven manuscripts, all of London origin and all but one dating from the last half of the fifteenth century. Its main sources are *Dives and Pauper* [45] and *Pore Caitif* (see the chapter on the Mystical Writings), which provide the allegorical framework of horse and armor, and *Three Arrows of Doomsday* (see Mystical Writings) and *Pains of Purgatory* (see [18] and bibliography) which provide the eschatalogical material. The central image derives from Ephesians 6. It is conflationary in character rather than original, in simple prose, and intended for a lay as well as a religious audience. Horstmann printed the text from MS Harley 1706. It has been re-edited with a full critical text and notes from MS Douce 322, of which Harley 1706 is a copy, by Dr. Valerie Murray.

Brother and sister, if you would be saved, bear in mind what our Lord said to Job(8): All men's life on earth is but a fight against spiritual enemies. These enemies are the world, the flesh, and the devil. Saint Paul bids you clothe yourself in the true armor of God that you may withstand the temptations of your enemies. Man's body is as a cloth in which the soul is enclosed. It is also likened to a horse, for as a well-trained horse bears his master over many perils, so does a well-disciplined body bear the soul over the many perils of this wretched world. Just as a man may not indulge in combat against his enemy unless his horse is meek and mild, so the soul may not fight against the deceit of the fiend unless its body is meek and mild. A horse must have a bridle—heavy and sharp if he is unruly, soft and smooth if he is obedient and mild. The bridle is called abstinence from fleshly desires and worldly affections in favor of the love of God and heavenly desires. The two reins of this bridle are the two parts of temperance, i.e., neither too little nor too much, and they are bound together by the knot of good discretion. If the rein is too slack, the flesh will have its will in drinking, speaking, sleeping, telling empty tales, ribaldry, lies, swearing, or other unprofitable speech. If the rein is too taut, the flesh will become too feeble to serve God's will. The horse's saddle is patience and meekness in adversity. The stirrups of the saddle are humility and "sadness," humility against pride and "sadness" against worldly avarice and fleshly lusts, so that you do not feel excessive sorrow for adversity or excessive joy for prosperity. God spoke of this saddle to Cain when he was angry at Abel, for he had fallen out of the saddle of patience into the foul pit of wrath. Saint Paul bids man to arm his body with the virtue of truth which is the habergeon of righteousness. And as the rings of the habergeon are closely joined together and harmonize with each other, so should truth harmonize with righteouness and be closely joined together. Saint Paul also bids you to protect your legs with spiritual poverty so that your hearts and affections and desires are drawn away from earthly things. See that your feet are shod in making ready the gospel of peace. If you are a priest, preach and teach it reverently and charitably with meekness and a life of perfection whereby simple people may be inspired by your example to remain firm in their faith, to increase in virtue, and to avoid sin. If you are a layman, help and support the clergy in their mission, hear sermons, believe in the sacraments and do not question them, obey the laws of God and Holy Church. Take up the shield of faith which by virtue of its triangular shape symbolizes the Trinity. Then take up the basinet of health, i.e., the hope of forgiveness, and the vambrace and rerebrace and gloves of plate, i.e., good occupations and business in corporal or spiritual works. Gird yourself with the girdle of chastity. Take with you the sword of God's word and the spear of Christ's Passion. A wise man of arms will choose a good ground to fight on, which is to say, see to it that the cause for which you fight is always right, just, clear, and undefiled by avarice. Be sure that your spurs, which are the love and dread of God, are sharp. A wise man of arms before he enters battle will know whether the cause for which he fights is right and what reward he will receive. You are engaged in a righteous battle to save the soul, and your sword is salvation. If you are of two minds about the cause, send your friend, i.e., your heart, to observe the alternative to salvation, i.e., hell, where it shall see the suffering and torments of the damned. Consider the day of doom when the Lord will shoot three arrows, the first calling to judgment, the second sharply reproving all false Christians, the third pronouncing endless damnation. Then send your heart into purgatory to observe its seven pains which are no less than those of hell but of limited duration. Once you have seen the pains of hell and purgatory, do penance without delay, and beware of venial sins which may lead to mortal sins. Send your heart into heaven to observe its joys. Viewing even the smallest bliss of heaven will turn the pleasures and delights of this world to bitterness, sorrow, and care. We may learn from the experiences of Peter, Paul, and Moses.

Therefore, take heed of your horse, which is your body, that it be submissive and mild to the soul, its master. See to it that the soul is well armed with spiritual armor, i.e., the virtues, and that it not leave behind its spear, sword, and shield. Think of the bliss of heaven and the pains of hell, and it will fortify you to withstand spiritual enemies and resist their wicked counsels.

MILICIA CHRISTI [174]. A text of Northern origin dating from the late fourteenth or early fifteenth century. Its sources are numerous and diverse. The basic framework derives from the pseudo-Anselmian *Similitudo militis.* Other materials are drawn from *Pore Caitif,* Edmund of Abingdon's

Speculum Ecclesiae, pseudo-Augustinian *Sermo CCXLV (De mysteriis Trinitatis et Incarnationis), Legenda Aurea, Vitas Patrum, Gesta Romanorum,* Bromyard's *Summa Praedicantium, Glossa Ordinaria,* and *Catena Aurea.* There are extensive citations from the Bible. It was apparently addressed to a well-educated lay audience. Its partially rhythmical and alliterative style connect it with the Katherine group and with the works associated with Rolle and the Rolle tradition.

Induite vos armatura ut possitis stare adversus insidias diaboli. Clothe you well with the armor of God that you may withstand the temptations and assaults of the devil. These are the words of Saint Paul (Ephesians 6) which every Christian must understand and follow. What armor does he require? First, he must have a good horse with a bridle to control him and a saddle and two good sharp spurs. For himself he needs a good and reliable habergeon, a helmet, a shield on his left side, a sharp spear in his hand, and a good sword by his side. The knight is our soul, our inner man, made in God's likeness. The horse is our flesh. As soon as man begins to forsake the wickedness of this world and bow under the holy and virtuous yoke of God, his enemies begin to attack him with their wiles. Therefore, he must stand strongly in righteousness and dread of God and serve Him and resist temptation. Thus will he triumph over the fiend. The trappings of the horse are important to victory. The bridle is abstinence; the saddle is meekness; the spurs are love and dread. Seven things stir us to the dread of sin: remembrance of the tears that Christ shed, the great enormity of sins, the great violence that God will do for sin, the great mercy of God to the sinner, the great power and might that God will show at the Judgment, the great vengeance that God out of righteousness has taken for sin, the great reproof and shame that shall befall man taken in sin. Dread can be likened to three kinds of men: a porter that keeps a gate, a just judge, a watchman who trumpets soldiers awake in a war. Dread serves man's soul as a religious chapter. As religious are accused in chapter, so does dread accuse the soul and urge it to penance. The habergeon stands for righteousness, the helmet for hope. Four things strengthen our hope—mindfulness of our Lord Jesus Christ, mindfulness of our Lady, mindfulness of the angels, mindfulness of holy saints. The shield stands for true faith which enables man to withstand pride and worldly worship to be above all other men. Follow the path of good deeds to God and keep true faith. Do not dispute the faith, but truly believe the points of the Creed, the Incarnation, Transubstantiation, and Trinity. Examine your conscience for sin and thank God for His blessings.

THE DESERT OF RELIGION [175]. An allegory of Northern origin in 940 four-stress couplets. It is preserved in three illustrated manuscripts of the first half of the fifteenth century in the British Library, MS Additional 37049, MS Cotton Faustina B.vi, pars II, and MS Stowe 39, which ascribe it incorrectly to Richard Rolle. Apart from the opening passage and incidental details relating to the forest, it is entirely derivative. Hope Emily Allen identified its main source as the *Speculum Vitae* [7]. Other materials come from the *Prick of Conscience, Legenda Aurea,* and *De Duodecim Abusionum Gradibus* attributed to St. Cyprian. The "twelve virtues" are the chapter titles of Rolle's *Emendatio Vitae.* The central image is developed from the Psalter 54.8: *Elongavi fugiens, et mansi in solitudine.*

The desert of religion is a wilderness betokening "Hard Penaunce." It is called the field of temptation. Within it grow trees with branches and boughs, some reaching upward to heaven, others downward to hell, each of which signifies virtues to follow or vices to avoid. Twenty trees are then described: Virtues rooted in Meekness; Vices rooted in Pride; Meekness; Pride; Twelve Abuses of Religion; Twelve Abuses of the World; Seven Points of Christ's Godhead and Seven Points of His Manhood; Seven Sacraments and Seven Virtues; Deeds of Bodily and Spiritual Mercy; Ten Commandments; Five Outer Wits; Confession; Six Things Good To Avoid; Chastity; Wicked Tongue; Prowess; Perfection; Twelve Virtues; Fourteen Pains of Hell; Seven Joys of Heaven.

THE QUATREFOIL OF LOVE [176]. 40 thirteen-line stanzas comprising eight four-stress alliterative lines riming abababab and a bob-and-wheel of five lines with a varying number of stresses and alliteration riming cdddc. It is a clerical composition of Northern origin glorifying the Virgin Mary. Its resemblance to a group of Northern stanzaic alliterative poems, particularly *Susannah* and *Summer Sunday*, suggests that it was written in the last half of the fourteenth century.

On a May morning, as I worked through a garden, I heard a maiden lamenting and beseeching Mary for succor. A turtle dove, perched on a tree above her, asked the reason for her distress. She replied that she had long sought in vain for a true-love flower. The turtle dove advised her to seek a true-love with four leaves representing the Trinity and Virgin Mary. There follows an account of the Creation, Fall, Incarnation, Passion, and Death of Christ, the Harrowing of Hell, and the Assumption of Mary. The maiden is urged to repentance. She thanks the turtle dove for his counsel. Man, too, is exhorted to seek Mary's intercession. After death it will be too late.

AN HONEST BEDE (or LECTUM BONUM) [177]. An interesting and ingenious prose allegorization of conscience as a bed developed from Canticles 1.15 is preserved in four fifteenth-century manuscripts. Copies are also found incorporated in *Disce Mori* [11] and its derivative, *Ignorancia Sacerdotum* [12]. It was composed, perhaps either at the Briggetine convent at Syon or at the Charterhouse at Sheen, about 1425. Jolliffe distinguishes two slightly different versions of the text. Dr. A. I. Doyle has an edition in hand.

Take heed how to make an honest bed pleasing to God and profitable to your soul. When the chamber of your soul is cleansed from sin through confession, you will array a bed in which our Lord Jesus Christ will be pleased to rest. First consider all the sins you have committed, and gather them together as in a litter of straw. Then shake out of this litter all the dust of your sins and evil thoughts with the shake-fork of kindness which contains two prongs, the will to amend and a prayer to God for grace to amend. The canvas atop the straw must be complete sorrow for your sins which will cause you to water the litter of your bed with tears. The mattress of your bed will be holy meditation which will put out of your soul all foul thoughts that defile it and incline it to sin. The two blankets of your bed shall be abstinence against gluttony and chastity against lechery and lust. The undersheet shall be true belief in the articles of the faith. The oversheet shall be sure hope of salvation through good works. The coverlet shall be charity, i.e., the love of God and neighbor. The pillows shall be pity of the poor and patience in adversity. The bolster supporting the pillows shall be zeal in good works lest torpor lead to despair. The tester at the head shall be *liberum arbitrium* that you choose nothing against God's Commandments. The curtains on the right side shall be righteousness and reason, on the left side understanding and wisdom. Let these curtains run on the rings of the Ten Commandments. Take care that the rings be unbroken lest the curtains sag and allow the devil to peer into the bed of Jesus. The curtain at the foot of the bed shall be your will. Let it run on the seven rings of the seven works of mercy. The canopy over your bed shall be silence that you slander neither man nor God with great oaths and avoid backbiting and foul words. Let the cords used to tie the canopy and on which the curtains run be made of double silk or twine of perseverance. The hooks in the walls supporting the cords and curtains shall be a firm resolve never to sin again. The boards of the bed shall be the four cardinal virtues nailed together at the corners by peace, truth, meekness, and right. See to it that the sheets are white in token of purity and powdered with red roses in token of Christ's Passion. The chamberlin shall be conscience, the usher dread who will admit no one at the door or at the window of your five wits to disturb the rest of our Lord Jesus Christ or defile the chamber. When He is in this bed, angels will sing about it the prophetic song, *Exulta et lauda habitacio Syon* etc.

THE CASTLE OF THE SOUL [178]. A short text of West Midland origin deriving from the *Ancrene Riwle*.

A soul is like a lady in a castle with four walls representing the four cardinal virtues and a tower representing the three theological virtues. In the tower are seven maidens representing the seven gifts of the Holy Ghost. The lady has a chamber made of reason, will, and mind. The oratory of the castle is contemplation of God and the four ministers are a strong desire for God, a prayer for mercy, contrition for sin, and enjoyment of God. The walls have five gates representing the five wits. Beside them are seven almoners, i.e., the seven works of bodily mercy. Seven knights, i.e., the seven virtues, are stationed there to keep out the seven deadly sins. Surrounding the soul are seven doctors, i.e., the seven works of spiritual mercy.

A MORALIZATION ON ARTICLES OF CLOTHING [179]. A text of Northern provenance comprising the last part of a sermon on the feast of the Assumption addressed to women in religion. It incorporates a version of the *Twelf Poyntes* and other material drawn from the *Revelations of Saint Bridget*. The central image is developed from Revelations 1.13.

Special feasts call for clean and honest clothing. As religious you wear next to your body a smock signifying contrition and confession which is the first and principal way of conversion to God. Your kirtle is trust in God. Your girdle is the bridle of your will that is in opposition to the will of God. The knives hanging from the girdle are the loving contemplation of everlasting joy. Your surplice is true knowledge of God and constant remembrance of His benefactions and close attention to His Commandments. Your mantle is your faith, and its seams are the signs of God's charity. The lace on your mantle is contemplation of Christ's Passion. Your wimple is abstinence from meat and drink and sin and peril. Your veil is true obedience to God and your religious vows. The ring on your finger is made of three things, gold, silver, and stone, which signify God's commandments to religious persons seeking salvation—the three things He bids us do, the three things He counsels us to do, the three things He commands us to do, the three things He suffers us to do. Here the treatise concludes with the *Twelf Poyntes* [143].

For a similar allegorization of liturgical vestments, see the *Meditations for Goostely Exercise in the Tyme of the Masse* [205] and *Speculum Christiani*, table 8 [15].

OF THE FLODE OF THE WORLD [180]. 218 lines in riming couplets probably based on the *Prick of Conscience,* Book 2, lines 1213 ff., or on Garner's *Gregorianum,* Book VII, Chapter 3 (Migne PL, 193.287). A copy of it is found inserted in British Library MS Additional 25013 of the *Prick of Conscience* [18]. It originated in the West Midlands.

It is a great wonder why men place their trust in the world and love it so much when it is unstable and uncertain. It offers no rest or ease, but travail and affliction. Its wisdom is nothing but folly, its worship nothing but deception. The enjoyment of it lasts but a little while. The world tosses men like a ball from hand to hand, from weal to woe, from joy to sorrow. It may be likened to nothing more appropriately than to the sea which ebbs and flows, waxes and wanes, daily. Storm and winds give rise to many great waves. Men who love the world are like the different kinds of fish that swim in the sea. Some swim amidst the waves, others at the bottom; some swim against the tide, while others follow it or are borne along by it; still others dwell amidst its worst filth. The sea is deep and powerful. Crossing it requires a ship guided by skillful and experienced mariners, and even then it is at times a perilous and frightening experience. So does the world cast men to and fro, up and down. When a man is cast down, the world seems to him at low tide; when he rises high with worldly goods, it seems at high tide. Just as fish swim about the sea seeking what they enjoy, so men seek worldly ends—high offices, honors, power, wealth. Hard-hearted, avaricious men who think only of worldly goods are like the fish that swim at the bottom of the sea. Rightly do such men dwell with the rich in hell. Unruly and rebellious men who resist the laws of God, their sovereigns, and Holy Church are like the fish that swim against the tide and are always grumbling and impatient. Those who flatter and fawn in the presence of their lords contrary to truth and good conscience are like the fish that swim with the tide. Lustful and slothful men are like the fish that dwell in filth and mud. Restless men lacking in stability and steadfastness are like the fish that swim up and down, to and fro. Some men afflicted by fortune are like the fish cast about on the waves or borne under by them. On the sea are sly fishermen, i.e., evil spirits who spread their nets and bait their hooks to catch men through sin and deceit. But a ship sails through the world laden with God's victuals. It is Holy Church, and its crew are men of religion and devout, unworldly men, each performing a different task, whom it leads to salvation. In the midst of the ship is a strong mast with a broad sail which is Christ and His mercy. Through His might an unfailing wind brings the ship to its haven. There are good fishermen aboard the ship—preachers of God's word who, in accordance with His injunction, spread their nets to draw men from the sea of worldliness to Holy Church.

THE LADDRE OF HEVYNE [181]. An early fifteenth-century moral treatise in prose uniquely preserved in Longleat (Marquis of Bath) MS 29. It bears a general similarity to two Latin works on this subject, Guigo II's *Scala paradisi* (or *Scala claustralium*) and Gobius' *Scala celi,* but neither is its source. Much of the text is derived from the Psalms, the Gospels, and the Books of Wisdom. The prose is lucid and fluent. Dr. Sarah Ogilvie-Thomson of St. Edmund Hall, Oxford, has an edition in preparation.

> The rungs of the ladder by which man climbs to heaven are these: (1) faith with good works; (2) steadfast hope in God; (3) perfect charity; (4) true patience; (5) humility; (6) meekness; (7) a spirit of forgiveness; (8) compunction; (9) prayer; (10) confession; (11) penance; (12) abstinence; (13) fear of the Lord; (14) chastity; (15) justice; (16) mercy; (17) almsdeeds; (18) hospitality; (19) honoring parents; (20) silence; (21) good counsel; (22) honest judgment; (23) good example; (24) visitation of the sick; (25) visitation of churches and shrines; (26) worthy offerings to God; (27) payment of tithes; (28) wit and wisdom to avoid evil; (29) benevolence; and (30) perseverance in good works. The two sides of the ladder are the holy sacrament of the Eucharist and the renunciation of the devil and his works in baptism.

VERSIONS OF GROSSETESTE'S CHATEAU D'AMOUR [182]. *The Chateau d'Amour,* a long allegorical account of the Creation, the Fall, and the Redemption, was composed by Robert Grosseteste in Anglo-Norman for the instruction of the laity generally, but immediately and specifically, perhaps, as Legge suggests, for the noble youths, among them, the sons of Simon de Montfort, in his episcopal household. It is 1168 lines long, in octosyllabic couplets, and is preserved in sixteen manuscripts, all but one from the last half of the thirteenth or the first half of the fourteenth century. Its date of composition is a matter of considerable dispute, ranging from the period before 1199 to that just before his death in 1253. Its chief sources are *Rex et Famulus,* a late twelfth-century, anonymous, prose sermon mainly concerned with the allegory of Four Daughters of God developed from Psalm 84.11, and various exegetical treatises on redemption. No specific source has been discovered for the allegory of the Castle of Love as it appears in the *Chateau.* Sajavaara points out that it contains "one of the richest, perhaps the richest, and most varied versions of the castle-of-the-body idea adapted to the Blessed Virgin" in the entire medieval figurative tradition on this subject. Its central theme, the legalization of atonement, represented through the allegory of the King and the Thrall, was, according to Creek, based on the theory of the Devil's rights, a topic much discussed in medieval theology up to the thirteenth century.

There are four extant Middle English versions of the *Chateau.* The most complete translation is the *Castle of Love* which was composed in the West Midlands about 1300. It runs to 1860 lines in short, rimed couplets and is preserved in three manuscripts. A second version entitled *Myrour of Lewed Men* was made by an unidentified monk of Sawley in a Northeast Midlands dialect during the second half of the fourteenth century. It is a free rendering of the *Chateau*, with much omission and condensation, expressly adapted to a popular audience. It runs to 1248 lines in irregular, rimed couplets and is preserved in a single manuscript associated with the Cistercian abbey where it was probably composed. A third version entitled *King and Four Daughters* contains only the allegory of the Four Daughters of God. It runs to 440 lines in short, rimed couplets and is preserved in a single manuscript. Its composition is assigned to the Northeast Midlands between 1400 and 1450. *Four Daughters,* preserved in British Library MS Cotton Appendix VII, is little more than a paraphrase of the same subject. It was composed in the Northeast Midlands between 1350 and 1400 and consists of 32 tail-rime stanzas (aabccb). Mention has already been made of an independent, fragmentary translation of the *Chateau* incorporated in four separate passages of the *Cursor Mundi* [31]. Other versions of the Four Daughters allegory stemming in part from the *Rex et Famulus* tradition may be found incorporated in the *Gesta Romanorum* and the *Court of Sapience.*

After an invocation to the Trinity and a resumé of the story, the author describes the fall of Lucifer and the rebel angels to hell, the creation of Adam and Eve, and the bestowal on Adam of the lordship of the world and the heritage of paradise. Heaven was his destination. God gave him two laws to observe in paradise: the natural law which obliged him to obey His commandments and the positive law which obliged him not to eat the fruit of the forbidden tree. If he observed the positive law, he would have all worldly bliss; if he broke it, he and his heirs would suffer death. All too soon he broke both laws because he preferred to do his wife's bidding rather than God's. Thus he lost his heritage, was driven from paradise, and became mortal. As the slave and servant of sin, he lost the right to his possessions. His heritage was taken from him. Only a man who was born free, had not eaten of the forbidden tree, and had not transgressed against the laws of paradise and Moses could claim back Adam's heritage. Where might such a man be found? Here the author relates the exemplary story of a mighty and wise king with a son who matched him in virtue. They were as one in all matters. The king governed through his son. He also had four daughters, to each of whom he gave a portion of his substance, power, and wisdom. He could not rule his kingdom properly without them. The first (and eldest) was called Mercy, the second Truth, the third Justice, and the fourth Peace. The king had a servant who had broken his laws and had been given to his enemies. They cast him into the prison of death and caused him great distress. Mercy, seeing this, was moved to pity and entreated the king to pardon him because he had been deceived by false promises and to arrange for his ransom. Truth asked the king to reject her sister's plea. Were Mercy to prevail, transgression would never be punished nor the king feared. The servant had been warned. Why should he receive mercy who was so heedless of his own welfare? Justice supported Truth, saying that the servant had had Mercy, Truth, Justice, and Peace with him but had forsaken them for wrath and woe. His death was just, for Truth had given evidence against him. Peace complained to the king that Truth and Justice could not prevail without the help of Mercy and herself. The end of Truth and Justice was to preserve peace. Mercy should be heard, and no judgment passed until all the daughters were in agreement. Only then would it be valid. Peace would remain abroad until her sisters reconciled. The king's son intervened to settle the quarrel. He was so moved by Mercy that he was prepared to don the servant's clothing and suffer punishment for him. Thus Justice would be done, Peace would return home and be reconciled with Justice, War would be banished, and the people of the country would be saved. So it is that only through God's death could Adam's sin be atoned. The prophets announced His coming, and Isaiah described Him as both God and man. But to become man, it was necessary for Him to be born of a woman. God could descend only in a beautiful and bright place—a comely castle "of all flour, of solas and of socour." The Castle of Love is then described with its tower surrounded by deep ditches and situated on a high rock. Around the tower are four smaller towers, three baileys, and seven barbicans with a gate to each. The castle is painted green, blue, and red. It is white within. In the middle of the tower is a well from which four streams run and an ivory throne with seven steps leading to it. The castle is the body of the Virgin Mary; the rock is her heart. The green, blue, and red colors stand for faith, hope, and charity. The four small towers are the four cardinal virtues; the baileys, Mary's maid-enhood, chastity, and wedding; the barbicans, the seven virtues that overcame the seven deadly sins. The well is the well of grace; the ditches are the Virgin's patient poverty.

When the author knocks at the castle and asks to be admitted, he is beset on all sides by the devil, the world, and the flesh. The devil attacks with pride, wrath, and sloth, the world with envy and avarice, and the flesh with lechery and gluttony. Jesus is born, and demands the return of man's heritage. Of man He asks only that he love God and his neighbor. The author praises the Redeemer's affection, sweetness, and humility. The devil demands a ransom for his prisoner. Jesus promises to give a just ransom—even His own body. The devil demands His death; Christ agrees. Could Christ have done more for mankind? The author describes Christ's suffering on the cross and the Virgin's compassion. She is asked to intercede for mankind. God redeemed us because He possesses two natures: He is true God and true man, as is evidenced by the miracles He performed at the marriage feast of Cana, the multiplication of the loaves and fishes, and the raising of Lazarus. So mighty was He that He burst the gates of hell and released all who believed in Him. He is father of the world to come. Adam was man's worldly father, but Christ his spiritual father. Through Christ man can claim his rights to heaven. Peace was restored to the world. He rose to heaven and will return to judge the world. The treatise concludes with a description of the Fifteen Tokens of Doomsday (see XVI [51] in *Manual*, vol. 6), the Judgment, the pains of hell, and the joys of heaven.

TEMPLUM DOMINI [183]. 784 lines in four-stress eight-line stanzas alternately riming abababab. It is uniquely extant in British Library MS Additional 32578 of the early fifteenth century. Its source is the first six chapters of Robert Grosseteste's *Templum Domini*, a popular confessional manual composed between 1220 and 1230, which survives in over 90 manuscripts. Cornelius notes correspondence with the *Abbey of the Holy Ghost*, [184] below, and Ailred of Rievaulx. The central image goes back to 1 Corinthians 3.16 and 6.19.

This matter is principally addressed to priests, although it is pertinent to all Christians. A priest shall have two temples, the bodily to receive God's manhood, the spiritual to receive His godhead. The bodily temple must have a foundation of temperance paved with abstinence, continence, and "gud thewes." Its four walls shall be will power, steadfastness, strength to withstand adversity, and faithfulness. Its roof shall be constructed of the wits covered by wisdom. The spiritual temple must be founded on faith with walls of hope and a roof of charity. The foundation shall be paved with the twelve articles of the faith. The hope shall be to obtain reward through good deeds and penance, fearing God's righteousness but trusting in His mercy. The roof of charity shall enclose the two commandments of the Gospel and the Ten Commandments. Care must be taken to protect these temples from the seven deadly sins through virtue, prayer, and grace.

THE ABBEY OF THE HOLY GHOST [184]. A translation of a French prose tract, *Abbaye du Saint Esprit*, extant in 24 manuscripts (plus a fragment) and three early prints. *The Charter of the Abbey of the Holy Ghost*, [186] below, an independent treatise, is appended to it in sixteen manuscripts and conflated with it in three others, Bodleian Library MS Douce 323, Bradfer-Lawrence, and Hopton Hall, as well as in the three early prints which are probably based on Bradfer-Lawrence. The English *Abbey*, as Allen and Consacro note, is closely related to a late redaction of the French text found in British Library MS Royal 16.E.xii, dating from the mid-fourteenth century. It is far from a slavish rendering, however, and it contains much rhetorical amplification and interpolative matter of a mystical nature not in the original. Consacro interprets it as a treatise on the Mixed Life addressed to devout men and women who cannot enter a religious community. It urges them to a spiritual life, with particular emphasis on contemplation, conceived as the exercise of charity and other virtues under the sanctifying power of the Holy Ghost. Its composition may be assigned to the third quarter of the fourteenth century. The dialect of the earliest and best manuscript—the Vernon—is Southwestern. Allen suggests that its author was a follower of Rolle.

My dear brothers and sisters, I observe that many of you would be in religion, but are prevented by age, poverty, fear of kin, or bond of marriage. I shall therefore write a book of the religion of the heart which is the Abbey of the Holy Ghost. Where is this abbey established? It is established in a place called Conscience which in the first instance must be cleansed of impurities. The Holy Ghost will send down two maidens, Righteousness and Love of Purity, to remove from Conscience all manner of filth. When this is done, two other maidens, Meekness and Poverty, will lay the foundation by the River of Tears or Repentance. Blessed is the religion that is founded in poverty and meekness. Obedience and Pity will rear the walls of almsdeeds cemented by Love-of-God and Steadfast Faith. Forbearance and Strength will raise the pillars. Confession will make the chapter house; Preaching, the refectory; Prayer, the chapel; Contemplation, the dormitory; Ruefulness, the infirmary; Devotion, the cellar; and Meditation, the storeroom. The Holy Ghost will be warden and visitor; Charity, the abbess; Wisdom, the prioress; Meekness, the sub-prioress; Discretion, the treasurer; Prayer, the preceptor; Devotion, the cellarer; Penance, the cook. Temperance shall serve in the frater, seeing that moderation prevails in food and drink. Sobriety shall read aloud from the lives of the Fathers at table. Pity is pittancer and her sister, Mercy, is almoner. Fear is the porter. Honesty is the mistress of novices teaching them honesty. Courtesy looks after the guests. Reason is provisioner; Loyalty, infirmarian; Meditation, in charge of the granary; Pity, in charge of pittances; and Watchfulness, the bell waking the nuns to matins.

When this abbey was established, a tyrant, i.e., the devil, came with his four daughters—Envy, Pride, Complaint, and Judging-Others-Unjustly—and lodged them by force within it. They were loathly and bad-mannered and did much harm to the convent. When Wisdom, Meekness, and others saw that it was being brought to ruin, they rang the chapel bell and sought counsel as to what was best to do. Discretion advised them to pray to the Holy Ghost for Grace. They all sang *Veni Creator Spiritus*, and the Holy Ghost immediately came and expelled the tyrant's daughters and made the abbey better than it was before. Imitate these ladies daily. If any of the fiend's four daughters seek to enter into your heart, follow Discretion's advice and pray for God's help. He shall deliver you through His mercy and grace.

EIGHT GHOSTLY DWELLING PLACES [185]. A brief prose passage analogous to *The Abbey of the Holy Ghost*, [184] above.

Every religious soul has eight ghostly dwelling places. The first is a temple of devout prayer; the second a school of truth; the third a cloister of silence; the fourth a chapter of rightful correction; the fifth a refectory of sobriety; the sixth a dormitory of rest and peace; the seventh an infirmary of pity and patience; the eighth a hostel of charity and generosity. Whoever has these eight ghostly dwelling places in his soul and follows them in practice achieves religious perfection. They who are disposed to these places eat, sleep, and live together in token of their spiritual accord.

THE CHARTER OF THE ABBEY OF THE HOLY GHOST [186]. A prose treatise symbolically linking the fortunes of *The Abbey of the Holy Ghost*, [184] above, with appropriate incidents in the Biblical narrative from the fall to the redemption. It is preserved in 24 manuscripts and three early prints. Although altogether independent of *The Abbey*, it follows it in sixteen manuscripts and is conflated with it in three others, Bodleian Library MS Douce 323, Bradfer-Lawrence, and Hopton Hall, as well as in the three early prints which are probably based on Bradfer-Lawrence. Its appearance in the Vernon manuscript (Bodleian Library MS Eng poet a.1)—the earliest and the best of the extant manuscripts—indicates that it was composed before 1380, probably in the Southwest of England. *The Charter* is not modelled on *The Abbey* despite their close relationship in the manuscript tradition. Although the figure of the spiritual abbey is taken from the earlier treatise, it is made to serve, as Dr. Brook notes, merely as a vehicle for an allegorical meditation on the spiritual implications of the scriptural events. Within the general allegory has been incorporated a version of the Four Daughters of God and a Carta Dei which bears a faint resemblance to the *Charter of Christ*, [187] below, and gives the work its misleading title. Some of the Biblical material has been taken from a Middle English devotional work, *The Life of the Virgin Mary and the Christ*, extant in Trinity College, Dublin, MS 423. *The Life* also incorporates a version of the Four Daughters nearly identical with *The Charter*'s. Their common source is the pseudo-Bonaventuran *Meditationes vitae*

Christi which itself is partly based on Saint Bernard's *Sermon on the Annunciation* (Migne PL, 183.283). Other versions of the Four Daughters in the Bernardine-pseudo-Bonaventuran tradition are found in *Vices and Virtues* (VII [26] in *Manual,* vol. 3), Love's *The Mirror of the Blessed Life of Jesus Christ, Jacob's Well* [9], *Piers Plowman* (see XVIII in this volume), *Mirror of Simple Souls, Ludus Coventriae* and *The Castle of Perseverance* (XII [12] and [27] in *Manual,* vol. 5), Walter Kennedy's *The Passioun of Christ,* Lydgate's *Life of Our Lady* (XVI [108] in *Manual,* vol. 6), and Thomas Chaundler's *Liber apologeticus de omni statu humanae naturae.*

Bloomfield rightly observes that *The Charter* is written in "excellent" prose.

Here is a book that speaks of a place that is called the Abbey of the Holy Ghost which should be founded in clean conscience. In it are 29 spiritual ladies, among whom Charity is abbess, Wisdom prioress, Meekness subprioress. The Father of Heaven is founder of this abbey, and the Holy Ghost is its warden and visitor. Yet an abbey must have deeds and charters to secure its property. So I shall make the abbess a book called *The Charter of the Abbey of the Holy Ghost* in which I shall relate when, where, and by whom the abbey was founded, when the abbey was destroyed, how the convent was expelled and later restored, and how God installed His four daughters in place of the devil's daughters driven out by the Holy Ghost. Know all present and to come that God granted Adam and Eve and their heirs a little precious place called conscience lying in their souls between reason and synderesis. God gave them this place unblemished and made a house of religion called The Abbey of the Holy Ghost in which He lodged many spiritual ladies, i.e., good virtues, among whom He made Love and Charity abbess, Wit and Wisdom prioress, Meekness and Humility subprioress. The abbey was so strongly walled about that no evil could have entered it if Adam and Eve had so willed. God gave them also the lordship of heaven and earth and all the world to maintain themselves with the noble ladies in their convent, to have and to hold freely forever so long as they resisted the temptations of the devil. But Satan was envious of the abbey and devised a scheme to destroy it. He came to the abbey gate as an adder, but Dread was unprepared, and Eve admitted him. As soon as Adam and Eve ate the forbidden fruit, he and his four tormentors—Pride, Gluttony, Avarice, and Folly—entered the abbey and despoiled it of its goods, including its charter, and expelled the convent. Adam and Eve covered their nakedness with leaves and wanted to enter the abbey, but they saw that it had been destroyed and pillaged because of their sin. God drove them out of paradise, promising that they would never be permitted to return until they had restored the abbey and convent. Then Adam went about the world seeking the Abbess, but he was unable to find her. He and Eve died, and their souls went to hell where they remained for many thousands of years until God took pity on them and sent down His Son to seek the abbey and convent. He sought them for 33 years and found them hanging on the rood. He took them down to hell to talk to Adam and Eve and then restored them all to paradise.

I shall tell you how He found the abbess and her convent. After Adam and Eve's death many patriarchs and prophets sought them in vain. God heard their anguished pleas for help and convened a council of the Holy Trinity in heaven and proposed to restore the abbey and deliver mankind from hell. His four daughters—Mercy, Truth, Peace, and Righteousness—debated the issue, and He finally decided to save mankind. So God became man to seek the abbess and her convent. He found Purity at His conception and Poverty at His birth. He found Righteousness and Wisdom in the Temple and Obedience at home with His parents. He found Temperance and Soberness, Penance and Fortitude in the desert, Shrift and Preaching in His ministry, and Generosity at the seashore. When He went from Mt. Olivet to preach in the Temple of Jerusalem, He found Mercy and Ruefulness and later Reason and Jealousy. At the Last Supper He found Courtesy, Honesty, Humility, and Meekness; later, Dread, Contemplation, and Prayer. During His Passion He found Devotion,

Contemplation, Fidelity, and Jubilation; at His arrest, Patience; at His trial, Simplicity; at His scourging and crowning with thorns, Meekness who accompanied Him to Calvary. And while He was hanging on the cross, He found the last member of the convent, the abbess Charity, and so the restoration of the Abbey was completed. Then He delivered the souls from hell and led them to paradise to dwell with the Abbey of the Holy Ghost in everlasting bliss, appointing His four daughters to serve as its chaplains. Whoever keeps the Abbey in this world shall have much mirth and bliss in the next.

THE CHARTER OF CHRIST (or CARTA CHRISTI or CARTA DEI or TESTAMENTUM CHRISTI or MAGNA CARTA DE LIBERTATIBUS MUNDI or CARTA REDEMPCIONIS HUMANE or TESTAMENTUM DOMINI or FEOFFEMENT IHESU or BONA CARTA GLORIOSE PASSIONIS DOMINI NOSTRI IHESU CHRISTI) [187]. A verse text of varying length, in short couplets, under the figure of a charter recording a grant of heaven's bliss to man on condition that he forswears sin and gives his love to God and his neighbor. It follows the structure and employs the formulae of its legal prototype. Over 40 extant manuscripts testify to its widespread popularity from the mid-fourteenth century onwards. It survives in three distinct versions: (A) the Carta Dei of 42 lines preserved in a single late fourteenth- or early fifteenth-century copy; (B) the "Short" Charter of 32 lines preserved in 24 manuscripts dating mainly from the fifteenth and sixteenth centuries; (C) the "Long" Charter subdivided into three groups (texts A, B, and C), the first of 234 lines preserved in nine manuscripts, the second of 418 lines preserved in nine manuscripts, and the third of 618 lines preserved in a single manuscript. All but two manuscripts of the Long Charter date from the fifteenth century. Texts B and C represent later redactions of A with the addition of familiar didactic materials. In addition to the Middle English, there are two Latin versions of *The Charter,* one in verse entitled *Carta libera Domini Nostri Ihesu Christi,* the other in prose entitled *Carta Domini Nostri Iesu Christi.* Their interrelationships, inconclusively discussed by Spalding, require further investigation. None of these versions either in Latin or in Middle English represents the original state of the text. It is clear, however, from linguistic and paleographical evidence that a vernacular form was in existence as early as the first half of the fourteenth century. The language of the charters is mixed. The Carta Dei derives from Kent, the Short Charter from the North, the A-Text of the Long Charter from the Midlands and the B- and C-Texts from the Midlands or South. The application of legal terminology to the Redemption by Saint Paul in the Epistle to the Ephesians and to human events by Saint Ambrose in his Exposition of the Gospel according to Luke, chapter 10, gave rise to the testamentory form of literature out of which *The Charter* developed. *The Charter of Christ* is, as Woolf aptly notes, "a distinctive and curious form," combining the traditions of the charter and the Passion complaint. Other instances of the allegorical charter in Middle English are the Charter of Favel in *Piers Plowman* (Chapter XVIII), *The Charter of the Abbey of the Holy Ghost*, [186] above, whose phraseology occasionally bears a faint resemblance to *The Charter of Christ*, and the *Pilgrimage of the Life of Man* (XVI [139] in *Manual*, vol. 6).

Version A: Carta Dei. Know all men present and to come that I, Jesus Christ, of My own free and good will, have granted, given, and by this present charter of My body hanging on the cross confirmed to mankind heaven's eternal bliss, to all [aforesaid] men that will flee sin to have and to hold that sweet place in peace through My favor. Further, I, Jesus of Nazareth, and My heirs shall be bound to this pledge in perpetuity. In testimony thereof I have set My seal made of My heart's blood on this My good and true charter. The witnesses being the crown of thorns on My head, the scourges and the long nails, the spear that pierced My heart, the beaker full of vinegar and gall, My laments, tears, bonds, pains, and many more. Granted and guaranteed at Calvary on Good Friday in the thirty-third-and-one-half year of My reign on earth (MS 1, Bodley Kent Charter).

Version B: Short Charter. Know all men present and to come that I, Jesus of Nazareth, Who for love of mankind suffered death upon the cross, have given and granted heaven's eternal bliss to all who claim it provided that they repent their sins and bestow their love upon Me and their neighbor. The witnesses being the earth that quaked, the great rocks that broke asunder, the veil that was rent in two, the men that rose from death to life, the sun that withdrew its light, My mother, St. John, and many others. In testimony and confirmation thereof I have set My seal on this charter—the seal of the wound in My side pierced by the soldier's sharp spear. Given at Calvary on the first day of the great mercy (MS 20, BL Addit 37049).

Version C: Long A-Text Charter. Man and woman, I, Jesus, King of Heaven and Hell, will relate what I did for you for love. What have you done for Me? I came down from My kingdom to bestow My heritage upon you. The deed was made at My birth and confirmed by My Passion and death. Since I could not find a durable parchment upon which to write the charter, I gave My own skin for this purpose. The ink was made of Jews' spittle, the pens were the scourge laid upon Me, the letters were the 5,460 wounds on My body. You that pass by the way, stop and read this parchment and judge if any sorrow compares with Mine. Know all men present and to come that I, Jesus Christ, made a gift to man at My birth and by this present charter grant and confirm that he may live with Me in heaven's eternal bliss on condition he be mindful of My loving deeds for him and that he give Me in return a four-leaved clover. One leaf represents true confession, the second sorrow for sin, the third a resolve to sin no more, and the fourth fear of the Lord. Five seals formed from the iron nails which pierced My body were affixed to the charter with wax made of My heart's blood. The witnesses were Matthew, Mark, Luke, and John, and many more, including particularly My sweet mother who never ceased to cry and lament. After My death I descended into hell to show this charter to Satan and later reappeared on earth. I have left for you an indenture of My flesh and blood in priestly hands as a surety for My gift. Pay your rent, keep from sin, and claim your inheritance when you will (MS 34, BL Addit 11307).

THE BRANCHES OF THE APPLE TREE [188]. A translation of *Palma contemplationis*, a contemplative text that circulated widely on the Continent in Latin, French, German, and Netherlandish, appears in the devotional compilation printed by Wynkyn de Worde in 1493/94 under the title *The Tretyse of Love*. For discussion of this work, the reader is referred to the chapter on English Mystical Writings in a later volume of this *Manual*.

2. Works Based on Personification

THE REBELLION OF PRIDE AND HER DAUGHTER ENVY [189]. A semi-alliterative allegory of 114 long lines in couplets with some internal rime. The text is preserved in a late fourteenth-century manuscript formerly belonging to Sir Fergus Graham of Netherby, Cumberland.

> When God completed the creation, Pride appeared in heaven with her daughter Envy to under-mine it. They brought down Lucifer and forced him to hell. A vivid portrait is drawn of their disgraceful conduct, obscene language, and excessive preoccupation with fine dress. Man, against whom they conspire, is warned to forego their blandishments and turn to God for salvation.

SPECULUM MISERICORDIE [190]. 976 four-stress lines in 81 stanzas riming abababababab. It is uniquely extant in the mid-fifteenth-century "De-lamere" manuscript of *The Canterbury Tales*. The dialect is mixed, showing both Midland and Northern features. Dr. R. H. Robbins aptly describes the work as a "tissue of many fifteenth-century doctrinal commonplaces bound together by a rather prosaic allegory." Nevertheless, although its theme of the encouraging of the dying sinner to hope for mercy is well-worn, the author has made an effort, not wholly without success, to adapt the chanson d'aventure conventions of secular love poetry to his religious purpose.

> The narrator who has been ill sets out for a walk on a May morning. He sees a young man fall from his horse and lie fatally injured, his carefree song of love turned to a bitter complaint of death. Suddenly, a comely lady (Discrecio) and her seven daughters (the seven virtues opposed to the deadly sins) appear to comfort the knight who despairs of salvation because of his sinful life. Discrecio urges him to contemplate Christ's Passion and to hope for mercy. He recounts his transgression against the seven deadly sins, but the seven virtues respond with examples of Biblical personages who, although they had committed the same transgressions, nevertheless received God's mercy. When the knight remains unconvinced, Discrecio introduces the example of Saint Peter who thrice denied Christ and was saved. He faints, and the ladies kneel at his side and pray for him. When he recovers consciousness, he cries out for God's mercy, recites a general confession, and beseeches Mary, angels, Apostles, confessors, and virgins for their aid and intercession on his behalf. Then, making his farewells to the world and kissing the maidens, he "yaf up the goost."

THE TESTAMENT OF LOVE [191]. A prose treatise, in three books, on the nature of love and its relationship to free will and grace. Its sole textual authority is William Thynne's 1532 edition of Chaucer to whom it was inaccurately ascribed until the middle of the nineteenth century. The discovery by Skeat of an acrostic (as corrected by Bradley) reading "Margarete of Virtw Have Merci on thin Usk" provided internal evidence of its author's identity as Thomas Usk, a member of Chaucer's circle, by profession a scrivener, whose involvement in the political intrigues of London, particularly his strong initial support and subsequent betrayal of the belligerent Mayor of London, John de Norhampton, in 1384 ultimately led to his own arrest and execution at the hands of the Merciless Parliament four years later. *The Testament*, which was composed between December 1384 and June 1385 when Usk was for a time in Nicholas Brembre's custody, awaiting his first trial for treason, is filled with autobiographical details, and its purpose in part was to substantiate and justify his conduct towards Norhampton. Its main sources are Boethius' *Consolation of Philosophy* on which it heavily relies, particularly in Book Two, and St. Anselm's *De Concordia praescientiae et praedestinationis*, from which the discussion of free will and foreknowledge in Book Three is derived. The image of the Tree of Charity comes from *Piers Plowman*. Use is also made of Gregory's *Homily XXVI*, Bartholomaeus Anglicus, Higden's *Polychronicon*, and Augustine's *Confessions*. Usk's text suffered serious corruption in transmission. Bradley, however, largely repaired the dislocation of chapters, and Skeat and Schaar emended many of the readings. Major improvements to the text have also been made by John Leyerle in a new edition of *The Testament* awaiting publication. Nevertheless numerous problems remain to be resolved, particularly in Book Three, and they are exacerbated both by the obscurity of the argument and by the awkwardness of the prose. *The Testament* has not fared well with most critics, yet the richness and complexity of the symbolism of the margaret-pearl and the subtle blending of autobiographical and philosophical elements compensate for the sometimes tedious dullness of the narrative and the tortuous and mannered style.

I shall compose this treatise in English in a familiar style so that my meaning may be more easily grasped. It will be concerned with the causes of love and the passion and distress of unfulfilled desire. Its title is *The Testament* (i.e., the witnessing) *of Love,* and its purpose is to bring us to a perfect love of our Maker. Boethius and other great clerks have already treated this subject, and I am a mere gleaner after them. If need be, I shall increase my portion out of their shock. "A slye servaunt in his owne helpe is often moche commended." (Prologue).

Separated from my Margaret, I endured penance in a dark prison, bewailing the sundry evils that had befallen me. Suddenly there appeared before me a lovely lady whose look gladdened me and gave me solace. It was my patroness, Love, who had come to comfort and reclaim me from error in order that I might win my lady's favor. I assured her of my constancy to Margaret and recounted my woes. Once, as I wandered through the woods, I was attacked by animals who had suddenly turned wild. I fled to the shore and boarded a ship called Travail with a captain, Will, and three crewmen, Sight, Lust, and Thought. It was driven by a storm to an island where I discovered Margaret, a pearl of great price in a blue shell, whom I immediately recognized as the object of my heart's desire. I had served her faithfully without success for seven years and asked for comfort in my eighth. Love bade me persevere in her service and endure the contumely of my detractors. I explained that I earned their odium when, having been threatened with imprisonment unless I revealed a certain plot and fearing that London would suffer unrest unless I remained silent, I made a declaration on the matter. But I spoke no untruth, and I deemed my oath in court to take precedence over my former oath of secrecy. Love supported my action, but she reproved me from straying from the right path and advised me to despise earthly fame and direct my thoughts to the fame that comes after death. Still I deplored my ill fortune and protested the loss of my worldly benefits—property, position, power and good reputation. Love explained that adversity teaches salutary lessons and that I might yet attain true wealth. Worldly goods are unstable and therefore unable to satisfy man's desire for happiness. Perfect bliss—"the knot in the herte"—can only be achieved through a life of reason rooted in virtue. How does the soul acquire virtue? Through love's service. What does love's service entail? The right use of the will freely exercised in the performance of good deeds. God's foreknowledge does not constrain the will to love. The Tree of Bliss is grounded in the freedom and rectitude of the will. Love and virtue are intertwined and in accord with reason and good will. Steadfast continuance in good service will in time produce the fruit of grace. Through the goodness and grace of the Margaret pearl, God will finally grant "wysdom and love in parfyte charite . . . to al tho that wel canne deserve." With that, Love took up her place in my heart.

The treatise ends with a recapitulation of Love's doctrine and an analysis of the function of grace in sustaining and strengthening the righteous will and in turning the degenerate will again to virtue. In a final statement Margaret is said to betoken "grace, lernyng, or wisdom of God, or els holy church."

3. Works Based on Allegorical Action

VERSIONS OF GUILLAUME DE GUILLEVILLE'S PÈLERINAGE DE LA VIE HUMAINE (THE PILGRIMAGE OF THE LYFE OF THE MAN-HODE) [192] and PÈLERINAGE DE L'AME (THE PILGRIMAGE OF THE SOUL or GRACE DIEU or GRACE DE DIEU) [193]. Guillaume de Guilleville entered the Cistercian monastery of Chaalis in 1316 at the age of 21 and remained there the rest of his life. His voluminous writings include a poetic trilogy consisting of the *Pèlerinage de la vie humaine* composed in 1330–31 and expanded in 1335, the *Pèlerinage de l'âme* composed in 1335–58, and the *Pèlerinage de Jesus Christ* composed about 1358. Tuve has demonstrated how highly his contemporaries valued the work. There are over 60 manuscripts of the *Vie* alone. A prose version was made of it in the fifteenth century, and it was translated into German, Dutch, Spanish, and English. A prose version of the *Ame* was made by Jean Gallopes at the request of John,

Duke of Bedford, between 1422 and 1431. All three *Pèlerinages* appeared in early prints.

Two Middle English translations were made of the *Vie*. Lydgate rendered the expanded version into verse at the request of Thomas Montacute, Earl of Salisbury, about 1426. For a discussion of it, and a detailed summary of its contents, the reader is referred to XVI [139] in volume 6 of the *Manual*. The original *Vie* had already been rendered into prose under the title *The Pilgrimage of the Lyfe of the Manhode* at the end of the fourteenth or the beginning of the fifteenth century. The anonymous translation is not without artistic merit; it is faithful to the French text and shows some concern for style. A new edition by Dr. Avril K. Henry based on a complete collation of the six extant manuscripts is in preparation. Two anonymous seventeenth-century abridgments are found in Magdalene College, Cambridge, MS Pepys 2258 and Cambridge University Library MS Ff.6.30.

The *Ame* was turned into English prose in 1413. Its source was the original French version and not, as is commonly asserted, the later prose redaction. It is of Southeast Midland, probably London, provenance and is partially or wholly preserved in thirteen manuscripts and Caxton's print. Interspersed throughout the English text are fourteen poems, all in rime royal, of which the first eight and the twelfth follow originals in the French. The remainder have no counterparts in the French text. One of them, *The Lamentation of the Green Tree* or the *Complaint of the Virgin,* is certainly by Thomas Hoccleve who wrote it for Joan FitzAlan, Countess of Hereford, the maternal grandmother of Henry V. He may have composed them all, as Furnivall originally suggested and Matthews (*Manual,* vol. 3, VIII [36–49]) thought probable. Seymour who, following Furnivall, believes that a strong case can be made for Hoccleve's authorship raises the additional probability that he translated the entire work for the Countess of Hereford. The translation is highly commendable for its accuracy, fluency, and ease. It deserves a critical edition.

As I lay in bed asleep on the Feast of Saint Lawrence, I had a marvelous dream. My earthly pilgrimage was nearly at an end, and I was approaching the heavenly city of Jerusalem. Death smote me with his venomous dart, and my soul and body parted. I felt my soul rise in the air. Satan immediately assailed it, claiming it as a prisoner and threatening to carry it off to Hell, but my Guardian Angel intervened and denounced his malice. I was taken to trial before St. Michael, the provost of Heaven. My Guardian Angel assured the court that I had kept the faith throughout my life, but Satan and Synderesis, the Worm of Conscience, presented such overwhelming evidence of my sinfulness that I made a complete confession and pleaded for mercy. Justice rejected my plea. Truth and Reason gave Witness against me and supported Justice. Suddenly Mercy appeared and appealed to the Judge on my behalf. During a delay in the proceedings she procured from Christ a charter of grace which, when put in the balance, outweighed my misdeeds. The Judge decided in favor of my salvation, but remanded me to Purgatory for the satisfaction of my sins. Justice and Mercy accepted the decision and were reconciled, but Satan departed to Hell in a rage.

As my Guardian Angel escorted me to Purgatory, I saw pilgrims on their way to Heaven singing the praises of God and Mary, and I heard the song of the angels in Heaven. I entered Purgatory and learned that the prayers, Masses, alms, and good deeds of friends, the pardons of Holy Church, and the charity and devotions of its ministers could shorten my stay there. My Guardian Angel led me to Hell where I witnessed the horrible punishments suffered by souls who died in deadly sin. In the lowest part of Hell called Abissus were pagans, heretics, disbelieving persecutors of Holy Church, and false Christians who broke God's Commandments and slandered the true teachers of His law. As we left Hell and rose above the earth, I beheld a fair plain where a multitude of pilgrims were playing with an apple between a green tree and a dry tree. My Guardian Angel explained that the apple was created in the green tree and carried to the dry tree in order to replace the one which Adam had eaten. The green tree is identified with Mary, the apple with Christ, and the dry tree with the Cross. The dry tree revived when the apple was "nailed" to it, i.e., when God expiated Adam's sin and released man from damnation at the crucifixion. Inserted into this narrative is an account of Seth's journey to Paradise for the oil of mercy and a brief history of the Cross (see *Manual*, 2.443). Then I met Doctrine who instructed me on the nature of the soul, and I saw two statues—the one a knight armed for battle, the other a figure with a head of gold, arms and breast of silver, stomach and thighs of brass, and legs of iron and earth—representing good government and social order. I was told the exemplary tale of a king who had banished Liberality and installed Covetousness in his court. A knight courageously defended Liberality in the lists and restored her to the king's favor. Rulers are warned to protect themselves from evil counsellors who would pervert them.

After my burden of guilt diminished, I was taken up into the heavenly city of Jerusalem and shown its mansions and feasts. In the midst of it, I saw the green tree with a high, dry branch. About it thronged Adam and Eve and many of their lineage thanking God for their redemption. A light shone in my eyes and made me open them. I awoke and found myself lying in bed. Midnight sounded, and I realized I had not slept three hours.

Piers Plowman is discussed in Chapter XVIII. Discussion of two monitory pieces, *Three Messengers of Death* and *The Enemies of Man,* which employ devices of moral allegory, are reserved for a later chapter of the *Manual*. In earlier volumes *Death and Liffe* (XIII [245]) has already been treated among the poems dealing with contemporary conditions, *The Dance of the Sevin Deidly Synnis* (X [78]) among the poems of Dunbar, the *Pearl* (II [2]) among the works of The Pearl Poet, the *Assembly of Gods* (XVI [7]) among the works of Lydgate, the *Conflict of Wit and Will* (VII [29]) among Dialogues, Debates, and Catechisms, and the *Castle of Perseverance* (XII [27]) among the dramatic pieces. See *Manual*, volumes 2–6.

V. Service and Service-Related Works

1. The Mass

ARA DEI [194]. A prose treatise in seventeen books, the first comprising a detailed commentary on the Mass, the last nine an encyclopedic compilation of general religious, philosophic, and scientific knowledge. Although it was written "in hoomli wise," Latin passages are frequently interspersed with the English, and it was clearly addressed to an educated, probably lay audience. The commentary on the Mass incorporates much familiar instruction and devotional material, including the *Virtues of the Mass* [202], *Sixtene Condiciouns of Charity* [58], *Four Tokens of Salvation* [146], the petitions of the Pater Noster [32], the levation prayers [204], the figural meaning of parts of the Mass, the treatise against despair (Jolliffe, no. I.32), the pains of purgatory and hell, and the joys of heaven. Authorities are drawn from Augustine, Ambrose, Jerome, and Hugh of St. Victor. The dialect is East Midland.

For a similar treatise composed for the nuns of Syon entitled *The Mirror of Our Lady*, see VI [8] in *Manual*, vol. 2.

LAY FOLKS' MASS BOOK [195]. 629 lines (abbreviated versions have as few as 358 lines) in short couplets save for the General Confession riming aabccb and the Creed riming abab. It was originally composed about 1150 in French by Jeremy, canon of Rouen and York and archdeacon of Cleveland, for a noble household with a private chapel. Deanesly suggests that it may have circulated for a time in its French form in England. Adapted to general usage, it was translated into Northern English early in the fourteenth century and recopied by Southern scribes late in the fourteenth century. The number of extant manuscripts, and their distribution, point to its considerable popularity as an aid to church service among the prosperous laity in the fifteenth century. Its title is the editor's invention.

(MS Royal version.) The Mass is the worthiest thing on earth. It has been profusely praised in church books, but even learned authors cannot convey so much as a fifth part of its worth to those who hear it with purity and sincere devotion. I shall now translate into English a book by Dan Jeremy which counsels against idle chatter at Mass and gives the following instructions for hearing it properly. The priest enters vested except for the chasuble which he takes from the altar and places about him. With his hands on high, he recites the liturgical confession and then absolves all present, including the lay congregation, who are exhorted to make, silently or aloud, a General Confession followed by an Ave Maria, Pater Noster, and Credo. After the General Confession the congregation shall stand as the priest begins the introit. The prayer to be said during the introit is an intercessory prayer for the succor and salvation of the priest, the congregation, their relatives and friends, and departed souls. On feast days, when the Gloria is sung, the congregation shall say it in English, beginning "Ioy be unto God in heaven," and then kneel and say the Pater Noster until the deacon or priest reads the Gospel which they shall hear standing, the while meditating on Christ's redemption and praying for the grace and strength to do His will. As the Mass Creed is said, they are to say an expanded English version of the Apostles' Creed, beginning "I trow in God, fader of might." They may now, if they wish, make an offering and beseech God to receive their prayers and offerings, fulfill their good desires, and help them in time of need. Let them then say Pater Nosters while the priest washes his hands and, when he turns to them and asks their prayers, smite their breasts and pray aloud for the Holy Ghost to light upon him and rule his heart and speech. As the priest recites the Secret, they should kneel and with uplifted hands beseech God to receive their sacrifice and the priest's. Let them stand as the priest moves to the middle of the altar and begins the Preface and silently recite a prayer of praise and thanksgiving to God. They are to kneel at the Canon and again offer thanks to God for His many benefactions, protection from perils, and the grace of redemption and pardon for sin, and recite an intercessory prayer for the Church and all estates of mankind. Finally, let them ask God for strength to avoid sin in the future and that He direct the course of this world for their good. When the sacring bell is rung, they shall kneel and do reverence to the presence of Christ, and, raising their hands in welcome as the Host is raised at the Levation, a prayer of their own choosing, concluding with an Ave Maria, Pater Noster, Credo, and a petition for God's mercy. After the consecration let them pray for the dead until they hear the priest intone *Per omnia secula* and then stand and listen to the Pater Noster, silently repeating it first in Latin, then in English, and attend to the priest as he says the Agnus Dei. When they hear the *pax*, they are to pray for peace and charity which is of three kinds—love of God, love of self, love of neighbor. The Pater Noster must be said again at the rinsing. When the ablution is over, they are to stand while the priest reads the common prayer and to ask God for protection from all peril and that in case of sudden death the Mass be their viaticum and absolution. At the conclusion of this prayer, let them kneel and say Pater Nosters until the end of Mass. Their final prayer is to thank God for His goodness, especially for the Mass, and to ask His acceptance and blessing.

THE MANNER AND MEDE OF THE MASS [196]. 57 twelve-line stanzas riming aabccbddbccb with a prefatory quatrain riming abab. Simmons, its editor, regards it as a "confused and very fragmentary copy" of a much older Northern original. It is a free paraphrase of the *Lay Folks' Mass Book*, [195] above, intended for recitation.

This treatise teaches men how to hear Mass and is needful to high and low. Hearing Mass is good for all Christians. It was made for the soul's health. Be silent, and listen to a discourse full of comfort on the meeds of the Mass. Every man should know how to say the service and to pray in private to God, Who is always ready to help us banish our sins and teach us the way to heaven. What man would be as long suffering as He? When we commit a mortal sin, we put Him through the same pain He endured before for our sake. Yet His mercy overcomes justice which would condemn us to death. May mercy be master through the power of the Holy Ghost and remain with us until we are delivered by prayer. Now I will begin to speak of the Mass. Every day you may see the same body Who died for you in the form of bread. Although it is a lofty subject, laymen may easily learn when to participate in the service and when to pray privately. Every man should pray as the priest, if he knows the words. I shall tell you the merits of the Mass not on my own authority but on that of Augustine, Ambrose, Bernard, and Bede. Our guardian angel notes every step of our way to and from hearing Mass. That day we shall not age, nor become blind. God will pardon our sins if we confess them. Mass will serve as a viaticum, if we die. It will make work lack vexation and help alleviate distress. For a prosperous journey hear Mass before setting forth. The unworthiness of the priest does not affect the validity of the Mass. Christ will judge him. Saint Ambrose says that no man, be he young or old, no matter how great his skill, and though he were to live forever, could expound the tenth part of the Mass, so vast is the subject. Saint Jerome says that, however many Masses are sung for several souls, each individual soul enjoys the benefit of a whole Mass. I advise you to go to church and do God's work. Have no doubt that every soul shall have a whole Mass with the aid of our Heavenly King. I cannot cite authorities for all the points I shall make. I shall be glad for you to know when to call on Christ. When the priest says his Confiteor, bowing before the altar, and you pray for him, if he remembers you [in the memento], you will merit a great reward. But if you pray only for yourself, you will not merit a great reward, for your nature inclines you to evil. If you would do well, join with the priest in mutual prayer. That is charity. When you enter the church and see the priest vesting, kneel and be still. Then rise at the service and serve God in this manner. Say the prayer beginning "Lord" and "Dear God Almighty" and "In Mary I place my trust" and follow them with a prayer for the forgiveness of your sins and life to complete your penance. You may pray for scores at Mass, either naming them or thinking of them, and each of them shall have a whole Mass, if he is not in hell. Were my own father in hell, I would no more pray for him than for a dead dog. But since we do not know who is in hell, we pray for all the faithful. Do not chatter in church after the priest begins to vest or the devil will record your words on a roll, as Saint Augustine of Canterbury bears witness. Assisting Pope Gregory at Mass one day, he saw the devil recording the words of two women who were talking together as he was reading the Gospel. So voluble were they that the devil soon used up the parchment on which he was writing and, in an effort to stretch it with his teeth, knocked his head against the wall. Augustine laughed, interrupting his reading, and was later rebuked by the Pope. Everyone should be silent at Mass. Consider that God may punish us for our speech and that if we distract the priest, the whole world may suffer for our action. Say the Pater Noster which should take precedence over all other prayers since the Redeemer Himself made it. It contains all we need to know in this world and the next. Stand at the Gospel and attend to it. You may not understand it, but God wrought it, and it is wisdom for unlearned men to honor His works. The Creed follows the Gospel. If you knew it, and had full faith in it and could say it with the priest, you would win much merit. Although faith without works is worthless, yet I would like more men to know their Creed, and I have done my best to render it in English. [The MS lacks the text of the Creed.] Before the priest's ablution, go up to him and make your offering. There is no obligation to make an offering, but it is beneficial, for it will keep you from sin and increase the silver in your coffer. At the offertory, say the devotion beginning "God that was born in Bethlehem, three kings kneeled before thee." After the ablution the priest returns to the altar, bows before it, crosses himself, and then turns to the congregation to ask their prayers. When he begins his private prayers, kneel until he completes them and intones *Sursum corda*, "Lift up your hearts to Him that is almighty." Stand from the Sanctus to the consecration, thereafter kneel and meditate on Christ's passion. You may pray as you will between the Sanctus and before the bell rings. At the elevation of the body and blood, kneel and say a prayer. Then the priest spreads his arms in token of the crucifixion. After the Pater Noster comes the Agnus Dei, a prayer for forgiveness of sins, strength, grace, and peace. When the priest has taken communion, he washes his hands again and says a special prayer for the congregation which should remain kneeling until the end of Mass. After the Mass you should kneel down and say a prayer by Saint Ambrose to our Lord, beginning "God that died upon the cross," and a prayer to Our Lady. Do not forget the Gospel according to Saint John after the Mass. Those who attend to it and kiss the ground when it is ended shall receive an indulgence of a year and 40 days at the least. Now I have finished *The Manner and Mede of the Mass*. The effort that I have put into it will not have been wasted if you benefit from it. Anyone may listen to it with profit. None has heard better things than I have told except the five words of consecration which only a priest should read. God that died upon the cross, give us grace by virtue of the Mass to save our souls. Father, Son, and Holy Ghost, save us from the torment of hell.

A similar treatise of Northern origin survives in two early fifteenth-century manuscripts, Bodleian Library Additional A.26 and British Library Royal 17.C.xvii. Shrewsbury School MS 3 (1484) contains "A Fruitful And a compendius tretyse specyally schewing wat meryte of pardon it is to hear a masse, and in specyall to see our Lord Jhesu Cryst in forme of breyd."

DE MERITIS MISSE [197]. An abridgment of *The Manner and Mede of the*

Mass [196] by John Audelay in 69 six-line stanzas riming aabccb. Audelay remains close to his original in content and frequently in expression. His few additions consist of exhortations to charity and prayer.

MERITA MISSE [198]. 203 lines in short couplets with some lacunae. Owst regards it as a versified sermon. It has been misascribed to Lydgate.

God of heaven, give me grace to instruct laymen. Keep silent, laymen, while I tell you how, when, and where to pray. Say your devotions at bedtime, midnight, and at rising. In the morning, say the Creed first, then the Pater Noster. Bless yourself and go to church. At the door, take holy water and say a prayer for the forgiveness of your venial sins. Then pray to the Blessed Sacrament above the high altar and worship the Trinity. When the priest rings the bell, be silent and attend to him. Listen to the Gospel and be prepared to fight for it. Pray for the priest when he bids you pray for him. At the elevation kneel and cry God's mercy. Show all the reverence you can at the consecration and at the fraction. Reflect on Christ's suffering and distress for your sake. Weep for Him Who wept for you. Let no worldliness drive His love out of your heart. When the priest takes communion, pray that the Mass may avail instead of viaticum in case of need. At the rinsing thank God that He has given you the opportunity to behold the Sacrament. You have seen the King Who made the world, the King Who made both night and day. Follow the example of Godfrey of Boulogne, Charlemagne, and Arthur who paid reverence to the Sacrament and not those fools who bring shame on themselves and their kindred by behaving like lions in church and lambs in battle. Envious, they want precedence in church, but run from the battlefield. Proud knaves who jest in church, I address you contemptuously as "thou."

All men must fight against the flesh and the devil. God give us grace to hear Mass, to fight, to pray that we may win salvation at the day of doom.

HOW TO SING MASS [199]. Ten lines of irregular length in couplets following the Trentalle Gregorii in British Library MS Harley 3810.

Son, I urge you to sing Mass well for the benefit of the living and the dead whose souls must be saved thereby. Do not desist until you are absolved of temporal punishment. May your soul never suffer the pain I have suffered.

THE SACRIFICE OF THE MASS [200]. Thirteen stanzas in rime royal.

This treatise is written to make you hear the Mass more devoutly. It is the highest sacrifice. It is prefigured in the Old Law by Melchisedech's offering of bread and wine to Abraham. As blood was once used to heal wounds, so Christ's blood, consecrated daily at Mass, heals and purifies the people. The church is called the spouse of Christ by virtue of Their marriage in the Mass. The celestial court reveres this sacrifice. It brings trouble and sorrow to infernal spirits. Saint Augustine in *The City of God* describes the benefits to be derived from attendance at Mass. The day you hear Mass you will not go hungry or blind, you will be forgiven your venial sins and oaths, you will not grow older and be afflicted by sudden death, and you will have shelter if you fall ill. The priest prays at Mass for all in attendance as well as for all Christians. If any of your relations are in purgatory, your prayers at Mass may deliver them, and they, in turn, shall pray for your redemption before the angels and saints in heaven. The number of the Masses you attend on earth is reported to the Trinity after your death. I advise you, man, to follow the priest to Mass and, unless you are ill, sit bareheaded and beat your breast, saying "Cor mundum crea in me, Deus, et spiritum."

PARTS OF THE MASS [201]. Two eight-line stanzas riming abababab on four parts of the Mass (introit, collects, readings, secrets) and their correspondences with scripture.

VIRTUES OF THE MASS (or VIRTUTES MISSARUM) [202]. A collection of pieces in verse and prose enumerating, on the spurious authority of the apostles and fathers and doctors of the Church, chiefly Saint Augustine, the extraordinary temporal benefits to be gained from attendance at Mass. They are of no literary merit and tastelessly exploit the simple piety of the laity. Similar works in Latin, French, and German owe their origin to the clergy's efforts from the twelfth century onwards to encourage regular and frequent attendance at the service. They elicited strong protests from Nicholas of Cusa and John Gerson among other reforming churchmen. The Middle English versions date from the late fourteenth and fifteenth centuries. Judging from the closing stanza of the version in Bodleian Library MS Rawlinson Poet 32, they may have been used in England to counter Wycliffite doctrine on the Mass. Seven versions are in verse: (A) British Library MS Harley 3954, misattributed to Lydgate, 134 short couplets; (B) Bodleian Library MS Rawlinson Poet 36, 24 rime royal stanzas with an envoy of two eight-line stanzas; (C) Cambridge University Library MS Ii.6.2 and Henry E. Huntington MS 26.A.13, one stanza rime royal; (D) Bodleian Library MS Rawlinson Poet 32, 31 quatrains and two concluding stanzas of six lines each; (E) Cambridge University Library MS Hh.3.13, thirteen eight-line stanzas riming ababbcbc; (F) Bodleian Library MS Rawlinson Poet 118 and Trinity College, Cambridge, MS 601, seventeen couplets of irregular length; and (G) a closely related version, Bodleian Library MS Ashmole 59. Prose versions appear in three fifteenth-century manuscripts. The virtues of the Mass are also to be found in *Ara Dei* [194], John Mirk's *Instructions for Parish Priests* [233], *The Manner and Mede of the Mass* [196], John Audelay's *De Meritis Misse* [197], and *The Sacrifice of the Mass* [200].

(MS Rawl poet 32; Version D.) Hearing Mass brings 30 rewards: that day you shall not go hungry;

you shall be forgiven your idle words; you shall not suffer sudden death; you shall not age; you shall remain steadfast in your faith and have strength to resist the devil; you shall not lose your sight; you shall have an opportunity to put aside your sins; the day you hear Mass shall serve as your viaticum if no priest is at hand; you shall have 40 days of pardon if you kneel and give a kiss at the Verbum Caro; you shall relieve souls in torment for as long as you stand at Mass; you shall be absolved of your venial sins; you shall travel in safety; you shall be forgiven your oaths; you shall be free of the devil; however wicked you may be, during the Mass you shall be absolved of forgotten sins; you shall know God is One whether whole or fractioned; you shall be accompanied to Mass by your good angel; you shall be free of evil temptation; you shall have faith in the Eucharist; you shall be healed of deadly sin and brought to confession; your commerce and other works will prosper; you shall have the occasion to meditate on Christ's passion; angels will come down to pay reverence to the sacrament; you shall have a good remedy for whatever afflicts you, if you hear Mass from beginning to end; you shall be made pure of soul; you shall release a soul from the pains of hell; God is born again at Mass; there is as much good in the Mass as there are beams in the sun or drops in the sea or stars in the sky or angels; he that hears daily Mass shall have a long life and a good end. The virtues of the Mass have been set forth by Saint Bernard, Saint Augustine, Saint Thomas Aquinas, and other holy doctors. Therefore, Lollards and heretics, put aside your errors and follow the love of Holy Church. Embrace the Mass with all your heart, and God will send you a good end.

BIDDING PRAYERS (or THE BIDDING OF THE BEDES) [203]. An intercessory prayer for all men in their various estates, as well as for departed souls, recited after the Gospel on Sundays and festivals. Its modern counterpart is the Prayer of the Faithful. There are many versions of it in manuscripts and early prints.

LEVATION PRAYERS [204]. Occasionally in prose, more often in verse, they flourished in England most prominently during the late fourteenth and early fifteenth centuries. Their content consists of effusive salutations and praises of Christ in the Eucharist combined with pleas for forgiveness of sins and against sudden death and supplications for salvation. According to Dr. R. H. Robbins, they are independent of Latin originals. The intention was for the laity to recite them immediately after the consecration of the Host at the Levation or occasionally perhaps in veneration of the Host during the procession for the Feast of Corpus Christi. It has also been suggested that the longer versions were used for private meditation. In addition to the Levation prayers occurring independently, others are found in the *Lay Folks' Mass Book* [195], Lydgate's *Interpretacio Misse* (XVI [87]), Mirk's *Instructions for Parish Priests* [233], *Ara Dei* [194], and John Audelay [197] and [29].

MEDITATIONS FOR GOOSTELY EXERCISE IN THE TYME OF THE MASSE [205]. A treatise consisting of a series of meditations on the Mass, each of which is related to episodes of the Passion, extant in two late fifteenth-century manuscripts, Bodleian Library Wood empt 17 and British Library Harley 494. It appears to derive from Innocent III's *De Mysterio Missae,* Durandus' *Rationale,* and other late medieval allegorizations of the Mass and liturgical vestments. A closely related and contemporary text, lacking the allegorizations, may be found in Columbia University MS Plimpton 263; it is mistitled in the colophon "The Medis off the Masse."

The priest on his way to Mass signifies the Savior coming from heaven to suffer for man's redemption. The process of the Mass represents the process of Christ's passion. The priest signifies Christ, the altar the cross, the vestments the white and purple garments with which Christ was clothed in derision. The right side of the altar represents the life of innocence which man lost by sin, the left side the miserable life he now leads. The chalice signifies the Lord's sepulchre, the paten the stone that covered it, the corporal, sudary, and sindon the shroud in which He was wrapped, the Host His body, the water and wine the water and blood that poured from His side. Let this be a daily meditation to stir you to a remembrance of Christ's passion. If you wish to thank Him for His incarnation, take note how at a sung Mass the bishop or priest, emerging in his garments from the vestry behind the deacon and subdeacon, goes to the altar and kisses it, then moves to the right of the altar and afterwards to the left where he reads the Gospel and finally back again to the right. All these movements signify great mysteries of the incarnation. The choir represents the holy fathers of the old law, the patriarchs and prophets, who insistently prayed and besought God to send His eternal Son into this world. The vested bishop or priest represents Christ Who clothed Himself in the garment of our nature in the vestry, i.e., in the womb of the Blessed Virgin Mary. The amice represents Christ's spiritual strength, the white alb His innocence, the chasuble His charity, the stole His freedom from original and mortal sin, the maniple His purity from venial sin. The two lights on either side of the vestry represent the law of Moses and holy charity, the deacon the apostles, the subdeacon the disciples of Christ, the altar in this instance the church, the kissing of the altar the marriage between Christ and the church. The right side of the altar to which the celebrant goes first represents the Jews to whom He preached first, the left side the Gentiles to whom He sent His apostles. That is why the Gospel containing the mysteries of the faith received by the Gentiles is read on the left side. The return of the priest to the right side of the altar signifies the conversion of the Jews at the end of the world. The bishop also has nine ornaments [ten are listed]—mitre, crosier, gloves, ring, hose, sandals, dalmatic, tunicle, chasuble, and succinctory—which represent his special duties, i.e., to confer orders, dedicate churches, consecrate nuns, bless the properties and vestments of the church, call synods, etc.

    When the fannell is placed on the priest's left hand, call to mind the ropes with which the soldiers bound our Savior's left hand when they led Him to Pilate. When the stole is cast over his neck, call to mind the ropes with which He was drawn on the cross. When he dons the chasuble, call to mind the purple mantle which was placed on Him and the beating and mockery He received. When the priest, vested, bows before the altar, call to mind the Savior Who humbled Himself for our salvation. When he begins Mass at the right side of the altar, call to mind the life of our Savior Who by His incarnation and death restored paradise to us. When he begins the *Gloria in excelsis,* call to mind the joy and glory of the angels at Christ's nativity. At the Collects and Sequence, call to mind that Christ prayed for us night and day. When the priest or deacon reads the Gospel facing north, call to mind that Christ preached for all mankind facing north, i.e., against the spiritual enemy. When the priest says *Credo in Deum,* join him in the act of faith. At the Oblation reflect on Christ's sacrifice for man and offer yourself to Him again body and soul. When the priest says the Secrets in silence, reflect on Christ's withdrawal from the company of Jews and His solitude in silence and contemplation. When the priest begins *Per omnia secula seculorum,* bear in mind how some of the Jews received Him joyfully into Jerusalem, singing *Benedictus qui venit in nomine domini Ozana filio David.* Say with the priest *Sanctus, sanctus,* and at the consecration honor the Blessed Sacrament, praying at the Levation, *Salve lux mundi* and *Ave precium redemptoris,* and recalling the events of the Passion. Let the Pater Noster bring to mind that Christ prayed for His enemies in the midst of His agony on the cross. See to it that you also forgive all injuries and wrongs you have suffered at the hands of others. Then shall you be His disciple and a chosen vessel worthy to receive His grace. When the priest touches the Host and kisses the paten, saying *Da pacem,* remember the peace between God and man—the peace our Savior won for us. At the Pax and Agnus Dei consider the mercy and humility of our Redeemer in taking our nature and suffering torment and death for us. [There is a lacuna in the manuscript here.]

The Mass betokens the joy and mirth of the Apostles on hearing of Christ's resurrection. We should give thanks with them for the most gracious gift of His resurrection and for the Mass. From the beginning of Mass to the consecration, you may meditate on Christ's incarnation and preaching; from the consecration to the post-communion on His passion and death; after the post-communion on His joyous resurrection; and at the *Ite missa est* on His glorious ascension. The five turnings of the priest toward the people at Mass, saying *Dominus vobiscum,* signifies the five appearances of our Savior after the Resurrection.

A GOOD CONTEMPLACION FOR A PRESTE OR HE GO TO MASSE

[206]. A translation of a text ascribed to Saint Bonaventure.

Before a priest says Mass, let him be aware of the fact that he will receive God and man. He must have devotion toward His holiness, reverence for His lordship, love and desire for His goodness, steadfastness and diligence for His nobility. He must examine his conscience and confess himself, if necessary, before receiving the sacrament and meditate devoutly before and after receiving the sacrament. He must not read the service too rapidly or skip passages.

PRAEPARATIO EUCHARISTIAE [207]. A treatise on matters for consideration before and after receiving the Eucharist.

Before receiving the Eucharist, six things must be taken into consideration. The communicant must know that he is receiving Jesus Christ in the form of bread and that he must put aside all malice and beastliness. He must receive the Eucharist with devotion, and in as holy a state as possible. He must receive it with reverence and a sense of his own unworthiness, although trusting in God's mercy. He must receive it with love and desire, considering His passion. He must receive it with prayer for pardon and grace. If he is a priest, he must take special care to abstain from distracting, worldly occupations. He must gather his thoughts wholly within himself, examine his conscience, and go to confession. Let him reflect on God's meekness and his own frailty and on His love for man in dying for him and giving Himself to him in the Eucharist. A priest, too, must reflect on his unworthiness to receive the Eucharist, but rely on Christ's mercy.

After receiving the Eucharist, the communicant should reflect on the vanity of the world and his own sinfulness and plead for mercy. Humbling himself before Christ, he should amend his life and await the benefits of the sacrament, acknowledging His goodness.

2. Festivals

THE FEASTS OF THE CHURCH [208]. A fragment of 334 lines, loosely alliterative, in 30 stanzas of irregular length. Pickering ascribes its authorship

to an East Anglian cleric writing in the mid-fourteenth century who composed the Eucharistic poem, "Alle ӡe mowyn be blyth and glade."

> The Lord is a generous householder. He clothes us with His garments and feeds us with His flesh and blood. He has ordained eight feasts for us—Christmas, New Year's, Epiphany, Easter, Holy Thursday, Whitsunday, Trinity, and Corpus Christi. An account of each feast seen in relation to the Eucharistic mystery follows with the text breaking off in the midst of the discussion of Easter.

OF THE SACRAMENT OF THE ALTAR [209]. Sixteen eight-line stanzas riming abababab. A translation of St. Thomas Aquinas' *Laude Sion* in celebration of the Feast of Corpus Christi.

> The church is an assembly of good men, and priests are to guide them to heaven. Church, glorify the Savior. This day commemorates the Last Supper. By this day we know that Easter is at hand. Christ taught us at the Last Supper to consecrate bread and wine to banish death. The bread is turned into flesh, the wine into blood. Faith alone, not the eyes, beholds this transubstantiation. Christ is present in both species as soon as the priest speaks God's words. When the wicked receive the Eucharist, they receive their endless damnation. When the good receive the Eucharist, they receive their endless salvation. The sacrament loses none of its efficacy if the recipient receives only a portion of the Eucharist. In the Old Law the Jews ate a lamb at Easter; we now eat living bread. Jesus, forgive us our sins, lead us to heaven, and feed us among the saints of heaven, at the feast of life. To our senses You seem bread, but in faith You are the living God. Isaac, manna, and the paschal lamb prefigured Christ in the Eucharist.

3. The Ceremonies of the Ritual

i. Baptism

THE SERVICE FOR BAPTISM [210]. The vernacular form of baptism is preserved in the York and Sarum Manuals, Mirk's *Instructions for Parish Priests* [233], *Sacerdos Parochialis* [22], and an unpublished Latin *Sacerdos parochialis* (ca. 1400) based on William of Pagula's *Oculus sacerdotis* and regularly appended to the *Pupilla oculi*.

ii. Confession

FORMS OF CONFESSION [211]. Guides to the penitent in self-examination for confession. They consist of a review, more often detailed than perfunctory, of the actions which constitute sin in the form of an interrogation or a series of self-accusations under the headings of the Seven Deadly

Sins, the Ten Commandments, the Five Wits, and the Seven Works of Mercy. Longer forms explore willful actions against the four cardinal virtues, the seven sacraments and the fourteen articles of the faith. Some also provide instructions in the method of making confession. The confession spuriously attributed to Saint Brendan enjoyed particular popularity and took an unusual form of a prayer. Prose and verse forms of confession, varying considerably in length and treatment, exist in large numbers in medieval manuscripts. Others are to be found in Mirk's *Instructions for Parish Priests* [233], *The Clensying of Mannes Sowle* [84], *Confessional Manuals* [88], Primers [225], the *Speculum Christiani* [15], and Visitations of the Sick (see [215–224] below). The evidence seems to support Jolliffe's observation that forms of confession were used not only as guides to confession but also "to help implement the decree of the Fourth Lateran Council and support the subsequent conciliar and episcopal efforts to instruct the laity as to which actions constitute sin and what their Christian profession demands of them." For Dunbar's *The Tabill of Confession,* see X [104] in *Manual,* vol. 4. There is a brief form of confession in Betson's *Tretyse* [27].

TRACTATUS DE MODO CONFITENDI [212]. A treatise by John Drury, schoolmaster of Beccles of Suffolk, composed about 1435 to instruct his students how to make confession in the season of Lent. It consists of a series of short summaries of the following topics: the three parts of Penance, the Ten Commandments, the seven deadly sins and their opposing virtues, the five wits, the seven deeds of mercy, the fourteen articles of the faith, the seven sacraments, and the seven principal virtues. The entire work has the appearance of a homily intended, as its editor, S. B. Meech suggests, "to sum up a long course of oral instruction."

iii. Marriage

THE MARRIAGE SERVICE [213]. Vernacular versions of the marriage rite, differing somewhat in phraseology and detail, are contained in a large number of service and service-related manuscripts and early prints. The pledge beginning "With this rynge I wedde the" is often given in monoriming lines.

BENEDICTA SIT SANCTA TRINITAS [214]. Seven eight-line stanzas riming ababbcbc on the indissolubility of marriage.

iv. Visitation of the Sick

DE VISITACIONE INFIRMORUM [215]. A prose treatise developed in varying ways from the pseudo-Augustinian *Visitatio infirmorum* and St. Anselm's *Admonitio morienti*. It was widely used by priests in ministering to the dying as part of the rite known as The Visitation of the Sick, which included prayer, exhortation, and interrogation, as well as the sacraments of Penance, the Eucharist, and Extreme Unction. The treatise exists in five Middle English versions. Version A was composed in the Southeast Midlands about 1400. It integrates both Latin texts, combining material from chapters 2, 4, 6, and 7 of the first book of the *Visitatio* and the first part of the *Admonitio*. Version B was composed in the Southwest Midlands about 1400. It is based on portions of the *Admonitio* alone. Version C was composed in the Southeast Midlands early in the fifteenth century. It survives in a single manuscript and consists of a summary and elaboration of chapters 2 and 6 of the first book of the *Visitatio*. Version D was also composed in the Southeast Midlands early in the fifteenth century. It is a close translation of chapters 6 and 7 of the first book of the *Admonitio*. One of the two extant manuscripts, Bodley 789, also appends the seven questions based on the examination in the *Admonitio*. Version E, the most popular, judging from the number of extant manuscripts, was also composed in the Southeast Midlands between 1400 and 1425. It derives from Version A which it expands with extensive interpolations.

(Version A.) My dear son in God, it seems that you are rapidly passing from this life Godward. There you shall behold the entire company of the saved. You must lay a stone on the wall of the heavenly city—a stone that must be prepared before you leave the world. The stone is your soul which you must cleanse. The din you make in preparing the stone is the reflection on your sins which you must confess to the priest. The hammer is penance that will smite your breast and make you sorry for your sins. Therefore I advise you to make your confession and prepare yourself for death. And this advice I give not only to sick men but also to well, for every day brings death nearer. Be ever ready for it. God visits men for their sins in different ways. Some are imprisoned; others are afflicted with illness. God said to ten lepers when he had cured them of leprosy: Go and sin no more lest worse befall you, as if to say, you suffered this illness because of your sins. And so it is ordained by law that a doctor may not prescribe a medicine for a sick man until he is spiritually healed and has taken his spiritual medicine, i.e., confession and the Eucharist. If he makes a good confession and repents of his sins, I have no doubt that his illness will either abate or bring him to greater bliss after death. If his illness does not abate, comfort him as follows: Son, do you love your Lord God? He will say yes. If you love God, you will have faith in His deeds. He scourges you, and you must suffer it gladly. As Solomon says, Son, do not complain about the chastisement of your Father for he is no son whom a father does not chastise. Do not object to your Heavenly Father's chastisements. He says Himself: Whom I love I chastise. A sick body makes for a healthy soul, and a healthy soul comes from God. Do not despise God for visiting these scourges upon you. Rather thank and love Him for amending your life. His mercy overcomes His great wrath. He is the Judge. It is not His will to damn you but to show you mercy. He chastises you out of mercy. Even though you have earned His wrath and eternal damnation, He puts aside His vengeance and mercifully punishes you here for a time. And so do not despise His rod of mercy and complain about it, but suffer it gladly, for all of God's judgments are righteous.

If you complain against God, you will weaken your soul, you will grieve God, and you will have less reward in heaven than if you had suffered patiently. Moreover, God does not punish a sin twice. If you cheerfully bear the illness He has sent you, you shall be relieved of the pain of purgatory and be admitted to the kingdom of heaven all the sooner.

If a man draws near to death, speak to him as follows: Man, if you consider and number the evils of this world, you should want to die and be with God. Holy Writ says: Blessed are they who die in God, for this life is but care and sorrow, travail and illness. Is it better to die well or live ill? Surely to die well. You cannot live completely well in this wretched world. For Holy Writ says: Every man is a liar, i.e., sinful, and even a just man falls seven times daily, and in the words of St. Paul, no living man is without sin. Ancient philosophers sorrowed when their children were born and rejoiced when they died and passed out of this woeful world. Saint Augustine, when he was about to die, spoke to Death in this manner. Ah, Death, end of all evil, end of travail, beginning of solace and joy, who can imagine the reward and bliss you bring with you? Welcome, Death, for a true Christian may live with Christ. When you have told him all this, or if you have no time to say this because his death is imminent, speak to him as follows: Brother, are you glad to die in the Christian faith? Reply: Yes. Do you acknowledge that you have not lived as you should? Reply: Yes. Are you repentant? Reply: Yes. Are you determined to amend your life if you are spared? Reply: Yes. Do you believe in God, Father Almighty, Creator of heaven and earth? Reply: Yes. Do you believe in the Father, Son, and Holy Ghost, three persons and one God? Reply: Yes. Do you believe that our Lord God, Jesus Christ, God's Son, was conceived of the Holy Ghost, took flesh and blood of Our Lady, Mary, and was born of her, a mother and maiden? Reply: Yes. Do you believe that He suffered death for our sins, that He died on the cross for you on Good Friday and was buried? Reply: Yes. Do you give Him thanks for that? Reply: Yes. Do you believe that you can be saved only through His death? Reply: Yes.

Then the priest shall say: While your soul is still in your body, place all your trust in His passion and death, reflecting on that and on nothing else. Give no thought to your wife, children, or wealth, but only to Christ's passion. Let the cross be before you and say: I place the cross between You, Lord, and my evil deeds. And again: Lord, I place the death of my Lord Jesus Christ between me and Your wrath. And add: In Your hands, Lord, I commend my spirit, for You, God of Truth, redeemed me. And repeat it thrice.

St. Augustine spoke to God in this manner. Ah, my Lord God, my mercy, my refuge, I desire You. I flee to You. Lord, do not despise me, though I be a wretched sinner, but help me in my great need. Bring me out of care and have mercy on me. I have no faith in my deeds; I trust more in Your mercy. You are my hope. I confess I have sinned against You. I beseech You of mercy—You Who have denied no man mercy.

BOKE OF CRAFT OF DYING [216]. A translation in six chapters of a Latin treatise generally known as *Ars moriendi* (or *Tractatus artis bene moriendi* or *Speculum artis bene moriendi* or *De arte bene moriendi*), extant in two principal versions which O'Connor styles CP and QS. The CP version upon which the Middle English translation is based survives in over 200 Latin manuscripts.

It is drawn from Part 3 of Jean Gerson's *Opusculum tripartitum* which comprises three treatises originally composed independently in French between 1400 and 1403, then brought together and supplied with a general introduction in 1404, and, finally, translated (probably by Gerson himself) into Latin between 1405 and 1410. The Middle English version may be dated about 1410. Judging from the extant manuscripts, it appears to have originated around London and to have circulated there mainly within a narrow lay circle. The only exceptions are a Northern manuscript and an abridged version in the Scottish dialect. Although its main source is Gerson's *Opusculum*, it has also drawn upon the *Ordo commendationis animae* for chapter 6, upon the *Quaestiones* in *Libros IV Sententiarum* of Duns Scotus for chapters 4 and 5, and upon Anselm's *Admonitio morienti* for chapter 3. Its purpose was to instruct the laity in the spiritual issues confronting them in time of death and to provide them with directions for administering to the dying in the absence of clergy.

This treatise in six chapters is intended to instruct and comfort men who are at the point of death. It is profitable to all Christian men generally who wish to learn how to die well. Although physical death is the most dreadful of all dreadful things, nevertheless the spiritual death of the soul is more horrible and detestable, for the soul is more precious than the body. But the death of good men is ever precious in the sight of God. Moreover, however wicked men may have been to the point of death, if they die in a state of true repentance and contrition, and in the true faith and unity and charity of Holy Church, their death is acceptable and precious in the sight of God. Therefore, a wise man says in commendation of the death of good men: Death is nothing but a departure from prison and an end of exile, a discharging of a heavy burden, an end of all infirmity, an escape from all perils, a destruction of all things evil, a breaking of all bonds, a payment of the debt of nature, a return to His country and an entry into bliss and joy. The day of man's death is better than the day of his birth. But this is said only of good men and the chosen people of God, for to evil men neither the day of their birth nor the day of their death is good. Therefore, every good, perfect, Christian man and every other man, although he be imperfect and but late converted from sin, so long as he is truly contrite and believes in God, should not be troubled by or dread the death of his body, but gladly and willingly, with the reason of his mind ruling his sensuality, take his death and bear it patiently, submitting his will to God's will. Moreover, no man can escape death. Therefore, we ought to accept it when God wills it without complaint or contradiction. To know how to die is to have a heart and soul ever ready to rise to God and to be prepared to receive death as a long-awaited, well-loved, and trusting friend. Every man should live in such a way that he may safely die any hour that God wills. And so he should have his life in patience and death in desire (chapter 1).

Men in their last illnesses experience the most grievous temptations of their whole lives. There are chiefly five temptations, the first of which is faith, which is the foundation of the soul's faith. Saint Paul says it is impossible to please God without faith. And Saint John says he who lacks faith is judged. Since no man is saved without it, the devil endeavors in man's last illness to subvert it or deceive him with superstitions and false errors. But every Christian must have faith not only in the principal articles of the faith but also in Holy Writ and obey the commandments of the Church and hold them firmly and die in them. Be advised that, in respect to this temptation and the rest, the devil cannot prevail against man so long as he has the use of his free will and reason. When a man is on his deathbed, he will profit from saying the Creed in a high voice often. It will fortify him in the faith and drive away the fiends who cannot bear to hear it. A double advantage should induce every sick man to remain firm in the faith: one is that all things are possible to the firm believer; the other is that he shall have all that he asks and prays for. The second temptation is despair, which is against hope and confidence that every man shall dwell with God, for when a man is gravely ill, the devil is busy to add sorrow on sorrow, confronting him with his sins, particularly the sins of which he was never absolved, to induce him to despair. A man should never despair in such circumstances—not even if he is incapable of oral confession. Contrition of heart is sufficient for everlasting salvation. Saint Bernard says: The pity and mercy of God transcend any evil. No man need despair, therefore, for that only offends God the more and his other sins become more grievous in His sight. To avoid despair, let him meditate on the spectacle of Christ on the cross, and take example of innumerable great sinners who have been saved. The third temptation is impatience which is against charity by which we are bound to love God above all things, for they who are on their deathbeds suffer great pain and sorrow because they are not dying generally of natural causes and old age, but of an accidental illness such as a fever, a postume, or other painful and long sickness. And so they die against their will and lack true charity and through sorrow and impatience become mad and witless. Therefore, it is essential for all dying men not to complain whatever illness befalls them, be it long or short, however painful or grievous. By your patience, says Saint Luke, you possess your souls. The physical suffering is a temporary punishment for sin. The fourth temptation is complacency or the pleasure that a man takes in himself, that is, spiritual pride. When the devil cannot shake a man's faith or bring him to impatience or despair, he assails him with complacence. "How stable you are in the faith, how strong in the faith, how resolute in patience! How many good deeds you have done!" Such are the thoughts he plants within the dying man. At such times let him take care to make himself meek by reflecting on his sins and realizing that he does not know whether he deserves everlasting love or hate, i.e., salvation or damnation. Lest he despair, he must lift up his heart to God in hope of His mercy. The fifth temptation is excessive occupation with temporal matters—wife, children, friends, riches. Let him put away all thoughts of worldly matters and commit himself to God (chapter 2).

Saint Anselm urges that the following questions be asked of the dying man who is not fully disposed for death: Brother, are you glad that you shall die in the faith of Christ? Do you realize that you have not conducted yourself as well as you should have? Do you repent of your conduct? Are you resolved to amend your life if you are spared? Do you believe that our Lord God Jesus Christ died for you? Are you grateful to Him? Do you believe that you can be saved only by Christ's death and passion? Then thank Him and put all your trust in His passion and death. And if it occurs to you, or the devil puts it into your mind, that you will be judged, say these words: Lord, I put the death of Our Lord Jesus Christ between me and my evil deeds, between me and Your judgment, between me and Your righteousness. These questions are appropriate for religious and devout people. Another set of questions posed by the Chancellor of Paris is appropriate for all men, both secular and religious: Do you believe the articles of the faith and holy scripture as interpreted by the doctors of the church, and are you glad that you shall die in the faith of Christ and in the obedience of Holy Church? Do you acknowledge that you have sinned often and grievously? Are you sorry for your sins, and do you ask the forgiveness of God? Do you purpose to amend your life if you are spared? Do you forgive those who have wronged you? Are you prepared to restore the goods you have acquired improperly, or even to forsake all your goods if you can make due satisfaction in no other way? Do you believe that Christ died for you and that you may never be saved but by the merit of Christ's passion, and do you thank God for it? Whoever responds affirmatively to these questions shall be saved (chapter 3).

Man at his last end should do the five things that Christ did on the cross: (1) pray; (2) cry out with his heart, i.e., desire forgiveness of sins and everlasting life; (3) weep for his sins; (4) commend his soul to God; (5) willingly surrender his spirit to God (chapter 4).

Man should prepare for death well in advance. He who is ill or in danger of death should receive the sacraments, make his testament, lawfully dispose of his household. Friends should not offer him the deceptive hope of recovery. Let him rather look for spiritual medicines through contrition and confession. If his illness is prolonged, let those who attend him read to him pious stories and prayers and rehearse before him the commandments of God. The image of the crucifix or Our Lady or a saint should ever be in his presence, and he should often be sprinkled with holy water to drive away the devils. He must pray intently, especially to Jesus Christ, and dispose himself to death without distraction of friends or family (chapter 5).

Friends and family or members of the community, if he be religious, should say prayers to God the Father, Christ, Mary, and Saint Michael over him for the repose of his soul (chapter 6).

THE ART AND CRAFT TO KNOW WELL TO DIE [217]. A translation by William Caxton of the *Ars moriendi* from a French original very closely related, according to Dr. G. R. Morgan, to Lille MS 127. Caxton adapts the text more specifically for the use of the ordinary laity, omitting many of the reflections on death and the passages urging spiritual preparations for death. For a summary of its contents and R. H. Wilson's commentary and bibliography, see IX [43] in *Manual,* vol. 3.

ARS MORIENDI [218]. A miscellany by William Caxton containing, in addition to the section on the craft of dying (see IX [42] in *Manual,* vol. 3), a devotion on the Eucharist, a list of the ways in which venial sins are removed (see [118] above), a passage from Gerson's *Opusculum* 1.16 on the three things men must do to obtain God's forgiveness, the twelve degrees of humility [77], the seven degrees of obedience [82], the seven degrees of patience [72], and the fifteen degrees of charity [59]. The section on the craft of dying is a considerably shortened version of the original with the elimination of much illustrative and devotional material. It probably derives from the same Lille manuscript Caxton used for the translation of *The Art and Craft to Know Well to Die* [217]. (See Malory and Caxton, IX [42], for R. H. Wilson's commentary and bibliography on *Ars Moriendi.*)

DE VISITACIONE INFIRMORUM ET CONSOLACIONE MISERO-RUM [219]. 31 thirteen-line stanzas riming ababbcbcdeeed by John Audelay [29]. Its source is ascribed to Saint Anselm whose *Admontio morienti* may have been used in part.

Saint Anselm made this treatise by God's grace. Have in mind, when you pass out of this world to place your hope in God, forsake your worldly possessions, desire eternal bliss. Make your confession by the commandments, five wits, works of mercy, and deadly sins. The world's bliss is transitory; it fades as a flower. Pope, king, duke, emperor, high or low, rich or poor—all shall die. He that lives most virtuously shall have the greatest reward in heaven. Each shall be rewarded according to his deserts. Sinful man, amend your life betimes, serve God, forsake the fiend, and you shall have forgiveness. Cursed is he who trusts in man and does not follow Christ's will. You can take no more with you after death than your good deeds, prayers, almsdeeds, and Masses. For God's love do good works and hear Mass. You will please God if you confess your sins to the priest and perform your penance. Do not oppose His will, Saint Anselm says, but accept adversity, for He will fulfill His mercy to you. It is better to suffer pain—to endure purgatory—in this world before your death. God will not punish you twice. Repent while you have time. God's mercy is above all. Consider how He forgave Mary Magdalene, Peter, and Thomas, and received them into heaven. Believe in Christ truly and foresake worldly lust and pleasure in order that you may attain everlasting bliss. Resolve, if you are spared, to amend your life and to serve God, and beseech Him to grant you grace to make a good end. Let Him be your comfort and consolation. He can cure your illness and grant forgiveness for your sins. Through Extreme Unction the priest has the power to absolve your sins if you are repentant. When you receive this sacrament, be assured that you will be saved at the Judgment. Keep the articles of the faith and ask God's mercy and grace. Make your last will and testament, and be prepared to join your Father when He sends for you, His child. These are not my words, but Saint Anselm's. Blind Audelay urges you, curates, to read them to the sick. Take good heed of your life. Beware lest you offend God, for He will judge you as He finds you. Amend your ways for fear of sudden death. All is well that ends well.

SEX OBSERVANDA OMNI CHRISTIANO IN EXTREMIS [220]. 24 quatrains in irregular lines riming abab. The Latin source precedes the expanded English text in the two extant manuscripts.

All men and women approaching death must take heed of six things: (1) that they pay their debts and restore any goods acquired unjustly; (2) that they make their last will and testament; (3) that they confess their sins; (4) that they receive Extreme Unction; (5) that they receive the Eucharist; (6) that they pray God for His mercy and contemplate the joys of paradise.

TO KUNNE TO DI3E (or SCIRE MORI) [221]. A translation of chapter 5 of Heinrich Suso's *Orologium sapientiae* on the preparation for death, extant in three versions. Two of the three versions appear to be related to the Middle English translation of Suso known as *The Seven Poyntes of Trewe Wisdom*. Full treatment of this work is reserved to the chapter on English Mystical Writings in a later volume of this *Manual*.

For other works in the Ars Moriendi tradition, see Hoccleve's *Ars Sciendi Mori* (VIII [6] in *Manual*, vol. 3), the versions of *Somme le Roi* [4–6] and *Miroir du Monde* [10], *Disce Mori* [11], and the *Craft to Live Well and Die* translated by Andrew Chertsey from the French and printed by Wynkyn de Worde in 1505.

THE V WYLES OF KING PHARAO [222]. A popular fifteenth-century treatise on the temptations of the devil added to the Middle English prose translation of Jean de Vignay's *Légende dorée* known as the *Gilte Legende*. It appears in manuscripts of the *Gilte Legende* and independently. It makes extensive use of Augustine, Gregory the Great, Rabanus Maurus, and Peter Lombard.

King Pharaoh perpetrated five wiles against the children of Israel. (1) He granted them permission to sacrifice to their God in order that they might remain in Egypt under his authority. Similarly, it is the devil's will that sinners publicly perform the penance enjoined by priests while they continue to sin privately. (2) He granted them permission to leave Egypt and make sacrifice to their God so long as they did not go far from Egypt and promptly returned to dwell in his power. Similarly, the devil allows men to leave their sins for a time—at Easter, for example—so long as they do not put aside the proximate occasions of sin and can promptly fall into sin again, even deeper than before. (3) He granted them permission to go far from Egypt and make sacrifice to their God so long as they left their children behind, thus assuring that they would return and remain in his power. Similarly, the devil allows men to perform penance in hypocrisy and vainglory, leaving their good works in the land of the fiend and rejecting God's grace. (4) He granted them permission to go far from Egypt and make sacrifice to their God and even to take their children with them so long as they left behind their sheep and cattle which they required for their livelihood, thus assuring that they would return and remain in his power. Similarly, the devil allows men to perform good works and penance so long as they leave their wits in sin, pursuing lust and failing to behave with reason and discretion. (5) He grants them permission to go far from Egypt with their children and beasts and make sacrifice to their God as long as they speak well of him and Egypt and resolve to come again to him later. Similarly, the devil allows men to forsake him, perform penance and good works, and chastise their flesh so long as they delight in recalling and recounting their old sins. They rejoice in rehearsing the sins of their youth. When they speak of sin, they call it mirth; when they speak of harlotry, they call it sport. Be wary of the wiles of the devil, and praise not the works of those men who rejoice in their misdeeds.

THE DIRECCION OF A MANNYS LYFE [223]. A short treatise in seven chapters on resisting temptation.

Every man who wishes to please and serve God must avoid three spiritual enemies—the world, the flesh, and the devil—who are busy night and day to bring him to evil through the seven deadly sins, to lead him to break the commandments, misuse his five wits, and deny the articles of the faith. A good remedy against such temptations is prayer or meditation on Christ's passion or on his own death and last end. A man who has fallen into great sin and wickedness should confess to a priest and perform penance, avoid despair, for God is merciful and patient. If a man wishes to live virtuously but often succumbs to sin again after confession, he should resolve to amend his life. For all his faults, he will eventually prevail over sin. God looks to his good purpose. As he improves, the devil's temptations will become more severe. He will bring old sins to mind and put a man in doubt whether he is completely absolved of them or not. Let him not attempt to resolve the matter himself, but trust in God's judgment and his confessor's and continue in prayer and good work. He must not grumble at temptation, for it is there to prove him, to keep him from taking pride in his virtue. He need only hope and trust in God, asking His help, to overcome all temptation.

THE THRE ARGUMENTIS THAT THE DEVEL WILL PUTTE TO MAN IN HIS DIINGE [224]. A brief dialogue between the devil and man.

1. You have committed countless horrible sins in the course of your life, and now you have no time to make satisfaction for them. Man's reply: God is righteous, but His mercy surpasses all.

2. I was damned for one sin only. You have committed innumerable sins and must needs be condemned by God's justice. Man's reply: You sinned of your own free will; I sin at the constant urging of the world, the flesh, and the devil. Moreover, God took flesh to save mankind.

3. I was the highest angel in heaven and know who is to be saved and who damned. You are to be damned. Man's reply: Liar! You did not even know of your own damnation. How can you know of mine?

4. Non-liturgical and Occasional Services and Devotions

PRIMER (or LAY FOLKS' PRAYER BOOK) [225]. English translations of the Latin *Horae* or *Hours of the Blessed Virgin Mary* were made from about 1380 to 1450 when, according to Deanesly, they fell under suspicion of Lollardry. They were produced for mainly lay readers as a book of private devotion and as a devotional aid during church services. Their basic corpus consists of the Hours of the Virgin, the Seven Penitential Psalms, the Fifteen Gradual Psalms, the Litany, the Office of the Dead, and Commendations. Other matter was often appended in the form of prayers and texts of spiritual guidance and instruction. Sixteen manuscripts (and a fragment) of the *Primer* survive, two of them (Glasgow University MS Hunter 512 and University College, Oxford, MS 179) in a parallel Latin-English text. Littlehales, who collated all but three of the *Primer* manuscripts, divided them according to their liturgical structure into a shorter and an extended group. Harris suggests a classification into earlier primers (e.g., St. John's College, Cambridge, MS 192) whose translation of the Psalms bears a resemblance either to Rolle's or to the English versions of St. Jerome's and later primers (e.g., British Library MS Additional 17010) which follow in part the Wycliffite version of the Bible. University College, Oxford, MS 179 is somewhat exceptional, differing from other manuscripts in its translation of the Hours and the Psalms. Much remains to be explored in the textual and structural relationship of the primers. A majority of the manuscripts localize in the Southwest Midlands; others show a more northerly or easterly provenance. Interest in primers revived in the sixteenth century, and it has been demonstrated that Cranmer among others made extensive use of them.

LITANY [226]. A supplicatory prayer based on the Litany of the Saints and used for both public and private devotion in the late Middle Ages. There are five vernacular versions in verse: (1) a litany to the cross, Trinity, Blessed

Virgin, angels, patriarchs, apostles, martyrs, confessors, religious orders, holy women, and saints in sixteen rime royal stanzas. Perhaps the most popular of the litanies and seemingly designed as an illustrated devotional poem, it is preserved in whole or in part in ten manuscripts and several early prints; (2) a litany to Christ, Blessed Virgin, angels, and saints in nine six-line stanzas in the form of a carol (see XIV [311] in *Manual,* vol. 6); (3) a litany to the Trinity, Blessed Virgin, angels, patriarchs and prophets, apostles, saints, and martyrs, concluding with a fervent appeal for peace between England and France, in 25 eight-line stanzas riming ababbcbc; (4) a litany to the Blessed Virgin, Saint Catherine, angels, patriarchs and prophets, apostles, martyrs, confessors, virgins, and saints in eight quatrains and a final couplet; (5) a litany to angels, patriarchs and prophets, apostles, martyrs, confessors, virgins, and saints in sixteen short couplets. Prose versions of the litany regularly appear in the *Primer* [225]. For a litany by Lydgate consisting of a series of prayers to ten saints, see XVI [155] in *Manual,* vol. 6.

HOURS OF THE CROSS [227]. A popular devotion linking the canonical hours to the various phases of Christ's passion. Its source is a fourteenth-century Latin hymn, *Patris sapientia,* attributed to Pope John XXII. It was turned into English many times. Audelay, William of Shoreham, and possibly Ryman made versions of it. Other versions are found in John of Grimestone's Preaching Book, the *Primer* [225], *Cursor Mundi* [31], and the Vernon and Worcestershire miscellanies. There is a "Meditations on the Hours of the Cross" in *The Tretyse of Love* (see the chapter on English Mystical Writings in a later volume of this *Manual*).

STATIONS OF THE CROSS [228]. A late medieval devotion, perhaps of Dominican origin, that is meant to recall the sacred sites of Christ's passion, is preserved in Lambeth Palace Library MS 546. It describes the fifteen "stations" or halting places along the Via Dolorosa which the Virgin Mary, according to a familiar tradition recounted in the headnote to the text, visited daily. The devotee is urged to follow her practice in his heart.

THE SENTENCE OF CURSING (also THE GREAT SENTENCE and THE GENERAL SENTENCE OF EXCOMMUNICATION) [229]. The form of excommunication in English is found in many manuscripts and early prints with considerable variations in matter and length. Directions for pronouncing the ban often introduce the text which typically consists of a list of offenses incurring excommunication followed by a formal curse. Parish priests were instructed to recite it to their parishioners in church three or four times a year. There are versions of it in the Sarum and York Manuals, Mirk's *Instructions for Parish Priests* [233], *Sacerdos Parochialis* [22], Caxton's *Quattuor Sermones* [21], and *Jacob's Well* [9]. Pickering has made a most valuable study of the interrelationships of these texts and their sources in canon law and episcopal legislation. Mirk's *Oculus sacerdotis*, and possibly other Latin manuals for parish priests, also influenced their composition.

HAVE MERCY UPON ME O LORD [230]. The Miserere psalm translated into couplets and arranged for use in the Asperges service of Salisbury Cathedral.

THE ROSARY [231]. A unique, half-obliterated text giving directions for saying the rosary is extant in Exeter College, Oxford, MS 47.

5. General Directions

DIRECTIONS FOR DEACONS AND SUBDEACONS AT CHURCH SERVICES [232]. Apparently three excerpts, the first imperfect at the beginning, on the duties of deacons and subdeacons assisting at Mass and evensong by John Gysborn, a Premonstratensian canon of Coverham and later curate of Allington in Lincolnshire.

VI. Tracts on the Duties of the Clergy

INSTRUCTIONS FOR PARISH PRIESTS [233]. 1934 lines in octosyllabic couplets together with a prose version of the Great Sentence. It survives in seven manuscripts, all of them at one or more removes from the original. Kristensson, its most recent editor, like his predecessors, Peacock and Furnivall, makes British Library MS Cotton Claudius A.ii the basis of his text with variants from Bodleian MSS Douce 60 and 103. A Northern copy of the *Instructions* in British Library MS Royal 17.C.xvii which differs from the

Cotton manuscript in dialect and detail is printed separately. It is in the main a free translation of portions of William of Pagula's *Oculus sacerdotis*. The interrogation of the sinner is based on Saint Anselm's *Admonitio morienti*. Other sources were used, but they remain to be explored. The colophon of the *Instructions* in the Cotton manuscript identifies its author as John Mirk, a canon-regular of Lilleshall in Shropshire, who also composed the *Festial*, a popular collection of sermons in vernacular prose for the principal feasts of the Christian year, and a Latin *Manuale sacerdotis*. The dialect of the *Instructions* is West Midland with an admixture of Northern forms. It was composed about 1400.

In addition to the complete text, 70 lines of the *Instructions* are found interspersed in a contemporary poem on the constitutions of masonry, *Constituciones Artis Geometriae Secundum Euclyde[m]*, extant in British Library MS Royal 17.A.i. A 126-line abstract of the *Instructions*, corresponding to lines 410–525 of the complete text and presenting the Pater Noster, Ave Maria, Creed, and Articles of the Faith, has been published by K. Bitterling from Trinity College, Dublin, MS 211.

The *Instructions* is not without interest to the church historian and liturgiologist, but it has little or no literary merit, and few would disagree with Pearsall's pungent observation that Mirk "works on a level of low expectation."

(MS Cotton text.) When the blind lead the blind, both fall into the ditch. Priests are so blind to God's law today that they lead their parishioners into sin. Therefore, priest, if you are unlearned, read this treatise. Your preaching, however, will be worth little if you lead an evil life. You must be chaste, conduct services without haste, and eschew lies, oaths, drunkenness, gluttony, pride, sloth, and envy. Stay away from taverns; take no part in trade. Do not play at wrestling, shooting, and the like. Forego hawking, hunting, and dancing. Avoid cutted clothes, piked shoes, markets, and fairs. Wear neither dagger nor sash. Shave your beard and head. Show hospitality, read the psalter, fear the day of doom, and return good for evil. Forsake the service of women lest they bring you into ill repute. The conversation of evil women often perverts good manners. Avoid foolish japes and ribaldry. Despise the world, and turn your thoughts to virtue. If you do this, you will be respected by all who see and hear you.

You must teach your parishioners to confess their sins promptly and women with child, when they are near their term, to go to confession and receive communion. It is the midwife's duty (and the parents', too, if no one else is at hand) to christen the child in case of necessity. The form of baptism may be said in Latin or English. Godparents are obliged to teach their godchildren the Pater Noster and Creed. Confirmation should take place in the fifth year. Marriage vows are irrevocable. Do not preside at irregular nuptials. After the proclamations of the banns, let the bride and groom be wed openly at the church door before witnesses. Teach your parishioners to go to confession and receive communion on Easter, believing that they receive God's body and blood in the form of bread, and to behave properly in church, avoiding idle chatter, putting away all vanity, and praying on their knees for God's grace. All are to stand at the Gospel, kneel at the consecration, and say the prayer at the Levation, "Ihesu, lord, welcome thou be, in forme of bred as I the se." According to St. Augustine, there are benefits to be derived from seeing the Host. The viewer on that day shall not want for food, shall be forgiven idle oaths and words, shall not die suddenly, nor lose his sight. Games should not be played in church or churchyard, nor courts be held there. Tithes are to be duly paid of all things great and small. Witchcraft and magic spells are forbidden; so, too, is usury which is a grievous sin. Husbands and wives must be advised not to make vows of penance, chastity, or pilgrimage (saving only the vow of a pilgrimage to Jerusalem) without each other's consent, nor wives to make vows unknown to their husbands. Two or three times a year teach your parishioners the Pater Noster, Ave Maria, Creed, Articles of the Faith, and the Seven Sacraments. Learn to administer the sacraments properly. If the baptism bestowed on a child at home appears to have been invalid, perform the rite again, using the form of conditional baptism as for a foundling. Do not baptize in an intoxicated state. Confirmation may be performed by a bishop only. The name given in confirmation cannot be changed. The Great Sentence of Excommunication is to be pronounced to the parish two or three times a year. Penance must be given discreetly, but it is of little value without confession. When a man comes to confession, you must first ask if he is a parishioner. If he is not, you may not hear his confession unless he has leave to come from his own parish priest or has valid grounds not to confess to him. You have authority to hear the confession of a scholar, sailor, traveller, person about to go into battle, or person at the point of death, even though he be not a parishioner. If the penitent is ignorant of the Pater Noster, Ave Maria, and Creed, set him a penance that will compel him to learn them. Examine him in the Articles of the Faith, the Ten Commandments, the Seven Deadly Sins, and the Venial Sins. Before you enjoin penance, you must know who the penitent is—young or old, bond or free, clerk or secular, single or married, rich or poor—as well as the circumstances and frequency of his sins. Take care not to impose a harsh penance that the penitent will not perform. Better to send him to purgatory with a light penance than to hell with overmuch penance. Contraries often cure contraries. The remedy for pride is meekness; the remedy for wrath is for a man to realize that it turns him from God's child to the devil's; the remedy for envy is love; the remedy for covetousness is restitution and charity; the remedy for gluttony is abstinence, almsgiving, and feeding the poor; the remedy for sloth is to say the Pater Noster morning, noon, and night, and to hear Mass daily, or, if work prevents attendance at church, to join in heart in the service when the Mass knell is heard; the remedy for lechery is chastity, or, if chastity is impossible, marriage. Since few will perform the legal penance for mortal sin, enjoin a light one. Let mercy prevail. Reserve certain cases for the bishop. After hearing confession and giving the penance, bid the penitent make an act of contrition and grant him absolution. Extreme Unction is to be administered when a man is near death, after an interrogation to determine the strength of his faith and his willingness to acknowledge and repent of his sins. You must visit the sick quickly, bearing the Host on your breast, in a clean surplice. If the sick man cannot receive the sacrament, store it securely in church again to protect it from rats or mice.

Now, dear priest, pray for the author and remember him in your Masses. Read this book often and let others read it. It is written to instruct those who have no books of their own and others of mean learning.

THE OFFICE OF A BISHOP OR PRIEST [234]. A single page on the duties of the clergy drawn from patristic authorities with the Latin initia in the margin.

The office of a bishop or priest consists in: (1) preaching Christ's gospel; (2) praying; (3) administering the sacraments; (4) studying scripture; (5) giving good example.

THE ORDER OF MELCHISEDECH [235]. Four eight-line stanzas riming ababbcbc in praise of the priesthood. Its source, a Latin poem beginning

"Mechisedech rex et sacerdos panem et vinum optulit," precedes it in the manuscript. The last stanza of the English text introduces, after an intervening Latin passage, the poem on the virtues of the Mass (see [202] above, Version E).

> Honor the priesthood, Christians, for, as scripture says, it is the worthiest of all orders. Witness Melchisedech, the king and priest who offered bread and wine, betokening the Blessed Sacrament. He prefigured the power of the priesthood. Through transubstantiation priestly power surpasses that of the patriarchs, prophets, and angels.

For additional material on the duties of the clergy, see the *Speculum Christiani* [15], table 8.

2. WORKS OF PHILOSOPHICAL INSTRUCTION

I. Translations of Cicero

CICERO'S OF OLD AGE AND OF FRIENDSHIP [236]. There are few works of philosophical instruction in Middle English. Two translations of Latin classics—Cicero's *Of Old Age* and *Of Friendship*—dating from the second half of the fifteenth century have already been discussed as dialogues (VII [44] in *Manual*, vol. 3). *Of Friendship* was executed by John Tiptoft, Earl of Worcester, about 1460. It is excessively slavish and marred by inaccuracies. *Of Old Age*, long attributed to Tiptoft, is actually by William Worcester, the antiquarian scholar and confidential secretary of Sir John Fastolf. Its direct source was not *De senectute*, but a popular French version, *Le livre de Tulle de viellesse*, made by Laurence de Premierfait about 1405. In 1481, William Caxton printed both translations in a composite volume which also included Tiptoft's expanded translation of Buonaccorso da Montemagno of Pistoia's *Dialogus de vera nobilitate* (see VII [43] in *Manual*, vol. 3). A corrected version of Tiptoft's translation of *De amicitia* attributed to William Rastell was printed about 1530. (See Dialogues, Debates, and Catechisms, VII [44], for F. L. Utley's commentary and bibliography on Cicero's *Of Old Age* and *Of Friendship*.)

II. The Tradition of Boethius

1. Translation of the *Consolation of Philosophy*

JOHN WALTON'S BOETHIUS TRANSLATION [237]. 7584 lines in two
meters, Books I to III, including a Translator's Preface paying tribute to
Chaucer and Gower and expressing a determination to remain faithful to
the original and a Prologue giving a brief biography of Boethius, in eight-
line stanzas with the rime scheme ababbcbc and Books IV and V in rime
royal. Over twenty extant manuscripts attest to its considerable popularity
in the fifteenth and early sixteenth centuries. It was printed in 1525 by
Thomas Rychard, a monk of Tavistock Abbey and graduate of Colchester
College, Oxford, to whom we owe the information that it was commissioned
by Elizabeth, daughter of Thomas Lord Berkeley, a celebrated fifteenth-
century patron of letters. Ten manuscript colophons and Rychard's print
date it 1410 and identify its author as John Walton, a papal chaplain and
Augustinian canon of Oseney, about whom little is known. He was grounded
in logic and rhetoric, knew French well, and judging from the large number
of references to the law, may have had legal training. The ascription to him
of the translation of Vegetius' *De re militari* has yet to be established. Although
he worked from the Latin original, he made extensive use of Chaucer's *Boece*
(Aldridge suggests that his copy may have contained French glosses) together
with Trevet's *Commentary* on the *De Consolatione* for the Prologue and incidental explanatory matter. His translation is the work of a skillful and determined craftsman. It is accurate, fluent, and often felicitous. In Pearsall's
view, it is "in every respect superior" to Chaucer's prose version. The dialect
is East Midland with a generous sprinkling of other forms. More than half
his vocabulary is of Romance origin.

2. Commentary on the *Consolation of Philosophy*

BOETHIUS—COMMENTARY [238]. A unique commentary on Book I
of the *Consolatio*, here called the *Book of Comfort*, is extant in Bodleian MS
Auct.F.3.5. It was designed to provide a popular introduction to the *Consolatio*, and its exposition is keyed to Chaucer's translation. An edition by B. S.
Donaghey of Sheffield University is in progress.

3. Works Partially Modelled on the *Consolation of Philosophy*

GEORGE ASHBY'S A PRISONER'S REFLECTIONS [239]. 50 rime royal stanzas. Little is known of the life of George Ashby. He was born about 1390 and from early youth served first King Henry VI and then Queen Margaret of Anjou as signet clerk. Later he appears to have assumed direction of the education of Edward, Prince of Wales, until his assassination in 1471. For Edward he composed two works, also in rime royal, *Active Policy of a Prince* (XIII [251] in *Manual*, vol.5), and a collection of moral saws, *Dicta et Opiniones Diversorum Philosophorum. A Prisoner's Reflections* was composed in 1463 during his confinement in Fleet Prison following the overthrow of King Henry VI. Baugh describes it as a "modest consolation of philosophy." Pearsall would accord him the title of poet "only by courtesy." His skills are indeed modest.

At the end of summer, towards Michaelmas, I was unjustly committed to Fleet Prison by order of a lord whose power commands obedience. I was despoiled of my property and reduced to poverty. My name is George Ashby. My imprisonment has lasted a year or more. I receive no comfort from friends who have forgotten my benefactions to them and disdain to visit me. My greatest distress is that I cannot free myself from debt. To whom can I complain? For 40 years I faithfully served the king, queen, and their uncle, the Duke of Gloucester, as writer to the Signet. Now, in old age, I have been thrown into prison and subjected to cruel treatment. My former prosperity and joy make my present circumstances even harder to bear. With God's grace I shall make the best of my life, knowing that His punishments are profitable to the soul. I write to counsel patience to those in trouble whether it be deserved or not. The soul is purified by adversity, worldly joys are fleeting. Wealth departs, family life brings sorrow and strife. All things go by contraries. Prosperity never endures long. There is no perfection on earth. Life is a pilgrimage to heaven. Meekly accept whatever trouble or distress God sends. Witness how much Christ suffered for our salvation. Witness the suffering of Mary, St. John the Evangelist, martyrs, confessors, holy virgins, St. John the Baptist, Job, innumerable saints. All classes of men have experienced adversity. Let them be an example to us of patience through which we can overcome adversity. I beseech Jesus to guide me to victory over my troubles and to grant me the grace to please Him. Go, little book, to people in adversity and teach them to bear it patiently. Written in prison, the sepulchre of the living, 1463.

A number of other works were also partially modelled on Boethius. They include *The Kingis Quair* (X [1]), Thomas Usk's *Testament of Love* ([191] above), *Adversite and Resoun* (VII [33]), Alain Chartier's *Le Traité de l'Esperance* (VII [34]]), now available in an edition by M. S. Blayney (EETS 270, 281), Henryson's *Orpheus and Eurydice* (X [5]), the *Prisoner's Complaint against Fortune* (XI [7]), and possibly Lydgate's *Serpent of Division* (XVI [167]). (See *Manual*, vols. 3, 4, and 6.)

DE LIBERO ARBITRIO [240]. A unique English version of St. Anselm's treatise on free will has been published in facsimile. It dates from the late fifteenth century and is of metropolitan provenance.

DIALOGUE ON TRUE NOBILITY [241] has been previously discussed in vol. 3 of the *Manual* (VII [43]). Schlauch finds additional evidence to support Mitchell's contention that Tiptoft worked from the original Latin of Buonaccorso rather than from the French of Mielot, and she argues that he expanded the Latin even more than the French translator. Willard, following the view that Tiptoft used Mielot, points to it as further proof of Burgundy's significant role in the transmission of humanist ideas and texts. (See Dialogues, Debates, and Catechisms, VII [43], for F. L. Utley's commentary and bibliography on *Dialogue on True Nobility*.)

III. Translations of Petrarch

PETRARCH'S SECRETUM [242]. A late fifteenth-century verse translation (908 pentameter lines riming alternately) of the Proem and Book One of the *Secretum*, Petrarch's dialogue with Saint Augustine on his inner struggle between asceticism and worldliness, appears in a recently acquired British Library manuscript, Additional 60577, closely associated with Winchester.

For an adaptation of Petrarch's *De remediis utriusque fortunae*, see *Adversite and Resoun* (VII [33] in volume 3 of the *Manual*).

3. UNDISTRIBUTED WORKS

I. The Joys of Paradise

DE QUATTUORDECIM PARTIBUS BEATUDINIS [243]. A unique, unprinted, Middle-English version of chapter 5 of the *Dicta Anselmi*, "De quattuordecim partibus aeternae commoditatis sive beatudinis," compiled by Alexander, a monk of Canterbury, secretary to the archbishop, about 1115. It is extant in Lichfield Cathedral MS 16 of the late fourteenth century preceded by the Latin text and followed by a unique, Anglo-Norman version.

THE DOWERS OF THE BODY AND THE SOUL [244]. A late fifteenth-century prose treatise, incomplete at the end, on the joys of paradise, possibly derived from a version of Archbishop Robert Grosseteste's *De Dotibus*.

This treatise speaks of joy in bliss—such joy as man has neither seen nor heard, such joy as he has only glimpsed through God's grace. Saint Augustine says that the blessed in heaven desire and receive nothing but good. The four blisses with which God endows the body are subtlety, agility, clarity (brightness), and immortality. He bestows four dowers upon the soul: knowledge of past, present, and future devoid of contradiction. . . .

A poem of 175 lines in long, riming couplets on the joys of paradise and how to achieve it is extant in British Library MS Harley 2383.

II. The Pains of Hell

FOUR MANERS OF HELLE [245].

There are four kinds of hell: (1) the eternal hell of fire, smoke, devils, etc.; (2) the hell of unbaptized children who feel no pain, but only joy in the goodness of God and in the knowledge that they have not sinned against Him and that they shall never come to eternal hell. What will become of them after the Judgment only God knows; (3) purgatory where the pain depends on the quality and quantity of the sins. Release from purgatory can be effected by Masses, almsgiving, prayer, fasting, indulgences, pardons, visiting the Holy Sepulchre of Christ, and penance; (4) limbo where saints dwelled before Christ's resurrection.

A poem of 29 lines in long, riming couplets on how to escape the pains of purgatory is extant in British Library MS Harley 2383.

XIV MANERIS OF HELLE [246]. A prose catalogue of torments ascribed to Saint Paul. The reference is undoubtedly to the *Vision of St. Paul* (see V [320] in *Manual*, vol. 2), the source from which many of its details ultimately derive. Its immediate source was probably *Les peines de purgatorie* ascribed to Archbishop Robert Grosseteste. Additional details may have come from St. Anselm's *De moribus*, chapters 48–49, or *De anima*, chapter 13, ascribed to Hugh of St. Victor.

The torments of hell are: (1) unquenchable fire; (2) chilling cold; (3) insufferable stench;

(4) unsatisfied hunger; (5) unremitting thirst; (6) thick darkness; (7) the horrible sight of the devil; (8) the biting and stinging of venomous snakes; (9) pummeling by devils with iron hammers; (10) bitter and endless remorse of conscience; (11) copious weeping; (12) surpassing shame; (13) burning bonds on hands and feet; (14) despair of mercy.

III. Prayer

THE VERTUE OF HOLY PRAYERE [247]. A collection of ten "notable saynges" by Augustine, Bernard, Isidore, Jerome, Ambrose, Chrisostom, Gregory, Cassiodorus, Bede, and Aquinas on the benefits of prayer.

THE XII LETTYNGIS OF PREYERE [248]. A fifteenth-century text based on Augustine, Bernard, and Biblical authorities. It is found both independently and as part of a composite work on faith, charity, etc., in the Durham, Rylands, and Trinity 601 manuscripts.

By this treatise men may learn why God does not hear their prayers. They mistakenly believe that faith alone without charity is sufficient for salvation. Faith alone, however, shall save no man. The lettings of prayer are: (1) the suppliant's sinfulness; (2) his doubt; (3) the inappropriateness of his request; (4) the unworthiness of the person for whom he prays; (5) his many evil and unclean thoughts; (6) his scorn of God's law; (7) his harsh attitude towards the poor and his unforgiving attitude towards those who do him harm; (8) the growing number of his sins; (9) the devil's distracting suggestions; (10) the paucity of his desire to pray; (11) his impatience; (12) his lack pf perseverance in prayer.

According to Aarts, there is a Latin tract on this subject in Emmanuel College, Cambridge, MS 46.

IV. Fasting

SEVEN FRIDAYS WHEN IT IS GOOD TO FAST [249]. A late medieval devotion actually listing twelve Fridays.

Pope St. Clement discovered this devotion in the canon of the Mass. The person who observes it will see his soul borne to heaven by angels provided that he makes a good confession on the eves of the twelve Fridays: the first Friday of March, the Friday before the Annunciation, Good Friday, the Friday before Holy Thursday, the Friday before Whitsun, the Friday of Whitsun Week, the Friday before St. John the Baptist's Day, the Friday before the Feast of Sts. Peter and Paul, the Friday before the Assumption of Our Lady, the Friday before the Nativity of Our Lady, the Friday after St. Andrew's Day, and the Friday before Christmas.

A LYTEL TREATYSE TO FASTE ON THE WEDNESDAY [250]. 70 long couplets. It appears to have been modelled on the *Virtues of the Mass* [202].

Every man and woman ought to abstain from flesh on Wednesday. Abstinence from flesh hallows men's souls, makes them chaste, and brings rest and joy. He who serves gluttony is prompt to sin, says Augustine. Authorities are spuriously drawn from the Bible, *De Esu Carnuum, Vitas Patrum,* Bede, saints' lives, and local legend to demonstrate the benefits of following this injunctive as well as the evils that can ensue from its neglect. The treatise is written in honor of God and Saints Catherine and Christopher.

Bibliography

TABLE OF ABBREVIATIONS

For abbreviations and shortened forms not appearing in this table consult the list of background books at the beginning of the appropriate chapter of the Bibliography.

AAGRP	Ausgaben und Abhandlungen aus dem Gebiete der romanischen Philologie
AC	Archaeologica Cantiana
Acad	Academy
AEB	Kölbing E, Altenglische Bibliothek, Heilbronn 1883–
AELeg 1875	Horstmann C, Altenglische Legenden, Paderborn 1875
AELeg 1878	Horstmann C, Sammlung altenglischer Legenden, Heilbronn 1878
AELeg 1881	Horstmann C, Altenglische Legenden (Neue Folge), Heilbronn 1881
AESpr	Mätzner E, Altenglische Sprachproben, Berlin 1867–
AF	Anglistische Forschungen
AfDA	Anzeiger für deutsches Alterthum
AHR	American Historical Review
AJ	Ampleforth Journal
AJA	American Journal of Archaeology
AJP	American Journal of Philology
ALb	Allgemeines Literaturblatt
ALg	Archivum linguisticum
Allen WAR	Allen H E, Writings Ascribed to Richard Rolle Hermit of Hampole and Materials for His Biography, MLA Monograph Series 3, N Y 1927
Angl	Anglia, Zeitschrift für englische Philologie
AnglA	Anglia Anzeiger
AnglB	Beiblatt zur Anglia
AN&Q	American Notes and Queries

Antiq	Antiquity
APS	Acta philologica scandinavica
AQ	American Quarterly
AR	Antioch Review
Arch	Archiv für das Studium der neueren Sprachen und Literaturen
Archaeol	Archaeologia
Ashton	Ashton J, Romances of Chivalry, London 1890
ASp	American Speech
ASR	American Scandinavian Review
ASt	Aberystwyth Studies
Athen	Athenaeum
BA	Books Abroad
BARB	Bulletin de l'Académie royal de Belgique
Baugh LHE	Baugh A C, The Middle English Period, in A Literary History of England, N Y 1948; 2nd edn 1967
BB	Bulletin of Bibliography
BBA	Bonner Beiträge zur Anglistik
BBCS	Bulletin of the Board of Celtic Studies (Univ of Wales)
BBGRP	Berliner Beiträge zur germanischen und romanischen Philologie
BBSIA	Bulletin bibliographique de la Société internationale arthurienne
Bennett OHEL	Bennett H S, Chaucer and the Fifteenth Century, Oxford 1947
Best BIP	Best R I, Bibliography of Irish Philology, 2 vols. Dublin 1913
BGDSL	Beiträge zur Geschichte der deutschen Sprache und Literatur
BHR	Bibliothèque d'humanisme et renaissance
BIHR	Bulletin of the Institute of Historical Research
Billings	Billings A H, A Guide to the Middle English Metrical Romances, N Y 1901
Blackf	Blackfriars

Bloomfield SDS	Bloomfield M W, The Seven Deadly Sins, Michigan State College of Agriculture and Applied Science Studies in Language and Literature, 1952
BNYPL	Bulletin of the New York Public Library
Böddeker AED	Böddeker K, Altenglische Dichtungen des MS Harl 2253, Berlin 1878
Bossuat MBLF	Bossuat R, Manuel bibliographique de la littérature française du moyen âge, Paris 1951; supplément Paris 1955; deuxième supplément Paris 1961 [the item numbers run consecutively through the supplement]
BPLQ	Boston Public Library Quarterly
BQR	Bodleian Quarterly Record (sometimes Review)
Brandl	Brandl A, Mittelenglische Literatur, in Paul's Grundriss der germanischen Philologie, 1st edn, Strassburg 1893, 2^1.609 ff, Index 2^2.345
Brown ELxiiiC	Brown C F, English Lyrics of the 13th Century, Oxford 1932
Brown Reg	Brown C, A Register of Middle English Religious and Didactic Verse, parts 1 and 2, Oxford (for the Bibliographical Society) 1916, 1920
Brown RLxivC	Brown C F, Religious Lyrics of the 14th Century, Oxford 1924
Brown RLxvC	Brown C F, Religious Lyrics of the 15th Century, Oxford 1939
Brown-Robbins	Brown C and R H Robbins, The Index of Middle English Verse, N Y 1943; see also Robbins-Cutler
Bryan-Dempster	Bryan W F and G Dempster, Sources and Analogues of Chaucer's Canterbury Tales, Chicago 1941
BrynMawrMon	Bryn Mawr College Monographs, Bryn Mawr 1905–
BSEP	Bonner Studien zur englischen Philologie
BUSE	Boston University Studies in English
CASP	Cambridge Antiquarian Society Publication
CBEL	Bateson F W, Cambridge Bibliography of English Literature, 5 vols, London and N Y 1941, 1957

CE	College English
CFMA	Les classiques français du moyen âge; collection de textes français et provençaux antérieurs à 1500, Paris 1910–
Chambers	Chambers E K, The Mediaeval Stage, 2 vols, Oxford 1903; rptd from corrected sheets 1925, 1948, 1954
Chambers OHEL	Chambers E K, English Literature at the Close of the Middle Ages, Oxford 1945
CHEL	Ward A W and A R Waller, The Cambridge History of English Literature, vols 1 and 2, Cambridge 1907, 1908; NY 1933
CHR	Catholic Historical Review
ChS	Publications of the Chaucer Society, London 1869–1924
Ch&Sidg	Chambers E K and F Sidgwick, Early English Lyrics, London 1907; numerous reprints
CJ	Classic Journal
CL	Comparative Literature
CMLR	Canadian Modern Language Review
Comper Spir Songs	Comper F M M, Spiritual Songs from English Manuscripts of Fourteenth to Sixteenth Centuries, London and N Y 1936
Conviv	Convivium
Courthope	Courthope W J, History of English Poetry, vol 1, London 1895
CP	Classical Philology
Craig HEL	Craig H, G K Anderson, L I Bredvold, J W Beach, History of English Literature, N Y 1950
Cross Mot Ind	Cross T P, Motif Index of Early Irish Literature, Bloomington Ind 1951
Crotch PEWC	Crotch W J B, The Prologues and Epilogues of William Caxton, EETS 176, London 1928
CUS	Columbia University Studies in English and in Comparative Literature, N Y 1899–

DA, DAI — Dissertation Abstracts, Dissertation Abstracts International

DANHSJ — Derbyshire Archaeological and Natural History Society Journal

de Julleville Hist — de Julleville L Petit, Histoire de la langue et de la littérature française, vols 1 and 2, Paris 1896–99

de Ricci Census — de Ricci S and W J Wilson, Census of Medieval and Renaissance Manuscripts in the United States of America and Canada, vols 1–3, N Y 1935, 1937, 1940

Dickins and Wilson — Dickins B and R M Wilson, Early Middle English Texts, Cambridge 1950

DLz — Deutsche Literaturzeitung

DNB — Stephen L and S Lee, Dictionary of National Biography, N Y and London 1885–1900, and supplements

DomS — Dominican Studies: An Annual Review, Blackfriars Publications, London

DUJ — Durham University Journal

EA — Études anglaises

EBEP — Erlanger Beiträge zur englischen Philologie

EC — Essays in Criticism

EETS — Publications of the Early English Text Society (Original Series), 1864–

EETSES — Publications of the Early English Text Society (Extra Series), 1867–

EG — Études germaniques

EGS — English and Germanic Studies

EHR — English Historical Review

EIE, EIA — English Institute Essays (Annual), N Y 1939–

EJ — English Journal

ELH — Journal of English Literary History

Ellis EEP — Ellis G, Specimens of Early English Poetry, 3 vols, London 1811

Ellis Spec — Ellis G, Specimens of Early English Metrical Romances, 3 vols, London 1805; rvsd Halliwell, 1 vol,

	Bohn edn 1848 (latter edn referred to, unless otherwise indicated)
Enc Brit	Encyclopaedia Britannica, 11th edn
Engl	English: The Magazine of the English Association
E&S	Essays and Studies by Members of the English Association, Oxford 1910–
E&S Brown	Essays and Studies in Honor of Carleton Brown, N Y 1940
Esdaile ETPR	Esdaile A, A List of English Tales and Prose Romances Printed before 1740, London 1912
EStn	Englische Studien
ESts	English Studies
ETB	Hoops J, Englische Textbibliothek, 21 vols, Heidelberg 1898–1935?
Expl	Explicator
Farrar-Evans	Farrar C P and A P Evans, Bibliography of English Translations from Medieval Sources, N Y 1946
FFC	Folklore Fellows Communications
FFK	Forschungen und Fortschritte: Korrespondenzblatt der deutschen Wissenschaft und Technik
Flügel NL	Flügel E, Neuenglisches Lesebuch, Halle 1895
FQ	French Quarterly
FR	French Review
FS	French Studies
Furnivall EEP	Furnivall F J, Early English Poems and Lives of Saints, Berlin 1862 (Transactions of Philological Society of London 1858)
Gautier Bibl	Gautier L, Bibliographie des chansons de geste, Paris 1897
Gayley	Gayley C M, Plays of Our Forefathers, N Y 1907
GdW	Gesamtkatalog der Wiegendrucke, Leipzig 1925–
Germ	Germania
Gerould S Leg	Gerould G H, Saints' Legends, Boston 1916
GGA	Göttingische gelehrte Anzeiger
GJ	Gutenberg Jahrbuch

GQ	German Quarterly
GR	Germanic Review
Greene E E Carols	Greene R L, The Early English Carols, Oxford 1935; 2nd edn 1977
GRM	Germanisch-Romanische Monatsschrift
Gröber	Gröber G, Grundriss der romanischen Philologie, Strassburg 1888–1902, new issue 1897–1906, 2nd edn 1904– (vol 2¹ 1902 referred to, unless otherwise indicated)
Gröber-Hofer	Hofer S, Geschichte der mittelfranzösischen Literatur, 2 vols, 2nd edn, Berlin and Leipzig 1933–37
Hall Selections	Hall J, Selections from Early Middle English 1130– 1250, 2 parts, Oxford 1920
Hammond	Hammond E P, Chaucer: A Bibliographical Manual, N Y 1908
Hartshorne AMT	Hartshorne C H, Ancient Metrical Tales, London 1829
Hazlitt Rem	Hazlitt W C, Remains of the Early Popular Poetry of England, 4 vols, London 1864–66
Herbert	Herbert J A, Catalogue of Romances in the Department of MSS of the British Museum, London 1910 (vol 3 of Ward's Catalogue)
Hermes	Hermes
Hibbard Med Rom	Hibbard L, Medieval Romance in England, N Y 1924
HINL	History of Ideas News Letter
Hisp	Hispania
HispR	Hispanic Review
HJ	Hibbert Journal
HLB	Harvard Library Bulletin
HLF	Histoire littéraire de la France, Paris 1733–; new edn 1865–
HLQ	Huntington Library Quarterly
Holmes CBFL	Cabeen D C, Critical Bibliography of French Literature, vol 1 (the Medieval Period), ed U T Holmes jr, Syracuse N Y 1949

HSCL	Harvard Studies in Comparative Literature
HSNPL	Harvard Studies and Notes in Philology and Literature, Boston 1892–
HudR	Hudson Review
IER	Irish Ecclesiastical Review
IS	Italian Studies
Isis	Isis
Ital	Italica
JAAC	Journal of Aesthetics and Art Criticism
JBL	Journal of Biblical Literature
JCS	Journal of Celtic Studies
JEGGP	Jahresbericht über die Erscheinungen auf dem Gebiete der germanischen Philologie
JEGP	Journal of English and Germanic Philology
JEH	Journal of Ecclesiastical History
JfRESL	Jahrbuch für romanische und englische Sprache und Literatur
JGP	Journal of Germanic Philology
JHI	Journal of the History of Ideas
JPhilol	Journal of Philology
JPhilos	Journal of Philosophy
JRLB	Bulletin of the John Rylands Library, Manchester
Kane	Kane G, Middle English Literature: A Critical Study of the Romances, the Religious Lyrics, Piers Plowman, London 1951
Kennedy BWEL	Kennedy A G, A Bibliography of Writings on the English Language from the Beginning of Printing to the End of 1922, Cambridge Mass and New Haven 1927
Kild Ged	Heuser W, Die Kildare-Gedichte, Bonn 1904 (BBA 14)
Körting	Körting G, Grundriss der Geschichte der englischen Literatur von ihren Anfängen bis zur Gegenwart, 5th edn, Münster 1910
KR	Kenyon Review

Krit Jahresber	Vollmüller K, Kritischer Jahresbericht über die Fortschritte der romanischen Philologie, Munich and Leipzig 1892–1915 (Zweiter Teil, 13 vols in 12)
KSEP	Kieler Studien zur englischen Philologie
Lang	Language
LB	Leuvensche Bijdragen, Periodical for Modern Philology
LC	Library Chronicle
Leeds SE	Leeds Studies in English and Kindred Languages, School of English Literature in the University of Leeds
Legouis	Legouis E, Chaucer, Engl trans by Lailvoix, London 1913
Legouis HEL	Legouis E and L Cazamian, trans H D Irvine and W D MacInnes, A History of English Literature, new edn, N Y 1929
LfGRP	Literaturblatt für germanische und romanische Philologie
Libr	The Library
Litteris	Litteris: An International Critical Review of the Humanities, New Society of Letters
LMS	London Medieval Studies
Loomis ALMA	Loomis R S, Arthurian Literature in the Middle Ages, A Collaborative History, Oxford 1959
LP	Literature and Psychology
LQ	Library Quarterly
Lund SE	Lund Studies in English
LZ	Literarisches Zentralblatt
MÆ	Medium ævum
Manly CT	Manly J M, Canterbury Tales by Geoffrey Chaucer, with an Introduction, Notes, and a Glossary, N Y 1928
Manly Spec	Manly J M, Specimens of the Pre-Shakespearean Drama, vol 1, 2nd edn, Boston 1900

Manly & Rickert	Manly J M and E Rickert, The Text of the Canterbury Tales Studied on the Basis of All Known Manuscripts, 8 vols, Chicago 1940
Manual	A Manual of the Writings in Middle English 1050–1500, New Haven 1967– (vols 1 and 2, ed J B Severs; vols 3–7, ed A E Hartung)
MBREP	Münchener Beiträge zur romanischen und englischen Philologie
MED	Kurath H, S M Kuhn, R E Lewis, Middle English Dictionary, Ann Arbor 1954– (for bibliography of ME texts see Plan and Bibliography 1954, p 15, and Plan and Bibliography Suppl I 1984, p 7)
MH	Medievalia et humanistica
MHRA	MHRA, Bulletin of the Modern Humanities Research Association
Migne PL	Migne, Patrologiae Latinae cursus completus
Minor Poems	Skeat W W, Chaucer: The Minor Poems, 2nd edn, Oxford 1896
MKAW	Mededeelingen van de Koninklijke akademie van wetenschappen, afdeling letterkunde
ML	Music and Letters
MLF	Modern Language Forum
MLJ	Modern Language Journal
MLN	Modern Language Notes
MLQ (Lon)	Modern Language Quarterly (London)
MLQ (Wash)	Modern Language Quarterly (Seattle, Washington)
MLR	Modern Language Review
Monat	Monatshefte
Moore Meech and Whitehall	Moore S, S B Meech and H Whitehall, Middle English Dialect Characteristics and Dialect Boundaries, University of Michigan Essays and Studies in Language and Literature 13, Ann Arbor 1935
Morley	Morley H, English Writers, vols 3–6, London 1890
Morris Spec	Morris R (ed part 1), R Morris and W W Skeat (ed

	part 2), Specimens of Early English, part 1, 2nd edn, Oxford 1887; part 2, 4th edn, Oxford 1898
MP	Modern Philology
MS	Mediaeval Studies
MSEP	Marburger Studien zur englischen Philologie, 13 vols, Marburg 1901–11
MUPES	Manchester University Publications, English Series
NA	Neuer Anzeiger
Neophil	Neophilologus, A Modern Language Quarterly
NEQ	New England Quarterly
New CBEL	Watson G, The New Cambridge Bibliography of English Literature, 4 vols, Cambridge 1969–74; Index, compiled J D Pickles, Cambridge 1977
NLB	Newberry Library Bulletin
NM	Neuphilologische Mitteilungen: Bulletin de la Société neophilologique de Helsinki
NMQ	New Mexico Quarterly
NNAC	Norfolk and Norwich Archaeological Society
N&Q	Notes and Queries
NRFH	Nueva revista de filologia hispánica
NS	Die neueren Sprachen, Zeitschrift für den neusprachlichen Unterrecht
O'Dell CLPF	O'Dell S, A Chronological List of Prose Fiction in English Printed in England and Other Countries, Cambridge Mass 1954
OMETexts	Morsbach L and F Holthausen, Old and Middle English Texts, 11 vols, Heidelberg 1901–26
Oxf Ch	Skeat W W, The Works of Geoffrey Chaucer, Oxford 1894–1900 (6 vols; extra 7th vol of Chaucerian Poems)
Palaes	Palaestra, Untersuchungen und Texte
PAPS	Proceedings of the American Philosophical Society
Paris Litt Franç	Paris G P B, La littérature française au moyen âge, 4th edn, Paris 1909

Patterson	Patterson F A, The Middle English Penitential Lyric, N Y 1911
Paul Grundriss	Paul H, Grundriss der germanischen Philologie, 3 vols, 1st edn, Strassburg 1891–1900; 2nd edn 1900–
PBBeitr	Paul H and W Braune, Beiträge zur Geschichte der deutschen Sprache und Literatur, Halle 1874–
PBSA	Papers of the Bibliographical Society of America
PBSUV	Papers of the Bibliographical Society, Univ of Virginia
PFMS	Furnivall F J and J W Hales, The Percy Folio MS, 4 vols, London 1867–69; re-ed I Gollancz, 4 vols, London 1905–10 (the earlier edn is referred to, unless otherwise indicated)
Philo	Philologus
PMLA	Publications of the Modern Language Association of America
PMRS	Progress of Medieval and Renaissance Studies in the United States and Canada
Pollard 15CPV	Pollard A W, Fifteenth Century Prose and Verse, Westminster 1903
PP	Past and Present
PPR	Philosophy and Phenomenological Research
PPS	Publications of the Percy Society
PQ	Philological Quarterly
PR	Partisan Review
PS	Pacific Spectator
PSTS	Publications of the Scottish Text Society, Edinburgh 1884–
PULC	Princeton University Library Chronicle
QF	Quellen und Forschungen zur Sprach- und Culturge-schichte der germanischen Völker
QQ	Queen's Quarterly
RAA	Revue anglo-américaine
RadMon	Radcliffe College Monographs, Boston 1891–

RB	Revue britannique
RC	Revue celtique
RCHL	Revue critique d'histoire et de littérature
REH	The Review of Ecclesiastical History
Rel Ant	Wright T and J O Halliwell, Reliquiae Antiquae, 2 vols, London 1845
Ren	Renascence
Renwick-Orton	Renwick W L and H Orton, The Beginnings of English Literature to Skelton 1509, London 1939; 2nd rvsd edn 1952; 3rd rvsd edn 1966
RES	Review of English Studies
RevP	Revue de philologie
RF	Romanische Forschungen
RFE	Revista de filología española
RFH	Revista de filología hispánica
RG	Revue germanique
RHL	Revue d'histoire littéraire de la France
Rickert RofFr, RofL	Rickert E, Early English Romances in Verse: Romances of Friendship (vol 1), Romances of Love (vol 2), London 1908
Ringler BEV	Ringler W, A Bibliography and First-Line Index of English Verse Printed through 1500, PBSA 49.153
Ritson AEMR	Ritson J, Ancient English Metrical Romances, 3 vols, London 1802, rvsd E Goldsmid, Edinburgh 1884 (earlier edn referred to, unless otherwise indicated)
Ritson APP	Ritson J, Ancient Popular Poetry, 2nd edn, London 1833
Ritson AS	Ritson J, Ancient Songs from the Time of Henry III, 2 vols, London 1790, new edn 1829; rvsd W C Hazlitt, Ancient Songs and Ballads, 1 vol, London 1877 (last edn referred to, unless otherwise indicated)
RLC	Revue de littérature comparée
RLR	Revue des langues romanes
RN	Renaissance News

Robbins-Cutler	Supplement to Brown-Robbins, Lexington Ky 1965
Robbins-HP	Robbins R H, Historical Poems of the 14th and 15th Centuries, Oxford 1959
Robbins SL	Robbins R H, Secular Lyrics of the 14th and 15th Centuries, 2nd edn, Oxford 1955
Robson	Robson J, Three Early English Metrical Romances, London (Camden Society) 1842
Rolls Series	Rerum Britannicarum medii aevi scriptores, Published by Authority of the Lords Commissioners of Her Majesty's Treasury, under the Direction of the Master of the Rolls, London 1857–91
Rom	Romania
RomP	Romance Philology
RomR	Romanic Review
Root	Root R K, The Poetry of Chaucer, Boston 1906
Rot	Rotulus, A Bulletin for MS Collectors
Roxb Club	Publications of the Roxburghe Club, London 1814–
RSLC	Record Society of Lancashire and Cheshire
RUL	Revue de l'Université Laval
SA	The Scottish Antiquary, or Northern Notes and Queries
SAQ	South Atlantic Quarterly
SATF	Publications de la Société des anciens textes français, Paris 1875–
SB	Studies in Bibliography: Papers of the Bibliographical Society of the University of Virginia
SBB	Studies in Bibliography and Booklore
ScanSt	Scandinavian Studies
Schipper	Schipper J, Englische Metrik, 2 vols, Bonn 1881–88
Schofield	Schofield W H, English Literature from the Norman Conquest to Chaucer, N Y 1906
SciS	Science and Society
Scrut	Scrutiny
SE	Studies in English

SEER	Slavonic and East European Review
SEP	Studien zur englischen Philologie
ShJ	Jahrbuch der deutschen Shakespeare-Gesellschaft
SHR	Scottish Historical Review
Skeat Spec	Skeat W W, Specimens of English Literature 1394–1579, 6th edn, Oxford 1892
SL	Studies in Linguistics
SN	Studia neophilologica: A Journal of Germanic and Romanic Philology
SP	Studies in Philology
Spec	Speculum: A Journal of Mediaeval Studies
SR	Sewanee Review
SRL	Saturday Review of Literature
SSL	Studies in Scottish Literature
STC	Pollard A W and G R Redgrave, A Short-Title Catalogue of Books Printed in England, Scotland, and Ireland and of English Books Printed Abroad 1475–1640, London 1926
StVL	Studien zur vergleichenden Literaturgeschichte
Summary Cat	Madan F and H H E Craster, A Summary Catalogue of Western Manuscripts Which Have Not Hitherto Been Catalogued in the Quarto Series, Oxford 1895–1953
SUVSL	Skriften utgivna av Vetenskaps-societeten i Lund
SWR	Southwest Review
Sym	Symposium
Ten Brink	Ten Brink B A K, Early English Literature, English Literature, trans Kennedy et al, vol 1, vol 2 (part 1–2), London and N Y 1887–92 (referred to as vols 1–3)
Texas SE	Texas Studies in English
Thompson Mot Ind	Thompson S, Motif Index of Folk-Literature, 6 vols, Helsinki 1932–36
Thoms	Thoms W J, A Collection of Early Prose Romances,

	London 1828; part ed Morley, Carlsbrooke Library, whole rvsd edn, London (Routledge); new edn, Edinburgh 1904
TLCAS	Transactions of Lancashire and Cheshire Antiquarian Society
TLS	[London] Times Literary Supplement
TNTL	Tijdschrift voor nederlandse taal- en letterkunde
TPSL	Transactions of the Philological Society of London
Trad	Traditio, Studies in Ancient and Medieval History, Thought, and Religion
TRSL	Transactions of the Royal Society of Literature
TTL	Tijdschrift voor taal en letteren
Tucker-Benham	Tucker L L and A R Benham, A Bibliography of Fifteenth-Century Literature, Seattle 1928
UKCR	University of Kansas City Review
UQ	Ukrainian Quarterly
Utley CR	Utley F L, The Crooked Rib: An Analytical Index to the Argument about Women in English and Scots Literature to the End of the Year 1568, Columbus O 1944
UTM	University of Toronto Monthly
UTQ	University of Toronto Quarterly
VMKVA	Verslagen en mededeelingen der Koninklijke vlaamsche academie
VOR	Virginia Quarterly Review
Ward	Ward H L D, Catalogue of Romances in the Department of MSS of the British Museum, 2 vols, London 1883–93 (see Herbert for vol 3)
Ward Hist	Ward A W, A History of English Dramatic Literature to the Death of Queen Anne, 3 vols, new edn, London 1899
WBEP	Wiener Beiträge zur englischen Philologie
Weber MR	Weber H W, Metrical Romances of the 13th, 14th, and 15th Centuries, 3 vols, Edinburgh 1810

Wehrle	Wehrle W O, The Macaronic Hymn Tradition in Medieval English Literature, Washington 1933
Wells	Wells J E, A Manual of the Writings in Middle English 1050–1400, New Haven 1916 (Supplements 1–9, 1919–51)
Wessex	Wessex
WHR	Western Humanities Review
Wilson EMEL	Wilson R M, Early Middle English Literature, London 1939
WMQ	William and Mary Quarterly
WR	Western Review
Wright AnecLit	Wright T, Anecdota literaria, London 1844
Wright PPS	Wright T, Political Poems and Songs from the Accession of Edward III to That of Richard III, 2 vols, London (Rolls Series) 1859–61
Wright PS	Wright T, Political Songs of England from the Reign of John to That of Edward III, Camden Society, London 1839 (this edn referred to, unless otherwise indicated); 4 vols, rvsd, privately printed, Goldsmid, Edinburgh 1884
Wright SLP	Wright T, Specimens of Lyric Poetry Composed in England in the Reign of Edward I, Percy Society, 2 vols, London 1896
Wülcker	Wülcker R P, Geschichte der englischen Literatur, 2 vols, Leipzig 1896
YCGL	Yearbook of Comparative and General Literature
YFS	Yale French Studies, New Haven 1948–
Yksh Wr	Horstmann C, Yorkshire Writers, Library of Early English Writers, 2 vols, London 1895–96
YR	Yale Review
YSCS	Yorkshire Society for Celtic Studies
YSE	Yale Studies in English, N Y 1898–
YWES	Year's Work in English Studies
YWMLS	Year's Work in Modern Language Studies

ZfCP	Zeitschrift für celtische Philologie (Tübingen)
ZfDA	Zeitschrift für deutsches Alterthum und deutsche Literatur
ZfDP	Zeitschrift für deutsche Philologie
ZfFSL	Zeitschrift für französische Sprache und Literatur
ZfÖG	Zeitschrift für österreichischen Gymnasien
ZfRP	Zeitschrift für romanische Philologie
ZfVL	Zeitschrift für vergleichende Literaturgeschichte, Berlin

Other Commonly Used Abbreviations

ae	altenglische	AN	Anglo-Norman	OF	Old French
af	altfranzösische	c	copyright	ON	Old Norse
engl	englische	ca	circa	pt	part
f	für	crit	criticized by	re-ed	re-edited by
me	mittelenglische	f, ff	folio, folios	rptd	reprinted
u	und	ME	Middle English	rvsd	revised
z	zu	n d	no date	unptd	unprinted

XVII. GOWER

by

John H. Fisher, R. Wayne Hamm,
Peter G. Beidler, and Robert F. Yeager

GENERAL TREATMENTS.

Tanner T, Bibliotheca Britannico-Hibernica, London 1748, p 335.

Cibber T, Lives of the Poets, London 1753, 1.20.

Biographia Britannica, London 1757, 4.2242.

Ritson J, Bibliographia Poetica, London 1802, p 24.

Brydges E, Censura Literaria, London 1809, 10. 346; British Bibliographer, London 1812, 2.1.

Campbell T, Specimens of the British Poets, London 1819, 1.73.

Warton T, Hist of Eng Poetry, 2nd edn, London 1824, 2.305.

Villemain A F, Littérature française au Moyen Age, Paris 1850, 2.184.

British Quart Rev 27(1858).1, John Gower and His Works; rptd Littell's Living Age, 57.163 (crit of Pauli, Coxe, Roxb Club Balades).

Marsh G P, Origin and Hist of the Eng Lang, N Y 1862, p 429.

Collier W F, Hist of Eng Lit, London 1865, p 61.

Craik G L, A Compendious Hist of Eng Lit, N Y 1866, 1.328.

Ellis EEP, 1.169.

Backus T J, Shaw's New Hist of Eng Lit, N Y 1875; 2nd edn rvsd 1884, p 59.

Corser T, Collectanea Anglo-poetica, London 1877, 7.36.

Taine H A, Histoire de la littérature anglaise, Paris 1877, 1.228.

Ward A W, Chaucer, London 1879, pp 17, 80.

Arnold T, Gower, in T H Ward's Eng Poets, London 1881, 1.102.

Körting, § 160.

Brandl, § 97.

Ten Brink B, Hist of Eng Lit, trans Robinson, N Y 1893, 2.38, 99, 132.

Courthope, 1.305.

Jusserand J J, A Literary Hist of the Eng People, London 1895, 1.364.

Stryienski, Un poète d'autrefois, Revue de l'enseignement des langues vivantes, August 1895 (n v).

Wülcker, 1.132.

Morley, 4.150.

Imbert-Terry H M, The Poetical Contemporaries of Chaucer, in Chaucer Memorial Lectures, ed P W Ames, London 1900 (crit H Spies, EStn 32 [1903].255).

Spies H, Bisherige Ergebnisse und weitere Aufgaben der Gower-Forschung, EStn 28(1900).161 (allusions and reputation; crit C S Northup, JEGP 4[1902].118); Goweriana, EStn 34(1904).169; EStn 35(1905).105 (allusions).

Macaulay, edn (see under Collected Editions below), 2.viii (allusions); CHEL, 2.133.

Moulton C W, Libr of Literary Crit, Buffalo 1901, 1.172.

Snell F J, Age of Chaucer, London 1901, p 101.

Ker W P, John Gower, Poet, Quart Rev 197 (1903).437; rptd Essays on Medieval Lit, London 1905, p 101 (crit of Macaulay edn, above).

Baldwin C S, An Introd to Eng Medieval Lit, N Y 1914, pp 212, 224.

Schofield, p 416.

Schneider R, Der Mönch in der engl Dichtung bis auf Lewis's Monk, 1795, Palaes 155(1928).46.

Naunin T, Der Einfluss der mittelalterlichen Rhetorik auf Chaucers Dichtung, Bonn 1929, p 57.

Street E, John Gower, London Mercury 24 (1931).230.

Baldwin C S, Three Medieval Centuries of Lit in England, 1100–1400, Boston 1932, p 220.

Kaplan, John Gower, TLS no 1594 (18 Aug 1932), p 573, John Gower Memorial Essay.

Bardi P, Storia della letteratura inglese, Bari 1933, p 23.

Schirmer W F, Geschichte der engl Literatur von den Anfang bis zur Gegenwart, Halle 1937, pp 144, 165.

Evans B I, A Short Hist of Eng Lit, Harmondsworth 1940, p 19.

Bland D S, The Poetry of John Gower, English 6(1947).286 (Gower's economical narrative style).

Baugh A C, A Literary Hist of England, N Y 1948, p 264.

Pattison B, Music and Poetry of the Eng Renaissance, London 1948, p 28.

Craig H, A Hist of Eng Lit, N Y 1950, pp 84, 89, 144.

Seaton E, Le songe vert, MÆ 19(1950).1 (proposes Gower as author on basis of comparison with his other poems).

Thomas M E, Medieval Skepticism and Chaucer, N Y 1950, pp 70, 108, 130.

Dwyer J B, The Tradition of Medieval Manuals of Religious Instruction in the Poems of John Gower, with Special Reference to the Development of the Book of Virtues, Univ of N Carolina Record, no 492, Research in Progress (1951), p 126.

Wickert M, Studien zu John Gower, Cologne 1953 (for an account of this book, see RES ns 8[1957].54; trans R J Meindl as Studies in John Gower, Washington D C 1982).

Rickert M, Painting in Britain: The Middle Ages, London 1954, p 181 (Herman Scheerre's illuminations of Confessio [7]).

Peter J, Complaint and Satire in Early Eng Lit, Oxford 1956, pp 47, 61, 70, 209.

Baldin Gabriele, Storia della letteratura inglese la tradizione letteraria dell' Inghiltaria Medioevale, Turin 1958, p 197 (Gower among his contemporaries).

Dédéyan C, Dante en Angleterre, Les Lettres Romanes 13(1959).45.

Daiches D, A Critical Hist of Eng Lit, N Y 1960, 1.121.

Basu N K, A Hist of Eng Lit, Calcutta 1963, 2.80.

Fisher J H, John Gower: Moral Philosopher and Friend of Chaucer, N Y 1964.

Esch A, John Gowers Erzälkunst, in Chaucer und seine Zeit: Symposion für Walter F Schirmer (Buchreihe der Anglia, Zeitschrift für engl Philologie 14), ed A Esch, Tübingen 1968, p 207.

Ito M, The Progress in Gower Studies, Shiron 10(1968).68 (in Japanese).

Pearsall D, Gower and Lydgate (WTW 211), London 1969.

Bolton W F, The Middle Ages, London 1970, 1.ix.

Cowling S T, The Personages in the Major Narrative Works of John Gower, diss Mich State; DAI 32(1971).384A.

Dean J, The World Grows Old: The Significance of a Medieval Idea, diss Johns Hopkins; DAI 32(1971).6924A.

Hussey S S, Chaucer: An Introd, London 1971, pp 196, 216.

Ito M, Gower and Rime Royal, Bulletin, Coll of General Education, Tohoku Univ (Sendai Japan), 12(1971).ii:47 (in Japanese; Eng summary, p ii).

Howard D R, Medieval Poems and Medieval Society, Mediaevalia et Humanistica ns 3(1972).99.

Willliams M, The Linguistic and Cultural Frontier in Gower, Archaeologia Cambrensis 121 (1972).61.

Kelly H A, Love and Marriage in the Age of Chaucer, Ithaca 1975, p 121.

Kim S S, Chaucer and Gower: A Comparative Study, diss S Carolina; DAI 36(1975).3732A.

Yeager R F, John Gower's Poetic, diss Yale; DAI 37(1976).4345A.

Dean J, Time Past and Time Present in Chaucer's Clerk's Tale and Gower's Confessio Amantis, ELH 44(1977).401.

Miller R P, Chaucer: Sources and Backgrounds, N Y 1977, p 192.

Otsuki H, Confessio Amantis (I), Ronshu 12(1978).22; (II), Ronshu 13(1979).16 (in Japanese).

PLACE IN SOCIAL AND INTELLECTUAL HISTORY.

Hearne T, ed, Historia vitae et regni Ricardi II, Oxford 1729, p xiv.

Gentleman's Magazine 21(1751).303 (interest in alchemy).

Brooks S W, Some Predecessors of Spenser, Poet-Lore 1(1889).214 (Spenser read Gower).

Alden R L, The Rise of Formal Satire in England under Classical Influence, Univ of Penn Series in Philology, Lit, and Archaeology 7(1899); rptd Hamden Ct 1962, p 151.

Fowler R E, Une source française des poèmes de Gower, Macon 1905 (Somme le roi tradition).

Baake W, Die Verwendung des Traummotivs in der engl Dichtung bis auf Chaucer, Halle 1906.

Walz G, Das Sprichwort bei Gower, Munich 1907.

Krollreuter M, Das Privatleben in England nach Chaucer, Gower, und Langland, Zurich 1908.

Gebhard H, Langlands und Gowers Kritik der kirchlichen Verhältnisse, Hornberg 1911.

Mosher J A, The Exemplum in the Early Religious and Didactic Lit of England, N Y 1911.

Garrett R M, Gower in Pericles, ShJ 48(1912).13 (Elizabethan allusions).

Cook A S, Dante and Gower, Archiv 132(1914).395.

Wedel T O, The Medieval Attitude toward Astrology, New Haven 1920, p 132.

Welter J T, L'Exemplum dans la littérature religieuse et didactique du Moyen Age, Paris 1927, p 207.

Schneider R, Der Mönch in der engl Dichtung, Palaes 155(1928).46.

Fox G G, The Medieval Sciences in the Works of Gower, Princeton 1931.

Byrne Sister M, Tradition of the Nun in Medieval England, Washington D C 1932 (see index).

Mohl R, The Three Estates in Medieval and Renaissance Lit, N Y 1933 (see index).

Glunz H H, Die Literarästhetik des europäischen Mittelalters, Bochum-Langendreer 1937, p 349 (function of the allegory).

Kleineke W, Engl Fürstenspiegel, Halle 1937, p 129.

Coulton G G, Medieval Panorama, London 1938 (see index).

Heather P J, The Seven Planets, Folklore 54 (1942).339 (Gower's star lore).

Utley CR, passim (antifeminism).

Coffman G R, John Gower in His Most Significant Role, Univ of Colorado Stud, B.2.52 (1945); rptd ME Survey, ed E Vasta, Notre Dame 1965.

Robertson D W Jr, The Cultural Tradition of Handlying Synne, Spec 22(1947).162.

Stillwell G, John Gower and the Last Years of Edward III, SP 45(1948).454.

Bland D S, Gower and His Critics, Journ of Southwest Essex Technical Coll and School of Art 2(1948).198 (assesses importance to Eng letters).

Clawson W H, The Framework of the Canterbury Tales, UTQ 20(1951).137 (Confessio Amantis [7] associated with narrative moral tales).

Bloomfield SDS, p 193.

Cazamian L, Development of Eng Humor, 2nd edn, Durham N C 1952, p 85.

Dulak R E, Gower's Tale of Constance, N&Q 198(1953).368 (treatment of baptism).

Coffman G R, John Gower, Mentor for Royalty, PMLA 69(1954).953 (critic of Richard II).

Siegmund-Schultze D, John Gower und seine Zeit, Zeitschrift für anglistik und amerikanistik 3 (1955).6 (Marxist interpretation).

Hazelton R M, Two Texts of the Disticha Catonis and Its Commentary, with Special Reference to Chaucer, Langland, and Gower, diss Rutgers; DA 16(1956).1899.

Cunningham J V, Tradition and Poetic Structure: Essays in Literary Hist and Criticism, Denver 1960, p 65.

Stockton E W, Major Latin Works of John Gower, Seattle 1962, p 4.

Fisher J H, John Gower, N Y 1964, p 1.

Fish S E, John Skelton's Poetry, New Haven 1965, p 231 (Gower's influence on Skelton).

Ferguson A B, The Articulate Citizen and the Eng Renaissance, Durham N C 1965, p 42 (political theory).

Weber E, Gower: Dichter eines ethisch-politischen Reformation, Bad Homberg 1965.

Brewer D S, Chaucer and Chaucerians: Critical Stud in ME Lit, Univ of Alabama 1966, p 5.

Greenfield T, A Re-examination of the "Patient" Pericles, Shakespeare Stud 3(1967).51.

Bennett J A W, ed, Selections from John Gower, Oxford 1968, p vii.

Gray D, Later Poetry: The Courtly Tradition, in The Middle Ages, ed W F Bolton, London 1970, p 316.

Gilroy-Scott N, John Gower's Reputation: Literary Allusions from the Early 15 Cent to the Time of Pericles, Yearbook of Eng Stud 1(1971).30.

Hertzig M J, The Early Recension and Continuity of Certain ME Texts in the 16 Cent, diss Univ of Penn; DAI 34(1973).1913A.

Gradon P, John Gower and the Concept of Righteousness, Poetica 8(1977).61.

Doyle A I and M B Parkes, The Production of Copies of the Canterbury Tales and the Confessio Amantis in the Early Fifteenth Century, in Medieval Scribes, Manuscripts and Libraries: Essays Presented to N R Ker, ed. M B Parks and A G Watson, London 1978, p 163.

Fitzpatrick J F, Courtly Love and the Confessional in Eng Lit from 1215 to John Gower, diss Indiana; DAI 39(1978).895A.

Green R F, Poets and Princepleasers: Literature and the English Court in the Late Middle Ages, Toronto 1980, pp 119, 142, 175, 208.

Kratzmann G, Anglo-Scottish Literary Relations 1430–1550, Cambridge 1980, pp 16, 37, 45, 77, 198 (Gower's influence on the Scots).

Kan T, The Literature and History of Middle English, Especially on Gower and Langland, English Education 38 (1979).2 (in Japanese).

BIBLIOGRAPHIES.

CHEL, 2.454.

Wells (Manual and Supplements, New Haven 1918–51).

CBEL, 1940, 1957 edns, 1.205.

Pickford T E, A Biblio of John Gower, 1925–72, Parergon 3(1972).27.

CBEL, 1974 edn, 1.553.

Yeager R F, A Biblio of John Gower Materials through 1975, Mediaevalia (1977); John Gower Materials: A Biblio through 1979, N Y 1981; The Poetry of John Gower: Important Studies, 1960–83, in 15-Cent Stud: Recent Essays, ed R F Yeager, Hamden Ct 1984, p 3.

LIFE.

Bale J, Scriptorium illustrium maioris Britannie, Basle 1557, p 524.

Pits J, De illustribus Britanniae scriptoribus, Paris 1619, p 575.

Fuller T, Worthies of England, 1662; Freeman edn, London 1952, p 648.

Aubrey J, Brief Lives, Chiefly of Contemporaries, Set Down between the Years 1669–95, ed A Clark, Oxford 1898, 1.271.

Phillips E, Theatrum poetarum, London 1675, p 109.

Winstanley W, Lives of the Eng Poets, London 1687, p 18.

Leland J, Commentarii de scriptoribus Britannicis, Oxford 1709, p 414; rptd S E Brydges, Restituta 2, 1816.

Jacob G, The Poetical Register, London 1723, 1.66.

Anstis J, Register of the Garter, London 1724, 2.116 (Gower's "SS" collar).

Godwin W, Life of Chaucer, London 1803, p 333.

Chalmers A, Works of the British Poets, London 1810, 2.3.

Brydges E and J Haslewood, The British Bibliographer, London 1812, 2.1.

Pauli, edn, 1.x (see below under [7] *Editions*).

Wright PPS, 1.lxxxiv.

Thomson K B [Wharton G], The Lit of Society, London 1862, 1.55.

Morley, 4.150.

DNB.

Macaulay G C, Athen 21 Sept 1901, p 385 (date of birth); edn (see under Collected Editions below), 4.vii.

Rickert E, Was Chaucer a Student at the Inner Temple? Manly Anniv Stud, Chicago 1923, p 20.

Buchan J, A Hist of Eng Lit, N Y 1932, p 26 (good, brief biography).

Fisher J H, A Calendar of Documents Relating to the Life of John Gower the Poet, JEGP 58 (1959).1; John Gower, pp 37 (life records), 70 (literary career).

Stockton E W, Major Latin Works, Seattle 1962, p 4.

Robertson D W Jr, Chaucer's London, N Y 1968, pp 150, 170, 212 (ties with Arundel family).

FAMILY AND TOMB.

Thynne F, Animadversions, 1599; Furnivall edn, ChS, London 1875, p xv.

Weever J, Ancient Funerall Monuments, London 1631, p 270.

Stow J, Survey of London, London 1633, p 450.

Selden J, Titles of Honour, London 1672, p 692.

Leland J, Itinerary, 1710; Smith edn, London 1909, 4.75.

Gough R, Sepulchral Monuments, London 1796, 2.24.

Todd H J, Illustrations of the Lives and Writings of Gower and Chaucer, London 1810 (crit Nicolas, John Gower, the Poet, below).

Gentleman's Magazine 83(1813).231; 85(1815).109 (the "SS" collar).

Blore E, Monumental Remains of Noble Persons, London 1826, n p.

Nicolas N H, John Gower, the Poet, Retrospective Rev 2s 2(1828).103 (reply to Todd, Illustrations, above).

Taylor W, Annals of St Mary Overy, London 1833, pp 26, 73.

Gunner W H, N&Q 1s 9(1854).487 (prints marriage license).

Wood A, Ecclesiastical Antiquities of London and Its Suburbs, London 1874, p 78.

Rendle W, Old Southwark, London 1878, p 227.

N&Q 8s 8(1895).87, 130, 317 (query and replies concerning inscriptions on tomb).

Thompson Canon, Hist and Antiquities of the Collegiate Church of St Saviour, London 1898, pp 8, 47.

Loomis R S, A Mirror of Chaucer's World, Princeton 1965, p 8 (tomb).

ASSOCIATIONS WITH CHAUCER AND THE COURT.

Speght T, Works of Chaucer, London 1598, b ii.

Thynne F, Animadversions, p 19.

Tanner T, Bibliotheca Britannico-Hibernica, p 335.

Tyrwhitt T, The Canterbury Tales of Chaucer, 1775 (London 1822, Introd Discourse, p xiv; first notice of altered conclusion to Confessio).

Marsh G P, Origin and Hist of the Eng Lang, N Y 1862, p 429.

Hales J W, The Confessio Amantis, Athen 24 Dec 1881, p 851; rptd Folia litteraria, London 1893, p 114.

Bech L, Quellen und Plan der Legende of Goode Women und ihr Verhältnis zur Confessio Amantis, Angl 5(1882).313.

Meyer K, John Gowers Bezeihungen zu Chaucer und Richard II, Bonn 1889 (crit H Spies, EStn 28[1900].174; Macaulay, edn [see under Collected Editions below]), 2.xxii).

Browning E B, Poetical Works, London 1890, 5.211.

Skeat W W, Acad 18 Mar 1893, p 246 (report of an address On Relations between the Works of Chaucer and Gower); OxfCh, 3.xli, 413.

Ten Brink B, Hist of Eng Lit, trans Robinson, N Y 1893, 2.99, 132.

Flügel E, Some Notes on Chaucer's Prologue, JEGP 1(1897).118; Chaucers kleinere Gedichte, Angl 23(1900).195.

Macaulay, CHEL, 2.133.

Maynadier G H, The Wife of Bath's Tale, London 1901, p 131.

Bilderbeck J B, Chaucer's Legend of Good Women, London 1902, p 81.

Fleay F G, On Neglected Facts Relating to Authors Buried in St Saviour's, Trans of the London and Middlesex Archaeological Soc, London 1905, p 392.

Lowes J L, The Prologue to the Legend of Good Women, PMLA 20(1905).780; The Date of Chaucer's Troilus, PMLA 23(1908).300.

Tatlock J S P, Development and Chronology of Chaucer's Works, ChS, London 1907, pp 128, 173.

Hammond, pp 75, 278.

Kittredge G L, The Date of Chaucer's Troilus, ChS, London 1909, p 77.

Holzknecht K J, Literary Patronage in the Middle Ages, Phila 1923, p 147.

Garrett R M, Cleopatra the Martyr, JEGP 22 (1923).64.

Brusendorff A, The Chaucer Tradition, London 1925, p 431.

Schlauch M, Constance and Accused Queens, N Y 1927, p 132.

Meech S B, Chaucer and the Ovide moralisé, PMLA 46(1931).202.

Brown C, The Man of Law's Headlink, SP 34 (1937).8.

Galway M, Chaucer's Sovereign Lady, MLR 33 (1938).145; Cancelled Tributes to Chaucer's Sovereign Lady, N&Q 193(1948).3.

Edwards A C, Knaresborough Castle and "The Kynges Moodres Court," PQ 19(1940).306.

Barker E, The Character of England, Oxford 1947, p 288.

Edwards H L R, Skelton: Life and Times of an Early Tudor Poet, London 1949, pp 35, 228.

Bland D S, Chaucer and the Inns of Court: A Reexamination, Eng Stud 33(1952).145 (Chaucer and Gower probably not at Inns of Court).

Sullivan W L, Chaucer's Man of Law as Literary Critic, MLN 68(1953).1.

Townsend F G, Chaucer's Nameless Knight, MLR 49(1954).1.

Brewer D S, Chaucer, London 1953; 3rd edn rvsd 1973, pp 40, 180, 210 (Gower and Chaucer); Chaucer in His Time, London 1963, pp 135, 195 (Gower and Chaucer compared); Chaucer and His World, London 1978, pp 69, 84, 138, 154, 209 (Gower as man and friend of Chaucer).

Ito M, Two Tales of Constance: Chaucer and Gower, Shiron 1(1958).60 (in Japanese).

Stockton E W, Major Latin Works, Seattle 1962 (see index).

Fisher J H, John Gower, N Y 1964, pp 1, 204 (Gower and Chaucer).

Mathew G, The Court of Richard II, N Y 1968, pp 68, 74, 133.

Culver T D, The Imposition of Order: A Measure of Art in the Man of Law's Tale, Yearbook of Eng Stud 2(1972).13 (Gower a model for the Man of Law).

Frank R W Jr, Chaucer and the Legend of Good Women, Cambridge Mass 1972, pp 47, 134 (Gower's tales which appear in LGW also).

Mann J, Chaucer and Medieval Estates Satire, Cambridge 1973.

Barnie J, War in Medieval Eng Society: Social Values and the Hundred Years' War 1337–99, London 1974, pp 22, 119.

Kirk E R, Chaucer and His Eng Contemporaries in Geoffrey Chaucer: A Collection of Original Articles, N Y 1975, p 111.

Miskimin A, The Renaissance Chaucer, New Haven 1975, pp 26, 231, 259.

Kelly D, Medieval Imagination: Rhetoric and the Poetry of Courtly Love, Madison Wis 1978, p 195.

Middleton A, The Idea of Public Poetry in the Reign of Richard II, Spec 53(1978).94.

Woolf R, Moral Chaucer and Kindly Gower, in J R R Tolkien, Scholar and Storyteller: Essays in Memoriam, ed M Salu and R T Farrell, Ithaca NY 1979, p 221.

Strohm P A, Form and Social Sentiment in Confessio Amantis and the Canterbury Tales, Stud in the Age of Chaucer 1(1979).17.

Green R F, Poets and Princepleasers: Literature and the Eng Court in the Late Middle Ages, Toronto 1980, pp 130, 161, 175.

Jones T, Chaucer's Knight: The Portrait of a Medieval Mercenary, Baton Rouge 1980, pp 19, 31, 52, 84, 236, 250.

Sugano M, Gower and Chaucer, Study Report of Aichi University of Education 29(1980).19 (in Japanese).

Collins M, Love, Nature, and Law in the Poetry of Gower and Chaucer, in Court and Poet, ed G S Burgess, Liverpool 1981, p 113.

Haman M S, The Introspective and Egocentric Quests of Character and Audience: Modes of Self-Definition in the New Corpus Christi Cycle and in Chaucer's Merchant's Tale, diss Rochester; DAI 42(1982).444A.

Lundberg M H C, The Chaucer-Gower Analogues: A Study in Literary Technique, diss Indiana; DAI 42(1982).3993A.

Doyle A I, Eng Books in and out of Court from Edward III to Henry VI, in Eng Court Culture in the Later Middle Ages, ed V J Scattergood, London 1983, p 163.

Hiscoe D W, "Equivocations of Kynde": The Medieval Tradition of Nature and Its Use in Chaucer's Troilus and Criseyde and Gower's Confessio Amantis, diss Duke; DAI 44(1983).1447A.

Yeager R F, Aspects of Gluttony in Chaucer and Gower, SP 81(1984).42; "O Moral Gower": Chaucer's Dedication of Troilus and Criseyde, Chaucer Rev 19(1985).87.

COLLECTED EDITIONS.

Macaulay G C, The Complete Works of John Gower, 4 vols, Oxford 1899–1902 (crit G L Hamilton, AJP 24[1903].204; Rom 29[1900].160; L T Smith,

Arch 110[1903].197; Athen 7 Sep 1901, p 305 [corrected by Macaulay, 21 Sep 1901, p 385]; EStn 32[1903].251 [Eng works]; EStn 35 [1905].104 [Latin works]; E Stengel, Krit Jahresber 6[1899–1901].330 [French works]; Athen 11 May 1901, p 597 [comment on genesis of Macaulay edn]).

Bennett J A W, ed, Selections from John Gower (Confessio Amantis, Peace, Balades 34, 35, 36, Mirour, Vox), Oxford 1968.

1. FRENCH WORKS.

[1] CINKANTE BALADES.

MS. BL Addit 59495, ff 11b–33a (1375–1425; originally the "Trentham" MS, a later transcript of which is now BL Addit 59496).
Macaulay, edn, 1.lxxix; CHEL, 2.452.
Hammond, p 431 (BL Addit 59495).
Fisher J H, John Gower, N Y 1964, p 71.
Editions. [Lord Gower] Roxb Club edn, Balades and Other Poems, London 1818 (from BL Addit 59495).
Stengel E, John Gowers Minnesang und Uhzuchtbüchlein, AAGRP 64, 1886 (Cinkante Balades from Roxb Club edn).
Macaulay, edn, 1.335.
Selections. Chalmers A, Works of the British Poets, London 1810, 2.viii (Balades 36, 34, 43, 20).
Ellis EEP, 1.170 (Balades 36, with 2nd stanza omitted).
Warton T, Hist of Eng Poetry, 2nd edn London 1824, 2.338 (Balades 36, 34, 43, 20).
Hartley A, ed, Penguin Book of French Verse, London 1961, pp 230 (Balade 37), 231 (Balade 24; both with Eng trans).
Bennett J A W, ed, Selections from John Gower, p 126 (Balades 34, 35, 36).
Translations. Brit Quart Rev 27(1858).3 (trans Balades 21, 30, and two stanzas of 48).
Morley H, Eng Writers: An Attempt toward a Hist of Eng Lit, London 1887, 4.162 (trans Balade 2).
Benham A R, Eng Lit from Widsith to the Death of Chaucer, New Haven 1916, p 601 (trans Balade 1, stanza 3).
Discussion. Koeppel E, Gowers französische Balladen und Chaucer, EStn 20(1895).154.
Ten Brink B, Hist of Eng Lit, trans Robinson, N Y 1893, 2¹.38.
Macaulay, edn, 1.lxxi.
Ker W P, John Gower, Poet, Quart Rev 197 (1903).437; rptd Essays on Medieval Lit, London 1905, p 101.

Tanneberger O A, Sprachliche Untersuchung der französischen Werke John Gowers, ZfFSL 36 (1910).1.
Dodd W G, Courtly Love in Chaucer and Gower, Cambridge 1913 (see index).
Cohen H L, The Ballade, N Y 1915, p 105.
Vising J, AN Lang and Lit, London 1923, p 82.
Audiau J, Les troubadours et l'Angleterre, Paris 1927, p 103.
Gröber-Hofer (1933 edn), 1.44.
Kar G, Thoughts on the Mediaeval Lyric, Oxford 1933, p 55.
Maynard T, The Connections between the Balade, Chaucer's Modification of It, Rime Royal, and the Spenserian Stanza, Washington D C 1934, pp 89, 129.
Legge M D, The Balades of John Gower, in AN Lit, Oxford 1963, p 357.
Stockton E W, Major Latin Works, Seattle 1962, p 3.
Fisher, John Gower, p 71.
Hagman L W, A Study of Gower's Cinkante Balades [portions of text in French and ME], diss Detroit; DA 29(1968).1207A.
Fyler J M, Chaucer and Ovid, New Haven 1979, pp 91, 177 (Balades 25 and 34).
Cressman R R, Gower's Cinkante Balades and French Court Lyrics, diss N Carolina-Chapel Hill; DAI 44(1983).1079A.

[2] TRAITIÉ POUR ESSAMPLER LES AMANTZ MARIETZ.

MSS. 1, Bodl 2449 (294), ff 197a–199a (1400–25); 2, Bodl 3883 (Fairfax 3), ff 186b–190b (1375–1400); 3, All Souls Oxf 98, ff 132a–135a (1375–1400); 4, Wadham Oxf 13, ff 442b–446b (1475–1500); 5, Trinity Camb 581 (R.3.2), ff 148a–152a (1400–25); 6, BL Addit 59495, ff 34a–39a (1375–1425; originally "Trentham" MS; see also BL Addit 59496); 7, BL Arundel 364, f 223 (1400–1500); 8, BL Harley 3869, ff 357b–361b (1440–50); 9, Glasgow, Hunterian T.2.17, ff 124b–128a

(1390–1410); 10, Nottingham Univ Libr Mi LM 8 (1400–25); 11, Geneva, Bodmer 178, ff 182[b]–186[a] (1400–25); 12, Yale, Beinecke Libr, Osborn Collection fa.1, ff 196[a]–199[a] (1400–50); 13, Princeton, Robert H Taylor Collection (Phillipps 8192), ff 184[a]–188[a] (1400–25).

Macaulay, edn, 1.lxxxv; CHEL, 2.452.

Fisher J H, John Gower, N Y 1964, p 72.

Quixley Translation—MS. BL Stowe 951, ff 313[a]–322[a] (1430–50).

Brown-Robbins, no 4105.

Editions. Roxb Club edn, Balades and Other Poems, London 1818 (leaf in MS 6 mutilated, so [2] incomplete).

Stengel E, John Gowers Minnesang, AAGRP 64, 1886 (text from MS 1).

Macaulay, edn, 1.379.

Quixley Translation—Edition. MacCracken H N, ed, Quixley's Ballades Royal, Leeds 1908; rptd Yorkshire Archaelogical Journ 20(1909).33.

Discussion. Macaulay, edn, 1.lxxxiii.

Hamilton G L, The Indebtedness of Chaucer's Troilus to Guido Delle Colonne's Historia Trojana, N Y 1903, p 97 ([2], 9.18; [7], 3.1885; and Guido).

Ker W P, John Gower, Poet, Quart Rev 197 (1903).437; rptd Essays on Medieval Lit, London 1905, pp 101.

Cohen H L, The Ballade, N Y 1915, p 264.

Stockton E W, Major Latin Works, Seattle 1962, p 34.

Fisher, John Gower, p 83.

[3] MIROUR DE L'OMME.

MS. Camb Univ Addit 3035, ff 1[a]–162[b] (1375–1400).

Macaulay, edn, 1.lxviii; CHEL, 2.452.

M[eyer] P, Rom 24(1895).620 (rediscovery of MS).

Fisher J H, John Gower, N Y 1964, p 91.

Editions. Macaulay, edn, 1.1.

Troendle D F, John Gower's Mirour de L'Omme, diss Brown; DA 28(1967).1797A (edited by author; portions of text in Norman-French, Old Eng, and Vulgate Latin).

Translation. Wilson W B, A Trans of John Gower's Mirour de l'Omme, diss Miami; DAI 31 (1970).1778A.

Language and Versification. Macaulay, edn, 1.xvi, xliii.

Toynbee P, Athen 18 May 1901, p 632 (line 6397, l'areine au mer = sea-spider).

Vising J, Frankaspråket i England, Gøteborgs Høgskolas Årsskrift 1902, 8.16; AN Lang and Lit, London 1923, p 82.

Tanneberger O A, Sprachliche Untersuchung der französischen Werke John Gowers, ZfFSL 36 (1910).1 (phonology).

Comtois C P, Rhetoric in John Gower's Speculum Meditantis, diss Fordham 1953.

Stockton E W, Major Latin Works, Seattle 1962, p 9.

Ito M, Gower's Use of Rime Riche in Confessio Amantis: As Compared with His Practice in Mirour de L'Omme and with the Case of Chaucer, Stud in Eng Lit (Japan) 46(1969).29.

Date. Macaulay, edn, 1.xlii.

Lowes J L, The Date of Chaucer's Troilus, PMLA 23(1908).285.

Kittredge G L, The Date of Chaucer's Troilus, London 1909, p 77.

Stockton, Major Latin Works, p 9.

Fisher, John Gower, p 95.

Authorship. Macaulay G C, Acad 13 Apr 1895, p 315; Acad 27 Jul 1895, p 71; Acad 3 Aug 1895, p 91; edn, 1.xxxiv.

Sources and Literary Relations. Macaulay, edn, 1.xlvi.

Kittredge G L, Nation 71(1900).254 (crit of Macaulay; lines 205–37 and Paradise Lost 2.649).

Spies H, Bisherige Ergebnisse und weitere Aufgaben der Gower-Forschung, EStn 28(1900).161.

Flügel E, Gowers MiRour und Chaucers Prolog, Angl 24(1901).437.

Fowler R E, Une source française des poèmes de Gower, Macon 1905 (crit Rom 34[1905].632).

Tatlock J S P, Milton's Sin and Death, MLN 21(1906).239 (lines 205–37, 841–948: see Kittredge above).

Mosher J A, The Exemplum in the Early Religious and Didactic Lit of England, N Y 1911, p 124.

Lowes J L, Spenser and the Mirour, PMLA 29(1914).388.

Rickert E, Manly Anniv Stud, Chicago 1923, p 31 (line 21,774 and pictures of lawyers in Archaeol 39[1862–63].358).

Gröber-Hofer (1933 edn), 1.80.

Owst G R, Literature and Pulpit in Medieval England, Cambridge 1933, p 230.

West C B, Courtoisie in AN Lit, Oxford 1938, p 123.

Huppé B F, The A-Text of Piers Plowman and the Norman Wars, PMLA 54(1939).37 (lines 22,811–12 and Alice Perrers).

Stillwell G, John Gower and the Last Years of Edward III, SP 45(1948).454 (allusions to contemporary events).

Dwyer J B, Gower's Mirour and Its French Sources, SP 48(1951).482 (crit of Fowler).

Neville M, Gower's Serpent and the Carbuncle, N&Q 197(1952).225.

Wenzel S, The Sin of Sloth: Acedia in Medieval Thought and Lit, Chapel Hill 1960, pp 114, 234.

Stockton, Major Latin Works, p 9.

Fisher, John Gower, p 93.
Badenyck J L, The Achievement of John Gower: A Reading of the Confessio Amantis, diss CUNY; DAI 33(1972).1157A.
Legge M D, Gower's Mirrour de l'Omme, in AN Lit, Oxford 1963, p 220.

Kloesel C J W, Medieval Poetics and John Gower's Vox Clamantis, diss Kansas; DAI 34 (1974).7709A.
Coleman J, Medieval Readers and Writers: 1350–1400, N Y 1981, p 131.

2. Latin Works.

[4] VOX CLAMANTIS.

MSS. 1, Bodl 1061 (Laud Misc 719), ff 1ᵃ–161ᵇ (1425–50); 2, Bodl 1739 (Digby 138), ff 1ᵃ–157ᵃ (1425–50); 3, All Souls Oxf 98, ff 6ᵃ–116ᵃ (1375–1400); 4, BL Cotton Tib A.4, ff 2ᵃ–151ᵇ (1375–1400); 5, BL Cotton Titus A.13, ff 105ᵃ–137ᵃ (16 cent); 6, BL Harley 6291, ff 1ᵃ–134ᵃ (1375–1400); 7, Glasgow, Hunterian T.2.17, ff 7ᵃ–103ᵇ (1390–1410); 8, Trinity Dublin D.4.6, ff 1ᵃ–142ᵃ (1400–25); 9, Lincoln Cathedral Libr A.72(235) (early 16 cent); 10, Hatfield House (Marquess of Salisbury), ff 3ᵃ–146ᵃ (1425–75); 11, Huntingon Libr Hm.150 (Ecton-Sotheby), ff 4ᵃ–183ᵇ (1375–1400).
Macaulay, edn, 4.lix; CHEL, 2.452.
Meyer K, John Gowers Beziehungen zu Chaucer und Richard II, Bonn 1889, p 66.
de Ricci Census (see index).
Stockton E W, Major Latin Poems, Seattle 1962, p 11.
Fisher J H, John Gower, N Y 1964, p 99.
Editions. Coxe H O, Roxb Club edn, London 1850 (crit Macaulay, edn, 4.lxxii).
Macaulay, edn, 4.1.
Selections. Fuller T, Church Hist, 1655 (Brewer edn, Oxford 1845, 2.353; trans 1.783f rustics' names).
Coulton G G, Europe's Apprenticeship, London 1940, p 259 (1.843–64 arming the rustics, with trans).
Bennett J A W, ed, Selections from John Gower, Oxford 1968, p 134 (1.783–816, Peasants' Revolt; 5.735–86, Fraud; 7.545–66, Creation of Man; 7.637–60, Man the Microcosm; 7.1289–1302, Amor Patriae).
Translation. Stockton, Major Latin Works, p 49 (selections from Stockton's trans are available in R P Miller, Chaucer: Sources and Backgrounds, N Y 1977, pp 194, 215, 233, 264; J Coleman, Medieval Readers and Writers: 1350–1400, N Y 1981, pp 68, 140; and M Ito, On the English Translation of Vox Clamantis by E W Stockton, Proceedings of the Liberal Arts Department of Tohoku University 18(1973).1 (in Japanese).

Date. Meyer, Gowers Beziehungen, p 34.
Stockton, p 11.
Fisher, p 106.
Discussion. Courthope, 1.308.
Spies H, Bisherige Ergebnisse, EStn 28(1900).161.
Flügel E, Zu Chaucers Prolog, line 218, Angl 23(1900).225 (Vox 4.18, friars and confession).
Macaulay, edn, 4.xxx.
Tucker S M, Verse Satire in England before the Renaissance, N Y 1908, p 84.
Eberhard O, Der Bauernaufstand in der engl Poesie, AF 51(1917).37.
TLS 18 Aug 1932, p 573 (Bk 1 and Spenser).
Marcus H, Chaucer der Freund des einfachen Mannes, Arch 172(1937).32.
Hussey R, N&Q 180(1941).386 (1.312, 7.479, and Shakespeare's Sonnet 64).
Wickert M, Studien zu John Gower, Cologne 1953, pp 11 (textual crit), 31 (Peasants' Revolt).
Coffman G R, John Gower, Mentor for Royalty, PMLA 69(1954).953.
Beichner P E, Gower's Use of Aurora in Vox Clamantis, Spec 30(1955).582.
Raymo R R, Gower's Vox Clamantis and the Speculum Stultorum, MLN 70(1953).315; Vox Clamantis, IV.12, MLN 71(1956).82.
Baum P F, Chaucer: A Critical Appreciation, Durham N C 1958, pp 72, 144, 163 (Gower in Vox a political conservative).
Kinney T L, Eng Verse of Complaint, 1250–1400, diss Michigan; DAI 20(1959).1767A.
Stockton, p 11.
Yunck J A, The Lineage of Lady Meed: The Development of Medieval Veniality Satire, South Bend 1963, p 262.
Fisher, p 99.
Kinney, The Temper of 14-Cent Eng Verse of Complaint, Annuale Mediaevale 7(1966).74.
Ito M, Paranomasia in Vox Clamantis, Proceedings of the Liberal Arts Department of Tohoku University 6(1967).21 (in Japanese).
Keller J R, The Triumph of Vice: A Formal Approach to the Times, Annuale Medievale 10 (1969).120.

Regan C L, John Gower and the Fall of Babylon: Confessio Amantis, Prol.II.670–686, Eng Lang Notes 7(1969).85.

Badenyck J L, The Achievement of John Gower: A Reading of the Confessio Amantis, diss CUNY; DAI 33(1972).1157A.

Harbert B, The Myth of Tereus in Ovid and Gower, MÆ 41(1972).208.

Kloesel C J W, Medieval Poetics and John Gower's Vox Clamantis, diss Kansas; DAI 34 (1974).7709A.

Mish F C, The Influence of Ovid on John Gower's Vox Clamantis, diss Minnesota; DAI 34 (1974).7198A.

Mann J, Chaucer and the Medieval Latin Poets, B: The Satirical Tradition in Geoffrey Chaucer: A Collection of Original Articles, ed G D Economou, N Y 1975, p 174.

Ito M, Nightmare on a Summer's Day: The Voice of One Crying, Shiron 12(1971).1 (in Japanese; Eng trans in Ito, John Gower the Medieval Poet, Tokyo 1976).

Coleman J, Medieval Readers and Writers: 1350–1400, N Y 1981, p 138.

Wawn A, Truth-telling and the Tradition of Mum and the Sothsegger, YWES 13(1983).270.

[5] CRONICA TRIPERTITA.

MSS. 1, Bodl 4073 (Hatton 92) Item 4, ff 103ª ff (1400–50); 2, All Souls Oxf 98, ff 116ª–126ᵇ (1375–1400); 3, BL Cotton Tib A.4, ff 153ª–167ª (1375–1400); 4, BL Harley 6291, ff 134ª–149ᵇ (1375–1400); 5, Glasgow, Hunterian T.2.17, ff 103ᵇ–119ª (1390–1410).

Macaulay, edn, 4.lxxv.

Stockton E W, Major Latin Works, Seattle 1962, p 36.

Fisher J H, John Gower, N Y 1964, p 99.

Editions. Gough R, Hist of Pleshy, London 1803, Appendix 4.

Coxe H O, Roxb Club edn, London 1850 (crit Macaulay, edn, 4.lxxii).

Wright PPS, 1.417.

Macaulay, edn, 4.314.

Discussion. Meyer K, John Gowers Beziehungen, Bonn 1889, p 29.

Coffman G R, John Gower, Mentor for Royalty, PMLA 69(1954).953.

Stockton, p 36.

Fisher, p 109.

Ito M, Omnia Vincit Amor: An Interpretation of Gower's Cronica Tripertita, Stud in Eng Lit (Japan) 59(1973).185.

Wawn A, Truth-telling and the Tradition of Mum and the Sothsegger, YWES 13(1983).270.

[6] MINOR LATIN POEMS.

Although Gower's minor Latin works are technically outside the scope of this series, it will be useful to list them here.

    a. Rex celi Deus.
    b. H. aquile pullus.
    c. O recolende.
    d. Carmen super multiplici viciorum pestilencia.
    e. De lucis scrutinio.
    f. Ecce patet tensus.
    g. Est amor.
    h. Quia unusquisque.
    i. Eneidon bucolis.
    j. O Deus immense.
    k. Quicquid homo scribat.
    l. Henrici quarti.
    m. Vnanimes esse.
    n. Presul, ouile regis.
    o. Cultor in ecclesia.
    p. Dicunt scripture.
    q. Ad mundum mitto.
    r. Quam cinxere.
    s. Inter saxosum.
    t. Epistola super huius.
    u. Explicit iste liber.

MSS. For information about the MSS of these minor poems in Latin, see J Griffiths, K Harris, and D Pearsall, A Descriptive Catalogue of MSS of the Works of John Gower. New York: Garland Press, forthcoming.

Editions. Roxb Club edn, Balades and Other Poems, London 1818 (poems a, f, l).

Coxe H O, Roxb Club edn, London 1850 (poems k, i, j).

Wright PPS, 1.346 (poems d, e, j).

Meyer K, John Gowers Beziehungen, Bonn 1889, p 67 (poems m, n, o, p).

Macaulay, edn, 3.492; 4.343.

Discussion. Meyer, p 29.

Macaulay, edn, 4.lvii.

Tucker S M, Verse Satire in England before the Renaissance, N Y 1908, p 93.

Raby F J E, A Hist of Secular Latin Poetry in the Middle Ages, Oxford 1934, 2.343.

Coffman G R, John Gower, Mentor for Royalty, PMLA 69(1954).953.

Stockton E W, Major Latin Works, Seattle 1962 (see index).

Fisher J H, John Gower, N Y 1964 (see index).

3. ENGLISH WORKS.

[7] CONFESSIO AMANTIS.

MSS. *Version A.* 1, Bodl 754 (Laud Misc 609), ff 1ᵃ–170ᵃ (1400–25); 2, Bodl 2875 (693), ff 1ᵃ–196ᵃ (1400–25); 3, Bodl 3357 (Selden B.11), ff 1ᵃ–169ᵃ (1425–75); 4, Bodl 6916 (Ashmole 35), ff 1ᵃ–181ᵇ (1400–25); 5, Bodl 27573 (902), ff 2ᵃ–183ᵇ (1400–25; R Tuve, SP 37[1940].152, availability to Spenser); 6, Christ Church Oxf 148, ff 1ᵃ–207ᵃ (1400–25; dedicated to Richard II, with MS 5 explicit; described by G W Kitchin, Catalogue Codicum Manuscriptorum Qui in Bibliothecae Aedis Christi apud Oxoniensis Adservantus, Oxford 1869, no 148); 7, Corpus Christi Oxf 67, ff 1ᵃ–209ᵃ (1400–25); 8, New Oxf 326, ff 1ᵃ–207ᵃ (1478); 9, Camb Univ Dd.8.19, ff 1ᵃ–130ᵇ (1400–1500; incomplete and misbound); 10, Camb Univ Mm.2.21 ff 1ᵃ–183ᵇ (1400–50); 11, Pembroke Camb 307, ff 1ᵃ–197ᵃ (1400–25); 12, St Catharine's Camb 7, ff 1ᵃ–188ᵇ (1425–75); 13, St John's Camb 34 (B.12), ff 1ᵃ–214ᵃ (1400–25); 14, BL Addit 22139, ff 1ᵃ–137ᵇ (before 1432); 15, BL Egerton 913, ff 1ᵃ–47ᵇ (Prol.1.1709; 1425–75); 16, BL Egerton 1991, ff 1ᵃ–214ᵃ (1400–25); 17, BL Harley 3490, ff 8ᵃ–215ᵇ (1425–75); 18, BL Royal 18.C.22, ff 1ᵃ–205ᵃ (1400–25); 19, BL Stowe 950, ff 2ᵃ–176ᵃ (1400–50); 20, London, Coll of Arms 65 (Arundel 45), ff 1ᵃ–167ᵇ (1425–50); 21, London, Soc of Antiquaries 134, ff 30ᵇ–249ᵃ (1425–75); 22, Manchester, Chetham's Libr 6696 (A.6.11), ff 2ᵃ–126ᵃ (an abridged text, same as in MS 25; 1500–25); 23, Glasgow, Hunterian S.1.7, ff 1ᵃ–174ᵇ (1390–1410); 24, Marquess of Bute, ff 1ᵃ–163ᵇ (sold at Sotheby's 13 June 1983, Lot 10; 1400–25); 25, Garrett 136 (Phillipps 2298), ff 1ᵃ–191ᵃ (Quaritch Cat, nos 193 [1899], Item 73; 211 [1902], Item 88; 220 [1903], Item 8, an abridged text, same as in MS 22; 1400–25); 26, Chicago, Newberry Libr Case +33.5, ff 1ᵃ–111ᵃ (1475–1500); 27, Columbia Univ Libr Plimpton 265, ff 1ᵃ–171ᵇ (G A Plimpton, Education of Chaucer, N Y 1935, p 147 and plate 47; Quaritch Cat, no 344 [1924], Item 16; 1400–25); 28, Morgan Libr M.125 (Loudoun), ff 1ᵃ–180ᵃ (1400–50); 29, Morgan Libr M.126 (Narford-Fontaine), ff 1ᵃ–204ᵃ + index 207ᵃ–212ᵇ (Quaritch Cat, no 217 [1902], Item 1; Athen 1902, 1.784; N&Q 150[1926].389; Arch 110[1903].103; Centl für Bibliothekeswesen 19.362; 1400–25); 30, Morgan Libr M.690 (Ravensworth), ff 2ᵃ–204ᵇ (E Charlton, Archaeol Aeliana 6.12; holograph: Maggs Cat, no 422, Item 742; Maggs Cat, no 434, Item 483 with plate; Maggs Cat, no 456, Item 184; 1400–25); 31,

Phila, Rosenbach Foundation 368 (1083–29) (Earl of Aberdeen), ff 1ᵃ–162ᵃ (Rosenbach, Cat of Eng Poetry to 1700 [1941], Item 368; 1400–60).

MSS. *Version B.* 32, Bodl 2449 (294), ff 1ᵃ–197ᵃ; 33, Sidney Sussex Camb 63 (Δ.4.1), ff 2ᵃ–202ᵇ (1425–75); 34, Trinity Camb 581 (R.3.2), ff 1ᵃ–147ᵇ (1400–25); 35, BL Addit 12043, ff 1ᵃ–155ᵃ (1400–25); 36, Nottingham Univ Libr Mi LM.8, ff 1ᵃ–200ᵇ (1400–25); 37, Huntington EL 26.A.17 (Ellesmere-Stafford), ff 1ᵃ–169ᵇ (1375–1400); 38, Princeton, Robert H Taylor Collection (Phillipps 8192), ff 1ᵃ–183ᵇ (Rosenbach, Cat of Eng Poetry to 1700 [1941], Item 369; 1400–25).

MSS. *Version C.* 39, Bodl 3883 (Fairfax 3), ff 2ᵃ–186ᵃ (1390–1410); 40, Bodl 4099 (Hatton 51), ff 2ᵇ–205ᵇ (from Caxton edn); 41, Bodl (Lyell 31), ff 1ᵃ–165ᵇ (Sotheby Cat 6 Dec 1937, Item 947; Maggs Cat, no 691, Item 242; Maggs Cat, no 687, Item 175 and plate 12; 1425–75); 42, Magdalen Oxf 213, ff 1ᵃ–180ᵃ (1450–1500); 43, New Oxf 266, ff 1ᵃ–183ᵃ (1400–50); 44, Wadham Oxf 13, ff 1ᵃ–442ᵃ (1475–1500); 45, BL Harley 3869, ff 5ᵃ–356ᵇ (1440–50); 46, BL Harley 7184, ff 1ᵃ–134ᵇ (1425–75); 47, Folger Libr Sm.1 (Phillipps 8942), ff 1ᵃ–174ᵃ (Sotheby Cat 16 Mar 1903, Item 690; 1425–75); 48, Geneva, Bodmer 178, ff 1ᵃ–182ᵃ (1400–25); 49, Yale, Beinecke Libr, Osborn Collection Fa.1, ff 1ᵃ–196ᵃ (1400–50).

MSS. *Selections and Fragments.* 50, Bodl 12900 (Rawl D.82), f 25ᵃ (8.2377–2970 Conclusion; 1450–1500; C version); 51, Bodl 12908 (Rawl D.82), ff 25ᵃ–33ᵇ (8.2377–2970 Venus' Conclusion; 1450–1500; B version); 52, Balliol Oxf 354, ff 55ᵃ–70ᵇ (8.271–2028 Apollonius), 70ᵇ–79ᵇ (2.587–1612 Constance), 79ᵃ–81ᵇ (2.1613–1865 Demetrius and Perseus), 81ᵇ–83ᵇ (5.4937–5162 Adrian and Bardus), 83ᵇ–86ᵇ (6.485–599 Pirithous, Galba and Vitellius), 84ᵇ–86ᵇ (6.975–1238 Dives, Delicacy of Nero), 86ᵇ–89ᵇ (2.3187–3507 Constantine and Silvester), 89ᵇ–91ᵇ (1.2785–3066 Nebuchadnezzar's Punishment), 91ᵇ–93ᵃ (3.1201–1300 Diogenes and Alexander), 93ᵃ–94ᵇ (3.1331–1680 Pyramus and Thisbe), 94ᵇ–96ᵃ (5.141–312 Midas), 171ᵇ–175ᵃ (1.3067–3402 Three Questions); B or C version (1520); 53, Trinity Oxf D.29, ff 189ᵃ–195ᵃ (Prol 567–1088 Nebuchadnezzar's Dream, etc.; 1500–25); 54, Camb Univ Ee.2.15, ff 38ᵃ (1.3124–3315 Three Questions), 44ᵃ (1.2083–2253 Trump of Death); Manly and Rickert, 1.126 (1475–1500); 55, Camb Univ Ff.1.6, ff 3ᵃ (5.5921–6052 Tereus), 5ᵃ (4.1114–1466 Idleness, Rosipheles), 45ᵃ (1.3067–3425 Three Questions), 81ᵃ (4.2745–2926 Somnolence), 84ᵇ

(8.271–846 Apollonius); B version (1450–1500); 56, Gonville and Caius Camb 176/97, p 23 (4.1622–34 Duties of a Knight); 57, Trinity Camb, MS Fragments Box 2 (single leaf containing 1.1816–32, 1861–77, 1897–1909, and Latin summary by 1.1911, 1938–54; 1400–50); 58, Univ Coll London, MS Frag Angl.1 (5.775–966, 1159–1592, 1735–1926 Religions of the World; 1400–25); 59, BL Addit 38181 (transcript of MS 61; 17 cent); 60, BL Harley 7333, ff 120ª–121ᵇ (5.5551–6052 Tereus), 122ª–125ᵇ (2.587–1608 Constance), 126ª–127ᵇ (1.3067–3625 Three Questions), 127ᵇ (2.291–372 Travellers and Angel), 127ᵇ–128ᵇ (5.2031–2272 Virgil's Mirror), 128ᵇ–129ª (5.2273–2390 Two Coffers), 129ª–ᵇ (5.2391–2498 Beggars and Pasties); Manly and Rickert, 1.207 (1450–1500); 61, Tokyo, Takamiya Collection 32, ff 3ª (1.3067–3402 Three Questions), 5ᵇ (5.5551–6047 Tereus), 8ᵇ (6.1789–2358 Nectanabus; transcript from MS 59: Brown-Robbins, no 2662), 11ᵇ (2.1613–1864 Demetrius and Perseus), 13ª (5.4937–5162 Adrian and Bardus), 158ª–162ᵇ (Prol.585–1087, Nebuchadnezzar's Dream, 1.2785–3042 Nebuchadnezzar's Punishment) (ca 1455; R H Robbins, PMLA 54 [1939].935; Manly and Rickert, 1.108; Sotheby Cat 16 Jul 1928, Item 558); 62, Shrewsbury School (single leaf containing Prol.188–95, 224–44, 274–95, 324–43; 1400–50); 63, Mertoun, Duke of Sutherland (single leaf containing 1.1136–1298; 1425–75); 64, Private collection, Robert C Pearson, Cat 13 (1953), Item 219 (8 leaves containing 1.1361–2602, a single quire from MS 49; 1400–50).

Meyer K, John Gowers Beziehungen, Bonn 1889, p 47.

Macaulay, edn, 2.cxxvii; CHEL, 2.452.

Brown-Robbins, no 2662.

Spies H, EStn 28(1900).191; 34(1904).175.

Bone G, Extant MSS Printed by Wynkyn de Worde, Libr 2s 12(1931).284 (MS 42).

de Ricci Census (see index).

Manly and Rickert, 1.93, 117 (scribal hands), 624 (lost MS).

Robbins R H, The Findern Anthology, PMLA 69(1954).610 (description of MS 55, a large anthology containing 5 stories from Confessio: Philomene 5.5920–6052, Lover's Complaint 4.1114–1244, Herypus 4.1245–1466, Three Questions 1.3067–3425, The Lover's Confession 4.2746–2926, Antiochus 8.271–846; suggests MS was begun by group of young ladies as diversion or exercise, and finished by professional scribes—all after 1450).

Fisher, p 303.

Spriggs G M, Unnoticed Bodleian MSS, Bodleian Libr Record 7(1964).193 (illuminations in 3 undated MSS of Confessio, MSS 32, 2, 5).

Doyle A I and M B Parkes, The Production of Copies of the Canterbury Tales and the Confessio Amantis in the Early 15 Cent, in Medieval Scribes, MSS and Libr: Essays Presented to N R Kerr, ed M B Parkes and A G Watson, London 1978, p 163.

Samuels M L and J J Smith, The Language of Gower, NM 82(1981).295.

Griffiths J, Confessio Amantis: The Poem and Its Pictures, in Gower's Confessio Amantis: Responses and Reassessments, ed A J Minnis, Woodbridge (Suffolk) 1983, p 163.

Harris K, John Gower's Confessio Amantis: The Virtues of Bad Texts, in MSS and Readers in 15-Cent England: The Literary Implications of MS Study, ed D Pearsall, Cambridge 1983, p 27; crit G Keiser, Papers of the Bibliographical Soc of America 79(1985).241.

Pearsall D S, The Gower Tradition in Gower's Confessio Amantis: Responses and Reassessments, ed A J Minnis, Woodbridge (Suffolk) 1983, p 179.

Harris K, The Origins and Make-Up of Cambridge Univ Libr MS Ff.1.6, Trans of Cambridge Biblio Soc 7(1983).299 (MS 55).

Griffiths J, Marginalia, Yale Univ Libr Gazette 59(1985).174 (MSS 49, 64).

Editions. Caxton, London 1483 (described by T F Dibdin, Typographical Antiquities, London 1810, 1.177; Macaulay, edn, 2.clxviii; sale copies described by W J Loftie, N&Q 4s 10[1872].165; J Piggot, N&Q 4s 10[1872].370).

Berthelette T, London 1532 and 1554; rptd A Chalmers, Works of the Eng Poets, London 1810, 2.1 (describes Dibdin, 3.278, 340; E Brydges, Censura Literaria, London 1809, 10.346; Pauli, edn, 1.xlii [incorrectly]; Macaulay, edn, 2.clxix; sale copy described Maggs Cat, no 691, Item 241).

Pauli R, ed, 3 vols, London 1857 (crit Athen 11 Apr 1857, p 467; W B D, Fraser's Magazine 59 [1859].571; Macaulay, edn, 2.clxix).

Macaulay, edn, vols 2 and 3 (also issued as EETSES 81 and 82, London 1900–01).

Spies H, Bisherige Ergebnisse, EStn 28(1900).161; EStn 34(1904).175 (edns discussed).

Wells W, The One Millionth Volume: The Poet and the Poem, the Printer and the Book, Chapel Hill 1960 (Caxton).

Fisher J H, John Gower, N Y 1964, pp 8 (Caxton), 12 (Berthelette), 13 (Pauli), 29 (Macaulay).

Blake N F, Caxton's Copytext of Gower's Confessio Amantis, Angl 85(1967).282.

Translation. Ito M, Confessio Amantis: Trial Translation, Study Reports of the Liberal Arts Department of Shizuoka University 26(1976).53 (part I), 27(1977).81 (part II), 28(1978).73 (part III) (trans into modern Japanese); Confessio Amantis, Tokyo 1983 (trans into modern Japanese).

MS. Confisyon del amante. Escorial g.II.19, ff 1ª–411ª (1400–25).

Editions. Confisyon del amante. Birch-Hirschfeld A, ed, Confision del amante, Leipzig 1909 (15-cent Spanish; based on transcript of H Knust; crit C P Wagner, RomR 2[1911].459).

Deyermond A D, ed, Apollonius of Tyre: Two 15-Cent Spanish Prose Romances, Historia de Apollonio and Confision del Amante, Apolonyo De Tyro, Exeter 1973.

Discussion. Confisyon del amante. Ebert A, NT, Jahrbuch für romanische und engl Literatur 4 (1862).69 (notes presence of Gower MS in Escorial Library).

Knust H, Ein Beitrag zur Kentniss der Escorialbibliothek, JfRESL 10(1869).165 (Book 7 and Secretum).

Manly J M, On the Portuguese Translation of Confessio Amantis, MP 27(1930).467 (authorship).

Pietsch K, Zur Frage nach der portugiesischen Übersetzung, Manly Anniv Stud, Chicago 1923, p 323 (traces of Portuguese in vocabulary).

Russell P E, Robert Payn and Juan de Cuenca, Translators of Gower's Confessio Amantis, MÆ 30(1961).26.

Hamm R W, An Analysis of the Confisyon del amante, the Castilian Translation of Gower's Confessio Amantis, diss Tennessee; DAI 36 (1975). 3651A; A Critical Evaluation of the Confisyon del Amante, the Castilian Trans of Gower's Confessio Amantis, MÆ 47(1978).91.

Martins M, Dum poema inglês de John Gower e da sua tradução do Português para o castelhano, Didaskalia 9(1979).413 (in Portuguese).

Selections. Ashmole E, Theatrum chemicum, London 1652, no 18 (4.2456 alchemy).

Chaucer's Ghost, London 1672 (selections from Confessio; described by T R Lounsbury, Stud in Chaucer, N Y 1892, 3.118).

Cooper E, The Muses' Libr, London 1737, p 19 (2.291 Travellers and Angel).

Todd H J, Illustrations of the Lives and Writings of Gower and Chaucer, London 1810, p 145 (5.2273 Two Coffers, Berthelette Pref).

Campbell T, Specimens of the British Poets, London 1819, 2.1 (5.2273 Two Coffers; 6.827 Love Delicacy).

Sanford E, The Works of the Eng Poets, Phila 1819, 1.225 (1.577 Vices; 1.1411 Florent).

Collier J P, Shakespeare's Libr, London 1843, 1.258 (8.271 Apollonius; from MSS 17, 45).

AESpr, 1.347 (Prol.1–100; 1.761 Mundus and Pauline; 4.77 Eneas and Dido; 7.1900 Alcestis; text from Pauli edn).

Ellis A J, Early Eng Pronunciation, London 1869, 3.728 (1.2786 Nebuchadnezzar); Ellis EEP, 1.169

(1.1411 Florent; text from Berthelette 1532 edn and MSS 32, 2, 39).

Corson H, Handbook of Anglo-Saxon and Early Eng, London 1871, p 316 (4.2927 Ceix and Alceone; Rosiphelee; text from Pauli edn).

Beeton S O and W Rosetti, Encyclopaedia of Eng and American Poetry from Caedmon and King Alfred's Boethius to Browning and Tennyson, London 1873, 1.29 (2.291 Travellers and the Angel; 4.1283 Rosiphelee; 5.2273 Two Coffers Text partially modernized from Pauli edn).

Wülker R P, Ae Lesebuch, Halle 1874, 2.36 (1.1 Introd; text from MS 45).

Buckley W E, Cephalus and Procris, London 1882 (1.2254; text from Pauli edn).

Clouston W A, Originals and Analogues, London 1888, p 483 (1.1407 Florent; text from MS 45).

Morris Spec, 6th edn 1892, 2.270 (5.2273 Two Coffers; 5.3827 Eson's Rejuvenation; text from MS 45).

Warner C D, Libr of the World's Best Lit, N Y 1897, 2.6579 (1.3067 Three Questions).

Macaulay G C, Selections, Oxford 1903 (omits Prologue and parts of each book; text from MS 39).

Hadow G E and W H, Oxford Treasury of Eng Lit, Oxford 1907, 1.131 (1.3067 Three Questions).

Of False Allegations, Cleveland 1913, privately printed by C C Bubb, Clerk in Holy Orders (5.*7105–*7192 Lucius and the Statue).

Cook A S, A Literary ME Reader, Boston 1915, p 35 (8.597 Apollonius; 5.3945 Eson's Rejuvenation).

Neilson W A and K G T Webster, Chief British Poets, Boston 1916, p 79 (1.407 Florent; 2.3187 Constantine and Silvester; 4.1245 Rosiphelee; 5.4937 Adrian and Bardus; text from Macaulay edn).

Sisam K, 14-Cent Verse and Prose, Oxford 1921, p 129 (4.2927 Ceix and Alceone; 5.4937 Adrian and Bardus; text from Macaulay edn).

Bennett H S, Gower: Confessio Amantis: Selections, Cambridge 1927 (1.93–228; 1.2458 Albinus and Rosemund; 2.291 Travellers and the Angel; 4.1083 Jason and Medea; 5.3247, 6.7030; text from Pauli edn, but line numbers from Macaulay edn; edits out all sexual references).

Brandl A and O Zippel, Me Sprach- und Literaturproben, 2nd edn, Berlin 1927, p 174 (Prol.1–90 from MSS 32, 39; 3.1331 Pyramus paralleled by Ovid).

Patterson R F, Six Cent of Eng Lit, London 1933, 1.28 (5.4243 Two Coffers).

Schlauch M, in Bryan-Dempster, p 181 (2.587 Constance; text from MS 39).

Spargo J W, in Bryan-Dempster, p 693 (4.2559 Philosopher's Stone; text from Macaulay edn).

Whiting B J, in Bryan-Dempster, p 224 (1.1396; text from Macaulay edn).

Work J A, in Bryan-Dempster, p 709 (3.768 Why the Raven is Black; text from Macaulay edn).

Mossé F, Manuel de l'anglais du moyen âge, Paris 1949, 2.346 (trans J A Walker, A Handbook of ME, Baltimore 1952, p 313 (5.3945 Eson's Rejuvenation, paralleled by Ovid).

Bullough G, Narrative and Dramatic Sources of Shakespeare, London 1966, 6.360 (Apollonius of Tyre, text from Berthelette).

Stevick R D, Five ME Narratives, N Y 1967, p 37 (Apollonius of Tyre).

Bennett J A W, ed, Selections from John Gower, Oxford 1968 (1.1–288 Love and the Lover; 1.1407–1861 Florent; 3.143–356 Canace; 4.1083–1501 Idleness in Love; 4.1615–1770 Rosiphelee; 5.2771–3258 Ceyx and Alcione; 5.3247–4174 Jason and Medea; 5.5551–6047 Tereus and Procne; 8.2013–14 Confessor's Final Counsel).

Peck R A, ed, Confessio Amantis (Rinehart), N Y 1968; rptd (Medieval Academy Reprints for Teaching) Toronto 1980 (an abridgment of Macaulay edn).

Weinberg C, ed, John Gower: Selected Poetry, Carcanet (Manchester) 1983 (lines renumbered from Macaulay edn and slightly modernized [e.g., sch = sh]; nearly 5000 lines selected from Books 1, 3–6, 8).

Modernizations. Morley H, Tales of the Seven Deadly Sins, London 1889 (crit Athen 4 May 1889, p 566; H Bradley, Athen 25 May 1889, p 663; Macaulay, edn, 2.clxx).

Benham A R, Eng Lit from Widsith to the Death of Chaucer: A Source Book, New Haven 1916.

Tiller T, trans, Confessio Amantis (The Lover's Shrift), John Gower, Penguin Classics, Baltimore 1963.

Byrd D G, Confessio Amantis: A Modern Prose Trans, diss S Carolina, DA 28(1967).620A.

Nakamura R and Y Nakamura, Apollonius of Tyre in John Gower's Confessio Amantis Translated into Modern English, Attempts 8 (Society for Linguistics and Literature, ICU) (1980).85.

Textual Comment. Nicholson E W B, Mispunctuation in Gower and Ronsard, Acad 3 Sep 1881, p 182 (correction of Pauli and Lowell, see below *Versification and Rhetoric*).

Easton M W, Readings in Gower, Boston 1895 (crit R Brotanek, AnglB 6[1896].324; G C Macaulay, Acad 31 Aug 1895, p 162).

Language. Johnson S, A Dictionary of the Eng Lang, London 1755, n p (remarks on Gower's innovations; French influence).

Pauli, edn, 1.xxxv.

AESpr, 1.349.

Child F J, Observations on the Language of Gower's Confessio Amantis, Boston 1868 (suppl of Observations on Language of Chaucer; final e and morphology; crit A Stimmung, Arch 47[1871].322).

Ellis A J, Early Eng Pronunciation 1.343 (heavily indebted to Child's Morphology).

Tiete G, Zu Gowers Confessio Amantis, I Lexikalisches, Breslau 1889.

Bradley H, Some Proper Names in the Confessio Amantis, Athenaeum 3213(May 1889).663.

Fahrenberg K, Zur Sprache der Confessio Amantis, Arch 89(1892).389 (chiefly phonology).

Lounsbury T R, Studies in Chaucer, N Y 1892, 2.189 (crit W W Skeat, Acad Mar 1892, p 230; OxfCh, 6.1, lvii).

Mayhew A L, The Word Artemage, Acad 18 Mar 1893, p 242 (see Chance and Krebs below).

Chance F, Artemage, Acad 8 Apr 1893, p 307 (see Mayhew above).

Krebs H, Artemage, Acad 8 Apr 1893, p 307 (see Mayhew above).

Macaulay, edn, 2.xcii.

Spies H, Engl Wörterbucharbeit, Arch 116(1906).111 (report of paper on method of compiling lexicon).

Förg F, Die Konjunktionen in Confessio Amantis, Heidelberg 1911.

Eichhorn E, Das Partizipium bei Gower, Kiel 1912.

Bihl J, Die Wirkungen des Rhythmus in der Sprache von Chaucer und Gower, AF 50(1916) (crit E Bjørkman, AnglB 28[1917].10; E Eckhardt, EStn 52[1918].94 [adds data on iambic variation]).

Steinhoff E, Über den Gebrauch des Artikels in den engl Werken John Gowers, Heidelberg 1916.

Narr A, Die Syntax in John Gower's Confessio Amantis, Vienna 1926.

Kaplan T H, Gower's Vocabulary, JEGP 31 (1932).395.

Burch J C H, Notes on the Language, EStn 69(1934).207 (lexicographical).

Casson L F, Diction of the Confessio Amantis, EStn 69(1934).184.

Wyld H C, A Hist of Modern Colloquial Eng, 3rd edn rvsd, Oxford 1936, p 56.

Mersand J, Chaucer's Romance Vocabulary, N Y 1939, pp 17, 44.

Homann E R, Chaucer's Use of "Gan," JEGP 53(1954).389.

Lawson D D, The Strong Verb in Gower's Confessio Amantis, N Y 1956.

Stockton E W, Major Latin Works, Seattle 1962, p 33.

Kanno M, Some Characteristics of the Verbal Substantive in Gower's Confessio Amantis, Hiroshima Stud in Eng Lang and Lit 9(1963).i, 90.

Kanno M, Expression in Confessio Amantis, Proceedings of the Gifu Pharmaceutical College 14(1964).64; Syntax of the Infinitive in John Gower's Confessio Amantis, 15(1965).51 (part I) and 16(1966).5 (part II); Verbs in John Gower's Confessio Amantis, 17(1967).53; Prepositions in Gower's Confessio Amantis, 18(1968).13 (all in Japanese).

Brook G L, A Hist of the Eng Lang, London 1968, pp 48, 55 (Gower's Kentish forms).

Peck (see under *Selections* above), p xxxiv.

Iwasaki H, A Peculiar Feature in the Word-Order of Gower's Confessio Amantis, Stud in Eng Lit (Japan) 45(1969).205.

Bauer G, Studien zum System und Gebrauch der "Tempora" in der Sprache Chaucers und Gowers, Vienna 1970.

Kanno M, Vocabulary of John Gower, Aichi University Studies in Foreign Languages 9(1971).117 (in Japanese).

Ito M, Wordplay in Confessio Amantis, Shiron 13(1973).1.

Kanno M, Gower's French Vocabulary, I: Adjectives, Aichi University Studies in Foreign Languages 10(1973).119.

Byrd D G, Gower's Confessio Amantis, VI.145, Expl 33(1975).Item 35 (Gower's creation of the nonce word newefot).

Kanno M, Gower's Historical Present, Study Report of Aichi University of Education 25(1976).45.

Nakane S, Grammatical Notes on John Gower's Confessio Amantis, Proceedings of Fukui University of Education 26(1976).123; 27(1977).43.

Otsuki H, On the Use of the Gerund in Confessio Amantis, Ronshu 14(1980).61.

Otsuki H, On the Use of the Present Participle in Confessio Amantis, Proceedings of the Baika Women's College Department of Literature (English/American Language and Literature Volume) 17(1981).61.

Phelan W S, Beyond the Concordance: Semantic and Mythic Structures in Gower's Tale of Florent, Neophil 61(1977).461.

Benskin M and M Laing, Translations and Mischsprachenen in Middle English Manuscripts, in So meny people langages and tonges: Philological Essays in Scots and Medieval English Presented to Angus McIntosh, ed M Benskin and M L Samuels, Edinburgh 1981, p 55.

Samuels M L and J J Smith, The Lang of Gower, NM 82(1981).295.

Shibata S, The Expletive "NE'" in John Gower and Some Middle English Writers, Tokyo University of the Arts, Proceedings 32(1981).75–82.

Porter E, Gower's Ethical Microcosm and Political Macrocosm, in Gower's Confessio Amantis: Responses and Reassessments, ed A J Minnis, Woodbridge (Suffolk) 1983, p 135.

Versification and Rhetoric. Schipper J, Ae Metrik, Bonn 1881, 1.279.

Lowell J R, Chaucer, in My Study Windows, Boston 1887, p 258.

Browning E B, Poetical Works, London 1890, 5.211 (versification).

Höfer P, Alliteration bei Gower, Leipzig 1890 (illuminating comp with Chaucer).

Easton M W, The Rhymes of Gower's Confessio Amantis, Phila 1895.

Macaulay, edn, 2.cxx.

Saintsbury G E B, Hist of Eng Prosody, London 1906, 1.139.

Hammond, p 152.

Bihl (see under *Language* above).

Naunin T, Der Einfluss der Rhetorik auf Chaucers Dichtung, Bonn 1929, p 57.

Oakden J P, Alliterative Poetry in ME, Manchester 1935, pp 368, 378 (draws upon Höfer, above).

Lewis C S, Allegory of Love, Oxford 1936, p 198 (Gower first master of the plain style).

Comtois C P, Rhetoric in John Gower's Speculum Meditantis, diss Fordham 1953.

Francis W N, Chaucer Shortens a Tale, PMLA 68(1953).1126 (Gower's use of rhetorical figures of abbreviation).

Southworth J G, Verses of Cadence: An Intro to the Prosody of Chaucer and His Followers, Oxford 1954, pp 17, 50.

Murphy J J, Chaucer, Gower, and the Eng Rhetorical Tradition, diss Stanford; DA 17(1957).849; John Gower's Confessio Amantis and the First Discussion of Rhetoric in the Eng Lang, PQ 41 (1962).401.

Spearing A C, Verbal Repetition in Piers Plowman Band C, JEGP 62(1963).722.

Daniels R B, Figures of Rhetoric in John Gower's Eng Works, diss Yale; DA 27(1966).1781A.

Davie D, Purity of Diction in English Verse, London 1967, pp 32, 59, 68.

Ito M, Gower's Use of Rime Riche in Confessio Amantis: As Compared with His Practice in Mirour de L'Omme and with the Case of Chaucer, Stud in Eng Lit (Japan) 46(1969).29; Gower's Knowledge of Poetria Nova, Stud in Eng Lit (Japan) 52(1975).3.

Cottle B, The Triumph of Eng 1350–1400, London 1969, pp 68, 120, 293.

Kloesel C J W, Medieval Poetics and John Gower's Vox Clamantis, diss Kansas; DAI 34 (1974). 7709A.

Gallick S, Medieval Rhetorical Arts in England and the MS Tradition, Manuscripta 18(1974).67 (availability to Gower).

Greene L L, Lust and Lore: Figures of Speech in John Gower's Confessio Amantis, diss Arkansas; DAI 39(1978).3567A.

Kelly D, The English Rhetoricians: Chaucer and Gower, in Medieval Imagination: Rhetoric and the Poetry of Courtly Love, Madison Wis 1978, p 195.

Date. Meyer K, John Gowers Beziehungen, Bonn 1889, p 12.

Hales J W, The Confessio Amantis, in Folia Litteraria, London 1893, p 114.

OxfCh, 3.xli.

Macaulay, edn, 2.xxi.

Spies H, Bisherige Ergebnisse, EStn 28(1900).174.

Tatlock J S P, Development and Chronology of Chaucer's Works, ChS, London 1907, p 220 and Appendix A.

Brown C, Man of Law's Headlink, SP 34(1937).10.

Fisher, p 116.

Sources and Literary Relations. Sandras E G, Étude sur Chaucer, Paris 1859, p 58 (7.1917 Alcestis from oriental sources).

Bartsch K, Albrecht von Halberstadt und Ovid, Leipzig 1861, pp 23, 39.

Knust H, Ein Beitrag zur Kentniss der Escorialbibliothek, JfRESL 10(1869).165 (Book 7 and Secretum).

Bech L, Quellen und Plan der Legende of Goode Women und ihr Verhältnis zur Confessio Amantis, Angl 5(1882).313 (crit OxfCh, 3.xli).

Clouston W A, Originals and Analogues, London 1888, p 497 (Florent).

Rumbaur O, Die Geschichte von Appius und Virginia, Breslau 1890, p 15 (7.5131 not Chaucer's source; crit L Fränkl, Estn 17[1892].122).

Hart G, Die Pyramus und Thisbe Sage in Holland, England, Italien, Spanien, Passau 1891 (3.1331 Pyramus).

Lücke E, Das Leben der Constanze bei Trivet, Gower und Chaucer, Angl 14(1892).77, 147 (crit OxfCh, 3.413).

OxfCh, 3.413 (2.587 Constance).

Courthope, 1.312.

Ewig W, Shakespear's Lucrece, Angl 22(1899).31.

Klebs E, Die Erzählung von Apollonius von Tyros: Eine geschichtliche Untersuchung über lateinische Urform und ihre Späteren Bearbeitungen, Berlin 1899, p 462.

Eichinger K, Die Trojasaga als Stoffquelle für Confessio Amantis, Munich 1900.

Flügel E, Chaucers kleinere Gedichte, Angl 23 (1900).195 (2.393 and Truth, line 2).

Görbing F, The Marriage of Sir Gawain und ihren Beziehungen zu Chaucer und Gower, Angl 23 (1900).405.

Neilson A, The Purgatory of Cruel Beauties, Romania 29(1900).89.

Maynadier G H, The Wife of Bath's Tale, London 1901, p 131.

Strollreither E, Quellen-Nachweise zu Gowers Confessio Amantis, Munich 1901.

Bilderbeck J B, Chaucer's Legend of Good Women, London 1902, p 81.

Gough A B, The Constance Saga, Palaes 23 (1902).84.

Hamilton G L, The Indebtedness of Chaucer's Troilus to Guido, N Y 1903, p 97 (Traitié 9.18, Confessio 3.1885, and Guido); Stud in the Sources, JEGP 26(1927).491 (Latin and French versions of Barlaam and Hist of Alexander); Notes on Gower, MLN 19(1904).51 (Mirour 23449, Confessio 5.6498, and Jacques de Vitry); Some Sources of the 7th Book of Confessio Amantis, MP 9(1912). 323 (Jofroi de Watreford's French trans of Secretum and Latini's Trésor); Gower's Use of the Enlarged Roman de Troie, PMLA 20(1905).179 (4.1968 and expanded Benoît).

Lowes J L, The Prologue to the Legend of Good Women, PMLA 20(1905).780.

Moorman F W, Interpretation of Nature in Eng Poetry, Strassburg 1905, p 122.

Baake W, Die Verwendung des Traummotivs in der engl Dichtung bis auf Chaucer, Halle 1906 (use of dream-vision).

Mosher J A, The Exemplum in the Early Religious Lit of England, N Y 1911, p 126.

Singer S and A Bockhoff, Heinrichs von Neustadt Apollonius Tyrland, Tübingen 1911 (reconstruction of lost version which Gower might have known).

Garrett R M, Gower in Pericles, ShJ 48(1912).13; Cleopatra the Martyr, JEGP 22(1923).64 (Confessio and LGW).

Dodd W G, Courtly Love in Chaucer and Gower, Boston 1913.

Cook A S, Dante and Gower, Arch 132(1914).395.

Berndt E, Dame Nature in der engl Lit, Palaes 110(1923).43.

Knowlton E C, Genius as an Allegorical Figure, MLN 39(1924).89.

Schlauch M, Constance and Accused Queens, N Y 1927, p 132.

Gilbert A H, Notes on the Influence of the Secretum Secretorum, Spec 3(1928).84 (Book 7).

TLS 25 Apr 1929, p 338 (3.1495 and Wordsworth).

Heather P J, Precious Stones in ME Verse of the 14 Cent, Folk-Lore 42(1931).217.

Meech S B, Chaucer and the Ovide Moralisé, PMLA 46(1931).202 (Confessio and LGW).

Krappe A H, La Thème de la science stérile chez Gower et chez Goethe, RLC 12(1932).821 (7.1564 and Faust 1.1988).

Patch H R, Boethius' Consolatio IV.m.vi 23–24 and Confessio 7.498–505, Spec 8(1933).41.

Grimes E M, Le Lay du Trot, Romanic Rev 26(1935).315.

Rosenthal G L, The Vitae Patrum in Old and ME Lit, Phila 1936, p 117.

Glunz H H, Die Literarästhetik des europäischen Mittelalters, Bochum-Langendrer 1937, p 349.

Galway M, Chaucer's Sovereign Lady, MLR 33 (1938).145 (Confessio and LGW); Cancelled Tributes to Chaucer's Sovereign Lady, N&Q 193(1948).3.

Jacobson J H, The Church of Love in the Works of John Gower, diss Yale; DAI(1939).2347A.

Tuve R, Spenser and Some Pictorial Conventions, SP 37(1940).152 (Spenser and MS 5).

Dilts D A, John Gower and De geneologia deorum, MLN 57(1942).23.

Heather, The Seven Planets, Folk-Lore 54 (1943).339.

Henkin L J, The Carbuncle in the Adder's Head, MLN 58(1943).34 (lapidaries and 1.463).

Leonhard Z B, Gower's Treatment of Classical Mythology in the Confessio Amantis, diss Northwestern; Summaries of Doctoral Diss, Northwestern Univ, 12(1944).20.

Callan N, Chaucer, Gower, and Ovid, RES 22 (1946).269.

Thorpe L, A Source of the Confessio Amantis, MLR 43(1948).175 (2.2501 and Roman de Marques de Rome).

Bennett J A W, Caxton and Gower, MLR 45 (1950).325 (Gower as source for lines in Caxton's trans of Ovid); Gower's Honeste Love, in J Lawlor, ed, Patterns of Love and Courtesy: Essays in Memory of C S Lewis, London 1966, p 107.

Neville M, Gower's Serpent and the Carbuncle, N&Q 197(1952).225 (reply to Henkin, above); The Vulgate and Gower's Confessio Amantis, diss Ohio State; Ohio State Univ Abstracts of Doctoral Diss no 64(1953).387.

Block E A, Originality, Controlling Purpose, and Craftsmanship in Chaucer's Man of Law's Tale, PMLA 68(1953).600.

Manzalaoui M, The Secreta Secretorum in Eng Thought and Lit from the 14 to the 17 Cent, diss Oxford 1954.

Cary G, The Medieval Alexander, ed D J A Ross, Cambridge 1956, pp 252, 278, 330.

Ames R M, The Source and the Significance of the Jew and the Pagan, MS 19(1957).37.

Eisner S, A Tale of Wonder: A Source Study of the Wife of Bath's Tale, Wexford 1957, p 62.

Isaacs N S, Constance in 14-Cent England, NM 58(1958).260.

Ackerman R W, Arthurian Lit in the Middle Ages: A Collaborative Hist, ed R S Loomis, Oxford 1959, p 501 (Tale of Florent in loathly lady tradition).

Mahoney J L, Ovid and Medieval Courtly Love Poetry, Classical Folia 15(1961).14.

Means M H, The Consolatio Genre in ME Lit, diss Florida; DA 29(1963).875A.

Fisher, John Gower, passim.

Jochums M C, As Ancient as Constantine, Stud in Eng Lit 4(1964).101.

McNally J J, The Penitential and Courtly Tradition in Gower's Confessio Amantis, in Stud in Medieval Culture, J R Sommerfeldt, ed, Kalamazoo 1964, p 74.

Prasad P, The Order of Complaint: A Study in Medieval Tradition, diss Wisconsin; DA 26 (1966).3930.

Byrd D G, Gower's Confessio Amantis, III.585, Expl 29(1967).Item 2.

Hieatt C B, The Realism of Dream Visions: The Poetic Exploitation of Dream-Vision in Chaucer and His Contemporaries, The Hague 1967, p 47.

Mainzer C, A Study of the Sources of the Confessio Amantis by John Gower, diss Oxford 1967.

Vinge L, The Narcissus Theme in Western European Lit up to the Early 19 Cent, Lund 1967, pp 45, 55.

Hoffman R L, An Ovidian Allusion in Gower, AN&Q 6(1968).127.

Williams L F, The Gods of Love in Ancient and Medieval Lit as Background of John Gower's Confessio Amantis, diss Columbia; DA 28 (1968).4193A.

Stanford W B, The Ulysses Theme: A Study in the Adaptability of a Traditional Hero, 2nd edn, Ann Arbor 1968, pp 182, 188.

Grellner Sister M A, John Gower's Confessio Amantis: A Critical Assessment of Themes and Structure, diss Wisconsin; DAI 30(1969).2483A.

Lord M L, Dido as an Example of Chastity: The Influence of Example Lit, HLB 17(1969).22, 216.

Regan C L, John Gower and the Fall of Babylon: Confessio Amantis, Prol II.670–686, Eng Lang Notes 7(1969).85.

Bauer G, Studien zum System und Gebrauch der Tempora in der Sprache Chaucers und Gowers, WBEP 73(Vienna 1970).

Economou G D, The Character Genius in Alain de Lille, Jean de Meun, and John Gower, Chaucer Rev 4(1970).203.

Speed D P, Gower's Narrative Technique as Revealed by His Adaptations of Source Material in the Tales of Confessio Amantis, diss London 1970.

Brumble H D, Genius and Other Related Allegorical Figures in the De Planctu Naturae, the Roman de la Rose, the Confessio Amantis and the Faerie Queene, diss Nebraska; DAI 31(1971).4113A.

Harder H L, Ovid and the Sentence of the Confessio Amantis, diss Maryland; DAI 31(1971).6057A.

Bargreen M L, The Author and His Work: The Priest/Pupil Narrative Topos, diss California-Irvine; DAI 33(1972).2884A.

Mainzer C, John Gower's Use of the Medieval Ovid in the Confessio Amantis, MÆ 41(1972).215.

Schueler D G, Gower's Characterization of Genius in the Confessio Amantis, MLQ 33(1972).243.

Harbert B, The Myth of Tereus in Ovid and Gower, MÆ 41(1972).208.

Klauser H A, The Concept of Kynde in John Gower's Confessio Amantis, diss Fordham; DAI 33(1973).4350A.

Pease R W III, The Genesis and Authorship of Pericles, diss Texas A&M; DAI 33(1973).4358A.

Pickford T E, John Gower and the Apollonius Tradition, diss Waikato (N Zealand) 1973.

Foster J J, The Influence of Medieval Mythography on John Gower's Confessio Amantis, diss Duke; DAI 34(1974).4259A.

Nitzsche J C, The Genius Figure in Antiquity and the Middle Ages, N Y 1975, pp 1, 63, 115, 125.

Price R C, Pauline Perils: A Religious Reading of Pericles, Prince of Tyre, diss California-Berkeley; DAI 35(1975).7266A.

Baker D N, The Priesthood of Genius: A Study of the Medieval Tradition, Spec 50(1976).277.

Weiher C, Chaucer's and Gower's Stories of Lucretia and Virginia, Eng Lang Notes 14(1976).7.

Shaw J D, Confessio Amantis: Gower's Art in Transforming His Sources into Exempla of the Seven Deadly Sins, diss Penn; DAI 38(1977).6709A.

Ito M, Gower's Use of Vita Barlaam et Josaphat in Confessio Amantis, Studies in English Lit, English number (1979).3.

Burke L B, The Sources and Significance of the Tale of the King, Wine, Woman and Truth in John Gower's Confessio Amantis, Greyfriar 21(1980).3.

Minnis A J, John Gower, Sapiens in Ethics and Politics, MÆ 49(1980).207.

Cresswell J, The Tales of Actaeon and Narcissus in the Confessio Amantis, Reading Medieval Stud 7(1981).32.

Ito M, The Use of the Roman de Troie in the Confessio Amantis, in Festschrift for Dr. Matsui Hasegawa on His 70th Birthday, Sendai (Japan) 1981, p 175.

Manzalaoui M A, Noght in the Registre of Venus: Gower's English Mirror for Princes, in Medieval Studies for J A W Bennett, Aetatis suae LXX, ed P L Heyworth, Oxford 1981, p 159.

Medcalf S, Inner and Outer, in The Later Middle Ages, ed S Medcalf, New York 1981, p 158.

Beidler P G, ed, John Gower's Literary Transformations in the Confessio Amantis: Original Articles and Translations, Washington D C 1982 (contains trans by P I De Bellis and E S deAngeli of two of Gower's sources for the Tale of Nectanabus).

Miller P S, The Medieval Literary Theory of Satire and Its Relevance to the Works of Gower, Langland and Chaucer, diss Queen's Univ (Belfast) 1982.

Braswell M F, The Medieval Sinner: Characterization and Confession in the Literature of the English Middle Ages, Rutherford NJ, 1983, p 93.

Ito M, Gower's Diogenes and Alexander in Its Philosophic-Literary Tradition, Poetica (Eng Literary Soc of Japan) 16(1983).66.

Minnis A J, ed, Gower's Confessio Amantis: Responses and Reassessments, Woodbridge (Suffolk) 1983 (various articles).

Burrow J A, The Portrayal of Amans in Confessio Amantis, in Minnis above, p 5.

Miller P S, John Gower, Satiric Poet, in Minnis above, p 79.

Minnis, Moral Gower and Medieval Literary Theory, in Minnis above, p 50.

Ricks C, Metamorphosis in Other Words, in Minnis above, p 24.

Runacres C A J, Art and Ethics in the Exempla of Confessio Amantis, in Minnis above, p 106.

Martins M, Como Apolonio de Tiro chegou até nós através de John Gower, in Estudos de Cultura Medieval 3, Lisbon 1983, p 133 (in Portuguese).

Criticism. Lowell J R, Chaucer, in My Study Windows, Boston 1887, p 258 (caustic criticism).

Ker W P, Eng Lit: Medieval, N Y 1912, p 222.

John Gower Memorial Essay, TLS 18 Aug 1932, p 573 (perceptive appreciation of poetry).

Lewis C S, Allegory of Love, Oxford 1936, p 198 (perceptive critical comment).

Leonhard Z B, Gower's Treatment of Classical Mythology in the Confessio Amantis, diss Northwestern; Summary of Doctoral Dissertations, Northwestern Univ 12(1944).20.

Bland D S, The Poetry of Gower, English 6 (1947).286 (Ceix and Alceone; Medea; Lucrece; frame technique).

Wickert M, Studien zu John Gower, p 174 (narrative technique; trans R J Meindl, as Stud in John Gower, Washington D C 1982).

Goolden P, Antiochus' Riddle in Gower and Shakespeare, RES ns 6(1955).245.

Fison P, The Poet in John Gower, Essays in Criticism 8(1958).16.

Fisher, John Gower, pp 1 (useful review of Gower's critical reputation), 204 (relationship with Chaucer).

Schueler D G, A Critical Evaluation of John Gower's Confessio Amantis, diss Louisiana State; DA 23(1963).4678; Some Comments on the Structure of John Gower's Confessio Amantis, in R D Reck, ed, Explorations of Lit (LSU Stud 18), Baton Rouge 1966, p 15; The Age of the Lover in Gower's Confessio Amantis, MÆ 36(1967).152; Gower's Characterization of Genius in the Confessio Amantis, MLQ 33(1972).240.

Chapin D F, Theme and Structure in John Gower's Confessio Amantis, diss Toronto; DA 31 (1964).2869A.

Meindl R J, A New Reading of John Gower's Confessio Amantis, diss Tulane; DA 26(1965).2727.

Yoshida S, Love and Reason in Gower's Confessio Amantis, Stud in Eng Lit (Japan) 42(1965).1.

Bennett J A W, Gower's Honeste Love, in J Lawlor below, p 107.

Lawlor J, On Romanticism in the Confessio Amantis, in J Lawlor, ed, Patterns of Love and Courtesy, London 1966, p 122.

Pearsall D, Gower's Narrative Art, PMLA 81 (1966).475.

Prasad P, The Order of Complaint: A Study of Medieval Tradition, diss Wisconsin; DA 26 (1966).3930.

Gallacher P J, The Structural Uses of the Theme of Speech in John Gower's Confessio Amantis, diss Illinois; DA 27(1967).3839A; Love, the Word, and Mercury: A Reading of John Gower's Confessio Amantis, Albuquerque 1975.

Oiji T, Chaucer and His Contemporary Poets, Tokyo 1968, p 273 (in Japanese).

Grellner Sister M A, John Gower's Confessio Amantis: A Critical Assessment of Themes and Structure, diss Wisconsin; DAI 30(1969).2483A.

Hoben Sister M W, John Gower's Confessio Amantis: An Analysis of the Criticism and a Critical Analysis, diss Penn; DAI 30(1969).1136A.

Ito M, Gower's Use of Rime Riche in Confessio Amantis, Stud in Eng Lit (Japan) 46(1969).37.

Olsson K O, The Poetry of John Gower: The Art of Moral Rhetoric, diss Chicago 1969.

Peck (see under *Selections* above), pp v, xi.

Burrow J A, Ricardian Poetry: Chaucer, Gower, Langland, and the Gawain Poet, New Haven 1971.

Badenyck J L, The Achievement of John Gower: A Reading of the Confessio Amantis, diss CUNY; DAI 33(1972).1157A.

Kiji T, Lamentation and Prayer: Gower in the Opening Song of Confessio Amantis, Bunka 36(1972).1 (in Japanese).

Phelan W S, The Conflict of Courtly Love and Christian Morality in John Gower's Confessio Amantis, diss Ohio State; DAI 32(1972).3961A.

Clogan P M, From Complaint to Satire: The Art of the Confessio Amantis, MH 4(1973).217.

Klauser H A, The Concept of Kynde in John Gower's Confessio Amantis, diss Fordham; DAI 33 (1973).4350A.

Tague W L, John Gower's Confessio Amantis: An Hypothesis of Structure, diss Wisconsin; DAI 33(1973).3604A.

Pickford T E, Fortune in Gower's Confessio Amantis, Parergon 7(1973).20.

Farnham A E, The Art of High Prosaic Seriousness: John Gower as Didactic Raconteur, in L D Benson, ed, The Learned and the Lewed: Stud in Chaucer and Medieval Lit (Harvard Eng Stud no 5), Cambridge 1974, p 161.

Ito M, On Jason and Medea by John Gower—A Story of Golden Love, Study Reports of the Liberal Arts Department of Shizuoka University 12(1974).79.

Norton-Smith J, Geoffrey Chaucer, London 1974, pp 69, 88, 158.

Schmitz G, The Middel Weie: Stil- und Aufbauformen in John Gowers Confessio Amantis, Bonn 1974.

Cowling S T, Gower's Ironic Self-Portrait in the Confessio Amantis, Annuale Mediaevale 16 (1975).63.

Davis N, Chaucer and 14-Cent England in Geoffrey Chaucer, ed D S Brewer, Athens, Ohio 1975 p 70 (Gower draws style from French and Latin).

Economou G D, The Two Venuses and Courtly Love, in In Pursuit of Perfection: Courtly Love in Medieval Lit, ed J M Ferrante and G D Economou, Port Washington N Y 1975, p 17.

Hatton T J, The Role of Venus and Genius in John Gower's Confessio Amantis: A Reconsideration, Greyfriar 16(1975).29.

Oiji T, Eng Lit in the 14 Cent, Tokyo 1976, p 29 (in Japanese).

Yeager R F, John Gower's Poetic, diss Yale; DAI 37(1976).4345A.

Burke L B, Women in John Gower's Confessio Amantis, Mediaevalia 3(1977).238.

Eberle P A, Vision and Design in John Gower's Confessio Amantis, diss Harvard 1977.

Cherniss M D, The Allegorical Figures in Gower's Confessio Amantis, Res Publica Litterarum 1 (1978).7.

Woolf R, Moral Chaucer and Kindly Gower, in J R R Tolkien, Scholar and Storyteller: Essays in Memoriam, ed M Salu and R T Farrell, Ithaca NY 1979, p 231.

Benson C D, The History of Troy in Middle English Literature, Woodbridge (Suffolk) 1980, pp 117, 162.

Grant K B, Kingship in John Gower's Confessio Amantis, diss Marquette; DAI 40(1980).5045A.

Minnis A J, John Gower, Sapiens in Ethics and Politics, MÆ 49(1980).207.

Burrow J A, The Poet as Petitioner, Stud in the Age of Chaucer 3(1981).61.

Coleman J, Medieval Readers and Writers: 1350–1400, N Y 1981, p 126.

Creswell J, The Tales of Actaeon and Narcissus in the Confessio Amantis, Reading Medieval Stud 7(1981).32.

Mangan R, Loves luste and lockes hore: Medieval Attitudes toward Aging and Sexuality, Human Values and Aging Newsletter 4(1981).5.

Manzalaoui M A, Nought in the Registre of Venus: Gower's Eng Mirror for Princes, in P L Heyworth and D Davin, edd, Medieval Stud for J A W Bennett, Aetatis Suae 70, Oxford 1981, p 159.

Yeager R F, "oure englisshe" and Everyone's Latin: the Fasciculus Morum and Gower's Confessio Amantis, South Atlantic Rev 46(1981).41.

Allen J B, The Ethical Poetic of the Later Middle Ages: A Decorum of Convenient Distinction, Toronto 1982, p 142.

Beidler P G, ed, John Gower's Literary Transformations in the Confessio Amantis: Original Articles and Translations, Washington D C 1982 (contains critical commentaries on a number of tales from [7]: on Acteon, on Acis and Galatea, and on Nectanabus by Beidler; on Deianira and Nessus and on Pygmalion by C K Brown; on Pyramus and Thisbe and on Midas by J C G Moran; on Phebus and Daphne and on Neptune and Cornix by N E Ruyak; on Iphis and on Iphis and Araxarathen by N Stasko; on Icarus and on Echo by K Zipf; on Ceyx and Alceone and on Leucothoe by J B Gaston; and on Argus and Mercury and on Tereus by D L Lepley).

Boitani P, Eng Medieval Narrative in the 13 and 14 Cents, trans J K Hall, N Y 1982, p 122.

Burrow J A, Medieval Writers and Their Work, Oxford 1982, pp 7, 40, 53, 110.

Hoeniger F D, Gower and Shakespeare in Pericles, Shakespeare Quart 33(1982).461.

Lynch K, The Medieval Dream-Vision: A Study in Genre Structure and Meaning, diss Virginia; DAI 43(1982).3314A.

Minnis A J, Chaucer and Pagan Antiquity, Woodbridge (Suffolk) 1982, pp 16, 18, 56, 77.

Olsson K, Natural Law and John Gower's Confessio Amantis, MH ns 11(1982).231.

Strohm P, A Note on Gower's Persona, in Acts of Interpretation: The Text in Its Contexts 700–

1600, Essays on Medieval and Renaissance Lit in Honor of E Talbot Donaldson, ed M J Carruthers and E Kirk, Norman (Oklahoma) 1982, p 293.

Wickert M, Stud in John Gower, trans R J Meindl, Washington D C 1982 (originally published in German in 1953).

Shaw J D, John Gower's Illustrative Tales, NM 84(1983).437.

Minnis A J, Medieval Theory of Authorship: Scholastic Literary Attitudes in the Later Middle Ages, London 1984, pp 167, 200.

[8] IN PRAISE OF PEACE.

MSS. 1, BL Addit 59495, ff 5ᵃ–10ᵇ (1375–1425); originally "Trentham" MS; see also 18-cent transcript of this MS, BL Addit 59496; 2, BL Cotton Julius F.VII, f 167ᵃ (Latin heading only).

Macaulay, edn, 1.lxxix.

Brown-Robbins, no 2587.

Fisher J H, John Gower, N Y 1964, p 73.

Editions. Thynne W, ed, Workes of Chaucer, London 1532, f 375ᵇ.

Urry J, Works of Chaucer, London 1721, p 540.

Bell R, Poetical Works of Geoffrey Chaucer with Poems Formerly Printed with His, or Attributed to Him, London 1782, n p.

Wright PPS, 2.4.

OxfCh, 7.205 (text from Wright PPS).

Macaulay, edn, 3.481.

Bennett J A W, ed, Selections from John Gower, Oxford 1968, p 124 (abridgment).

Discussion. OxfCh, 7.xxxviii (authorship).

Skeat W W, The Chaucer Canon, Oxford 1900, p 100.

Daniels R B, Rhetoric in Gower's In Praise of Peace, SP 32(1935).62.

Stockton E W, Major Latin Works, Seattle 1962, p 42.

Fisher, p 127.

Barnie J, War in Medieval Society, London 1974, p 138.

Yeager R F, "oure englisshe" and Everyone's Latin, South Atlantic Rev 46(1981).41.

[9] BALADE MORAL.

MSS. 1, Bodl 6943 (Ashmole 59), f 17ᵇ (1400–1500); 2, Bodl 11951 (Rawl C.86), f 89ᵇ (1450–1500); 3, BL Addit 29729, f 6ᵇ (handwriting of John Stowe; ca 1600).

Macaulay, edn, 2.clxxiii.

Brown-Robbins, no 2737.

Editions. Meyer K, John Gowers Beziehungen, Bonn 1889, p 72.

Förster M, Über Benedict Burghs Werks, Arch 101(1898).50 (prints [9] from MS 3 as Burgh's work).

Macaulay, edn, 2.clxxiii.

Authorship. Förster, Arch 102(1898).213 (evidence of MS Harley 2251 that [9] is by Gower); Arch 103(1900).149 (casts doubt on evidence of MS Harley 2251).

Macaulay, edn, 2.clxxiii.

XVIII. PIERS PLOWMAN

by

Anne Middleton

BACKGROUND BOOKS: The following important, frequently listed entries, here given full statement, are referred to in abbreviated form in the pages that follow. For abbreviations not appearing in this list, consult the general Table of Abbreviations.

Donaldson C-Text Poet	Donaldson E T, Piers Plowman: The C-Text and Its Poet, YSE 113, New Haven 1949; rptd Hamden Conn 1966, with revised list of MSS
Kane A-Text	Kane G, ed, Piers Plowman: The A-Version, London 1960 (vol 1, Athlone edn)
Kane-Donaldson B-Text	Kane G and E T Donaldson, edd, Piers Plowman: The B-Version, London 1975 (vol 2, Athlone edn)
Knott-Fowler A-Text	Knott T A and D C Fowler, edd, Piers Plowman: A Critical Edition of the A-Version, Baltimore 1952
Skeat A-Text	Skeat W W, ed, Piers Plowman A-Text, EETS 28, London 1867
Skeat B-Text	Skeat W W, ed, Piers Plowman B-Text, EETS 38, London 1869
Skeat C-Text	Skeat W W, ed, Piers Plowman C-Text, EETS 54, London 1873
Skeat Notes	Skeat W W, ed, Notes to Piers the Plowman, Indexes, EETS 67, London 1877
Skeat Glossary	Skeat W W, ed, General Preface, Indexes, Glossary, EETS 81, London 1884
Skeat Oxford	Skeat W W, ed, Piers Plowman in Three Parallel Texts, 2 vols, Oxford 1886 (EETS texts printed in parallel with selected variants, notes, glossary)

(Bibliographical Note: For over a century, the standard modern edition of all three versions of *Piers Plowman*, to which nearly all critical and historical notices of the poem have referred, has been that of Skeat. Yet during much of that period, vigorous study of the extremely complex textual history of the poem has continued, examining and re-assessing the relations among manuscripts, some of which were unknown to Skeat, and offering different principles for evaluating this evidence and presenting it in an edition. While this work has involved several scholars and editors for more than 50 years (see [2–4] below), its chief editorial monument is of fairly recent date, and has only in the last few years figured in critical citations. This is the four-volume Athlone edition, of which the A version (Kane A-Text) and the B version (Kane-Donaldson B-Text) have been published. The C version, edited by G. H. Russell, and a volume containing notes and a glossary, are in preparation. The Athlone edition makes the most exhaustively reasoned and documented attempt to date to restore and approximate what the fourteenth-century poet wrote, and when complete will become the fundamental text of reference.

There have also been several careful re-editions of each of the three versions made in the last generation. While these do not always agree in detail or in principle with the work of the Athlone editors, they too have benefited from the textual scholarship postdating Skeat. This state of affairs now requires the committed reader or scholar to consult more than one "standard" text in surveying past work on the poem, and dictates the mixed citation procedure followed in this bibliography.

In MANUSCRIPTS [1], the Kane A-Text and the Kane-Donaldson B-Text are the editions to which the line numbers refer, since these volumes are the source of the most detailed account of the manuscripts. In the descriptions of the C-text manuscripts, the passus and line numbers refer to Skeat's edition, since G. H. Russell's C version has not yet been published. (Professor Russell has kindly supplied the corresponding line and passus numbers from his forthcoming text, however; these follow the Skeat numbers in parentheses.) Because Skeat's was the reference text of most past criticism, citations in the remainder of the bibliography refer to that text unless otherwise noted.

In compiling the bibliography, I have made some exceptions to the general practice of the *Manual*, of two main kinds. First, I have included some unpublished works. Several of these have greatly influenced the course of published scholarship, particularly on textual matters. A few unpublished critical and historical studies have also made valuable contributions to *Piers Plowman* studies. To one of these and its author, in fact, Professor Donaldson—my predecessor in this project—and I are particularly indebted: S. S. Hussey's critical review of 80 years of *Piers Plowman* scholarship, a most informative and thorough London University M.A. thesis, unequalled in the published literature.

Second, I have listed a few items—many, but by no means all, of them under MISCELLANEOUS [20]—which were intended for a popular, general, even occasionally deeply partisan audience, for the "common reader" rather than the literary scholar. These are customarily excluded from the *Manual*, and fall outside the ordinary purposes of its users. Their inclusion seems justified, however, by their role, past and present, in informing readers' taste and affection for this poem, and the idea of it with which more specialized studies must sometimes contend. Though they may contribute little to editorial choices or to scholarly interpretation, they may help to illuminate the textual and critical fortunes of the poem, and show its continued vitality and importance in both literary and historical debate.)

[1] MANUSCRIPTS.

(Note: Sigils in parentheses are, unless otherwise noted, those of the Athlone Press edition, under the general editorship of George Kane: Kane A-Text, Kane-Donaldson B-Text, and the still unpublished C-Text, edited by G. H. Russell.)

A-Text. 1, (K) Bodl 1746 (Digby 145), ff 2ª–130ª (1531–32); continues as C-text from end of A Pas

11; 2, (V) Bodl 3938 (Vernon), ff 394ᵇ–401ᵇ (ca 1400); ends at Pas 11.180; 3, (A) Bodl 7004 (Ashmole 1468), ff 307–78 (1450–75); begins at Pas 1.142 and has serious gaps; 4, (R) Bodl 14631 (Rawlinson Poet 137), ff 1ª–41ᵇ (ca 1450); contains Pas 12; 5, (D) Bodl 21897 (Douce 323), ff 102ª–140ª (1450–1500); 6, (U) Univ Coll Oxf E.45, ff 1ª–36ᵇ (1400–25); contains Pas 12; 7, (T) Trinity Camb 594 (R.3.14), ff 2ª–74ᵇ (ca 1400); continues as C-text from end of A Pas 11; [7a,

Pembroke Camb; fragment of about 140 lines preserved in a binding (Kane A-Text, p 13)]; 8, (H) Harley 875, ff 1ª–22ᵇ (1400–50); ends at Pas 8.142; 9, (H³) Harley 3954, ff 92ª–123ᵇ (1400–50); begins as B-text, becoming A-text at Pas 5.106; 10, (H²) Harley 6041, ff 1ª–96ª (post 1425); continues as C-text from end of A Pas 11; 11, (L) Lincoln's Inn 150, ff 109ª–125ᵇ (1400–25); ends at Pas 8.158; 12, (Ch) Liverpool Univ F.4.8 (Chaderton), ff 1ª–101ᵇ (ca 1425); continues as C-text from end of A Pas 11; 13, (N) Nat Libr Wales Addit 733.B, pp 1–176 (1400–50); begins at Pas 1.76 and becomes C-text after A Pas 8, ending at C Pas 22.456; 14, (M) Society of Antiquaries London 687 (Bright), pp 470–549 (ca 1425); 15, (E) Trinity Dublin 213 (D.4.12), ff 1ª–26ᵇ (1475–1500); ends at Pas 7.45; 16, (W) Westminster (now owned by a British private collector; Lot 233 at Sotheby's, 11 July 1966), ff 1ª–76ª (1450–75); continues as C-text from end of A Pas 11; 17, (J) Morgan Libr M.818 (Ingilby), ff 16ª–54ᵇ (ca 1450); contains Pas 12.1–88. MSS 19, 28, and 29 of the B-class are A-text from A Pas 2.90–212 (see Kane-Donaldson B-Text, pp 35, 40). MS 38 (Skeat's Z) of the C-class begins as an extremely corrupt A-text, becoming C at Pas 11 (see Kane-Donaldson B-Text, p 14).

B-Text. 18, (L) Bodl 987 (Laud Misc 581), ff 1ª–91ᵇ (1400–25); 19, (Bo) Bodl 2683 (Bodl 814), ff 1ª–92ª (ca 1400); begins as C-text, Prologue 1–Pas 2.131, followed by A 2.90–212, becoming B-text at B Pas 3; 20, (R) Bodl 15563 (Rawlinson Poet 38), ff 1ª–105ª (1400–25); begins at Pas 2.41; see next item; [20a, (R) BL Lansdowne 398, ff 77–80 (1400–25); originally ff 3–6 of preceding item, containing Prologue 125–1.140]; 21, (F) Corp Christi Oxf 201, ff 1ª–93ª (1400–50); 22, (O) Oriel Oxf 79, ff 1ª–88ª (1400–50); missing leaves in Pas 17 and 19; 23, (C) Camb Univ Dd.1.17, vol 3, ff 1ª–31ª (ca 1400); 24, (G) Camb Univ Gg.4.31, ff 1ª–101ª (1500–50); 25, (C²) Camb Univ L1.4.14, ff 1ª–107ª (ca 1450); [25a, Caius Camb 201, ff 1ª–119ᵇ (after 1561); transcript of Owen Rogers' edn of 1561]; 26, (Y) Newnham Camb (Yates-Thompson), ff 1ª–104ᵇ (1400–50); 27, (W) Trinity Camb 353 (B.15.17), ff 1ª–130ᵇ (ca 1400); 28, (Cot) Cotton Calig A.xi, ff 170ª–286ª (1400–50); begins as C-text, Prologue 1–Pas 2.131, followed by A 2.90–212, becoming B-text in Pas 3; 29, (Bm) BL Addit 10574, ff 1ª–91ᵇ (ca 1400); begins as C-text, Prologue 1–Pas 2.131, followed by A 2.90–212, becoming B-text in Pas 3; 30, (M) BL Addit 35287 (Ashburnham 129), ff 1ª–104ᵇ (1400–50); 31, (called Ht by Donaldson C-Text Poet, p 229) Huntington HM 114 (Phillipps 8252), ff 1ª–129ᵇ (1400–25); mixture of ABC

texts; 32, (Hm) Huntington HM 128 (Ashburnham 130), ff 113ª–205ª (1400–25); fragment (Hm²) containing Pas 2.209–3.72 on ff 95ª–96ᵇ; 33, (S) Takamiya 23 (Prof Toshiyuki Takamiya, Keio Univ, Tokyo; formerly Sion Coll Arc. L.40 2/E76, Lot 74 at Sotheby's, 13 June 1977), ff 1–182 (ca 1550); 34, (Cr¹) Crowley R, London 1550 (STC, no 19906) reproduces a lost MS; its two successive printings (Cr², Cr³) in that year (STC, nos 19907, 19907a) are corrected from a second MS. See also MS 9 (H³) above, which is B-text (called H in Kane-Donaldson B-Text) to Pas 5.105.

C-Text. 35, (E) Bodl 1059 (Laud Misc 656), ff 19ᵇ–114ª (ca 1400); 36, (Y) Bodl 1703 (Digby 102), ff 1ª–97ᵇ (1400–25); begins at Pas 3.160 (2.159); 37, (K) Bodl 1772 (Digby 171), ff 3ª–62ª (ca 1400); contains Pas 3.217–16.65 (2.220–15.65); 38, (Z) Bodl 3041 (Bodley 851), ff 124ª–208ᵇ (1425–50); not reliable as C-text until Pas 11 (10.1) (see Kane-Donaldson B-Text, p 14); 39, (D) Bodl 21678 (Douce 104), ff 1ª–112ᵇ (1427); 40, (G) Camb Univ Dd.3.13, ff 1ª–99ᵇ (1375–1400); contains Pas 1.154–23.39 (Prologue 152–22.39); 41, (F) Camb Univ Ff.5.35, ff 49ᵇ–152ª (1400–50); 42, (Q) Camb Univ Addit 4325, ff 3ª–83ᵇ (1400–25); 43, (S) Corp Christi Camb 293, ff 1ª–64ᵇ (ca 1425); [43a, Caius Camb 669, f 210ª (15 cent; transcript of 17 lines from Pas 17)]; 44, (M) Cotton Vesp B.xvi, ff 6ª–95ª (ca 1400); 45, (N) Harley 2376, ff 1ª–124ª (ca 1425–35); 46, (R) Royal 18.B.xvii, ff 14ª–122ᵇ (1525–50); 47, (P²) BL Addit 34779 (Phillipps 9056), ff 1ª–93ᵇ (ca 1400); 48, (U) BL Addit 35157, ff 7ª–124ª (very early 15 cent); 49, (A) Univ of London Libr V.17 (Sterling), ff 1ª–98ᵇ (1400–25); ends at Pas 23.87 (22.87); 50, (I) Univ of London Libr V.88 (Ilchester), ff 1ª–125ᵇ (126ª offset; ca 1400); 51, (V) Trinity Dublin 212 (D.4.1), ff 1ª–89ᵇ (1375–1400); ends at Pas 23.87 (22.87); 52, (P) Huntington HM 137 (Phillipps 8231), ff 1ª–89ᵇ (ca 1400); 53, (X) Huntington HM 143, ff 1ª–106ᵇ (ca 1400); 54, Fragment owned by Prof John Holloway, Queen's College, Cambridge (ca 1400); contains Pas 2.201–3.44 (1.200–2.46), Pas 4.123–75 (3.123–76). See also items listed above: MS 1, which is C-text from C Pas 12.297 (11.296) and lacks the Latin quotation following Pas 12.296; MSS 7, 10, and 12, which are C-texts from C Pas 12.296 (11.295) and contain the Latin line following Pas 12.296; MS 13, which is C-text from C Pas 11.1 (10.1); MS 16, which is C-text from C Pas 13.1 (12.1); MSS 19, 28, and 29, which are C-texts to C Pas 3.127 (2.130); and Donaldson C-Text Poet, p 229.

MS Listings. Skeat Glossary, p 832; Skeat Oxford, 2.lxii.

Kron R, W Langleys Buch von P dem P, Erlangen 1885, p 11.

Brown Reg, nos 477, 880, 881.

Chambers R W and J H G Grattan, The Text of P P, MLR 26(1931).50.

Donaldson C-Text Poet, p 227.

Knott-Fowler A-Text, p 23 (A MSS).

Kane A-Text, p 1 (A MSS).

Kane-Donaldson B-Text, p 1 (B MSS).

Brown-Robbins, nos 745, 1458, 1459; Robbins-Cutler, no 1459.

For information about MSS, see [3] and [4] below.

[2] EDITIONS.

(Note: For full bibliographic statement of the editions here listed, see the Table of Abbreviations at the beginning of the *Piers Plowman* bibliography.)

ABC-Texts. Skeat A-Text, Skeat B-Text, Skeat C-Text, Skeat Notes, and Skeat Glossary (critical edns with variants of many MSS; crit C H Pearson, North British Rev 52.241; J J Jusserand, Revue Critique, Oct 25 and Nov 1 1879, pp 313, 321).

Skeat Oxford (ABC-texts printed in parallel form with selected variants; crit H Bradley, Athen, Jan 29 1887, p 70).

A-Text. Skeat A-Text (from MS 2).

Knott-Fowler A-Text (from MS 7, with selected variants from all MSS; crit S Brook, RES ns 5.179; G H Gerould, Spec 29.108; B von Lindheim, Angl 71.495; F Mossé, EA 6.56; R Quirk, JEGP 52.400).

Kane A-Text (critical edn based on MS 7, corrected from other MSS, with variant readings; crit J A W Bennett, RES 14.68; J B Bessinger, JEGP 60.571; M W Bloomfield, Spec 36.133; G Bourquin, EA 14.141; N Davis, N&Q ns 8.115; A I Doyle, ESts 43.55; D C Fowler, MP 58.212; P M Kean, Library 16.218; J Lawlor, MLR 56.243; G Mathew, MÆ 30.126; T F Mustanoja, Angl 80.172; J Swart, Neophil 45.249; C L Wrenn, MLN 76.856).

Rigg A G and C Brewer, P P: The Z Version, Toronto 1983 (presents text of Prologue–Pas 8 of MS 38; argues that it is an early version of the A-text; dates MS before 1388; crit R Adams, Stud in the Age of Chaucer 7.233; G Kane, Spec 60.910).

B-Text. Crowley R, London 1550 (STC, no 19906; from MS now lost); 2nd and 3rd issues (STC, nos 19907, 19907a; same year with revisions from other MSS).

Rogers O, London 1561 (STC, no 19908; reprint of Crowley's 3rd impression).

Wright T, London 1842 (from MS 27); 2nd rvsd edn 1856.

Skeat B-Text (from MS 18).

Skeat W W, Oxford 1869 (Prologue and Pas 1–7 of Skeat B-Text; students' edn, often rptd; see J A W Bennett below).

Davis J F, London 1896 (Prologue and Pas 1–7 from MS 18); rvsd by E S Olszewska 1928.

O'Kane H M, ed and illustr, New Rochelle 1901 (Prologue and Pas 1–7 of Skeat B-Text).

Onions C T, London 1904 (B Prologue).

Drennan C M, London 1914 (Prologue and Pas 1).

Pamely C D, London 1928 (Prologue and Pas 5–7 from MS 18).

Petrushevsky D V, Moscow 1941.

Kane G, M A thesis London Univ 1946 (Pas 18–20).

Wilcockson C, London and N Y 1965 (from Skeat B-Text, parts of Prologue and Pas 1, 5, 6, 16–18, 20; students' edn).

Oiji T, Tokyo 1968 (Skeat B-Text Prologue and Pas 1–7 and C-Text 6.1–108, with introd and notes in Japanese compiled from various edns); rvsd edn: vol 1 (text), 1973; vol 2 (notes and glossary), 1978.

Bennett J A W, Oxford 1972 (Prologue and Pas 1–7 of B from MS 18; supplants Skeat's 1869 student edn with new notes, glossary, selected variants; crit TLS Jan 4 1973, p 9; S Wenzel, Spec 49.745).

Casieri S, Milan 1973 (selections from Skeat B-Text, with introd and notes in Italian).

Brook S, N Y 1975 (selections from MS 18, with parallel modernization).

Kane-Donaldson B-Text (critical edn based on MS 27, corrected and restored, with all substantive variants; crit J Alford, Spec 52.1002; J A W Bennett, RES 69.323; G Bourquin, EA 30.474; J Burrow, TLS Nov 21 1975, p 1380; B Cottle, JEGP 75.589; D C Fowler, YES 7.23; D Pearsall, MÆ 46.278; E G Stanley, N&Q 23.435; T Turville-Petre, SN 49.153).

Schmidt A V C, London and N Y 1978 (critical edn from MS 27, with selected variants, introd, glosses, commentary; crit S Barney, Spec 56.161; D Fowler, Review 2.211; N Jacobs, English 28. 151; T Turville-Petre, RES 30.454; C Wilcockson, MÆ 50.166).

C-Text. Whitaker T D, London 1813 (from MS 52; crit [T Wright,] Gentleman's Magazine, April 1834, p 385).

Skeat C-Text (from MS 52).

Parish E L, M A thesis London Univ 1933 (critical edn of Pas 9 and 10).

Carnegy F A R, An Attempt to Approach the C-Text of P P, London 1934 (critical edn of Pas 3–5, based on MS 48).

Mitchell A G, diss London Univ 1939 (critical edn of Prologue and Pas 1–4).

Salter E and D Pearsall, London and Evanston Ill 1967 (students' edn of selections from C, based on MS 53, with selected variants).

Pearsall D, Berkeley and Los Angeles 1979 (based on MS 53, with selected variants, introd, notes, glossary; crit S Barney, Spec 56.161; D Fowler, Review 2.211; N Jacobs, English 28.151; A V C Schmidt, N&Q 27.102; T Turville-Petre, RES 30.454).

[3] INFORMATION ABOUT MSS.

Facsimiles. Skeat C-Text (MS 35; C 7.196–240).

Skeat W W, 12 Facsimiles of Old English MSS, Oxford 1892 (MS 18; B 7.115–47).

Greg W W, Facsimiles of 12 Early English MSS in the Libr of Trinity Coll Camb, Oxford 1913 (MS 27; B Prologue 227–1.17).

Chambers R W, R B Haselden and H C Schulz, P P: The Huntington Libr MS (HM 143), San Marino 1936 (entire C-text MS).

Haselden R B, The Fragment of P P in Ashburnham 130, MP 29(1932).391 (MS 32; B 2.208–3.10; also fragmentary text in same MS of B 2.208–3.9).

Chambers R W, A P P MS, Nat Libr of Wales Journ 2(1942).42 (MS 13; A 8.175–9.15).

Kane G, P P: The Evidence for Authorship, London 1965 (MS 51; C 23.40–86, ff 88^b–89^b; also MS 32, front endpaper containing mid-16th-cent authorship ascription. See [11] and [12] below).

Bennett J A W, ed, The Vision of Pierce Plowman, London 1976 (facs of Crowley's 1st impression 1550).

Excerpts. Skeat W W, Parallel Extracts from 29 MSS of P P, EETS 17, London 1866; augmented to 45 MSS, Skeat Glossary, p 831.

Description. Skeat A-Text, p xv (A MSS); Skeat B-Text, p vi (B MSS); Skeat C-Text, p xix (C MSS); Skeat Glossary, p 831 (ABC MSS); Skeat Oxford, 2.lxi (ABC MSS).

Kron R, W Langleys Buch von P dem P, Erlangen 1885.

Chambers R W, The MSS of P P in the Huntington Libr, and Their Value for Fixing the Text of the Poem, Huntington Libr Bull 8(1935).1 (BC MSS 31, 32, 52, 53); material on C MSS rptd as introd to Chambers, Haselden, and Schulz, P P: The Huntington Libr MS (HM 143).

Mitchell A G, A Newly-Discovered MS of the C-Text of P P, MLR 36(1941).243 (MS 49).

Chambers, Nat Libr of Wales Journ 2(1942).42 (MS 13).

Grattan J H G, The Text of P P: A Newly Discovered MS and Its Affinities, MLR 42(1947).1 (MS 12).

Bennett J A W, A New Collation of a P P MS, MÆ 18(1948).21 (MS 52).

Brooks E StJ, The P P MSS in Trinity Coll Dublin, Libr 5s 6(1951).141 (MSS 51 and 15).

Knott-Fowler A-Text, p 22 (A MSS).

Kane A-Text, p 1.

Russell G H and V Nathan, A P P MS in the Huntington Libr, HLQ 26(1963).119 (MS 31).

Tanaka Y, C-Text no MSS ni tsuite (On the MSS of the C-Text), Gifu Univ (Gifu, Japan) Research Report 1(1966).120 (in Japanese).

Dwyer R A, The Appreciation of Handmade Literature, Chaucer Rev 8(1974).221 (MS 11).

Seymour M C, The Scribe of Huntington Libr MS HM 114, MÆ 43(1974).139 (MS 31).

Kane-Donaldson B-Text, p 1.

Rigg A G, Medieval Latin Poetic Anthologies (II), MS 40(1978).387 (contents of MS 38).

Brewer C, A Study of MS Bodley 851, Univ of Toronto thesis 1979 (describes MS 38).

Pearsall D, The 'Ilchester' MS of P P (Univ of London Lib V.88), NM 82(1981).181.

Production and Dissemination. Brandl A, Zu W Langland, Arch 100(1898).334.

(anon), The First Edition of P P, 1550: Notes on Sales, TLS May 11 1922, p 312.

Bennett H S, The Production and Dissemination of Vernacular MSS in the 15th Cent, Libr 5s 1(1946).177.

Illston O, A Literary and Bibliographical Study of the Work of Robert Crowley: Printer, Puritan, and Poet, M A thesis London Univ 1953.

Crawford W R, Robert Crowley's Editions of P P: A Bibliographical and Textual Study, diss Yale Univ 1957.

Doyle A I, ESts 43(1962).55 (Kane A-Text).

Samuels M L, Some Applications of ME Dialectology, ESts 44(1963).81 (36 P P MSS localized by dialect; finds A, B and C texts differ in regional distribution).

Gordan J D, The First Edition of P the P, Printed on Vellum, in J D Gordan, An Anniv Exhibition: The Henry W and Albert A Berg Collection 1940–65, Pt I, Bull of the N Y Public Libr 69(1965).537 (MS 34, Cr^1, printed on vellum).

Hudson A, A Lollard Sermon Cycle and Its Implications, MÆ 40(1971).142.

Doyle A I, The MSS, in ME Alliterative Poetry and Its Literary Background, ed D A Lawton, Cambridge 1982, pp 88, 142n; Eng Books in and out of Court from Edward III to Henry VII, in Eng Court Culture in the Later Middle Ages, ed V J Scattergood and J W Sherborne, London 1983, p 165.

Russell G H, Some Early Responses to the C-Version of P P, Viator 15(1984).275.

Scattergood J, An Unrecorded Fragment of the Prose Lancelot in Trinity Coll Dublin MS 212 (MS 51), MÆ 53(1984).301.

Wood R A, A 14-Cent Owner of P P, MÆ 53(1984).83.

Adams R, The Reliability of the Rubrics of P P B, MÆ 54(1985).208.

[4] CLASSIFICATION OF MSS AND PROBLEMS OF EDITING.

ABC-Texts. [Wright,] Gentleman's Magazine, April 1834, p 385.

Kron R, W Langleys Buch von P dem P, Erlangen 1885, p 18.

Teichmann E, Zum Texte von W Langlands Vision, Angl 15(1893).223.

Carnegy F A R, Problems Connected with the Three Texts of P P, M A thesis London Univ 1923; publ in part in Carnegy, An Attempt to Approach the C-Text, London 1934.

Chambers R W and J H G Grattan, The Text of P P, MLR 26(1931).1; rptd Folcroft Pa 1969.

Grattan J H G, The Text of P P: Critical Lucubrations with Special Reference to the Independent Substitution of Similars, SP 44(1947).593.

Kane G, Textual Criticism of P P, TLS Mar 17 1950, p 176.

A-Text. Chambers R W and J H G Grattan, The Text of P P, MLR 4(1909).357.

Chambers R W, The Original Form of the A-Text of P P, MLR 6(1911).302.

Knott T A, An Essay toward the Critical Text of the A-Version of P the P, MP 12(1914).389.

Chambers R W and J H G Grattan, The Text of P P: Critical Methods, MLR 11(1916).257.

Grattan, MLR 42(1947).1.

Fowler D C, Contamination in MSS of the A-Text of P the P, PMLA 66(1951).495.

Knott-Fowler A-Text, p 22.

Kane A-Text, p 53.

B-Text. Chick E, A Preliminary Investigation of the Pedigree of the B-Text MSS of P P, M A thesis London Univ 1914; results summarized in E Blackman, Notes on the B-Text MSS of P P, JEGP 17(1918).489.

Kane G, P P: Problems and Methods of Editing the B-Text, MLR 43(1948).1.

Donaldson E T, MSS R and F in the B-Tradition of P P, Trans of the Conn Acad of Arts and Sciences 39(1955).177.

Kane-Donaldson B-Text, pp 16, 128.

C-Text. Allen B F, The Genealogy of the C-Text MSS of P P, M A thesis London Univ 1923.

Chambers R W, Huntington Libr Bull 8(1935).1.

Mitchell A G, MLR 36(1941).243.

Bennett J A W, MÆ 18(1948).21.

Donaldson C-Text Poet, p 232 (crit J A W Bennett, MÆ 21.51; M W Bloomfield, MLQ (Wash) 12.230; G R Coffmann, Spec 24.422; N K Coghill, RES ns 2.268; J R Hulbert MP 47.207; B von Lindheim, Angl 71.352; A G Mitchell, MLR 45.3; TLS Feb 10 1950, p 87; H W Wells, Thought 24.707); rptd with new pref and rvsd MS lists, Hamden Conn 1966; excerpt (chap 6, pp 156–98), rptd in E Vasta, ed, Interpretations of P P, Notre Dame Ind 1968, p 130.

Miscellaneous. Coffman G R, The Present State of a Critical Edn of P P, Spec 20(1945).482.

Russell G H, The Evolution of a Poem: Some Reflections on the Textual Tradition of P P, Arts 2(1962).33.

Donaldson E T, The Psychology of Editors of ME Texts, Eng Stud Today 4, Rome 1966, p 45; rptd in Speaking of Chaucer, London 1970, p 102; P P: Textual Comparison and the Question of Authorship, Chaucer u seine Zeit: Symposion für W Schirmer, and A Esch, Tübingen 1968, p 241.

Kane G, Conjectural Emendation, in Medieval Lit and Civilization: Stud in Memory of G N Garmonsway, ed D A Pearsall and R A Waldron, London 1969, p 155; rptd in Medieval MSS and Textual Criticism (Univ of N Carolina Stud in Romance Languages and Lit 173), ed C Kleinhenz, Chapel Hill N C 1976, p 211.

Russell G H, Some Aspects of the Process of Revision in P P, in P P: Critical Approaches, ed S S Hussey, London and N Y 1969, p 27.

Poole E, The Computer in Determining Stemmatic Relationships, Computers and the Humanities 8(1974).207 (applied to P P A-Text 5.105–88).

Hudson A, Middle English, in Editing Medieval Texts, ed A G Rigg, N Y 1977, p 41 (criticizes Kane-Donaldson B-Text).

Kane G, A Short Report on the Athlone Press Edn of P P, Chaucer Newsletter 2(1980).15 (progress of vol III, C-Text, and vol IV, glossary, description of syntax, versification).

Fowler D C, Editorial 'Jamming': Two New Edns of P P, Review 2(1980).211 (rev art on Schmidt B Text 1978, Pearsall C Text 1979).

Russell G H, The Poet as Reviser: The Metamorphosis of the Confession of the Seven Deadly Sins in P P, in Acts of Interpretation: Essays in Honor of E T Donaldson, ed M Carruthers and E D Kirk, Norman Okla 1982, p 53.

Brewer C, Z and the A-, B-, and C-Texts of P P, MÆ 53(1984).194.

Pearsall D, Texts, Textual Criticism, and 15-Cent MS Production, in 15-Cent Stud: Recent Essays, ed R F Yeager, Hamden Conn 1984, p 121.

Schmidt A V C, The Authenticity of the Z Text of P P: A Metrical Examination, MÆ 53(1984).295.

White H, The Z-Text: A New Version of P P?, MÆ 53(1984).290.

Patterson L, The Logic of Textual Criticism and the Way of Genius: The Kane-Donaldson P P in Historical Perspective, in Textual Criticism and Literary Interpretation, ed J J McGann, Chicago 1985, p 55 (see next entry).

Pearsall D, Editing Medieval Texts: Some Developments and Some Problems, in Textual Criticism and Literary Interpretation, p 98.

[5] SELECTIONS.

AESpr, p 327.

Wülcker R P, Ae Lesebuch, Halle 1874–79, 2.29.

Morris Spec, 2.175.

Kluge F, Me Lesebuch, Halle 1904, p 110; 2nd edn 1912, p 98.

Cook A S, A Literary ME Reader, Boston 1915, p 334.

Brandl A and O Zippel, Me Sprach- und Literaturproben, Berlin 1917, p 163; 2nd edn 1927, rptd as ME Lit, N Y 1947.

Sisam K, 14-Cent Verse and Prose, Oxford 1921, p 76; rvsd edns 1937, 1955.

Brunner K and R Hittmair, Me Lesebuch für Anfänger, Heidelberg 1928; 2nd edn 1957, p 35.

Patterson R F, Six Cents of Eng Lit, London 1933, 1.35.

Lieder P R, R M Lovett and R K Root, edd, British Poetry and Prose, Cambridge Mass 1938; 3rd edn 1950, 1.87.

Mossé F, Manuel de l'anglais du moyen age: Pt 2, Moyen anglais, Paris 1949, 1.289; Eng trans, J A Walker, A Handbook of ME, Baltimore 1952, p 258.

Ford B, The Age of Chaucer, London and Baltimore 1954, p 334; rvsd and expanded as Medieval Lit: Chaucer and the Alliterative Tradition, London 1982, p 418.

Kaiser R, Alt- und me Anthologie, Berlin 1954, p 256; 3rd edn rvsd and enlarged 1958; 5th impression (rvsd) 1961, p 305.

Haskell A S, A ME Anthology, N Y 1969, p 140.

Sisam C, The Oxford Book of Medieval Eng Verse, Oxford 1970, p 237.

Dunn C W and E T Byrnes, ME Lit, N Y 1973, p 277.

Kermode F and J Hollander, The Oxford Anthology of Eng Lit, N Y London and Toronto 1973, 1.348.

Burrow J A, ed, Eng Verse 1300–1500, London and N Y 1977.

[6] TRANSLATIONS AND MODERNIZATIONS.

Warren K M, The Vision of P P, London and N Y 1895 (B Prologue and Pas 1–7; crit E Teichmann, AnglB 6.166); rvsd edn 1899.

Skeat W W, The Vision of P P, London 1905 (B Prologue and Pas 1–7).

Pancoast H S and J D Spaeth, Early Eng Poems, N Y 1911, p 155 (selections from B).

Burrell A, P P: The Vision of a People's Christ, London 1912; rvsd 1931 (complete B).

Weston J L, Romance, Vision and Satire, Boston 1912, p 241 (B Prologue and A Pas 1–8).

Neilson W A and K G T Webster, The Chief British Poets of the 14 and 15 Cents, Boston 1916, p 48 (A Prologue and Pas 1–8); rptd in Sir Gawayne and the Green Knight, Boston 1917, p 30.

Attwater D, A Version of the Vision of William Concerning P the P, London 1930 (B Prologue and Pas 1–7); new trans D and R Attwater, London and N Y 1957.

Klett W, trans, The Vision of William Concerning P the P, Bonn 1935 (German trans of B-text).

Wells H W, W Langland: The Vision of P P, N Y 1935 (B-text, with additions from C-text); rptd 1945.

Loomis R S and R Willard, Medieval Eng Verse and Prose, N Y 1948, p 294 (selections from ABC texts).

Coghill N K, Visions from P P, London 1949 (selections chiefly from B).

Spencer H et al, British Lit: Old Eng to 1800, Lexington Mass 1952; 3rd edn 1974, p 96 (A Prologue and part of B Pas 13).

Goodridge J F, ed, P the P, Baltimore 1959; rvsd 1966; rptd (Prologue and Pas 1–7) in The Lit of Medieval England, ed D W Robertson, N Y 1970, p 423.

Oiji T, trans, P P A-Text (trans into Japanese), Banjō 8(1960).47; 9(1961).61; 10(1962).34; 12 (1963).17.

Abrams M H, gen ed, Norton Anthology of Eng Lit, N Y 1962; 4th edn 1979, 1.329 (verse modernization by E T Donaldson of B Prologue and Pas 5).

Ikegami T, trans, Nōfu Piers no Meisō (P P's Meditations), Shi to Sanbun (Poetry and Prose, Tokyo) 16–22 (1967–70); translator's note, Shinsensha, Feb 1975, p 245 (crit Y Terasawa, Eigo Seinen [The Rising Generation] 121.170).

Williams M R, trans, P the P by William Langland, N Y 1971 (alliterative verse trans, with introd).

Oiji, trans, P P B-Text (trans into Japanese), Tokyo 1974 (crit S Ono, Shūkan Dokushojin [Weekly: The Reader] 1040.6; Eigo Seinen 120.288).

Brook S, P P, N Y 1975 (selections from B with parallel modernization).

Tiller T, The Vision of P P: A Trans into Modern Eng Verse, London 1982.

[7] TEXTUAL NOTES.

Kölbing E, EStn 5(1882).150 (B 5.328, atte newe faire).

Brown W H, MLN 7(1892).268 (A 5.70, vernisch).

Shute H W, Arch 100(1898).155 (B 1.41, sueth/ seeth).

Bradley H, MLR 2(1906–07).163 (A 2.87 and 101, moillere).

Onions C T, MLR 3(1908).170; MLR 4(1909).507 (C 1.215, reed/reik); see also: G T Flom, MLN 23(1908).156; C T Onions, MLN 23(1908).231 (reply to Flom); A G Mitchell, MÆ 8(1939).118.

Fisher A W, MLN 23(1908).231 (B 5.28–29).

Bradley H, MLR 5(1910).340 (B 6.328–29; also 13.150–51, half a laumpe lyne ex vi transicionis); on B 13.151, see also B H Smith Jr, MLN 76(1961).675; R E Kaske, JEGP 62(1963).32, rptd in Style and Symbolism in P P, ed R J Blanch, Knoxville 1969, p 228; A Middleton, ELH 39(1972).179; E C Schweitzer, JEGP 73(1974).313.

Hemingway S B, MLN 32(1917).57 (B 15.281).

Fairchild H N, MLN 41(1926).378 (B 6.124, aliri); see also: C Brett, MLR 22(1927).260; E Colledge, MÆ 27(1958).111; M Jeremy, ELN 1(1964).250.

A R K, Amer Speech 2(1927).215 (C 7.144, ypar-roked/parked).

Withycombe E G, TLS Apr 7 1927, p 251 (B 5.402, Robin Hood); see also: R M Wilson, The Lost Lit of Medieval England, London 1952, rvsd edn 1970, p 117; R B Dobson and J Taylor, Rymes of Robyn Hood, Pittsburgh 1976.

Balogh J, Spec 3(1928).580 (B Prologue 141, rex a recte regendo).

von Bonsdorff I, MP 26(1928).57 (Haukyn/Han-kyn).

Day M, MLR 26(1931).336 (A 2.183, din/doom; reply to Chambers and Grattan, MLR 26.29).

Coghill N K, RES 8(1932).303 (A 7.212, naket; B 6.226, nauȝty); see also M Day, RES 8(1932).445 (B 6.226; C 9.233).

Day, MLR 27(1932).317 (B 5.500, mele tyme of seintes).

Coghill, MÆ 4(1935).83 (B 10.291, 317–26, Abbot of Abingdon); see also G D G Hall, MÆ 28(1959).91.

Ashton J W, ELH 5(1938).195 (B 5.402, Randolph Earl of Chester); see also R M Wilson, The Lost Lit of Medieval England, p 117.

Hort G, P P and Contemporary Religious Thought, N Y 1938 (appendix identifies 216 Biblical quotations as from the Breviary).

Richardson M E, TLS Mar 11 1939, p 149 (B 5.226, Rose); TLS Jan 13 1940, p 24 (B 5.189, Heruy); N&Q 180(1941).116 (B 15.538, Bishop of Bethlehem); see also D C Fowler, MP 77(1979).158 (B 15.554–56, Bishop is Simon Sudbury).

Sledd J, MLN 55(1940).379 (C 6.65–69).

Spencer H, MLN 58(1943).48 (B Prologue 78, worth both his eres; B 5.194; C 7.201); on B Prologue 78, see also: A G Mitchell, MLN 59(1944).222; G K W Johnston, N&Q ns 6(1959).243.

Bennett J A W, MLR 40(1945).309 (B 5.251, Lombards' letters).

Mitchell A G, LMS 1(1948, for 1939).483 (C 2.95, lordene; on 3.16–18, 4.140–42, 4.77–120 disputes readings and punctuation of Carnegy 1934 and Skeat).

Cassidy F G, MLN 63(1948).52 (B 1.182, Malkyn's merit).

Kellogg A L, Spec 24(1949).413, and Trad 14 (1958).385 (C 2.111, pedem/sedem); both rptd in Chaucer, Langland, Arthur: Essays in ME Lit, New Brunswick N J 1972, pp 29, 32; see also R G Risse Jr, PQ 45(1966).712.

Kaske R E, PQ 31(1952).427 (B 3.195, brass).

Mustanoja T, NM 55(1954).57 (Knott-Fowler A-Text, Pas 1.92–93, riden and rappen doun, and variant ryden at randoun).

Bloomfield M W, PQ 35(1956).60 (B 17.252; C 20.218, pardons of Pamplona).

Orrick A H, PQ 35(1956).213 (A 4.33, declynede).

Kaske, JEGP 56(1957).177 (B 18.249–51, Gigas the Giant); MLN 72(1957).481 (B 10.300–05, paradisus claustralis); JEGP 58(1959).650 (B 11.251–53, kirnelle of conforte).

Kellogg A L, Langland's Canes Muti (B 10.287), Essays in Literary Hist in Honor of Milton French, ed R Kirk and C F Main, New Brunswick N J 1960, p 25; rptd in Chaucer, Langland, Arthur: Essays in ME Lit, p 51.

Bennett J A W, N&Q ns 7(1960).364 (B Prologue 132–38, sum rex, sum princeps, etc); see also B M H Strang, N&Q ns 7(1960).436 (variants: vestiri for vestire, nudum vis for nudum ius).

Oliphant R, N&Q ns 7(1960).167 (B 5.321, Sire Piers of Pridie).

Bowers R H, N&Q 8(1961).327 (C 22.247, foleuyles laws).

Fuller A H, Scripture in P P B, MS 23(1961).352 (revises and augments list of Vulgate quotations in Skeat Notes, p 503).

Schoeck R J, Harvard Theol Rev 54(1961).21 (B 15.115ff, use of pseudo-Chrysostom Opus Imperfectum).

Johnston G K W, AN&Q 1³ (Nov 1962).35 (B 3.160–61).

Strang B M H, N&Q ns 10(1963).286 (B 5.491–92).

Jochums M C, N&Q ns 11(1964).44 (C 18.222; also B Prologue 128, voice from heaven).

d'Ardenne S T R O, ESts 45 suppl(1964).143 (A Prologue 6, ferly/feyrie).

Schmidt A V C, N&Q ns 14(1967).365 (A 10.91–94; suggests Summa de Vitiis of Jean de la Rochelle as source); N&Q ns 15(1968).168 (C 11.51, free wit); N&Q ns 16(1969).285 (C 4.335–409, mede, mercede; B 4.275, donum dei); on C 4.335–409, see also M Amassian and J Sadowsky, Mede and Mercede: A Study of the Grammatical Metaphor in P P, NM 72(1971).457.

Polak L, N&Q 17(1970).282 (A 6.8–16, Babylon and Armenia).

Baird J, Secte and Suit Again: Chaucer and Langland, Chaucer Rev 6(1971).117 (B 5.495–504); see also T D Hill, RES 24(1973).444 (B 5.503).

Taitt P, N&Q 18(1971).284 (C 2.25–28, Lot and his daughters).

Alford J A, MP 69(1972).323 (B 18.390, til parce it hote).

Middleton A, Two Infinites: Grammatical Metaphor in P P, ELH 39(1972).169 (B 13.119–32).

Hill T D, The Light That Blew the Saints to Heaven, RES 24(1973).444 (B 5.495–503).

Alford, MÆ 43(1974).133 (B 14.22–27, Haukyn's coat); Some Unidentified Quotations in P P, MP 72(1974).390 (sources for over 35 Latin quotations; refers to Skeat with cross refs to Kane A-Text).

Demedis P, Expl 33(1974), item 27 (B Prologue 196, mase); see also T J Wertenbaker, Expl 34(1975), item 51.

Hill, NM 75(1974).92 (B 11.161–67; B 1.115–24); N&Q ns 22(1975).531 (B 16.88; liturgical source); N&Q ns 23(1976).291 (B 19.95–103).

Lupack A C, Expl 34(1975), item 31 (B 7.116, pure tene).

Lindemann E C D, Analogues for Latin Quotations in Langland's P P, NM 78(1977).359 (finds 13 non-Biblical Latin quotations accounting for 35 occurrences of Latin in P P).

St-Jacques R, N&Q ns 24(1977).483 (B 17.1, Spes, a spy).

Regan C L, John Gower, John Barleycorn, and William Langland, AN&Q 16(1977).102.

Hill, N&Q ns 25(1978).200 (C 11.193, Christ's thre clothes).

Matheson L M, An Example of Ambiguity and Scribal Confusion in P P, ELN 15(1978).263 (scribal treatment of word misshapes, B 7.94, etc).

Fowler D C, Review 2(1980).211 (cruces and emendations in Schmidt B Text 1978, Pearsall C Text 1979).

Olmert M, Troilus in P P: A Contemporary View of Chaucer's Troilus, Chaucer Newsletter 2, ii(1980).13 (C 21.321, troyledest).

Harley M P, The Derivation of Hawkin and Its Application in P P, Names 29(1981).97 (Hawkyn; relationship to David K of Israel).

Schmidt A V C, Langland, Chrysostom, and Bernard: A Complex Echo, N&Q 30(1983).108 (Kane-Donaldson B-Text, 1.188–89).

Alford, More Unidentified Quotations in P P, MP 81(1984).278.

Biggs F M, Aungeles Peeris: P P B 16.67–72 and C 18.85–100, Angl 102(1984).426 (cites Kane-Donaldson B-Text, Pearsall C-Text).

Heffernan C F, P P B 1.153 (Kane-Donaldson B-Text), Eng Lang Notes 22(1984).1.

Schmidt A V C, A Covenant More than Courtesy: A Langlandian Phrase in Its Context, N&Q 31(1984).153.

Whatley G, P P B 12.277–94: Notes on Language, Text, and Theology, MP 82(1984).1 (Kane-Donaldson B-Text, 12.290, allowed).

[8] LANGUAGE.

Bernard E, W Langland: A Grammatical Treatise, Bonn 1874.

Teichmann E, Die Verbalflexion in W Langleys Buch von P dem P, diss Tübingen, Aachen 1887.

Wandschneider W, Zur Syntax des Verbums in Langleys Vision of W, diss Kiel, Leipzig 1887.

Klapprott L, Das ende -e in W Langlands Buch von P dem P, Text B, Göttingen 1890.

Dobson M, An Examination of the Vocabulary of the A-Text of P the P, Angl 33(1910).391.

Chambers R W, The Three Texts of P P and Their Grammatical Forms, MLR 14(1919).129 (argues with Manly; see [12] below).

Schiff E, Studien zur Syntax Langlands, diss Wien 1926.

Oakden J P, Alliterative Poetry in ME, Manchester 1930–35, 1.61.

Kittner H, Studien zum Wortschatz W Langlands, Halle 1937.

Klett W, Wörter im Sinnbereich der Gemeinschaft bei W Langland, Bonn 1939.

Mossé F, Un cas d'ambiguite syntactique en Moyen Anglais: I Was Wery For Wandred, EA 5 (1952).289; L Spitzer, Le type Moyen Anglais I Was Wery for Wandred et ces paralleles romans,

NM 55(1954).161; reply M L Samuels, ESts 36(1955).310.

Grant C M, A Vocabulary Study of Skeat's Edition of the A-Text of P P, diss Univ of Okla 1956; DA 17.850.

Ryan W M, Modern Idioms in P P, Amer Speech 34(1959).67.

Käsmann H, Studien zum kirchlichen Wortschatz des Me 1100–1350: Ein Beitrag zum Problem der Sprachmischung, Tübingen 1961.

Miura T, P P no Ing-Form Oboegaki (Notes on the Ing-form in P P), Pt 1, Research (Kōbe Univ Lit Group) 23(1961).19; Pt 2, Prelude (Kōbe) 5 (1961).1 (in Japanese).

Swieczkowski W, Word Order Patterning in ME, The Hague 1962 (quantitative analysis comparing P P and a group of ME sermons).

Samuels M L, ESts 44(1963).81 (dialect of ABC MSS).

Tajima S, Langland ni Okeru Verbals (Verbals in Langland), Pt 1, Participles, Cairn (Kyūshū Univ) 8(1966).76; Pt 2, Gerund, and Pt 3, Infinitive, Bungei to Shisō (Literary Art and Thought, Fukoaka Women's College) 31(1968).29 and 32 (1968).1 (in Japanese).

Jordan R, Handbuch der me Grammatik, 3rd edn Heidelberg 1968; trans E J Crook, Handbook of ME Grammar: Phonology, The Hague 1974, p 11 (West Midland dialect illustrated by Staffordshire MSS of P P).

Itō K, P P B ni Mochirareta Kankeidaimeishi ni tsuite (On the Use of the Relative Pronoun in P P B), Osaka Women's Junior Coll Bull 19 (1975).99; P P B ni Mochirareta Futeishi ni tsuite (On the Use of the Infinitive in P P B), Aisen Women's Junior Coll Bull 12, 13(1978).1 (in Japanese).

Blake N F, The Eng Language in Medieval Lit, SN 48(1975).59; also The Eng Language in Medieval Lit, London 1977.

Kane G, Poetry and Lexicography in the Translation of P P, Medieval and Renaissance Stud 9(1982).33.

Samuels M L, Langland's Dialect, MÆ 54(1985).232.

[9] VERSIFICATION.

PFMS, 3.xi.

Rosenthal F, Die alliterierende engl Langzeile im 14 Jahrhundert, Angl 1(1878).418.

Luick K, Die engl Stabreimzeile im 14, 15, und 16 Jahrhundert, Angl 11(1889).429.

Kaluza M, Strophische Gliederung in der me rein alliterierenden Dichtung, EStn 16(1892).169; M Day, Strophic Division in ME Alliterative Verse,

EStn 66(1931–32).245; J R Hulbert, Quatrains in ME Alliterative Poems, MP 48(1950).73 (agrees with Kaluza, arguing that P P A composed in quatrains); H N Duggan, Strophic Patterns in ME Alliterative Poetry, MP 74(1977).223.

Teichmann E, Zur Stabreimzeile in Langlands Buch von P dem P, Angl 13(1891).140.

Lawrence J, Chapters on Alliterative Verse, London 1893, p 101.

Schipper J, Grundriss der engl Metrik, Vienna and Leipzig 1895, p 83; A Hist of Eng Versification, Oxford 1910, p 93.

Fischer J and F Mennicken, Zur me Stabzeile, BBA 11(1901).133.

Schneider A, Die me Stabzeile im 15 und 16 Jahrhundert, BBA 12(1902).103.

Saintsbury G, A Hist of Eng Prosody, London 1906, 1.179; Historical Manual of Eng Prosody, London 1910, rptd N Y 1966, p 153.

Deakin M, The Alliteration of P P, MLR 4(1908–09).478.

Schumacher K, Studien über den Stabreim in der me Alliterationsdichtung, Bonn 1914.

Leonard W E, The Scansion of ME Alliterative Verse, Wisconsin Univ Stud 11(1920).72 (P P compared to metrical romances).

Day M, Alliteration of the Versions of P P in Its Bearing on Their Authorship, MLR 17 (1922).403.

Stewart G R, The Meter of P P, PMLA 42(1927).113.

Oakden J P, Alliterative Poetry in ME, Manchester 1930–35, 1.153; A Survival of a Stylistic Feature of Indo-European Poetry in Germanic, Especially in ME, RES 9(1933).50.

Hulbert J R, A Hypothesis Concerning the Alliterative Revival, MP 28(1931).413.

Koziol H, Zur Frage der Verfasserschaft einiger me Stabreimdichtungen, EStn 67(1932).165; Grundzüge der Syntax der me Stabreimdichtungen, Vienna 1932.

Stüdl J, Das Versmass in Langlands Vision Concerning P the P, diss Wien 1936.

Stobie M M R, The Influence of Morphology on ME Alliterative Poetry, JEGP 39(1940).319.

Clemoes P, Liturgical Influence on Punctuation in Late Old English and Early ME MSS, Occasional Papers, Dept of Anglo-Saxon, Cambridge 1952, 1.21.

Ivy G S, The Make-Up of ME Verse MSS, PhD thesis London Univ 1954 (copyists' practices with prose and verse lines).

Southworth J G, Verses of Cadence: An Introd to the Prosody of Chaucer and His Followers, Oxford 1954; suppl Oxford 1962, p 25 (punctuation in P P MSS).

Waldron R A, Oral-Formulaic Technique and ME Alliterative Poetry, Spec 32(1957).792.

Salter E, The Alliterative Revival, MP 64(1966).146 (Pt 1), 233 (Pt 2); P P and the Simonie, Arch 203(1966–67).241.

Blake N F, Rhythmical Alliteration, MP 67 (1970).122.

Covella F D, Formulaic Second Half-Lines in Skeat's A-Text of P P: Norms for a Comparative Analysis of the A, B and C texts, diss N Y Univ 1972; DAI 33.2887A.

Eby J A, The Alliterative Meter of P P A, diss Univ of Mich 1972; DAI 32.3948A.

Kane-Donaldson B-Text, p 131, and crit (see above under [2], *B-Text*).

Sapora R W, A Theory of ME Alliterative Meter, with Critical Applications, diss Univ of Conn 1976; DAI 36.7395A; publ in Spec Anniv Monographs 1, Cambridge Mass 1977.

Lawton D A, Form and Style in ME Unrhymed Alliterative Verse: Studies in the Formal Corpus, diss Univ of York 1977; DAI 37.674C.

Turville-Petre T, The Alliterative Revival, Cambridge and Totowa N J 1977.

Neufeldt V E, The Metric of Eng Alliterative Verse: P P and Beowulf, diss Univ of Toronto 1978; DAI 39.2226A.

Salter, Alliterative Modes and Affiliations in the 14 Cent, NM 79(1978).25.

Lawton, Gaytryge's Sermon, Dictamen, and ME Alliterative Verse, MP 76(1979).329.

Beckwith M A, The Alliterative Meter of P P, Comitatus 12(1981).31.

Kane G, Music Neither Unpleasant nor Monotonous, Medieval Stud for J A W Bennett, ed P L Heyworth, Oxford 1981, p 43.

Lawton, ME Alliterative Poetry: An Introd, in Lawton, ed, Middle English Alliterative Poetry and Its Literary Background, Cambridge 1982, pp 1, 125n.

Pearsall D, The Alliterative Revival: Origins and Social Backgrounds, in Lawton, ed, 1982, pp 34, 132n.

Schmidt A V C, The Authenticity of the Z-Text of P P: A Metrical Examination, MÆ 53(1984).295.

[10] DATE.

A-Text. Skeat A-Text, p xxxi; Skeat Oxford, 2.ix (1362).

Cargill O, The Date of the A-Text of P P, PMLA 47(1932).354 (1376).

Huppé B F, The A-Text of P P and the Norman Wars, PMLA 54(1939).37 (1373).

Bennett J A W, The Date of the A-Text of P P, PMLA 58(1943).566 (completed by 1370).

Bloomfield M W, P P as a 14-Cent Apocalypse, New Brunswick N J 1961, p 89 (1362–65).

B-Text. Skeat B-Text, p ii; J J Jusserand, Revue Critique, Oct 25 1879, p 313; Skeat Glossary, p 877; Skeat Oxford, 2.xi (1377).

Kellogg E H, Bishop Brunton and the Fable of the Rats, PMLA 50(1935).57.

Devlin M A, The Chronology of Bishop Brunton's Sermons, PMLA 51(1936).300; on the relation of Brunton's sermons to P P, see below under [13], *General Themes*.

Huppé B F, The Date of the B-Text of P P, SP 38(1941).34 (1377–81); P P: The Date of the B-Text Reconsidered, SP 46(1949).6 (1377–79).

Gwynn A, The Date of the B-Text of P P, RES 19(1943).1 (1376–77).

Bennett J A W, The Date of the B-Text of P P, MÆ 12(1943).55 (1377–79).

C-Text. Skeat C-Text, p xi; Skeat Oxford, 2.xxxiv (1393).

Jusserand J J, L'Epopée mystique de W Langland, Paris 1893; Eng trans, rvsd and enlarged, P P: A Contribution to the Hist of Eng Mysticism, London 1894, reissued 1965, p 56 (1398–99).

Devlin M A, The Date of the C Version of P the P, Univ of Chicago Abstracts of Theses, Humanistic Series 1925–26, Chicago 1928, 4.317 (before 1387).

Coghill N K, Two Notes on P P, MÆ 4(1935).83 (1393–94).

Bennett J A W, MÆ 21(1952).51.

[11] AUTHORSHIP.

Author's Name. Ritson J, Bibliographica Poetica, London, 1802, p 26.

Silverstone, The Vision of P P, N&Q 2s 6(1858).229 (transcribes annotations dated 1577 in Rogers' 1561 edn; these name Robertus Langland as the poet).

Skeat A-Text, p xxxiv; Skeat Glossary, p xxii; Skeat Oxford, 2.xxvii.

Pearson C H, North British Rev 52(1870).244.

Skeat W W, William Langley or Langland, The Eng Poets, ed T H Ward, London 1881, 1.91; John of Malvern and P the P, Acad Mar 18 1893(vol 43, no 1089).242.

Macaulay G C, The Name of the Author of P P, MLR 5(1910).195.

Bright A H, New Light on P P, Preface by R W Chambers, London 1928 (crit M Day, RES 6.92; J R Hulbert, MLN 45.203; H R Patch, EStn 68.112; H Schöffler, AnglB 41.295; TLS Feb 7 1929, p 94).

Cargill O, The Langland Myth, PMLA 50(1935).36.

Haselden R B and H C Schulz, Note on the Inscription in HM 128, Huntington Libr Bull 8(1935).26.

Chambers R W, Robert or William Longland?, LMS 1(1948, for 1939).430.

Brooks E StJ, Libr 5s 6(1951).141.

Kane G, The Autobiographical Fallacy in Chaucer and Langland Studies, London 1965; P P: The Evidence for Authorship, London 1965 (crit TLS Aug 12 1965, p 698; G Bourquin, EA 19.439; D F Chapin, Humanities Assoc Bull 17.71; D C Fowler, ELN 3.295; R E Kaske, JEGP 65.583; P M Kean, RES 17.303; J Lawlor, MLR 61.268; B Raw, N&Q ns 12.470; T A Stroud, MP 65.366; P J Verhoeff, Neophil 51.312).

Author's Life and Opinions. Hiatt C T J, W Langland, N&Q 7s 11(1891).108; St Swithin, N&Q 7s 11(1891).235.

Jusserand J J, L'Epopée mystique de W Langland, Paris 1893; Eng trans, rvsd and enlarged, P P: A Contribution to the Hist of Eng Mysticism, London 1894, reissued 1965, p 59.

Hopkins E M, The Character and Opinions of W Langland, Kansas Univ Quart 2(1894).233; The Education of W Langland, Princeton Coll Bull 7(1895).41; Who Wrote P P?, Kansas Univ Quart 7(1898).1; Notes on P P, Kansas Univ Quart 8(1899).29.

Mensendieck O, Characterentwicklung und ethisch-theologischen Anschauungen des Verfassers von P the P, Leipzig and London 1900.

Jack A S, The Autobiographical Elements in P the P, JEGP 3(1901).393.

Bannister A T, W Langland's Birthplace, TLS Sep 7 1922, p 569; A H Bright, TLS Mar 12 1925, p 172.

Bright A H, W Langland's Early Life, TLS Nov 5 1925, p 739; TLS Sep 9 1926, p 596; New Light on P P, London 1928, p 58; Langland and the Seven Deadly Sins, MLR 25(1930).133.

Day M, RES 8(1932).445.

Krog F, Autobiographische oder typische Zahlen in P P, Angl 58(1934).318.

Peregrinus, Langland at Great Malvern, N&Q 181(1941).121; A R Bayley, N&Q 181(1941).181.

Bloomfield M W, Was W Langland a Benedictine Monk?, MLQ (Wash) 4(1943).57.

Donaldson C-Text Poet, p 199; see crit TLS Feb 10 1950, p 87.

[12] AUTHORSHIP CONTROVERSY.

"Lost Leaf" and "Misplaced Lines." Manly J M, The Lost Leaf of P the P, MP 3(1906).359 (rptd EETS 135B); P P and Its Sequence, CHEL, 2.1 (rptd EETS 135B).

Bradley H, The Misplaced Leaf of P the P, Athen Apr 21 1906 (rptd EETS 135B).

Furnivall F J, Foreword to the reprinting of preceding items, EETS 135B, London 1908.

Brown C E, The Lost Leaf of P the P, Nation 88(1909).298; H Bradley, Nation 88(1909).436; T A Knott, Nation 88(1909).482.

Hall T D, The Misplaced Lines, P P A 5.236–41, MP 7(1909–10).327.

Chambers R W, The Authorship of P P, MLR 5(1910).1 (rptd EETS 139e); H Bradley, MLR 5(1910).202 (rptd EETS 139f).

Coulton G G, P P: One or Five, MLR 7(1912).102, 372.

John But. Bradley H, MLR 5(1910).202; Who Was John But?, MLR 8(1913).88.

Chambers, The Original Form of the A-Text of P P, MLR 6(1911).302.

Rickert E, John But, Messenger and Maker, MP 11(1913).107.

Style and Thought. Manly, CHEL, 2.1.

Hall T D, Was Langland the Author of the C-Text of the Vision of P P?, MLR 4(1908–09).1.

Deakin M, The Alliteration of P P, MLR 4(1908–09).478.

Jusserand J J, P P: The Work of One or of Five, MP 6(1909).271; J M Manly, The Authorship of P P, MP 7(1909).83; Jusserand, P P: The Work of One or of Five: A Reply, MP 7(1910).289 (items rptd as EETS 139b, c, and d).

Mensendieck O, Die Verfasserschaft der drei Texte des P the P, ZfVL 18(1910).10; The Authorship of P P, JEGP 9(1910).404.

Dobson M, An Examination of the Vocabulary of the A-Text of P the P, Angl 33(1910).391.

EETS Extra Vol 139b–e, The P P Controversy, London 1910 (reprinting of: Jusserand, MP 6, 7; Manly, MP 7; Chambers, MLR 5; Bradley, MLR 5, sometimes bound in as EETS 139f).

Moore S, Studies in P the P, MP 11(1913).177; MP 12(1914).19.

Görnemann G, Zur Verfasserschaft und Entstehungsgeschichte von P the P, diss Marburg, Heidelberg 1915 (crit R W Chambers and J H G Grattan, MLR 26.1; E Eckhardt, EStn 50.428; B Fehr, LfGRP 37.173).

Manly J M, The Authorship of P the P, MP 14(1916).315.

Knott T A, Observations on the Authorship of P the P, MP 14(1916).531; MP 15(1917).23.

Chambers R W, The Three Texts of P P and Their Grammatical Forms, MLR 14(1919).129.

Day M, Alliteration of the Versions of P P in Its Bearing on Their Authorship, MLR 17(1922).403.

Chambers, Long Will, Dante, and the Righteous Heathen, E&S 9(1924).50.

Day, Duns Scotus and P P, RES 3(1927).333; G Sanderlin, The Character Liberum Arbitrium in the C-Text of P P, MLN 56(1941).449.

Adams M R, The Use of the Vulgate in P P, SP 24(1927).556.

Day, The Revisions of P P, MLR 23(1928).1.

Krog F, Studien zu Chaucer und Langland, Heidelberg 1928 (crit J Koch, LfGRP 50.19).

Chambers R W and J H G Grattan, The Text of P P, MLR 26(1931).1.

Chambers, Incoherencies in the A- and B-Texts of P P and Their Bearing on the Authorship, LMS 1(1948 for 1939).27.

Dunning T P, P P: An Interpretation of the A-Text, Dublin and London 1937 (crit J A W Bennett, MÆ 7.232; N Coghill, MLR 33.577; H Koziol, EStn 73.263; F Krog, AnglB 49.202); excerpts rptd in E Vasta, ed, Interpretations of P P, Notre Dame Ind 1968, p 87; 2nd edn rvsd and ed by T P Dolan, Oxford 1980 (crit J A Alford, Spec 57.367).

Huppé B F, The Authorship of the A- and B-Texts of P P, Spec 22(1947).578.

Hulbert J R, P the P after Forty Years, MP 45(1948).215.

Donaldson C-Text Poet.

Stroud T A, Manly's Marginal Notes on the P P Controversy, MLN 64(1949).9.

Meroney H, The Life and Death of Longe Wille, ELH 17(1950).1.

Fowler D C, The Relationship of the Three Texts of P the P, MP 50(1952).5; E T Donaldson, The Texts of P P: Scribes and Poets, MP 50(1952).269; A G Mitchell and G H Russell, The Three Texts of P the P, JEGP 52(1953).445.

Fowler, John Trevisa and the Eng Bible, MP 58(1960).81; New Light on John Trevisa, Trad 18(1962).289.

Fowler, P the P: Literary Relations of the A and B Texts, Seattle 1961 (crit M W Bloomfield, Spec 37.120; G Bourquin, EA 15.277; S S Hussey, RES 14.277; G Kane, MÆ 32.230; R E Kaske, JEGP 62.208; P Mertens-Fouck, Moyen Age 70.590; D W Robertson Jr, MLQ 23.84; R M Wilson, MLR 57.627).

Kane G, P P: The Evidence for Authorship, London 1965, p 1.

Donaldson E T, P P: Textual Comparison and the Question of Authorship, Chaucer u seine Zeit: Symposion für W Schirmer, ed A Esch, Tübingen 1968, p 241.

Covella F D, Formulaic Second Half-Lines in Skeat's A-Text of P P: Norms for a Comparative Analysis of the A, B and C Texts, diss N Y Univ 1972; DAI

33.2887A; Grammatical Evidence of Multiple Authorship in P P, Language and Style 9(1976).3.

Fowler, A Pointed Personal Allusion in P P, MP 77(1979).158 (date and authorship).

DiMarco V, 18-Cent Suspicions Regarding the Authorship of P P, Angl 100(1982).124.

[13] SOURCES.

Specific Works. Skeat W W, Fragments of Yorkshire Mysteries, Acad Jan 4 1890 (vol 37, no 922), pp 11, 27 (source of B Pas 18.1–68).

Owen D L, P P: A Comparison with Some Earlier and Contemporary French Allegories, London 1912; rptd Folcroft Pa 1971.

Gollancz I, ed, Winner and Waster, London 1920 (Select Early Eng Poems 3), preface.

Adams M R, The Use of the Vulgate in P P, SP 24(1927).556.

Day M, Duns Scotus and P P, RES 3(1927).333; G Sanderlin, The Character Liberum Arbitrium in the C-Text of P P, MLN 56(1941).449.

Cornelius R D, P P and the Roman de Fauvel, PMLA 47(1932).363.

Sullivan C, The Latin Insertions and the Macaronic Verse in P P, Washington 1932; G Hort, P P and Contemporary Religious Thought, N Y 1938, appendix; A H Fuller, Scripture in P P B, MS 23(1961).352; J A Alford, Some Unidentified Quotations in P P, MP 72(1974).390; E C D Lindemann, Analogues for Latin Quotations in P P, NM 78(1977).359; Alford, MP 81(1984).278.

Hazelton R M, Two Texts of the Disticha Catonis and Its Commentary with Special Reference to Chaucer, Langland and Gower, diss Rutgers Univ 1956; DA 16.1899.

Quick A W, Langland's Learning: The Direct Sources of P P, diss Univ of Toronto 1982; DAI 43.3905A.

Schmidt A V C, Langland's 'Book of Conscience' and Alanus de Insulis, N&Q 29(1982).482.

Alford, MP 81(1984).278.

Allen J B, Langland's Reading and Writing: Detractor and the Pardon Passus, Spec 59(1984).342.

See also [7] above.

General Themes. Traver H, The Four Daughters of God, Phila 1907, p 147; The Four Daughters of God: A Mirror of Changing Doctrine, PMLA 40(1925).44.

Spalding M C, The ME Charters of Christ, BrynMawrMon 15, Baltimore 1914 (A Pas 2.60–82).

Eberhard O, Der Bauernaufstand vom Jahre 1381 in der engl Poesie, Heidelberg 1917, p 16.

Baum P F, The Fable of Belling the Cat, MLN 34(1919).462.

Powell C L, The Castle of the Body, SP 16 (1919).197.

Knowlton E C, Nature in ME, JEGP 20(1921).197.

Owst G R, The Angel and the Goliardys of Langland's Prologue, MLR 20(1925).270 (crit C Brett, MLR 22.261); restated in Owst, Lit and Pulpit in Medieval England, Cambridge 1933, p 576; 2nd edn rvsd Oxford 1961; rptd N Y 1966; excerpt (pp 548–75) rptd in E Vasta, ed, Interpretations of P P, Notre Dame Ind 1968, p 22.

Owst, Preaching in Medieval England, Cambridge 1926.

Schneider R, Der Mönch in der engl Dichtung, Leipzig 1928, p 43.

Pantin W A, A Medieval Collection of Latin and Eng Proverbs and Riddles, JRLB 14(1930).101; see also: B G Hall, Sources of P P, TLS May 1 1930, p 370; A H Bright, TLS Apr 24 1930, p 352.

Cornelius R D, The Figurative Castle, Bryn Mawr 1930.

Gaffney W, The Allegory of the Christ Knight in P P, PMLA 46(1931).155; M LeMay, The Allegory of the Christ-Knight in Eng Lit, diss Catholic Univ, Washington DC 1932.

Byrne M, The Tradition of the Nun in Medieval England, Washington 1932, p 168.

Mohl R, The Three Estates in Medieval and Renaissance Lit, N Y 1933, p 103.

Kirk R, References to the Law in P the P, PMLA 48(1933).322.

Kleinecke W, Engl Fürstenspiegel von Policraticus ... zum Basilikon Doron König Jacobs I, Halle 1937, p 127.

Marcett M E, Uhtred de Boldon, Friar William Jordan and P P, N Y 1938; M D Knowles, The Censured Opinions of Uthred de Boldon, Proc Brit Acad 37(1951).305; M W Bloomfield, Piers Plowman as a 14-Cent Apocalypse, New Brunswick N J 1962, ch 3; G H Russell, The Salvation of the Heathen: The Exploration of a Theme in P P, Journ Warburg and Courtauld Institutes 29(1966).101.

Devlin M A, The Angel of the B-Text Prologue: Bishop Thomas Brunton and his Sermons, Spec 14(1939).324; Devlin, ed, The Sermons of Thomas Brinton, Bishop of Rochester 1373–89, Camden 3s vols 85–86, London 1954; M W Bloomfield, Apocalypse, ch 3; M A Gallemore, The Sermons of Bishop Thomas Brinton and the B-Text of P P, diss Univ of Wash 1967; DA 27.3008A.

Freyhan R, The Evolution of the Caritas Figure in the 13 and 14 Cents, Journ Warburg and Courtauld Institutes 11(1948).68.

Maguire C, Franciscan Elements in the Thought of P P, diss Fordham Univ 1951; abstr Fordham Univ Diss 18.63.

Bloomfield M W, The Seven Deadly Sins: An Introd to the Hist of a Religious Concept, East Lansing Mich 1952 (crit D Fowler, MLN 69.289).

Freyhan, Joachim and the Eng Apocalypse, Journ Warburg and Courtauld Institutes 18(1955).211.

Hussey S S, Langland, Hilton, and the Three Lives, RES ns 7(1956).132; rptd in E Vasta, ed, Interpretations of P P, Notre Dame Ind 1968, p 232; C K Pankhurst, The Active Life, the Contemplative Life, and the Mixed Life: A Study of the Three Lives with Special Reference to Walter Hilton, diss Univ of York 1976; DAI 37.473C; Steele F J, Definitions and Depictions of the Active Life in ME Religious Lit of the 13, 14, and 15 Cents, including Special Reference to P P, diss Oxford Univ 1977.

Bloomfield, Joachim of Flora: A Critical Survey of His Canon, Teachings, Sources, Biography and Influence, Trad 12(1957).247; P P and the Three Grades of Chastity, Angl 76(1958).227.

O'Grady G L, P P and the Medieval Tradition of Penance, diss Univ of Wisc 1962; DA 23.2117.

Yunck J A, The Lineage of Lady Meed: The Development of Medieval Venality Satire, Notre Dame Publications in Medieval Stud 8, South Bend Ind 1963.

Spearing A C, The Art of Preaching and P P, in Criticism and Medieval Poetry, London 1964; 2nd edn 1972, p 107; rptd in Chaucer and His Contemporaries, ed H Newstead, N Y 1968, p 255.

DiPasquale P Jr, The Form of P P and the Liturgy, diss Univ of Pittsburgh 1965; DA 26.4626.

Owen N H, Thomas Wimbledon's Sermon, Redde rationem villicationis tue, Medieval Stud 28 (1966).176; I K Knight, ed, Wimbledon's Sermon, Duquesne Stud, Philological Ser 9, Pittsburgh Pa 1967.

St-Jacques R, Langland's Christ-Knight and the Liturgy, Revue de l'Université d'Ottawa 37 (1967).144.

Wenzel S, The Sin of Sloth: Acedia in Medieval Thought and Literature, Chapel Hill N C 1967; The Seven Deadly Sins: Some Problems for Research, Spec 43(1968).1.

Beale W H III, The Medieval Topic of Active and Contemplative Life, diss Columbia Univ 1969; DA 32.6365A.

Dunning T P, Action and Contemplation in P P, in S S Hussey, ed, P P: Critical Approaches, London and N Y 1969, p 213.

St-Jacques R, The Liturgical Associations of Langland's Samaritan, Trad 25(1969).217; Conscience's Final Pilgrimage and the Cyclical Structure of the Liturgy, Revue de l'Université d'Ottawa 40(1970).210.

Alford J A, P P and the Tradition of Biblical Imitatio, diss Univ of N C Chapel Hill 1970; DAI 32.3536A.

Barney S A, The Plowshare of the Tongue: The Progress of a Symbol from the Bible to P P, MS 35(1973).261.

Birnes W J, Patterns of Legality in P P, diss N Y Univ 1974; DAI 35.1040A.

Bond R B, A Study of Invidia in Medieval and Renaissance Eng Lit, diss Univ of Toronto 1974; DAI 35.1087A.

Taitt P S, The Quest Theme in Representative Eng Works of the 13 and 14 Cents, diss Univ of British Columbia 1974; DAI 35.3703A.

Harvey E R, The Inward Wits: Psychological Theory in the Middle Ages and Renaissance, Warburg Institute Surveys 6, London 1975.

Adams R, Langland and the Liturgy Revisited, SP 73(1976).266.

Smith M, P P and the Tradition of the Medieval Life of Christ, diss Princeton Univ 1976; DAI 37. 1571A.

Tristram P, Figures of Life and Death in Medieval Lit, London 1976, p 197 (Harrowing of Hell).

Alford, Lit and Law in Medieval England, PMLA 92(1977).944 (Harrowing of Hell).

Coolidge S A, The Grafted Tree in Lit: A Study of Medieval Iconology and Theology, diss Duke Univ 1977; DAI 38.2107A.

Emmerson R K, The Coming of Antichrist: An Apocalyptic Tradition in Medieval Lit, diss Stanford Univ 1977; DAI 37.7739A.

St-Jacques, Langland's Bells of the Resurrection and the Easter Liturgy, Eng Stud in Canada 3 (1977).129.

Dronke P, Arbor Caritatis, in Medieval Stud for J A W Bennett, ed P L Heyworth, Oxford 1981, p 207.

Emmerson R K, Antichrist in the Middle Ages: A Study of Medieval Apocalypticism, Art, and Lit, Seattle 1981 (crit R E Lerner, Spec 57.601; R B Herzman, Stud in the Age of Chaucer 5.164).

Lindquist M A, P P and Manuals of Religious Instruction, diss Indiana Univ 1981; DAI 42.3992A.

Alford, The Grammatical Metaphor: A Survey of Its Use in the Middle Ages, Spec 57(1982).728.

Ashley K, The Guiler Beguiled: Christ and Satan as Theological Tricksters in Medieval Religious Lit, Criticism 24(1982).126.

Sears E L, The Ages of Man in Medieval Art, diss Yale Univ 1982; DAI 45.1560A.

Braswell M F, The Medieval Sinner: Characterization and Confession in the Lit of the Eng Middle Ages, London and Toronto 1983.

Carlson P J, The Grammar of God: Grammatical Metaphor in P P and Pearl, diss Columbia Univ 1983; DAI 44.2467A.

Emmerson R K, The Prophetic, the Apocalyptic, and the Study of Medieval Lit, in Poetic Prophecy in Western Lit, ed R-J Frontain and J Wojcik, London and Cranbury NJ 1984, p 40.

Fowler D C, The Bible in ME Lit, Seattle 1984.

Whatley G, The Uses of Hagiography: The Legend of Pope Gregory and the Emperor Trajan in the Middle Ages, Viator 15(1984).35.

Adams R, Some Versions of Apocalypse: Learned and Popular Eschatology in P P, in The Popular Lit of Medieval England, ed T J Heffernan, Knoxville Tenn 1985, p 194.

Allen J B, Reading and Looking Things Up in Chaucer's England, Chaucer Newsletter 7(1985).1 (on Langland's reading).

[14] COMPARISONS AND LATER RELATIONSHIPS.

Skeat W W, PFMS, 3.49 (influence on Death and Life).

Thomas M C, Sir Gawayne and the Green Knight, Zurich 1883, p 27 (relationship to Pearl poet).

Bellezza P, Langland and Dante, N&Q 8s 6(1894). 81; Di alcune notevoli coincidenzie tra la Divina Comedia e la Visione di Pietro l'Aratore, Rendicanti del Regio Instituto Lombardo di Scienze e Littere, Ser II, 29, Milano 1897; Langlands Figure des Plowman in der neuesten engl Literatur, EStn 21(1895).325 (Tennyson, Macaulay).

Schofield W H, The Nature and Fabric of the Pearl, PMLA 19(1904).202.

Keiller M M, The Influence of P P on the Macro Play of Mankind, PMLA 26(1911).339.

Burdach K, Über den Ursprung des Humanismus, Deutsche Rundschau 159(1914).72 (P P and German Protestantism).

M[onroe] H, Chaucer and Langland, Poetry 6 (1917).297.

Bateson H, ed, Patience, 2nd rvsd edn, Manchester 1918, p xxiv.

Hanford J H, Dame Nature and Lady Life, MP 15(1918).121 (Death and Life).

Hanford J H and J M Steadman, Death and Liffe: An Alliterative Poem, SP 15(1918).246.

Gollancz I, ed, Saint Erkenwald, London 1922 (Select Early Eng Poems 4), p liv.

Chambers R W, Long Will, Dante, and the Righteous Heathen, E&S 9(1924).50.

Iijima I, Langland and Chaucer, Boston 1925.

Patch H R, Characters in Medieval Lit, MLN 40(1925).10 (comparison with Chaucer).

Gollancz I and M Day, edd, Death and Liffe, London 1930 (Select Early Eng Poems 5), p 12.

Marx K, Das Nachleben von P P bis zu Bunyans The Pilgrim's Progress, diss Freiburg, Quakenbrück 1931.

McGinnis E, P P in Eng Lit to 1625, unpubl diss Yale Univ 1932.

Lucas F L, Studies French and Eng, London 1934, p 23 (Langland and Hesiod).

Coghill, MÆ 4(1935).83.

Day M and R Steele, edd, Mum and the Sothsegger, EETS 199, London 1936, p xiv.

Chambers R W, Robert or William Longland?, LMS 1(1948 for 1939).430; Poets and Their Critics: Milton and Langland, Proc Brit Acad 27 (1941).109.

White H C, Social Criticism in Popular Religious Lit of the 16 Cent, N Y 1944, p 1 (influence of P P).

Donna R B, Despair and Hope: A Study in Langland and Augustine, Washington 1948.

Kane G, The ME Verse in MS Wellcome 1493, LMS 2(1951).54 (verbal and formal influence of P P).

Smith A H, The ME Lyrics in Addit MS 45896, LMS 2(1951).33 (similarities to P P).

Peter J D, Complaint and Satire in Early Eng Lit, Oxford 1956 (comparison with Chaucer).

Burrow J, The Audience of P P, Angl 75(1957).373.

Hamilton A C, Spenser and Langland, SP 55 (1958).533.

Burrow J A, An Approach to Dream of the Rood, Neophil 43(1959).132 (compares poem to Harrowing of Hell in P P).

Elliott R W V, Landscape and Rhetoric in ME Alliterative Poetry, Melbourne Crit Rev 4(1961).65.

Fisher J H, Wyclif, Langland, Gower, and the Pearl-Poet on the Subject of Aristocracy, Stud in Medieval Lit in Honor of A C Baugh, ed M Leach, Phila and London 1961, p 139.

Hamilton A C, The Visions of P P and the Faerie Queene, in Form and Convention in the Poetry of Spenser, EIE, N Y 1961, p 1.

Woolf R, Some Non-Medieval Qualities of P P, EC 12(1962).111.

Yoshida S, Chiyosa no Shukyosei—Chiyosa to Rangurando (Chaucer's Religious Character; Chaucer and Langland), Jinbunkenkyū (Studies in Humanities; Osaka City College) 13(1962).1 (in Japanese).

Kratins O, P P and Arthurian Romance, EC 13(1963).304.

Muscatine C, The Locus of Action in Medieval Narrative, RomP 17(1963).122.

Anderson J H, Aspects of Allegory in P P and the Faerie Queene, diss Yale Univ 1965; DA 26.4622; The Growth of a Personal Voice: P P and The Faerie Queene, New Haven 1976.

Higgs E D, The Dream as a Literary Framework in the Works of Chaucer, Langland, and the Pearl Poet, diss Univ of Pittsb 1965; DA 27.1030A.

Hussey S S, Langland's Reading of Alliterative Poetry, MLR 60(1965).163.

Kane G, The Autobiographical Fallacy in Chaucer and Langland Studies, London 1965.

Howard D, The Three Temptations: Medieval Man in Search of the World, Princeton N J 1966, p 163.

Kinney T L, The Temper of 14-Cent Eng Verse of Complaint, Annuale Mediaevale 7(1966).74.

Tuve R, Allegorical Imagery: Some Medieval Books and Their Posterity, Princeton N J 1966.

Heyworth P L, Jack Upland's Rejoinder: A Lollard Interpolator and P P B Pas 10.249ff, MÆ 36 (1967).242.

Hieatt C, The Realism of Dream Visions: The Poetic Exploitation of the Dream Experience in Chaucer and His Contemporaries, The Hague and Paris 1967, p 89.

Oiji T, P P no Shūhen—tokuni Death and Liffe, Der Ackermann, Jack Upland ron so ni tsuite (On the Periphery of P P, particularly Death . . . Jack Upland Debate), Bull of the Coll of Liberal Arts of Tōhoku Univ (Sendai) 6(1967).1 (in Japanese).

Jones F, Dickens and Langland in Adjudication upon Meed, Victorian Newsletter 33(1968).53.

McNamara J F, Responses to Ockhamist Theology in the Poetry of the Pearl-Poet, Langland and Chaucer, diss Louisiana State Univ 1968; DA 29.3148A.

Bennett J A W, Chaucer's Contemporary, in S S Hussey, ed, P P: Critical Approaches, London and N Y 1969, p 310.

Elliott T J, Complaint as a ME Genre: A Survey of the Tradition Culminating in the School of P P, diss Univ of Mich 1970; DAI 31.4116A.

Blythe J H, Images of Wrath: Lydgate and Langland, diss Univ of N C Chapel Hill 1971; DAI 32.908A.

Burrow J A, Ricardian Poetry: Chaucer, Gower, Langland and the Pearl-Poet, New Haven and London 1971 (crit M W Bloomfield, Spec 48.345; G C Britton, N&Q ns 20.29; D Farley-Hills, RES 23.325; A B Friedman, ELN 11.126; J B Friedman, JEGP 73.241; M C Seymour, ESts 54.274; T A Stroud, MP 71.71; R M Wilson, MLR 67.612).

Calì P, Allegory and Vision in Dante and Langland, Cork 1971.

Globe A V, Apocalyptic Themes in the Sybilline Oracles, the Revelation, Langland, Spenser and Marvell, diss Univ of Toronto 1971; DAI 32.918A.

Shepherd G, The Nature of Alliterative Poetry in Late Medieval England, Proc Brit Acad 57 (1971).57.

Matlock C M, An Interpretation of P P Based on the Medieval Dream Background, diss SUNY Albany 1972; DAI 33.2940A.

Means M, The Consolatio Genre in Medieval Eng Lit, Univ of Fla Monographs 36, Gainesville 1972, p 66.

Muscatine, Poetry and Crisis in the Age of Chaucer, Notre Dame Ind and London 1972, p 71.

Tsuru H, Dōjidai no Futari no Sakka—Chaucer to Langland (Two Contemporaries: Chaucer and Langland), Yokahama National Univ Humanities Bull, Section 2: Language and Lit 19(1972).1 (in Japanese).

Hertzig M J, The Early Eng Recension and Continuity of Certain ME Texts in the 16 Cent, diss Univ of Penn 1973; DAI 34.1913A.

Mann J, Chaucer and Medieval Estates Satire, Cambridge 1973, p 207.

Medcalf S, P P and the Ricardian Age in Lit, Lit and Western Civilization, vol 2: The Medieval World, general edd D Daiches and A Thorlby, London 1973, p 643.

Faris D E, Symbolic Geography in ME Lit: Pearl, P P, Ywain and Gawain, diss Yale Univ 1974; DAI 34.7228A.

Fries M, Images of Women in ME Lit, CE 35(1974).851 (Lady Meed).

Hill J M, ME Poets and the Word: Notes toward an Appraisal of Linguistic Consciousness, Criticism 16(1974).154.

Holloway J B, The Figure of the Pilgrim in Medieval Poetry, diss Univ of Calif Berkeley 1974; DAI 35.2225A (Dante, Langland, Chaucer).

Blamires A G, Mum and the Sothsegger and Langlandian Idiom, NM 76(1975).583.

Carriere J L, Boethian Narrative Structure in 14-Cent Eng Lit, diss UCLA 1975; DAI 36.5273A.

King J N, Robert Crowley's Editions of P P: A Tudor Apocalypse, MP 73(1975).342.

Mussetter S A, The Reformation of the Pilgrim to the Likeness of God: A Study of the Tropological Level of the Divine Comedy and P P B, diss Cornell Univ 1975; DAI 36.8035A.

Anhorn J S, Sermo Poematis: Homiletic Traditions in Purity and P P, diss Yale Univ 1976; DAI 37.3605A.

Isaacson M K, The Unachieved Quest for Social Reformation from the Roman de Carité to P P, diss Stanford Univ 1976; DAI 36.6076A.

McCully J R Jr, Conceptions of P P: 1550s through 1970s, diss Rice Univ 1976; DAI 37.2164A.

Schotter A H, The Sacramental and Satirical Use of Formulas of Luxury in ME Alliterative Poetry (Gawain, P P, Pearl, Purity), diss CUNY 1976; DAI 37.4344A.

Spearing A C, Medieval Dream Poetry, Cambridge 1976, p 138.

Stock L K, Patience and Sloth in Two ME Works: Mankind and P P C, diss Cornell Univ 1976; DAI 36.7446A.

Wenzel S, Chaucer and the Language of Contemporary Preaching, SP 73(1976).138.

Keenum K G, 14-Cent Allegory: Radical, Descriptive and Mixed, diss Univ of Texas Austin 1977; DAI 37.7740A.

Kelly R L, Hugh Latimer as P P, Stud in Eng Lit 17(1977).13.

Möske B, Caritas: Ihre figurative Darstellung in der engl Literatur des 14 bis 16 Jahrhunderts, Bonn 1977.

Nolan B, The Gothic Visionary Perspective, Princeton 1977, p 205.

Oiji T, Tudor Ōchiyō no Okeru Nōfu Piers no Unmei (The Fate of P P in the Tudor Period), Middle Ages and Renaissance, ed T Oiji and P Milward, Tokyo 1977, p 105 (in Japanese).

Braswell M F, Confession and Characterization in the Lit of the Late Middle Ages, diss Emory Univ 1978; DAI 39.2246A; The Medieval Sinner, London and Toronto 1983.

Russell J S, The Grammar of the Dream Vision, diss Johns Hopkins Univ 1978; DAI 39.2250A.

Erzgräber W, Langland, Chaucer, Gower, in Europäisches Spätmittelalter (Neues Handbuch der Literaturwissenschaft 8), ed W Erzgräber, Wiesbaden 1978, p 221.

Palmer B D, 'To speke of wo that is in mariage': The Marital Arts in Medieval Lit, in Human Sexuality in the Middle Ages and Renaissance, ed D Radcliffe-Umstead, Pittsb 1978, p 3.

Caie G, Engelsk poesi mod slutningen af det 14 århundrede med særligt henblik på P P, in Kulturblomstring og samfundskrise i 1300-tallet, ed B P McGuire, Copenhagen 1979, p 40.

Ovitt G O Jr, Time as a Structural Element in Medieval Lit, diss Univ of Massachusetts 1979; DAI 40.4587A, chap 2.

Aers D, Chaucer, Langland, and the Creative Imagination, London and Boston 1980 (crit V Rothschild, TLS 6 Aug 1980, p 901; P Strohm, Criticism 22.376; B Harwood, Review 3.323; E D Higgs, Stud in the Age of Chaucer 3.121; J D Burnley, RES 33.309; B Nolan, Spec 58.139).

Mills D, The Dreams of Bunyan and Langland, in The Pilgrim's Progress: Critical and Historical Views, ed V Newey, Totowa N J 1980, p 154.

Schmidt A V C, Langland and the Mystical Tradition, in The Medieval Mystical Tradition in England 1, ed M Glasscoe, Exeter 1980, p 17.

Burrow J, Langland Nel Mezzo del Cammin, in Medieval Stud for J A W Bennett, ed P L Heyworth, Oxford 1981, p 21.

Holloway J B, Medieval Liturgical Drama, the Commedia, P P, and the Canterbury Tales, American Benedictine Rev 32(1981).114.

Kane G, Langland and Chaucer: An Obligatory Conjunction, in New Perspectives in Chaucer Criticism, ed D L Rose, Norman Okla 1981, p 5.

Perry S P, 'Trewe Wedded Libbynge Folk': Metaphors of Marriage in P P and the Canterbury Tales, diss Northwestern Univ 1981; DAI 42.2125A.

Boitani P, Eng Medieval Narrative in the 13 and 14 Cents, trans J K Hall, Cambridge 1982, p 72.

Bourquin G, The Dynamics of the Signans in the Spiritual Quest, in The Medieval Mystical Tradition in England 2, ed M Glasscoe, Exeter 1982, p 182 (P P, mystics, religious drama).

Lawton D A, ed, ME Alliterative Poetry and Its Literary Background, Cambridge 1982 (collection of original essays, listed separately).

Middleton A, The Audience and Public of P P, in Lawton, ed, 1982, pp 101, 147n.

Miller P S, The Medieval Literary Theory of Satire and Its Relevance to the Works of Gower, Langland, and Chaucer, diss Queen's Univ Belfast 1982; DAI 44.9/68c.

Johnson B A, From P P to Pilgrim's Progress: The Generic and Exegetical Contexts of Bunyan's 'Similitude of a Dream,' diss Brown Univ 1983; DAI 44.2154A.

Lawton, The Unity of ME Alliterative Poetry, Spec 58(1983).72.

Salter E, Alliterative Verse and P P, in 14-Cent Eng Poetry: Contexts and Readings, Oxford 1983, pp 86, 199n.

Schmidt A V C, The Treatment of the Crucifixion in P P and in Rolle's Meditations on the Passion, in Spiritualität heute und gestern, Analecta Cartusiana 35, Salzburg 1983, p 174.

Baker D N, Dialectic Form in Pearl and P P, Viator 15(1984).263.

Baldwin A, The Tripartite Reformation of the Soul in the Scale of Perfection, Pearl, and P P, in The Medieval Mystical Tradition in England 3, ed M Glasscoe, Woodbridge, Suffolk 1984, p 136.

Braswell M F, Poet and Sinner: Literary Characterization and the Mentality of the Late Middle Ages, 15-Cent Stud 10(1984).39.

Bridges M, The Sense of an Ending: The Case of the Dream-Vision, Dutch Quart Rev of Anglo-American Letters 14(1984).81.

Economou G D, Self-Consciousness of Poetic Activity in Dante and Langland, in Vernacular Poetics in the Middle Ages, ed L Ebin, Kalamazoo Mich 1984, p 177.

Lawes R W, The Heaven of the 14-Cent Eng Poets: An Examination of the Paradisaical References in the Eng Works of Chaucer, Gower, Langland, and the Pearl Poet, diss Univ of Mississippi 1984; DAI 45.111A.

Ralston M E, A Typology of Guides in Medieval Lit, diss Auburn Univ 1984; DAI 45.111A.

[15] GENERAL INTERPRETATION.

Gilman A, Our Earliest Allegory, Appleton's Journal 6(1871).243.

Hanscom E D, The Argument of the Vision of P P, PMLA 9(1894).403.

Jusserand J J, L'Epopée mystique de W Langland, Paris 1893; Eng trans, rvsd and enlarged, P P: A Contribution to the Hist of Eng Mysticism, London 1894, reissued 1965, p 153.

Burdach K, Der Dichter des Ackermann aus Böhmen und seine Zeit, Berlin 1926–32, 1.140.

Wells H W, The Construction of P P, PMLA 44(1929).129; rptd in Middle English Survey, ed E Vasta, Notre Dame Ind 1965, p 147, and in E Vasta, ed, Interpretations of P P, Notre Dame Ind 1968, p 1.

Nishiwaki J, Langland, Eibei Bungaku Hyōden Sōsho (Eng Lit Critical Biography Ser) 2, Tokyo 1933 (in Japanese).

Carnegy F A R, The Relation between the Social and Divine Order in . . . P the P, Breslau 1934 (crit H Caplan, MLN 51.561; N Coghill, MÆ 4.47; TLS Sept 20 1934, p 639).

Dawson C, Medieval Religion, London 1934, p 157; rptd Medieval Essays, N Y 1954, p 239.

Saito T, Langland no Seishijidai (The Age of Langland), Eigo Seinen (The Rising Generation) 71(1934).265 (in Japanese).

Coghill N K, Introd to H W Wells, W Langland: The Vision of P P, N Y 1935; rptd 1945 (modernization).

Traversi D A, The Vision of P P, Scrut 5(1936).276; rvsd and rptd in The Age of Chaucer, ed B Ford, p 129; rvsd in rvsd edn of Ford, Medieval Lit: Chaucer and the Alliterative Tradition, London 1982, p 188.

Dunning T P, P P: An Interpretation of the A-Text, Dublin and London 1937.

Glunz H H, Literarästhetik des europäischen Mittelalters, Bochum-Langendreer 1937, p 520.

Hort G, P P and Contemporary Religious Thought, N Y 1938 (crit M Deanesley, History 23.160).

Stone G W, An Interpretation of the A-Text of P P, PMLA 53(1938).656.

Wells H W, The Philosophy of P P, PMLA 53(1938).339; rptd in E Vasta, ed, Interpretations of P P, Notre Dame Ind 1968, p 115.

Chambers R W, Man's Unconquerable Mind, London 1939, p 88.

Coulton G G, Medieval Panorama, Cambridge 1939; 2nd edn 1946, p 534.

Gerould G H, The Structural Integrity of P P B, SP 45(1948).60.

Donaldson C-Text Poet.

Kane G, ME Lit, London 1951, p 182.

Robertson D W Jr and B F Huppé, P P and Scriptural Tradition, Princeton 1951 (crit TLS July 25 1952, p 477; M W Bloomfield, Spec 27.245; S Brook, RES 4.150; T P Dunning, MÆ 24.23; R W Frank, MLN 68.194; F Mossé, EA 6.57; S Neuijen, ESts 34.79; R Quirk, JEGP 52.253); excerpts rptd in E Vasta, Interpretations of P P, p 190.

Smith A H, P P and the Pursuit of Poetry, London 1951; rptd in R J Blanch, ed, Style and Symbolism in P P, Knoxville 1969, p 26.

Spiers J, Chaucer the Maker, London 1951, p 208.

Tillyard E M, The Eng Epic and Its Background, London 1954, p 151.

Cejp L, An Interpretation of P the P, Philologica 7(1955).17 (suppl to Časopis pro Moderni Filologii, Československa Akademie, vol 37).

Erzgräber W, W Langlands P P im Lichte der mittelalterlichen Philosophie und Theologie, Angl 73(1955).127.

Suddaby E, The Poem P P, JEGP 54(1955).91.

Cejp, An Introd to the Study of Langland's P P, B-Text, Acta Universitatis Palackianae Olomucensis 9, Olomouc 1956 (in Eng with summary in Czech).

Dunning T P, The Structure of the B-Text of P P, RES ns 7(1956).225; rptd in: E Vasta, Interpretations of P P, p 259; R J Blanch, Style and Symbolism in P P, p 87.

Erzgräber W, William Langlands P P: Eine Interpretation des C-Textes, Frankfurter Arbeiten aus dem Gebiete der Anglistik und Amerika-Studien 3, Heidelberg 1957 (crit M W Bloomfield, Angl 76.550; D C Fowler, MLQ 20.285).

Frank R W Jr, P P and the Scheme of Salvation: An Interpretation of Dowel, Dobet and Dobest, New Haven 1957 (crit G Bourquin, EA 11.245; T P Dunning, RES 11.67; W Erzgräber, Angl 77.83; D C Fowler, MLQ 20.285; S S Hussey, MLR 54.84; R E Kaske, MLN 74.730; J Lawlor, MÆ 28.215; S Neuijen, ESts 42.248; D W Robertson Jr, Spec 33.395; T Silverstein, MP 56.204); excerpt rptd in E Vasta, Interpretations of P P, p 298.

Lawlor J, The Imaginative Unity of P P, RES ns 8(1957).113; rptd in: E Vasta, Interpretations, p 278; R J Blanch, Style and Symbolism, p 101.

Tanaka Y, Nōfu Piers Kenkyūjyuron (Introd to P P Studies), Iwate Univ (Morioka Japan) Research Annual 12(1957).19 (in Japanese).

Zeeman (Salter) E, P P and the Pilgrimage to Truth, E&S ns 11(1958).1; rptd in: E Vasta, ed, ME Survey, Notre Dame Ind 1965; rptd 1968, p 195; R J Blanch, Style and Symbolism, p 117.

Adams J F, The Dreamer's Quest for Salvation in P P, diss Univ of Wash 1960; DA 21.1553.

Bloomfield M W, P P as a 14-Cent Apocalypse, Centennial Review of Arts and Sciences (Mich State Univ) 5(1961).281; rptd in E Vasta, Interpretations, p 339; Bloomfield, P P as a 14-Cent Apocalypse, New Brunswick N J 1961 (crit G Bourquin, EA 16.70; T P Dunning, RES 16.188; D C Fowler, MLQ 24.410; S Greenfield, Comp Lit 15.374; S S Hussey, N&Q 10.232; R E Kaske, JEGP 62.202; J Lawlor, MLR 57.89; G Mathew, MÆ 32.72; E Standop, Arch 201.134; R E Sullivan, Spec 39.121).

Cejp, The Methods of Medieval Allegory and Langland's P the P, Acta Universitatis Palackianae Olomucensis, Facultas Philosophica, Philologica 5, Prague 1961 (in Czech, summarized in Eng).

Fowler D C, P the P: Literary Relations of the A and B Texts, Seattle 1961.

Yoshida S, Nōfu Piers no Meiso (The Meditations of P P), Jinbunkenkyū (Studies in the Humanities, Osaka City Coll) 12(1961).1 (in Japanese).

Coghill N K, God's Wenches and the Light That Spoke: Some Notes on Langland's Kind of Poetry, Eng and Medieval Stud Presented to J R R Tolkien, ed N Davis and C L Wrenn, London 1962, p 200; rptd in H H Newstead, Chaucer and His Contemporaries, Essays on Medieval Literature and Thought, Greenwich Conn 1968, p 236.

Lawlor J, P P: An Essay in Criticism, London 1962 (crit M W Bloomfield, Spec 38.369; G Bourquin, EA 17.289; D S Brewer, Listener 68.1061; J Burrow, Critical Quart 5.380; S S Hussey, N&Q 10.351; P M Kean, RES 14.395; TLS Nov 1 1963, p 888).

Salter E, P P: An Introd, Cambridge Mass 1962 (crit M W Bloomfield, MP 62.62; D S Brewer, Listener 67.567; B Cottle, JEGP 62.213; T P Dunning, MÆ 33.147; R W Frank Jr, Spec 40.751; S S Hussey, RES 14.279).

Ōyama T, Langland, Lecture on the Hist of Eng Lit I: Middle Ages, Tokyo 1962, p 51 (in Japanese).

Bruneder H, Personifikation und Symbol in William Langlands P P, Wien 1963.

Sen Gupta J, P P, Essays in Criticism 13(1963).201.

Thimmesh H, A Synoptic Reading of Central Themes in P P, diss Cornell Univ 1963; DA 24.3733.

Coghill N, Langland: P P, Writers and Their Work 174, London and N Y 1964.

Colledge E and W O Evans, P P, Month 32 (1964).304.

Davlin M C, Treuthe in P P: A Study in Style and Sensibility, diss Univ of Calif Berkeley 1964; DA 25.1905.

Vasta E, The Spiritual Basis of P P, The Hague 1965.

Carruthers M J, The Mind of Will: A Pref to P P, diss Yale Univ 1965; DA 26.4625.

Holleran J V, The Role of the Dreamer in P P, Annuale Mediaevale 7(1966).33.

Saito I, A Study of P P with Special Reference to the Pardon Scene of the Visio, Tokyo 1966.

Case A M, The Pursuit of Wisdom: A Study of the Knowledge of Good and Evil in P P, diss Yale Univ 1968; DA 29.562A.

Engels H, P P: Eine Untersuchung der Textstruktur mit einer Einleitung zur mittelalterlichen Allegorie, diss Köln 1968; abstr in Eng and American Stud in German, ed W Habicht, Tübingen 1968, p 26.

Hammond D F, The Narrative Art of P P, diss Univ of Fla 1968; DA 29.870A.

Ryan W M, William Langland, Twayne's Eng Authors Ser 66, N Y 1968.

Vasta E, ed, Interpretations of P P, Notre Dame Ind 1968 (collects previously published essays).

Blanch R J, ed, Style and Symbolism in P P, Knoxville 1969 (collects previously published essays).

Hussey S S, ed, P P: Critical Approaches, London and N Y 1969 (collection of original essays, introd by Hussey; crit J Lawlor, Yearbook of Eng Stud 2.237).

Milowicki E J, P P and the Ways of Providence: A Study of Structure in Relation to Content, diss Univ of Oregon 1969; DA 29.3582A.

Murtaugh D M, P P and the Image of God, diss Yale Univ 1969; DA 29.876A; book of same title, Gainesville Fla 1978.

Trower K B, The Plowman as Preacher: The Allegorical and Structural Significance of P the P in P P, diss Univ of Ill 1969; DAI 30.712A.

Ames R M, The Fulfillment of the Scriptures: Abraham, Moses, and Piers, Evanston Ill 1970.

Harwood B J, P P and the Ways of Knowing, diss SUNY Buffalo 1970; DAI 31.4772A.

Chessell D, The Word Made Flesh: The Poetry of Langland, Critical Rev 14(1971).109.

Crewe J V, Langland's Vision in P P, Theoria 39(1971).1.

Kirk E, The Dream Thought of P P, New Haven and London 1972 (crit D C Fowler, MP 71.393; P M Kean, RES 25.72; J Kerling, ESts 56.256; J Lawlor, MLR 69.369; D Pearsall, JEGP 72.543; B Raw, N&Q ns 20.437; K Trower, Costerus ns 1.151; D J Williams, YWES 53.90).

Lichstein D P, P P: An Image of Neo-Platonic Christendom, diss Univ of Penn 1972; DAI 33.1690A.

Malard S G, The Rhetorical Structure of P P C, diss Univ of Mich 1972; DAI 33.2334A.

Adams I R, Narrative Techniques and the Apocalyptic Mode of Thought in P P, diss Univ of Va 1973; DAI 33.3627A.

Carruthers M, The Search for St Truth: A Study of Meaning in P P, Evanston Ill 1973.

Cull F C D, P P as a Christocentric Poem: The Rule of Christ as Prophet, Priest, and King, unpubl MPhil thesis Univ of York 1973.

Curran S T, The Dreamer and His Visions: Rhetorical Determinants of Structure in P P B, diss Univ of Wisc Madison 1973; DAI 34.3339A.

Higgs E D, The Path to Involvement: The Centrality of the Dreamer in P P, Tulane Stud Eng 21 (1974).1.

Aers D, P P and Christian Allegory, London 1975.

Arn M J, The Function of Duality and Trinity in the Structure of P P, diss SUNY Binghamton 1975; DAI 35.6088A.

Baker D N, Langland's Artistry: The Strategy and Structure of P P, diss Univ of Va 1976; DAI 36.6109A.

Martin P E, Studies in Modes of Allegorical Discourse in Langland's P P, diss Univ of East Anglia 1976.

Radigan J D, The Clouded Vision: Satire and the Way to God in P P B, diss Syracuse Univ 1976; DAI 36.6712A.

Pritchard G W, Law, Love, and Incarnation: An Interpretation of P P, diss Yale Univ 1977; DAI 38.286A.

Bourquin G, P P: Études sur la genèse littéraire des trois versions, Paris 1978 (crit G Kane, Spec 55.526; R W Lister, RES 31.336; D Pearsall, MLR 77.915).

Johnson W T, The Prophecy of William Langland, diss Univ of Calif Irvine 1978; DAI 38.5451A.

Bonner J H, The Half-Acre and the Barn: Structural and Thematic Unity in the Visio and Vita of P P, diss Indiana Univ 1979; DAI 40.839A.

Martin P, P P: The Field and the Tower, N Y 1979 (crit M Carruthers, Stud in the Age of Chaucer, 3.161; B Harwood, Review 3.323).

Murtaugh D M, P P and the Image of God, Gainesville Fla 1978 (crit B Harwood, Review 3.323).

Bertz D, Langland's P P and Poetic Time: Time, History, and Temporal Aspects of Narrative in the

B-Text, diss Univ of Toronto 1981; DAI 42. 1156A.

Goldsmith M E, The Figure of P P: The Image on the Coin (P P Stud 2), Cambridge and Totowa N J 1981 (crit P Neuss TLS 23 April 1982, p 470; R Adams, Stud in the Age of Chaucer 5.141; J A Alford, Spec 59.146).

Harwood B J, Subtlety and Sabotage in P P, Review 3(1981).323 (rev art on Murtaugh 1978, Martin 1979, Aers 1980).

Carruthers M J, Time, Apocalypse, and the Plot of P P, in Acts of Interpretation, ed Carruthers and Kirk, 1982, p 175.

Kee J M, P P and the Limits of Mediation, diss Univ of Virginia 1982; DAI 43.2680A.

Middleton A, MAPping the Field: P P at Claremont, Chronica no 30(Spring 1982).2 (report on P P papers read at Feb 1982 meeting of Medieval Assoc of the Pacific, Claremont Calif).

Norton-Smith J, William Langland, Leiden 1983.

Stokes M, Justice and Mercy in P P: A Reading of the B Text Visio, London 1984.

[16] DISCUSSION OF PARTICULAR PROBLEMS.

Sellert F, Das Bild in P the P, Rostock 1904.

Jones H S V, Imaginatif in P P, JEGP 13(1914).583.

Döring G, Die Personennamen in Langlands P the P, Leipzig 1922.

Troyer H W, Who is P P?, PMLA 47(1932).368; rptd in R J Blanch, ed, Style and Symbolism in P P, Knoxville 1969, p 156.

Coghill N K, The Character of P P Considered from the B-Text, MÆ 2(1933).108; rptd in E Vasta, ed, Interpretations of P P, Notre Dame Ind 1968, p 54.

Durkin J T, Kingship in the Vision of P P, Thought 14(1939).413.

Dunning T P, Langland and the Salvation of the Heathen, MÆ 12(1943).45.

Coghill, The Pardon of P P, Proc Brit Acad 30(1944).303; rptd in Blanch, Style and Symbolism, p 40.

Mathew G, Justice and Charity in the Vision of P P, Dominican Stud 1(1948).360.

Maguire S, The Significance of Haukyn, Activa Vita, in P P, RES 25(1949).97; rptd in Blanch, Style and Symbolism, p 194.

Huppé B F, Petrus Id Est Christus: Word-Play in P P, the B-Text, ELH 17(1950).163; W M Ryan, Word-Play in Some Old Eng Homilies and a Late ME Poem, Stud in Lang, Lit and Culture of the Middle Ages and Later, ed E B Atwood and A A Hill, Austin Tex 1969, p 265.

Lawlor J, P P: The Pardon Reconsidered, MLR 45(1950).449.

Frank R W, The Conclusion of P P, JEGP 49 (1950).309; The Pardon Scene in P P, Spec 26(1951).317; rptd in E Vasta, ed, ME Survey, Notre Dame Ind 1965; rptd 1968, p 169; The Number of Visions in P P, MLN 66(1951).309.

Hench A L, The Allegorical Motif of Conscience and Reason, Counsellors, Eng Stud in Honor of J S Wilson, Univ of Va Stud 4, Charlottesville 1951, p 193.

Kaske R E, The Nature and Use of Figurative Expression in P P B, Univ of N C Record 492, Research in Progress (1951).131; The Use of Simple Figures of Speech in P P B, SP 48(1951).571.

Bloomfield SDS, p 196.

Fowler D C, The Forgotten Pilgrimage in P the P, MLN 67(1952).524.

Maisack H, William Langlands Verhältnis zum zisterziensischen Mönchtum, diss Tübingen, Balingen 1953.

Quirk R, Langland's Use of Kind Wit and Inwit, JEGP 52(1953).182; Vis Imaginativa, JEGP 53(1954).81; both rptd in Quirk, Essays on the Eng Lang, Medieval and Modern, London 1968, pp 20, 27.

Cejp L, Zum Probleme der Anagramme in Langlands P der P, Zeitschr f Anglistik u Amerikanistik 4(1954).444 (included in Cejp, An Introd to the Study of Langland's P P, B-Text, Acta Universitatis Palackianae Olomucensis 9, Olomouc 1956; in Eng with summary in Czech).

Knight D J, The Relation between Symbolic and Dramatic Characterization in P P (Considered from the B-Text), diss Yale Univ 1954; DA 31.2885.

Manning S, That Dreamer Once More, PMLA 71(1956).541.

Mitchell A G, Lady Meed and the Art of P P, London 1956; rptd in Blanch, Style and Symbolism, p 174.

Patch G K, The Allegorical Characters in P P, diss Stanford Univ 1957; DA 17.2598.

Cejp, Some General Meanings of Langland's Fundamental Concepts, Philologica Pragensa 2 (1959).20 (Petrus id est Christus).

Kaske, The Speech of Book in P P, Angl 77 (1959).117; R L Hoffman, The Burning of the Boke in P P, MLQ 25(1964).57; E T Donaldson, The Grammar of Book's Speech in P P, Stud in Lang and Lit in Honour of M Schlauch, ed M Brahmer et al, Warszawa 1966, p 103; rptd in Blanch, Style and Symbolism, p 264.

Harrington D V, Techniques of Characterization in P P, diss Univ of Wash 1960; DA 21.1554.

Oiji T, Why Did Piers Rend His Pardon Asunder? A Personal Approach to the Pardon Scene, Liberal Arts Rev (Tōhoku Univ) 5(1960).1.

Spearing A C, The Development of a Theme in P P, RES 11(1960).241 (bread, hunger, lyflode).

Orsten E M, The Ambiguities in Langland's Rat Parliament, MS 23(1961).216.

Sudō J, W Langland: P P no Allegory—Tokuni Gengo no Kanten Kara (Allegory in P P, Especially from a Linguistic Perspective), Kōbe Gaidaironso (Kōbe Colloquium) 11(1961).93 (in Japanese).

Adams J F, P P and the Three Ages of Man, JEGP 61(1962).23.

Martin J, Will as Fool and Wanderer in P P, Texas Stud in Lit and Lang 3(1962).535.

Pančenko A M, Srednevekovyj allegorizm i istoričeskij smysl P P (Medieval Allegory and Its Historical Significance) Izvestia Akademii Nauk SSSR, Otdelenie Literatury i Jazyka (Moscow) 22(1963).151.

Saito I, On the Three Biblical Quotations in the Pardon Scene in P P, Jinbungaku (Humanities) 67(1963).1; Piers no Haneika Kosakuno Imi—P the P Pas 6 no Megutte (The Meaning of the Cultivation of Piers' Half-Acre: P P 6), Festschrift for Dr Naokura Ueno on ... His 60th Birthday, Tokyo 1963, p 244 (in Japanese).

Spearing, Verbal Repetition in P P B and C, JEGP 62(1963).722.

Spitzbart G, Das Gewissen in der me Literatur, diss Köln 1963 (Conscience).

Kean P M, Love, Law, and Lewte in P P, RES ns 15(1964).241; rptd in Blanch, Style and Symbolism, p 132.

Longo J A, P P and the Tropological Matrix, Pas 11 and 12, Angl 82(1964).291.

Saito, A Study of the Pardon Scene of P P (in Japanese), diss Doshisha Univ, Jinbunkenkyū (Stud in the Humanities) 57(1964).1; 81(1965).1.

Lattin L, Some Aspects of Medieval Number Symbolism in Langland's P P, A-Text, Emporia State Research Stud 14(1965).5.

Mroczkowski P, P P: The Allegory in Motion, Prace historycznoliterackiez (Kracow) 8(1965).7.

Burrow J, The Action of Langland's Second Vision, EC 15(1965).247; rptd in Blanch, Style and Symbolism, p 209.

Kean P M, Langland on the Incarnation, RES 16(1965).349.

Reidy J, Peris the Ploughman, Which a Pardoun He Hadde, Publ of the Mich Acad of Science Arts and Letters 50(1965).534.

Vasta E, Truth, the Best Treasure, in P P, PQ 44(1965).17 (Holichurche's speech).

Walker M, P P's Pardon: A Note, Eng Stud in Africa 8(1965).64 (interprets Pardon scene).

Wilkes G, The Castle of Unite in P P, MS 27 (1965).334.

Mroczkowski, Piers and His Pardon: A Dynamic Analysis, Stud in Lang and Lit in Honour of M Schlauch, ed M Brahmer et al, Warszawa 1966, p 273.

Russell G H, The Salvation of the Heathen (see M E Marcett, 1938, in [13] above).

Saito, Mede to Mercede—Lady Mede no Seikaku ni tsuite (Mede and Mercede: The Life of Lady Meed), Jinbungaku (Humanities) 90(1966).1 (in Japanese); Piers' Destruction of the Pardon: A Critical Comparison of the B and C Texts of P P, Dōshisha Literature (Kyoto) 23(1966).1.

Smith Ben H Jr, Traditional Images of Charity in P P, The Hague 1966.

Orsten E M, The Treatment of Caritas, Justitia and Related Theological Themes in the B-Text of P P, diss Univ of Toronto 1967; DA 28.2218A.

Kaske, P P and Local Iconography, Journ Warburg and Courtauld Institutes 31(1968).159.

Schmidt A V C, A Note on Langland's Conception of Anima and Inwit, N&Q ns 15(1968).363 (A 10.43–45, 49–54).

Strange W C, The Willful Trope: Some Notes on Personification with Illust from P P (A-Text), Annuale Mediaevale 9(1968).26.

Wesling D, Eschatology and the Lang of Satire in P P, Criticism 10(1968).277.

Brian B D, Satire in P P, diss Duke Univ 1969; DA 30.4936A.

Burrow J A, Words, Works, and Will: Theme and Structure in P P, in S S Hussey, ed, Critical Approaches, London and N Y 1969, p 111.

Elliott R W V, The Langland Country, in Hussey, Approaches, p 226.

Evans W O, Charity in P P, in Hussey, Approaches, p 245.

Jenkins (Martin) P, Conscience: The Frustration of Allegory, in Hussey, Approaches, p 125.

Kean, Justice, Kingship, and the Good Life in the Second Pt of P P, in Hussey, Approaches, p 76.

Knight S, Satire in P P, in Hussey, Approaches, p 279.

Mills D, The Role of the Dreamer in P P, in Hussey, Approaches, p 180.

Orsten E M, Patientia in the B-Text of P P, MS 31(1969).317.

Palmer B D, The Guide and Leader: Stud in a Narrative Structural Motif, diss Mich State Univ 1969; DA 31(1970).1236A.

Raw B, Piers and the Image of God in Man, in Hussey, Approaches, p 143.

Riach M, Langland's Dreamer and the Transformation of the Third Vision, EC 19(1969).6.

Saito, Haukyn and His Way of Life in P P, Eibungaku Kenkyū (Stud in Eng Lit), Eng Issue 1969, p 1.

Wittig J S, P P B, Pas 9–12: Elements in the Design of the Inward Journey, diss Cornell Univ 1969; DAI 30.5425A.

Woolf R, The Tearing of the Pardon, in Hussey, Approaches, p 50.

Harwood B J and R F Smith, Inwit and the Castle of Caro in P P, NM 71(1970).648.

Orsten E M, Heaven on Earth: Langland's Vision of Life within the Cloister, Amer Benedictine Rev 21(1970).526.

Prince H M, Long Will: The First-Person Narrator in P P, diss Northwestern Univ 1970; DA 30.4423A.

Schroeder M C[arruthers], P P: The Tearing of the Pardon, PQ 49(1970).8; The Character of Conscience in P P, SP 67(1970).13.

Bowers R H, The Comic in Late Medieval Sensibility (P P B Pas 5), Amer Benedictine Rev 22 (1971).353.

Davlin M C, Kynde Knowyng as a Major Theme in P P B, RES 22(1971).1; Petrus, id est, Christus: P the P as the Whole Christ, Chaucer Rev 6 (1971).280.

Gradon P, Form and Style in Early Eng Lit, London 1971, pp 60 (personification allegory, B Pas 18), 99 (Piers).

Kaulbach E N, The Imagery and Theory of Synderesis in P P B Pas 5.544ff and Pas 19, diss Cornell Univ 1971; DAI 31.4720A.

Lee B S, Antichrist and the Allegory in Langland's Last Passus, Univ of Capetown Stud in Eng 2(1971).1.

Mullaney C A, P P: A Study of Voice and Address Relationships in the Confessions of the Deadly Sins, diss Catholic Univ 1971; DAI 32.2063A.

Oiji T, Four Figures of P the P, Bull Coll of Liberal Arts, Tōhoku Univ (Sendai Japan) 12(1971).23.

Palmer B, The Guide Convention in P P, Leeds SE 5(1971).13.

Bowers A J, The Tree of Charity in P P: Its Allegorical and Structural Significance, Literary Monographs (Wisc) 6(1972).1.

Dale J, The Poet in P P, Parergon 4(1972).3.

Lindemann E C D, Translation Techniques in W Langland's P P, diss Univ of N C Chapel Hill 1972; DAI 34.279A.

Lunz E, The Valley of Jehosophat in P P, Tulane Stud Eng 20(1972).1.

Middleton A, ELH 39(1972).169 (grammatical metaphor).

Paull M R, Mahomet and the Conversion of the Heathen in P P, ELN 10(1972).1.

Ryan T A, The Poetry of Reform: Christian Socialism in the First Dream of Dowel, diss Brown Univ 1972; DAI 32.5750A.

Tanaka Y, W Langland no Inaka (Langland's Countryside), Bull of Chūkyō Univ Literary Group 6(1972).112 (in Japanese).

Van't Hul B, Didactic and Mimetic Ambivalence in the A-Visio of P P, diss Northwestern Univ 1972; DAI 32.5205A.

Whitworth C W Jr, Changes in the Roles of Reason and Conscience in the Revisions of P P, N&Q 19(1972).4.

Wittig, P P B Pas 9–12: Elements in the Design of the Inward Journey, Trad 28(1972).211.

Asakura B, P P zakkō—words, works, and will ni tsuite (General Thoughts about P P: Words, Works, and Will), Japanese and Eng Lit, ed H Akaba and B Asakura, Tokyo 1973, p 236 (in Japanese).

Harwood, Clergye and the Action of the Third Vision in P P, MP 70(1973).279; Liberum Arbitrium in the C-Text of P P, PQ 52(1973).680.

Saito A, The Half-Acre no Kōsaku ikkōsatsu (One Point of View on the Harvest of the Half-Acre), Tōhoku (Tōhoku Univ Graduate Research in Lit) 8(1973).26 (in Japanese); The Pardon Scene ni Okeru Piers—Saiko (The Pardon Scene in P P: Reconsiderations), Hempei 9(1973).23 (in Japanese).

Trower K B, The Figure of Hunger in P P, Amer Benedictine Rev 24(1973).238; Temporal Tensions in the Visio of P P, MS 35(1973).389.

Asakura B, P P zakkō—if hevene be on this erthe (General Thoughts about P P . . .), Bull 9, Research in Eng Lit, Notre Dame Sacred Heart Women's Coll (Okayama Japan) 1974, p 1 (in Japanese).

Birnes W J, Patterns of Legality in P P; diss N Y Univ 1974; DAI 35.1040A; Christ as Advocate: The Legal Metaphor of P P, Annuale Mediaevale 16(1975).71.

Kaske, Holy Churche's Speech and the Structure of P P, Chaucer and ME Stud in Honour of R H Robbins, ed B Rowland, London 1974, p 320.

Schweitzer E C Jr, Kynde Love and Caritas in the B-Text of P P, diss Cornell Univ 1974; DAI 35.4555A.

Vaughan M F, The Tropological Context of the Easter Awakening: P P B 16–20, diss Cornell Univ 1974; DAI 34.7205A.

Harwood, Imaginative in P P, MÆ 44(1975).249.

Wittig, The Dramatic and Rhetorical Development of Long Will's Pilgrimage, NM 76(1975).52.

Baldwin A P, The Law of the King in the C-Text of P P, diss Cambridge Univ 1976.

Benson C D, An Augustinian Irony in P P, N&Q 23(1976).51 (B 10, learning and good works).

Brosamer J J, The Personae of P P: Narrator, Dreamer, and Will, diss Univ of Oregon 1976; DAI 37.1559A.

Harwood, Langland's Kynde Wit, JEGP 75 (1976).330.

Saito A, An Interpretation of the Episode of Lady Meed in The Vision of P P, Aichi Univ Lit Soc Bull, Special Issue for the 30th Anniv of the Univ, 56/57(1976).563.

Thompson C A, Structural, Figurative, and Thematic Trinities in P P, Mosaic 9(1976).105.

Tristram P, Figures of Life and Death in Medieval Lit, p 197 (Harrowing of Hell).

Alford J A, PMLA 92(1977).944 (Harrowing of Hell); The Role of the Quotations in P P, Spec 52(1977).80.

Clutterbuck C, Hope and Good Works: Leaute in the C-Text of P P, RES 28(1977).129.

McLeod S H, The Tearing of the Pardon in P P, PQ 56(1977).14.

Adams R, The Nature of Need in P P 20, Trad 34(1978).273.

Bowers J M, Acedia and the Crisis of Will in Langland's P P, diss Univ of Va 1978; DAI 39.4930A.

Dale J, Making the Kingdom Come: The Poet and 'P the P,' in From Dante to Solzhenitsyn: Essays on Christianity and Lit, Wellington N Z 1978, p 55.

Finkel A J, Lang and Allegory in P P, diss UCLA 1978; DAI 38.4841A.

Jennings M, P P and Holychurch, Viator 9 (1978).367.

Kaulbach E N, P P B 9: Further Refinements of Inwitte, in Linguistic and Literary Stud in Honor of A A Hill, IV, ed M A Jazayery, E C Polomé, and W Winter, The Hague 1978, p 103.

Kirk E, Who Suffreth More than God?: Narrative Redefinition of Patience in Patience and P P, The Triumph of Patience: Medieval and Renaissance Stud, ed G Schiffhorst, Orlando Fla 1978, p 88.

Martindale M A, The Treatment of the Life of Christ in P P, MLitt thesis, Oxford Univ 1978.

Quilligan M, Langland's Literal Allegory, EC 28 (1978).95.

Schleusener J, Langland's Inward Argument: The Poetic Intent of P P B 15–18, diss Columbia Univ 1978; DAI 41.4028A.

Bennett J A W, Langland's Samaritan, Poetica (Tokyo) 12(1979).10.

Bissell B L, The Continuity of the Folk on the Field: Langland's Allegory of the Polity, diss City Univ of N Y 1979; DAI 40.839A.

Braswell M F, Langland's Sins: A 'True' Confession?, AN&Q 18(1979).154.

Clopper L M, Langland's Trinitarian Analogies as Keys to Meaning and Structure, MH 9(1979).87 (Kane-Donaldson B-Text, 17.143–203, 206–98).

Davlin M C, A Genius-Kynde Illustration in Codex Vaticanus Palatinus Latinus 629, Manuscripta 23(1979).149 (Kane-Donaldson B-Text, 11.325–31, 9.26–29).

Lawler T, The Gracious Imagining of Redemption in P P, Engl 28(1979).203.

Mander M N K, Grammatical Analogy in Langland and Alan of Lille, N&Q 26(1979).501 (see [7] above, Schmidt, 1969).

Mann J, Eating and Drinking in P P, E&S 32 (1979).26.

Baker D N, From Plowing to Penitence: P P and 14-Cent Theology, Spec 55(1980).715 (pardon scene).

Benson C D, The Function of Lady Meed in P P, ESts 61(1980).193.

Cree E G, 'Forþi i conseille alle': A Study of Direct Address in P P, diss Indiana Univ 1980; DAI 41.4027A.

Finke L A, 'Crabbed Eloquence': Dialectics of Style and Structure in P P, diss Univ of Penn 1980; DAI 41.1052A.

Lotto E E, The Web of Experience: A Study of the Epistemological Function of the Comparisons in P P, diss Indiana Univ 1980; DAI 41.4028A.

Ovitt G O Jr, The Structure of the 'Visio' of P P, Massachusetts Stud in Eng 7(1980).26.

Schmidt A V C, Langland's Structural Imagery, EC 30(1980).311.

Selzer J L, Topical Allegory in P P: Lady Meed's B-Text Debate with Conscience, PQ 59(1980).257.

Allen D G, Begging the Question in P P B: William Langland's Impossible Pedagogy, diss Duke Univ 1981; DAI 43.448A.

Ames R H, The Pardon Impugned by the Priest, in The Alliterative Tradition in the 14 Cent, ed B S Levy and P E Szarmach, Kent O 1981, p 47.

Arn M-J, Langland's Characterization of Will in the B-Text, Dutch Quart Rev of Anglo-American Letters 11(1981).287.

Baldwin A, The Double Duel in P P B 18 and C 21, MÆ 50(1981).64.

Bloomfield M W, The Allegories of Dobest (P P B 19–20), MÆ 50(1981).30.

Davlin M C, Kynde Knowyng as a ME Equivalent for 'Wisdom' in P P B, MÆ 50(1981).5.

Dillon J, P P: A Particular Example of Wordplay and Its Structural Significance (Will-Dowel), MÆ 50(1981).40.

Gilbert B B, 'Civil' and the Notaries in P P, MÆ 50(1981).49.

Lawton D A, On Tearing—and Not Tearing—The Pardon, PQ 60(1981).414.

Minnis A J, Langland's Ymaginatif and Late-Medieval Theories of Imagination, Comp Criticism 3(1981).71.

O'Driscoll P, The Dowel Debate in P P B, MÆ 50(1981).18.

Pickett J P, The Narrator's Persona in P P B, diss Univ of Mich 1981; DAI 42.715A.

Arn M-J, Langland's Triumph of Grace in Dobest, Eng Studies 63(1982).506.

Donaldson E T, Langland and Some Scriptural Quotations, in The Wisdom of Poetry: Essays . . . in Honor of Morton W Bloomfield, ed L D Benson and S Wenzel, Kalamazoo Mich 1982, pp 67, 277n.

Kane G, The Perplexities of William Langland, in Bloomfield festschrift (above), ed Benson and Wenzel, 1982, pp 73, 278n.

Middleton A, Narration and the Invention of Experience: Episodic Form in P P, in Bloomfield festschrift (above), ed Benson and Wenzel, 1982, pp 91, 280n.

Tavormina M T, 'Bothe two ben gode': Marriage and Virginity in P P C 18.68–100, JEGP 81 (1982).320; Kindly Similitude: Langland's Matrimonial Trinity, MP 80(1982).117.

Donaldson, Apocalyptic Style in P P B 19–20, in Essays in Memory of Elizabeth Salter, ed D Pearsall, Leeds SE ns 14(1983).74.

Gradon P, Trajanus Redivivus: Another Look at Trajan in P P, in ME Stud Presented to Norman Davis, ed D Gray and E G Stanley, Oxford 1983, p 93.

Harwood B J, Langland's Kynde Knowing and the Quest for Christ, MP 80(1983).242.

Spearing A C, Langland's Poetry: Some Notes in Critical Analysis, in Salter Memorial Essays (above), Leeds SE ns 14(1983).182.

Baker D N, The Pardons of P P, NM 85(1984).462.

Dove M, Perfect Age and P P, Parergon 1(1983).55.

Finke L, Dowel and the Crisis of Faith and Irony in P P, in Kierkegaard and Lit: Irony, Repetition, and Criticism, edd R Schleifer and R Markley, Norman Okla 1984, p 119.

Frost M H, Symbolic Buildings in P P, diss SUNY Binghamton 1984; DAI 45.190A.

Godden M, Plowmen and Hermits in Langland's P P, RES 35(1984).129.

Whatley G, P P B 12.277–94: Notes on Language, Text, and Theology, MP 82(1984).1 (cites Kane-Donaldson B-Text).

Adams R, The Reliability of the Rubrics of P P B, MÆ 54(1985).208.

Bertz D, Prophecy and Apocalypse in Langland's P P B 16–19, JEGP 84(1985).313.

Griffiths L, Personification in P P (P P Stud 3), Woodbridge Suffolk 1985.

Kaulbach E N, The 'Vis Imaginativa' and the Reasoning Powers of Ymaginatif in the B-Text of P P, JEGP 84(1985).16.

[17] CONTEMPORARY RELATIONSHIPS, MAINLY NON-LITERARY.

Günther C E, Engl Leben in 14 Jahrhundert, Leipzig 1889.

Gibbins H DeB, Eng Social Reformers, London 1892.

Mackail J W, P P and Eng Life in the 14 Cent, Cornhill Magazine ns 3(1897).42.

Scudder V D, Social Ideals in Eng Letters, Boston and N Y 1898; enlarged edn 1922, p 7.

Dale E, National Life and Character in the Mirror of Early Eng Lit, Cambridge 1907.

Köllrütter M, Das Privatleben in England nach den Dichtungen von Chaucer, Gower und Langland, Halle 1908.

Gebhard H, Langlands und Gowers Kritik der kirchlichen Verhältnisse ihrer Zeit, diss Strassburg 1910, Hornberg 1911.

Moore S, Patrons of Letters in Norfolk and Suffolk c 1450, PMLA 27(1912).188; 28(1913).79 (compares patronage in E Anglia 1450 to that of W Midl 1350), 103 (P P discussed); views extended by Hulbert, MP 28(1931).405.

Tristram E E, P P in Wall-Painting, Burlington Magazine 31(1917).135; C D'Evelyn, P P in Art, MLN 34(1919).247; E Breitenbach and T Hillman, Das Gebot der Feiertagsheiligung, Anzeiger für schweizerische Altertumskunde 39(1937).23 (Christ and the implements); A Caiger-Smith, Eng Medieval Mural Paintings, Oxford 1963, p 55 (corrects Tristram).

Manning B L, The People's Faith in the Time of Wyclif, Cambridge 1919.

Wedel T O, The Medieval Attitude toward Astrology, YSE 60, New Haven 1920.

Chadwick D, Social Life in the Days of P P, Cambridge 1922 (crit B Fehr, AnglB 34.87; C L Kingsford, EHR 308.105).

Burdach K, Antgaben über weitere Hinweises auf Langland, Euphorion 26(1925).33.

Hittmair R, Der Begriff der Arbeit bei Langland, Festgabe Karl Luick, NS 6(1925) Beiheft, p 204.

Tout T F, Lit and Learning in the Eng Civil Service in the 14 Cent, Spec 4(1929).381.

Wiehe H, P P und die sozialen Fragen seiner Zeit, diss Münster, Emsdetten 1935.

Bennett H S, The Author and His Public in the 14 and 15 Cents, E&S 23(1937).1.

Helming V P, Medieval Pilgrimages in Eng Lit to 1400, diss Yale Univ 1937; DA 31.2826A.

Pepler C, The Spirituality of W Langland, Blackfriars Magazine 20(1939).846.

Stillwell G, Chaucer's Plowman and the Contemporary Eng Peasant, ELH 6(1939).285.

Gwynn A, The Eng Austin Friars in the Time of Wyclif, London 1940.

Petrushevsky D V, edn, Moscow 1941, introd.

Kent M, A 14-Cent Poet Surveys the Eng Scene, HJ 40(1942).381.

Rauch R W, Langland and Medieval Functionalism, Annual Report of the Amer Historical Assoc 3(1942).39; rptd in Rev of Politics 5(1943).441.

Heather P J, The Seven Planets, Folklore 54 (1943).351.

Burton D J, The Compact with the Devil in the ME Vision of P the P, Calif Folklore Quart 5 (1946).179.

Pepler, The Beginning of the Way, in The Life of the Spirit 1(1946).101 (includes: Conversion in Langland, p 136; The Way Opens, p 169; Langland's Way to Unity, p 198); collected and rptd as The Eng Religious Heritage, St Louis Mo 1958.

Thrupp S, The Merchant Class of Medieval London, Ann Arbor 1948.

Hilton R H and H Fagan, The Eng Rising of 1381, London 1950.

Lindsay P and R Groves, The Peasants' Revolt of 1381, London 1950, pp 112, 135.

Eliason M, The Peasant and the Lawyer, SP 48(1951).506.

Wilson R M, The Lost Lit of Medieval England, London 1952 (copies of P P mentioned in wills).

Rutledge D, Langland and the Liturgical Tradition, Dublin Rev 228(1954).405.

Pantin W A, The Eng Church in the 14 Cent, Cambridge 1955.

Róna É, P the P és az 1381-es paraszforradalom (P the P and the 1381 Peasant Revolt), diss Budapest 1956, Libr of the Hungarian Acad of Sciences, Budapest 1956.

Schlauch M, Eng Medieval Lit and Its Social Foundations, Warszawa 1956, p 213.

Burrow J, Angl 75(1957).373 (audience).

Palmer W P, The Intellectual Background of the Vision of P P, with Particular Reference to the Eng and Latin Writings of Wyclif, diss Univ of Kansas 1957; DA 20.1769.

Saito T, Nōkōsha Piers (Farmer Piers), Fukuin no Sekai (The Gospel and the World), Tokyo 1957, p 46; rptd in Eikokushū Kyōshi Kanshyō (The Appreciation of Eng Religious Poetry), Tokyo 1958, p 1 (in Japanese).

Moe H A, The Vision of P P and Law of Foundations, PAPS 102(1958).371; The Power of Poetic Vision, PMLA 74(1959).37.

McKisack M, The 14 Cent 1307–99, Oxford 1959.

Langenfeld G, The Attitude to Villeins and Laborers in Eng Lit until c 1600, Zeitschr f Anglistik u Amerikanistik 8(1960).337.

Robbins R H, ME Poems of Protest, Angl 78 (1960).193.

Yunck J, The Venal Tongue: Lawyers and Medieval Satirists, Amer Bar Assoc Journ 46(1960).267.

Biggar R G, Langland's and Chaucer's Treatment of Monks, Friars, and Priests, diss Univ of Wisc 1961; DA 22.1992.

Gewirth A, Philosophy and Political Thought in the 14 Cent, in The Forward Movement of the 14 Cent, ed F L Utley, Columbus Ohio 1961.

Warren W L, The Peasants' Revolt of 1381, History Today Dec 12 1962, p 845; Jan 13 1963, p 44.

Ikegami T, P P and Monastic Tradition, Eigo Seinen 109(1963).217 (in Japanese).

Samuels M L, Some Applications of ME Dialectology, ESts 44(1963).81.

Kesteven G R, The Peasants' Revolt, London 1965, p 94.

Obermann H A, ed, Forerunners of the Reformation: The Shape of Late Medieval Thought, N Y 1966.

Roth F, The Eng Austin Friars 1249–1538, N Y 1966, 1.359.

Roush G J, The Political Plowman: The Expression of Political Ideals in P P and Its Successors, diss Univ of Calif Berkeley 1966; DA 27.752A.

Aston M, Thomas Arundel: A Study of Church Life in the Reign of Richard II, Oxford and N Y 1967.

McNamara J F, Responses to Ockhamist Theology in the Poetry of the Pearl-Poet, Langland and Chaucer, diss Louisiana State Univ 1968; DA 29.3148A.

Mathew G, The Court of Richard II, London 1968, p 83.

Fowler D C, Poetry and the Liberal Arts: The Oxford Background of P P, Arts libéraux et philosophie au moyen âge: Actes du quatrième congrès international de philosophie médiévale, Montreal and Paris 1969, p 715.

Moorman C, The Origins of the Alliterative Revival, The Southern Quart 7(1969).345.

Reeves M, The Influence of Prophecy in the Later Middle Ages, Oxford 1969.

Schmidt A V C, Langland and Scholastic Philosophy, MÆ 38(1969).134.

Dobson R B, ed, The Peasants' Revolt of 1381, London 1970 (collects and translates contemporary documents).

Zacher C K, Curiositas and the Impulses for Pilgrimage in 14-Cent Eng Lit, diss Univ of Calif Riverside 1970; DA 30.4429A.

Coleman J, Sublimes et Litterati: The Audience for the Themes of Grace, Justification and Predestination, Traced from the Disputes of the 14-Cent Moderni to the Vernacular P P, diss Yale Univ 1971; DAI 32.382A.

Harwood B J, P P: 14-Cent Skepticism and the Theology of Suffering, Bucknell Rev 19(1971).119.

Hudson A, A Lollard Sermon Cycle and Its Implications, MÆ 40(1971).142.

Jones W R, Lollards and Images: The Defense of Religious Art in Later Medieval England, JHI 34(1972).27.

Lyons T R, ME Political Poetry: The Poet's Call for Stability, diss Wash Univ 1972; DAI 33.1144A.

Szittya P R, Caimes Kynde: The Friars and the Exegetical Origins of Medieval Antifraternalism, diss Cornell Univ 1972; DAI 33.287A.

Elliott T L, ME Complaints against the Times: To Condemn the World or to Reform It?, Annuale Mediaevale 14(1973).22.

Flood D, Poverty in the Middle Ages, Collectanea Franciscana 43(1973).409.

Hilton R, Bond Men Made Free: Medieval Peasant Movements and the Eng Rising of 1381, London and N Y 1973, pp 178, 221.

Mann J, Chaucer and Medieval Estates Satire, Cambridge 1973.

Parkes M B, The Literacy of the Laity, Lit and Western Civilization, ed Daiches and Thorlby, 2.555.

Pearsall D and E Salter, Landscapes and Seasons of the Medieval World, London and Toronto 1973.

Krochalis J and E Peters, edd, The World of P P, Phila 1975 (collects and translates source and contemporary documents).

Krumme R D, Wealth and Reform in P P, diss Claremont Grad School 1975; DAI 36.2848A.

Taitt P S, Incubus and Ideal: Ecclesiastical Figures in Chaucer and Langland, Elizabethan and Renaissance Stud 44, Salzburg Univ 1975.

Dobson R B and J Taylor, Rymes of Robyn Hood: An Introd to the Eng Outlaw, Pittsb Pa 1976.

Parkes, The Influence of the Concepts of Ordinatio and Compilatio on the Development of the Book, Medieval Learning and Lit: Essays Presented to R W Hunt, ed J J G Alexander and M T Gibson, Oxford 1976, p 115.

Seehase G, Zu W Langlands Poems P der P, Renaissanceliteratur und frühbürgerliche Revolution, ed R Weimann et al, Berlin 1976, p 106.

Lawton D, Eng Poetry and Eng Society 1370–1400, The Radical Reader, ed S Knight and M Wilding, Sydney 1977, p 145.

Levy L H, P P and the Concept of Poverty, diss Univ of Okla 1977; DAI 37.7740A.

Aers D, Imagination and Ideology in P P, Lit and Hist 7(1978).2.

Crews C D, P P and 14-Cent Ecclesiology, diss Univ of N C Greensboro 1978; DAI 39.4266A.

Boyle L, Aspects of Clerical Education in 14-Cent England, Acta 4: The 14 Cent, Center for Medieval and Early Renaissance Stud, SUNY Binghamton 1979, p 19.

St-Jacques R, ME Lit and the Liturgy: Recent Research and Future Possibilities, Mosaic 12 (1979).1.

Salter E, Langland and the Context of P P (compilatio as genre) E&S 32(1979).19.

Gradon P, Langland and the Ideology of Dissent, Proc Brit Acad 66(1980).179.

Baldwin A P, The Theme of Government in P P (P P Stud 1), Cambridge 1981 (crit P Neuss, TLS 15 Jan 1982, p 56; R Adams, Stud in the Age of Chaucer 5.141).

Coleman J, P P and the Moderni, Rome 1981 (crit J Simpson, MÆ 53.125).

Lawton D A, Lollardy and the P P Tradition, MLR 76(1981).780.

Baldwin A, Reference in P P to the Westminster Sanctuary, N&Q 29(1982).106.

Lister R, The Peasants of P P and Its Audience, in Peasants and Countrymen in Lit, ed K Parkinson and M Priestman, London 1982, p 71.

Pearsall D, Origins and Social Backgrounds, in D A Lawton, ed, ME Alliterative Poetry and Its Literary Background, Cambridge 1982, pp 34, 132n.

Wenzel S, Pestilence and ME Lit: Friar John Grimestone's Poems on Death, in The Black Death: The Impact of the 14-Cent Plague, ed D Williman, Binghamton N Y 1982, p 131 (comparison to P P).

Aers D, P P and Problems in the Perception of Poverty: A Culture in Transition, Salter Memorial Essays, Leeds SE ns 14(1983).5; Representations of the Third Estate: Social Conflict and Its Milieu around 1381, Southern Rev (Adelaide Australia) 16(1983).335.

Shepherd G, Poverty in P P, in Social Relations and Ideas: Essays in Honour of R H Hilton, ed T H Aston, P R Coss, C Dyer, and J Thirsk, Cambridge 1983, p 169.

Martinet M-M, Wyclif et P P sous le petit Josias: le radicalisme médiéval transmis par Robert Crowley au temps d'Edouard VI, in Radicaux a l'anglaise, intro Olivier Lutaud, Paris 1984, p 1.

[18] GENERAL REFERENCES.

Webbe W, A Discourse of Eng Poetry (1586), ed E Arber, Westminster 1895, p 32.

Warton T, Hist of Eng Poetry, ed W C Hazlitt, London 1871, 2.244.

Marsh G P, Origin and Hist of the Eng Lang, N Y 1872, p 295.

Ten Brink, 1.351.

Morley, 4.285.

Brandl, 21.654.

Courthope, 1.200.

Jusserand J J, A Literary Hist of the Eng People, London and N Y 1895, 1.373.

Wülcker, 1.136.

Brook S A, Eng Lit, London 1897, p 52.

Saintsbury F, A Short Hist of Eng Lit, London and N Y 1898, p 131.

Snell F J, The 14 Cent, N Y 1899, p 379; The Age of Chaucer, London 1901, p 30.

Pollard A W, in Chambers' Cyclopedia of Eng Lit, 1901 edn, 1.55.

Schofield, passim.

Coulton G G, Chaucer and His England, London 1908, p 10.

Tucker S, Verse Satire in England before the Renaissance, N Y 1908, p 35.

Körting, §145.

Ker W P, Eng Lit: Medieval, London and N Y 1912, p 194; rptd 1948, p 144.

Cazamian L, Études de psychologie littéraire, Paris 1913.

Baldwin C S, An Introd to Medieval Eng Lit, N Y 1914, p 177.

Benham A R, Eng Lit from Widsith to the Death of Chaucer, New Haven 1916, p 595.

Deanesley M, Vernacular Books in England in the 14 and 15 Cents, MLR 15(1920).349.

Thomas P G, Eng Lit before Chaucer, London 1924, p 141.

Legouis E and L Cazamian, A Hist of Eng Lit, 650–1650, London and N Y 1926, p 71.

Quiller-Couch A T, The Age of Chaucer, London 1926, pp 74, 123.

Hecht H and L Schücking, Die engl Literatur im Mittelalter, Wildpark-Potsdam 1927, p 94.

Cazamian, The Development of Eng Humor, N Y 1930, 1.85.

Baldwin C S, Moral Allegory: P P, in Three Medieval Centuries of Lit in England 1100–1400, N Y 1932; rptd 1968, p 158.

Coghill N K, The Secentenary of W Langland, London Mercury 26(1932).40.

Osgood C G, The Voice of England, N Y 1935, p 87.

Lewis C S, The Allegory of Love, Oxford 1936, p 158.

Schirmer W F, Geschichte der engl Literatur von den Anfängen bis zur Renaissance, Halle 1937, p 129.

Evans B I, Tradition and Romanticism, London 1940, p 28.

Sampson G, The Concise Cambridge Hist of Eng Lit, London 1941, p 60.

Chaytor H J, From Script to Print, Cambridge 1945.

Bennett H S, Chaucer and the 15 Cent, Oxford 1947, p 15.

Baugh A C, A Literary Hist of England, N Y 1948, p 240.

Bloom E A, The Allegorical Principle, ELH 18 (1951).163.

Frank R W Jr, The Art of Reading Medieval Personification Allegory, ELH 20(1953).237; rptd in E Vasta, ed, Interpretations of P P, Notre Dame Ind 1968, p 217.

Speirs J, Medieval Eng Poetry: The Non-Chaucerian Tradition, London 1957; N Y 1958, p 35.

Donaldson E T, Patristic Exegesis in the Criticism of Medieval Lit: The Opposition; and R E Kaske, Patristic Exegesis . . . : The Defense, in Critical Approaches to Medieval Lit, EIE 1958–59, ed D Bethurum, N Y 1960, pp 1, 27; Kaske essay rptd in Vasta, Interpretations, p 319.

Bowers R H, P P and the Literary Historians, CE 21(1959).1.

Alekseyev M P, Iz istorija anglijskoi literatury (A Hist of Eng Lit), Moscow and Leningrad 1960, p 7 (chap 1 on P P).

Tillyard E M W, Myth and the Eng Mind: From P P to Edward Gibbon, N Y 1962, p 126.

Fletcher A, Allegory: The Theory of a Symbolic Mode, Ithaca N Y 1964.

Lubac H de, Exégèse médiévale: Les quatre sens de l'ecriture, Paris 1964.

Kahrl S T, Allegory in Practice: A Study of Narrative Styles in Medieval Exempla, MP 63 (1965).105.

Tuve R, Allegorical Imagery: Some Medieval Books and Their Posterity, Princeton 1966.

Engels H, P P: Eine Untersuchung der Textstruktur mit einer Einleitung zur mittelalterlichen Allegorie, diss Köln 1968; abstr in Eng and American Stud in German, ed W Habicht, Tübingen 1968, p 26 (allegory).

Salter E, Medieval Poetry and the Figural View of Reality, Proc Brit Acad 54(1968).73.

Hallmundsson M N, A Collection of Materials for a Study of the Literary Scene at the End of the 14 Cent, diss N Y Univ 1970; DAI 31.4120A.

MacQueen J, Allegory, The Critical Idiom 14, London 1970.

Sinclair L R Jr, The Evidence for an Aesthetic Theory in 14-Cent Vernacular Poetry, diss Univ of Wash 1970; DA 31.1772A.

Wimsatt J I, Allegory and Mirror: Tradition and Structure in Medieval Lit, N Y 1970, p 36.

Allen J B, The Friar as Critic: Literary Attitudes in the Later Middle Ages, Nashville Tenn 1971.

Gradon P, Form and Style in Early Eng Lit, p 60.

Piehler P, The Visionary Landscape: A Study in Medieval Allegory, London 1971.

Cantarow E, A Wilderness of Opinions Confounded: Allegory and Ideology, CE 34 (1972).215.

Delany S, Undoing Substantial Connection: The Late Medieval Attack on Analogical Thought, Mosaic 5(1972).31.

Hanson-Smith E A, Be Fruitful and Multiply: The Medieval Allegory of Nature, diss Stanford Univ 1972; DAI 33.2892A.

Robinson I, Chaucer and the Eng Tradition, Cambridge 1972, p 201 (comparison with Chaucer's narrative).

Clifford G, The Transformations of Allegory, London 1974.

Delany S, Substructure and Superstructure: The Politics of Allegory in the 14 Cent, Science and Society 38(1974).257.

Elliott R W V, Chaucer's Eng, London 1974, p 241.

Harper J F, Style in Medieval Art and Lit: Three Essays in Criticism, diss SUNY Stony Brook 1974; DAI 35.3682A.

Klein M, The Apocalyptic Configuration in Lit: A Study of Fragmentation and Contradiction in P P and Its Implications for Modern Lit, diss Univ of Sussex 1974.

Kirk E, Chaucer and His Eng Contemporaries, in Geoffrey Chaucer: A Collection of Original Articles, ed G Economou, N Y 1975, p 111.

Loftin A C, Such Shaping Fantasies: Visionary Narrative of the 14 through 17 Cents, diss Univ of Mich 1977; DAI 38.6715A.

Pearsall D, Old and ME Poetry, London Henley and Boston 1977, p 176 (crit A Hudson, RES 29.191).

Collar M L, Ties That Bind: Lit, Lang and the Idea of Man, diss Penn State Univ 1978; DAI 38.6139A.

Barney S A, Allegories of Hist, Allegories of Love, Hamden Conn 1979.

Allen J B, The Ethical Poetic of the Later Middle Ages: A Decorum of Convenient Distinction, Toronto 1982.

Coleman J, Eng Lit in Hist 1350–1400: Medieval Readers and Writers, London 1981.

[19] BIBLIOGRAPHY.

Bloomfield M W, The Present State of P P Stud, Spec 14(1939).215; rptd in R J Blanch, ed, Style and Symbolism in P P, Knoxville 1969, p 3.

Renwick-Orton, p 293.

CBEL, 1.197.

Hussey S S, Eighty Years of P P Scholarship: A Study of Critical Methods, M A thesis London Univ 1952.

Zesmer D M and S B Greenfield, Guide to Eng Lit from Beowulf through Chaucer and Medieval Drama, N Y and London 1961, pp 166, 347 (annotated OE and ME biblios by Greenfield).

Ackerman R W, ME Lit to 1400, The Medieval Lit of Western Europe: A Rev of Research, Mainly 1930–1960, ed J H Fisher, N Y and London 1966, p 75.

Oizumi A, A Classified Biblio of Writings in Eng Philology and Medieval Eng Lit, Tokyo 1966 (Japanese ME scholarship).

Fowler D C, P P, Recent ME Scholarship and Crit: Survey and Desiderata, ed J B Severs, Pittsb Pa 1971, p 9.

Proppe K, P P: An Annotated Biblio for 1900–1968, Comitatus 3(1972).33.

Bourquin G, P P: Études sur la genèse littéraire des trois versions, Paris 1978, 2.825.

Colaianne A J, A Companion to P P Studies: Authorship, Editions, Backgrounds, and Critical Interpretation, diss Univ of Cincinnati 1977; DAI 38.1206A; publ as P P: An Annotated Biblio of Edns and Crit, 1550–1977, N Y and London 1978.

Terasawa Y, ed, Chūsei Eigo Eibungaku Kenkyū Gyōseki Lisuto (Academic Research in ME Lit), ME Research Data Center, Tokyo 1979 (biblio in Japanese of ME research in Japan).

DiMarco V, P P: A Reference Guide, Boston 1982 (annotated, chronological list of 'writings about and records of' P P to 1979).

[20] MISCELLANEOUS.

Converse F, Long Will, a Romance, Boston 1903; 2nd edn 1908.

Chester F A, P P's Pilgrimage: A Morality Play, with music arranged and composed by B Muller, London 1925.

James S B, The Mad Poet of Malvern: W Langland, Month 159(1932).221; Back to Langland, London [1935]; The Neglect of Langland, Dublin Rev 196(1935).115.

Bennett J A W, W Langland's World of Visions, Listener 43(1950).381.

Brooke-Rose C, Ezra Pound: P P in the Modern Wasteland, Rev Eng Lit 1(1961).74.

Lawlor J, Two Scenes from The Vision of P P: To Nevill Coghill from Friends, ed W H Auden and J Lawlor, London 1966, p 43 (adaptation for modern theatre).

Hobsbawm P, P P through Modern Eyes, Poetry Rev 61(1970–71).335.

Oiji T, Langland Kenkyū no Senku, Ikuzo Iijima (Pioneer of Langland Studies, Ikuzo Iijima), Eigo Seinen 120(1975).468.

Glazier L, An Americanized P P: William Langland's Prologue Translated into American Idiom, Journ of Eng (Sana's Univ) 7(1980).1.

Donaldson E T, A Vision of Will, Spec 56(1981).707 (Presidential address in verse, Medieval Acad meeting 1981).

XIX. TRAVEL AND GEOGRAPHICAL WRITINGS

by

Christian K. Zacher

BACKGROUND BOOKS: The following important, frequently listed entries, here given full statement, are referred to in abbreviated form in the pages that follow. For abbreviations not appearing in this list, consult the general Table of Abbreviations.

Mitchell	Mitchell R J, The Spring Voyage: The Jerusalem Pilgrimage in 1458, London 1964
MT	Mandeville's Travels
Parker	Parker J, Books to Build an Empire: A Bibliographical History of English Overseas Interests to 1620, Amsterdam 1965
Parks ETI	Parks G B, The English Traveler to Italy, 1. The Middle Ages (to 1525), Rome 1954
Prescott	Prescott H F M, Friar Felix at Large: A Fifteenth-century Pilgrimage to the Holy Land, New Haven 1950; rptd Jerusalem Journey: Pilgrimage to the Holy Land in the Fifteenth Century, London 1954
Röhricht	Röhricht R, Bibliotheca Geographica Palaestinae: Chronologisches Verzeichnis der von 333 bis 1878 verfassten Literatur über das Heilige Land, Berlin 1890; rvsd D H K Amiran, Jerusalem 1963
Seymour MV	Seymour M C, The Metrical Version of Mandeville's Travels, EETS 269, London N Y and Toronto 1973
Sumption	Sumption J, Pilgrimage: An Image of Mediaeval Religion, Totowa N J 1975
Taylor	Taylor E G R, Tudor Geography 1485–1583, London 1930

GENERAL TREATMENTS OF MEDIEVAL
TRAVEL AND GEOGRAPHICAL WRITINGS.

Early Travels in Palestine, ed T Wright, London 1848.

Peregrinatores Medii Aevi Quatuor, ed J C M Laurent, Leipzig 1864.

The Libr of the Palestine Pilgrims' Text Soc, 13 vols, London 1885–97; rptd N Y 1971.

Beazley C R, The Dawn of Modern Geography, 3 vols, London 1897–1906; rptd N Y 1949, vol 2 (10–13 cent); vol 3 (13–15 cent).

Jusserand J J, Eng Wayfaring Life in the Middle Ages (XIVth Cent), trans L T Smith, London 1890 (crit W J Ashley, Political Science Quart 4.685).

Barwick G F, Some Early Guide-Books, Trans of the Bibliographical Soc 7(1904).191.

Newett M M, Canon Pietro Casola's Pilgrimage to Jerusalem in the Year 1494, Univ of Manchester Publs No 26, Manchester 1907.

Heath S H, Pilgrim Life in the Middle Ages, Boston and N Y 1911; rvsd, In the Steps of the Pilgrims, London and N Y 1950.

Howard C, Eng Travellers of the Renaissance, London N Y and Toronto 1914.

Hulbert J R, Some Medieval Advertisements of Rome, MP 20(1923).403.

Stretton G, Some Aspects of Medieval Travel, Trans of the Royal Historical Soc 4s 7(1924).77.

Wright J K, The Geographical Lore of the Time of the Crusades, N Y 1925.

Travel and Travellers of the Middle Ages, ed A P Newton, London 1926.

Parks G B, Richard Hakluyt and the Eng Voyages, ed J A Williamson, N Y 1930.

Taylor (crit J A W, EHR 47.151).

Rice W G, Early Eng Travelers to Greece and the Levant, Essays and Stud in Eng and Comp Lit, Univ of Mich Publs in Lang and Lit 10 (1933).205.

A XVth Cent Guide-Book to the Principal Churches of Rome Compiled c 1470 by William Brewyn, ed and trans C E Woodruff, London 1933; rptd N Y 1980.

Atiya A S, The Crusade in the Later Middle Ages, London 1938.

Kimble G H T, Geography in the Middle Ages, London 1938 (crit L Thorndike, AHR 44.868; D Durand, Isis 30.540).

Meech S B and H E Allen, The Book of Margery Kempe, EETS 212, London N Y and Toronto 1940; rptd 1961 (crit G Coffman, Spec 17.138).

Bennett H S, Science and Information in Eng Writings of the 15th Cent, MLR 39(1944).1.

Hennig R, Terrae Incognitae, 4 vols, Leiden 1936–39.

Burwash D, Eng Merchant Shipping 1460–1540, Toronto 1947 (crit F Mood, Journ of Economic Hist 9.69; T S Willan, Economic Hist Rev 2s 2.335).

Rickert E, Chaucer's World, edd C C Olson and M M Crow, N Y 1948.

Prescott.

Boyer M N, A Day's Journey in Mediaeval France, Spec 26(1951).597.

de Beer E S, The Development of the Guide-Book until the Early 19 Cent, British Archaeological Assoc Journ 3s 15(1952).35.

Penrose B, Travel and Discovery in the Renaissance 1420–1620, Cambridge Mass 1952.

Bennett H S, Eng Books and Readers 1475 to 1557, Cambridge 1952; 2nd edn 1969.

Parks ETI (crit J C Russell, AHR 60.593).

A Hist of Technology, edd C Singer, E J Holmyard, A R Hall and T L Williams, 7 vols, Oxford 1954–78, 2.493; 3.471, 513.

Carus-Wilson E M, Medieval Merchant Venturers: Collected Stud, London 1954; 2nd edn 1967.

A Hist of the Crusades, ed K M Setton, 6 vols, Phila and Madison 1955–, 3.

Barber M J, The Englishman Abroad in the 15 Cent, MH 11(1957).69.

Perry J H, The Age of Reconaissance, London 1963.

Mitchell (crit TLS, 10 Sept 1964, p 839).

Parker (crit T Colbourn, AHR 72.575).

Storrs C and C Carrete, Peregrinos Ingleses a Santiago en el siglo xiv, Cuadernos de estudios Gallegos 20(1965).193.

Hall D J, Eng Mediaeval Pilgrimage, London 1966.

Harvey J H, ed, William Worcestre Itineraries, Oxford 1969.

Seymour MV, p 126n (ME fragment of Inventio fortunata).

Sumption (crit G Constable, TLS 22 Aug 1975, p 949).

Zacher C K, Curiosity and Pilgrimage: The Lit of Discovery in 14-Cent England, Baltimore and London 1976 (crit P Adams, Comp Lit Stud 15.341; M C Seymour, RES ns 29.79).

Finucane R C, Miracles and Pilgrims: Popular Beliefs in Medieval England, Totowa N J 1977 (crit C N L Brooke, History 63.442).

Metlitzki D, The Matter of Araby in Medieval England, New Haven and London 1977 (crit S G Armistead, Hispanic Rev 46.235; M C Seymour, ESts 61.556).

Seymour M C, Medieval America and Sir John Mandeville, An Eng Misc Presented to W S Mackie, ed B S Lee, London N Y and Capetown 1977, p 51 (ME fragment of Inventio fortunata).

Hyde J K, Navigation of the Eastern Mediterranean in the 14 and 15 Cents According to Pilgrims' Books, Papers in Italian Archaeology, 1, British Archaeological Reports, Supplementary Ser 41(1978).521.

Turner V and E Turner, Image and Pilgrimage in Christian Culture, N Y 1978, p 172.

Howard D R, Writers & Pilgrims: Medieval Pilgrimage Narratives and Their Posterity, Berkeley Los Angeles and London 1980 (crit A S G Edwards, MP 79.421; D W Rowe, Spec 57.135).

Friedman J B, The Monstrous Races in Medieval Art and Thought, Cambridge Mass and London 1981 (crit S Wenzel, JEGP 81.551; T A Shippey, TLS 13 Nov 1981, p 1321; L Patterson, Criticism 24.70).

Richard J, Les Récits de voyages et de pèlerinages, Typologie des sources du moyen âge occidental no 38, Turnhout Belgium 1981 (crit D R Howard, Spec 58.558).

Hyde J K, Real and Imaginary Journeys in the Later Middle Ages, JRLB 65(1982).125.

Adams P G, Travel Literature and the Evolution of the Novel, Lexington 1983, p 38.

Richard J, Croisés, Missionnaires et voyageurs: les perspectives orientales du monde latin médiéval, London 1983.

General Bibliographies. Röhricht, pp 1 (Holy Land itineraries), 598 (maps of the Holy Land).

Parks G B, Richard Hakluyt and the Eng Voyages, N Y 1930, p 269 (Eng bks on geography and travel to 1600).

Taylor, p 163 (Eng geographical and travel works to 1583).

Cox E G, A Reference Guide to the Lit of Travel, Univ of Washington Publs in Lang and Lit, nos 9, 10 and 12, 3 vols, Seattle 1935–49.

Parks ETI, p xvii.

Parker, p 243 (printed bks 1481–1620).

New CBEL, 1.467, 2109.

Heninger S K jr, Eng Prose, Prose Fiction, and Criticism to 1660, Detroit 1975, p 61.

Sumption, p 355.

Dansette B, Les pèlerinages occidentaux en Terre Sainte: une pratique de la Dévotion Moderne à la fin du Moyen Age? Relation inédite d'un pèlerinage effectué en 1486, Archivum Franciscanum Historicum 72(1979).128 (14–15 cent Holy Land pilgrimage accounts).

[1] THE SHIRES AND HUNDREDS OF ENGLAND.

MS. Jesus Oxf 29, ff 194ᵃ–195ᵃ [alias 267ᵃ–268ᵃ] (ca 1275).

Coxe H O, Catalogus Codicum MSS qui in Collegis Aulisque Oxoniensibus hodie adservantur, Oxford 1852, pars 2, Jesus Coll, p 9 (MS described).

Wrenn C L, Curiosities in a Medieval MS, E&S 25(1939).101 (MS provenance and marginalia).

Sisam C, The Broken Leaf in MS Jesus Coll Oxford 29, RES ns 5(1954).337 (MS contents).

Hill B, The Hist of Jesus Coll Oxford MS 29, MÆ 32(1963).203 (MS described).

The Owl and the Nightingale: Reproduced in Facsimile from the Surviving MSS Jesus Coll Oxford 29 and BM Cotton Calig A.ix, introd N R Ker, EETS 251, London N Y and Toronto 1963, p xi (MS foliation).

Editions. Morris R, An Old Eng Misc, EETS 49, London 1872, p 145.

Kluge F, Me Lesebuch, 2nd edn, Halle 1912, p 19.

Date. Paues A C, A Newly Discovered MS of the Poema Morale, Angl 30(1907).222.

Brown Reg, 1.144.

Hill, MÆ 32.204.

The Owl and the Nightingale, pp ix, xvi.

General Reference. Braswell L, Utilitarian and Scientific Prose, in ME Prose: A Critical Guide to Major Authors and Genres, ed A S G Edwards, New Brunswick N J 1984, pp 345, 372.

[2] A LIST OF 108 ENGLISH TOWNS.

MS. Bodl 21672.4 (Douce 98), ff 194ᵇ–195ᵇ (1295–1330).

Summary Cat, 4.520.

Edition. Bonnier C, List of Eng Towns in the 14 Cent, EHR 16(1901).501.

Date. Liebermann F, Reimer von Worcester, Arch 107(1901).386.

Literary Relations. Hyde J K, Medieval Descriptions of Cities, JRLB 48(1966).308.

Rigg A G, The Stores of the Cities, Angl 85 (1967).127.

Palmer R, The Folklore of Warwickshire, Totowa N J 1976, p 17 (other town rimes).

Robbins R H, Manual, 5.1473 (XIII [173]).

General References. Reynolds S, An Introd to the Hist of Eng Medieval Towns, Oxford 1977 rvsd 1982, p 50.

Braswell, Utilitarian and Scientific Prose, p 345.

[3] A GEOGRAPHY IN VERSE.

MSS. 1, Royal 13.D.xii, f 246ᵇ (1375–1400); 2, two MSS, whereabouts unknown.

Brown-Robbins, Robbins-Cutler, no 3653.

The Phillipps MSS, introd A Munby, London 1968, p 39 (one of the lost MSS).

Edition. Rel Ant, 1.271 (MS 1).

Date. Warner G F and J P Gilson, Catalogue of the Western MSS in the Old Royal and King's Collections, London 1921, 2.109.

[4] THE STATIONS OF ROME.

MSS. 1, Bodl 3938 (Vernon), ff 314ª–315ᵇ (lines 1–734; ca 1385); 2, BM Addit 22283 (Simeon), ff 123ª–124ᵇ (lines 1–811; 1380–1400); 3, BM Addit 37787, f 18ª (last seven lines; ca 1386); 4, Cotton Calig A.ii, ff 83ª–86ᵇ (lines 1–553, incomplete; 1400–50); 5, Cotton Vesp D.ix, ff 183ª–188ª (lacks lines 1–100; early 15 cent); 6, Public Record Office, SC 6/956/5, roll (lines 1–667; after line 19, verse copied as prose; 15 cent); 7, Nat Libr Wales Deposit Porkington 10, ff 132ª–135ᵇ (prose; 1453–1500); 8, Lambeth 306, ff 152ᵇ–165ª (lines 1–914; 15 cent); 9, Newberry Gen Add 12 (Condover Hall), roll (late 14 cent).

Brown-Robbins, Robbins-Cutler, no 1172; Brown-Robbins, no 1962.

Brown Reg, pt 2, nos 715, 1216, 2641.

Summary Cat, vol 2, pt 2, p 789 (MS 1 described).

New CBEL, 1.470.

Catalogue of Additions to the MSS in the BM in the Years 1854–60, London 1875, p 623 (MSS 1 and 2 described).

Gairdner J ed, Three 15-Cent Chronicles, Camden Soc ns 28, Westminster 1880, p i (MS 8 described).

Ward, 1.180 (MS 4 dated).

James M R and C Jenkins, A Descriptive Catalogue of the MSS in the Libr of Lambeth Palace, Cambridge 1930, p 421 (MS 8 described and dated).

Greene R L, The Early Eng Carols, Oxford 1935, p 334 (MS 8 described).

Serjeantson M S, The Index of the Vernon MS, MLR 32(1937).222 (MS 1 described).

Kurvinen A, ed, Sir Gawain and the Carl of Carlisle in Two Versions, Annales Academiae Scientiarum Fennicae, B 71, 2, Helsinki 1951, p 28 (MS 7 dated); MS Porkington 10, Description with Extracts, NM 54(1953).33 (MS 7 described).

Faye C U and W H Bond, Supplement to the Census of Medieval and Renaissance MSS in the U S and Canada, N Y 1962, p 149 (MS 9 described).

Sajavaara K, The Relationship of the Vernon and Simeon MSS, NM 68(1967).428 (interrelations of MSS 1, 2 and 3); The ME Translations of Robert Grosseteste's Chateau d'Amour, Mémoires de la Société Néophilologique de Helsinki 32 (1967).103 (MS 1), 121 (MS 2).

Scattergood V J, An Inedited MS of The Stacions of Rome, Eng Philological Stud 11(1968).51 (MS 6 described; unique passages printed); Politics and Poetry in the 15 Cent, London 1971, p 168 (MS 8 dated).

Doyle A I, The Shaping of the Vernon and Simeon MSS, Chaucer and ME Stud in Honour of Rossell Hope Robbins, ed B Rowland, London 1974, p 328 (MS 1 and parallels between MSS 1 and 2 described).

Editions. Furnivall F J, Political, Religious, and Love Poems, EETS 15, London 1866; rvsd 1903, pp xxi (notes on stational churches by Rossetti), 143 (MSS 4 and 8); The Stacions of Rome, EETS 25, London 1867, pp xi (further notes by Rossetti), 1 (MS 1 minus prologue), 30 (MS 7); The Minor Poems of the Vernon MS, Pt 2, EETS 117, London 1901, p 609 (MS 1, prologue only).

Baugh N S, A Worcestershire Misc Compiled by John Northwood, c 1400, Phila 1956, introd, passim (date and scribe), pp 40 (other MSS and affiliations), 106 (MS 3).

Date. Schofield, p 461.

Sources and Literary Relations. Hulbert J R, Some Medieval Advertisements of Rome, MP 20(1923).411 (selections from another guide), 420 (additions to Rossetti's notes).

A XVth Cent Guide-Book to the Principal Churches of Rome Compiled c 1470 by William Brewyn, trans C E Woodruff, London 1933.

de Beer E S, The Stacions of Rome, N&Q 184(1943).126 (further notes on churches); An Eng XV-Cent Pilgrimage Poem, N&Q 187 (1944).244 (a passage recurring in [9]); The Development of the Guide-Book until the Early 19 Cent, British Archaeological Assoc Journ 3s 15(1952).39 (guides to Rome).

Parks ETI, p 243 (guides to Rome).

Scattergood V J, An Unpublished ME Poem, Arch 203(1967).277 (a 70-line description of Rome found with MS 6).

Sumption, p 225 (guides to Rome).

See [9], [12], [13], [14], [17], and [18] below.

General References. Sumption, p 243.

Scattergood, review, ELN 15(1977).125.

Robbins R H, Manual, 5.1473.

Bibliography. New CBEL, 1.470.

[5] MANDEVILLE'S TRAVELS.

MSS. Defective Version (prose): 32 MSS (after 1375; for description of MSS, see M C Seymour, Edinburgh Biblio Soc Trans 4, pt 5, p 178); *Cotton Version (prose)*: 33, Cotton Titus C.xvi (early 15 cent); *Egerton Version (prose)*: 34, Egerton 1982 (early 15 cent); *Bodley Version (prose)*: 35, Bodl 12917 (Rawlinson D.99) (1400–50); 36, Bodl 3617 (e Musaeo 116), ff 6ᵇ–49ᵇ (1390–1450); *Metrical Version (verse)*: 37, Coventry Record Office, ff 77ᵇ–95ᵇ (imperfect; 1425–50); *Stanzaic Fragment (verse)*: 38, Bodl 3692 (e Musaeo 160), ff 113ᵇ, 109ᵃ–112ᵇ, 115ᵃ (imperfect; early 16 cent); *Epitome (prose)*: 39, BM Addit 37049, ff 3ᵃ–9ᵃ (ca 1450); *Ashmole Extracts (prose)*: 40, Bodl 8193 (Ashmole 751), ff 48ᵃ–50ᵇ, 142ᵇ–143ᵃ (early 15 cent); *Digby Extracts (prose)*: 41, Bodl 1689 (Digby 88), ff 28ᵃ⁻ᵇ (ca 1500); *Ripon Fragment (prose)*: 42, 99 lines on vellum binding of 16-cent printed book.

Brown-Robbins, no 3843 (MS 38); Robbins-Cutler, nos 248.5 (MS 37), 3117.6 (MS 38).

Summary Cat, vol 2, pt 1, p 73 (MS 41); vol 2, pt 2, pp 703 (MS 36 described), 732 (MS 38 described), 1154 (MS 40); vol 3, p 226 (MS 35).

Vogels J, Handschriftliche Untersuchungen über die engl Version Mandevilles, Crefeld 1891.

Sisam K, 14-Cent Verse & Prose, Oxford 1921, p 239.

Letts M, N&Q 192(1947).46 (MSS and edns); N&Q 193(1948).200 (translators' errors); Sir John Mandeville: The Man and His Book, London 1949, pp 127 (MS 33 described; MSS 33 and 34 compared), 133 (MS 34 described), 167 (MSS of Eng versions).

Bennett J W, The Rediscovery of Sir John Mandeville, N Y 1954; rptd N Y 1971, p 287 (MSS 1–36, 39, 40 described).

Wright C E, Eng Vernacular Hands from the 12 to the 15 Cents, Oxford 1960, p 17 (MS 33 described), plate 17 (facsimile of MS 33, f 60ᵇ).

Seymour M C, A Medieval Redactor at Work, N&Q 206(1961).169 (MSS 35, 36 as abridgements); The Eng MSS of Mandeville's Travels, Edinburgh Biblio Soc Trans 4, pt 5.169 (all MSS of Eng versions described), 178 (MSS 1–32).

Smith K L, A 15-Cent Vernacular MS Reconstructed, The Bodleian Libr Record 7(1966).234 (MS 35).

Doyle A I and G B Pace, A New Chaucer MS, PMLA 83(1968).22 (MS 37 described).

Seymour M C, The Scribal Tradition of MT in England, in Seymour MV, p 193 (relation of Eng and nonEng insular versions); The Scribe of Huntington Libr MS HM.114, MÆ 43(1974).139 (MS of Defective Version).

Ker N R, Medieval MSS in British Librs, 2 vols, Abbotsford-Keele Oxford 1977, 2.411 (MS 37 described).

Friedman J B, The Monstrous Races in Medieval Art and Thought, Cambridge Mass and London 1981, pp 28, 34 (MS illuminations).

Hanna R III, Mandeville, in ME Prose: A Critical Guide to Major Authors and Genres, ed A S G

Edwards, New Brunswick N J 1984, p 129 (MSS of prose versions).

Editions. (Note: The editions of each version are listed separately below.)

a. Defective Version.

None, but see pre-modern edns listed in:

Esdaile A, A List of Eng Tales and Prose Romances Printed before 1740, London 1912, p 98.

Bennett J W, The Rediscovery of Sir John Mandeville, p 346.

Seymour, The Early Eng Printed Edns of MT, Libr 5s 19(1964).202.

The Travels of Sir John Mandeville: Facsimile of Pynson's Edn of 1496, introd M C Seymour, Exeter 1980, p x.

b. Cotton Version.

Hamelius P, Mandeville's Travels, 2 vols, EETS 153 and 154, London 1919 and 1923, 1.212 (prints from MS 34 passage missing in Defective Version); 2.1 (author), 14 (date), 16 (MS), 19 (sources), 21 (alphabets).

Seymour M C, Mandeville's Travels, Oxford 1967, pp xiii (author), xiv and 276 (sources), xxi (MS 33 described), 272 (MSS of French, Latin, Eng, Irish versions) (crit TLS, 11 Jan 1968, p 32; A C Cawley, N&Q 213.15; B D H Miller MÆ 37.336; C Sisam, RES ns 20.524).

c. Egerton Version.

Warner G F, The Buke of John Maundeuill, Roxb Club 119, Westminster 1889, pp x (MSS of French version), xi (MSS 33, 34 described), xv and passim (sources), xxx (author) (crit H Cordier, T'oung Pao, edd G Schlegel and H Cordier, Leiden 1891, 2.288).

d. Bodley Version.

Letts M, Mandeville's Travels: Texts and Translations, Hakluyt Soc, 2 vols, London 1953, 2.419 (MS 35), xxx (MSS 1–32), lxi (MS 34), 416 (MS 35 described); includes E G R Taylor, The Cosmographical Ideas of Mandeville's Day, 1.li.

Seymour M C, The Bodley Version of Mandeville's Travels, EETS 253, London N Y and Toronto 1963, pp 3 (MS 36), xi (relation to MS 35, date), xii (source), xvi (MSS 35, 36 described), xx (language and scribe), 176 (author) (crit A C Cawley, N&Q 209.194; N-O Jönsson, ESts 46.205; P Gradon, RES ns 16.411; B D H Miller, MÆ 35.71).

e. Metrical Version.

Seymour MV, pp xi (sources and origins), xvi (date, language), xviii (author), xx (MS 37 described) (crit B D H Miller, MÆ 43.302; A Leyland, ESts 56.259; W Arens, Angl 94.510).

f. Stanzaic Fragment.

Rel Ant, 2.113 (lines 185–282).

Hazlitt Rem, 1.155 (lines 185–282).

Seymour M C, Mandeville and Marco Polo: A Stanzaic Fragment, Journ of the Australasian Univs Lang and Lit Assoc 21(1964).39 (MS 38 described).

g. Epitome.

Seymour M C, The Eng Epitome of Mandeville's Travels, Angl 84(1966).27 (MS 39 described).

h. Ashmole Extracts.

Seymour M C, Secundum Iohannem Maundvyle, Eng Stud in Africa 4(1961).148 (MS 40 and relation to other versions described).

i. Digby Extracts.

Horner P J, Mandeville's Travels: A New MS Extract, Manuscripta 24(1980).171 (MS 41 and relation to Defective Version described).

j. Ripon Fragment.

Cawley A C, A Ripon Fragment of Mandeville's Travels, ESts 38(1957).262 (MS 42 and relation to Defective Version described).

Modernizations. See lists in: Bennett J W, The Rediscovery of Sir John Mandeville, N Y 1954; rptd N Y 1971, p 346 (to 1953); The Travels of Sir John Mandeville: Facsimile of Pynson's Edn of 1496, introd M C Seymour, Exeter 1980, p x (to 1973).

Moseley C W R D, trans, The Travels of Sir John Mandeville, Harmondsworth Eng 1983 (MS 34), pp 9 (author), 18 (sources), 22, 29 (influences and reputation), 35 (versions compared).

Selections. AESpr, 1(pt 2).155 (from MS 33).

Morris Spec, p 164 (MS 33).

Kluge F, Me Lesebuch, 2nd edn, Halle 1912, p 33 (MS 33).

Cook A S, A Literary ME Reader, Boston 1915, p 248 (MS 34).

Sisam K, 14-Cent Verse & Prose, Oxford 1921, p 94 (MS 33).

Guildford E L, Travellers & Travelling in the Middle Ages, London 1924, pp 10, 17, 35 (MS 33).

Patterson R F, Six Cents of Eng Lit, London 1933, 1.49 (MS 33).

Kaiser R, Medieval Eng, 3rd edn rvsd, Berlin 1958, p 512 (MS 33).

Matthews W, Later Medieval Eng Prose, N Y 1963, p 217 (MS 33).

Haskell A, A ME Anthology, Garden City N Y 1969, p 158 (MS 33).

Textual Matters. Hinton J, Notes on Walter Map's De Nugis Curialium, SP 20(1923).460 (a reading in MS 34 preferable to MS 33).

Letts M, The Source of the Woodcuts in Wynkyn de Worde's Edn of MT, 1499, Libr 5s 6(1951).154 (largely from 1481 German edn).

Bennett J W, The Woodcut Illusts in the Eng Edns of MT, PBSA 47(1953).59.

Seymour M C, The Origin of the Egerton Version of MT, MÆ 30(1961).159; Libr 5s 19(1964).202.

See MSS above.

Language. Gesenius [F W], Sir John Maundevylle, Arch 27(1860).399 (grammatical analysis).

Fife R H, Der Wortschatz des Engl Maundeville nach der Version der Cotton Handschrift Titus C.XVI, Leipzig 1902 (crit C G Osgood, AJP 28.90).

Van der Meer H J, Main Facts Concerning the Syntax of MT, Utrecht 1929 (crit D Everett, YWES 11.124; F Karpf, NS 40.311; R Hittmair, ESts 69.393).

Date. Steiner A, The Date of Composition of MT, Spec 9(1934).144.

Thomas J D, The Date of MT, MLN 72(1957).165.

Moseley C W R D, Sir John Mandeville's Visit to the Pope: The Implications of an Interpolation, Neophil 54(1970).77.

Author. Hamelius P, The Travels of Sir John Mandeville, Quart Rev 227(1917).331.

Singer D W, Note, Libr 3s 9(1918).275.

Jackson I, Who was Sir John Mandeville? A Fresh Clue, MLR 23(1928).466.

Cameron K W, A Discovery in John de Mandevilles, Spec 11(1936).351.

Braaksma M H, Travel and Lit: An Attempt at a Literary Appreciation of Eng Travelbooks about Persia, Groningen 1938, pp 21, 33.

Letts, N&Q 191(1946).202; N&Q 193(1948).52; Sir John Mandeville, pp 13, 107.

Fazy R, Jehan de Mandeville: ses voyages et son séjour discuté en Egypte, Etudes asiatiques 4 (1950).30.

Bennett, Rediscovery, p 89.

Mosse F, Du Nouveau sur le Chevalier Jean Mandeville, EA 8(1955).321.

Mourin L, Les lapidaires attribués à Jean de Mandeville et à Jean à la Barbe, Romanica Gandensia 4(1956).159 (includes edns of both).

Goosse A, Les lapidaires attribués à Mandeville, Les Dialectes Belgo-Romans 17(1960).63.

Lejeune R, Jean de Mandeville et les Liégeois, Mélanges de linguistique romane et de philologie médiévale offerts à Maurice Delbouille, 2 vols, Gembloux 1964, 2.409 (theories of identity reviewed).

Metlitzki D, The Matter of Araby in Medieval England, New Haven and London 1977, p 220 (Mandeville's possible firsthand knowledge of Egypt and vicinity).

Sources. Bovenschen A, Untersuchungen über Johann von Mandeville und die Quellen seiner Reisebeschreibung, Zeitschrift der Gesellschaft für Erdkunde zu Berlin 23(1888).177 (author), 206 (sources).

Beazley C R, The Dawn of Modern Geography, 3 vols, London 1897–1906; rptd N Y 1949, 3.319.

Esposito M, A New Mandeville Source, N&Q 11s 10(1914).505 (Alexander tale).

Peebles R J, The Dry Tree: Symbol of Death, Vassar Mediaeval Stud, ed C F Fiske, New Haven 1923, p 63.

Braaksma, Travel and Literature, p 12.

Letts, N&Q 192(1947).46; Sir John Mandeville, pp 29, 41.

Hennig R, Terrae Incognitae, 4 vols, Leiden 1936–39, 3.199.

Moule A C, N&Q 192(1947).152 (borrowing from Odoric).

Loomis R S, The Fier Baiser in MT, Arthurian Romance and Irish Saga, Studi Mediaevali 17 (1951).104 (tale of Hippocrates' daughter).

Bernheimer R, Wild Men in the Middle Ages: A Study in Art, Sentiment, and Demonology, Cambridge Mass 1952, pp 92, 107, 110 (heritage and appearance in MT).

Cawley A C, MT: A Possible New Source, N&Q 217(1972).47 (Macrobius); slightly rvsd as, Down Under: A Possible New Source for MT, Iceland and the Mediaeval World: Stud in Honour of Ian Maxwell, ed G Turville-Petre and J S Martin, Victoria Australia 1974, p 144.

Seymour M C, Medieval America and Sir John Mandeville, An Eng Misc Presented to W S Mackie, ed B S Lee, Capetown London and N Y 1977, p 46 (other circumnavigation stories).

Contemporary Literary Relations and Influences. Brown C F, Note on the Dependence of Cleanness on the Book of Mandeville, PMLA 19(1904).149.

Lowes J L, The Dry Sea and the Carrenare, MP 3(1905).1 (Chaucer's partial indebtedness).

Cawley R R, The Voyagers and Elizabethan Drama, Boston and London 1938, passim (literary relations); Unpathed Waters: Stud in the Influence of the Voyagers on Elizabethan Lit, Princeton 1940, passim (sources and influences).

Lange H, Die Paradiesvorstellung in MT im Lichte mittelalterlicher Dichtung, EStn 72(1938).312 (Chaucer's different depiction of earthly paradise); Chaucer und MT, Arch 174(1938).79.

Letts, N&Q 192(1947).224 (d'Outremeuse's debt to Mandeville).

Bennett, Chaucer and MT, MLN 68(1953).531 (allusion in Squire's Tale); Rediscovery, p 221 (influence on Chaucer and Pearl-poet).

Hertz J A, Chapters toward a Study of Chaucer's Knowledge of Geography, diss Lehigh Univ 1958, DAI 19(1959).2600 (debt to Mandeville).

Goosse A, Jean d'Outremeuse et Jean de Mandeville, Festschrift Walther von Wartburg zum 80 geburtstag, ed K Baldinger, 2 vols, Tübingen 1968, 1.235.

Morrall E J, Michel Velsers Mandeville und Petrarcas geographische Schriften: Bemerkungen zu der Mandeville-Handschrift Supersaxo 94 der Kantonsbibliothek zu Sitten im Wallis, Vallesia 26(1971).111 (their shared interests in travel and marvels).

Moseley, Chaucer, Sir John Mandeville, and the Alliterative Revival: A Hypothesis Concerning Relationships, MP 72(1974).182.

Influences in the Renaissance. Parr J, More Sources of Rastell's Interlude of the Four Elements, PMLA 60(1945).49 (Mandeville's account of Prester John and India).

Letts, Sir John Mandeville, p 34.

Bennett, Rediscovery, p 230.

York E C, Nashe and Mandeville, N&Q 202 (1957).159.

Moseley, The Lost Play of Mandeville, Libr 5s 25(1970).46 (possible 16-cent play based on Mandeville); The Availability of MT in England, 1356–1730, Libr 30(1971).125; Richard Head's The Eng Rogue: A Modern Mandeville? Yearbook of Eng Stud 1(1971).102 (debt to Mandeville).

Ginzburg C, Il formaggio e i vermi: Il cosmo di un mugnaio del '500, Torino 1976, trans J and A Tedeschi, The Cheese and the Worms: The Cosmos of a 16-Cent Miller, Baltimore 1980 (Mandeville's influence on popular thought).

Hahn T, Indians East and West: Primitivism and Savagery in Eng Discovery Narratives of the 16 Cent, Journ of Medieval and Renaissance Stud 8(1978).83 (Mandeville's image of virtuous Indians).

Moseley, Behaim's Globe and MT, Imago Mundi 33(1981).89.

Later Reputation. Letts, N&Q 191(1946).275.

Bennett, Rediscovery, p 250.

Moseley, Stitched Ships and Loadstone Rocks, N&Q 213(1968).323 (effect of a mistaken Mandevillian explanation on reception of other travellers' accounts).

Foster B, Wooden Ships and Loadstone Rocks: An Old French Example, N&Q 214(1969).403 (adds to Moseley).

Beckingham C F, The Near East: North and Northeast Africa, The Hakluyt Handbook, ed D B Quinn, 2 vols, London 1974, 1.180 (Hakluyt's opinion of Mandeville's reliability).

Moseley, The Metamorphosis of Sir John Mandeville, Yearbook of Eng Stud 4(1974).5 (changing texts and reputation to 1750).

Seymour, A Letter from Sir John Mandeville, N&Q 219(1974).326 (late medieval Eng reputation).

Tadie A A, Hakluyt's and Purchas's Use of the Latin Version of MT, Acta Conventus Neo-Latini Turonensis, ed J-C Margolin, Paris 1980, p 537.

Billingsley D B, Gulliver, Mandeville and Capital Crime, N&Q 228(1983).32 (crit H Real and H Vienken, Gulliver and Mandeville, N&Q 228 .512).

Non-English Versions. Vogels J, Das Verhältnis der italienischen Version der Reisebeschreibung Mandevilles zur französischen, Festschrift dem Gymnasium Adolfinum zu Moers, Bonn 1882, p 37; Die ungedruckten lateinischen Versionen Mandevilles, Crefeld 1886.

Stokes W, ed and trans, The Gaelic Maundeville, Zeitschrift für celtische Philologie 2(1899).1, 226.

Cordier H, Jean de Mandeville, T'oung Pao, edd G Schlegel and H Cordier, 2 vols, Leiden 1891, 2.299 (early Latin and vernacular edns).

Cestopis tzv Mandevilla, ed F Šimek, Prague 1911; rptd Prague 1963 (Czech version).

Entwistle W J, The Spanish Mandevilles, MLR 17(1922).251.

Letts, N&Q 192(1947).300 (German version), 494 (earliest MS); Sir John Mandeville, pp 135 (German version), 166 (Latin MSS), 172 (French, Italian, German, Irish, Dutch MSS), 177 (early non-Eng edns).

Haraszti Z, The Travels of Sir John Mandeville, Boston Pub Libr Quart 2(1950).306 (German versions, author, sources).

Bennett, Rediscovery, pp 265 and 298 (non-Eng MSS), 337 and 359 (early non-Eng edns).

Letts, A German MS of MT dated 1433, MLR 50(1955).57.

de Poerck G, La tradition manuscrite des Voyages de Jean de Mandeville, Romanica Gandensia 4(1956).125.

Morrall E J, Michel Velser, Übersetzer einer deutschen Version von Sir John Mandevilles Reisen, Zeitschrift für deutsche Philologie 81(1962).82; Michel Velser and His German Trans of MT, The Durham Univ Journ ns 24(1962).16.

Schepens L, Au sujet de deux manuscrits de Jean de Mandeville, Scriptorium 16(1962).377.

Seymour, The Irish Version of MT, N&Q 208 (1963).364; and R A Waldron, The Danish Version of MT, N&Q 208(1963).406; The Scribal Tradition of MT: The Insular Version, Scriptorium 18(1964).34 (crit L Schepens, Quelques observations sur la tradition manuscrite du Voyage de Mandeville, Scriptorium 18[1964].49).

Lejeune R, Jean de Mandeville et les Liégeois, 2.409.

de Kock J, Quelques copies aberrantes des Voyages de Jean de Mandeville, Le Moyen Age 71 (1965).521 (MSS of French version).

Morrall E J, Oswald von Wolkenstein and MT, Mediaeval German Stud Presented to Frederick Norman, London 1965, p 262.

Doyle M and M C Seymour, The Irish Epitome of MT, Éigse: A Journ of Irish Stud 12, pt 1(1967).29.

Morrall, The Text of Michel Velser's Mandeville Trans, Probleme Mittelalterlicher Überlieferung und Textkritik, edd P F Ganz and W Schröder, Berlin 1968, p 183.

Bradley S A J, The Translator of Mandevilles Rejse: a new name in 15-cent Danish Prose? Medieval Lit and Civilization: Stud in Memory of G N Garmonsway, edd D A Pearsall and R A Waldron, London 1969, p 146 (Peder Hare).

Sir John Mandevilles Reisebeschreibung in deutscher Übersetzung von Michel Velser, ed E J Morrall, Deutsche Texte des Mittelalters 66, Berlin 1974 (crit Seymour, MÆ 45.329).

Montañes P L, ed, Libro de las maravillas del mundo de Juan de Mandevilla, Zaragoza 1979.

Seymour, The Czech Version of MT, N&Q 224 (1979).395.

The Travels of Sir John Mandeville: A MS in the British Libr, introd J Krása, trans P Kussi, N Y 1983 (reprods of MS BM Addit 24189, containing no text but 28 illusts of the Czech trans).

Literary Criticism. CHEL, 2. 91, 96 (sources), 92 (author), 94 (versions).

Hamelius, Quart Rev 227.345 (Mandeville's religious views).

Powys L, Sir John Mandeville, The Freeman 7(1923).132 (technique of imaginary traveller).

Atiya A S, The Crusade in the Later Middle Ages, London 1938, p 161 (authentic and fictional mixed).

Braaksma, Travel and Literature, pp 18, 23.

Patch H R, The Other World According to Descriptions in Medieval Lit, Cambridge Mass 1950, pp 164, 172 (book as synthesis of journey to paradise).

Bloomfield M W, Chaucer's Sense of Hist, JEGP 51(1952).310 (Mandeville's tolerance and relativism).

Bennett, Rediscovery, p 15.

Schlauch M, Eng Medieval Lit and Its Social Foundations, Warsaw 1956; rptd 1967, p 196 (Mandeville's religious parody).

Howard D R, The World of MT, Yearbook of Eng Stud 1(1971).1 (originality and structure).

Butturff D R, Satire in MT, Annuale Mediaevale 13(1972).155.

Zacher C K, Curiosity and Pilgrimage: The Lit of Discovery in 14-Cent England, Baltimore and London 1976, p 130 (motives and structure).

Howard D R, Writers & Pilgrims: Medieval Pilgrimage Narratives and Their Posterity, Berkeley Los Angeles and London 1980, p 53 and passim.

Friedman J B, The Monstrous Races in Medieval Art and Thought, Cambridge Mass and London 1981, pp 154 and 158 (persona), 55, 143 and 166 (genre).

Mezciems J, 'Tis not to divert the Reader: Moral and Literary Determinants in Some Early Travel Narratives, Prose Stud 5(1982).5 (narrator).

Moseley, trans, Travels of Sir John Mandeville, pp 13, 16 (persona), 22 (genres).

Adams P G, Travel Literature and the Evolution of the Novel, Lexington 1983, pp 73 (sources and popularity), 95 and 172 (influence), 168 (persona).

Hanna, Mandeville, p 121 (textual tradition, genre, style).

Bibliography. Röhricht, p 79.

Hennig, Terrae Incognitae, 3.199.

Bennett H S, Chaucer and the 15 Cent, Oxford 1947; rvsd 1948, p 293.

Letts, Sir John Mandeville, p 182.

The Medieval Lit of Western Europe: A Rev of Research, Mainly 1930–60, gen ed J H Fisher, London 1966, pp 88, 189.

New CBEL, 1.471.

Lidman M J, The Travels of Sir John Mandeville: A Checklist, Thoth 15(1974–75).13.

Moseley, trans, Travels of Sir John Mandeville, p 194.

Hanna, Mandeville, p 130.

[6] ADVICE FOR EASTBOUND TRAVELLERS.

MS. Cotton Append VIII, ff 108^b–112^b (begins imperfectly; 15 cent).

Planta J, A Catalogue of the MSS in the Cottonian Libr Deposited in the British Museum, London 1802, p 615.

Blades W, The Life and Typography of William Caxton, 2 vols, London 1861 and 1863, 2.172 (MS dated).

Lauritis J A, R A Klinefelter and V F Gallagher, edd, A Critical Edn of John Lydgate's Life of Our Lady, Duquesne Stud, Philological Ser 2, Pittsb 1961, p 44 (MS described).

Edition. Horstmann, C, Rathschläge für eine Orientreise, EStn 8(1885).277.

Modernization. Parks ETI, p 550 (selections).

General References. Meech and Allen, EETS 212. 284n, 288n.

Bennett H S, MLR 39.6; Chaucer and the 15 Cent, Oxford 1947; rvsd 1948, p 199.

Braswell, Utilitarian and Scientific Prose, p 345.

[7] THE BOOK OF MARGERY KEMPE.

MS. BL Addit 61823 (Colonel W Butler-Bowdon; ca 1450).

Edition. Meech S B and H E Allen, The Book of Margery Kempe, EETS 212, London N Y and Toronto 1940; rptd 1961, pp xxxii (MS described), xxxiii (date), xlvi (de Worde 1501, selections), 284n (date of Jerusalem pilgrimage), 308n (date of Compostella pilgrimage), 343n (date of continental pilgrimage).

Selection. Matthews W, Later Medieval Eng Prose, N Y 1963, p 79 (Jerusalem pilgrimage).

Modernization. The Book of Margery Kempe 1436, ed and trans W Butler-Bowdon, introd R W Chambers, London and Toronto 1936; rptd N Y 1944.

Discussions of Kempe's Pilgrimage. Prescott, p 7 (Kempe's egotism).

Bennett H S, Six Medieval Men and Women, Cambridge 1955; rptd N Y 1962, p 124.

Howard D R, Writers & Pilgrims, Berkeley Los Angeles and London 1980, p 34 (lack of description).

Atkinson C W, Mystic and Pilgrim: The Book and the World of Margery Kempe, Ithaca and London 1983, p 51.

Parks ETI, p 523 (Kempe's Alpine route), 537 (mode of travel), 545 (dangers of travel), 547 (stay in Rome).

Fries M, Margery Kempe, An Introd to the Medieval Mystics of Europe: 14 Original Essays, ed P E Szarmach, Albany 1984, p 217 (pattern of Kempe's quests).

See The Book of Margery Kempe in the chapter on English Mystical Writers.

General References. Mitchell, pp 17, 105.

Sumption, pp 197, 269, 272, 299.

Bibliography. Lagorio V M and R Bradley, The 14 Cent Eng Mystics: A Comprehensive Annotated Biblio, N Y and London 1981, p 127.

Hirsh J C, Margery Kempe, in Middle Eng Prose: A Critical Guide to Major Authors and Genres, ed A S G Edwards, New Brunswick N J 1984, p 116.

[8] THE PILGRIMAGES OF THE HOLY LAND.

MS. Bodl 1414 (Laud Misc 622), f 64a–b (1400–25). Summary Cat, vol 2, pt 1, p 61.

Coxe H O, Bodleian Libr Quarto Catalogues, II: Laudian MSS, Oxford 1860; rvsd Oxford 1973, col 447 (MS described, dated).

Adam Davy's 5 Dreams about Edward II, ed F J Furnivall, EETS 69, London 1878, p 7 (MS described).

Smithers G V, Kyng Alisaunder, 2 vols, EETS 227, 237, London 1947, 1952, 1.1 (MS described, dated).

General Reference. Webb J, A Survey of Egypt and Syria, Undertaken in the Year 1422, by Sir Gilbert de Lannoy, Knt, Archaeol 21(1827).415.

See also the Holy Land itineraries in [13] and [14] below.

[9] PURCHAS'S PILGRIM ITINERARY.

MSS. No MS extant.
Robbins-Cutler, no 1557.5.

Edition. Purchas S, Purchas His Pilgrimes, London 1625, ii, p 1230; rptd Glasgow and N Y 1905, 20 vols, 7.527.

Selections. Webb J, Archaeol 21.375n (lines 1507–10).

King G G, The Way of Saint James, N Y and London 1920, 3 vols, 3.568 (lines 1–198).

Hartley D, ed, The Old Book: A Mediaeval Anthology, London 1930, p 134 (inaccurate selections from Purchas edn, misdated; crit C Coulter, Spec 7.131).

Language. Dunlap A R, A Pilgrimage to the Holy Land, MLN 63(1948).57 (northern dialect).

Date. de Beer E S, An Eng XV-Cent Pilgrimage Poem, N&Q 187(1944).244 (identifies two Eng companions, annotates place names, suggests [4] as source).

Parks ETI, pp 352, 381.

Other Scholarly Problems. Parks G B, The Route of Chaucer's First Trip to Italy, ELH 16(1949).174 (usual Eng route).

Emden A B, A Biographical Register of the Univ of Oxford to A D 1500, Oxford 1957–59, p 1252 (Medford).

Richard J, Les récits de voyages et de pèlerinage, Typologie des sources du moyen âge occidental no 38, Turnhout Belgium 1981, p 19 (mixed genres).

General References. Barwick G F, Trans of the Bibliographical Soc 7.191.

Lowes J L, The Dry Sea and the Carrenare, MP 3(1905).5n.

Robbins R H, Manual, 5.1473.

[10] THE WAY UNTO ROME AND SO TO VENICE AND TO JERUSALEM.

MS. Huntington Libr EL 26.A.13 (Bridgwater House), f 120b (1444–56).

Brown Reg, 1.467 (MS described).

de Ricci Census, p 132 (MS described).

Guide to Medieval and Renaissance MSS in the Huntington Libr, San Marino, forthcoming (MS described, dated).

Selection. Parks ETI, p 526 (first 60 names on list transcribed); illust no 19 (reduced facsimile of folio).

Date. Troilus and Criseyde: Geoffrey Chaucer, a Facsimile of Corpus Christi Coll Cambridge MS 61, introd M B Parkes and E Salter, Cambridge 1978, p 11n.

See [19] below.

[11] GUIDE TO THE HOLY LAND.

MS. Queen's Oxf 357, ff 8b–43b (15 cent).

Coxe H O, Catalogus Codicum MSS qui in Collegis Aulisque Oxoniensibus hodie adservantur, Oxford 1852, pars 1, Queen's College, p 83 (MS described).

General Reference. Hakluyt Handbook, 1.182.

[12] THE SOLACE OF PILGRIMS.

MSS. 1, Bodl 2322(E), ff 355a–414b (imperfect; ca 1451); 2, All Souls Oxf 17, f ia–b and pp 223–224 (fragment, corresponding to MS 1, ff 364a–365a; mid-15 cent); 3, Balliol Oxf 190, ff 118a–119b (fragment, corresponding to MS 1, ff 365a–366b; mid-15 cent).

Summary Cat, vol 2, pt 1, p 309 (MS 1 described).

Mynors R A B, Catalogue of the MSS of Balliol Coll Oxf, Oxford 1963, p 191 (MSS 2 and 3 described).

Lucas P J, A 15-cent Copyist at Work under Authorial Scrutiny: an Incident from John Capgrave's Scriptorium, SB 34(1981).67 (MSS 1, 2 and 3 described, related, dated); plate I (reduced reprod of MS 1, f 365a); plate II (partial reprods of MS 2, f ib and MS 3, f 118a).

Braswell, Utilitarian and Scientific Prose, p 371 (MSS 1, 2, 3).

Editions. Mills C A, Ye Solace of Pilgrims, Journ of the British and American Archaeological Soc of

Rome, introd H M Bannister, London 1911; rptd
N Y 1980, frntspc (reduced reprod of MS 1, f
387ᵃ), p xi (MS 1 described) (crit G Rushforth,
EHR 27.777; E S de Beer, N&Q 184.130).

Hingeston F C, The Chronicle of England by John
Capgrave, Rolls Series 1, London 1858, p 357
(MSS 2 and 3).

Selection. Codice Topografico della Città di Roma, a
cura di R Valentini e G Zucchetti, Instituto Storico
Italiano per il Medio Evo, vol 91, Roma 1953,
pp 330 (with Italian trans), 325 (sources).

Date. Meijer A de, John Capgrave OESA, Augustiniana 5(1955).422.

Emden A B, A Biographical Register of the Univ of
Cambridge to 1500, Cambridge 1963, p 122.

Lucas P J, ed, John Capgrave's Abbreuiacion of
Cronicles, EETS 285, Oxford 1983, p ci; John
Capgrave, OSA (1393–1464), Scribe and Publisher, Trans of the Cambridge Biblio Soc 5
(1969).3n.

Fredeman J C, The Life of John Capgrave, OESA
(1393–1464), Augustiniana 29(1979).231.

Author. Meijer, Augustiniana 5.400; 7.118.

Emden, Biographical Register, p 121.

Roth F, OSA, The Eng Austin Friars, 1249–1538,
vols i–ii, Cassiciacum vi–vii, N Y 1961–66, i.111,
413, 523.

Lucas, EETS 285.xix.

Sources and Literary Criticism. Mills, edn, p 440.

James M R and C Jenkins, A Descriptive Catalogue
of the MSS in the Libr of Lambeth Palace, Pt 1,
Cambridge 1930, p 50 (use of Dominicus de Ban-
dinis).

Parks ETI, p 596 (style).

Fredeman E J, The Life and Eng Writings of John
Capgrave, diss Univ of British Columbia 1970,
pp 312 (style), 363n (sources).

See [5] above.

Other Scholarly Problems. Lucas, Trans of the Cambridge Biblio Soc 5.1 (Capgrave's scriptorium);
6.137 (response to Lucas by E Colledge).

Beadle R, The East Anglian 'game-place': a Possibility for Further Research, Records of Early Eng
Drama 1(1978).2 (Capgrave on theater), 24 (response to Beadle by D Galloway).

General References. Hulbert, MP 20.415.

Gwynn A, The Eng Austin Friars in the Time of
Wyclif, London 1940, p 280.

Meech S B and H E Allen, The Book of Margery
Kempe, EETS 212, London N Y and Toronto
1940; rptd 1961, pp 305n, 306n, 312n.

Bennett H S, Chaucer and the 15 Cent, Oxford
1947; rvsd 1948, p 200.

Barber, MH 11.72.

Seymour MV, see notes on pp 81–91, 93.

Sumption, passim.

Braswell, Utilitarian and Scientific Prose, p 345.

On other Capgrave works, see R H Robbins, Manual, 5.1395, 1480; L Muir, Manual, 2.412, 426.

See [4] above.

Bibliography. Meijer, Augustiniana 5.420; 7.566.

Roth, Eng Austin Friars, i.527.

New CBEL, 1.663.

[13] THE ITINERARIES OF WILLIAM WEY.

MSS. 1, Bodl 2351 (text; after 1462); 2, Bodl 21964
(map).

Brown-Robbins, Robbins-Cutler, no 883.

Brown Reg, 2.549.

Summary Cat, vol 2, pt 1, p 323 (MS 1 described).

Aungier G J, The Hist and Antiquities of Syon Monastery, London 1840, p 527 (MS 1 described).

New CBEL, 1.2121.

Edition. [Williams G], The Itineraries of William
Wey, Fellow of Eton College, to Jerusalem, A D
1458 and A D 1462; and to Saint James of Compostella, A D 1456, 2 vols, Roxb Club 76 (text); 88
(map facsimile), London 1857, 1867.

Selections. Webb J, Archaeol 21.409 (25 pts of "A
preuysyoun"), 415n (lines 1–6 of verse itinerary).

Guildford E L, Travellers & Travelling in the Middle
Ages, London 1924, p 24 (25 pts of "A preuysyoun").

Matthews W, Later Medieval Eng Prose, N Y 1963,
p 224 (25 pts of "A preuysyoun").

Author. Emden A B, A Biographical Register of the
Univ of Oxford to A D 1500, Oxford 1957–59,
p 2028.

Sources and Literary Relations. Brown-Robbins, no 986
(but see [13] below).

Howard C, Eng Travellers of the Renaissance, London N Y and Toronto 1914, p 4 (source for [16]
below).

Blackie E M, ed, The Pilgrimage of Robert Langton,
Cambridge Mass 1924, p xxiv (Wey's description
superior to Langton's).

Mitchell, Robert Langton's Pilgrimage, Libr 5s
8(1953).43 (Wey's use of Compostella guidebook).

Parks ETI, pp 524 (Wey's routes), 582 (Wey in Venice).

See [6] above and [14], [17] and [19] below.

Literary Criticism. Matthews W, Later Medieval Eng
Prose, N Y 1963, p 217 (style).

Mitchell, pp 19 (narration); 20 (map); 45, 94, 123
(author); 190 (source for [17]); 42b-c (map partly
illust).

Other Scholarly Problems. Bateson M, Catalogue of the
Libr of Syon Monastery Isleworth, Cambridge
1898, p 162 (MS of Wey's Latin sermons).

Röhricht R, Die Palästinakarte des William Wey, Zeitschrift der Deutschen Palästina-Vereins 27 (1904).188.

Summary Cat, 4.617 (map predates Wey).

Prescott, pp 68 (map), 222 (Wey's pilgrimage souvenirs).

Adams P G, Travel Lit and the Evolution of the Novel, Lexington 1983, p 260 (interest in language).

General References. Ellis H, ed, The Pylgrymage of Sir Richard Guylforde to the Holy Land, A D 1506, Camden Soc no 51, London 1851, p xv.

Röhricht, p 116.

Heath S H, Pilgrim Life in the Middle Ages, Boston and N Y 1911; rvsd, In the Steps of the Pilgrims, London and N Y 1950, p 159.

Rice, Univ of Mich Publs in Lang and Lit 10.207.

Meech S B and H E Allen, The Book of Margery Kempe, EETS 212, London N Y and Toronto 1940; rptd 1961, passim.

Prescott, p 17.

Seymour MV, p xx.

Beckingham C F, The Near East: North and Northeast Africa, The Hakluyt Handbook, ed D B Quinn, 2 vols, London 1974, 1.182.

Sumption, passim.

Dansette, Archivum Franciscanum Historicum 72. 389, 390.

Howard D R, Writers & Pilgrims: Medieval Pilgrimage Narratives and Their Posterity, Berkeley Los Angeles and London 1980, p 20.

Friedman J B, The Monstrous Races in Medieval Art and Thought, Cambridge Mass and London 1981, p 219n.

Richard J, Les récits de voyages et de pèlerinages, Typologie des sources du moyen âge occidental no 38, Turnhout Belgium 1981, p 52.

Braswell, Utilitarian and Scientific Prose, p 345.

Robbins R H, Manual, 5.1473.

[14] THE STATIONS OF JERUSALEM.

MSS. 1, Bodl 6922 (Ashmole 61), ff 128ᵃ–135ᵇ (848 lines; late 15 cent); 2, Huntington Libr HM.144 (Huth 7), ff 67ᵃ–80ᵇ (870 lines; 1480–1500).

Brown-Robbins, Robbins-Cutler, no 986.

Brown Reg, 1.472 (MS 2).

Black W H, A Descriptive, Analytical, and Critical Catalogue of the MSS Bequeathed unto the Univ of Oxford by Elias Ashmole, Oxford 1845, p 106 (MS 1 described).

de Ricci Census, p 58 (MS 2 described; foliation and number of lines mistaken).

Manly & Rickert, 1.289 (MS 2 described).

Lauritis J A et al, A Critical Edn of Lydgate's Life of Our Lady, Duquesne Stud, Philological Ser 2, Pittsb 1961, p 42 (MS 2 described).

Silvia D S, Some 15-Cent MSS of the Canterbury Tales, Chaucer and ME Stud in Honour of Rossell Hope Robbins, ed B Rowland, London 1974, p 159 (MS 2).

Sullens I, ed, Robert Mannyng of Brunne Handlyng Synne, Medieval & Renaissance Texts & Stud, Binghamton N Y 1983, p xxiii (MS 1 described and dated).

Guide to Medieval and Renaissance MSS in the Huntington Libr, San Marino, forthcoming (MSS 1 and 2 compared; 80 interpolated lines from Lydgate identified).

Edition. AELeg 1881, p 355 (MS 1).

Date and Author. Brown J T T, The Poems of David Rate, Confessor of King James the First of Scotland, The Scottish Antiquary 11(1897).145.

Girvan R, Ratis Raving and Other Early Scots Poems on Morals, PSTS 3s no 11, Edinburgh and London 1939, p xxxii (disputes Brown).

Sources and Literary Relations. Brown-Robbins, Robbins-Cutler, no 883 (on similarity to Wey [13]).

Brown Reg, 2.549 (on similarity to Wey [13]).

Ker N R, Medieval MSS in British Librs, Oxford 1977, 2.310 (Brewyn's lost Eng Stations of Jerusalem and the Holy Land).

See [4] and [8] above.

Bibliography. New CBEL, 1.470.

[15] A RUTTER OF THE ENGLISH COAST.

MSS. 1, Lansdowne 285, ff 138ᵃ–142ᵃ (ca 1470); 2, Morgan Libr 775 (Hastings), ff 130ᵇ–138ᵇ (before 1461); 3, Bodl 15444 (Rawlinson D.328), f 183ᵃ (imperfect; 15 cent).

Ellis H and F Douce, A Catalogue of the Lansdowne MSS in the British Museum, London 1819; rptd London 1974, p 99 (MS 1 described).

Way A, Illustrations of Medieval Manners and Costume from Original Documents, Archaeological Journ 4(1847).226 (MSS 1 and 2 described).

Macray W D, Catalogi Codicum Manuscriptorum Bibliothecae Bodleianae . . . Pars V . . . Viri Munificentissimi Ricardi Rawlinson Codicum Classes Complectens, 5 vols, Oxford 1862–1900, 3.165 (MS 3 described).

Steele R, ed, Lydgate and Burgh's Secrees of Old Philisoffres, EETSES 66, London 1894, p xv (MS 1 dated).

Arthur H [Viscount Dillon], On a MS Collection of Ordinances of Chivalry of the 15 Cent, Belonging to Lord Hastings, Archaeol 57, pt 1 (1900), p 29 (MS 2 described); plate III, figures 1–2 (reprods of MS 2, ff 130ᵇ and 138ᵇ).

de Ricci Census, p 1501 (MS 2 described).

Buhler C F, Sir John Paston's Grete Booke, a 15-cent Best-Seller, MLN 56(1941).345 (MS 2 described).

Doyle A I, The Work of a Late 15-Cent Eng Scribe, William Ebesham, JRLB 39(1957).298, 301 (MS 1 described), 306 (date, relation of MSS), plate IIa (reprod of MS 2, f 136ᵃ), passim (scribe).

Medieval & Renaissance MSS: Major Acquisitions of The Pierpont Morgan Libr 1924–1974, N Y 1974, catalogue no 35 (MS 2 described).

Bornstein D, Mirrors of Courtesy, Hamden CT 1975, pp 98 (MSS 1 and 2), 104 (reprod of MS 2, f 130ᵇ).

Shrader C R, A Handlist of Extant MSS Containing the De Re Militari of Flavius Vegetius Renatus, Scriptorium 33(1979).303 (MSS 1 and 2).

Thompson D, A Descriptive Catalogue of ME Grammatical Texts, N Y and London 1979, p 311 (MS 3).

Lester G A, Sir John Paston's Grete Boke: A Descriptive Catalogue, with an Introd, of British Libr MS Lansdowne 285, Cambridge and Totowa N J 1984, pp 9 and 164 (MS 1 described), 16 and 36 (scribe), 27 (MS 3), 31 (MS 2 described, dated), 164 (biblio), 165 (crit).

Braswell, Utilitarian and Scientific Prose, p 373 (MSS 1 and 2; specious MS adduced).

Editions. Gairdner J, Sailing Directions for the Circumnavigation of England, and for a Voyage to The Straits of Gibraltar, Hakluyt Soc 79, London 1889 (MS 1).

Waters D W, The Rutters of the Sea, New Haven and London 1967, frntspc (reprod of MS 2, f 138ᵇ), pp 4, 7 (sources and literary relations), 187 (MS 1; crit C Koeman, Imago Mundi 21.126; J H Parry, Spec 44.504).

Date. Taylor, p 4.

Marcus G J, A Naval Hist of England, I. The Formative Centuries, London 1961, p 12.

Author. Burwash D, Eng Merchant Shipping 1460–1540, Toronto 1947, p 24.

Literary Relations. Arthur H, Archaeol 57, pt 1, p 31.

Sheppard L A, The Rutter of the Sea, The Brit Mus Quart 11(1936–37).18 (other 15-cent rutters).

Stephens A E, The Booke of the Sea Carte: A Seaman's Manual of the 16 Cent, Imago Mundi 2(1937).55 (16-cent borrowing from Copland).

Waters, The Art of Navigation in England in Elizabethan and Early Stuart Times, New Haven 1958, p 11 (contents of rutters).

See [18] below.

General References. Robinson A H W, Marine Cartography in Britain: A Hist of the Sea Chart to 1855, Leicester 1962, p 23.

Lang A, On the Beginnings of the Oldest Descriptions and Sea-charts by Seamen from North-West Europe, Proc of the Royal Soc of Edinburgh 73(1971–72).53.

Parry J H, The Discovery of the Sea, Berkeley Los Angeles and London 1981, p 34.

Braswell, Utilitarian and Scientific Prose, p 345.

[16] THE CABOT VOYAGES AND BRISTOL DISCOVERIES.

Documents. Quinn D B, Edward IV and Exploration, Mariner's Mirror 21(1935).275.

Hay D, ed, The Anglia Historia of Polydore Vergil A D 1485–1537, Publ Royal Historical Soc 74, London 1950, p 116 (Cabot's 2nd voyage).

Hennig R, Terrae Incognitae, 4 vols, Leiden 1936–39, 4.318.

Vigneras L A, New Light on the 1497 Cabot Voyage to America, Hispanic American Historical Rev 36(1956).503 (Day letter transcribed); The Cape Breton Landfall: 1494 or 1497; Note on a Letter from John Day, Canadian Historical Rev 38 (1957).219 (Day letter translated).

Quinn, The Argument for the Eng Discovery of America between 1480 and 1494, The Geographical Journ 127(1961).277 (facsimile of Day letter).

Skelton R A, Eng Knowledge of the Portuguese Discoveries in the 15 Cent: A New Document, Congresso Internacional de História dos Descobrimentos, Actas 2, Lisbon 1961, p 365 (William Worcestre).

Williamson J A, The Cabot Voyages and Bristol Discovery under Henry VII, Hakluyt Soc 120, 2s, Cambridge 1962, p 175; p 295 (Skelton, The Cartography of the Voyages) (crit E G R Taylor, The Geographical Journ 129.339; W E Washburn, AHR 68.1016).

Ruddock A A, John Day of Bristol and the Eng Voyages across the Atlantic before 1497, The Geographical Journ 132(1966).225 (John Day identified).

Harvey J H, ed, William Worcestre Itineraries, Oxford 1969, pp 309 (1480 Bristol voyage), 372 (Atlantic islands).

Quinn D B, ed, New American World: A Documentary Hist of North America to 1612, 5 vols, N Y 1979, 1.91.

Selected Scholarship. Williamson J A, The Voyages of the Cabots and the Eng Discovery of North America, London 1929.

Ganong W F, Crucial Maps in the Early Cartography and Place-nomenclature of the Atlantic Coast of Canada, Trans of the Royal Soc of Canada 3s 23(1929); rptd Toronto 1964, p 3 (Cabot voyages and La Cosa map).

Burwash D, Eng Merchant Shipping, 1460–1540, Toronto 1947.

Taylor E G R, A Letter Dated 1577 from Mercator to John Dee, Imago Mundi 13(1956).56 (Inventio fortunata).

Williamson, The Cabot Voyages and Bristol Discovery.

Parker, p 25 (importance of Bristol).

Skelton R A, The Vinland Map, in R A Skelton, T E Marston and G D Painter, The Vinland Map and the Tartar Relation, New Haven and London 1965, p 235 (Bristol and Iceland).

Carus-Wilson E M, Medieval Merchant Venturers: Collected Stud, London 1954; 2nd edn 1967, pp 1 (15-cent Bristol trade), 98 (Bristol and Iceland).

Quinn, John Day and Columbus, The Geographical Journ 133(1967).205 (Inventio fortunata); England and the Discovery of America, 1481–1620, N Y 1974, p 5 (explorations to 1536; crit A A Ruddock, The Geographical Journ 141.109).

McGrath P, Bristol and America, 1480–1631, The Westward Enterprise: Eng Activities in Ireland, the Atlantic, and America 1480–1650, edd K R Andrews, N P Canny and P E H Hair, Liverpool 1978, p 81.

Andrews K R, Trade, Plunder and Settlement: Maritime Enterprise and the Genesis of the British Empire, 1480–1630, Cambridge 1984, p 41.

Davies A, Prince Madoc and the Discovery of America in 1477, The Geographical Journ 150(1984).363 (possible Eng voyage).

Bibliography. Winship G P, Cabot Biblio, N Y 1900.

Hennig, Terrae Incognitae, 4.318.

Read C, ed, Biblio of British Hist: Tudor Period, 1485–1603, 2nd edn, Oxford 1959, p 268.

[17] INFORMATION FOR PILGRIMS
UNTO THE HOLY LAND.

MSS. No MS extant. PRINTS: 1, Informacõn for pylgrymes vnto the holy londe, [de Worde, 1500?] (STC, no 14081); 2, The way to the holy lande, de Worde, 1515 (STC, no 14082); 3, (wants title), de Worde, 1524 (STC, no 14083).

New CBEL, 1.2121.

Duff E G, 15-Cent Eng Books, London 1917, p 62 (PRINT 1 described).

Editions. Nicol W, Informacon for Pylgrymes vnto The Holy Londe, Roxb Club 138, London 1824 (facsimile of PRINT 1).

Duff E G, Information for Pilgrims unto the Holy Land, London 1893; rptd N Y 1980 (facsimile of PRINT 1), pp ix (date, author), xii (Wey and others as sources), xviii (PRINTS 1, 2, 3 described).

Selection. Taylor, p 244 (on Mediterranean climate).

Author. Mitchell R J, Libr 5s 8.45 (suggests Larke); The Spring Voyage: The Jerusalem Pilgrimage in 1458, London 1964, pp 19, 190.

Prescott, p 17.

Emden A B, A Bibliographical Register of the Univ of Cambridge to 1500, Cambridge 1963, p 353 (Larke?)

Sources. Howard C, Eng Travellers of the Renaissance, London N Y and Toronto 1914, p 4 (uses Wey).

Taylor, p 5 (Latin original).

Bennett H S, Chaucer and the 15 Cent, Oxford 1947; rvsd 1948, p 306 (Latin original).

Prescott, p 17 (uses Wey).

Mitchell, pp 19, 190 (uses Wey).

Howard D R, Writers & Pilgrims: Medieval Pilgrimage Narratives and Their Posterity, Berkeley Los Angeles and London 1980, p 20 (uses Wey).

Adams P G, Travel Lit and the Evolution of the Novel, p 39 (uses Wey).

Braswell, Utilitarian and Scientific Prose, p 345 (uses [6]).

See [4], [6] and [13] above and [19] and [22] below.

Other Scholarly Problems. Parks ETI, passim (pilgrimage routes).

Literary Criticism and Literary Relations. Rice, Univ of Mich Publs in Lang and Lit 10.208 (curiosity about ancient world).

Howard, Writers & Pilgrims, pp 23 (piety and worldliness), 92 (verisimilitude).

Harris K, John Gower's Confessio Amantis: The Virtues of Bad Texts, in MSS and Readers in 15-Cent England: The Literary Implications of MS Study, ed D Pearsall, Woodbridge Suffolk and Totowa N J 1983, p 32 (portions of Latin account from PRINT 1 trans in MS Trinity Oxf D.29).

General References. Röhricht, p 170.

Barwick, Trans of the Bibliographical Soc 7.203.

Heath S H, Pilgrim Life in the Middle Ages, Boston and N Y 1911; rvsd, In the Steps of the Pilgrims, London and N Y 1950, pp 163, 320.

Parker, p 23.

Bennett H S, Eng Books & Readers 1475 to 1557, Cambridge 1952; 2nd edn 1969, p 122.

Robbins R H, Manual, 5.1473.

[18] THE COPY OF A CHART COMPASSING
THE CIRCUIT OF THE WORLD.

MSS. No MS extant. PRINTS: 1, ["Arnold's Chronicle," A van Berghen, 1503?] (STC, no 782); 2, [another edn, P Treveris, 1525?] (STC, no 783); 3, Mappa mundi. Otherwyse called the compasse, and cyrcuet of the worlde, R Wyer [ca 1550] (STC, no 17297); 4a, Here begynneth the Compost of Ptholomeus, tr oute of French, R Wyer [1530?]

(STC, no 20480); 4b, (another edn) The Compost, of Ptholomeus, R Wyer [1540?] (STC, no 20480a); 4c, (another edn) The Compost of Ptholomeus, R Wyer [1550?] (STC, no 20481); 4d, (another edn) R Wyer [1552?] (STC, no 20481.3); 4e, (another edn) T Colwell [1562?] (STC, no 20481.7); 4f, (another edn, corr) M P[arsons] f H Gosson [1638?] (STC, no 20482).

New CBEL, 1.2203.

Taylor, pp 13, 166 (relations among PRINTS).

Parker, pp 28, 244 (relations among PRINTS 1–4c).

Edition. [Douce F,] The Customs of London, Otherwise Called Arnold's Chronicle, London 1811, pp vi (author), vii (sources), 140 (PRINTS 1 and 2).

Author and Date. DNB, 1.582.

Sources and Literary Relations. Busch W, England unter den Tudors, I. König Heinrich VII, Stuttgart 1892, trans A M Todd, London 1895, p 401.

Read C, ed, Biblio of British Hist: Tudor Period, 1485–1603, 2nd edn, Oxford 1959, pp 26, 29.

Parker, p 20.

Williams C H, ed, Eng Hist Documents 1485–1558, London 1967, p 93.

Bennett H S, Eng Books & Readers 1475–1557, Cambridge 1952; 2nd edn 1969, pp 121, 126.

Meale C M, The Compiler at Work: John Colyns and BL MS Harley 2252, in Manuscripts and Readers in 15-Cent England: The Literary Implications of MS Study, ed D Pearsall, Woodbridge Suffolk and Totowa N J 1983, p 100 (borrowings in Balliol 354 and Lansdowne 762).

See [1], [4], [5] and [15] above.

General References. Kingsford C L, Eng Hist Lit in the 15 Cent, Oxford 1913, p 106.

Taylor, p 6 (misdescribes itinerary).

de Beer, British Archaeological Assoc Journ 3s 15(1952).37n.

Parker, pp 17, 19n.

Utley F L, Manual, 3.730.

[19] THE WAY TO ITALY.

MS. Bodl 9822 (Tanner 2), ff 139^a–140^b (ca 1520).

Summary Cat, 3.82.

Hackman A, Catalogi Codicum Manuscriptorum Bibliothecae Bodleianae, pars quarta, Oxford 1860; rvsd Oxford 1966, col 2 (MS described and dated).

Date and Scribe. Ker N R, The Virgin and Child Binder, LVL, and William Horman, Libr 5s 17(1962).85.

Literary Relations. [Williams G, ed], The Itineraries of William Wey, Roxb Club 76.xix (resemblance to Wey's itinerary).

Parks ETI, p 524 (Wey duplicates route).

See [10], [13] and [17] above.

[20] THE PILGRIMAGE OF SIR RICHARD GUYLFORDE TO THE HOLY LAND.

MSS. No MS extant. PRINT: This is the begynnynge and contynuaunce of the pylgrymage of sir R. Guylforde knyght. And howe he went towardes Jherusalem, R Pynson, 1511 (STC, no 12549).

New CBEL, 1.2121.

Edition. Ellis H, The Pylgrymage of Sir Richard Guylforde to the Holy Land, A D 1506, Camden Soc 51, London 1851.

Selection. Salzman L F, Eng Trade in the Middle Ages, Oxford 1931, p 246 (the return voyage).

Author. DNB 8.770.

Sources and Literary Relations. Duff E G, Information for Pilgrims unto the Holy Land, London 1893; rptd N Y 1980, p xi (uses von Breydenbach).

Prescott, p 179 (uses von Breydenbach).

Seymour M C, The Early Eng Printed Edns of MT, Libr 5s 19(1964).207n (uses Mandeville).

Moseley C W R D, trans, The Travels of Sir John Mandeville, Harmondsworth Eng 1983, p 23 (uses Mandeville).

See [21] below.

Other Scholarly Problems. Parks ETI, pp 499 (route of itinerary), 583 (description of Venice).

General References. Röhricht, p 167.

Heath S H, Pilgrim Life in the Middle Ages, Boston and N Y 1911; rvsd, In the Steps of the Pilgrims, London and N Y 1950, p 160.

Taylor, pp 6 (mistakes date of PRINT), 167.

Rice, Univ of Mich Publs in Lang and Lit 10.208.

Meech S B and H E Allen, The Book of Margery Kempe, EETS 212, London N Y and Toronto 1940; rptd 1961, pp 284n, 285n, 289n.

Mitchell, p 102.

Seymour MV, p 98n.

Beckingham C F, The Near East: North and Northeast Africa, The Hakluyt Handbook, ed D B Quinn, 2 vols, London 1974, 1.182.

[21] THE PILGRIMAGE OF SIR RICHARD TORKINGTON TO THE HOLY LAND.

MSS. 1, BM Addit 28561 (early 16 cent); 2, BM Addit 28562 (1812 transcript).

Catalogue of Additions to the MSS in the British Museum, 1861–75, London 1877; rptd 1966, p 507.

New CBEL, 1.2121.

DNB, 19.987.

Edition. Loftie W J, Ye Oldest Diarie of Englysshe Travell: Being the Hitherto Unpublished Narrative of the Pilgrimage of Sir Richard Torkington to Jerusalem in 1517, London 1884, p ii (author, date, MSS).

Selection. Wheeler R B, Torkington's Pilgrimage to Jerusalem in 1517, The Gentleman's Magazine 82(1812).316.

Guylforde as Source. Duff E G, Information for Pilgrims unto the Holy Land, London 1893; rptd N Y 1980, p xi (and use of [17]).

Rice, Univ of Mich Publs in Lang and Lit 10.210n.

Parks ETI, p 584.

Seymour M C, Libr 5s 19.207n (and use of Mandeville); Mandeville's Travels, Oxford 1967, p 236; A 15-Cent East Anglian Scribe, MÆ 37(1968). 173n.

Moseley C W R D, trans, The Travels of Sir John Mandeville, Harmondsworth Eng 1983, p 23.

Other Scholarly Problems. Parks ETI, pp 499 and 533 (route of itinerary), 536 (return-trip delays).

General References. Ellis H, The Pylgrymage of Sir Richard Guylforde, Camden Soc 51(1851).xv.

Röhricht, p 172.

Heath S H, Pilgrim Life in the Middle Ages, Boston and N Y 1911; rvsd, In the Steps of the Pilgrims, London and N Y 1950, pp 64, 162.

Taylor, pp 6, 167.

Prescott, pp 81, 176.

Beckingham C F, The Near East: North and Northeast Africa, The Hakluyt Handbook, ed D B Quinn, 2 vols, London 1974, 1.182.

See [20] above.

[22] THE PILGRIMAGE OF ROBERT LANGTON.

MSS. No MS extant. PRINT: The pylgrimage of M Robert Langton clerke to saynt Iames in Compostell, etc, R Coplande, 1522 (STC, no 15206).

New CBEL, 1.2121.

Prescott H F M, Jerusalem Journey: Pilgrimage to the Holy Land in the 15 Cent, London 1954, figure I (facsimile of PRINT woodcut).

Edition. Blackie E M, The Pilgrimage of Robert Langton, Cambridge Mass 1924, pp vii (PRINT described), ix (author; crit F P S, EHR 41.149).

Author. Thompson J, Portrait of Dr Robert Langton, N&Q 2s 6(1858).347 (supposed lost portrait).

Mitchell, Eng Law Students at Bologna in the 15 Cent, EHR 51(1936).284.

Emden A B, A Biographical Register of the Univ of Oxford, Oxford 1957–59, 2.1100.

DNB, 11.562.

Date. Mitchell, Robert Langton's Pylgrimage, Libr 5s 8(1953).42 (after 1498; misdates PRINT); de Beer, Libr 5s 10(1955).58 (response to Mitchell; after 1506).

Information for Pilgrims as Source. Mitchell, Libr 5s 8(1953).42.

Parker, p 26 (and Compostella guidebook).

General References. Taylor, pp 6 (alleges MS survives), 167.

Seymour MV, p 99n.

Bennett H S, Eng Books & Readers 1475–1557, Cambridge 1952; 2nd edn 1969, p 122.

[23] MEDIEVAL MAPS WITH ENGLISH INSCRIPTIONS.

General Studies. Fordham H G, Stud in Carto-Biblio, Oxford 1914; rptd 1969 (crit W, EHR 30.574).

Andrews M C, The Boundary between Scotland and England in the Portolan Charts, Proc of the Soc of Antiquaries of Scotland 5s 12(1925–26).36; The Study and Classification of Medieval Mappae Mundi, Archaeol 75(1925–26).61; The British Isles in the Nautical Charts of the XIV and XV Cents, The Geographical Journ 68(1926).474.

Durand D B, The Vienna-Klosterneuburg Map Corpus of the 15 Cent: A Study in the Transition from Medieval to Modern Science, Leiden 1952, p 13.

Price D J and E G R Taylor, Cartography, Survey, and Navigation to 1400, A Hist of Technology, edd C Singer, E J Holmyard, A R Hall and T L Williams, 7 vols, Oxford 1954–78, 3.513.

Crone G R, Early Maps of the British Isles A D 1000–A D 1579, London 1961 (with reprods); Early Cartographic Activity in Britain, The Geographical Journ 128(1962).406; Early Mapping of the British Isles, Scottish Geographical Magazine 78(1962).73 (influence of itineraries on maps).

Bagrow L, Hist of Cartography, rvsd R A Skelton, London 1964; rptd 1966.

Destombes M, Mappemondes A D 1200–1500: Monumenta Cartographica Vetustioris Aevi, vol 1, Amsterdam 1964.

Shirley R V, Early Printed Maps of the British Isles 1477–1650: A Biblio; Pt I, 1477–1555, The Map Collectors' Circle 90, London 1973.

Crone G R, Maps and Their Makers: an Introd to the Hist of Cartography, 5th edn, Folkestone Kent and Hamden Conn 1978.

Bibliography. Destombes, Mappemondes, p 257.

Shirley, Early Printed Maps, p 17.

Graves E B, A Biblio of Eng Hist, Oxford 1975, p 72.

Crone, Early Maps, p 30.

Harvey P D A, The Hist of Topographical Maps: Symbols, Pictures and Surveys, London 1980, p 187.

a. Hereford World Map.

MS. Hereford Cathedral (ca 1290).

Studies. Bevan W L and H W Phillott, Medieval Geography: An Essay in Illust of the Hereford Mappa Mundi, London 1873 (reprod).

Letts M, Sir John Mandeville: The Man and His Book, London 1949, p 101 (resemblance between map and Mandeville's Travels); The Pictures in the Hereford Mappa Mundi, N&Q 200(1955).2.

The World Map by Richard of Haldingham in Hereford Cathedral circa A D 1285, introd G R Crone, Royal Geographical Soc, London 1954 (reprod).

Denholm-Young N, The Mappa Mundi of Richard of Haldingham at Hereford, Spec 32(1957).307 (identity of artist).

Destombes, Mappemondes, p 197; plates xxiv, xxv (reprod).

Bagrow, Hist of Cartography, p 50; plate xxiv (reprod).

Crone, New Light on the Hereford Map, The Geographical Journ 131(1965).447 (influence of itineraries).

b. The Matthew Paris Maps of Great Britain (ca 1250).

MSS 1, Cotton Claudius D.VI, f 8^b; 2, Corp Christi Camb 16, f v^b (incomplete); 3, Cotton Julius D.VII, ff 50^b–53^a; 4, Royal 14.C.vii, f 5^b.

Mitchell J B, The Matthew Paris Maps, The Geographical Journ 81(1933).27 (geography, names, interrelations of four maps); facing p 32 (partial reprods of maps).

Studies. Gough R, British Topography, 2 vols, London 1780, 1.62 (reprod of MS 4 map), 64 (MS 2), 66 (MS 1).

Beazley C R, The Dawn of Modern Geography, 3 vols, London 1897–1906, 2.584, 638; facing p 584 (reprod of MS 1 map).

Four Maps of Great Britain Designed by Matthew Paris about A D 1250, ed J P Gilson, London 1928 (reprods of all maps).

Lynam E, The Mapmaker's Art, London 1953, p 1.

Vaughan R, Matthew Paris, Cambridge 1958; rptd Cambridge 1979, p 241.

Crone, Early Maps, pp 7, 14; plate 4 (reprod of MS 1 map).

Bagrow, Hist of Cartography, p 143; plate B (reprod of MS 3 map).

Harvey, The Hist of Topographical Maps, pp 140; 141 (reprod of MS 1 map).

c. The Gough Map of Great Britain (anonymous).

MS. Bodl 17610 (Gough Gen Top 16) (ca 1360).

Summary Cat, 4.171 (MS described).

Studies. Gough, British Topography, 1.76; plate VI (reprod).

Pelham R A, The Gough Map, The Geographical Journ 81(1933).34.

Lynam, Mapmaker's Art, p 2.

Parsons E J S, The Map of Great Britain circa A D 1360 Known as the Gough Map: An Introd to the Facsimile, Bodleian Libr and Royal Geographical Soc, Oxford 1958, pp 16 (F Stenton on roads), 21 (list of place names; crit R A Skelton, The Geographical Journ 125.237).

Crone, Early Maps, pp 7, 16; plate 6 (reprod).

Harvey, The Hist of Topographical Maps, pp 142, 143 (partial reprod).

Salter E, 14-Cent Eng Poetry: Contexts and Readings, Oxford 1983, p 54.

d. Totius Britanniae Tabula Chorographica (anonymous).

MS. Harley 1808, f 9^b (ca 1400).

Studies. Reinhard W, Eine Manuskriptkarte der britischen Inseln aus dem 16 Jahrhundert, Globus 96(1909).1.

Crone, Early Maps, p 19; plate 8 (reprod).

Bagrow, Hist of Cartography, p 162.

e. Hardyng's Map of Scotland.

MSS. 1, Lansdowne 204, ff 226^b–227^a (ca 1457); 2, Harley 661, endleaves (late 15 cent); 3, Bodl 3356 (Selden B.10), ff 184^a–185^a (1470–80).

Ellis H and F Douce, A Catalogue of the Lansdowne MSS in the British Museum, London 1819, p 73 (MS 1).

Summary Cat, vol 2, pt 1, p 617 (MS 3 described).

Studies. Gough, British Topography, 2.579 (reprod of MS 3 map).

Ellis H, ed, The Chronicle of Iohn Hardyng, London 1812, pp xiv (maps), 417 (reprod of inscriptions in MS 2).

Kingsford C L, The First Version of Hardyng's Chronicle, EHR 27(1912).462, 476 (maps).

The Early Maps of Scotland to 1850, vol 1, introd D G Moir, The Royal Scottish Geographical Soc, 3rd edn, Edinburgh 1973, pp 6, 163; illust 2 (reprod of MS 1 map).

f. Local English Maps and Plans.

Studies. Price D J, Medieval Land Surveying and Topographical Maps, The Geographical Journ 121(1955).1; plate 2 (reprod of Harvey-Skelton map no 10); plate 7 (reprod of no 8).

Maps and Plans in the Public Record Office: I. British Isles, c 1410–1860, London 1967.

Harvey P D A H and R A Skelton, Medieval Eng Maps and Plans, Imago Mundi 23(1969).101; Local Maps and Plans before 1500, Journ of the Soc of Archivists 3(1969).496 (printed reprods listed).

Harvey, The Hist of Topographical Maps, pp 84, 140.

Harvey and Skelton, edd, Local Maps and Plans from Medieval England, forthcoming.

XX. WORKS OF RELIGIOUS AND PHILOSOPHICAL INSTRUCTION

by

Robert R. Raymo

BACKGROUND BOOKS: The following important, frequently listed entries, here given full statement, are referred to in abbreviated form in the pages that follow. For abbreviations not appearing in this list, consult the general Table of Abbreviations.

Arnould	Arnould E J, Le Manuel des Péchés, Paris 1940
Blake	Blake N F, Middle English Religious Prose, London and Evanston 1972
Doyle Survey	Doyle A I, A Survey of the Origins and Circulation of Theological Writings in English in the Fourteenth, Fifteenth and Early Sixteenth Centuries with special consideration to the part of the clergy therein, unpubl Cambridge Univ doct diss 1953
Jolliffe	Jolliffe P S, A Check-List of Middle English Prose Writings of Spiritual Guidance, Toronto 1974
Ker Manuscripts	Ker N R, Medieval Manuscripts in British Libraries, I: London, II: Abbotsford-Keele, III: Lampeter-Oxford, Oxford 1969, 1977, 1983
Maskell	Maskell W, Monumenta Ritualia Ecclesiae Anglicanae, 3 vols, 2nd edn, Oxford 1882
Pantin	Pantin W A, The English Church in the Fourteenth Century, Cambridge 1955; rptd Notre Dame 1962
Pfander Manuals	Pfander H G, Some Medieval Manuals of Religious Instruction in England and Observations on Chaucer's *Parson's Tale,* JEGP 35(1936).243
Revell	Revell P, Fifteenth Century English Prayers and Meditations. A Descriptive List of Manuscripts in the British Library, N Y and London 1975

Russell Vernacular Instruction	Russell G H, Vernacular Instruction of the Laity in the Later Middle Ages in England: Some Texts and Notes, Journ of Religious History 2(1962).98
Serjeantson Index	Serjeantson M, The Index of the Vernon Manuscript, MLR 32(1937).222
Wenzel	Wenzel S, The Sin of Sloth: Acedia in Medieval Thought and Literature, Chapel Hill 1960; rptd 1967
Woolf	Woolf R, The English Religious Lyric in the Middle Ages, Oxford 1968

GENERAL TREATMENTS: LITERARY AND HISTORICAL.

Wilkins D, Concilia Magnae Britanniae et Hiberniae, A D 446–1718, 4 vols, London 1737.

Maskell.

Ten Brink, p 280.

Maitland F W, Canon Law in England: I. William Lyndwood; II. Church, State and Decretals, EHR 11(1896).446, 641; 16(1901).35.

Gasquet F A, The Old Eng Bible and Other Essays, London 1897, p 179.

Cutts E L, Parish Priests and Their People in the Middle Ages, London 1898; rptd London and N Y 1914.

Capes W W, The Eng Church in the 14 and 15 Cents, London 1900; rptd 1903, 1909, 1920.

Schofield, p 403.

Patterson.

Richardson H G, The Parish Clergy of the 13 and 14 Cents, Trans of the Royal Historical Soc 3s 6(1912).118, 124.

Hefele C J and H Leclercq, edd, Histoire des Conciles, vol 5, pt 2, Paris 1913.

Tupper F, Chaucer and the Seven Deadly Sins, PMLA 29(1914).93.

Lowes J L, Chaucer and the Seven Deadly Sins, PMLA 30(1915).237.

Manning B L, People's Faith in the Age of Wycliff, Cambridge 1919.

Deanesly M, Vernacular Books in England in the 14 and 15 Cents, MLR 15(1920).349; The Lollard Bible and Other Medieval Biblical Versions, Cambridge 1920, pp 211, 343.

Owst G R, Preaching in Medieval England. An Introd to Sermon MSS of the Period ca 1350–1430, Cambridge 1926.

Welter T, L'Exemplum dans la littérature religieuse et didactique en Moyen Âge, Paris 1927.

Coulton G G, Ten Medieval Studies, Cambridge 1930; rptd Gloucester 1967, p 108.

Chambers R W, On the Continuity of Eng Prose from Alfred to More and His School, An Extract from the Introd to Nicholas Harpsfield's Life of Sir Thomas More, ed E V Hitchcock and R W Chambers, London 1932.

Wilmart A, Auteurs spirituels et textes dévots du Moyen Âge Latin, Paris 1932; rptd 1971.

Owst G R, Literature and Pulpit in Medieval England, Cambridge 1933; rptd N Y 1961.

Gibbs M and J Lang, Bishops and Reform 1215–72, Oxford 1934; rptd London 1962.

Peckham J L, Archbishop Peckham as a Religious Educator, Yale Stud in Religion no 7, Scottdale Pa 1934, pp 83, 98.

Pfander Manuals.

Weiss R, Humanism in England during the 15 Cent, Medium Ævum Monographs no 4, Oxford 1940; 2nd edn 1957; 3rd edn 1967.

Arnould.

Workman S K, 15-Cent Translation as an Influence on Eng Prose, Princeton 1940.

Cheney C R, Eng Synodalia of the 13 Cent, Oxford 1941.

Chambers OHEL.

Moorman J R H, Church Life in England in the 13 Cent, Cambridge 1946, p 90.

Bennett H S, The Production and Dissemination of Vernacular MSS in the 15 Cent, Libr 5s 1(1946–47).167.

Bennett OHEL.

Baugh LHE, p 200.

Knowles M D, The Religious Orders in England, 3 vols, Cambridge 1948–59.

McHugh H V, Eng Devotional Prose, 1200–1535, diss Stanford Univ 1948.

Craig HEL, p 107.

Kane, p 104.

Bennett H S, Eng Books and Readers 1475–1557, Cambridge 1952; 2nd edn 1969, p 65.

Bloomfield SDS.

Douie D L, Archbishop Pecham, Oxford 1952, p 133.

Wilson R M, The Lost Lit of Medieval England, 2nd edn, London 1952; rvsd London 1970.

Doyle Survey.

Powicke M, The 13 Cent 1216–1307, Oxford 1953, p 445.

Pantin.

Boyle L E, A Study of the Works Attributed to William of Pagula with Special Reference to the Oculus Sacerdotis and Summa Summarum, diss Oxford Univ 1956.

Pepler C, The Eng Religious Heritage, London 1958, p 13.

Wenzel.

Knowles D, The Eng Mystical Tradition, London and N Y 1961, p 39.

Boyle L E, The Constitution "Cum ex eo" of Boniface VIII. Education of Parochial Clergy, MS 24(1962).263.

Manning S, Wisdom and Number, Lincoln 1962.

Miner J N T, Schools and Literacy in Late Medieval England, British Journ of Educational Stud 11(1962–63).16.

Russell Vernacular Instruction.

Knowles M D, The Monastic Order in England, 2nd edn, Cambridge 1963.

Legge M D, Anglo-Norman Lit and Its Background, Oxford 1963, p 206.

Tuve R, Notes on the Virtues and Vices, Journ of the Warburg and Courtauld Institutes 26(1963).264; 27(1964).

Schirmer W F, Der Engl Frühhumanismus, 2nd edn, Tübingen 1963.

Katzenellenbogen A, Allegories of the Virtues and Vices in Mediaeval Art, N Y 1964.

Powicke F M and C R Cheney, edd, Councils & Synods, II (A D 1205–1313), Oxford 1964.

Schlauch M, Eng Medieval Lit and Its Social Foundations, Warsaw 1965, pp 191, 299.

Ackerman R W, Popular Christian Doctrine, in Backgrounds to Medieval Eng Lit, N Y 1966, p 80.

Edwards K, The Eng Secular Cathedrals in the Middle Ages, 2nd edn, Manchester 1967, p 187.

Jauss H R, La littérature didactique, allégorique et satirique, Grundriss der Romanischen Literaturen des Mittelalters, vol 6, 2 pts, Heidelberg 1968–70.

Woolf.

Haines R M, The Education of the Eng Clergy during the Later Middle Ages: Some Observations on the Operation of Pope Boniface VIII's Constitution Cum ex eo (1298), Canadian Journ of Hist 4(1969).1.

Heath P, The Eng Parish Clergy on the Eve of the Reformation, London and Toronto 1969, p 70 (clerical learning and preaching).

Weber S A, Theology and Poetry in the ME Lyric, Columbia 1969.

Du Boulay F R H, An Age of Ambition, Eng Society in the Late Middle Ages, London 1970, p 143.

Fischer N, Handlist of Animal References in ME Religious Prose, Leeds SE 4(1970).49.

Wimsatt J I, Allegory and Mirror: Tradition and Structure in ME Lit, N Y 1970, p 137.

Constable G, The Popularity of 12-Cent Spiritual Writers in the Late Middle Ages, in Renaissance Stud in Honor of Hans Baron, ed A Molho and J A Tedeschi, DeKalb 1971, p 3.

Constable G, 12-Cent Spirituality and the Late Middle Ages, Medieval and Renaissance Stud 5 (1971).27.

Gradon P, The Allegorical Picture, in Form and Style in Early Eng Lit, London 1971, p 32.

Haines R M, Education in Eng Ecclesiastical Legislation of the Later Middle Ages, in Councils and Assemblies, ed G J Cuming and D Baker, Cambridge 1971, p 161.

Blake, p 1.

Cheney C R, Medieval Texts and Studies, Oxford 1973, pp 158 (on Lyndwood's Provinciale), 185 (13-cent diocesan legislation).

McFarlane K B, The Nobility of Later Medieval England, Oxford 1973, p 228.

Blake N F, Varieties of ME Religious Prose, in Chaucer and ME Stud in Honour of Rossell Hope Robbins, ed B Rowland, London and Kent 1974, p 348.

Hay D, England and the Humanities in the 15 Cent, in Itinerarium Italicum, ed H O Oberman, Leiden 1975, p 305.

Ball R M, The Education of the Eng Parish Clergy in the Later Middle Ages with Particular References to the Manuals of Instruction, diss Camb Univ 1977.

Ruh K, Geistliche Prosa, in Europäische Spätmittelalters, ed W Erzgräber, Wiesbaden 1978, p 565.

Coleman J, Eng Lit in Hist 1350–1400, Medieval Readers and Writers, London 1981.

Boyle L E, The Fourth Lateran Council and Manuals of Popular Theology, in The Popular Lit of Medieval England, ed T J Heffernan, Tenn Stud in Lit 28, Knoxville 1985, p 30.

Shaw J, The Influence of Canonical and Episcopal Reform on Popular Books of Instruction, in The Popular Lit of Medieval England, ed Heffernan, p 44.

BIBLIOGRAPHICAL.

Booker J M, A ME Biblio, Heidelberg 1912; rptd Folcroft 1972.

Vising J, Anglo-Norman Lang and Lit, London 1923, pp 50, 56, 63, 66, 72.

Boussuat MBLF, pp 332, 466; Suppl I, pp 76, 101; Suppl II, pp 79, 99.

Ackerman R W, ME Lit to 1400, in The Medieval Rev of Western Lit: A Rev of Research, Mainly 1930–60, ed J F Fisher, N Y 1966, p 83.

Whiting B J, Proverbs, Sentences and Proverbial Phrases from Eng Writings Mainly before 1500, Cambridge 1968.

Tubach F C, Index Exemplorum A Handbook of Medieval Religious Tales, FFC no 204, Helsinki 1969.

Wilson E, A Descriptive Index of the Eng Lyrics in John of Grimestone's Preaching Book, Medium Ævum Monographs ns 2, Oxford 1973.

Jolliffe.

Preston M J, A Concordance to the ME Shorter Poem, 2 pts, Leeds 1975.

Revell.

Bloomfield M W, B-G Guyot, D R Howard, and T B Kabealo, Incipits of Latin Works on the Virtues and Vices, 1110–1500 A.D., Including a Selection of Incipits of Works on the Pater Noster, Cambridge 1979.

Sinclair K V, French Devotional Texts of the Middle Ages, A Bibliographic MS Guide, Westport and London 1979.

Edwards A S G and D Pearsall, edd, ME Prose Essays on Bibliographical Problems, N Y and London 1981.

Lagorio V M and R Bradley, The 14-Cent Eng Mystics, A Comprehensive Annotated Biblio, N Y and London 1981.

Edwards A S G, ed, ME Prose, New Brunswick 1984.

Lester G A, The Index of ME Prose, Handlist II, A Handlist of MSS containing ME Prose in the John Rylands University Library of Manchester and Chetham's Library, Manchester, Woodbridge 1985 (appeared too late for use in this chapter).

1. WORKS OF RELIGIOUS INSTRUCTION

I. Long Compilations of Religious Instruction

1. Versions of *Manuel des péchés*

[1] HANDLYNG SYNNE.

MSS. 1, Bodl 2313 (Bodley 415), ff 1ª–79ᵇ (1400–25); 2, Bodl 3938 (Eng poet a.1), ff 197ª–199ª (1380–1400; lines 9899–10,818, in a late redaction of the Northern Homily Cycle with the title: Septem Miracula de Corpore Christi); 3, Bodl 6922* (Ashmole 61), ff 26ᵇ–27ᵇ (1475–1500; an extract, lines 3799–3912); 4, Camb Univ Ii.4.9, ff 97ª–142ª (1475–1500); 5, BL Harley 1701, ff 1ª–84ᵇ (1400–50); 6, BL Addit 22283, ff 2ᵇ–4ª (1380–1400; same as MS 2); 7, Dulwich Coll 24, ff 1ª–21ᵇ (ca 1450); 8, Yale Univ Osborn a.2 (olim Bowes Midland), ff 1ª–142ᵇ (1460–1500); 9, Folger V.6.236 (olim Clopton), ff 1ª–84ª (ca 1450). *Continuation*: 10, Camb Univ Ii.4.9, ff 142ᵇ–190ª (1475–1500); 11, BL Harley 3954, ff 78ᵇ–86ᵇ (1400–50).

Brown-Robbins, nos 516, 778, 937 (Handlyng Synne) and 215, 976, 1901, 2045, 2059, 2062; Robbins-Cutler, nos 215, 778, 2059.

MSS Commentary. A Catalogue of the Harleian MSS in the British Museum, London 1808, 2.176 (MS 5); 3.98 (MS 11).

Black W H, A Descriptive, Analytical, and Critical Catalogue of the MSS Bequeathed unto the Univ of Oxford by Elias Ashmole, Oxford 1845, p 106 (MS 3).

A Catalogue of the MSS Preserved in the Libr of the Univ of Cambridge, Cambridge 1859, 3.448 (MS 4).

Catalogue of Additions to the MSS in the British Museum in the Years MDCCCLIV–MDCCCLX, London 1875, p 623 (MS 6).

Warner G F, Catalogue of the MSS and Muniments of Alleyn's Coll of God's Gift at Dulwich, London 1881, p 347 (MS 7).

Summary Cat, 2.303 (MS 1), 789 (MS 2).

Herbert, 3.272, 303, 310.

Serjeantson Index, p 245.

Schulz H C, The Monastic Libr and Scriptorium at Ashridge, HLQ 1(1938).305 (MS 1).

de Ricci Census, 3.97 (MS 8), 108 (MS 9).

Seymour M C, The Eng MSS of Mandeville's Travels, Edinburgh Biblio Soc Trans 4(1966).187 (MS 11).

Sajavaara K, The Relationship of the Vernon and Simeon MSS, NM 68(1967).428 (MSS 2, 6).

Ker Manuscripts, 1.46 (MS 7), 420 (Westminster Diocesan Archives).

Doyle A I, The Shaping of the Vernon and Simeon MSS, in Chaucer and ME Stud in Honour of R H Robbins, ed B Rowlands, London 1974, p 328 (MSS 2, 6).

Guddat-Figge, G, Catalogue of MSS Containing ME Romances, Munich 1976, pp 145 (MS 6), 186 (MS 5), 268 (MS 2).

Benskin M, Local Archives and ME Dialects, Journ of the Soc of Archivists 5(1977).513 (MS 7 scribe also wrote St John's Coll Cambridge MS 28).

Editions. Furnivall F J, Robert of Brunne's Handlyng Synne, Roxb Club 1862 (MS 3 with partial collation of MS 1 and corresponding parts of Manuel de péchés).

AELeg 1881, p 339 (MS 3).

Horstmann C, Die Evangelium-Geschichten der Homiliensammlung des MS Vernon, Arch 57 (1877).282 (MS 2); Sermo in festo Corporis Christi, Arch 82(1889).188 (MS 2); The Minor Poems of the Vernon MS, Vol I, EETS 98, London 1892, p 198 (MS 2).

Furnivall, Robert of Brunne's Handlyng Synne, EETS 119, 123, London 1901, 1903 (parallel Eng and French texts; base text MS 5 with incomplete collations of MSS 1 and 7; crit ?P Meyer, Rom 32.479; 33.142).

Fosgate H E, Stud in Robert of Mannyng's Handlyng Synne with an Edn of the 13 Original Stories, Mount Holyoke Coll MA thesis 1914.

Naish G H, A New Edn of Handlyng Synne and Medytacyons, diss Univ of London 1936 (base text: MS 1).

Bowers R H, A ME Poem on the Seven Gifts of the Holy Ghost, MLN 70(1955).250 (part of Continuation).

Schulz S A, An Edn of Robert Mannyng of Brunne's Handlyng Synne (Osborn MS), diss N Y Univ 1973 (MS 8, lines 1–3859 only).

Braekman W L, The Seven Virtues as Opposed to the Seven Vices, NM 74(1973).247 (part of Continuation); A ME Didactic Poem on the Works of Mercy, NM 79(1978).145 (part of Continuation).

Vanderschaaf B M, An Edn of Robert Mannyng's Handlyng Synne, diss Univ Iowa 1978 (base text: MS 1 with readings from MS 8).

Braekman, Of Ye Sacrementys Sevene, NM 82 (1981).194 (part of Continuation).

Sullens I, Robert Mannyng of Brunne, Handlyng Synne, Binghamton 1983 (base text: MS 1).

Selections. Halliwell J O, A Dictionary of Archaic and Provincial Words, 4th edn, London 1860, passim (quotes from MS 8).

Morris Spec, 2.50.

Emerson O F, A ME Reader, London 1905, p 88.

Cook A S, Literary ME Reader, Boston 1915, p 300.

Sisam K, 14-Cent Verse and Prose, Oxford 1921, p 1.

Funke O, A ME Reader, Berne 1944, p 59.

Brandl A and O Zippel, ME Lit, 2nd edn, N Y 1949, p 155.

Mossé F, A Handbook of ME, Baltimore 1952, p 211.

Ford B, ed, Medieval Lit: Chaucer and the Alliterative Tradition, Harmondsworth 1954, p 260.

Kaiser R, Medieval Eng, 3rd edn, Berlin 1958, p 251.

Haskell A S, A ME Anthology, Garden City 1969, p 443.

Sisam C and K, The Oxford Book of ME Verse, Oxford 1970, p 145.

Modernizations. Segar M G, A Medieval Anthology, London 1915, p 117.

Neilson W A and K G T Webster, Chief British Poets of the 14 and 15 Cents, Boston 1916, p 1.

Loomis R G and R Willard, Medieval Eng Verse and Prose, N Y 1948, p 104.

Corrigan F X, ME Readings in Trans, Boston 1965, p 106.

Textual Matters. McIntosh A, Some Notes on the Dancers of Colbeck—James Osborn: In Memoriam, N&Q ns 24(1977).196 (notes superior readings in MS 8).

Van der Schaaf B M, The MS Tradition of Handlyng Synne, Manuscripta 24(1980).119.

Besserman J J, The Dancers of Colbeck, MÆ 42(1980).260.

Language. Kington Oliphant T L, Old and ME, London 1878, pp 447, 575.

Hellmers G H, Über die Sprache Roberd Mannyngs of Brunne und über die autorschaft der ihm zugeschriebenen Meditations on the Supper of our Lord, Göttingen 1885.

Börner O L, Die Sprache Roberd Mannyngs of Brunne und ihr Verhältnis zur neuenglischen Mundart, SEP 12(1904); Reimuntersuchung über die Qualität der betonten langen E-Vokale bei Robert of Brunne, SEP 50(1913).298.

Schlutter O B, Weitere Beiträge zur ae Wortforschung, Angl 37(1913).52 n2 (lines 9863–9866); Zu Robert Brunne, Handlyng Synne, Angl 38 (1914).251 (lines 9863–9866).

Moore S, Robert Mannyng's Use of Do as Auxiliary, MLN 33(1918).385.

Moore Meech and Whitehall, p 55.

Prins A A, French Influence in Eng Phrasing, Leiden 1952, p 296.

Käsmann H, Studien zum kirchlichen Wortschatz des Me 1100–1350, Tübingen 1961, passim.

Gburek H, Der Wortschatz des Robert Mannyng of Brunne in Handlyng Synne, Bamberg 1977 (a complete concordance with a list of Furnivall's misreadings).

Stanley E G, A Concordance to Handlyng Synne, N&Q ns 25(1978).99 (rev of article of Gburek).

Bitterling K, Anoyntyng in Robert Mannyng's Handlyng Synne, N&Q ns 26(1979).8 (mistrans of anoitement meaning "increase").

Date. Doyle Survey, 1.60.

Sullivan, p 12 (see under *Literary and Cultural Relations* below).

Author. Furnivall, edn, Roxb Club, p v.

Hales J W, Robert of Brunne, Acad 31(1887).27 (on Brymwake).

DNB, 12.965 (sv Mannyng, Robert).

Graham R, S Gilbert of Sempringham and the Gilbertines, London 1901, pp 139, 158, 159, 161.

Foster C W, ed, Lincoln Wells, I, Publications of the Lincoln Record Soc 5(1914).15.

Crosby R, Robert Mannyng of Brunne: a New Biblio, PMLA 57(1942).15.

Seaton E, Robert Mannyng of Brunne in Lincoln, MÆ 12(1943).77.

Emden A B, A Biographical Register of the Univ of Cambridge to 1500, Cambridge 1963, p 388.

Source. Meyer P, Les manuscrits français de Cambridge, Rom 8(1879).332 (MSS of Manuel).

Paris G, Wilham de Wadington, Auteur de Manuel des péchés, HLF 28(1881).179.

Meyer, Les manuscrits français de Cambridge, Rom 15(1886).312, 348, 351 (MSS of Manuel); Notice du MS Rawlinson Poetry 241, Rom 29(1900).5, 47 (selections from Manuel des péchés).

Allen H E, Two ME Trans from the Anglo-Norman, MP 13(1916).167; The Manuel des Pechiez and Its Scholastic Prologue, RomR 8(1917).434; Mystical Lyrics of the Manuel des Pechiez, RomR 9(1918).154 (relation of Anglo-Norman lyrics to Eng mysticism).

Russell J C, Some 13-Cent Anglo-Norman Writers, MP 28(1931).261 (William of Wadington); Dictionary of Writers of 13-Cent England, London 1936, p 203 (William of Waddington).

Pfander Manuals, p 249.

Arnould E J, Un manuscrit partiel du Manuel des péchés, Rom 63(1937).226; On Two Anglo-Norman Prologues, MLR 34(1939).248.

Arnould, p 60.

Laird C G, The Source of Robert Mannyng of Brunne's Handlying Synne. A Study of the Extant MSS of the Anglo-Norman Manuel des Pechiez, diss Stanford Univ 1940; A 14-Cent Scribe, MLN 55(1940).601 (Huntington HM 903 copy of Manuel); MSS of the Manuel des Pechiez, in Stanford Stud in Lang and Lit, ed H Craig, Stanford 1941, p 99; Palatinus Latinus 1970, A Composite MS, MLR 38(1943).177.

Thomson S H, The Writings of Robert Grosseteste Bishop of Lincoln, Cambridge 1940, p 253 (denies Grosseteste's authorship of Manuel).

Robertson D W Jr, The Manuel des Péchés and an Eng Episcopal Decree, MLN 60(1945).43; The Manuel des Péchés, MLN 61(1946).144.

Laird C, Character and Growth of the Manuel des Péchés, Trad 4(1946).253.

Legge M D, Anglo-Norman Lit and Its Background, Oxford 1963, p 213.

Platts, Robert Mannyng of Brunne's Handlying Synne, as below, p 24 (thinks Grosseteste may have written Manuel).

Literary and Cultural Relations. Schröder E, Die Tänzer von Kölbigk, Zeitschrift für Kirchengeschichte 17(1897).125.

Gerould G H, The Northern Eng Homily Collection, Lancaster 1902, p 30.

Chambers E K, The Medieval Stage, London 1903, 1.90.

Crane T F, Mediaeval Story Books, MP 9(1911).228.

Mosher J A, The Exemplum in Early Eng Religious and Didactic Lit of England, N Y 1911, pp 119, 120, 126, 127, 129, 138.

Kunz A, Robert Mannyng of Brunne's Handlying Synne vergleichen mit der anglonormanischen Vorlage, William of Wadington's Manuel des Pechiez, Königsberg 1913.

Gerould, Saints' Legends, Boston 1916, pp 171, 200.

Crane, Mediaeval Sermon-Books and Stories and Their Study since 1883, PAPS 56(1917).376.

Deanesly M, The Lollard Bible and Other Medieval Biblical Versions, Cambridge 1920, pp 204, 214; Vernacular Books in England in the 14 and 15 Cents, MLR 15(1920).351.

Baskerville C R, Dramatic Aspects of Mediaeval Folk Festivals in England, SP 17(1920).54, 61, 70 (on popular amusements).

Owst G R, Preaching in Medieval England, Cambridge 1926, pp 45, 227, 276, 284, 286, 289.

Welter J T, L'Exemplum dans la littérature religieuse et didactique du Moyen Age, Paris 1927, pp 171, 433.

Verrier P, La plus vieille citation de carole, Rom 58(1932).380.

Os A B van, Religious Visions, Amsterdam 1932, p 224.

Owst, Literature and Pulpit in Medieval England, Cambridge 1933, pp 4, 378, 399, 412, 427, 479, 481.

Oakden J R, Alliterative Poetry in ME, Manchester 1935, 2.364 (alliterative phrases).

Rosenthal C L, The Vitae Patrum in Old and ME Lit, Phila 1936, pp 39, 64, 65, 85, 91, 111, 116, 121, 125, 141, 142, 143.

McGarry L, The Holy Eucharist in ME Homiletic and Devotional Verse, Washington D C 1936, p 90.

Pfander Manuals, p 250.

Pfander H G, The Popular Sermon of the Medieval Friar in England, N Y 1937, pp 23, 30.

Coulton G G, Social Life in Britain from the Conquest to the Reformation, Cambridge 1938, pp 47, 84, 136, 137, 207, 364, 365, 401.

Wilmart A, La Légende de Ste Edith en prose et vers par le moin Goscelin, Analecta Bollandiana 56(1938).5, 265 (Dancers of Colbek).

Heather P J, Seven Planets, Folklore 54(1943).354, 356.

Utley CR, pp 88, 108, 118, 207, 208.

Robertson D W Jr, A Study of Certain Aspects of the Cultural Tradition of Handlyng Synne, diss Univ of N C 1945; Certain Theological Conventions in Mannyng's Treatment of The Commandments, MLN 61(1946).505; The Cultural Tradition of Handlyng Synne, Spec 22(1947).162.

Berry F, Mannyng's Dancers of Colbeck, Life and Letters 60(1949).122.

Pecheux M C, Aspects of the Treatment of Death in ME Poetry, Washington D C 1951, pp 49, 89, 93.

McNeill J T, A Hist of the Cure of Souls, N Y 1951, p 154.

Cazamian L F, Development of Eng Humour, 2nd edn, N Y 1952, p 52.

Bloomfield SDS, p 171.

Pantin, p 224.

Moorman J R L, Church Life in England in the 13 Cent, Cambridge 1955, pp 69, 73, 82, 85, 88.

Peter J, Complaint and Satire in Early Eng Lit, Oxford 1956, pp 3, 45, 74, 100, 189, 268.

Owst, Sortilegium in Eng Homiletic Lit of the 14 Cent, in Stud Presented to Sir Hilary Jenkinson, ed J Conway Davies, London 1957, p 274.

Wenzel S, Sloth in ME Devotional Lit, Angl 79(1961).289.

Wenzel, pp 75, 84, 90, 113, 118, 229, 231, 235.

Woolf, pp 109 n3, 174, 248 n4, 377 n4, 396.

Whiting B J and H W, Proverbs, Sentences, and Proverbial Phrases from Eng Writings before 1500, Cambridge 1968, index.

Tubach F C, Index Exemplorum, FFC 204, Helsinki 1969, passim.

Priscandaro M T, ME Eucharistic Verse: Its Imagery, Symbolism, and Typology, diss St John's Univ 1975, p 26.

Harvey J, Gelwez Gebende: the Kulturmorphologie of a Topos, German Life and Letters ns 28(1975).253 (yellow articles of feminine attire).

Marchalonis S, Three Medieval Tales and Their Modern American Analogues, Journ of the Folklore Institute 13(1976).173.

Turville-Petre T, The Alliterative Revival, Cambridge and Totowa 1977, p 74.

Sullivan S A, Handlyng Synne in Its Tradition: A Study of Robert Mannyng of Brunne's Handlyng Synne and Its Relation to Other Instructional Works, in Order to Establish the Place of the Poem in Its Genre, diss Cambridge Univ 1978.

Relihan R L Jr, Les Peines de Purgatorie: The Anglo-Norman and Latin MS Traditions, Manuscripta 22(1978).166.

Patterson L W, The Parson's Tale and the Quitting of the Canterbury Tales, Trad 34(1978).337.

Platts G C, South Lincolnshire at the Beginning of the 14 Cent: the Social, Economic and Cultural Environment of Robert Mannyng's Handlyng Synne, diss Univ of Birmingham 1978; Robert Mannyng of Bourne's Handlyng Synne and South Lincolnshire Soc, Lincolnshire Hist and Archaeology 14(1979).23.

Hanning R W, Many Turned Tyme: The Cycle of the Year as a Religious Symbol in Two Medieval Texts, in Saints, Scholars and Heroes: Stud in Medieval Culture in Honour of C W Jones, ed M H King and W M Stevens, Ann Arbor 1979, 1.281.

Burke L, Women in the Medieval Manuals of Religious Instruction and John Gower's Confessio Amantis, diss Columbia Univ 1982, pp 36, 52, 64, 72 n105.

Sullens, edn, p 383 (complete list of Tubach numbers).

Literary Criticism. Furnivall, edn, Roxb Club, p xiv.

Arnould, p 295.

Laird G G, Robert Mannyng: A Critical Re-estimate, PMLA 59(1944).1333.

Usis C M, The Narrative and Homiletic Technique of Robert Mannyng, diss Univ of Calif 1950.

Sinclair L Jr, The Evidence for an Aesthetic Theory in 14-Cent Vernacular Poetry, diss Univ of Washington 1970, chaps 1–4.

Wimsatt J I, Allegory and Mirror, N Y 1970, pp 30, 140, 150, 160, 161, 171.

Boitani P, Eng Medieval Narrative in the 13 and 14 Cents, Cambridge 1982, p 23.

Burrow J A, Medieval Writers and Their Work, Oxford 1982, pp 76, 112.

General References. Ten Brink, 1.299.
Brandl, p 647, § 55.
Schofield, p 411.
CHEL, 1.384.
Körting, p 138.
Manning B L, The People's Faith in the Time of Wyclif, Cambridge 1919, p 71 and passim.
Amos F R, Early Theories of Trans, N Y 1920, p 42.
Thomas P G, Eng Lit before Chaucer, London 1924, pp 68, 95, 121.
Legouis HEL, p 81.
Renwick-Orton, p 280.
Baugh LHE, pp 139, 140, 204.
Schlauch M, Eng Medieval Lit and Its Social Foundations, Warsaw 1956, p 195.
Robbins R H, ME Carols as Processional Hymns, SP 56(1959).577.
Dubois M-M, La Littérature anglaise du Moyen Age, Paris 1962, p 107.
Ackerman R W, Backgrounds to Medieval Eng Lit, N Y 1966, pp 49, 89, 93.
Pearsall D, OE and ME Poetry, London 1977, pp 108, 242, 295, 313.
Speirs J, A Survey of Medieval Verse and Drama, in B Ford, ed, Medieval Lit: Chaucer and the Alliterative Tradition, Harmondsworth 1982, p 80.
Brewer D, Eng Gothic Lit, N Y 1983, p 37.
Bibliography. Booker J M, A ME Biblio, Heidelberg 1912, p 38.
Vising J, Anglo-Norman Lang and Lit, London 1923, p 57.
Doyle Survey, 1.58.
Bossuat MBLF, 1.334.
New CBEL, 1.503, 504.

[2] OF SHRIFTE AND PENANCE.

MS. St John's Camb 197, ff 1ᵃ–87ᵃ (1425–50).
Jolliffe, p 65, no A.7.
MS Commentary. James M R, A Descriptive Catalogue of the MSS in the Libr of St John's Coll Cambridge, Cambridge 1913, p 232.
Editions. Farkas C R, Of Shrifte and Pennance: The ME Prose Trans of the Manuel Des Pechiez, diss Univ of Maryland 1969.
Singer T S, A Critical Edn of Of Shrifte and Penance, diss N Y Univ 1972.
Selection. Arnould, p 399.
Source, Content, and Style. Allen H E, Two ME Trans from the Anglo-Norman, MP 13(1915–16).743; The Manuel des Pechiez and the Scholastic Prologue, RomR 8(1917).449.
Arnould, p 319.
Laird C G, The Source of Robert Mannyng of Brunne's Handlyng Synne, A Study of the Extant

MSS of the Anglo-Norman Manuel des Pechiez, diss Stanford Univ 1940, pp 67, 476.
Sullivan S A, Handlyng Synne in Its Tradition, diss Cambridge Univ 1979, p 99.
Date and Language. Arnould, pp 326, 332, 334.
Laird, p 480.
General Reference. Pantin, p 225.
Bibliography. Doyle Survey, 1.65.
New CBEL, 1.504.

[3] PETER IDLE'S (or IDLEY'S) INSTRUCTIONS TO HIS SON.

MSS. 1, Bodl 1479 (Laud misc 416), ff 1ᵃ–64ᵇ (1459); 2, Bodl 1782 (Digby 181), ff 10ᵇ–30ᵇ (1475–1500); 3, Bodl 11951 (Rawl C.86), f 31ᵃ (1450–1500); 4, Bodl Eng theol d.45, ff 1ᵃ–37ᵇ (1450–1500); 5, Camb Univ Ee.4.37, ff 1ᵃ–109ᵃ (ca 1460); 6, Magdalene Camb Pepys 2030, ff 19ᵃ–134ᵇ (1475–1500); 7, BL Arundel 20, ff 35ᵃ–70ᵇ (1450–1500); 8, BL Harley 172, ff 21ᵃ–51ᵇ (1450–1500); 9, BL Addit 57335, ff 1ᵃ–94ᵇ (1500–25); 10, Trinity Dublin 160, ff 14ᵃ–55ᵇ (1450–1500).
Brown-Robbins, Robbins-Cutler, nos 1287, 1540, 3847; Robbins-Cutler, no 4258.6 (Idle's epitaph).
MSS Commentary. A Catalogue of the Harleian MSS in the British Museum, London 1808, 1.60 (MS 8).
Catalogue of MSS in the British Museum ns 1, Pt I: The Arundel MSS, London 1840, p 6 (MS 7).
A Catalogue of the MSS Preserved in the Libr of the Univ of Cambridge, Cambridge 1857, 2.169 (MS 5).
Coxe H O, Catalogi Codicum Manuscriptorum Bibliothecae Bodleianae, Oxford 1858, 2.305 (MS 1).
Macray W D, Catalogi Codicum Manuscriptorum Bibliothecae Bodleianae, Oxford 1883, 9.194 (MS 2).
Abbott T K, Catalogue of the MSS in the Libr of Trinity Coll Dublin, Dublin 1900, p 8 (MS 10).
Herbert, p 313 (MS 7).
Root R K, The MSS of Chaucer's Troilus, ChS 1s, London 1914, p 9 (MS 2 and facsimile).
James M R, A Descriptive Catalogue of the Libr of Samuel Pepys, Pt III, Medieval MSS, London 1923, p 67 (MS 6).
Scott K L, A Mid-Fifteenth-Cent Eng Illuminating Shop and Its Customers, Journ of the Warburg and Courtauld Institute 31(1968).187 (MS 5).
Sotheby Sale Catalogue, 14 June 1971, Lot 1524 (MS 9).
Editions. D'Evelyn C, Peter Idley's Instructions to His Son, Boston 1935, p 81 (base text: MS 5); introd: pp 1 (author), 36 (content, sources), 58 (date, dialect, MSS) (crit TLS Sept 5 1935, p 554; H R Patch, Spec 11.295; K Brunner, AnglB

47.323; J R H[ulbert], MP 34.98; G D Wilcock, MLR 32.86).

Selections. Rel Ant, 2.27.

Furnivall F J, ed, Queen Elizabethes Achademy, EETSES 9, London 1869, p 109.

Miessner F, Peter Idle: Instructions to His Son, Griefswald 1903, pp 33, 34.

Heuser W, Die Kildare Gedichte, BBA 14 (1904).207.

Förster M, Kleine Mitteilungen zur me Lehrdichtung, Arch 104(1909).293.

Furnivall F J, ed, Early Eng Meals and Manners, EETS 32, rvsd edn, London 1931, p 219.

Jones H C, Peter Idley's Instructions to His Son, NM 74(1973).686 (prints lost leaf from MS 6 now in Univ of Missouri).

Gburek H, Der Wortschatz des Robert Mannyng of Brunne in Handlyng Synne, Bamberg 1977 (suggests Idle used Dulwich MS).

Sources and Literary Relations. Miessner, p 24.

Förster, p 293.

D'Evelyn, edn, p 36.

Rosenthal C L, The Vitae Patrum in Old and ME Lit, Phila 1936, p 112.

Arnould, p 335.

Utley CR, pp 107, 117, 146.

Authorship. St John Brooks E, Peter Idley, TLS Sept 12 1935, p 565.

General References. Brandl, § 107, p 690.

Owst G R, Preaching in Medieval England, Cambridge 1926, p 45 n1.

Bennett OHEL, p 158.

Bloomfield SDS, p 217.

Baugh LHE, p 303.

Pearsall D, OE and ME Poetry, London 1977, pp 226, 242, 299.

Scattergood V J and J W Sherborne, edd, Eng Court Culture in the Later Middle Ages, N Y 1983, pp 67, 81.

Bibliography. Doyle Survey, 1.66.

New CBEL, 1.504, 686.

2. Versions of
Somme le roi

[4] AYENBITE OF INWYT.

MS. BL Arundel 57, ff 2ᵃ–4ᵃ, 13ᵃ–94ᵃ (1340).

Jolliffe, p 61, no A.1(a).

Brown-Robbins, Robbins-Cutler, nos 1227, 2034, 2331, 3579; Robbins-Cutler, nos 539.5, 1961.3, 3578.5.

MS Commentary. Catalogue of MSS in the British Museum ns I, Pt I: The Arundel MSS, London 1840, p 12.

Wright C E, Eng Vernacular Hands from the 12 to the 15 Cents, Oxford 1960, no 12.

Parkes M B, Eng Cursive Book Hands 1250–1500, Oxford 1969, p xvii n1.

Editions. Stevenson J, Dan Michel The Ayenbite of Inwyt, Roxb Club 72(1885).

Morris R and P Gradon, Dan Michel's Ayenbite of Inwyt, EETS 26 (text), London 1866 (rvsd 1965), p 278 (introd, notes, and glossary); London 1979, introd: pp 1 (MS), 14 (Language).

Child C G, Verse as Prose in the Ayenbite, MLN 10(1895).127 (Prayer to the Blessed Virgin).

Selections. AESpr, 2.58.

Morris Spec, 2.98.

Zupitza J and J Schipper, Alt- und me Übungsbuch, Vienna 1899, p 89.

Wülcker, 1.112.

Kluge F, Me Lesebuch, Halle a S 1904, p 27.

Emerson O F, A ME Reader, London 1905, p 215.

Brandl A and O Zippel, Me Sprach- und Literaturproben, Berlin 1917, p 236.

McLean G E, An Old and ME Reader, N Y 1922, p 97.

Brown RLxivC, p 49.

Funke O, A ME Reader, Berne 1944, p 25.

Mossé F, A Handbook of ME, Baltimore 1952, p 221.

Baugh A, A Hist of the Eng Lang, 2nd edn, N Y 1957, p 476.

Kaiser R, Medieval Eng, 3rd edn, Berlin 1958, p 198.

Sisam K, 14-Cent Verse and Prose, Oxford 1962, p 33.

Fisher J H and D Bornstein, In Forme of Speche is Chaunge, Englewood Cliffs 1974, p 113.

Modernizations. Wyatt A J, The Ayenbite of Inwyt (Remorse of Conscience) A Trans of Parts into Modern Eng, London 1889.

Corrigan F X, ME Readings in Trans, Boston 1965, p 242.

Textual Matters. Varnhagen H, Beiträge zur Erklärung und Textkritik von Dan Michel's Ayenbite of Inwyt, EStn 1(1877).379; 2(1879).27.

Stratman F H, Verbesserungen zu ae Texten, EStn 2(1879).120.

Evers R W, Beiträge zur Erklärung und Textkritik von Michel's Ayenbite of Inwyt, Erlangen 1887.

Manly J M, Lok-Sounday, HSNPL 1(1892).88.

Language. Danker O, Die Laut- und Flexionslehre der mittelkentischen Denkmäler, Strassburg 1879.

Bülbring K D, Geschichte des Ablauts der Starken Zeitwörter innerhalb des Südenglischen, QF 63 (1889).27.

Konrath M, Zur Laut- und Flexionslehre des Mittelkentischen, Arch 88(1892).47, 157; 89 (1892).153.

Heuser W, Zum kentischen Dialekt im Me, Angl 17(1894).73.

Jensen H, Die Verbalflexion in Ayenbite of Inwyt, Kiel 1908.

Dolle R, Graphische und lautliche Untersuchung von Dan Michels Ayenbite of Inwyt, Bonn 1912.

Glahn N von, Zur Geschichte des grammatischen Geschlechts im Me, AF 53(1918).62.

Wyld H C, South-eastern and South-east Midlands Dialects in ME, E&S 6(1920).112.

Wallenberg J K, The Vocabulary of Dan Michel's Ayenbite of Inwyt, Uppsala 1923.

Taylor A B, On the Hist of Old Eng ēa, ēo in Middle Kentish, MLR 19(1924).1.

Flasdieck H W, Studien zur me Grammatik, AnglB 34(1924).21; Über die mkent Ordinalia, AnglB 39(1928).357.

Moore Meech and Whitehall, p 51.

Senff H, Die Nominalflexion im Ayenbite of Inwyt, Jena 1937.

Kaiser R, Zur Geographie des me Wortschatzes, Palaes 205(1937).143.

Schwede I, Die Bezeichnungen der Numeri, Kasus und Genera des Nomens in Dan Michel's Ayenbite of Inwyt, Berlin 1942.

Bliss A J, Vowel-Quantity in ME Borrowings from Anglo-Norman, ALg 4(1952).142, 144.

Prins A A, French Influence in Eng Phrasing, Leiden 1952, p 297.

Käsmann H, Studien zum kirchlichen Wortschatz des Me 1100–1500, Tübingen 1961, passim.

Magnusson U, Stud in the Phonology of the Ayenbite of Inwyt, Lund Theses in Eng 1, Lund 1971.

Freeman L H, Dialect Characteristics of Late ME Prepositions in Two Parallel Prose Works: Ayenbite of Inwyt and Vices and Virtues, diss Oregon Univ 1973.

Sources and Literary Relations. Konrath M, Die lateinische Quelle zu Ayenbite und zu Sawles Warde, EStn 12(1888).459.

Meyer R, Notice sur le Manusrit 27 de la Bibliothèque D'Alençon, SATF 2(1892).68.

Child C G, Verse as Prose in the Ayenbite, MLN 10(1895).64.

Peterson K O, The Sources of the Parson's Tale, Boston 1901, p 1.

Förster M, Die Bibliothek des Dan Michael von Northgate, Arch 115(1905).167.

Mosher J A, The Exemplum in Early Eng Religious and Didactic Lit of England, N Y 1911, p 122.

Lowes J L, Chaucer and the Seven Deadly Sins, PMLA 30(1915).237.

Deanesly M, The Lollard Bible and Other Medieval Biblical Versions, Cambridge 1920, pp 204, 214.

Owst G R, Preaching in Medieval England, Cambridge 1926, pp 289, 290; Lit and Pulpit in Medieval England, Cambridge 1933, pp 11, 26, 30, 32, passim.

Messenger R E, Ethical Teachings in the Latin Hymns of Medieval England, N Y 1930, pp 30, 71, 178.

Cornelius R D, The Figurative Castle, Bryn Mawr 1930, p 29.

Os A B van, Religious Visions, Amsterdam 1931, pp 147, 165.

Pfander Manuals, p 250.

Rosenthal C L, The Vitae Patrum in Old and ME Lit, Phila 1936, pp 110, 141, 143.

Francis W N, The Original of the Ayenbite of Inwyt, PMLA 53(1937).893.

Arnould, pp 36, 136, 158, 239.

O'Connor M C, The Art of Dying Well: the Development of the Ars Moriendi, N Y 1942, p 18 n35.

Bloomfield SDS, pp 182, 248, passim.

Pecheux M C, Aspects of the Treatment of Death in ME Poetry, Washington D C 1951, pp 21, 41.

Douie D L, Archbishop Peckam, Oxford 1952, p 140.

Morse J M, Augustine, Ayenbite, and Ulysses, PMLA 70(1955).1143.

Brayer E, Contenu, structure et combinaisons du Miroir du Monde et de la Somme le Roi, Rom 79(1958).1, 433.

Wenzel, pp 75, 80, 89, 152, 193, 230, 247.

Wenzel S, Sloth in ME Devotional Lit, Angl 79(1961).298.

Yunck J A, The Lineage of Lady Meed, Notre Dame 1963, pp 231, 232, 261.

Sachs A, Religious Despair in Mediaeval Lit and Art, MS 26(1964).231.

Gordon J D, The Articles of the Creed and the Apostles, Spec 40(1965).638.

Fischer N, Handlist of Animal References in ME Religious Prose, Leeds SE 4(1970).passim.

Blake N F, ME Prose and Its Audience, Angl 90(1972).453.

Doob P, Nebuchadnezzar's Children, New Haven and London 1974, pp 22, 28, 51, 151, 176, 177.

Sullivan S A, Handlyng Synne in Its Tradition, diss Cambridge Univ 1979, p 189.

Carruthers L M, La Somme le Roi de Lorens D'Orleans et ses traductions anglaises: Etude comparative, diss Univ of Paris 1980, p 69.

General References. Ten Brink, 1.283.

Brandl, p 633, § 34.

Schofield, pp 386, 409.

CHEL, 1.395.

Körting, p 150, § 137.

Patch H R, Characters in Medieval Lit, MLN 40(1925).7.

Wilson EMEL, pp 121, 142.

Reese G, Music in the Middle Ages, N Y 1940, p 243.

Baugh LHE, p 204.

Thurston H, Familiar Prayers: Their Origin & Hist, London 1952, p 27.

Pantin, p 225.

Schlauch M, Eng Medieval Lit and Its Social Foundations, Warsaw 1956, p 193.

Taylor J, Notes on the Rise of Written Eng in the Late Middle Ages, Proc of the Leeds Philosophical and Literary Soc 8(1956).129.

Dubois M-M, La Littérature anglaise du Moyen Age, Paris 1962, p 108.

Ackerman R W, Backgrounds to Medieval Eng Lit, N Y 1966, pp 89, 93, 142.

Brewer D, Eng Gothic Lit, N Y 1983, p 260.

Bibliography. Booker J M, A ME Biblio, Heidelberg 1912, p 4.

Ives D V, The Seven Deadly Sins in Eng Lit, Univ of London MA thesis 1931, p 42.

Doyle Survey, 1.69.

New CBEL, 1.502.

Barratt A, Works of Religious Instruction, in ME Prose, ed A S G Edwards, New Brunswick 1984, p 416.

[5] THE BOOK OF VICES AND VIRTUES.

MSS. 1, Univ Oxford 97, ff 125ᵃ–127ᵃ (1400–25; Articles of the Faith only); 2, BL Addit 17013, ff 2ᵃ–85ᵇ (1400–50); 3, BL Addit 22283, ff 92ᵃ–115ᵇ (1380–1400); 4, Henry E Huntington HM 147, ff 1ᵃ–113ᵇ (ca 1400).

Jolliffe, p 61, no A.1(b).

Robbins-Cutler, no 1436.5 (a quatrain against the sins of the tongue inserted in MSS 2, 4).

MSS Commentary. Catalogue of Additions to the MSS in the British Museum in the Years MDCCCXLVI–MDCCCXLVII, London 1864, p 347 (MS 2).

Catalogue of Additions to the MSS in the British Museum in the Years MDCCCLIV–MDCCCLX, London 1875, p 623 (MS 3).

de Ricci Census, 1.59 (MS 4).

Kosmer E V, A Study of the Style and Iconography of a 13-Cent Somme le Roi (British Museum MS Add 54180) with a Consideration of Other Illustrated Somme MSS of the 13, 14 and 15 Cents, diss Yale Univ 1973, Pt 2, p 188.

Doyle A I, The Shaping of the Vernon and Simeon MSS, in B Rowland, ed, Chaucer and ME Stud in Honour of R H Robbins, Kent 1974, p 328 (MS 3).

Guddat-Figge G, Catalogue of MSS Containing ME Romances, Munich 1976, p 145 (MS 3).

Doyle, Univ Coll Oxford MS 97 and Its Relationship to the Simeon MS (BL Add 22283), in M Benskin and M L Samuels, edd, So meny people longages and tonges philological Essays in Scots and Mediaeval Eng Presented to Angus McIntosh, Edinburgh 1981, p 265 (MSS 1, 3).

Hanna R III, The Index of ME Prose, Handlist I, A Handlist of Manuscripts containing ME Prose in the Henry E. Huntington Library, Woodbridge 1984, p 20.

Edition. Francis W N, The Book of Vices and Virtues, EETS, London 1942, p 1 (base text: MS 4); introd: pp xi (French original), xxxii (other Eng versions), xlvii (The Book of Vices and Virtues: MSS, language of MSS 2 and 4, authorship and date, relationship of MSS, the text) (crit J P Oakden MLR 39.404; G D Wilcock, YWES 23.79; TLS May 8 1943, p 228).

Selections. Matthews W, ed, Later ME Prose, N Y 1963, p 116.

Blake N F, ed, ME Religious Prose, Evanston 1972, p 132.

Sources and Literary Relations. Francis, edn, p xxi.

Bloomfield SDS, p 182.

Douie D L, Archbishop Pecham, Oxford 1952, p 139.

Hussey M, The Petitions of the Paternoster in Mediaeval Eng Lit, MÆ 27(1958).12.

Wenzel, pp 75, 80, 116, 193, 231, 237, 238, 247.

Gordon J D, The Articles of Creed and the Apostles, Spec 40(1965).634.

Tuve R, Allegorical Imagery, Princeton 1966, pp 23 n9, 57 n1, 86 n24.

Carruthers L M, La Somme le Roi de Lorens D'Orleans et ses traductions anglaises: Etude comparative, diss Univ of Paris 1980, p 99.

Burke L, Women in Medieval Manuals of Religious Instruction and John Gower's Confessio Amantis, diss Columbia Univ 1982, pp 20, 22, 24, 36, 41, 44, 47, 52, 66.

Date and Authorship. Francis, edn, p lx.

Language. Deanesly M, The Lollard Bible and Other Medieval Biblical Versions, Cambridge 1920, pp 96, 214, 342, 393.

Francis, edn, p liii.

Bühler C F, The Apostles and the Creed, Spec 28(1953).335.

Milosh J E, The Scale of Perfection, Madison 1966, p 145.

Freeman L H, Dialect Characteristics of Late ME Prepositions in Two Parallel Prose Works: Ayenbite of Inwyt and Book of Vices and Virtues, diss Univ of Oregon 1973.

Blake, The Eng Lang in Medieval Lit, London 1977, p 133.

General References. Workman S K, 15-Cent Trans as an Influence on Eng Prose, Princeton 1940, p 185.

Pantin, p 226.

Wenzel S, Sloth in ME Devotional Lit, Angl 79(1961).289.

Ackerman R W, Background to Medieval Eng Lit, N Y 1966, p 89.

Fischer N, Handlist of Animal References in ME Religious Prose, Leeds SE 4(1970).passim.

Wilson R M, The Lost Lit of Medieval England, 2nd edn, London 1970, p 146 (lost copies of [5]).

Pearsall D and E Salter, Landscapes and Seasons of the Medieval World, London 1973, pp 61, 71.

Blake, Varieties of ME Religious Prose, in B Rowland, ed, Chaucer and ME Stud in Honour of R H Robbins, London 1974, p 349.

Scattergood V J and J W Sherborne, edd, Eng Court Culture in the Later Middle Ages, N Y 1983, pp 35, 36.

Bibliography. Doyle Survey, 1.70.

Barratt A, Works of Religious Instruction in ME Prose, ed A S G Edwards, New Brunswick 1984, p 416.

[6] OTHER VERSIONS OF SOMME LE ROI.

MSS. Version A: 1, BL Royal 18.A.x, ff 16^a–55^b (1400–50); *Version B*: 2, BL Addit 37677, ff 61^b–83^b (1400–50); *Version C*: 3, BL Harley 6571, ff 1^a–73^b (1400–50); *Version D*: 4, Bodl 8174 (Ashmole 1286), ff 110^a–203^a, 236^a–251^b (1400–50); *Version E*: 5, Corpus Christi Camb 494, ff 1^a–117^b (1475–1500); *Version F*: 6, Bodl 3493 (e.Mus.23), pp 1–161 (1450–75); *Version G*: 7, Bodl 21896 (Douce 322), ff 25^b–26^b (1475–1500); 8, Camb Univ Ff.5.45, ff 23^a–24^b (1450–1500); 9, BL Harley 1706, ff 24^b–25^b (1475–1500). PRINTS: *Version H*: 10, William Caxton, Westminster 1484/85 (STC, no 21429); 11, Wynkyn de Worde, London 1507 (STC, no 21430); 12, Richard Pynson, London 1507 (STC, no 21430a).

Jolliffe, pp 61, nos A.1(c–d, f–i); 122, no L.1.

MSS Commentary. A Catalogue of the Harleian MSS in the British Museum, London 1808, 2.178 (MS 9); 3.376 (MS 3).

Black W H, A Descriptive, Analytical, and Critical Catalogue of the MSS Bequeathed unto the Univ of Oxford by Elias Ashmole, Oxford 1845, p 1051 (MS 4).

A Catalogue of the MSS Preserved in the Libr of the Univ of Cambridge, Cambridge 1857, 2.501 (MS 8).

Summary Cat, 2.656 (MS 6); 4.593 (MS 7).

James M R, A Descriptive Catalogue of the MSS in the Libr of Corpus Christi Coll Cambridge, Cambridge 1912, 2.446 (MS 5).

Catalogue of Additions to the MSS in the British Museum in the Years MDCCCCVI–MDCCCCX, London 1912, p 102 (MS 2).

Warner G F and J P Gilson, Catalogue of Western MSS in the Old Royal and King's Collections, London 1921, 2.265 (MS 1).

Francis W N, ed, The Book of Vices and Virtues, EETS 217, London 1942, p xxxii (description of Somme material in all MSS, except MSS 3, 8, and PRINTS).

Editions. Crotch W J B, The Prologues and Epilogues of William Caxton, EETS 176, London 1928, p 2 (PRINTS).

Blake N F, Caxton's Own Prose, London 1973, p 134 (PRINTS: Prologue and Epilogue).

Modernization. Comper F M, ed, The Book of the Craft of Dying and Other Early Eng Tracts Concerning Death, London 1917, p 127 (Version G: Toure).

Sources and Literary Relations. Pfander Manuals, p 250.

Bloomfield SDS, p 182.

Bühler C F, The Apostles and the Creed, Spec 28(1953).338 (PRINTS).

Pantin, p 226.

Gallagher J E, The Sources of Caxton's Ryal Book and Doctrinal of Sapience, SP 72(1965).40.

Tuve R, Allegorical Imagery, Princeton 1966, pp 41, 42 n19, 52, 57.

Blake, ME Prose and Its Audience, Angl 90 (1972).451.

Chené-Williams A, Vivre sa mort et mourir sa vie: l'art de mourir au XVe siècle, in Le Sentiment de la mort au Moyen Age, ed C Sutto, Quebec 1979, p 179 (Version G: Toure).

Carruthers L M, La Somme le Roi de Lorens d'Orleans et ses traductions anglaises: Etude comparative, diss Univ of Paris 1980, pp 83, 84, 85, 86, 90.

Authorship. Doyle Survey, 2.215.

Wilson E, Sir Robert Shottesbrook (1400–71): Translator, N&Q ns 28(1981).303 (MS 6).

General Reference. Workman S K, 15-Cent Trans as an Influence on Eng Prose, Princeton 1940, p 29 n3 (PRINTS).

Bibliography. Blades W, The Biography and Typography of William Caxton, London 1861, 1.187.

Gasquet F A, The Biblio of Some Devotional Books Printed by the Earliest Eng Printers, Trans of the Biblio Soc of London 7(1902–04).185 (PRINTS).

Duff E G, William Caxton, Chicago 1905, p 68.

de Ricci S, A Census of Caxtons, London 1909, p 89, no 89.

Duff E G, 15-Cent Eng Books, Oxford 1917, p 101, no 366 (PRINTS).

Aurner N S, Caxton: Mirror of 15-Cent Letters, N Y 1926, p 214.

Doyle Survey, 1.70.

Doyle A I, Books Connected with the Vere Family and Barking Abbey, Trans of the Essex Archaeological Soc 25(1958).222.

Blake, Caxton and His World, London 1969, pp 87, 96, 169, 236 (PRINT 10); Caxton: England's First Publisher, N Y 1976, pp 75, 77, 82, 139, 150, 181, 194, 208.

3. Works Derived from
Somme le roi

[7] SPECULUM VITAE.

MSS. 1, Bodl 1885 (Bodl 48), ff 47ᵃ–325ᵇ (1400–25); 2, Bodl 2685 (Bodl 446), ff 1ᵃ–207ᵇ (1400–50); 3, Bodl 3815 (Greaves 43), ff 1ᵃ–47ᵇ (ca 1400); 4, Bodl 3938 (Eng poet a.1), ff 231ᵃ–265ᵃ (1380–1400); 5, Bodl 4109 (Hatton 18), ff 2ᵃ–210ᵇ (1475–1500); 6, Bodl 4110 (Hatton 19), ff 3ᵃ–94ᵇ (1400–50); 7, Bodl 12718 (Rawl C.884), ff 1ᵃ–303ᵇ (1450–1500); 8, Bodl 12724 (Rawl C. 890), ff 1ᵃ–146ᵇ (ca 1400); 9, Bodl 31040 (Eng poet d.5), ff 1ᵃ–218ᵃ (1375–1400); 10, Bodl Lyell 28, ff 1ᵃ–79ᵇ (ca 1400); 11, Camb Univ Ff.4.9, ff 1ᵃ–83ᵇ (1475–1500); 12, Camb Univ Gg.1.7, ff 12ᵃ–277ᵇ (1400–25); 13, Camb Univ Gg.1.14, ff 2ᵃ–242ᵇ (ca 1400); 14, Camb Univ Ii.1.36, ff 1ᵃ–225ᵃ (1400–25); 15, Camb Univ Ll.1.8, ff 1ᵃ–200ᵇ (1375–1400); 16, Camb Univ Addit 2823, ff 1ᵃ–200ᵇ (ca 1450); 17, Gonville and Caius Camb 160, ff 1ᵃ–412ᵃ (1450–1500); 18, Trinity Camb 593 (R.3.13), ff 3ᵃ–85ᵇ (1400–25); 19, Trinity Camb 603 (R.3.23), ff 1ᵃ–179ᵇ (ca 1400); 20, Fitzwilliam Mus Camb McClean 130, ff 1ᵃ–200ᵃ (1400–25); 21, BL Cotton Tiberius E.vii, ff 1ᵃ–81ᵇ (1400–25); 22, BL Harley 435, ff 1ᵃ–102ᵃ (ca 1450); 23, BL Harley 2260, ff 1ᵃ–183ᵇ (1400–50); 24, BL Harley 6718, ff 16ᵃ–33ᵃ (1450–1500); 25, BL Royal 17.C.viii, ff 2ᵃ–336ᵇ (ca 1450); 26, BL Sloane 1785, ff 30ᵃ–60ᵇ (1450–1500); 27, BL Stowe 951, ff 32ᵃ–312ᵃ (ca 1440); 28, BL Addit 8151, ff 3ᵃ–199ᵃ (1475—1500); 29, BL Addit 22283, ff 33ᵃ–61ᵇ (1380–1400); 30, BL Addit 22558, ff 1ᵃ–212ᵇ (ca 1450); 31, BL Addit 33995, ff 1ᵃ–96ᵃ (ca 1375); 32, Glasgow Univ Hunter 89, ff 1ᵃ–73ᵇ (ca 1400); 33, Marlborough Vicarage (Marlborough Coll Libr Deposit), a single sheet (83 lines; 1400–25); 34, Nat Libr of Wales Peniarth 395.D (Hengwrt 226), ff 1ᵃ–326ᵇ (1400–25); 35, Liverpool Univ 23 (F.4.9), ff 1ᵃ–203ᵃ (1400–25); 36, Nottingham Univ Middleton Mi LM.9, no pagination (ca 1450); 37, Trinity Dublin 76, ff 1ᵃ–4ᵃ (15 cent; a fragment); 38, Trinity Dublin 423, ff 1ᵃ–4ᵃ (1450–1500); 39, Robert Taylor (Princeton), ff 1ᵃ–96ᵇ (ca 1400); 40, Takamiya (?Tokyo) 15 (Sotheby Sale, Dec 10, 1969, lot 43) (1400–50).

Brown-Robbins, nos 245, 3648; Robbins-Cutler, nos 245, *827.8, 1197.4.

MSS Commentary. A Catalogue of the MSS in the Cottonian Libr Deposited in the British Museum, London 1802, p 40 (MS 21).

A Catalogue of the Harleian MSS in the British Museum, London 1808, 1.311 (MS 22); 2.595 (MS 23); 3.389 (MS 24).

A Catalogue of the MSS Preserved in the Libr of the Univ of Cambridge, Cambridge 1857, 2.441 (MS 11); 3(1858).19 (MS 12), 23 (MS 13), 365 (MS 14); 4(1861).4 (MS 15).

Catalogue of Additions to the MSS in the British Museum in the Years MDCCCLIV–MDCCCLX, London 1875, pp 623 (MS 29), 672 (MS 30).

Macray W D, Catalogi Codicum Manuscriptorum Bibliothecae Bodleianae, Oxford 1878, 5.461 (MS 7), 463 (MS 8).

Catalogue of Additions to the MSS in the British Museum in the Years MDCCCLXXXVIII–MDCCCXCIII, London 1894, p 156 (MS 31).

Catalogue of the Stowe MSS in the British Museum, London 1895, 1.634 (MS 27).

Summary Cat, 2.97 (MS 1), 493 (MS 2), 746 (MS 3), 789 (MS 4), 844 (MSS 5, 6); 6.8 (MS 9).

Abbott T K, Catalogue of the MSS in the Libr of Trinity Coll Dublin, Dublin 1900, pp 10 (MS 37), 65 (MS 38).

James M R, The Western MSS in the Libr of Trinity Coll Cambridge A Descriptive Catalogue, Cambridge 1901, 2.63 (MS 18), 96 (MS 19); A Descriptive Catalogue of the MSS in the Libr of Gonville and Caius Coll Cambridge, Cambridge 1907, 1.184 (MS 17); A Descriptive Catalogue of the McClean Collection of MSS in the Fitzwilliam Museum, Cambridge 1912, p 277 (MS 20).

Young J and P H Aitken, A Catalogue of the MSS in the Hunterian Museum in the Univ of Glasgow, Glasgow 1908, p 96 (MS 32).

Warner G F and J P Gilson, Catalogue of Western MSS in the Old Royal and King's Collections, London 1921, 2.240 (MS 25).

Handlist of MSS in the National Libr of Wales, Pt 1, Aberystwyth 1940, p 9 (MS 34).

A Guide to the MSS Collections in Liverpool Univ Libr, Liverpool 1962, no 23 (MS 35).

de la Mare A, Catalogue of the Collection of Medieval MSS Bequeathed to the Bodleian Libr by James P R Lyell, Oxford 1971, p 59 (MS 10).

Doyle A I, The Shaping of the Vernon and Simeon MSS, in B Rowland, ed, Chaucer and ME Stud in Honour of R H Robbins, Kent 1974, p 328 (MSS 4, 29).

Guddat-Figge G, Catalogue of MSS Containing ME Romances, Munich 1976, pp 145 (MS 29), 269 (MS 4).

Ker Manuscripts, 3.308 (MS 35).

Editions. Rel Ant, 2.38 (50 lines from MS 26).

Cowper J M, Meditations on the Supper of Our Lord, EETS 60, London 1875, p 252 (MS 33).

Ullmann J, Studien zu Richard Rolle de Hampole, EStn 7(1884).417, 468 (lines 1–370 with analysis of the rest of the poem).

Brown Reg, 1.255, 360 (four lines adapted from [7], 11.372–73, 376–77).

Wordsworth C, Horae Eboracenses, Surtees Soc 132(1920).165 (MS 33).

Gunn A D, Accidia and Prowess in the Vernon Version of Nassyngton's Speculum Vitae: An Edn of the Text and a Study of the Ideas, diss Univ of Pennsylvania 1969 (MS 4).

Nelson V C, The ME Speculum Vitae: A Critical Edn of Part of the Text from 35 MSS, diss Univ of Sydney 1974 (an edn of lines 3359–7322; base text: MS 31).

Smeltz J W, Speculum Vitae: An Edn of British Museum MS Royal 17.C.viii, diss Duquesne Univ 1977 (MS 25).

Textual Matters. Zupitza J, Zu dem Anfang des Speculum Vitae, EStn 12(1888).468 (corrections of Ullmann edn).

Watson G, ME Poem: Identification, N&Q 147 (1924).371 (identification of MS 33).

Nelson V, The Vernon and Simeon Copies of the Speculum Vitae, ESts 57(1976).390 (MSS 4, 29); Problems of Transcription in the Speculum Vitae MSS, Scriptorium 31(1977).254; Cotton Tiberius E.VII: A MS of the Speculum Vitae, ESts 59(1978).97 (MS 21).

Authorship. Ritson J, Bibliotheca Poetica: A Catalogue of Eng Poets of the 12, 13, 14, 15, and 16 Cents, London 1802, p 91 (ascribes [7] to Nassyngton).

Ullmann, edn, p 470.

DNB, 14.120 (sv Nassyngton, William).

Allen H E, The Authorship of the Prick of Conscience, RadMon 15(1916).163 (Nassyngton as possible author of [18]); The Speculum Vitae: Addendum, PMLA 32(1917).133.

Sources and Literary Relations. Allen, RadMon 15 (1916).262, 309, 371, 381, 384, 390.

Fischer E, Ein nordenglisches moralisch-religiöses Versfragment aus dem 15 Jahrhundert, EStn 60(1925–26).252 (relationship to [9]).

Bradley R, Backgrounds of the Title Speculum in Mediaeval Lit, Spec 29(1954).100.

Pantin, p 228.

Wenzel, pp 75, 226, 228.

Gordon J D, The Articles of the Creed and the Apostles, Spec 40(1965).635.

Tuve R, Allegorical Imagery, Princeton 1966, p 114.

Hussey M, The Petitions of the Paternoster in Mediaeval Eng Lit, Papers on Lang and Lit 5 (1969).15.

Grabes H, The Mutable Glass Mirror—Imagery in Titles and Texts of the Middle Ages and Eng Renaissance, Cambridge 1973, pp 28, 265.

Nelson V, An Introd to the Speculum Vitae, Essays in Lit 2(1974).75.

General References. Warton T, The Hist of Eng Poetry, London 1840, 2.367.

Furnivall F J, Early Eng Games, N&Q 4s 3 (1869).169.

Brandl, p 668, §78.

Deanesly M, The Lollard Bible and Other Medieval Biblical Versions, Cambridge 1920, pp 204, 215.

Owst G R, Preaching in Medieval England, Cambridge 1926, pp 226, 266, 275, 277, 289, 290; Lit and Pulpit in Medieval England, Cambridge 1933, pp 13, 15.

Bloomfield SDS, p 178.

Bibliography. Doyle Survey, 1.77.

New CBEL, 1.520.

Barratt A, Works of Religious Instruction, in ME Prose, ed A S G Edwards, New Brunswick 1984, p 417.

[8] A MYROUR TO LEWDE MEN AND WYMMEN.

MSS. 1, Bodl 3615 (e.Mus.35), pp 221–452 (1425–50); 2, Bodl 11242 (Rawl A.356), ff 1ᵃ–83ᵃ (1450–1500); 3, BL Harley 45, ff 1ᵃ–167ᵇ (1400–25); 4, Univ of Pennsylvania Eng.3, ff 1ᵃ–168ᵇ (1400–25).

Jolliffe, p 63, no A.3.

MSS Commentary. A Catalogue of the Harleian MSS in the British Museum, London 1808, 1.12 (MS 3).

Macray W D, Catalogi Codicum Manuscriptorum Bibliothecae Bodleianae, Oxford 1862, 5.370 (MS 2).

Summary Cat, 2.702 (MS 1).

Stover E V, A Myrour to Lewde Men and Wymen. A Note on a Recently Acquired MS, LC 16 (1950).81 (MS 4).

Editions. Stover E V, A Myrour to Lewde Men and Wymmen, diss Univ of Pennsylvania 1951 (base text: MS 3).

Lubbe L, A Myrour to Lewde Men and Women, diss UCLA 1956.

Nelson V, A Myrour to Lewde Men and Wymmen, Heidelberg 1981, introd: pp 11 (relationship of [7] and [8] to Somme le Roi), 15 (relationship between [7] and [8]), 24 (date and authorship), 25 (stylistic comparison of [7] and [8]), 36 (comparison of [8] and [9]), 39 (place of [8] in later ME prose), 41 (description of MSS), 48 (language of MSS), 51 (classification of MSS).

Selection. Bowers R H, A ME Mnemonic Poem on Usury, MS 17(1955).228 (De Usura section).

Sources and Literary Relations. Allen H E, The Speculum Vitae: Addenum, PMLA 32(1917).138.

Owst G R, The Angel and Goliardys in Langland's Prologue, MLR 20(1925).271 n4 (mistakenly suggests [8] is an expansion of [4] and direct source of [9]); Preaching in Medieval England, Cambridge 1926, p 290; Lit and Pulpit in Medieval England, Cambridge 1933, pp 103, 151, 575.

Bloomfield SDS, p 141.

Pantin, p 228.

Wenzel, pp 75, 226, 228.

Gordon J D, The Articles of the Creed and the Apostles, Spec 40(1965).634.

Aarts F G A M, ed, The Pater Noster of Richard Ermyte, The Hague 1967, p cxii.

Bibliography. Doyle Survey, 1.89.

Barratt A, Works of Religious Instruction, in ME Prose, ed A S G Edwards, New Brunswick 1984, p 417.

[9] JACOB'S WELL.

MS. Salisbury Cath 174 (olim 103), ff 5ᵃ–23ᵃ (ca 1450).

MS Commentary. A Catalogue of the Cathedral Church of Salisbury, London 1880, p 21.

Ker N, Salisbury Cathedral MSS and Patrick Young's Catalogue, Wiltshire Archeological and Natural Hist Magazine 53(1949–50).172.

Edition. Brandeis A, Jacob's Well, Pt I, EETS 115, London 1900, p 1 (chaps 1–50 only; Pt II, chaps 51–95, has not been published).

Modernized Selections. Bennett H S, England from Chaucer to Caxton, N Y 1928, pp 78, 133, 150.

Matthews W, ed, Later Medieval Eng Prose, N Y 1963, p 274.

Sources and Literary Relations. Mosher J, The Exemplum in the Early Religious and Didactic Lit of England, N Y 1911, pp 5, 7, 126, 129, 132.

Crane T, Medieval Sermon Books and Stories and Their Study since 1883, Proc of the American Philosophical Soc 56(1917).379, 380.

Barnicle M E, The Exemplum of the Penitent Usurer, PMLA 33(1918).413.

Owst G R, Preaching in Medieval England, Cambridge 1926, pp 74, 87, 88, 94, passim; Lit and Pulpit in Medieval England, Cambridge 1933, pp 11, 13, 32, 40, 42, passim.

Peckham J L, Archbishop Peckham as a Religious Educator, YSE 7(Scottdale Pa 1934).109.

Rosenthal C L, The Vitae Patrum in Old and ME Lit, Phila 1936, pp 64, 65, 96, 104, 110, 120, 122, 124, 125, 141, 142, 143.

Lloyd D J, An Edn of the Prose and Verse in the Bodleian MS Laud Misc 23, diss Yale Univ 1943, p xxiii (indebtedness of [9] to [106]).

Douie D L, Archbishop Pecham, London 1952, p 141.

Zutphen J P W M Van, ed, A Litil Tretys on the Seven Deadly Sins, Rome 1956, p xxiii (relation of [106] to [9]).

Wenzel, pp 75, 80, 85, 93, 105, 111, 115, 152, 235, 245.

Wenzel S, Sloth in ME Devotional Lit, Angl 79(1961).299, 302.

Yunck J A, The Lineage of Lady Meed, Notre Dame 1963, pp 239, 242, 245, 246, 249, 250, 261.

Tubach F, Index Exemplorum: A Handbook of Medieval Religious Tales, FFC 86, Helsinki 1969, nos 141, 2143, 2440, 4216, 5015, etc.

Fischer N, Handlist of Animal References in ME Religious Prose, Leeds SE 4(1970).49 and passim.

Gregg J Y, The Narrative Exempla of Jacob's Well: A Source Study with an Index for Jacob's Well to Index Exemplorum, diss N Y Univ 1973, p 30.

Doob P, Nebuchadnezzar's Children, New Haven and London 1974, pp 214 n10, 215.

Gregg J Y, The Exempla of Jacob's Well: A Study in the Transmission of Medieval Sermon Stories, Trad 33(1977).359.

Möske B, Caritas, Bonn 1977, p 52.

Nelson V, ed, A Myrour to Lewde Men and Wymmen, Heidelberg 1981, p 36 (a comparison of [9] and [8]).

Pickering O S, Notes on the Sentence of Cursing in ME; or, A Case for the Index of ME Prose, Leeds SE 12(1981).229 (use of [9] by author of [229] found in Dulwich MS 22).

General References. Furnivall F J, Jacob's Well and Its Skeat, Acad Aug 27 1892, p 171 (first notice with summary of contents).

Workman S K, 15-Cent Trans as an Influence on Eng Prose, Princeton 1940, p 43.

Chew S, The Virtues Reconciled, Toronto 1947, p 42.

Bennett OHEL, pp 20, 186, 307.

Baugh LHE, pp 203, 205.

Pecheux M C, Aspects of the Treatment of Death in ME Poetry, Washington D C 1951, pp 10, 13, 21, 28.

Bloomfield SDS, pp 23, 245, 420.

Schlauch M, Eng Medieval Lit and Its Social Foundations, Warsaw 1956, p 299.

Russell Vernacular Instruction, p 101.

Blench J W, Preaching in England in the Late 15 and 16 Cents, N Y 1964, pp 133 n129.

Ackerman R W, Backgrounds to Medieval Eng Lit, N Y 1966, p 94.

Patterson L W, The Parson's Tale and the Quitting of the Canterbury Tales, Trad 34(1978).336.

Bibliography. Doyle Survey, 1.93.

4. Version of
Miroir du monde

[10] MIRROURE OF THE WORLD.

MS. Bodl 2338 (Bodley 283), ff 1ᵃ–180ᵇ (1470–80). Jolliffe, p 62, no A.1(e).

MS Commentary. Summary Cat, 2.316.

Francis W N, ed, The Book of Vices and Virtues, EETS 217, London 1942, p xxxviii.

Smith [Scott] K L, An Archaeological Analysis of MS Bodley 283, The Mirroure of the World, Produced by a Publishing House of Vernacular Lit in Mid-15-Cent England, diss Univ of Calif Berkeley 1965.

Pächt O and J J G Alexander, Illuminated MSS in the Bodleian Libr Oxford, I: German, Dutch, Flemish, French and Spanish Schools, Oxford 1966, no 222, plate 16; III: British, Irish, and Icelandic Schools, Oxford 1973, no 1082, plate 101.

Scott K L, A Mid-15-Cent Eng Illuminating Shop and Its Customers, Journ of the Warburg and Courtauld Institutes 31(1968).182.

Delaissé L M J, A Cent of Dutch MS Illumination, Berkeley 1968, fig 144.

Hobson A R L, Great Libraries, London 1970, p 167.

Pollard G, The Names of Some 15-Cent Binders, Libr 5s 25(1970).198.

Kosmer E V, A Study of the Style and Iconography of a 13-Cent Somme le Roi (Brit Mus MS Add 54180) with a Consideration of Other Illustrated Somme MSS of the 13, 14 and 15 Cents, diss Yale Univ 1973, Pt I, pp 46 n35, 276, 279 n20; Pt II, pp 40, 188.

Tudor-Craig P, Richard III, National Portrait Gallery, Exhibition Catalogue, London 1973, no 17 (entry contributed by K Scott).

Scott K L, The Caxton Master and His Patrons, Cambridge Biblio Soc Monograph no 8, Cambridge 1976, p 25.

The Mirroure of the Worlde the Physical Composition Decoration and Illustration, with an Introd by K L Scott, Roxb Club 1980.

Edition. Whitaker E, A Critical Edn of The Mirroure of the World, diss N Y Univ 1971.

Facsimile of Somme le Roi Illustrations. An Illuminated MS of La Somme le Roy Attributed to the Parisian Miniaturist Honoré, with an Introd by E G Millar, Roxb Club 219(1953).

Sources and Literary Relations. Langlois C V, La Vie en France au moyen âge du XIIe au milieu de XIVe siècle, IV: La vie spirituelle, Paris 1928, p 123.

Dondaine A, Guillaume Peyraut, vie et oeuvres, Archivum Fratrum Praedicatorum 18(1948).162.

Brayer E, Contenu, structure et combinaisons du Miroir du monde et de la Somme le roi, Rom 79(1958).1, 434.

Wenzel, pp 75, 80, 226, 231, 232, 237.

Tuve R, Notes on Virtues and Vices, Pt II, Journ of the Warburg and Courtauld Institutes 27 (1964).44; Allegorical Imagery: Some Medieval Books and Their Posterity, Princeton 1966, p 103.

Fischer N, Handlist of Animal References in ME Religious Prose, Leeds SE 4(1970).49 and passim.

Carruthers L M, La Somme le Roi de Lorens d'Orleans et Ses Traductions Anglaises: Etude Comparative, diss Univ of Paris 1980, p 93.

Burke L, Women in Medieval Manuals of Religious Instruction and John Gower's Confessio Amantis, diss Columbia Univ 1982, pp 22, 24, 27, 28, 66, 70, 73, 76, 78, 79, 80.

General References. Tinbergen D C, Dex Coninx Summe, Bibliotheek van Middelnederlandsche Letterkunde, Leiden 1900, p 76.

Owst G R, Preaching in Medieval England, Cambridge 1926, p 289 n6.

Bibliography. Doyle Survey, 1.70.

5. Works Derived from
Miroir du monde

[11] DISCE MORI.

MSS. 1, Bodl 1123 (Laud misc 99), ff 1ᵇ–257ᵇ (ca 1500); 2, Jesus Oxford 39, ff 1ᵃ–645ᵃ (1450–1500); 3, ?Hopton Hall (Chandos-Pole-Gell) (1400–25; a fragment).

Jolliffe, p 64, no A.6.

Brown-Robbins, nos 3327, 3786.

MSS Commentary. Coxe H O, Catalogus Codicum MSS qui in Collegiis Aulisque Oxoniensibus Hodie Adservantur, Oxford 1852, 2.14 (MS 2);

Catalogi Codicum Manuscriptorum Bibliothecae Bodleianae, Oxford 1878, 2.104 (MS 1).

Historical MSS Commission. 9th Report of the Royal Commission on Historical MSS, pt 2, London 1883, app, p 384 (MS 3).

Bazire J and E Colledge, edd, The Chastising of God's Children, Oxford 1957, pp 6 (description of MSS), 26 (relationship of MSS).

Editions. Chadwick N A, An Edn of Disce Mori (pp 1–177): Introd and Seven Deadly Sins, diss Liverpool Univ 1966.

Rigg A G, Jam Nunc in Proximo: A Latin Mortality Poem, MÆ 36(1967).249.

Sources and Literary Relations. Allen WAR, p 399.

Wager W, Fleshly Love in Chaucer's Troilus, MLR 34(1939).62.

Francis W N, ed, The Book of Vices and Virtues, EETS 217, London 1942, p xxxix.

Hudson A, A Chap from Walter Hilton in Two ME Compilations, Neophil 52(1968).416.

Fischer N, Handlist of Animal References in ME Religious Prose, Leeds SE 4(1970).49 and passim.

Patterson L W, Ambiguity and Interpretation: A 15-Cent Reading of Troilus and Criseyde, Spec 54(1979).297.

Carruthers L M, La Somme le Roi de Lorens d'Orleans et Ses Traductions Anglaises: Etude Comparative, diss Univ of Paris 1980, p 87.

General References. Allen WAR, p 399.

O'Connor M C, The Art of Dying Well, N Y 1942, p 18 n35.

Pace G B, Cotton Otho A.XVIII, Spec 26 (1951).315.

Howard D, The Three Temptations: Medieval Man in Search of the World, Princeton 1966, p 124 n74.

Woolf, pp 75, 219 n6.

Bibliography. Doyle Survey, 1.74.

[12] IGNORANCIA SACERDOTUM.

MS. Bodl Eng theol c.57, ff 3ᵃ–141ᵃ (1475–1500). Jolliffe, p 63, no A.2.

MS Commentary. Bazire J and E Colledge, edd, The Chastising of God's Children, Oxford 1957, pp 6 (description of MS), 26 (relationship of MS).

Sources and Literary Relations. Hodgson P, Ignorancia Sacerdotum: a 15-cent Discourse on the Lambeth Constitutions, RES 24(1948).1.

Douie D L, Archbishop Pecham, Oxford 1952, p 141.

Bazire and Colledge, p 25 (relationship to [11]).

Hudson A, A Chap from Walter Hilton in Two ME Compilations, Neophil 52(1968).412 n26.

Bibliography. Doyle Survey, 1.75.

Barratt A, Works of Religious Instruction, in ME Prose, ed A S G Edwards, New Brunswick 1984, p 417.

6. Versions of
Livre des bonnes meurs

[13] VERSIONS OF LIVRE DES BONNES MEURS.

MSS. 1, BL Harley 149, ff 183ᵃ–252ᵃ (ca 1450); 2, BL Addit 5467, ff 92ᵃ–211ᵃ (ca 1440); 3, Glasgow Univ Hunter 78, ff 1ᵃ–39ᵇ (1430–40); 4, Henry E Huntington HM 39872 (olim Beaumont College), ff 1ᵃ–122ᵇ (ca 1470; same version as MS 3). PRINTS: 5, William Caxton, Westminster 1487 (STC, no 15394); 6, R Pynson, London 1494 (STC, no 15395), 1500 (STC, no 15396); 7, Wynkyn de Worde, Westminster 1498 (STC, no 15397), London 1507 (STC, no 15398), ?1526 (STC, no 15399); 8, R Wyer, London 1531–34 (STC, no 15399.5; an extract only).

MSS Commentary. A Catalogue of the Harleian MSS in the British Museum, London 1808, 1.44 (MS 1).

Young J and P H Aitken, A Catalogue of the MSS in the Hunterian Museum in the Univ of Glasgow, Glasgow 1908, p 86 (MS 3).

Brusendorff A A, The Chaucer Tradition, London 1924, pp 213, 453 (MS 2).

Hammond E P, Eng Verse between Chaucer and Surrey, Durham 1927, p 191 (MS 2).

Bond M J, Some Early Books at Beaumont Coll, Berkshire Archaeological Journ 54(1954–55).54 (now MS 4).

Doyle A I, More Light on John Shirley, MÆ 30(1961).93 (MS 2).

Hanna R III, The Index of ME Prose, Handlist I, A Handlist of Manuscripts containing ME Prose in the Henry E Huntington Library, Woodbridge 1984, p 45.

Edition. Campbell B R, A Partial Edn of The Book of Good Condicions: A ME Trans of Le Livre des bonnes meurs of Jacques Legrand, diss Univ of Ottawa 1978 (first half of MS 3).

Selection. Blake N F, Caxton's Own Prose, London 1973, p 60.

Authorship. Colville A, De Jacobi Magni vita et operibus, Paris 1889.

Roth F, Jacques Legrand (Jacobus Magni), Augustiniana 7(1957).485.

Fox D, Stephen Scrope, Jacques Legrand, and the Word Mankyndely, N&Q ns 29(1982).400 (suggests Scrope was translator of MS 3 version).

Sources and Literary Relations. Duff E G, William Caxton, Chicago 1905, p 10 (Caxton's French source).

Combes A, Jacques Legrand, Alfred Coville and le Sophilogium, Augustiniana 7(1957).327, 493; 8(1958).129.

Lucas R H, Two Notes on Jacques Legrand, Augustiniana 7(1962).196 (relation of Sophilogium to Archiloge sophie).

Tuve R, Allegorical Imagery, Princeton 1966, pp 92, 114.

Literary Criticism. Gaertner O, John Shirley. Sein Leben und Werke, Halle a S 1904, p 48.

Lindström B, Some Remarks on Two Eng Trans of Jacques Legrand's Livre de bonnes meurs, ESts 58(1977).304; The Eng Versions of Jacques Legrand's Livre de Bonnes Meurs, Libr 6s 1 (1979).247.

Greenberg C, John Shirley and the Eng Book Trade, Libr 6s 4(1982).369.

General References. Workman S K, 15-Cent Trans as an Influence on Eng Prose, Princeton 1940, pp 185, 186.

Bradley R, The Background of the Title Speculum in Medieval Lit, Spec 29(1954).100.

Jacob E F, The 15 Cent 1399–1485, Oxford 1961, p 306.

Chew S C, The Pilgrimage of Life, New Haven 1962, pp 89 n12, 104, 106 n6.

Wilson R M, The Lost Lit of Medieval England, 2nd edn, London 1970, p 155.

Bibliography. Gasquet F A, The Biblio of Some Devotional Books Printed by the Earliest Eng Printers, Trans of the Biblio Soc of London 7(1902–04).176, 184.

de Ricci S, A Census of Caxtons, London 1909, p 73, no 65.

Duff E G, 15-Cent Eng Books, Oxford 1917, pp 69, 70, nos 248 (PRINT 5), 249 (PRINT 6, 1494), 250 (PRINT 6, 1500), 251 (PRINT 7, 1498).

Manual, 3.942 (IX [40]).

Blake N F, Caxton: England's First Publisher, N Y 1976, pp 50, 75, 78, 115, 195.

7. Version of
L'Ordinaire des Chrétiens

[14] THE ORDINARYE OF CRYSTYANYTE (or OF CRYSTEN MEN).

MSS. No MS extant. PRINT: Wynkyn de Worde, London 1502 (STC, no 5198); 1506 (STC, no 5199) (a 19-cent transcript is in MS BL Addit 26675).

Robbins-Cutler, no 3481.5.

Source. le Tailleur G, Paris ?1485.

Literary Relations. Tuve R, Allegorical Imagery, Princeton 1966, p 114.

Language. Prins A A, French Influence in Eng Phrasing, Leiden 1952, p 302.

Bibliography. Gasquet F A, The Biblio of Some Devotional Books Printed by the Earliest Eng Printers, Trans of the Biblio Soc of London 7(1902–04).185.

Short-title Catalogue of Books Printed in France and of French Books Printed in Other Countries from 1476 to 1600 in the British Museum, London 1924, p 108.

Bennett H S, Eng Books & Readers 1475 to 1557, 2nd edn, Cambridge 1969, p 261.

8. Native Compilations

[15] SPECULUM CHRISTIANI.

MS. BL Harley 6580, ff 2ᵃ–64ᵇ (ca 1450; Articles of the Faith in a later hand).

Jolliffe, p 112, no I.27 (listing two copies of the Fifth Tabula of [15]), additional copies are in Henry E Huntington Library HM.124 and elsewhere, as noted by Holstedt, below, and Hanna R III, The Index of ME Prose, Handlist I, A Handlist of Manuscripts containing ME Prose in the Henry E Huntington Library, Woodbridge 1984, p 61.

Brown-Robbins, Robbins-Cutler, nos 750 (exemplum); 1342 (exhortation); 2119 (orison to BVM); 2167 (four philosophers); 1286, 4150 (seven deadly sins); 1491, 3685, 3887 (Ten Commandments); Brown-Robbins, no 1111 (Ten Commandments); Robbins-Cutler, no 2233.5 (introd to Table 5).

Ringler BEV, nos 33, 46, 47, 60, 93.

MS Commentary. A Catalogue of the Harleian MSS in the British Museum, London 1808, 3.377.

Editions. Holmstedt G, Speculum Christiani, EETS 182, London 1929, p 2; introd, pp xix (description and language of the MSS, both Latin and Eng), cxxix (printed edns), cxxxiii (relation of the printed edns), clxxv (date and authorship), clxxx (composition and contents) (crit A Kihlbom, SN 4.84; TLS Apr 26 1934, p 306; K Brunner, AnglB 46.22; A Brandl, Arch 165.302; O Everett, YWES 14.139; N&Q 166.358; O L Wrenn, RES 11.331; D Hamer, MLR 30.512).

For editions of the Eng verses of [15], see Brown-Robbins, Robbins-Cutler numbers listed above.

Language. Laing M, Stud in the Dialect Material of Mediaeval Lancashire, diss Univ of Edinb 1978.

Date. Brown C, The Towneley Play of the Doctors and the Speculum Christiani, MLN 31(1916).223.

Holmstedt, edn, p clxxv.

Sources and Literary Relations. Taylor G C, The Relation of the Eng Corpus Christi Play to the ME Religious Lyric, MP 5(1907–08).28 (influence of Commandments on Towneley Cycle).

Deanesly M, The Lollard Bible and Other Medieval Biblical Versions, Cambridge 1920, p 346.

Owst G R, Preaching in Medieval England, Cambridge 1926, pp 4, 227, 232, 284, 286 n1, 291.

Allen WAR, p 404.

Peckham J L, Archbishop Peckham as a Religious Educator, Yale Stud in Religion 7, Scottdale Pa 1934, p 110.

Pfander Manuals, p 247.

Pfander H G, The Popular Sermon of the Medieval Friar in England, N Y 1937, p 51.

Pecheux M C, Aspects of the Treatment of Death in ME Poetry, Washington D C 1951, pp 21, 33, 122.

Bloomfield SDS, pp 186, 207, 246, 247, 425.

Douie D L, Archbishop Pecham, Oxford 1952, p 141.

Boyle L E, A Study of the Works Attributed to William of Pagula with Special Reference to Oculus Sacerdotis and Summa Summarum, diss Oxford Univ 1956, p 379.

Hackett M B, William Flete and the De Remediis Contra Temptaciones, in Medieval Stud Presented to Aubrey Gwynn, S J, ed J A Watt, J B Morrall, F X Martin, Dublin 1961, p 377 n25 (notes a quotation from Flete's De Remediis in [15]).

Tuve R, Allegorical Imagery, Princeton 1966, p 114.

Fischer N, Handlist of Animal References in ME Prose, Leeds SE 4(1970).49 and passim.

Doob P, Nebuchadnezzar's Children, New Haven and London 1974, p 28.

Jeffrey D L, The Early Eng Lyric and Franciscan Spirituality, Lincoln 1975, pp 197, 198, 207, 209, 210, 273.

Gillespie V, Doctrina and Praedicacio: The Design and Function of Some Pastoral Manuals, Leeds SE 11(1980 for 1979).36.

Gillespie V A, The Literary Form of the ME Pastoral Manual with Particular Reference to the Speculum Christiani and Some Related Texts, diss Oxford Univ 1981.

Gillespie N G, A Syon MS Reconsidered, N&Q ns 30(1983).203 (indebtedness of [15] to a Treatise on the Priesthood in BL Royal 5.A.vi).

General References. Deanesly M, Vernacular Books in England in the 14 and 15 Cents, MLR 15 (1920).349 (on owners of MSS of [15]).

Baugh LHE, p 203.

Edwards A S G, Toward an Index of ME Prose, in ME Prose Essays in Bibliographical Problems, ed A S G Edwards and D Pearsall, N Y 1981, p 31.

Bibliography. Gasquet F A, The Biblio of Some Devotional Books Printed by the Earliest Eng Printers, Trans of the Biblio Soc of London 7(1902–04).183.

Allen WAR, p 404.

Bloomfield M W, A Preliminary List of Incipits of Latin Works on the Virtues and Vices, Trad 11(1955).306.

Pantin, p 230.

Bloomfield M W, B-G Guyot, D R Howard and T B Kabealo, Incipits of Latin Works on the Virtues and Vices, 1100–1500 AD, Cambridge 1979, nos 1552 (Cibus animae), 2363 ([15] with additions to Holmstedt).

Barratt A, Works of Religious Instruction, in ME Prose, ed A S G Edwards, New Brunswick 1984, p 417.

[16] BOOK TO A MOTHER.

MSS. 1, Bodl 1292 (Laud misc 210), ff 20^a–93^b (1400–25); 2, Bodl 2315 (Bodley 416), ff 1^a–105^a (1400–25); 3, BL Egerton 826, ff 1^a–55^b (1400–25); 4, BL Addit 30897, ff 78^a–137^b (1400–25).

Jolliffe, p 64, nos A.5(a–b).

MSS Commentary. List of Additions to the MSS in the British Museum in the Years MDCCCXXXVI–MDCCCXL, London 1843, p 16 (MS 3).

Coxe H O, Catalogi Codicum Manuscriptorum Bibliothecae Bodleianae, Oxford 1858, 2.181 (MS 1).

Catalogue of Additions to the MSS in the British Museum in the Years MDCCCLXXVI–MDCCCLXXXI, London 1882, p 126 (MS 4).

Summary Cat, 2.304 (MS 2).

Edition. McCarthy A J, Book to a Mother, Salzburg 1981, introd, pp iii (MSS), xix (contents), xxv (author and destination), xxx (date), xxxv (sources), xlvi (problem of orthodoxy), lviii (style).

Selections. Rel Ant, 1.38 (extract from MS 3).

Kirchberger C, Coasts of the Country, London n d, pp 12, 73, 243.

Modernization. Kirchberger, p 12 (modernized extracts from MS 2).

General Reference. Deanesly M, The Lollard Bible and Other Medieval Biblical Versions, Cambridge 1920, p 345.

Bibliography. Doyle Survey, 1.56 n11.

[17] MEMORIALE CREDENCIUM.

MSS. 1, Bodl 10027 (Tanner 201), ff 7^a–106^b (1400–25); 2, Bodl 11954 (Rawl C.89), ff 1^a–16^a (1400–50; fragment); 3, Camb Univ Dd.1.1, ff 251^a–294^a (1400–50); 4, BL Harley 211, ff 69^b–84^b, 86^a–100^b, 100^b–101^a (1400–25; sections on sins, remedies, and penance only); 5, BL Harley 535, ff 4^a–

116ᵇ (1425–75); 6, BL Harley 2250, ff 88ᵃ–93ᵇ, 95ᵃ–108ᵃ (ca 1477; sections on Commandments, sins, virtues, penance, shrift); 7, BL Harley 2398, ff 1ᵃ–69ᵃ (1400–25); 8, BL Sloane 1009, ff 2ᵃ–16ᵇ (1475–1500; sections on penance, confession, and the obstacles to them, the degrees of contemplation, the gifts of the Holy Ghost).

Jolliffe, p 63, no A.[4](i–iii).

MSS Commentary. A Catalogue of the Harleian MSS in the British Museum, London 1808, 1.66 (MS 4), 343 (MS 5); 2.577 (MS 6), 685 (MS 7).

A Catalogue of the MSS Preserved in the Libr of the Univ of Cambridge, Cambridge 1856, 1.1 (MS 3).

Hackman A, Catalogi Codicum Manuscriptorum Bibliothecae Bodleianae, Oxford 1860, 4.637 (MS 1).

Macray W D, Catalogi Codicum Manuscriptorum Bibliothecae Bodleianae, Oxford 1878, 5(2).32 (MS 2).

Edition. Kengen J H L, Memoriale Credencium, Nijmegen n d [ca 1979], p 37 (base text: MS 1); introd, pp 3 (contents and description of MSS), 11 (interrelation of the four complete MSS), 13 (sources), 18 (localization of the MSS), 22 (date and authorship) (crit R Hanna, Spec 56.151; S Wenzel, Angl 99.511).

Textual Matters. Hanna R, The Text of Memoriale Credencium, Neophil 67(1983).284.

Literary Relations. Owst G R, Preaching in Medieval England, Cambridge 1926, pp 194, 285, 288; Literature and Pulpit in Medieval England, Cambridge 1933, pp 143, 151, 327.

Pfander Manuals, p 252.

Bloomfield SDS, p 432.

Douie D L, Archbishop Pecham, Oxford 1952, p 141.

General References. Deanesly M, The Lollard Bible and Other Medieval Biblical Versions, Cambridge 1920, p 216.

Robbins R H, Popular Rhyme in ME Verse, MP 36(1939).345.

Bibliography. Doyle Survey, 1.56 n11.

Barratt A, Works of Religious Instruction, in ME Prose, ed A S G Edwards, New Brunswick 1984, pp 417, 419.

Wenzel S, ed, Summa Virtutum de Remediis Animae, Athens 1984, p 34.

[18] PRICK OF CONSCIENCE (or STIMULUS CONSCIENCIE or KEY OF KNOWING or THE FLOURE OF CONSCIENCE or SPECULUM HUIUS VITE).

MSS. Version A (Main Version): 1, Bodl 1186 (Laud Misc 486), ff 1ᵃ–122ᵃ (1400–25); 2, Bodl 1615

(Digby 14), ff 2ᵃ–158ᵇ (1400–50); 3, Bodl 1688 (Digby 87), ff 1ᵃ–133ᵇ (ca 1400); 4, Bodl 1700 (Digby 99), ff 8ᵇ–156ᵇ (ca 1400); 5, Bodl 1944 (Bodley 99), ff 1ᵃ–120ᵇ (ca 1400); 6, Bodl 3509 (e Mus 88), ff 1ᵃ–92ᵃ (1400–50); 7, Bodl 3679 (e Mus 76), ff 1ᵃ–127ᵃ (1400–50); 8, Bodl 3938 (Eng poet a.1), ff 265ᵃ–284ᵃ (1380–1400); 9, Bodl 5167* (Junius 56), ff 1ᵃ–120ᵇ (1400–50); 10, Bodl 6921 (Ashmole 41), ff 1ᵃ–130ᵃ (ca 1400); 11, Bodl 6922 (Ashmole 60), ff 1ᵃ–138ᵇ (ca 1400); 12, Bodl 6936 (Ashmole 52), ff 1ᵃ–65ᵃ (1350–1400); 13, Bodl 11901 (Rawl C.35), ff 1ᵃ–117ᵇ (1400–50); 14, Bodl 12143 (Rawl C.285), f 39ᵃ (1400–50; an extract of 28 lines); 15, Bodl 12175 (Rawl C.319), ff 1ᵃ–140ᵃ (1400–50); 16, Bodl 12725 (Rawl C.891), ff 1ᵃ–127ᵃ (1400–50); 17, Bodl 13679 (Rawl D.913), ff 9ᵃ–ᵇ, 62ᵃ–ᵇ (1350–1400; fragments only); 18, Bodl 14632 (Rawl poet 138), ff 1ᵃ–112ᵇ (1400–50); 19, Bodl 14633 (Rawl poet 139), ff 1ᵃ–55ᵇ (1350–1400); 20, Bodl 14667 (Rawl poet 175), ff 1ᵃ–55ᵇ (1350–1400); 21, Bodl 15460 (Rawl A.366), pp 1–250 (1400–25); 22, Bodl 21700 (Douce 126), ff 1ᵃ–68ᵇ (1400–50); 23, Bodl 21715 (Douce 141), ff 1ᵃ–129ᵇ (1400–50); 24, Bodl 21730 (Douce 156), pp 1–172 (ca 1400); 25, Bodl 21731 (Douce 157), ff 1ᵃ–114ᵇ (ca 1400); 26, Bodl Selden Supra 102*, ff 15ᵃ–16ᵇ (1450–1500); 27, St John's Oxford 57, ff 1ᵃ–137ᵃ (1450–1500); 28, St John's Oxford 138, ff 1ᵃ–126ᵇ (1400–50); 29, Trinity Oxford 15, ff 1ᵃ–203ᵇ (1400–50); 30, Trinity Oxford 16A, ff 1ᵃ–116ᵇ (1400–50); 31, Trinity Oxford 16B, ff 3ᵃ–114ᵃ (ca 1400); 32, Univ Oxford 142, ff 4ᵃ–125ᵇ (1400–25); 33, Camb Univ Dd.5.55, f 101ᵇ (ca 1400; an extract of 28 lines); 34, Camb Univ Dd.11.89, ff 9ᵃ–162ᵃ (ca 1400); 35, Camb Univ Dd.12.69, ff 37ᵃ–97ᵇ (ca 1400); 36, Camb Univ Ff.5.40, ff 113ᵇ–114ᵃ (1400–50; extract of 28 lines); 37, Camb Univ L1.2.17, ff 2ᵃ–145ᵃ (1450–1500); 38, Camb Univ Addit 6693, ff 1ᵃ–17ᵃ (ca 1400); 39, Cambridge Fitzwilliam Mus McClean 131, ff 1ᵃ–113ᵇ (ca 1400); 40, Gonville and Caius Camb 386, ff 1ᵃ–96ᵃ (1400–50); 41, Magdalene Camb 18, ff 1ᵃ–110ᵇ (ca 1400); 42, St John's Camb 80, ff 1ᵃ–118ᵃ (ca 1400); 43, St John's Camb 137, ff 1ᵃ–113ᵇ (1400–25); 44, Trinity Camb 1144 (0.2.0), ff 104ᵃ–105ᵃ, 119ᵃ–ᵇ (1475–1500; three extracts); 45, BL Arundel 140, ff 41ᵇ–146ᵇ (1400–50); 46, BL Cotton Galba E.IX, ff 76ᵃ–113ᵃ (1400–25); 47, BL Cotton App VII, ff 3ᵃ–145ᵇ (1400–25); 48, BL Egerton 657, ff 1ᵃ–95ᵇ (1350–1400); 49, BL Egerton 3245, ff 2ᵃ–156ᵃ (ca 1400); 50, BL Harley 1205, ff 1ᵃ–106ᵃ (ca 1400); 51, BL Harley 2377, ff 1ᵃ–106ᵇ (ca 1400); 52, BL Harley 2394, ff 1ᵃ–129ᵃ (15 cent); 53, BL Harley 4196, ff 215ᵇ–258ᵇ (ca 1400); 54, BL Harley 6923, ff 2ᵃ–117ᵇ (ca

1400); 55, BL Lansdowne 348, ff 2ᵃ–127ᵇ (1400–25); 56, BL Royal 17.C.xvii, ff 117ᵃ–124ᵃ (1400–25); 57, BL Sloane 1044, item 235 (1400–50); 58, BL Sloane 2275, ff 150ᵃ–183ᵇ (1350–1400); 59, BL Addit 11304, ff 71ᵇ–194ᵃ (1350–1400); 60, BL Addit 22283, ff 243ᵃ–259ᵇ (1380–1400); 61, BL Addit 24203, ff 1ᵃ–150ᵇ (ca 1400); 62, BL Addit 25013, ff 1ᵃ–136ᵃ (1400–50); 63, BL Addit 32578, ff 1ᵃ–103ᵃ (1405); 64, BL Addit 33995, ff 102ᵃ–155ᵃ (ca 1375); 65, BL Addit 36983, ff 159ᵃ–174ᵇ (1400–50; extract of nearly all of Book 5); 66, BL Addit 37049, ff 36ᵃ, 69ᵃ, 72ᵃ (1400–50; three brief extracts); 67, Coll of Arms London 57, ff 133ᵃ–175ᵇ (ca 1400); 68, Lambeth Palace 260, ff 101ᵃ–139ᵇ (1400–25); 69, Lambeth Palace 491, ff 296ᵃ–323ᵃ (1400–50); 70, Lambeth Palace 492, ff 1ᵃ–56ᵇ (ca 1400); 71, Sion Coll London Arc L.40.2/E.25, ff 48ᵃ–133ᵇ (ca 1400); 72, Soc of Antiquaries London 288, ff 1ᵃ–120ᵇ (1400–50); 73, Soc of Antiquaries London 687, pp 5–358 (1400–50); 74, Canterbury Cath 66, ff 1ᵃ–144ᵇ (ca 1350); 75, Lincoln Cath 91, ff 276ᵇ–277ᵃ (ca 1430; an extract of 111 lines); 76, Leeds Univ Brotherton 500, ff 1ᵃ–147ᵇ (ca 1400); 77, Leeds Univ Brotherton 501, ff 1ᵃ–58ᵇ (1400–50); 78, Chetham's Hospital Manchester Mun A.4.103 (8008), ff 1ᵃ–115ᵇ (ca 1400); 79, John Rylands Manchester Eng 50, pp 1–204 (ca 1400); 80, John Rylands Manchester Eng 51, ff 5ᵃ–116ᵇ (1400–25); 81, John Rylands Manchester Eng 90, ff 2ᵃ–62ᵇ (ca 1400); 82, Arundel Castle (Duke of Norfolk), ff 1ᵃ–141ᵇ (ca 1400); 83, Beeleigh Abbey, Maldon (Foyle), ff 1ᵃ–131ᵇ (ca 1465); 84, Douai Abbey 7, ff 2ᵃ–150ᵃ (ca 1400); 85, Hatfield House (Marquis of Salisbury), Deeds 59/1, covers (1400–50); 86, Holkham Hall (Earl of Leicester) 668, ff 1ᵃ–134ᵇ (ca 1400); 87, Longleat House (Marquis of Bath) 31, ff 1ᵃ–146ᵇ (1400–25); 88, Shrewsbury School 3, ff 1ᵃ–27ᵇ (1475–1500); 89, Nat Libr of Wales Porkington 20, ff 1ᵃ–94ᵇ (1400–50); 90, Bibliothèque Royale Albert I, Brussels, IV.998, ff 1ᵃ–105ᵇ (1400–25); 91, Trinity Dublin 156, ff 2ᵃ–136ᵇ (1400–25); 92, Trinity Dublin 157, ff 1ᵃ–89ᵃ (1400–25); 93, Trinity Dublin 158, ff 1ᵃ–81ᵇ (1400–50); 94, Harvard Univ English 515, ff 1ᵃ–77ᵃ (1350–1400); 95, Univ of Virginia Hench 10, ff 1ᵃ–136ᵇ (ca 1370); 96, Newberry Libr 32.9, ff 1ᵃ–99ᵃ (1350–1400); 97, Newberry Libr 33, pp 1–198 (1350–1400); 98, Yale Univ Osborn a.13, ff 2ᵃ–139ᵃ (1400–50); 99, Pierpont Morgan Bühler 13, ff 1ᵃ–107ᵃ (ca 1400); 100, Univ of Pennsylvania English 1, ff 13ᵃ–118ᵃ (ca 1400); 101, Univ of Pennsylvania English 8, ff 147ᵃ–159ᵇ (1400–25); 102, Henry E Huntington HM 139, ff 144ᵃ–187ᵃ (ca 1450); 103, Wellesley Coll 8, pp 13–247 (1400–25); 104, Robert Taylor (Princeton), ff 1ᵃ–126ᵇ (1350–1400); 105, Sothe-by's Sale Catalogue, 20–22 December 1920, lot 515 (olim Halliwell; present location unknown); *Version B (the Southern Recension)*: 106, Bodl 1491 (Laud misc 601), ff 1ᵃ–115ᵇ (ca 1400); 107, Bodl 2322 (Bodley 423), ff 244ᵃ–351ᵃ (1400–50); 108, Bodl Lyell empt 6, ff 1ᵃ–116ᵇ (1400–25); 109, Camb Univ Ee.4.35, ff 1ᵃ–96ᵇ (1350–1400); 110, Pembroke Camb 272, ff 1ᵃ–143ᵇ (ca 1450); 111, St John's Camb 29, ff 5ᵃ–119ᵇ (ca 1450); 112, BL Harley 1731, ff 1ᵃ–133ᵇ (1400–50); 113, BL Harley 2281, ff 1ᵃ–64ᵇ (1400–25); 114, BL Royal 18.A.v, ff 2ᵃ–126ᵇ (1400–50); 115, BL Addit 11305, ff 3ᵃ–126ᵇ (1400–50); 116, Lichfield Cath 16, ff 35ᵃ–189ᵇ (1375–1400); 117, Lichfield Cath 50, ff 1ᵃ–109ᵇ (1350–1400); 118, Trinity Dublin 69, ff 65ᵃ–72ᵇ, 83ᵇ–123ᵇ (ca 1400); 119, Princeton Univ Garrett 138, ff 1ᵃ–130ᵇ (1400–25); 120, Henry E Huntington HM 125, ff 1ᵃ–100ᵃ (ca 1400); 121, Henry E Huntington HM 128, ff 1ᵃ–94ᵃ (1400–25); 122, Henry E Huntington HM 130, pp 1–240 (ca 1400); 123, H P Kraus (olim Beaumont Coll, Old Windsor 9), ff 3ᵃ–158ᵃ (1350–1400); *Version C (Speculum Huius Vite)*: 124, Bodl 29387 (Add.A.268), ff 117ᵃ–139ᵇ (1400–25); 125, Trinity Dublin 155, pp 149–238 (1400–25); *Version D (the Latin translation)*: 126, Bodl 2009 (Bodley 159), ff 161ᵃ–179ᵃ (1400–25); 127, Merton Oxford 68, ff 74ᵇ–88ᵇ (ca 1450); 128, Camb Univ Dd.4.50, ff 57ᵃ–99ᵃ (1400–50); 129, Magdalene Camb 14, ff 14ᵃ–31ᵇ (1400–50); 130, Pembroke Camb 273, ff 1ᵃ–29ᵇ (1375–1400); 131, BL Harley 159, ff 138ᵇ, 344ᵇ (1400–50). PRINTS: 132, R Wyer, Boke of Purgatorye, London ca 1532–33 (STC, no 3360; Book 4 of [18]); 133, R Wyer, A Newe Treatyse (attributed to Myles Hogarde), London ca 1542–43 (STC, no 24228; Books 1–3 of [18]).

Brown-Robbins, Robbins-Cutler, nos 484, 672, 790, 806, 2753, 3428, 3429, 3866; Brown-Robbins, nos 812, 1193, 3561; Robbins-Cutler, nos 1197.1, 3769.8.

For related texts see the poems on the joys of paradise [243–244], the pains of hell [245–246] and Brown-Robbins, no 3476.

MSS Commentary. Cave W, Scriptorum Ecclesiasticorum Historia Literaria, with app by H Wharton, London 1720, p 26 (MS 70).

Hearne T, ed, Peter Langtoft's Chronicle, Oxford 1725, 2.527, 581 (MS 21).

Ayscough S, A Catalogue of the MSS Preserved in the British Museum Hitherto Undescribed, London 1782, 1.384, 399 (MS 57).

A Catalogue of the MSS in the Cottonian Libr Deposited in the British Museum, London 1802, pp 363 (MS 46), 614 (MS 47).

A Catalogue of the Harleian MSS in the British Museum, London 1808, 1.31 (MS 131), 597 (MS 50); 2.191 (MS 112), 641 (MS 113), 673 (MS 51), 682 (MS 52); 3.124 (MS 53), 449 (MS 54).

Walter W J, An Account of a MS of Ancient Eng Poetry, Entitled Clavis Scientiae, or, Bretayne's Skyll—Kay of Knawing, by John de Wageby, Monk of Fountains Abbey, London 1816 (MS 61).

A Catalogue of the Lansdowne MSS in the British Museum, Pt II, London 1819, p 107 (MS 55).

Yates J B, An Account of an Unprinted Eng Poem, Written in the Early Part of the 14 Cent, by Richard de Hampole, and Entitled Stimulus Conscientiae or the Pricke or Conscience, Archaeologia 19(1821).314 (MS 119).

Hood E [J Haslewood], Stimulus Conscientie, The Gentleman's Magazine and Historical Chronicle 97(1827).216 (MS 23).

Black W H, Catalogue of the Arundel MSS in the Libr of the Coll of Arms, London 1829, p 101 (MS 67).

Catalogue of MSS in The British Museum, ns I, Pt I: The Arundel MSS, London 1834, p 38 (MS 45).

Halliwell J O, An Account of the European MSS in the Chetham Libr Manchester, Manchester 1842, p 16 (MS 78).

List of Additions to the MSS in the British Museum in the Years MDCCCXXXVI–MDCCCXL, London 1843, pp 2 (MSS 59, 115), 26 (MS 48).

Black, A Descriptive, Analytical, and Critical Catalogue of the MSS Bequeathed unto the Univ of Oxford by Elias Ashmole, Oxford 1845, pp 62 (MS 10), 91 (MS 12), 104 (MS 11).

Coxe H O, Catalogus Codicum MSS qui in Collegiis Aulisque Oxoniensibus Hodie Adservantur, Oxford 1852, 1.39 (MS 32), 41 (MS 127); 2.7 (MSS 29, 30, 31), 16 (MS 27), 42 (MS 28).

A Catalogue of the MSS Preserved in the Libr of the Univ of Cambridge, Cambridge 1856, 1.243 (MS 128), 275 (MS 33), 481 (MS 34), 506 (MS 35); 2(1857).167 (MS 109), 498 (MS 36); 4(1861).44 (MS 37).

Coxe, Catalogi Codicum Manuscriptorum Bibliothecae Bodleianae, Oxford 1858, 1.350 (MS 1), 428 (MS 106).

Catalogue of the MSS at Ashburnham Palace Appendix, London 1861, item 136.

R M, Hampole's Works, N&Q 3s 2(1862).386 (MS 82).

Skeat W W, The Pricke of Conscience, N&Q 4s 1(1868).65 (MS 40).

Horwood A J, The MSS of the Most Honorable Marquis of Bath, at Longleat, Co Wilts, Third Report of the Royal Commission on Historical MSS, London 1872, Appendix, p 181 (MS 87).

Catalogue of Additions to the MSS in the British Museum in the Years MDCCCLIV–MDCCCLX, London 1875, p 623 (MS 60).

Catalogue of Additions to the MSS in the British Museum in the Years MDCCCLIV–MDCCCLXXV, London 1877, pp 22 (MS 61), 140 (MS 62).

Horwood, The MSS of J R Ormsby-Gore, Esq, MP, of Brogyntyn, Co Salop, Second Report of the Royal Commission on Historical MSS, London 1874, Appendix, no 20, p 84 (MS 89).

Macray W D, Catalogi Codicum Manuscriptorum Bibliothecae Bodleianae, Oxford 1878, 5.11 (MS 13), 123 (MS 14), 140 (MS 15), 464 (MS 16); 5(1983).136 (MS 17); 5(1862).374 (MS 21); Catalogi Codicum Manuscriptorum Bibliothecae Bodleianae, Oxford 1883, 9.10 (MS 2), 97 (MS 3), 113 (MS 4).

Andreae P, Die Handschriften des Pricke of Conscience von Richard Rolle de Hampole im Britischen Museum, Berlin 1888.

Gibbs H H, A Catalogue of Some Printed Books and MSS at St Dunstan's, Regents Park, and Aldenham House, Herts, London 1888, p 159 (MS 95).

Catalogue of Additions to the MSS in the British Museum in the Years MDCCCLXXXII–MDCCCLXXXVII, London 1889, p 157 (MS 63).

Bülbring K D, ed, The Earliest Complete Eng Prose Psalter, EETS 97, London 1891, pp vii, x (MS 118); Über die Handschrift Nr 491 der Lambeth-Bibliothek, Arch 86(1891).383 (MS 69); On 25 MSS of Richard Rolle's Pricke of Conscience, 18 of Them in the British Museum, 4 in the Libr of Trinity Coll Dublin, the Corser MS, and 2 in Lichfield Cathedral Libr, Trans of the Philological Soc 1888–90(1891).261.

Catalogue of Additions to the MSS in the British Museum in the Years MDCCCLXXXVIII–MDCCCXCIII, London 1894, p 156 (MS 64).

Calvert E, Extracts from a 15-Cent MS, Trans of the Shropshire Archaeological and Natural Hist Soc 2s 6(1894).99 (MS 88).

Yksh Wr, 1.129.

Herbert J A, Catalogue of the Early MSS of Shrewsbury School, Trans of the Shropshire Archaeological and Natural Hist Soc 2s 9(1897).294 (MS 88).

Bülbring, Zu den Handschriften von Richard Rolle's Prick of Conscience, EStn 23(1897).1.

Abbott T K, Catalogue of the MSS in the Libr of Trinity Coll Dublin, Dublin 1900, pp 9, 20, 21 (MSS 91, 92, 93).

Summary Cat, 1.126 (MS 5); 2.308 (MS 107), 665 (MS 6), 728 (MS 7), 789 (MS 8), 977 (MS 9); 3.311 (MS 18), 312 (MS 19), 321 (MS 20); 4.529 (MS 22), 535 (MS 23), 540 (MSS 24, 25); 5.610 (MS 124).

James M R, The Western MSS in the Libr of Trinity Coll Cambridge A Descriptive Catalogue, Cambridge 1902, p 142 (MS 44); A Descriptive Catalogue of the MSS in the Libr of Pembroke Coll Cambridge, Cambridge 1905, p 248 (MSS 110, 130).

Campbell K, A Neglected MS of The Prick of Conscience, MLN 20(1905).210 (MS 20).

de Ricci S, A Hand-List of a Collection of Books and MSS Belonging to The Right Hon Lord Amherst of Hackney at Didlington Hall, Norfolk, Cambridge 1906, p 135 (MS 83).

Catalogue of Additions to the MSS in the British Museum in the Years MDCCCC–MDCCCCV, London 1907, pp 265 (MS 65), 324 (MS 66).

James, A Descriptive Catalogue of the MSS in the Libr of Gonville and Caius Coll Cambridge, Cambridge 1908, 2.446 (MS 40); A Descriptive Catalogue of the MSS in the College Libr of Magdalene Coll Cambridge, Cambridge 1909, pp 37, 45 (MS 41).

Allen H E, RadMon 15(1910).121, 123 n4, 124 n2 and n3, 125 n1, 126, 128 n5, 168, 169.

James, A Descriptive Catalogue of the McClean Collection of MSS in the Fitzwilliam Museum, Cambridge 1912, p 278 (MS 39); A Descriptive Catalogue of the MSS in the Libr of St John's Coll Cambridge, Cambridge 1913, pp 38 (MS 111), 107 (MS 41), 173 (MS 43).

Allen, The Speculum Vitae: Addendum, PMLA 32(1917).162 n67 (MS 60).

Warner G F and J P Gilson, Catalogue of Western MSS in the Old Royal and King's Collections, London 1921, 2.243 (MS 56), 263 (MS 114).

Allen WAR, pp 307, 372, 373, 374, 375, 376, 377, 379, 380, 385, 386, 388, 389, 393, 395, 397.

Tyson M, Hand-List of the Collections of Eng MSS in the John Rylands Libr, 1928, JRLB 13 (1929).163 (MSS 79, 80), 169 (MS 81).

Powicke F M, The Medieval Books of Merton Coll, Oxford 1931, p 206, item 971 (MS 127).

A Handlist of the MSS in the Libr of the Earl of Leicester at Holkham Hall Abstracted from the Catalogues of William Roscoe and Frederic Madden and Annotated by Seymour de Ricci, Oxford 1932, p 56 (MS 86).

James M R and C Jenkins, A Descriptive Catalogue of the MSS in the Libr of Lambeth Palace, Cambridge 1932, pp 406 (MS 68), 681 (MS 69), 684 (MS 70).

Haselden R B, The Fragment of Piers Ploughman in Ashburnham No CXXX, MP 29(1932).391 (MS 121).

Brunner K, Der Streit der vier Himmelstöchter, EStn 68(1933–34).188 (MS 47).

Hooper A G, The Lambeth Palace MS of the Awntyrs of Arthure, Leeds SE 3(1934).37 (MS 69).

Dickens B, The Ireland Blackburne MS of the Seven Penitential Psalms, the Pricke of Conscience and Lamentacio Sancti Anselmi, Leeds SE 3(1934).30 (MS 100).

de Ricci Census, 1.53, 54 (MSS 120, 121, 122), 56ʹ (MS 102), 541 (MS 97), 892 (MS 119), 966 (MS 94), 1068 (MS 103); 3.100 (MS 98), 389 (MS 99), 479 (MSS 100, 101), 515 (MS 95).

Serjeantson Index, p 245.

Robbins R H, The Gurney Series of Religious Lyrics, PMLA 54(1939).389 (MS 49).

Manly & Rickert, 1.52 (MS 45).

Schulz H C, MS Printer's Copy for a Lost Early Eng Book, Libr 4s 22(1942).138 (MSS 120, 121, 122).

Ker N S, Fragments of Medieval MSS Used as Pastedowns in Oxford Bindings, Oxford Biblio Soc Publ ns 5(1951–52).157, item 1744.

Humphreys K W and J Lightbown, Two MSS of the Pricke of Conscience in the Brotherton Collection, Univ of Leeds, Leeds SE 7–8(1952).29 (MSS 76, 77).

Quinn J, Earlier Owners of the Vernon MS, The Bodleian Libr Record 4(1952–53).133 (MS 8).

Doyle Survey, 1.106, 123; 2.46, 47, 57, 115, 116, 162, 164.

Steer F W, Bibliotheca Norfolciana, n p 1961, p 25 (MS 82).

Zacour N P and R Hirsch, Catalogue of the MSS in the Libraries of the Univ of Pennsylvania to 1800, Phila 1965, pp 49, 50 (MSS 100, 101).

Schulz, A ME MS Used as Printer's Copy, HLQ 29(1966).325 (MSS 120, 122).

Sajavaara K, The Relationship of the Vernon and Simeon MSS, NM 68(1967).428 (MSS 8, 60).

Ker Manuscripts, 1.289 (MS 71), 310 (MS 72), 314 (MS 73); 2.281 (MS 74), 416 (MS 84); 3.67 (MSS 76, 77), 116 (MS 116), 125 (MS 117), 361 (MS 78), 401 (MS 79), 402 (MS 80), 413 (MS 81).

Catalogue of Additions to the MSS in the British Museum in the Years 1936–45, London 1970, 1.358 (MS 49).

De la Mare A, Catalogue of the Collection of Medieval MSS Bequeathed to the Bodleian Libr Oxford by James P R Lyell, Oxford 1971, p 287 (MS 108).

Nevanlinna S, ed, The Northern Homily Cycle, Mémoires de la Société Néophilologique de Helsinki 38(1972).5 (MS 53).

Wright C E, Fontes Harleiani: A Study of the Sources of the Harleian Collection of MSS Preserved in the Department of Manuscripts in the British Museum, London 1972, pp 85 (MS 53), 198 (MS 51), 195, 296 (MS 54), 284 (MS 112).

Doyle A I, The Shaping of the Vernon and Simeon MSS, in Chaucer and ME Stud in Honour of R H Robbins, ed B Rowland, Kent 1974, p 328 (MSS 8, 60).

Hunt R, Donors of MSS to St John's Coll Oxford During the Presidency of William Laud 1611–21, in Stud in the Book Trade in Honour of Graham Pollard, Oxford Biblio Soc Publ ns 18(1975).63, 66 (MS 28).

Owen A E B, The Collation and Descent of the Thornton MS, Trans of the Cambridge Biblio Soc 6(1975).218.

Guddat-Figge G, Catalogue of MSS Containing ME Romances, Munich 1976, pp 145 (MS 60), 269 (MS 8), 297 (MS 32).

Britton D, MSS Associated with Kirby Bellars Priory, Trans of the Cambridge Biblio Soc 6(1976).267, 277 (MS 44).

Fleming J V, Medieval MSS in the Taylor Libr, Princeton Univ Libr Chronicle 38(1977).116 (MS 104).

Krochalis J E, Contemplations of the Dread and Love of God: Two Newly Identified Pennsylvania MSS, LC 42(1977).11 (MSS 100, 101).

Benedikz B S, Lichfield Cathedral Libr: A Catalogue of the Cathedral Libr MSS, rvsd version, Birmingham 1978, pp 9, 28 (MSS 116, 117).

Britton D, Unnoticed Fragments of the Prick of Conscience, NM 80(1979).327.

Hogg J, Unpublished Texts in the Carthusian Northern ME Religious Miscellany British Libr MS Add 37049, in Essays in Honour of Erwin Stürzl on His 60th Birthday, ed J Hogg, Salzburg 1980, 1.241 (MS 66).

Benskin and Laing, see under *Language* below, p 99 (MS 91).

Lewis R E and A McIntosh, A Descriptive Guide to the MSS of the Prick of Conscience, Medium Aevum Monographs ns 12, Oxford 1982.

Hanna R, III, Leeds Univ Brotherton 501: A Redescription, Manuscripta 26(1982).38 (MS 77).

Preston J F, The Pricke of Conscience Pts I–III and Its First Appearance in Print, Libr (forthcoming) (MS 122 and PRINTS 132, 133).

Editions. Halliwell J O, The Thornton Romances, London 1844, p 259 (MS 11 interpolation from [31]).

Morris R, The Pricke of Conscience (Stimulus Conscientiae) a Northumbrian Poem by Richard Rolle de Hampole, Philological Soc, Berlin 1863, p 1 (base text: MS 46).

Furnivall F J, Ballads from MSS I, London 1868–72, p 62 (excerpt from MS 11).

Yksh Wr, 1.129, 372; 2.36, 67, 70.

James, St John's Catalogue, as above, p 174 (tag in MS 43).

Ross T W, Five 15-Cent Emblem Verses from Brit Mus Addit MS 37049, Spec 32(1957).274 (MS 66).

Person H A, Cambridge ME Lyrics, rvsd edn, N Y 1962, pp 22, 23.

Doty B L, An Edn of Brit Mus MS Addit 37049: A Religious Miscellany, diss Michigan State Univ 1963 (MS 66).

Waters S, The Pricke of Conscience: The Southern Recension, Book V, diss Univ of Edinburgh 1976.

McIntosh A, Two Unnoticed Interpolations in Four MSS of the Prick of Conscience, NM 77(1976).63.

Hogg, as above, pp 266, 271.

Selections. AESpr, 1.286.

Morley, 4.264.

Morris Spec, 2.107.

Brandl A and O Zippel, Me Sprach- und Literaturproben, Berlin 1917, p 159.

Kaiser R, ed, Medieval Eng, 3rd edn, Berlin 1958, p 234.

Sisam C and K, Oxford Book of Medieval Verse, Oxford 1970, p 172.

Facsimiles. Wright C E, Eng Vernacular Hands from the 12 to the 15 Cents, Oxford 1960, item 16 (MS 63).

The Thornton MS (Lincoln Cathedral MS 91) with introds by D S Brewer and A E B Owen, London 1975 (MS 75).

Hogg T, ed, An Illustrated Yorkshire Carthusian Religious Miscellany BL London Addit MS 37049, Vol 3: The Illustrations, Analecta Carthusiana 95(1981).49, 109 (facsimiles of MS 66, ff 36ᵃ, 39ᵃ).

Textual Matters. D'Evelyn C, An East Midland Recension of The Pricke of Conscience, PMLA 45 (1930).180.

Lightbown J, The Pricke of Conscience: A Collation of MSS Galba E.IX and Harley 4196, Leeds SE 4(1935).58 (MSS 46, 53).

Baugh N S, ed, A Worcestershire Miscellany, Compiled by John Northwood, ca 1400, Edited from BM MS Add 37787, Phila 1956, p 39 (provenance of MS 60).

McIntosh A, Scribal Profiles from ME Texts, NM 76(1975).218.

Lewis R E, The Relationship of the Vernon and Simeon Texts of the Pricke of Conscience, in M Benskin and M L Samuels, edd, So many people longages and tonges, Philological Essays in Scots and Mediaeval Eng Presented to Angus McIntosh, Edinburgh 1981, p 251; Editorial Technique in the Index of ME Prose, in ME Prose: Essays on Biblio Problems, ed A S G Edwards and D Pearsall, N Y 1981, p 52.

Language. Lightbown J, The Dialect of the Pricke of Conscience, Together with a Collation of MSS Galba E.ix and Harley 4196, Leeds Univ MA thesis 1935 (MSS 46, 53).

Lindheim B von, Studien zur Sprache des Manu-skriptes Cotton Galba E.IX, Wiener Beiträge zur engl Philologie 59(1937) (MS 46); Sprachliche Studien zu Texten des MS Cott Galba E.IX, Angl 61(1937).65 (MS 46).

McIntosh A, A New Approach to ME Dialectology, ESts 44(1963).7 (MS 50).

Dareau M G and A McIntosh, A Dialect Word in Some West Midland MSS of the Prick of Con-science, in Edinburgh Stud in Eng and Scots, ed A J Aitken, A McIntosh, and H Pálsson, London 1971, p 20.

Benskin M and M Laing, Translations and Misch-sprachen in ME MSS, in M Benskin and M L Sam-uels, edd, So meny people longages and tonges, Philological Essays in Scots and Mediaeval Eng Presented to Angus McIntosh, Edinburgh 1981, p 99 (MS 91).

Sources and Literary Relations. Köhler R, Quellen-nachweise zu Richard Rolle's von Hampole Ged-icht The Pricke of Conscience, JfRESL 6(1865).196.

Hahn A, Quellenuntersuchungen zu Richard Rolles engl Schriften, Halle a/S 1900, p 16.

Hahn A, Zu Pricke of Conscience V.7651–86, Arch 106(1901).349.

Mosher J A, The Exemplum in the Early Religious and Didactic Lit of England, N Y 1911, pp 106, 122.

Powell C L, The Castle of the Body, SP 16 (1919).197.

Deanesly M, Vernacular Books in England in the 14 and 15 Cents, MLR 15(1920).353; The Lollard Bible and Other Medieval Biblical Versions, Cam-bridge 1920, pp 86, 204, 214, 333, 368, 392.

Allen WAR, p 372 (similarity to [7]).

Cornelius R D, The Figurative Castle, Bryn Mawr 1930, p 15.

Os A B van, Religious Visions, Amsterdam 1931, pp 151, 169.

Coffman G R, Old Age from Horace to Chaucer: Some Literary Affinities and Adventures of an Idea, Spec 9(1934).264 (argues erroneously that [18] influenced [31]).

Pfander H G, The Popular Sermon of the Medieval Friar in England, N Y 1937, p 25.

Pecheux M C, Aspects of the Treatment of Death in ME Poetry, Washington D C 1951, pp 18, 19, 32, 94 n18.

Heist W W, The 15 Signs before Doomsday, East Lansing 1952, pp 30, 31, 32, 38, 40, 41, 131, 140, 141, 148, 158, 174, 197, 208.

Bloomfield SDS, pp 176, 220, 415.

Pantin, p 231.

Woolf, pp 4, 77 n1, 103 n9, 106.

Sinclair L Jr, The Evidence for an Aesthetic Theory in 14-Cent Vernacular Poetry, diss Univ of Wash-ington 1970, chaps 1–4.

Lewis R E, Medieval Popularity, Modern Neglect: The Case of the Pricke of Conscience, 14-Cent Eng Mystics Newsletter 2(1976).3.

Aston M, Lollardy and Literacy, History 62 (1977).362, 364.

Relihan R J Jr, A Critical Edn of the Anglo-Norman and Latin Versions of Les Peines de Purgatorie, diss Univ of Iowa 1978, p 71 (evidence of indebt-edness to French rather than Latin version of Grosseteste's De Penis Purgatorii).

Wilson E, Langland's Book of Conscience: Two ME Analogues and Another Possible Latin Source, N&Q ns 30(1983).387.

Authorship. Ullmann J, Studien zu Richard Rolle de Hampole I, EStn 7(1884).419, 468.

Bale J, Index Britanniae Scriptorum, ed R L Poole and M Bateson, Anecdota Oxoniensia, Mediaeval and Modern Series, Pt IX, Oxford 1902, p 348 (first post-medieval writer to ascribe the work to Rolle).

Allen H E, The Authorship of the Prick of Con-science, RadMon 15(1910).115; Two ME Trans-lations from the Anglo-Norman, MP 13(1916).745 (argues against the ascription of the Latin trans to Richard Methley); PMLA 32(1917).133.

Allen WAR, pp 371, 372.

Comper F M M, The Life of Richard Rolle, London and N Y 1928, p 224.

Boner G, Über den Dominikanertheologen Hugo von Strassburg, Archivum Fratrum Praedicato-rum 24(1954).276, 283.

Britton, NM 80(1979).330 n12 (suggests [18], [7], Band of Loving, and Stimulus Conscientie Minor were the work of one man).

General References. Pits J, Relationum Historicarum de Rebus Anglicis, Paris 1619, 1.466.

Oudin C, Commentarius de Scriptoribus Ecclesiae Antiquis Illorumque Scriptis Tam Impressis Quam Manuscriptis, Frankfurt am Main and Leipzig 1722, 3.928.

Tanner T, Bibliotheca Britannico-Hibernica, Lon-don 1748, p 375.

Ritson J, Bibliographica Poetica: A Catalogue of Eng Poets of the 12, 13, 14, 15 and 16 Cents, London 1802, pp 17, 34, 36.

Warton T, The Hist of Eng Poetry from the Close of the 11 to the Commencement of the 18 Cent, new edn by R Price, London 1824, 2.91, 96.

Guest E, A Hist of Eng Rhythms, London 1838, 2.418.

Warton, Hist of Eng Poetry from the 12 to the Close of the 16 Cent, ed W C Hazlitt, London 1871, 2.239, 240 n1, 242.

Ten Brink, 1.295.

Brandl, p 651, § 61.

Wülcker, p 104.

Schofield, pp 105, 388.

CHEL, 2.49, 55.

Körting, p 152, § 138.

Fowler J T, The 15 Last Days of the World in Medieval Art and Lit, The Yorkshire Archaeological Journ 23(1915), Plate II.

Deanesly, Lollard Bible, p 214.

Owst G R, Preaching in Medieval England, Cambridge 1926, pp 277, 280, 289.

Linn I, Dean Swift, Pope Innocent, and Oliver Wendell Holmes, PQ 16(1937).317.

Baugh LHE, pp 205, 207, 228.

Woodforde C, Eng Stained and Painted Glass, Oxford 1954, Plate 34.

Wenzel, p 108.

Ackerman R W, Backgrounds to Medieval Eng Lit, N Y 1966, p 100.

Gee E A, The Painted Glass of All Saints' Church, North Street, York, Archaeologia 102(1969).158 (quotations from [18] in stained-glass window depicting 15 signs before Doomsday).

Wilson R M, The Lost Lit of Medieval England, 2nd edn, London 1970, p 146.

Pearsall D, OE and ME Poetry, London 1977, pp 120, 139, 208, 296.

Coleman J, Eng Lit in Hist 1350–1400, London 1981, pp 23, 69, 71.

Brewer D, Eng Gothic Lit, N Y 1983, p 38.

Bibliography. Booker J M, A ME Biblio, Heidelberg 1912, p 37.

New CBEL, 1.503.

Waters S A, A Hist of Pricke of Conscience Stud, SN 55(1983).147 (a rev of early scholarship and stud of the Southern Recension).

II. Manuals of Instruction in the Elements of the Faith

1. Compilations of Elementary Instruction

[19] THE LAY FOLKS CATECHISM (or JOHN GAYTRYGE'S SERMON).

MSS. 1, Bodl 2643 (Bodley 789), ff 52ᵃ–68ᵇ (1400–50; with Wycliffite interpolations); 2, Bodl 12143 (Rawl C.285), ff 61ᵇ–63ᵇ (1400–25; Ten Commandments only); 3, Bodl 12146 (Rawl C.288), ff 85ᵃ–91ᵇ (1400–50); 4, Bodl Don C.13, ff 162ᵇ–165ᵇ (1400–50); 5, Corpus Christi Oxf 155, ff 239ᵃ–250ᵃ (1425–50); 6, Queen's Oxf 389A, ff 245ᵃ–246ᵇ (15 cent; Ten Commandments and seven deadly sins only); 7, Camb Univ Dd.12.39, ff 1ᵃ–3ᵃ (1475–1500; seven virtues only); 7a, Camb Univ Ff.5.40, ff 117ᵇ–119ᵃ (1400–50; Ten Commandments only); 8, Camb Univ Ii.4.9, ff 95ᵇ–96ᵃ (1425–50; articles of the Creed only); 9, Camb Univ Addit 6686, pp 362–364 (1400–50; articles of the Creed, seven Sacraments, seven works of mercy, seven virtues only); 10, Sidney Sussex Camb 55, ff 41ᵃ–49ᵇ (ca 1450; lacks prologue); 11, Trinity Camb 223 (B.10.12), ff 56ᵃ–67ᵃ (1400–50); 12, BL Arundel 507, ff 50ᵃ–54ᵃ (ca 1400); 13, BL Harley 1022, ff 66ᵃ–73ᵇ (1400–25; begins imperfectly); 14, BL Harley 6615, ff 127ᵃ–140ᵇ (1450–1500); 15, BL Addit 24202, ff 35ᵇ–36ᵇ (ca 1400; fragment of seven virtues only);

16, BL Addit 25006, ff 1ᵃ–9ᵇ (1475–1500); 17, Lambeth Palace 408, ff 1ᵃ–17ᵃ (1400–50; with Wycliffite interpolations); 18, Lincoln Cath 91, ff 213ᵇ–218ᵇ (ca 1440); 19, York Minster XVI.L.12, ff 1ᵃ–50ᵃ (1400–50); 20, Borthwick Institute of Historical Research, York, Register of Archbishop Thoresby, ff 295ᵃ–297ᵇ (1357); 21, Hopton Hall (Chandos-Pole-Gell); 22, Bibliothèque Ste Geneviève Paris 3390, ff 37ᵇ–57ᵃ (1400–25). Related Text: Univ Oxford 28, ff 119ᵃ–125ᵇ (1400–25; the concluding portion of a Northern English prose commentary on the seven deadly sins).

Brown-Robbins, Robbins-Cutler, no 406.

Jolliffe, pp 85, no G.1; 88, no G.16 (Wycliffite version of Three Good Vertues [53] incorporated in MSS 19, 22).

MSS Commentary. A Catalogue of the Harleian MSS in the British Museum, London 1808, 1.511 (MS 13); 3.380 (MS 14).

Catalogue of MSS in the British Museum ns I, Pt I: The Arundel MSS, London 1840, p 143 (MS 12).

Coxe H O, Catalogus Codicum MSS qui in Collegiis Aulisque Oxoniensibus Hodie Adservantur, Oxford 1852, 2.63 (MS 5), 89 (MS 6).

A Catalogue of the MSS Preserved in the Libr of the Univ of Cambridge, Cambridge 1856, 1.489 (MS 7); 2(1857).498 (MS 7a); 3(1858).448 (MS 8).

Catalogue of Additions to the MSS in the British Museum in the Years MDCCCLIV–

MDCCCLXXV, London 1877, pp 22 (MS 15), 139 (MS 16).

Macray W D, Catalogi Codicum Manuscriptorum Bibliothecae Bodleianae, Oxford 1878, 5(2).123 (MS 2), 125 (MS 3).

James M R, A Descriptive Catalogue of the MSS in the Libr of Sidney Sussex Coll Cambridge, Cambridge 1895, p 39 (MS 10); The Western MSS in the Libr of Trinity Coll Cambridge, A Descriptive Catalogue, Cambridge 1900, 1.307 (MS 11).

Summary Cat, 2.467 (MS 1).

Wooley R M, Catalogue of the MSS of Lincoln Cathedral Chap Libr, Oxford 1927, p 149 (MS 18).

Cumming W P, A ME MS in the Bibliothèque Ste Geneviève Paris, PMLA 42(1927).862 (MS 22).

James M R and C Jenkins, A Descriptive Catalogue of the MSS in the Libr of Lambeth Palace, Cambridge 1932, p 561 (MS 17).

Brown B D, Religious Lyrics in MS Don C.13, BQR 7(1932).1 (MS 4).

Bazire J and E Colledge, edd, The Chastising of God's Children, Oxford 1957, p 4 n6 (MS 14).

Owen A E B, The Collation and Descent of the Thornton MS, Trans of the Cambridge Biblio Soc 6(1975).218 (MS 18).

Guddat-Figge G, Catalogue of MSS Containing ME Romances, Munich 1976, p 135 (MS 18).

Editions. Perry G G, Religious Pieces in Prose and Verse, EETS 26, London 1867; rvsd 1914, p 1 (MS 18).

Simmons T F and H E Nolloth, The Lay Folks' Catechism, EETS 118, London 1901, p 1 (includes on facing pages Thoresby's and Peckham's Latin instructions, Gaytryge's Sermon from Thoresby's Register, and the Wycliffite Lambeth and York versions).

Blake N F, ME Religious Prose, Evanston 1972, p 73 (MS 18).

Facsimiles. Gregg W W, Facsimiles of Twelve Early Eng MSS in the Libr of Trinity Coll Cambridge, Oxford 1913, plate ix (MS 11).

The Thornton MS (Lincoln Cathedral MS 91), introd by D S Brewer and A E B Owen, London 1975 (MS 18).

Selections. Halliwell J O, Yorkshire Anthology, London 1851, p 287 (MS 20).

Arnold T, ed, Select Eng Works of John Wyclif, Oxford 1871, 3.114 (MS 17).

Simmons T F, ed, The Lay Folk's Mass Book, EETS 71, London 1879, p 118 (excerpt from the Seven Sacraments).

Yksh Wr, 1.104, 108.

Modernization. Watts N H, Love Songs of Sion: A Selection of Devotional Verse from Old Eng Sources, London 1924, p 24.

Language. Moore Meech and Whitehall, p 51.

Blake N F, The Eng Lang in Medieval Lit, London 1977, pp 91, 109.

Style and Form. Skeat W W, An Essay on Alliterative Poetry, in Bishop Percy's Folio MS, ed J W Hales and F J Furnivall, London 1868, 3.xxxviii.

Krapp G P, The Rise of Eng Literary Prose, N Y 1915, p 23.

Salter E, Alliterative Modes and Affiliations in the 14 Cent, NM 79(1978).29.

Lawton D A, Gaytryge's Sermon, Dictamen, and ME Alliterative Verse, MP 76(1979).329.

Authorship. DNB, 19.760 (sv Thoresby, John).

Sources and Literary Relations. Vicaria Leodensis, or The Hist of the Church of Leeds in Yorkshire, London 1724, p 213.

Tupper F, Chaucer's Bed Head, MLN 30(1915).5 ([19] and Parson's Tale).

Allen WAR, p 190.

Owst G R, Preaching in Medieval England, Cambridge 1926, pp 46, 53, 146, 147, 227, 275, 282, 289, 291, 357; Literature and Pulpit in Medieval England, Cambridge 1933, p 543.

Messenger R E, Ethical Teaching in the Latin Hymns of Medieval England, N Y 1930, p 28.

Peckham J L, Archbishop Peckham as a Religious Educator, Yale Studies in Religion 7, Scottdale Pa 1934, p 106.

Pfander Manuals, p 250.

Arnould, p 36.

Bloomfield SDS, pp 184, 185, 186.

McNeill J T, A Hist of the Cure of Souls, N Y 1951, p 155.

Douie D L, Archbishop Peckham, Oxford 1952, p 139.

Taylor J, Notes on the Rise of Written Eng in the Late Middle Ages, Proc of the Leeds Philosophical and Literary Soc 8(1956).129.

Pantin, pp 212, 214, 233.

Kellogg A L and E W Talbert, The Wycliffite Pater Noster and Ten Commandments, with Special Reference to Eng MSS 85 and 90 in the John Rylands Libr, JRLB 42(1960).356.

Wenzel, pp 225, 229, 231, 232, 247.

Gillespie V, Doctrina and Predicacio: The Design and Function of Some Pastoral Manuals, Leeds SE 11(1980 for 1979).36.

General References. Paues A C, A 14-Cent Biblical Version, Cambridge 1902, p lxxi note.

Mosher J A, The Exemplum in the Early Religious and Didactic Lit of England, N Y 1911, p 118.

Manning B L, The People's Faith in the Time of Wyclif, Cambridge 1919, passim.

Deanesly M, The Lollard Bible and Other Medieval Biblical Versions, Cambridge 1920, pp 141 n3, 346.

Workman H B, John Wyclif, Oxford 1926, 2.157.

Rushforth G M, Seven Sacraments Compositions in Eng Medieval Art, Antiquaries Journ 9 (1929).83.

McGarry L, The Holy Eucharist in ME Homiletic and Devotional Verse, Washington D C 1936, p 62.

Smith H M, Pre-Reformation England, London 1938, p 125.

Arnould, p 37.

Rouse E C, Wall Paintings in the Church of St John the Evangelist, Corby, Lincolnshire, Archaeological Journ 100(1945 for 1943).160 (Peckhamite influence on pictorial representations of the seven deadly sins).

Moorman J R H, Church Life in England in the 13 Cent, Cambridge 1946, pp 72 n1, 79 n2, 81, 87.

Bennett OHEL, p 19.

Baugh LHE, pp 203, 207.

Douie D L, Archbishop Peckham, Oxford 1952, pp 139, 141.

Dugmore C W, The Mass and the Eng Reformers, London 1958, p 73.

Ackerman R W, Backgrounds to Medieval Eng Lit, N Y 1966, pp 90, 91.

Blake N F, Varieties of ME Religious Prose, in B Rowland, ed, Chaucer and ME Stud in Honour of R H Robbins, London 1974, p 349.

Priscandaro M T, ME Eucharistic Verse: Its Imagery, Symbolism, and Typology, diss St John's Univ 1975, p 28.

Dolan T P and V J Scattergood, ME Prose, in B Ford, ed, Medieval Lit: Chaucer and the Alliterative Tradition, Harmondsworth 1982, p 114.

Brewer D, Eng Gothic Lit, N Y 1983, p 260.

Bibliography. New CBEL, 1.496.

Doyle Survey, 1.30.

[20] TRINITY COLLEGE CAMBRIDGE MS 305 (B.14.19).

MS. Trinity Camb 305 (B.14.19), ff 194ª–237ᵇ (1400–25).

MS Commentary. James M R, The Western MSS in the Libr of Trinity Coll Cambridge, A Descriptive Catalogue, Cambridge 1900, 1.418.

General Reference. Blake N F, ed, Quattuor Sermones, Heidelberg 1975, p 16.

[21] QUATTUOR SERMONES.

MSS. No MS extant. PRINTS: 1, William Caxton, Westminster, ca 1483–84, ca 1484 (STC, nos 17957, pts 2 and 3); ca 1491 (STC, no 17959); 2, T Rood, Oxford 1486 (STC, no 17958); 3, Wynkyn de Worde, Westminster 1493 (STC, no

17962); 4, R Pynson, London 1493 (STC, nos 17960–61).

MSS Commentary. Karmowitz J H, A Newly Identified Copy of Mirk's Liber Festivalis and Quatuor Sermones (STC, no 17970.5), PBSA 76(1982).221 (a copy in Watkinson Libr incorrectly listed as 1532 de Worde edn, STC, no 17975).

Editions. Blades W, Quatuor Sermones, London 1883.

Blake N F, Quattuor Sermones Printed by William Caxton, Heidelberg 1975, p 19 (crit K Sperk, GRM 28.493).

Textual Matters. Webb C A, Caxton's Quattuor Sermones: a Newly Discovered Edn, in D A Rhodes, ed, Essays in Honor of Victor Scholderer, Mainz 1970, p 407.

Blake N F and L Reffkin, Caxton's First Edn of Quattuor Sermones, GJ(1974).77.

Blake, edn, p 7.

Blake N F, Caxton: England's First Publisher, N Y 1976, pp 58, 60, 63, 70, and passim.

Sources and Literary Relations. Douie D L, Archbishop Pecham, Oxford 1952, p 142.

Blake, edn, p 14.

Bibliography. Blades W, The Life and Typography of William Caxton, London and Strassburg 1863, 2.137.

Gasquet F A, The Biblio of Some Devotional Books Printed by the Earliest Eng Printers, Trans of the Biblio Soc of London 7(1902–04).172.

de Ricci S, A Census of Caxtons, London 1909, p 86.

Duff E G, 15-Cent Eng Books, Oxford 1917, pp 84, 85, 86 (nos 298–99, 300–02, 304, 306–08).

Barratt A, Works of Religious Instruction, in A S G Edwards, ed, ME Prose, New Brunswick 1984, p 417.

[22] SACERDOS PAROCHIALIS and
[23] EXORNATORIUM CURATORUM.

MSS. Sacerdos Parochialis: 1, Bodl 1963 (Bodley 110), ff 155ª–167ᵇ (ca 1450); 2, Bodl 11263 (Rawl A.381), ff 112ª–115ª (ca 1450); 3, Bodl 13679 (Rawl D.913), ff 10ª–19ª (1400–50); 3a, Bodl 2326 (Bodley 554), ff 88ᵇ–89ª (15 cent; sins of thought, mouth and deed as in MS 3); 4, Trinity Oxf 7, ff 165ª–176ᵇ (1400–25; with Wycliffite version of Pater Noster); 5, Camb Univ Dd.12.69, ff 25ª–34ᵇ (1400–25); 6, Pembroke Camb 285, ff 49ª–72ᵇ (1400–25); 7, BL Addit 10036, ff 91ᵇ–96ª (1400–50); 8, BL Addit 10053, ff 99ª–114ª (1400–25); 9, BL Burney 356, ff 43ᵇ–55ᵇ (1400–50); 10, BL Harley 4172, ff 1ª–16ᵇ (1426); 11, BL Royal 1.A.x, f 238ª (15 cent); 12, Durham Univ Cosin V.iv.2, ff 136ª–140ª (1477).

MSS. Exornatorium Curatorum: 13, BL Lansdowne 4843, ff 260ᵃ–262ᵃ (17 cent; excerpt only). PRINTS: 14, Wynkyn de Worde, London 1515? (STC, no 10628); 15, J Notary, London 1519 (STC, no 10629); 16, R Pynson, London 1520? (STC, no 10630); 17, Wynkyn de Worde, London 1520? (STC, no 10631); 18, H Treveris, London 1530? (STC, no 10633); 19, H Pepwell, London 1530? (STC, no 10632); 20, T Godfray, London 1532? (STC, no 10634). BL Lansdowne MS 379, ff 23ᵃ–37ᵇ, contains a copy of a de Worde print with the last two leaves (36ᵃ–37ᵇ) supplied in a 16-cent hand.

Jolliffe, pp 77, no E.11; 80, no F.4; 83, no F.20 (all unidentified portions of [22]); 123, L.3 (unidentified portion of [23]).

MSS Commentary. A Catalogue of the Harleian MSS in the British Museum, London 1808, 3.121 (MS 10).

List of Additions to the MSS in the British Museum in the Years MDCCCXXXVI–MDCCCXL, London 1843, pp 5 (MS 7), 7 (MS 8).

Raine J, Catalogues of the Libr of Durham Cathedral, Surtees Soc 7(1838).174 (MS 12).

Catalogue of MSS in the British Museum ns I, Pt 2: The Burney MSS, London 1840, p 95 (MS 9).

Coxe H O, Catalogus Codicum MSS qui in Collegiis Aulisque Oxoniensibus Hodie Adservantur, Oxford 1852, 2.34 (MS 4).

Macray W D, Catalogi Codicum Manuscriptorum Bibliothecae Bodleianae, Oxford 1852, 5(1).380 (MS 2); 5(4)(1898).136 (MS 3).

A Catalogue of the MSS Preserved in the Libr of the Univ of Cambridge, Cambridge 1856, 1.506 (MS 5).

Summary Cat, 2.135 (MS 1), 311 (MS 3a).

James M R, A Descriptive Catalogue of the MSS in the Libr of Pembroke Coll Cambridge, Cambridge 1905, p 258 (MS 6).

Warner G F and J P Gilson, Catalogue of Western MSS in the Old Royal and King's Collections, London 1921, 1.4 (MS 11).

Pantin, pp 277 (MS 9), 279 (MS 1).

Guddat-Figge G, Catalogue of MSS Containing ME Romances, Munich 1976, p 143 (MS 7).

Pickering O S, Notes on the Sentence of Cursing in ME; or, A Case for the Index of ME Verse, Leeds SE 12(1981).230 (MS 9 versions).

Edition. Arnold T, Select Eng Works of John Wyclif, Oxford 1871, 3.93 (MS 4 Pater Noster).

Literary Relations. Pfander Manuals, p 252.

Peckham J L, Archbishop Peckham as a Religious Educator, Yale Stud in Religion 7, Scottdale Pa 1934, p 110.

Douie D L, Archbishop Peckham, Oxford 1952, p 141.

General References. Gasquet F A, The Eve of the Reformation, London 1900, p 286.

Janelle P, L'Angleterre catholique à la veille du Schesme, Paris 1935, p 19.

Bloomfield SDS, p 216.

Bibliography. Gasquet F A, The Biblio of Some Devotional Books Printed by the Earliest Eng Printers, Trans of the Biblio Soc of London 7(1902–04).173.

Doyle Survey, 1.37.

Doyle A I, Early Printed Tracts, Durham Philobiblon 1(1954).68.

Bennett H S, Eng Books & Readers 1475 to 1557, Cambridge 1969, p 249.

[24] MISCELLANEOUS MANUALS.

MSS. Prose: 1, Bodl 655 (Laud misc 23), ff 41ᵃ–65ᵃ (1400–25; Seven Virtues Opposed to Seven Deadly Sins; Seven Principal Virtues; Five Inner and Outer Wits; Seven Works of Bodily and Spiritual Mercy; Seven Gifts of Holy Ghost; How Man schal ȝelde a streit rekenyng of thre goods; Seven Sacraments; Twelve Lettynges of Prayere; A treatise on prayer; Mirror of Sinners; Fourteen Manneris of Peynes of Helle; An Anselmian meditation; Three Arrows; Faith, here called A Short Declaration of Belief; Exposition of Ten Commandments); 2, Bodl 1049 (Laud misc 524), ff 11ᵃ–20ᵇ (1400–25; Two Expositions of Ten Commandments, Five Inner and Outer Wits, Seven Principal Virtues, Seven Works of Bodily and Spiritual Mercy); 2a, Bodl 1700 (Digby 99), f 139ᵃ (ca 1400; Pater Noster, Creed); 3, Bodl 2289 (Bodley 85), ff 110ᵃ–122ᵃ (after 1410; Exposition of Ten Commandments, Seven Deadly Sins, The World is Contrarie to God, Five Wits, Seven Virtues, Seven Works of Bodily and Spiritual Mercy, How Man schal ȝelde a streit rekenyng of thre goods, Seven Gifts of Holy Ghost, A Hard Word, Words of St Paul); 4, Bodl 2643 (Bodley 789), ff 97ᵃ–123ᵃ, 150ᵃ–152ᵃ (1400–50; Exposition of Pater Noster and Ave Maria, Apostles Creed, Form of Confession, Expositions of Ten Commandments and Pater Noster [some items with Wyclif-fite interpolations]); 5, Bodl 3054 (Bodley 938), ff 1ᵃ–10ᵇ, 243ᵇ–247ᵇ, 267ᵃ (1400–50; ff 1ᵃ–10ᵇ: Creed, Ten Commandments, Seven Deadly Sins, Seven Virtues Opposed to the Seven Vices, Seven Works of Bodily and Spiritual Mercy, Seven Gifts of Holy Ghost, Seven Principal Virtues, Five Inner and Outer Wits, Pater Noster, Ave Maria, Seven Deadly Sins; ff 243ᵇ–247ᵇ: Five Inner and Outer Wits, Seven Deadly Sins; f 267ᵃ: Seven Sacraments); 6, Bodl 10027 (Tanner 201), ff 1ᵃ–6ᵃ (1400–25; Contrition, Seven Deadly Sins, Seven

Virtues Opposed to Seven Deadly Sins, Seven Works of Bodily and Spiritual Mercy, Five Inner and Outer Wits, Ten Commandments, Prayer in Praise of God's Goodness to Man); 7, Bodl 10234 (Tanner 407), f 35^{a-b} (1475–1500; Ten Commandments, Seven Deadly Sins, Seven Works of Bodily Mercy, Seven Principal Virtues, Seven Sacraments [lists only]); 8, Bodl 12071 (Rawl C.209), ff 1^a–22^a (1400–25; Pater Noster, Ave Maria, Creed [incomplete], Ten Commandments [incomplete], Seven Deadly Sins, Seven Virtues Opposed to Seven Deadly Sins, Five Inner and Outer Wits, Seven Gifts of Holy Ghost, Seven Works of Bodily and Spiritual Mercy, Four Cardinal Virtues, Eight Tokenes of Mekeness, Sixtene Condicions of Charity, Four Tokens of Salvation); 9, Bodl 21820 (Douce 246), ff 3^b–4^a, 15^a, 101^b–107^a (1400–50; ff 3^b–4^a: Creed, Form of Confession; f 15^a: Pater Noster, Ave Maria; ff 101^b–107^a: Ten Commandments, Lists of Five Wits, Seven Deadly Sins, Seven Gifts of Holy Ghost and Seven Works of Bodily Mercy, Six Manner Consentis to Synne, Seven Works of Ghostly Mercy); 10, Bodl 21849 (Douce 275), f 5^a (ca 1400; Pater Noster, Ave Maria); 11, Bodl Lyell 29, ff 99^b–106^a (ca 1400; Seven Deadly Sins, Five Inner and Outer Wits, Seven Works of Bodily and Spiritual Mercy); 12, St John's Oxford 94, ff 119^a–126^b (1420–36; Seven Deadly Sins, Five Inner and Outer Wits, Seven Deeds of Bodily and Spiritual Mercy, Ten Commandments, Seven Sacraments, Seven Principal Virtues, Seven Gifts of Holy Ghost, Seven Petitions of the Pater Noster, Creed [the last two items listed in the heading but lacking in the text], Seven Washings of Sin); 13, New Oxford 67, ff 1^a–2^a (ca 1400; Sixtene Condicions of Charity, Ten Commandments, Seven Virtues Opposed to Seven Deadly Sins, Five Inner and Outer Wits; perhaps of Wycliffite origin); 14, Trinity Oxford E.86, ff 30^a–71^b (1475–1500; Ten Commandments, Seven Deadly Sins, Seven Devils Who Stir Men to the Seven Deadly Sins, Seven Virtues Opposed to the Seven Deadly Sins, Seven Works of Bodily and Spiritual Mercy, Five Inner and Outer Wits, Four Cardinal Virtues, Seven Gifts of Holy Ghost, Seven Sins against Holy Ghost, Sixtene Condicions of Charity, Beatitudes, St Augustine wonders about human behavior, Four Tokens of Salvation, Seven Things that prevent men from reading the book of their conscience, Four Needful Things, Biblical proverbs, Visitation of the Sick, Marriage Service, Excommunication [short and long form], List of those who must be absolved by the bishop or his suffragan, form of confession); 15, Univ Oxford 97, ff 85^a–93^b, 123^b–127^a (1400–25; ff 85^a–93^b: Ten Command-

ments, Seven Commandments of New Testament; ff 123^b–127^a: Pater Noster, Creed); 16, Univ Oxford 179, ff 9^{a-b}, 96^{a-b} (1400–25; f 9^{a-b}: Pater Noster, Ave Maria, Creed, Misereatur, Confiteor, Doxology; f 96^{a-b}: Athanasian Creed); 17, Camb Univ Dd.14.26(3), ff 36^a–41^a (ca 1450; Pater Noster, Ave Maria, Creed as in MS 44); 18, Camb Univ Hh.3.13, f 109^a (15 cent; Ten Commandments, Seven Deadly Sins, Five Inner and Outer Wits, Seven Principal Virtues, Seven Works of Bodily and Spiritual Mercy); 19, Camb Univ Ii.4.9, ff 60^b–63^a (ca 1450; Ten Commandments, Seven Deadly Sins, Seven Virtues Opposed to the Seven Deadly Sins, Five Inner and Outer Wits, Seven Works of Bodily and Spiritual Mercy, Seven Sacraments, Seven Principal Virtues, Sixtene Condicions of Charity, Doxology, Pater Noster, Ave Maria, Creed); 20, Camb Univ Ii.6.43, ff 3^a–16^a (1400–25; Ten Commandments, Seven Deadly Sins, Seven Deeds of Bodily and Spiritual Mercy, Seven Gifts of Holy Ghost, Seven Principal Virtues, Five Inner and Outer Wits, Sixtene Condicions of Charity, Beatitudes); 21, Camb Univ Kk.1.3, article 22, ff 1^a–12^b; article 23, a single parchment leaf (1475–1500; article 22: Ten Commandments [two versions], Pater Noster, Ave Maria, Creed, Seven Deadly Sins, Seven Virtues Opposed to the Seven Deadly Sins; article 23: Seven Works of Bodily and Spiritual Mercy, Five Inner and Outer Wits); 22, Camb Univ Nn.4.12, ff 39^a–40^a (ca 1450; Five Outer Wits, Seven Deadly Sins, Seven Virtues Opposed to the Seven Deadly Sins, Seven Gifts of Holy Ghost, Seven Works of Bodily and Spiritual Mercy, Six Manner Consentis to Synne; lists only in an otherwise Wycliffite manuscript); 23, Camb Univ Addit 4120, ff 47^a–49^b, 56^a–57^b (ca 1500; ff 47^a–49^b: Pater Noster, Ave Maria, Creed; ff 56^a–57^b: Ten Commandments); 23a, Emmanuel Camb 246, ff 57^b–60^b (ca 1400; Seven Deadly Sins, Ten Commandments, Seven Gifts of the Holy Ghost); 24, Gonville and Caius Camb 52, f 43^a (14 cent; Pater Noster, Ave Maria); 25, Sidney Sussex Camb 55, ff 49^b–50^a (1400–50; Pater Noster, Ave Maria, Creed, Ten Commandments, Seven Sacraments, Seven Gifts of Holy Ghost); 26, St John's Camb 256, pp 252–253 (1300–50; Pater Noster, In Manus tuas, Seven Deadly Sins, Ten Commandments, Seven Works of Mercy); 27, St John's Camb 257, ff 78^b–79^b (15 cent; Ten Commandments, Seven Mortal Sins, Seven Works of Bodily and Spiritual Mercy, Five Inner and Outer Wits, Seven Gifts of Holy Ghost, Seven Principal Virtues); 28, Trinity Camb 601 (R.3.21), ff 1^a–12^a (1475–1500; Pater Noster; Ave Maria; Creed; Five Outer Wits; Ten Commandments; Five Inner and Outer Wits;

Seven Principal Virtues; Ten Commandments; Seven Deadly Sins; How Many Maners Weyes Synne is Foryeve; Seven Works of Bodily and Spiritual Mercy; Seven Gifts of Holy Ghost; Creed; Faith, here called A Short Declaration of Belief; Seven Sacraments; Twelve Lettynges of Prayere; How Man schal ȝelde a streit rekenyng of thre goods); 29, Trinity Camb 1099 (0.1.74), ff 17ᵃ–70ᵃ (1450–1500; Five Inner and Outer Wits, Seven Principal Virtues, Seven Works of Bodily and Spiritual Mercy, Seven Sacraments, How Man schal ȝelde a streit rekenyng of thre goods, Twelve Lettynges of Prayere, A Form of Confession); 30, BL Arundel 57, ff 81ᵃ, 96ᵇ (1340; f 81ᵃ: Pater Noster, Ave Maria, Creed; f 96ᵇ: Ave Maria (2)); 31, BL Cotton Titus D.xix, ff 161ᵇ–168ᵃ (1400–50; Ten Commandments, Seven Works of Bodily and Spiritual Mercy, Five Inner and Outer Wits, Seven Principal Virtues, Sixtene Condicions of Charity, Seven Deadly Sins); 32, BL Harley 2343, ff 1ᵃ–12ᵃ, 78ᵇ–96ᵇ (1400–50; ff 1ᵃ–12ᵃ: Pater Noster, Ave Maria, Creed; ff 78ᵇ–96ᵇ: Seven Deadly Sins, Seven Virtues Opposed to the Seven Deadly Sins, Five Inner and Outer Wits, Seven Works of Bodily and Spiritual Mercy, Seven Virtues, Beatitudes, Sixtene Condicions of Charity, Four Tokens of Salvation, Five Wonders of St Augustine, An Exhortation to a Good Life, Four Needful Things, Magnificat); 33, BL Harley 2406, ff 1ᵃ–8ᵇ, 8ᵇ–9ᵃ (1475–1500; ff 1ᵃ–8ᵇ: Pater Noster, Ave Maria, Creed, Ten Commandments, Seven Deadly Sins, Seven Works of Bodily and Spiritual Mercy, Seven Principal Virtues, Seven Gifts of Holy Ghost, Twelve Articles of the Faith, Five Inner and Outer Wits, Seven Virtues Opposed to the Seven Deadly Sins, How Many Maners Weyes Synne is Foryeve; ff 8ᵇ–9ᵃ: Ten Commandments, Seven Deadly Sins, Seven Works of Bodily and Spiritual Mercy, Five Outer Wits in a different hand); 34, BL Lansdowne 388, ff 368ᵃ–369ᵇ (1475–1500; Seven Gifts of Holy Ghost, Five Sins against Holy Ghost, Sixtene Condicions of Charity, Beatitudes, St Augustine wonders about human behavior, Four Tokens of Salvation, Seven Things that prevent men from reading the book of their conscience, Four Needful Things); 35, BL Royal 8.A.xv, f 184ᵃ (1350–1400; Pater Noster, Creed); 36, BL Royal 17.A.xxvi, ff 4ᵃ–30ᵃ (1400–50; Ten Commandments, Seven Deadly Sins, Works of Bodily and Spiritual Mercy, Five Outer Wits, Seven Gifts of Holy Ghost, Four Cardinal Virtues, Seven Sacraments, Six Manner Consentis to Synne, Four Needful Things); 37, BL Addit 17010, ff 77ᵇ–80ᵃ (1400–25; Pater Noster, Ave Maria, Creed, Ten Commandments, Seven Deadly Sins, Form of Confession [in later hand]); 38, BL

Addit 27592, ff 42ᵃ–52ᵇ (1400–25; Ten Commandments, Seven Deadly Sins, Five Inner and Outer Wits, Seven Works of Bodily and Spiritual Mercy, Seven Gifts of Holy Ghost, Seven Words of Christ, St Augustine speaks to sinful man, Sixtene Condicions of Charity); 39, BL Addit 28026, ff 187ᵃ–188ᵃ, 188ᵇ–189ᵃ (1400–50; ff 187ᵃ–188ᵃ: Pater Noster, Ave Maria, Creed, Ten Commandments, Twelve Articles of the Faith, Seven Works of Bodily and Spiritual Mercy, Seven Deadly Sins, Seven Virtues Opposed to the Seven Deadly Sins, Five Inner and Outer Wits, Three Enemies of Man [World, Flesh, Devil], Four Cardinal Virtues, Sixtene Condicions of Charity, Beatitudes, Seven Gifts of Holy Ghost; ff 188ᵇ–189ᵃ: Ten Commandments, Five Wits and how men fall by them because of the fiend, Seven Deadly Sins, Seven Virtues Opposed to the Seven Deadly Sins [a list only], Seven Works of Bodily and Spiritual Mercy, Twelve Articles of the Faith, Seven Sacraments Opposed to Seven Deadly Sins [last two items in a later hand]); 40, BL Addit 50577, ff 120ᵃ–178ᵇ (1475–1550; Pater Noster, Ave Maria, Creed, Ten Commandments, Seven Works of Bodily and Spiritual Mercy, Five Inner and Outer Wits, Seven Deadly Sins [imperfect], Seven Virtues Opposed to Seven Deadly Sins, Seven Gifts of Holy Ghost, Four Cardinal Virtues, Sixtene Condicions of Charity, Seven Sacraments, Twelve Articles of the Faith, Pater Noster, Eight Tokenes of Mekenes, How Spiritual Love is turned to Earthly Love, Sayings of St Augustine and St Ambrose, Four Tokens of Salvation, St Augustine wonders about the behavior of people, Beatitudes, Form of Confession); 41, Soc of Antiquaries London 687, p 3 (ca 1400; Pater Noster, Ave Maria, Creed); 42, Dr Williams's Libr London Anc.3, ff 130ᵃ–133ᵇ (1450–1500; Ten Commandments, Seven Works of Bodily and Spiritual Mercy, Seven Deadly Sins, Three Enemies, Three Friends, Three Good Virtues, Five Inner and Outer Wits); 43, St Alban's Cath, ff 1ᵃ–4ᵇ (1400–25; Pater Noster, Seven Principal Virtues, Seven Works of Bodily and Spiritual Mercy, Five Outer Wits, Seven Gifts of Holy Ghost, Sixtene Condicions of Charity, Beatitudes); 44, Lincoln Cath 66, ff 137ᵃ–138ᵃ (ca 1450; Pater Noster, Ave Maria, Creed, Exhortation to Easter Communion); 45, John Rylands Manchester Eng 85, ff 2ᵃ–64ᵇ (1400–25; Pater Noster, Ave Maria, Creed, Doxology, Ten Commandments, Seven Deadly Sins, Five Inner and Outer Wits, Seven Principal Virtues, Seven Works of Bodily and Spiritual Mercy, Twelve Lettynges of Prayere, Eight Parts of Charity, Pater Noster); 46, Durham Univ Cosin V.iv.2, ff 133ᵇ–135ᵇ (1477; Pater Noster, Ave Maria, Creed, Ten Commandments, Seven Deadly Sins, Five Wits, Seven Works of Bodily Mercy, Seven Sacraments, Seven Principal Virtues, Fourteen Articles of the Faith); 47, Edinburgh Univ 93, ff 1ª–103ᵇ (1430–50; Ten Commandments, Seven Sacraments, Five Inner and Outer Wits, Seven Gifts of Holy Ghost, Six Manner Consentis to Synne, Beatitudes, Three Maner Goods, Seven Sacraments, Four Needful Things, Four Cardinal Virtues, Sixtene Condicions of Charity, Rolle's Emendatio Vitae, Seven Works of Bodily Mercy, Twelve Articles of the Faith, Eight Tokenes of Mekenes, Sixtene Tokens of Love, Four Errors, Seven Gifts of Holy Ghost, Magnificat, Lords and Husbandmen, Meditation I of St Anselm, The Stathel of Sin, Biblical Passages [some Wycliffite material]); 48, Glasgow Univ Gen 223, ff 213ª–223ª (1400–25; Ten Commandments, Seven Deadly Sins, Seven Works of Bodily and Spiritual Mercy, Three Good Virtues, Five Inner and Outer Wits, Seven Gifts of Holy Ghost, Four Cardinal Virtues, Seven Sacraments, Six Manner Consentis to Synne [the last five items lists only], Four Things Needful); 49, Glasgow Univ Hunter 472, ff 1ª–5ª, 71ᵇ–80ᵇ (ca 1382; ff 1ª–5ª: Pater Noster, Ave Maria, Creed, Confiteor, Seven Sacraments [list only]; ff 71ᵇ–80ᵇ: Ten Commandments, Seven Deadly Sins, Seven Gifts of the Holy Ghost); 50, Glasgow Univ Hunter 512, ff 11ª–33ª (1400–25; Ten Commandments, Seven Deadly Sins, Seven Works of Bodily and Spiritual Mercy, Three Theological Virtues, Five Inner and Outer Wits [lists only], Seven Gifts of Holy Ghost, Four Cardinal Virtues, Seven Sacraments, Seven Consents to Sin, Four Things Needful [the last four items lists only], Articles of the Faith, Words of St John XV, Sixtene Condicions of Love, Translation of Leviticus XIX, Doxology, Pater Noster, Ave Maria, Creed); 51, Glasgow Univ Hunter 520, pp 337–352 (1450–1500; Five Outer Wits, Ten Commandments, Seven Works of Bodily and Spiritual Mercy); 52, Bibliothèque Ste Geneviève 3390, ff 1ª–37ª (1400–25; Ten Commandments, Pater Noster, Three Theological Virtues [with Wycliffite interpolations in last two items]); 53, Pierpont Morgan 861, ff 1ª–6ᵇ (ca 1450; Ten Commandments, Ten Vengeaunces of God, Seven Deadly Sins, Seven Works of Bodily and Spiritual Mercy, Five Inner and Outer Wits, Four Cardinal Virtues, Seven Sacraments, Eight Tokenes of Mekenes); 54, Princeton Univ Dep 1459 (Garrett 143), ff 1ª–35ᵇ (1400–25; Ten Commandments, Seven Works of Bodily and Spiritual Mercy); 55, Sotheby's Sale, December 10 1969, lot 43, f 80ª–ᵇ (1400–50; Pater Noster, Ave Maria, Creed, Ten Commandments, Seven Virtues Opposed to the Seven Deadly Sins, Five Inner and Outer Wits,

Seven Works of Bodily and Spiritual Mercy, Ten Commandments [fragment only]); 56, Columbia Univ Plimpton 258, ff 1ª–8ª (ca 1400; Pater Noster, Ave Maria, Ten Commandments, Seven Deadly Sins, Seven Works of Bodily and Spiritual Mercy, Five Inner and Outer Wits, Four Cardinal Virtues, Seven Gifts of Holy Ghost, Sixtene Condicions of Charity, Beatitudes, St Augustine Marvels at five things, Four Tokens of Salvation); 57, Univ of Penn 2, ff 146ª–147ᵇ (1450–1500; Seven Virtues Opposed to Seven Deadly Sins, Works of Mercy, Seven Gifts of the Holy Ghost). *Verse:* 58, Bodl 1596 (Laud misc 463), f 157ª–ᵇ (1400–25; Seven Deadly Sins, Ten Commandments); 59, Bodl 2298 (Bodley 549), f 78ª–ᵇ (1400–25; Creed, Ten Commandments, Seven Deadly Sins, Seven Works of Bodily and Spiritual Mercy, Pater Noster, Seven Sacraments, Seven Gifts of Holy Ghost, Seven Principal Virtues); 60, Bodl 3938 (Eng poet a.1), ff 115ᵇ–116ª, 408ᵇ (1380–1400; ff 115ᵇ–116ª: Prayer for Seven Gifts of Holy Ghost, Confession of Negligence of Deeds of Mercy, Prayer for saving of Five Wits, Prayer for Negligence of Ten Commandments; f 408ᵇ: Exhortation to Keep Ten Commandments); 61, Bodl 4127 (Hatton 12), ff 211ᵇ–212ª (1375–1400; prose Creed, Seven Principal Virtues, Ten Commandments, Seven Deadly Sins, Seven Sacraments, Seven Works of Bodily and Spiritual Mercy); 62, Bodl 21715 (Douce 141), ff 130ª–139ª (1400–25; Pater Noster, Ten Commandments, Seven Deadly Sins); 63, Corpus Christi Oxf 155, f 248ª–ᵇ (1400–50; Creed, Ave Maria); 64, Camb Univ Ee.4.35, ff 5ᵇ–6ª (1500–25; Seven Virtues Opposed to the Seven Deadly Sins, Ten Commandments); 65, Camb Univ Ff.2.38, ff 31ᵇ–33ᵇ (ca 1450; Ave Maria, Ten Commandments, Seven Works of Bodily and Spiritual Mercy, Five Inner and Outer Wits, Seven Deadly Sins, Wounds of Christ as Remedies for the Seven Deadly Sins, Seven Virtues Opposed to the Seven Deadly Sins, Twelve Articles of the Faith, Seven Sacraments [last two items in prose from [36], The Mirror of St Edmund]); 66, Camb Univ Gg.4.32, ff 21ª–23ᵇ (14 cent; Pater Noster, Ave Maria, Creed [prose], Creed, Ave Maria); 67, Camb Univ Hh.6.11, f 70ᵇ (ca 1400; Ave Maria, Pater Noster); 68, Camb Univ Addit 5943, ff 167ᵇ–168ᵇ (1400–25; Pater Noster, Ave Maria, Creed); 69, Emmanuel Camb 27, ff 111ᵇ, 162ª–ᵇ (1250–1300; f 111ᵇ: Ten Commandments, Seven Deadly Sins; f 162ª–ᵇ: Pater Noster, Ave Maria, Creed [prose], Ten Commandments, Seven Deadly Sins, Seven Works of Bodily Mercy); 70, Magdalene Camb Pepys 1584, ff 102ᵇ–108ᵇ (1475–1500; Ave Maria, Ten Commandments, Seven Works of Bodily and Spiritual

Mercy, Five Inner and Outer Wits, Seven Deadly Sins, Seven Virtues Opposed to the Seven Deadly Sins); 71, BL Arundel 292, f 3ᵃ⁻ᵇ (1400–25; Creed, Pater Noster, Ave Maria); 72, BL Cotton Cleopatra B.vi, f 204ᵇ (14 cent; Pater Noster, Ave Maria, Creed [prose]); 73, BL Harley 1704, ff 48ᵇ–49ᵃ (ca 1465; Ten Commandments, Seven Deadly Sins, Seven Principal Virtues); 74, BL Harley 1706, ff 205ᵃ–209ᵃ (1450–1500; Ten Commandments, Seven Deadly Sins, Seven Virtues Opposed to the Seven Deadly Sins, Seven Works of Bodily and Spiritual Mercy, Five Inner and Outer Wits, Three Theological Virtues, Four Cardinal Virtues, Beatitudes); 75, BL Harley 2339, ff 116ᵃ–121ᵇ (1400–50; Ten Commandments, Seven Deadly Sins, Wounds of Christ as remedies for the Seven Deadly Sins, Seven Works of Bodily and Spiritual Mercy, Seven Sacraments, Five Inner and Outer Wits); 76, BL Harley 2391, f 134ᵃ (1475–1500; Ten Commandments, Seven Deadly Sins); 77, BL Harley 3724, f 49ᵃ⁻ᵇ (1300–50; Creed [prose], Pater Noster); 78, BL Addit 37787, ff 157ᵇ–159ᵃ (1400–25; Prayer for Seven Gifts of Holy Ghost, Confessions of Negligence of Deeds of Mercy, Prayer for saving of Five Wits, Prayer for Negligence of Ten Commandments); 79, Lambeth Palace 491, f 295ᵃ⁻ᵇ (1475–1500; Creed, Five Outer Wits, Seven Works of Bodily and Spiritual Mercy); 80, Lambeth Palace 853, pp 39–53 (1400–50; Creed, Sixtene Condicions of Charity, two versions of Ten Commandments); 81, Salisbury Cath 126, f 5ᵃ⁻ᵇ (1400–50; Seven Deadly Sins, Ten Commandments, Seven Works of Bodily and Spiritual Mercy, Creed [prose]); 82, Nat Libr of Scotland Advocates 18.7.21, ff 95ᵃ, 124ᵃ, 128ᵇ 130ᵇ (1372; f 95ᵃ: Pater Noster; f 124ᵃ: Wounds of Christ as Remedies for Seven Deadly Sins; f 128ᵇ: Ten Commandments; f 130ᵇ: Wounds of Christ as Remedies for Seven Deadly Sins); 83, Nat Libr of Scotland Advocates 19.2.1, ff 70ᵃ–72ᵇ (1330–40; a poem treating Seven Deadly Sins, Ten Commandments, Pater Noster, Creed, Ave Maria, Pater Noster); 84, Univ of Edinburgh 205, f 87ᵃ⁻ᵇ (after 1477; Pater Noster, Ave Maria, Creed). A metrical compendium consisting of Forms of Confession, Ten Commandments, Seven Works of Mercy, Articles of the Faith, and Seven Principal Virtues is incorporated in a prose work in: 85, BL Addit 37049, f 87ᵃ (1400–50).

Brown-Robbins, nos *30, 197, 206, 214, 254, 453, 475, 505, 645, 660, 662, 744, 784, 802, 804, 880, 945, 958, 1012, 1013, 1065, 1067, 1069, 1282, 1283, 1284, 1324, 1376, 1393, 1416, 1503, 1570, 1658, 1746, 1748, 1760, 1776, 1856, 1945, 2291, 2344, 2352, 2535, 2569, 2694, 2702, 2705, 2706, 2708, 2738, 3040, 3263, 3340, 3356, 3400, 3486,

3555, 3731. Brown-Robbins, Robbins-Cutler, nos 469, 787, 975, 1026, 1041, 1062, 1064, 1126, 1129, 1326, 1374, 1379, 1602, 1815, 1959, 1969, 2100, 2703, 2704, 2769, 2770, 2776, 3100, 3262, 3685, 3686, 3810, 4200.

Robbins-Cutler, no 851.6.

MSS Commentary. A Catalogue of the MSS in the Cottonian Libr Deposited in the British Museum, London 1802, pp 565 (MS 31), 578 (MS 72).

A Catalogue of the Harleian MSS in the British Museum, London 1808, 2.177 (MS 73), 178 (MS 74), 658 (MS 75), 660 (MS 32), 680 (MS 76), 688 (MS 33); 3.55 (MS 77).

A Catalogue of the Lansdowne MSS in the British Museum, London 1819, p 12 (MS 34).

Raine J, Catalogues of the Libr of Durham Cathedral, Surtees Soc 7(1838).174 (MS 46).

Catalogue of MSS in the British Museum ns I, Pt I: The Arundel MSS, London 1840, pp 12 (MS 30), 86 (MS 71).

Catalogue of Additions to the MSS in the British Museum in the Years MDCCCXLVI–MDCCCXLVII, London 1864, p 346 (MS 37).

Coxe H O, Catalogus Codicum MSS qui in Collegiis Aulisque Oxoniensibus Hodie Adservantur, Oxford 1852, 1.19 (MS 13), 28 (MS 15), 49 (MS 16); 2.26 (MS 12), 35 (MS 14), 63 (MS 63).

A Catalogue of the MSS Preserved in the Libr of the Univ of Cambridge, Cambridge 1856, 1.530 (MS 17); 2(1857).124 (MS 64), 404 (MS 65); 3(1858).117 (MS 66), 280 (MS 18), 448 (MS 19), 540 (MS 20), 551 (MS 21); 4(1861).499 (MS 22).

Coxe H O, Catalogi Codicum Manuscriptorum Bibliothecae Bodleianae, Oxford 1858, 2.65 (MS 1), 331 (MS 58), 378 (MS 2).

Hackman A, Catalogi Codicum Manuscriptorum Bibliothecae Bodleianae, Oxford 1860, 4.637 (MS 6), 764 (MS 7).

Catalogue of Additions to the MSS in the British Museum in the Years MDCCCLIV–MDCCCLXXV, London 1877, pp 334 (MS 38), 339 (MS 39).

Macray W D, Catalogi Codicum Manuscriptorum Bibliothecae Bodleianae, Oxford 1878, 5.209 (MS 8).

A Catalogue of the Libr of the Cathedral Church of Salisbury, London 1880, p 24 (MS 81).

James M R, A Descriptive Catalogue of the MSS in the Libr of Sidney Sussex Coll Cambridge, Cambridge 1895, p 39 (MS 25); The Western MSS in the Libr of Trinity Coll Cambridge A Descriptive Catalogue, Cambridge 1901, 2.83 (MS 28); 3(1902).74 (MS 29).

Summary Cat, 2.291 (MS 3), 295 (MS 59), 467 (MS 4), 578 (MS 5), 789 (MS 60), 855 (MS 61); 4.535 (MS 62), 566 (MS 9), 577 (MS 10).

James M R, The Western MSS in the Libr of Emmanuel Coll A Descriptive Catalogue, Cambridge 1904, p 22 (MS 69); A Descriptive Catalogue of the MSS in the Libr of Gonville and Caius Coll Cambridge, Cambridge 1907, 1.44 (MS 24).

Young J and P H Aitken, A Catalogue of the MSS in the Hunterian Museum in the Univ of Glasgow, Glasgow 1908, pp 149 (MS 49), 419 (MS 50).

Catalogue of Additions to the MSS in the British Museum in the Years MDCCCCVI–MDCCCCX, London 1912, p 140 (MS 78).

James M R, A Descriptive Catalogue of the MSS in the Libr of St John's Coll Cambridge, Cambridge 1913, pp 291 (MS 26), 293 (MS 27).

Borland C R, A Descriptive Catalogue of the Western Mediaeval MSS in Edinburgh Univ Libr, Edinburgh 1916, p 291 (MS 84).

Warner G F and J P Gilson, Catalogue of Western MSS in the Old Royal and King's Collections, London 1921, 1.214 (MS 35); 2.220 (MS 36).

James M R, A Descriptive Catalogue of the Libr of Samuel Pepys, Pt III, Medieval MSS, London 1923, p 19 (MS 70).

Owst G R, A 15-Cent MSS in St Alban's Abbey, St Albans and Hertfordshire Architectural and Archaeological Soc Trans (1924), p 43 (MS 43).

Wooley R M, Catalogue of the MSS of Lincoln Cathedral Chapter Libr, Oxford 1927, p 35 (MS 44).

Cumming W P, A ME MS in the Bibliothèque Ste Geneviève, Paris, PMLA 42(1927).862 (MS 52).

James M R and C Jenkins, A Descriptive Catalogue of the MSS in the Libr of Lambeth Palace, Cambridge 1932, pp 681 (MS 79), 809 (MS 80).

de Ricci Census, 1.894 (MS 54); 3.365 (MS 53).

Serjeantson Index, pp 255, 260.

Bühler C F, The ME Texts of Morgan MS 861, PMLA 69(1954).692 (MS 53).

Wolpe B, Florilegium Alphabetum: Alphabets in Medieval MSS, in Calligraphy and Palaeography Essays Presented to Alfred Fairbank, ed A S Osley, N Y 1966, p 70 (MSS 50, 51).

Ker Manuscripts, 1.314 (MS 41), 426 (MS 42); 2.904 (MS 48); 3.409 (MS 45).

De La Mare A, Catalogue of the Collection of Medieval MSS Bequeathed to the Bodleian Libr by James P R Lyell, Oxford 1971, p 59 (MS 11).

Guddat-Figge G, Catalogue of MSS Containing ME Romances, Munich 1976, pp 94 (MS 65), 100 (MS 19), 121 (MS 83).

Krochalis J E, Contemplation of the Dread and Love of God: Two Newly Identified Pennsylvania MSS, LC 42(1977).16 (MS 57).

Doyle A I, Univ Coll Oxf MS 97 and Its Relationship to the Simeon MSS (BL Addit 22283), in M Benskin and M L Samuels, edd, So meny people longages and tonges, Philological Essays in Scots and Medieval Eng Presented to Angus McIntosh, Edinburgh 1981, p 265 (MS 15).

Editions. Weever J, Ancient Funerall Monuments, London 1631, p 152 (Brown-Robbins, no 2703).

Haupt M and A H Hoffmann, Altdeutsche Blätter, Leipzig 1836, 2.141, 142 (Brown-Robbins, nos 787 and 1326; 2100).

Rel Ant, 1.282 (MS 24); 22 (Brown-Robbins, nos 1062 and 2706); 38 (MS 32), 57 and 159 (Brown-Robbins, no 2703); 160 (Brown-Robbins, no 1282); 169 (Brown-Robbins, nos 2705 and 1067); 234, 235 (Brown-Robbins, nos 1326, 2100, 787).

Laing D, A Penni Worth of Wit, Abbotsford Club (1857), pp 89, 92 (Brown-Robbins, nos 1760, 206).

Heurtley C A, Harmonica Symbolica, Oxford 1858, pp 94 (MS 72), 96 (MS 32).

Furnivall EEP, p 15 (Brown-Robbins, no 2344).

AESpr, 1.49, 50, 60, 128 (Brown-Robbins, nos 1326, 2100, 787, 2344); 2.4.

Black W H, Paraphrase of Seven Penitential Psalms, PPS 7(1842).61 (Brown-Robbins, no 2770).

Furnivall F J, Hymns to the Virgin and Christ, EETS 24, London 1867, pp 101, 104, 106 (Brown-Robbins, nos 1570, 744, 1379).

Ellis A E, Early Eng Pronunciation, Pt 2, EETSES 7, London 1869, pp 442, 443, 444 (Brown-Robbins, nos 1062 and 2706; 2703; 1326, 787, and 2100); On Early Eng Pronunciation, ChS 2s 4, London 1869, pp 442, 443, 444 (Brown-Robbins, nos 2706; 2703 and 1062; 1326, 787, and 2100).

Camden W, Remains Concerning Britain, London 1870, pp 28, 29 (Brown-Robbins, nos 787, 2703).

Thompson E M, Scraps from ME MSS, EStn 1(1877).214 (Brown-Robbins, nos 2776, 3731, 3263).

Maskell, 2.240 (MS 72), 241 (MSS 32, 9); 3.248, 254 (Brown-Robbins, nos 2706; 3685 and 2770).

Kölbing E, Kleine Publikationen aus den Auchinleck-HS, EStn 9(1885).43, 47 (Brown-Robbins, nos 1760, 206).

Zupitza J, Zwei Umschreibungen der Zehn Gebote in me Versen, Arch 85(1890).45 (Brown-Robbins, no 744).

Bülbring K D, Über die Handschrift Nr 491 der Lambeth-Bibliothek, Arch 86(1891).387, 388, 389 (MS 79; Brown-Robbins, nos *30; 1815; 3040 and 3262).

Horstmann C, Minor Poems of the Vernon MS, Vol I, EETS 98, London 1892, pp 34, 35, 36 (Brown-Robbins, nos 1959, 1969, 1602).

Zupitza J, Die Gedichte des Franziskaners Jakob Ryman, Arch 89(1892).247 (Brown-Robbins, no 2535).

Yksh Wr, 2.454 (MS 15); 1.111 (Brown-Robbins, no 1856).

Furnivall F J, Minor Poems of the Vernon MS, Vol II, EETS 117, London 1901, p 680 (Brown-Robbins, no 1379).

Heuser W, Die Kildare Gedichte, BBA 14 (1904).114, 185, 197, 205 (Brown-Robbins, nos 2344; 1776; 3685 and 2770); Ave Maria, Angl 27(1904).325 (Brown-Robbins, no 1062).

Clark A, The Eng Register of Godestow Nunnery, EETS 129, London 1905, pp 5, 7, 8 (Brown-Robbins, nos 2702; 1069 and 1283; 1324).

Mayers L S, Music Cantilenas and Songs, London 1906, nos 13, 14, 15, 16 (Brown-Robbins, nos 2738, 453, 662).

Patterson, pp 48, 108, 128 (Brown-Robbins, nos 1324; 2702 and 2703; 975).

Garrett R M, Religious Verses from MS Arundel 292, Arch 128(1912).368 (MS 71; Brown-Robbins, nos 1326, 787, 2100).

Patterson F A, Sermon on the Lord's Prayer, JEGP 15(1916).406 (Brown-Robbins, no 958).

Stevenson G S, Pieces from the Makculloch and the Gray MSS, PSTS 65, Edinburgh 1918, pp 17, 18, 19 (Brown-Robbins, nos 254, 1065, 1376).

Brown RLxivC, pp 148, 227, 230 (Brown-Robbins, nos 1379, 4200, 1062).

Seymour S-J D, Anglo-Irish Lit, 1200–1582, Cambridge 1929, p 67 (Brown-Robbins, no 3400).

Brown ELxiiiC, pp 127, 129, 181 n23 (Brown-Robbins, nos 2706, 2291, 1129).

Holmstedt G, Speculum Christiani, EETS 182, London 1933, p lxxiv (Brown-Robbins, no 3685).

Thomson S H, A XIII-Cent Oure Fader in a Pavia MS, MLN 49(1934).236 (Brown-Robbins, no 2704).

Brown RLxvC, pp 30, 84 (Brown-Robbins, nos 1026; 254 and 2738).

Lloyd D J, An Edn of the Prose and Verse in the Bodleian MS Laud Misc 23, diss Yale Univ 1943 (MS 1).

Utley F L, How Iudicare Came in the Creed, MS 8(1946).304 (Brown-Robbins, no *30; Robbins-Cutler, no 851.6).

Bloomfield SDS, pp 169, 208 (Brown-Robbins, nos 802 and 2769; 2776).

Bowers R H, Three ME Poems on the Apostles' Creed, PMLA 70(1955).213 (Brown-Robbins, no 1374).

Baugh N S, A Worcestershire Miscellany, Phila 1956, pp 145, 146, 147, 148 (Brown-Robbins, nos 975, 1959, 1969, 1602).

Hussey M, The Petitions of the Pater Noster in Mediaeval Eng Lit, MÆ 27(1958).10 (Brown-Robbins, no 2704).

Kaiser R, Medieval Eng, 3rd edn, Berlin 1958, p 296 (Brown-Robbins, no 469).

Person H A, Cambridge ME Lyrics, rvsd edn, N Y 1962, pp 11, 14, 21, 24, 27, 29, 68 (Brown-Robbins, nos 1041; 1064; 469; 1126; 2769, 2704, and 1062; 3100; 4200).

Russell Vernacular Instruction, pp 103 (Brown-Robbins, no 1760, excerpt only), 105 (Brown-Robbins, no 206, excerpt only), 108 (Brown-Robbins, nos 1376, 1282), 114 (Brown-Robbins, nos 1284, 1393, 1945, 945, 1012, 784, 1658, 2569, 1013), 116 (Brown-Robbins, nos 3810, 3686, 802, 3340, 3486, 660).

Doty B L, An Edn of British Museum MS Addit 37049: A Religious Miscellany, diss Michigan State 1963 (MS 85).

Wilson E, A Descriptive Index of the Eng Lyrics in John of Grimestone's Preaching Book, Oxford 1973, pp 29, 49, 56 (Brown-Robbins, nos 2708, 3356, 197).

Reichl K, Religiöse Dichtung in Engl Hochmittelalter, Munich 1973, pp 334, 335, 336 (Brown-Robbins, nos 1129, 2694).

Martin C A, Edinburgh Univ Libr 93: An Annotated Edn of Selected Devotional Treatises, diss Univ of Edinburgh 1978 (MS 47).

Hirsch J, Prayer and Meditation in Late Medieval England: MS Bodley 789, MÆ 48(1979).63, 64 (MS 4; Brown-Robbins, nos 505, 475, 1746).

Louis C, The Commonplace Book of Robert Reynes of Acle, N Y and London 1980, p 243 (MS 7).

Facsimiles. Plimpton G A, The Education of Chaucer, London and N Y 1935 (MS 56).

The Auchinleck Manuscript. Nat Libr of Scotland Advocates' MS 19.2.1 with an introd by D Pearsall and I C Cunningham, London 1979 (MS 83).

The Winchester Anthology, with an introd by E Wilson and I Fenlon, Woodbridge 1981 (MS 40).

Literary and Cultural Relations. Spencer H L, Eng Vernacular Sunday Preaching in the Late 14 Cent and 15 Cent, with Illustrative Texts, diss Oxford Univ 1982, p 118 (on the preaching of the pastoralia).

General References. Bloomfield SDS, pp 162 (MS 83), 167 (MS 59), 169 (MSS 61, 69), 208 (MSS 74, 81), 215 (MS 54).

Edwards K, The Eng Secular Cathedrals in the Middle Ages, 2nd edn, Manchester 1967, p 213 (Cyreter, author and scribe of poems in MS 81).

Bibliography. Booker J M, A ME Biblio, Heidelberg 1912, pp 30, 43.

[25] A GOOD AND A PROFITABLE TABLE OF THE FEYTH OF CHRISTIAN PEOPLE.

MS. BL Addit 10106, ff 3ᵇ–44ᵃ (1475–1500).

MS Commentary. List of Additions to the MSS in the British Museum in the Years MDCCCXXXVI–MDCCCXL, London 1843, p 12.

General References. Doyle A I, The Work of a Late 15-Cent Eng Scribe, William Ebesham, JRLB 39 (1957).313.

Kellogg A L and E W Talbert, The Wyclifite Pater Noster and Ten Commandments, with Special Reference to Eng MSS 85 and 90 in the John Rylands Libr, JRLB 42(1960).349.

Gillespie V, Doctrina and Predicacio: The Design and Function of Some Pastoral Manuals, Leeds SE 11(1980 for 1979).43.

[26] BACULUS VIATORIS.

MS. BL Royal 8.F.vii, ff 45^b–51^b (1450–1500).

Brown-Robbins, nos 1479, 2692, 3116; Robbins-Cutler, no 2692.

MS Commentary. Warner G F and J P Gilson, Catalogue of Western MSS in the Old Royal and King's Collections, London 1921, 1.165.

General References. Bloomfield SDS, p 169.

Doyle Survey, 1.37.

[27] A RYGHT PROFYTABLE TREATYSE.

MS. St John's Camb 109, ff 10^b–11^b (ca 1500; partial copy in Betson's hand). PRINT: Wynkyn de Worde, Westminster 1500 (STC, no 1978).

MS Commentary. James M R, A Descriptive Catalogue of the MSS in the Libr of St John's Coll Cambridge, Cambridge 1985, p 142.

Facsimile. Betson 1905 facsimile, rptd Norwood N J, 1977.

Authorship. Bateson M, Catalogue of the Libr of Syon Monastery, London 1898, p xxiii n5.

Doyle A I, Thomas Betson of Syon Abbey, Libr 5s 11(1956).115.

Emden A B, A Biographical Register of the Univ of Cambridge, Cambridge 1963, p 59.

Ker Manuscripts, 1.243 (St Paul's Cathedral MS 5 partially in Betson's hand).

General References. Workman S K, 15-Cent Translation as an Influence on Eng Prose, Princeton 1940, p 176.

Bennett OHEL, p 265.

Bibliography. Doyle A I, Early Printed Tracts, Durham Philobiblon 1(1954).66.

Bennett H S, Notes on Two Incunables: The Abbey of the Holy Ghost and A Ryght Profytable Treatise, Libr 5s 10(1955).120; Eng Books & Readers 1475–1557, Cambridge 1969, p 244.

New CBEL, 1.689.

[28] THE POEMS OF WILLIAM OF SHOREHAM.

MS. BL Addit 17376, ff 150^a–220^b (ca 1350).

Brown-Robbins, nos 1495, 2107, 2226, 3107, 3199, 3417, 3681; Robbins-Cutler, nos 2107, 2226.

MS Commentary. Catalogue of Additions to the MSS in the British Museum in the Years MDCCCXLVIII–MDCCCLIII, London 1868, p 11.

Hunt R W, A Dismembered MS Bodleian MS Lat th.e.32 and British Musuem Add MS 17376, Bodleian Libr Record 7(1966).271.

Editions. Wright T, The Religious Poems of William de Shoreham, PPS 28, London 1849, p 1.

Konrath M, Poems of William of Shoreham, EETSES 86, London 1902, p 1 (crit J Koch, EStn 33.406; W Dibelius, Arch 113.194).

Brown RLxivC, p 46 (Hymn to BVM; Brown-Robbins, no 2107).

Brandl A L and O Zippel, Me Sprach- und Literaturproben, 2nd edn, Berlin 1927, p 100 (Five Joys of BVM; Brown-Robbins, no 2226).

Sisam C and K, The Oxford Book of Medieval Eng Verse, Oxford 1970, p 164 (Hymn to BVM; Brown-Robbins, no 2107).

Selections and Modernizations. AESpr, 1.260.

Wülker R P, ed, Ae Lesebuch, Halle 1874, 1.21.

Morris Spec, 2.63.

Watts N H, Love Songs of Sion; A Selection of Devotional Verse from Old Eng Sources, London 1924, p 131.

Sampson G, The Cambridge Book of Prose and Verse, Cambridge 1924, p 361.

Kaiser R, Medieval Eng, 3rd edn, Berlin 1958, p 246.

Textual Matters. Konrath M, Beiträge und Textkritik des William von Shoreham, Berlin 1878 (crit K Bödekker, LfGRP 1.60; E Kölbing, EStn 3.164; H Varnhagen, AfDA 5.257).

Varnhagen H, Zu William von Shoreham, Angl 4(1881).200.

Manly J M, Lok-Sounday, HSNPL 1.88.

Kölbing E, Textkritische Bemerkungen zu Williams von Schoreham, EStn 21(1895).154.

Kock E A, Interpretations and Emendations of Early Eng Texts, Angl 26(1903).365.

Holthausen F, Zur Textkritik der Dichtungen Williams von Shoreham, EStn 42(1910).205.

Konrath, Zur Textkritik der Dichtungen Williams von Shoreham, EStn 43(1911).1.

Holthausen, Zu William of Shoreham, EStn 57 (1923).307.

Language. Danker O, Die Laut- und Flexionslehre der Mittelkentischen Denkmäler, Strassburg 1879.

Bülbring K D, Geschichte des Ablauts der Starken Zeitwörter innerhalb des Südenglischen, QF 63(1889).25.

Heuser W, Zum Kent Dialekt im Me, Angl 17 (1895).80.

Glahn N, Zur Geschichte des grammatischen Geschlechts im Me, AF 53(1918).93.

Seidel W, William of Shorehams Laut- und Formenlehre seiner Gedichte, Leipzig 1929 (crit E Fischer, AnglB 42.8).

Prins A A, French Influence on Eng Phrasing, Leiden 1952, p 296.

Versification. Schipper, 1.386; 2.605.

Authorship. Konrath, Beiträge, p 3 (denies Shoreham's authorship of Psalter in MS Addit 17376).

Deanesly M, The Lollard Bible and Other Medieval Biblical Versions, Cambridge 1920, p 146 n3.

Russell J C, Dictionary of Writers of 13-Cent England, London 1936, p 201.

Sources and Literary Relations. Jacoby M, Vier me geistliche Gedichte des XIII Jahrhunderts, Berlin 1890, p 29 (relation to other Patris sapientia poems).

McGarry L, The Holy Eucharist in ME Homiletic and Devotional Verse, Washington D C 1936, p 65.

Wenzel, pp 167, 169, 232.

Woolf, pp 236, 377 n4, 378.

General References. Ten Brink, 1.281.

Brandl, § 34, p 633.

Schofield, p 387.

CHEL, 1.394.

Körting, § 129, p 141.

Renwick-Orton, p 301.

Baugh LHE, p 215.

Pecheux M C, Aspects of the Treatment of Death in ME Poetry, Washington D C 1951, pp 108, 114, 124.

Bloomfield SDS, p 174.

Pantin, p 230.

Schlauch M, Eng Medieval Lit and Its Social Foundations, Warsaw 1956, p 193.

Dubois M-M, La Littérature anglaise du Moyen Age, Paris 1962, p 108.

Ackerman R W, Backgrounds to Medieval Eng Lit, N Y 1966, pp 97, 118.

Pearsall D, Old Eng and ME Poetry, London 1977, p 135.

Bibliography. CBEL, 1.271.

New CBEL, 1.710.

[29] THE POEMS OF JOHN AUDELAY.

MS. Bodl 21876 (Douce 302), ff 27ᵇ–28ᵃ (1425–50). Brown-Robbins, nos 304, 792, 858, 2173, 3346.

MS Commentary. Summary Cat, 4.585.

Editions. See Manual, 6.1994 (XIV [327–331]).

Language. Rasmussen J, Die Sprache John Audelays Laut- und Flexionlehre, Bonn 1914.

Authorship. Bennett M, John Audelay: Some New Evidence on His Life and Work, Chaucer Rev 16(1982).344.

Literary Relations. Priebsch P, John Audelay's Poem on the Observance of Sunday and Its Source, in An Eng Miscellany Presented to Dr Furnivall in Honour of His 75th Birthday, Oxford 1901, p 397.

General References. Bennett OHEL, pp 109, 161.

Baugh LHE, p 216.

Bloomfield SDS, p 224.

Woolf, pp 220, 335, 377.

McIntosh A, Some Notes on the Text of the ME Poem De Tribus Regibus Mortuis, RES 28 (1977).386.

Pearsall D, Old Eng and ME Poetry, London 1977, p 249.

Stevens J, Medieval Lyrics and Music, in B Ford, ed, Medieval Lit: Chaucer and the Alliterative Tradition, rvsd edn, Harmondsworth 1982, p 265.

[30] AN ABC OF DEVOCIONE.

MSS. 1, Bodl 11755 (Rawl B.408), ff 3ᵃ–6ᵇ (1400–50); 2, Bodl 21803 (Douce 229), f 8ᵃ (15 cent).

Brown-Robbins, nos 121, 664, 1069, 1283, 1324, 1340, 1557, 1600, 1972, 2316, 2702; Robbins-Cutler, no 664.

MSS Commentary. Summary Cat, 4.562 (MS 2).

Macray W D, Catalogi Codicum Manuscriptorum Bibliothecae Bodleianae, Oxford 1862, 5(1).665.

Editions. Clark A, The Eng Register of Godstow Nunnery, EETS 129, London 1905, p 4.

Patterson, pp 71, 108, 137.

MacCracken H N, John Lydgate: The Minor Poems, vol I, The Religious Poems, EETSES 107, London 1911 (for 1910), p 376.

Brown RLxvC, pp 73, 149.

Davies R T, Medieval Eng Lyrics, Evanston 1964, p 209.

[31] CURSOR MUNDI (or THE CURSOR O THE WORLD).

MSS. 1, Bodl 1479 (Laud misc 416), ff 65ᵃ–181ᵇ (ca 1450); 2, Bodl 3894 (Fairfax 14), ff 4ᵃ–109ᵇ (ca 1400); 3, Bodl 14667 (Rawl poet 175), ff 80ᵇ–93ᵃ (ca 1350); 4, Bodl 29003 (Add A.106), ff 15ᵇ–27ᵇ (1450–1500; Cato's Distichs); 5, Trinity Camb 588 (R.3.8), ff 1ᵃ–142ᵇ (1400–50); 6, BL Cotton Vespasian A.iii, ff 2ᵃ–162ᵃ (ca 1350); 7, BL Cotton Galba E.ix, ff 67ᵃ–75ᵃ (1400–25); 8, BL Addit 31042, ff 3ᵃ–32ᵇ (ca 1450); 9, BL Addit 36983, ff

1ᵃ–117ᵇ, 127ᵇ–174ᵇ (1442); 10, Coll of Arms London Arundel 57, ff 1ᵃ–175ᵇ (ca 1400); 11, Royal Coll of Physicians Edinburgh, ff 1ᵃ–50ᵇ (1300–50); 12, Göttingen Univ Theol 107, ff 2ᵃ–169ᵇ (ca 1400); 13, Wellesley de Ricci Census No 8, pp 3–12 (1450–1500; fragment of Book of Penance). A similar version of the Dialogue between Christ and Man is in 14, Hopton Hall (Chandos-Pole-Gell), pp 25–26 (1400–25). 56 lines from the Prologue to [31] are incorporated in four MSS of Prick of Conscience [18] with Wycliffite associations.

Brown-Robbins, Robbins-Cutler, nos 2153 (Cursor Mundi), 694 (Book of Penance), 780 (Prayer to the Trinity), 1885 (Conception), 3208 (Dialogue between Virgin and St Bernard). Brown-Robbins, nos 169 (Cato's Distichs), 788 (Exposition of the Pater Noster), 959 (Exposition of the Creed), 1029 (Song of the Five Joys of the Blessed Virgin), 1375 (an independent poem on the Creed incorporated in MS 3), 1775 (Hours of the Cross), 1786 (Dialogue between Christ and Man), 3976 (Assumption).

MSS Commentary. A Catalogue of the MSS in the Cottonian Libr Deposited in the British Museum, London 1802, pp 363 (MS 7), 433 (MS 6).

Black W H, Catalogue of the Arundel MSS in the Libr of the Coll of Arms, London 1829, p 101 (MS 10).

Coxe H O, Catalogi Codicum Manuscriptorum Bibliothecae Bodleianae, Oxford 1858, 2.305 (MS 1).

Catalogue of Additions to the MSS in the British Museum in the Years MDCCCLXXVI–MDCCCLXXXI, London 1882, p 148 (MS 8).

Historical MSS Commission, 9th Report of the Royal Commission on Historical MSS, Pt II, London 1883, appendix, p 384 (MS 14).

Hupe H, EETS 101 (see below under Morris edn), pp 59*, 124*.

Die Handschriften in Göttingen. II Universitäts-Bibliothek, Berlin 1893, p 353 (MS 12).

Summary Cat, 2.777 (MS 2); 3.321 (MS 3); 5.540 (MS 4).

James M R, The Western MSS in the Libr of Trinity Coll Cambridge A Descriptive Catalogue, Cambridge 1901, 2.55 (MS 5).

Hörning W, Die Schreibung der HS E des Cursor Mundi, Berlin 1906 (MS 11).

Catalogue of Additions to the MSS in the British Museum in the Years MDCCCC–MDCCCCV, London 1907, p 265 (MS 9).

Herbert, 3.307 (MS 9).

Brunner K, Hs Brit Mus Addit 31042, Arch 132(1914).316 (MS 8).

Allen WAR, pp 374, 380.

de Ricci Census, 1.1068 (MS 13).

Pace G B, Four Unpubl Chaucer MSS, MLN 63(1948).457 (MS 9).

Doyle Survey, 2.47.

Wright C E, Eng Vernacular Hands from the 12 to the 15 Cents, Oxford 1960, p 11 (with facing facsimile; MS 6).

Dareau M G and A McIntosh, A Dialect Word in Some West Midland MSS of the Pricke of Conscience, in A J Aitken, A McIntosh, and H Palsson, edd, Edinb Stud in Eng and Scots, London 1971, p 21 (MS 10).

Ker Manuscripts, 2.539 (MS 11).

Owen A E B, The Collation and Descent of the Thornton MS, Trans of the Cambridge Biblio Soc 6(1975).218 (MS 8).

Stern K, The London "Thornton" Miscellany. A New Description of British Museum Addit MS 31042, Scriptorium 30(1976).26, 201 (MS 8).

Guddat-Figge G, Catalogue of MSS Containing ME Romances, Munich 1976, pp 169 (MS 7), 159 (MS 8), 166 (MS 9).

Horrall S M, The London Thornton MS: A New Collation, Manuscripta 23(1979).99 (MS 8).

Lewis R E and A McIntosh, A Descriptive Guide to the MSS of the Prick of Conscience, Oxford 1982, pp 7 n18 (interpolations from [31] in MSS 7, 11, 72 and 80 of [18]), 128 (MS 13 of [31]).

Editions. Ellis H, Liber Censualis vocati Domesday Book, London 1811, 2.99 (Founding of the Feast of the Conception from MS 6).

Mancel G and G S Trebutien, L'Etablissement de la fête de la conception Notre-Dame dite la fête aux Normands, Caen 1842, p 90 (reprint of Ellis edn).

Small J, Eng Metrical Homilies from MSS of the 14 Cent, Edinburgh 1862, pp xiv (excerpts of Dialogue between Virgin and St Bernard), xv (Founding of the Feast of the Conception from MS 11).

Morris R, The Seven Deadly Sins, JfRESL 6 (1865).332 (from MS 6).

Furnivall F J, How Cato was a Paynym and a Christian too, N&Q 4s 2(1868).176 (excerpt from Cato's Distichs).

Morris R, Cursor Mundi, EETS 57, 59, 62, 66, 68, 99, 101, London 1874–93, rptd 1961–66 (parallel texts of MSS 6, 2, 12, and 5, with excerpts from MSS 1, 9, 10, 11).

Horstmann C, Canticum de Creatione, Angl 1 (1878).391 (A Song of the Five Joys of the Blessed Virgin from MS 12).

Brown RLxivC, pp 37 (A Prayer to the Trinity from MS 6), 39 (Hours of the Cross from MS 2), 44 (A Song of the Five Joys of the Blessed Virgin from MS 12).

Ross C C V, An Edn of Part of the Edinburgh Fragment of the Cursor Mundi, Oxford Univ thesis 1971 (MS 11).

Horrall S M, The Southern Version of Cursor Mundi, I, Ottawa 1978, p 33 (lines 1–9228; base text: MS 10 with variants from MSS 1, 5, 9); edn in progress.

Selections. Morris R and W W Skeat, edd, Specimens of Early Eng, 2nd edn, Oxford 1889, 2.69.

MacLean G E, Old and ME Reader, N Y 1893, p 91.

Emerson O F, ME Reader, London 1915, p 126.

Zupitza J, Alt- und Me Übungsbuch, 12th edn, Vienna and Leipzig 1922, p 84.

Sampson G, The Cambridge Book of Prose and Verse, Cambridge 1924, p 352.

Brandl A and O Zippel, ME Lit, 2nd edn, N Y 1949, p 100.

Dickens B and R M Wilson, edd, Early ME Texts, London 1951, p 115.

Baugh A C, A Hist of the Eng Lang, 2nd edn, N Y 1957, p 467.

Kaiser R, Medieval Eng, 3rd edn, Berlin 1958, p 222.

Bennett J A W and G V Smithers, Early ME Verse and Prose, Oxford 1966, p 184.

Fisiak J, An Early ME Reader, Warsaw 1969, p 32.

Fisher J H and D Bornstein, In Forme of Speeche is Chaunge: Readings in the Hist of the Eng Lang, Englewood Cliffs 1974, p 162.

Modernizations. MacLean, N Y 1922, p 91.

Adamson M R, A Treasury of ME Verse, London 1930, p 37.

Corrigan F X, ME Readings in Translation, Boston 1965, p 145.

Textual Matters. Hupe H, Genealogie und Überlieferung der Handschriften des me Gedichtes Cursor Mundi, Altenberg 1886 (crit M Kaluza, EStn 11.235 and 12.451; replies H Hupe, Angl 11.121 and AnglB 1.133).

Hupe, On the Filiation and the Text of the MSS of the ME Poem Cursor Mundi, EETS 101, pp 59*; Cursor Studies and Criticism on the Dialects of Its MSS, EETS 101, p 113*.

Bülbring K D, Zu den Handschriften von Richard Rolle's Pricke of Conscience, EStn 23(1897).24.

Kock E A, Interpretations and Emendations of Early Eng Texts, Angl 26(1903).365.

Menner R J, Two Notes on Medieval Euhemerism, Spec 3(1928).247 (Ninus and Nimrod).

Olszewska E S, ME Isked 'longed,' Leeds SE 6(1937).65.

Larsen H, Cursor Mundi 1291, in T A Kirby and H Bosley, edd, Philologica: The Malone Anniversary Studies, Baltimore 1949, p 164.

Lamberts J J, The Noah Story in Cursor Mundi (lines 1625–1916), MS 24(1962).217.

Language. Hupe, EETS 101, p 135*.

Bowen E W, The ie Sound in Accented Syllables, AJP 15(1894).58.

Barth C, Der Wortschatz des Cursor Mundi, Königsberg 1903.

Cox E G, The Pronominal Forms of the Cursor Mundi, diss Cornell Univ 1906.

Strandberg O, The Rime-Vowels of Cursor Mundi, Uppsala 1919.

Arend K M, Linking in Cursor Mundi, TPSL (1925–30).200.

Orton H, The Medial Development of ME ō₁ (tense), FR ü [= ÿ] and ME eu (OE ēow) in the Dialects of the North of England, EStn 63(1928–29).229.

Moore Meech and Whitehall, p 53.

Lindheim B von, Studien zur Sprache des Manuskriptes Cotton Galba E.ix, Wiener Beiträge zu engl Philologie 59(1937).

Kaiser R, Zur Geographie des me Wortschatzes, Palaes 205(1937).5.

Prins A A, French Influence on Eng Phrasing, Leiden 1952, pp 295, 297, 300.

Lamberts J J, The Dialect of Cursor Mundi (Cotton MS Vespasian A.iii), diss Univ of Mich 1953 (MS 6).

Fausboll E, A Study of the Phonology and Accidence of the Fairfax MS of Cursor Mundi, diss Univ of Manchester 1954 (MS 2).

McIntosh A, A New Approach to ME Dialectology, ESts 44(1963).6 (MS 5).

Kivimaa K, Bitwix and in Cursor Mundi, in Studies Presented to Tauno F Mustanoja on the Occasion of His 60th Birthday, NM 73(1972).134.

Snouffer E J, Verbal Syntax of Cursor Mundi (Cotton Vespasian A.iii), diss Univ of North Carolina 1972 (MS 6).

Murray J A H, The Dialect of the Southern Counties of Scotland, London 1873, p 30.

Versification. Hupe, EETS 101, p 253*.

Crow C L, Zur Geschichte des kurzen Reimpaars in me Harrowing of Hell, Cursor Mundi, Chaucer's House of Fame, Göttingen 1892, § 14.

Sources and Literary Relations. Reinsch R, Die Pseudoevangelium von Jesus und Marias Kindheit in der germanischen und romanischen Literatur, Halle 1879.

Haenisch H C, Inquiry into the Sources of the Cursor Mundi, Breslau 1884; EETS 101(1892).3* (omitted from 1962 reprint of this volume).

Cook A S, A Literary Motive Common to Old, Middle and Modern Eng, MLN 7(1892).270 (Christ's address to sinner).

Traver H, Four Daughters of God, Phila 1907, p 39.

Brown C, The Cursor Mundi and the Southern Passion, MLN 26(1911).15.

Gerould G H, Saints' Legends, Boston 1916, p 199, 213, 219.

D'Evelyn C, The ME Metrical Versions of the Revelations of Methodius, PMLA 33(1918).147.

Durrschmidt H, Die Sage von Kain in der Mittelalterlichen Literatur Englands, Bayreuth 1919, p 91.

Lyle M C, The Original Identity of the York and Towneley Cycles, Minneapolis 1919 (parallels between [31] and cycle plays).

Bonnell J K, Cain's Jaw Bone, PMLA 39(1924).140.

Cooke J D, Euhemerism: A Medieval Interpretation of Classical Paganism, Spec 2(1927).405.

Emerson O F, Legends of Cain, Especially in Old and ME, PMLA 43(1928).79.

Faverty F E, Legends of Joseph in Old and ME, PMLA 43(1928).79.

Borland L, The Cursor Mundi and Herman's Bible, diss Univ of Chicago 1929; Herman's Bible and the Cursor Mundi, SP 30(1933).427.

Cornelius R D, The Figurative Castle, Bryn Mawr 1930, p 46.

Os A B van, Religious Visions, Amsterdam 1932, pp 149, 166.

Coffman G, Old Age from Horace to Chaucer. Some Literary Affinities and Adventures of an Idea, Spec 9(1934).249.

McGarry L, The Holy Eucharist in ME Homiletic and Devotional Verse, Washington D C 1936, pp 58, 109.

Pfander H G, The Popular Sermon of the Medieval Friar in England, N Y 1937, p 25.

Creek M, The Sources and Influence of the Chasteau d'Amour, diss Yale Univ 1941, p 222.

Whiting C E, Cursor Mundi, Yorkshire Archaeological Journ 36(1944–47).297.

Chew S C, The Virtues Reconciled, Toronto 1947, p 38 (Cursor Mundi and Four Daughters of God).

Whiting B J, Notes on the Fragmentary Fairfax Version of The Disticha Catonis, MS 10(1948). 212.

Larsen H, Origo Crucis, in If by Your Art: Testament to Percival Hunt, Lancaster 1948, p 27 (comparison of true cross in Cursor Mundi with that in Old Norse Hausbok).

Beichner P E, The Cursor Mundi and Petrus Riga, Spec 24(1949).239 (use of Riga's De quattuor Evangelistarum proprietatibus).

Douie D L, Archbishop Pecham, Oxford 1952, p 140.

Wenzel S, Sloth in ME Eng Devotional Lit, Angl 79(1961).290, 303, 308.

Quinn E C, The Quest of Seth for the Oil of Life, Chicago 1962, pp 2, 133.

Buehler P, The Cursor Mundi and Herman's Bible—Some Additional Parallels, SP 61(1964).485.

Kolve V A, The Play Called Corpus Christi, Stanford 1966, pp 9, 17, 84, 91, 126, 176, 177, 218.

Sajavaara K, The Use of Robert Grosseteste's Chateau d'Amour as a Source of the Cursor Mundi, NM 68(1967).184.

Woolf, pp 2, 103 n9, 141, 147, 235, 248.

Mardon E G, The Finding of the Cross Episode in the Cursor Mundi, Eglise et Théologie 1 (1970).83.

Kelly H A, The Metamorphoses of the Eden Serpent during the Middle Ages and Renaissance, Viator 2(1971).301.

Goodring J M, Some Vernacular Sources for the ME Mystery Cycles, diss Univ of London 1973, pp 15, 276 (influence of [31] on four cycles).

Doob P, Nebuchadnezzar's Children, New Haven and London 1974, pp 103, 160, 189, 195.

Tristram P, Figures of Life and Death in Medieval Eng Lit, N Y 1976, pp 57, 63, 142.

Fowler D C, The Bible in Early Eng Lit, Seattle 1976, p 165.

Jones C E, Cursor Mundi and Post Peccatum Adae: A Study of Textual Relationships, diss Florida Univ 1976.

Horrall S M, The Cursor Mundi Creation Story and Hugh of St Victor, N&Q ns 23(1976).99; An Old French Source for the Genesis Section of Cursor Mundi, MS 40(1978).361; 'A Schippe Behoves þe to Dight': Woven Arks of Noah in the 14 Cent, Proceedings of the 6th Annual Symposium of the Ottawa-Carleton Medieval Renaissance Club, Ottawa 1978 (not seen).

Patterson L W, The Parson's Tale and the Quitting of The Canterbury Tales, Trad 34(1978).339, 340, 345 (Book of Penance).

Horrall S M, An Unknown ME Trans of the Distichs of Cato, Angl 99(1981).25 (Bodl MS Eng misc C.291; independent of MS 2).

Lewis and McIntosh, as above, p 7 n18 (notes a treatise in reproof of worldliness in the clergy [Brown-Robbins, no 1425] is partially based on [31]).

Bitterling K, William Dunbar's The Maner of Passyng to Confession and the Circumstances of the Medieval Confession, N&Q ns 30(1983).390.

Horrall, William Caxton's Biblical Trans, MÆ 53(1984).91 (Caxton's use of [31] in Golden Legend).

Other Scholarly Problems. Heather P J, Seven Planets, Folklore 54(1943).357, 358, 361.

Heist W W, The Fifteen Signs before Doomsday, East Lansing 1952, pp 30, 31, 32, 38, 48, 179, 199, 201.

Bonfield J P M, The Penitence of the Medieval Magdalen: A Study in the Meanings of Her Appelation "Penitent" as Reflected in Vernacular Lit of the British Isles c 1250–c 1500, diss Univ of Texas 1969.

Literary Criticism. Mardon E G, The Narrative Unity of the Cursor Mundi, Glasgow 1970.

Crepin A, Tradition et innovation: Contexture de la poèsie vieil-anglaise in Tradition et innovation, littérature et paralittérature, Actes du Congrès de Nancy (1972), Paris 1975, p 25.

Boitani P, Eng Medieval Narrative in the 13 and 14 Cents, Cambridge 1982 p 5.

General References. Ten Brink, 1.287.

Morley, 4.121.

Brandl, § 60, p 649.

Schofield, p 375.

CHEL, 1.381.

Körting, § 125, p 130.

Mosher J A, The Exemplum in the Early Religious and Didactic Lit of England, N Y 1911, p 92.

Deanesly M, The Lollard Bible and Other Medieval Biblical Versions, Cambridge 1920, p 147.

Amos F R, Early Theories of Translation, N Y 1920, p 10.

Thomas P G, Eng Lit before Chaucer, London 1924, pp 58, 67, 110, 114.

Owst G R, Preaching in Medieval England, Cambridge 1926, p 277; Literature and Pulpit in Medieval England, Cambridge 1933, pp 91, 114, 196, 474, 476.

Legouis HEL, p 82.

Wilson EMEL, pp 181, 235.

Renwick-Orton p 278.

Baugh LHE, p 206.

Pecheux M C, Aspects of the Treatment of Death in ME Poetry, Washington D C 1951, pp 13, 40, 93, 97, 100, 114, 136.

Bloomfield SDS, pp 141, 175, 353.

Schlauch M, Eng Medieval Lit and Its Social Foundations, Warsaw 1956, p 193.

Wenzel, pp 84, 86, 140, 167, 230, 236, 245.

Ackerman R W, Backgrounds to Medieval Eng Lit, N Y 1966, p 101.

Turville-Petre T, The Alliterative Revival, Cambridge 1977, p 74.

Pearsall D, Old Eng and ME Poetry, London 1977, pp 106, 253.

Brewer D, Eng Gothic Lit, N Y 1983, p 38.

Bibliography. Booker J M, A ME Biblio, Heidelberg 1912, p 7.

New CBEL, 1.500.

2. Translations, Paraphrases, and Expositions of the Individual Elements of the Faith

i. Pater Noster

[32] PATER NOSTER.

MSS. Verse: Version A: 1, Nat Libr of Scotland Advocates 18.7.21, f 95ᵃ (1372); *Version B*: 2, Salisbury Cath 82, f 271ᵇ (1250–1300); *Version C*: 3, Edinburgh Univ 205 (Laing 149), f 87ᵃ (1477); *Version D*: 4, Bibl Univ Pavia 69, f 41ᵇ (13 cent); *Version E*: 5, Camb Univ Ee.1.12, f 61ᵇ (1475–1500; Pater Noster and Ave Maria in a single poem).
Prose: Version A: 6, BL Cotton Vitellius A.xii, f 184ᵇ (1175–1200); *Version B*: 7, Fairfax-Blakeborough, f 1ᵃ (1339).

Brown-Robbins, nos 2535, 2704, 2708, 2710; Robbins-Cutler, no 2704.

MSS Commentary. A Catalogue of the MSS in the Cottonian Libr Deposited in the British Museum, London 1802, p 379 (MS 6).

A Catalogue of the MSS Preserved in the Libr of the Univ of Cambridge, Cambridge 1857, 2.11 (MS 5).

A Catalogue of the Libr of the Cathedral Church of Salisbury, London 1880, p 17 (MS 2).

Borland C R, A Descriptive Catalogue of the Western Mediaeval MSS in Edinburgh Univ Libr, Edinburgh 1916, p 291 (MS 3).

Ker N R, Catalogue of MSS Containing Anglo-Saxon, Oxford 1957, p 279 (MS 6).

Editions. Rel Ant, 1.204 (MS 7).

Thomson E M, Scraps from ME MSS, EStn 1(1877).215 (MS 2).

Zupitza J, Die Gedichte des Franziskaners Jakob Ryman, Arch 89(1982).247 (MS 5).

Onions C T, A 13-Cent Paternoster by an Anglo-French Scribe, MLR 3(1907).69 (MS 2).

Stevenson G, Pieces from the Makculloch and the Gray MSS, PSTS 65, Edinburgh 1918, p 117 (MS 3).

Fairfax-Blakeborough J, Fountains Abbey Parchments, N&Q 12s 10(1922).128 (MS 7).

Morey A, Bartholomew of Exeter, Bishop and Canonist, Cambridge 1937, p 300 (MS 6).

Thompson S H, A xiiith Cent Oure Fader in a Pavia MS, MLN 49(1934).235 (MS 4).

Brown RLxvC, p 84 (MS 3).

Hussey M, The Petitions of the Pater Noster in Medieval Eng Lit, MÆ 27(1958).10 (MS 4).

Person H A, Cambridge ME Lyrics, rvsd edn, N Y 1969, p 27 (Emmanuel Coll 27 version of MS 4 text).

Wilson E, A Descriptive Index of the Eng Lyrics in John of Grimestone's Preaching Book, Oxford 1973, p 29 (MS 1).

Modernization. Adamson M R, A Treasury of ME Verse, London 1930, p 128 (MS 3).

General Discussion. Thurston H, Familiar Prayers Their Origin and History, London 1953, p 22.

[33] STANDARD EXPOSITION OF
THE PATER NOSTER.

MSS. 1, Bodl 2643 (Bodley 789), ff 97ª–102ᵇ (1400–50); 2, Camb Univ Dd.12.39, ff 72ª–74ᵇ (1475–1500); 3, BL Harley 2385, ff 1ª–4ᵇ (1400–25); 4, BL Addit 17013, f 36ᵃ⁻ᵇ (1400–25); 5, Lambeth Palace 408, ff 1ᵇ–2ᵇ (1400–50); 6, York Minster 16.L.12, ff 32ª–36ᵇ (1400–25); 7, Trinity Dublin 69, ff 79ª–83ᵇ (ca 1400); 8, Bibliothèque Ste Geneviève Paris 3390, ff 27ª–30ᵇ (1400–25). A copy of it is found incorporated in BL Addit 10053, which is MS 8 of the Sacerdos Parochialis; see [22] above.

MSS Commentary. A Catalogue of the Harleian MSS in the British Museum, London 1808, 2.676 (MS 3).

A Catalogue of the MSS Preserved in the Libr of the Univ of Cambridge, Cambridge 1856, 1.489 (MS 2).

Catalogue of Additions to the MSS in the British Museum in the Years MDCCCXLVI–MDCCCXLVII, London 1864, p 347 (MS 4).

Summary Cat, 2.467 (MS 1).

Abbott T K, Catalogue of the MSS in the Libr of Trinity Coll Dublin, Dublin 1900, p 9 (MS 7).

Cumming W P, A ME MS in the Bibliothèque Ste Geneviève, Paris, PMLA 42(1927).862 (MS 8).

James M R and C Jenkins, A Descriptive Catalogue of the MSS in the Libr of Lambeth Palace, Cambridge 1932, p 561 (MS 5).

Editions. Arnold T, Select Eng Works of John Wyclif, Oxford 1871, 3.93 (MS 1).

Simmons T F and H E Nolloth, Lay Folks Catechism, EETS 118, London 1901, p 7 (MS 5 with variants from MS 6).

Francis W N, The Book of Vices and Virtues, EETS 217, London 1942, p 336 (MS 4).

General Discussion. Kellogg A L and E W Talbert, The Wycliffite Pater Noster and Ten Commandments, with Special Reference to Eng MSS 85 and 90 in the John Rylands Libr, JRLB 42(1960).345 (defend orthodoxy of treatise).

[34] TRACT IN HARLEY AND
NORWICH CASTLE MUSEUM.

MSS. 1, BL Harley 1197, ff 28ᵇ–48ᵇ (1425–50); 2, Castle Museum Norwich 158.926.4g.5, ff 58ᵇ–88ª (1400–50).

Jolliffe, p 128, no M.9.

MSS Commentary. A Catalogue of the Harleian MSS in the British Museum, London 1808, 1.595 (MS 1).

Ker Manuscripts, 3.523 (MS 2).

[35] THE PATER NOSTER OF
RICHARD ERMYTE.

MSS. 1, Bodl 1244 (Laud Misc 104), ff 22ª–42ª (ca 1450); 2, Camb Univ Ii.6.40, ff 95ª–191ª (1450–1500); 3, Trinitiy Camb 1053 (0.1.29), ff 18ª–66ᵇ (1400–50); 4, Sidney Sussex Camb 74, ff 143ª–167ᵇ (1400–25); 5, Westminster School 3, ff 1ª–76ᵇ (1400–25); 6, Durham Cath A.iv.22, ff 1ª–97ᵇ (1400–25).

Jolliffe, p 127, no M.4.

MSS Commentary. Rud T, Codicum Manuscriptorum Cathedralis Dunelmensis Catalogus Classicus, ed J Raine, Durham 1825, p 72 (MS 6).

A Catalogue of the MSS Preserved in the Libr of the Univ of Cambridge, Cambridge 1858, 3.538 (MS 2).

Coxe H O, Catalogi Codicum Manuscriptorum Bibliothecae Bodleianae, Oxford 1858, 1.65 (MS 1).

James M R, A Descriptive Catalogue of the MSS in the Libr of Sidney Sussex Cambrdige, Cambridge 1895, p 52 (MS 4); The Western MSS in the Libr of Trinity Coll Cambridge, A Descriptive Catalogue, Cambridge 1902, 3.33 (MS 3).

Allen WAR, p 358 (MS 5).

Ker Manuscripts, 1.422 (MS 5).

Editions. Aarts F G A M, The Pater Noster of Richard Ermyte, The Hague 1967, p 3; and see Introd, pp xi (description of the MSS), xx (relationship of the MSS and the choice of MS 5 as the basic text), xxviii (language), lxxxii (literary background, including author and style, audience and purpose, composition and sources), cii (the Pater Noster in medieval Eng lit) (crit T P Dunning, SN 41.465; J J Vaissier, Levende Talen 248.375; J Simon, EA 1.87; G C Britton, YWES 48.84).

Authorship. Allen WAR, p 155 (rejects Rolle's authorship).

Literary Relations. Hussey M, The Petitions of the Pater Noster in Medieval Eng Lit, MÆ 27(1958).8.

Aarts, The Pater Noster in Medieval Eng Lit, Papers on Lang and Lit 5(1969).3.

Bibliography. Doyle Survey, 1.90.

Barratt A, Works of Religious Instruction, in A S G Edwards ed, ME Prose, New Brunswick 1984, p 420.

[36] THE MIRROR OF SAINT EDMUND AND OTHER SHORT VERSIONS.

MSS. Verse: Version A: 1, Bodl 21715 (Douce 141), ff 130ᵃ–138ᵃ (1400–25); 2, Camb Univ Dd.11.89, ff 186ᵃ–196ᵃ (ca 1400); *Version B*: 3, Bodl 30314 (Add E.6), a roll (verso) (1250–1300); *Version C*: 4, St John's Camb 28, ff 39ᵃ–41ᵇ (1375–1400); 5, Trinity Camb 605 (R.3.25), f 270ᵃ⁻ᵇ (1400–25); *Version D*: 6, Lambeth Palace 487, ff 21ᵇ–24ᵇ (ca 1200).
Prose: Version A (Mirror of Saint Edmund): 7, Bodl 3657 (e Mus 232), ff 44ᵃ–45ᵇ (1400–25); 8, Queen's Oxford 324, ff 78ᵇ–81ᵇ (1400–25); 9, Camb Univ Ii.6.43, ff 16ᵃ–18ᵇ (1400–25); 10, BL Harley 665, ff 296ᵇ–297ᵇ (1475–1500); 11, BL Harley 2398, ff 153ᵃ–155ᵇ (1400–25); 12, BL Addit 60577, ff 141ᵃ–145ᵃ (1475–1550); *Version B*: 13, Univ Oxford 97, ff 123ᵇ–124ᵇ (1400–25); 14, BL Addit 22283, ff 101ᵃ⁻ᵇ (1380–1400); *Version C*: 15, Bodl 2643 (Bodley 789), ff 150ᵃ–152ᵃ (1400–50); *Version D*: 16, Camb Univ Ff.6.33, ff 31ᵇ–32ᵇ (ca 1500); *Version E*: 17, Camb Univ Kk.1.3, article 9 (16 cent); *Version F*: 18, Magdalene Camb Pepys 2125, ff 119ᵃ–123ᵇ (ca 1450); *Version G*: 19, Sidney Sussex Camb 55, ff 50ᵃ–51ᵇ (ca 1450); *Version H*: 20, BL Burney 30, ff 86ᵃ–105ᵃ (1400–25); *Version I*: 21, Lincoln Cath 91, ff 209ᵇ–211ᵇ (ca 1440); *Version J*: 22, St Cuthbert's Coll Ushaw 28, ff 16ᵇ–21ᵃ (ca 1450); *Version K*: 23, Camb Univ Ff.6.33, ff 27ᵃ–31ᵇ (ca 1500).
Brown-Robbins, nos 958, 1904, 2707, 2709; Robbins-Cutler, nos 958, 1904.
MSS Commentary. A Catalogue of the Harleian MSS in the British Museum, London 1808, 1.400 (MS 11); 2.684 (MS 12).
Catalogue of MSS in the British Museum ns I, Pt 2: The Burney MSS, London 1840, p 30 (MS 21).
Coxe H O, Catalogus Codicum MSS qui in Collegiis Aulisque Oxoniensibus Hodie Adservantur, Oxford 1852, 1.28 (MS 14), 77 (MS 8).
A Catalogue of the MSS Preserved in the Libr of the Univ of Cambridge, Cambridge 1856, 1.481 (MS 2); 2(1857).34 (MSS 9, 17; both in Camb Univ Ff.6.33); 3(1858).540 (MS 10), 551 (MS 18).
Catalogue of Additions to the MSS in the British Museum in the Years MDCCCLIV–MDCCCLX, London 1875, p 623 (MS 15).
James M R, A Descriptive Catalogue of the MSS in the Libr of Sidney Sussex Coll Cambridge, Cambridge 1895, p 39 (MS 20).

Summary Cat, 2.467 (MS 16), 722 (MS 7); 4.535 (MS 1), 585 (Douce 302); 5.786 (MS 3).
James M R, The Western MSS in the Libr of Trinity Coll Cambridge A Descriptive Catalogue, Cambridge 1901, 2.97 (MS 5); A Descriptive Catalogue of the MSS in the Libr of St John's Coll Cambridge, Cambridge 1913, p 37 (MS 4); A Descriptive Catalogue of the Libr of Samuel Pepys, Pt III, Medieval MSS, London 1923, p 72 (MS 19).
Wooley R M, Catalogue of the MSS of Lincoln Cathedral Chap Libr, Oxford 1927, p 149 (MS 22).
James M R and C Jenkins, A Descriptive Catalogue of the MSS in the Libr of Lambeth Palace, Cambridge 1932, p 673 (MS 6).
Owen A E B, The Collation and Descent of the Thornton MS, Trans of the Cambridge Biblio Soc 6(1975).218 (MS 22).
Guddat-Figge G, Catalogue of MSS Containing ME Romances, Munich 1976, p 135 (MS 22), 145 (MS 15).
Doyle A I, Univ Coll Oxford MS 97 and Its Relationship to the Simeon MS (BL Add 22283), in M Benskin and M L Samuels, edd, Philological Essays in Scots and Mediaeval Eng Presented to Angus McIntosh, Edinburgh 1981, p 265 (MSS 14, 15).
Editions. Morris R, Old Eng Homilies and Homiletic Treatises, First Series, EETS 29, London 1858, p 55 (MS 6).
Yksh Wr, 1.261 (MS 22).
Patterson F A, A Sermon on the Lord's Prayer, JEGP 15(1916).406 (MS 2).
Pfander H G, The Popular Sermon of the Medieval Friar, N Y 1937, p 41 (MS 3).
Francis W N, The Book of Vices and Virtues, EETS 217, London 1942, p 334 (MS 15).
Facsimile. The Thornton MS (Lincoln Cath MS 91), introd by D S Brewer and A E N Owen, London 1975 (MS 22).
The Winchester Anthology, with an introd by E Wilson and I Fenlon, Woodbridge 1981 (MS 13).
Sources and Literary Relations. Hussey M, The Petitions of the Paternoster in Mediaeval Eng Lit, MÆ 27(1958).8.
Bibliography. Booker J M, A ME Biblio, Heidelberg 1912, p 30.

ii. Ave Maria

[37] THE AVE MARIA.

MSS. Version A: 1, Camb Univ Addit 5943, f 168ᵃ (1400–25); *Version B*: 2, Camb Univ Gg.4.32, f 15ᵇ (14 cent); 3, Emmanuel Camb 27, f 162ᵃ (15 cent);

4, Cotton Cleopatra B.vi, f 204[b] (14 cent); *Version C*: 5, BL Royal 17.A.xvi, ff 3[a]–4[b] (1475–1500); *Version D*: 6, Camb Univ Gg.4.32, f 13[a] (14 cent); *Version E*: 7, Edinburgh Univ 205, f 87[a] (1477); *Version F*: 8, Camb Univ Hh.6.11, f 70[b] (14 cent); *Version G*: 9, BL Arundel 292, f 3[b] (1400–25).

Brown-Robbins, nos 453, 1062, 1063, 1064, 1065, 1067, 2100; Robbins-Cutler, nos 1062, 1064, 2100.

MSS Commentary. A Catalogue of the MSS in the Cottonian Libr Deposited in the British Museum, London 1802, p 578 (MS 4).

Catalogue of MSS in the British Museum ns I, Pt I: The Arundel MSS, London 1840, p 86 (MS 9).

A Catalogue of the MSS Preserved in the Libr of the Univ of Cambridge, Cambridge 1858, 3.117 (MSS 2, 6; both in Camb Univ Gg.4.32), 305 (MS 8).

James M R, The Western MSS in the Libr of Emmanuel Coll A Descriptive Catalogue, Cambridge 1904, p 22 (MS 3).

Borland C R, A Descriptive Catalogue of the Western Mediaeval MSS in Edinb Univ Libr, Edinburgh 1916, p 291 (MS 7).

Warner G F and J P Gilson, Catalogue of Western MSS in the Old Royal and King's Collections, London 1921, 2.217 (MS 5).

Editions. Haupt M and A H Hoffmann, Altdeutsche Blätter, Leipzig 1840, 2.142 (Version G).

Rel Ant, 1.22 (Version B: MS 4), 169 (Version F), 235 (Version G).

Mätzner E, Ae Sprachproben, I. Poesie, Berlin 1867, p 50 (Version G).

Ellis A J, On Early Eng Pronunciation, EETSES 7, London 1869, pp 442 (Version B: MS 4), 444 (Version G); On Early Eng Pronunciation, ChS 2s 4.443 (Version B: MS 4), 444 (Version G).

Heuser W, Ave Maria, Angl 27(1904).325 (Version B: MS 2).

Mayers L S, Music, Cantilenas and Songs, London 1906, nos 14, 15 (Version A).

Garrett R M, Religious Verses from MS Arundel 292, Arch 128(1912).368 (Version G).

Stevenson G, Pieces from the Makculloch and the Gray MSS, PSTS 65, Edinburgh 1918, p 18 (Version E).

Brown RLxivC, p 230 (Version B: MS 2).

Person H A, Cambridge ME Lyrics, rvsd edn, N Y 1969, pp 14 (Version D), 27 (Version B: MS 3).

Literary Relations. Woolf, pp 117, 120, 377.

iii. Creed

[38] CREED.

MSS. Apostles' Creed: Verse: 1, Bodl 3692 (e Mus 160), f 139[a] (1500–25); 2, Bodl 13679 (Rawl D.913), ff 7[a]–8[b] (1400–25); 3, Bodl 14667 (Rawl Poet 175), f 84[a] (ca 1350; a unique version of [38] incorporated in one MS of the Book of Penance from Cursor Mundi [31]); 4, Camb Univ Gg.4.32, f 21[b] (14 cent); 5, BL Arundel 292, f 3[a] (1400–25); 6, Lambeth Palace 853, pp 39–41 (1400–50); 7, Edinburgh Univ 205, f 87[b] (1477).

Prose: 8, Bodl 21820 (Douce 246), f 3[b] (1400–50); 9, Camb Univ Ff.2.38, f 33[a–b] (ca 1450; from St Edmund's Speculum Ecclesiae); 10, Camb Univ Gg.4.12, f 12[a] (15 cent); 11, Emmanuel Camb 27, f 162[a] (13 cent); 12, St John's Camb 121, ff 65[a]–67[b] (14 cent); 13, BL Addit 60577, ff 139[a]–141[a] (1475–1550; from St Edmund's Speculum Ecclesiae); 14, BL Arundel 292, f 49[a] (1400–25); 15, BL Cotton Nero A.xiv, f 131[a] (13 cent); 16, BL Harley 3724, f 49[a] (1300–50); 17, BL Harley 6580, ff 64[b]–66[a] (1475–1500); 18, Edinburgh Univ 93, ff 80[b]–81[b] (1430–50; from St Edmund's Speculum Ecclesiae); 19, Glasgow Univ Hunter 512, ff 26[b]–28[a] (1400–25); 20, Blickling Hall, f 35[a] (1250–1300).

MSS. Athanasian Creed: Verse: 21, Bodl 2325 (Bodley 425), f 69[b] (ca 1350).

Prose: 22, BL Addit 36683, ff 173[a]–175[a] (1400–25); 23, Univ Oxford 179, f 96[a–b] (1400–25); 24, Trinity Dublin 70, ff 171[a]–173[b] (15 cent); 25, Trinity Dublin 195, ff 105[b]–107[b] (1400–50).

MS. Nicene Creed: Prose: 26, SC 5232 (Junius 121), f vi (13 cent).

Brown-Robbins, nos 934, 1282, 1285, 1326, 1375, 1376, 1570, 4147; Robbins-Cutler, no 1326.

MSS Commentary. A Catalogue of the MSS in the Cottonian Libr Deposited in the British Museum, London 1802, p 205 (MS 15).

A Catalogue of the Harleian MSS in the British Museum, London 1808, 3.55 (MS 16), 377 (MS 17).

Catalogue of MSS in the British Museum ns I, Pt I: The Arundel MSS, London 1840, p 86 (MS 14).

Macray W D, Catalogi Codicum Manuscriptorum Bibliothecae Bodleianae, Oxford 1898, 5(4).136 (MS 2).

Coxe H O, Catalogus Codicum MSS qui in Collegiis Aulisque Oxoniensibus Hodie Adservantur, Oxford 1852, 1.49 (MS 23).

A Catalogue of the MSS Preserved in the Libr of the Univ of Cambridge, Cambridge 1857, 2.404 (MS 9); 3(1858).152 (MS 10), 177 (MS 4).

Summary Cat, 2.310 (MS 21), 732 (MS 1), 989 (MS 26); 3.321 (MS 3); 4.566 (MS 8).

Abbott T K, Catalogue of the MSS in the Libr of Trinity Coll Dublin, Dublin 1900, pp 9 (MS 24), 27 (MS 25).

James M R, The Western MSS in the Libr of Emmanuel Coll A Descriptive Catalogue, Cambridge 1904, p 22 (MS 11).

Borland C R, A Descriptive Catalogue of the Western Mediaeval MSS in Edinb Univ Libr, Edinburgh 1906, pp 149 (MS 18), 291 (MS 7).

Catalogue of Additions to the MSS in the British Museum in the Years MDCCCC–MDCCCCV, London 1907, p 189 (MS 22).

Young J and P H Aitken, A Catalogue of the MSS in the Hunterian Museum in the Univ of Glasgow, Glasgow 1908, p 419 (MS 19).

James M R, A Descriptive Catalogue of the MSS in the Libr of St John's Coll Cambridge, Cambridge 1913, p 155 (MS 12).

James M R and C Jenkins, A Descriptive Catalogue of the MSS in the Libr of Lambeth Palace, Cambridge 1932, p 809 (MS 6).

Ker N R, Catalogue of MSS Containing Anglo-Saxon, Oxford 1957, p 412 (MS 26).

Editions. Hickes G, Linguarum Veterum Septentrionalium Thesaurus Grammatico-Criticus et Archaeologicus, Oxford 1705, 1.233 (MS 21).

Haupt M and A H Hoffmann, Altdeutsche Blätter, Leipzig 1836, 2.141 (MSS 5, 14; both in Arundel 292).

Rel Ant, 1.160 (MS 4), 234 (MSS 5, 14; both in Arundel 292).

Heurtly C A, Harmonia Symbolica, Oxford 1858, pp 93 (MS 15), 95 (MS 16), 163 (MS 26).

AESpr, 1.49 (MSS 5, 14; both in Arundel 292).

Furnivall F J, Hymns to the Virgin and Christ, EETS 24, London 1867 (rptd 1973), p 101 (MS 6).

Morris R, Old Eng Homilies and Treatises, 1s, EETS 29, London 1868, p 217 (MS 15).

Ellis A E, Early Eng Pronunciation, EETSES 7, London 1869, p 444 (MSS 5, 14; both in Arundel 292); On Early Eng Pronunciation, ChS 2s 4, London 1869, p 444 (MSS 5, 14; both in Arundel 292).

Zupitza J, Das Nicaeische Symbolum in engl Aufzeichnung Des 12 Jhds, Angl 1(1878).286 (MS 26).

Maskell, 3.304 (MS 8).

Maskell W, The Ancient Liturgy of the Church of England, 3rd edn, Oxford 1882, p 16 (MS 8).

Napier A S, Odds and Ends, MLN 4(1889).276 (MS 20).

Heuser W, Eine Vergessene Handschrift des Surtuspsalter, Angl 29(1906).405 (MS 21).

Garrett R M, Religious Verses from MS Arundel 292, Arch 128(1912).367 (MSS 5, 14).

Stevenson G, Pieces from the Makculloch and the Gray MSS, PSTS 65, Edinburgh 1918, p 19 (MS 7).

Crawford S J, The Worcester Marks and Glosses of the Old Eng MSS in the Bodleian, Together with the Worcester Version of the Nicene Creed, Angl 52(1928).5 (MS 26).

Martin C A, Edinb Univ Libr 93: An Annotated Edn of Selected Devotional Treatises, diss Univ of Edinburgh 1978 (MS 18).

Facsimile. The Winchester Anthology, with an Introd by E Wilson and I Fenlon, Woodbridge 1981 (MS 14).

Modernization. Adamson M R, A Treasury of ME Verse, London 1930, p 128 (MS 7).

Bibliography. Booker J M, A ME Biblio, Heidelberg 1912, p 7.

[39] HOW JUDICARE CAME
INTO THE CREED.

MS. Lambeth Palace 491, Pt 2, f 295^a (1475–1500).
Brown-Robbins, no *30; Robbins-Cutler, no 851.6.

MS Commentary. James M R and C Jenkins, A Descriptive Catalogue of the MSS in the Libr of Lambeth Palace, Cambridge 1932, p 681.

Editions. Bülbring K, Über die Handschrift Nr. 491 der Lambeth-Bibliothek, Arch 86(1891).387.

Utley F L, How Judicare Came in the Creed, MS 8(1946).304.

General Reference. Bloomfield SDS, p 204.

[40] HOW THE APOSTLES
MADE THE CREED.

MSS. Verse: 1, Corpus Christi Oxford 155, f 250$^{a–b}$ (1425–50); 2, BL Addit 39996, ff 51^b–52^b (ca 1450); 3, BL Addit 32578, ff 104^a–105^b (1405); 4, Shrewsbury School 3, ff 45^b–46^b (1484).
Prose: 5, Bodl 1699 (Digby 98), f 255^b (1400–25); 6, Bodl 4127 (Hatton 12), f 211^b (1375–1400); 7, Bodl 8193 (Ashmole 751), f 85^b (1375–1400); 8, Camb Univ Dd.14.26(3), ff 40^a–41^a (ca 1450); 9, Camb Univ Ff.6.33, ff 32^b–33^b (ca 1500); 10, Camb Univ Gg.4.32, f 21^a (14 cent); 11, Trinity Camb 337 (B.14.54), ff 1^a–33^b (15 cent); 12, Trinity Camb 601 (R.3.21), f 1$^{a–b}$ (1475–1500; Apostles listed in margin); 13, Trinity Camb 987 (R.17.1), ff 281^b–282^a (12 cent); 14, BL Burney 30, ff 105^a–106^a (1400–25); 15, BL Harley 2403, ff 191^b–194^a (1475–1500); 16, BL Harley 3724, f 49^b (1300–50); 17, Lambeth Palace 487, ff 25^b–27^a (ca 1200); 18, Lincoln Cath 66, f 137^a (15 cent); 19, St Cuthbert's Coll Ushaw 28, ff 22^a–23^a

(ca 1450); 20, Norwich Castle Mus 158.926/4.g.3, ff 78ᵇ–82ᵇ (ca 1450; possibly identical with MS 11).

Brown-Robbins, nos 311, 1374, 2700; Robbins-Cutler, nos 311, 1374, 2700, 662.5.

MSS Commentary. A Catalogue of the Harleian MSS in the British Museum, London 1808, 2.686 (MS 15); 3.55 (MS 16).

Catalogue of MSS in the British Museum ns I, Pt 2: The Burney MSS, London 1840, p 30 (MS 14).

Black W H, A Descriptive, Analytical, and Critical Catalogue of the MSS Bequeathed unto the Univ of Oxford by Elias Ashmole, Oxford 1845, p 362 (MS 7).

Coxe H O, Catalogi Codicum MSS qui in Collegiis Aulisque Oxoniensibus Hodie Adservantur, Oxford 1852, 2.63 (MS 1).

A Catalogue of the MSS Preserved in the Libr of the Univ of Cambridge, Cambridge 1856, 1.530 (MS 8); 2(1857).534 (MS 9); 3(1858).177 (MS 10).

Macray W D, Catalogi Codicum Manuscriptorum Bibliothecae Bodleianae, Oxford 1883, 9.108 (MS 5).

Catalogue of Additions to the MSS in the British Museum in the Years MDCCCLXXXII–MDCCCLXXXVII, London 1889, p 157 (MS 3).

Summary Cat, 2.855 (MS 6).

James M R, The Western MSS in the Libr of Trinity Coll Cambridge A Descriptive Catalogue, Cambridge 1900, 1.463 (MS 11); 2(1901).83 (MS 12); 987 (MS 13).

Wooley R M, Catalogue of the MSS of Lincoln Cathedral Chap Libr, Oxford 1927, p 35 (MS 18).

James M R and C Jenkins, A Descriptive Catalogue of the MSS in the Libr of Lambeth Palace, Cambridge 1932, p 673 (MS 17).

British Museum: Catalogue of Additions to the MSS 1916–1920, London 1933, p 272 (MS 2).

Wakelin M F, The MSS of John Mirk's Festial, Leeds SE 1(1967).97 (MS 15).

Ker Manuscripts, 3.521 (MS 20).

Editions. Morris R, Old Eng Homilies and Treatises, 1s, EETS 29, London 1868, p 72 (MS 17).

Calvert E, Extracts from a 15-Cent MS, Shropshire Archaeological and Natural Hist Soc Trans 2s 6(1894).102 (MS 4).

Bowers R H, Three ME Poems on the Apostles' Creed, PMLA 70(1955).210 (MSS 1, 2, 3).

Source. Migne PL, 39.2190 (De Symbolo).

Literary Relations. Bühler C F, The Apostles and the Creed, Spec 28(1953).335.

Brady M T, The Apostles and the Creed in MSS of The Pore Caitiff, Spec 32(1957).323.

Gordon J B, The Articles of the Creed and the Apostles, Spec 40(1965).634.

[41] A CHRISTIAN MANNES BILEEVE.

MSS. 1, Camb Univ Ii.1.2, ff 112ᵇ–135ᵇ (ca 1450); 2, BL Harley 4012, ff 83ᵇ–100ᵇ (1475–1500); 3, Coughton Court (Throckmorton), ff 79ᵇ–89ᵇ (1450–75); 4, Libr of Congress 4, ff 64ᵃ–78ᵃ (1400–25).

MSS Commentary. A Catalogue of the MSS Preserved in the Libr of the Univ of Cambridge, Cambridge 1858, 3.314 (MS 1).

de Ricci Census, 1.180 (MS 4).

Wilson E, A ME MS at Coughton Court, Warwickshire, and BL MS Harley 4012, N&Q ns 24 (1977).295 (MSS 2, 3).

iv. Ten Commandments

[42] TEN COMMANDMENTS.

MSS. 1, Bodl 4061 (Hatton 26), f 211ᵃ (1200–50); 2, Bodl 6922 (Ashmole 61), ff 16ᵇ–17ᵃ (1500–25); 3, Bodl 6943 (Ashmole 59), f 72ᵇ (1450–1500); 4, Bodl 8741 (Bodley 841), f iiᵇ (1475–1500); 5, Bodl 1596 (Laud misc 463), ff 158ᵇ–159ᵇ (ca 1400); 6, Bodl 11263 (Rawl A.381), ff 107ᵃ–111ᵇ (ca 1450); 7, Bodl 12146 (Rawl C.288), ff 92ᵃ–95ᵃ (1400–50); 8, Bodl 12143 (Rawl C.285), f 61ᵇ (1400–50); 9, Bodl 14526 (Rawl poet 32), f 55ᵃ (1450–1500); 10, Bodl 3938 (Eng poet a.1), f 408ᵇ (1380–1400); 11, Bodl 15839 (Rawl liturg e.7), f 14ᵃ (1425–50); 12, Exeter Oxford 47, f 127ᵇ (ca 1500); 13, New Oxford 88, f 490ᵇ (ca 1300); 14, Univ Oxford E.96, f 109ᵇ (1450–1500); 15, Camb Univ Ff.6.15, f 21ᵃ (ca 1300); 16, Emmanuel Camb 27, f 111ᵇ (13 cent); 17, Magdalene Camb Pepys 1584, art 9 (1475–1500); 18, Sidney Sussex Camb 55, f 3ᵇ (1400–50); 19, Trinity Camb 43 (B.1.45), f 42ᵃ (13 cent); 20, Trinity Camb 323 (B.14.39), f 29ᵃ (13 cent); 21, BL Cotton Caligula A.ii, f 58ᵃ (1400–50); 22, BL Harley 78, f 86ᵃ (1450–1500); 23, BL Harley 665, f 90ᵃ⁻ᵇ (1475–1500); 24, BL Harley 1704, ff 48ᵇ–49ᵃ (ca 1465); 25, BL Harley 2391, f 134ᵃ (1400–25); 26, BL Harley 5396, f 285ᵇ (1450–1500); 27, BL Royal 8.F.vii, f 145ᵇ (1450–1500); 27a, BL Sloane 1313, f 127ᵃ⁻ᵇ (15 cent); 28, BL Addit 22283, f 130ᵃ (1380–1400); 29, BL Addit 25031, f 5ᵇ (13 cent); 30, Lambeth Palace 853, pp 47–49, 49–53 (1400–50); 31, Gray's Inn London 15, f 72ᵇ (15 cent); 32, St George's Chapel Windsor E.1.1, ff 29ᵃ–32ᵇ (1450–1500); 33, Nat Libr Scotland Advocates 18.7.21, f 128ᵇ (1327); 34, St Cuthbert's Coll Ushaw 28, pp 25ᵃ–27ᵃ (ca 1450); 35, Bodl Lat liturg e.17, f 53ᵃ (15 cent).

Brown-Robbins, nos 176, 744, 1129, 1379, 2000, 2286, 3345, 3483, 3684, 3685; Robbins-Cutler, nos 176, 1129, 1379, 1856.5, 3685. For a tag on the Ten Commandments from the Fasciculus Morum, see Brown-Robbins, Robbins-Cutler, no 3254, and Wenzel, Verses in Sermons, as below, p 156.

MSS Commentary. A Catalogue of the MSS in the Cottonian Libr Deposited in the British Museum, London 1802, p 42 (MS 21).

A Catalogue of the Harleian MSS in the British Museum, London 1808, 1.20 (MS 22), 400 (MS 23); 2.777 (MS 24), 680 (MS 25); 3.264 (MS 26).

Black W H, A Descriptive, Analytical, and Critical Catalogue of the MSS Bequeathed unto the Univ of Oxford by Elias Ashmole, Oxford 1845, pp 95 (MS 3), 106 (MS 2).

Coxe H O, Catalogus Codicum MSS qui in Collegiis Aulisque Oxoniensibus Hodie Adservantur, Oxford 1852, 1.18 (MS 12), 28 (MSS 13, 14).

A Catalogue of the MSS Preserved in the Libr of the Univ of Cambridge, Cambridge 1857, 2.522 (MS 15).

Coxe, Catalogi Codicum Manuscriptorum Bibliothecae Bodleianae, Oxford 1858, 2.331 (MS 5).

Catalogue of Additions to the MSS in the British Museum in the Years MDCCCLIV–MDCCCLX, London 1875, p 623 (MS 28).

Catalogue of Additions to the MSS in the British Museum in the Years MDCCCLIV–MDCCCLXXV, London 1877, p 142 (MS 29).

Macray W D, Catalogi Codicum Manuscriptorum Bibliothecae Bodleianae, Oxford 1862, 5(2).380 (MS 6); 1878, 5(2).123 (MS 8), 125 (MS 7).

James M R, A Descriptive Catalogue of the MSS in the Libr of Sidney Sussex Coll Cambridge, Cambridge 1895, p 39 (MS 18).

Summary Cat, 2.789 (MS 10), 1216 (MS 4), 4061 (MS 1); 3.290 (MS 9), 514 (MS 11).

James, The Western MSS in the Libr of Trinity Coll Cambridge A Descriptive Catalogue, Cambridge 1900, 1.56 (MS 19), 438 (MS 20); The Western MSS in the Libr of Emmanuel Coll A Descriptive Catalogue, Cambridge 1904, p 22 (MS 16).

Warner G F and J P Gilson, Catalogue of Western MSS in the Old Royal and King's Collections, London 1921, 1.265 (MS 27).

James, A Descriptive Catalogue of the Libr of Samuel Pepys, Pt III, Medieval MSS, London 1923, p 19 (MS 17).

James M R and C Jenkins, A Descriptive Catalogue of the MSS in the Libr of Lambeth Palace, Cambridge 1932, p 809 (MS 30).

James, The MSS of St George's Chapel Windsor, Libr 4s 13(1933).72.

Serjeantson Index, p 260.

Guddat-Figge G, Catalogue of MSS Containing ME Romances, Munich 1976, pp 145 (MS 28), 169 (MS 21), 269 (MS 10).

Editions. A Catalogue of the MSS Preserved in the Libr of the Univ of Cambridge, Cambridge 1857, 2.522 (MS 15).

Furnivall F J, Hymns to the Virgin and Christ, EETS 24, London 1867 (rptd 1895), pp 104 (MS 30), 106 (MSS 30, 10).

Morris R, An Old Eng Miscellany, EETS 49, London 1872, p 200 (MS 15).

Catalogue of Additions to the MSS in the British Museum in the Years MDCCCLIV–MDCCCLXXV, London 1877, p 142 (MS 29).

Zupitza J, Zwei Umschreibungen der Zehn Gebote im me Versen, Arch 85(1890).45 (MS 23); The Proverbis of Wysdom, Arch 90(1893).247 (MS 9).

Yksh Wr, 1.111 (MS 24).

Förster M, Kleine Mitteilungen zur me Lehrdichtung, Arch 104(1900).302 (MS 19).

Furnivall, The Minor Poems of the Vernon MS, Vol II, EETS 117, London 1901, p 680 (MS 10).

Brown RLxivC, p 148 (MS 10).

Brown ELxiiiC, p 33 (MS 20), 129 (MS 19), 181 (MS 13), 219 (MS 14).

Brown RLxvC, p 211 (MS 11).

Hoffman D L, The Chevalere Assigne: an Edn with Introd, Notes, and Glossary Together with the Legend of the Swan-Knight from Bodleian MS Rawlinson Misc 358 and the Previously Unedited The First Introyte of Sapyens, from Cotton Caligula A.ii, diss N Y Univ 1967, p 263 (MS 21).

Reichl R, Religiöse Dichtung im engl Hochmittelalter, Munich 1973, pp 334 (MSS 20, 16), 335 (MSS 13, 33, 4), 336 (MSS 24, 25, 27).

Wilson E, A Descriptive Index of the Eng Lyrics in John of Grimestone's Preaching Book, Oxford 1973, p 56 (MS 33).

Wenzel S, Verses in Sermons, Cambridge 1978, p 155 (text from Fasciculus Morum similar to MS 31).

Literary Relations. Cawley A C, ME Metrical Versions of the Decalogue with Reference to the Eng Corpus Christi Cycles, Leeds SE 8(1975).133.

[43] STANDARD ORTHODOX EXPOSITION OF THE TEN COMMANDMENTS.

MSS. 1, Bodl 1049 (Laud misc 524), ff 11ª–17ᵇ, 18ª⁻ᵇ (compressed version; 1400–25); 2, Bodl 1292 (Laud misc 210), f 117ª⁻ᵇ (1400–25; fragment); 3, Bodl 1428 (Laud misc 699), ff 79ª–80ᵇ (1400–50); 4, Bodl 2289 (Bodley 85), ff 110ª–115ᵇ (1375–1400); 5, Bodl 11263 (Rawl A.381), ff 107ª–111ᵇ (ca 1450); 5a, Bodl 11303 (Rawl A.423), ff 1ª–6ᵇ (ca 1400); 6, Bodl 10027 (Tanner 201), ff 3ᵇ–4ª (compressed version; 1400–25); 7, Univ Oxford 97, ff 85ᵃ–94ᵇ (1400–25); 8, Camb Univ Kk.1.3, art 22, ff 10ᵇ–11ᵃ (?compressed version; 1450–1500); 8a, Camb Univ Nn.4.12, ff 1ᵃ–7ᵇ (ca 1450); 8b, Sidney Sussex Camb 74, ff 181ᵃ–189ᵇ (1425–50); 9, Trinity Camb 601 (R.3.21), ff 2ᵇ–6ᵃ (1475–1500; mixed orthodox and Wycliffite elements); 9a, BL Arundel 286, ff 179ᵃ–191ᵇ (1400–25); 10, BL Harley 218, ff 159ᵃ–167ᵃ (ca 1400); 11, BL Harley 2346, ff 34ᵃ–47ᵇ (1400–50); 12, BL Royal 17.A.xxvi, ff 4ᵃ–22ᵃ (1400–25); 13, BL Addit 22283, ff 92ᵃ–93ᵇ (1380–1400); 14, BL Addit 27592, ff 42ᵃ–45ᵇ (ca 1400; mixed orthodox and Wycliffite elements); 15, Westminster School London 3, ff 73ᵃ–88ᵃ (1400–50); 16, Soc of Antiquaries London 687, pp 412–420 (ca 1400); 17, Edinburgh Univ 93, ff 4ᵃ–10ᵇ (1430–50; mixed orthodox and Wycliffite elements); 18, Bibliothèque Ste Geneviève Paris 3390, ff 1ᵃ–23ᵇ (1400–25); 19, Princeton Univ Garrett 143, ff 1ᵃ–21ᵇ (1400–25); 20, Henry E Huntington HM.744, ff 13ᵇ–24ᵇ (ca 1450).

MSS. Related Versions: Version A: 21, Leeds Univ Brotherton 501, ff 74ᵇ–81ᵃ (ca 1450); *Version B:* 22, BL Cotton Vespasian A.xxiii, ff 107ᵃ–115ᵇ (1400–25).

MSS Commentary. A Catalogue of the MSS in the Cottonian Libr Deposited in the British Museum, London 1802, p 437 (MS 22).

A Catalogue of the Harleian MSS in the British Museum, London 1808, 1.69 (MS 10); 2.662 (MS 11).

Catalogue of MSS in the British Museum, ns I, Pt I: The Arundel MSS, London 1840, p 84 (MS 9a).

Macray W D, Catalogi Codicum Manuscriptorum Bibliothecae Bodleianae, Oxford 1852, 5(1).380 (MS 5), 405 (MS 5a).

A Catalogue of the MSS Preserved in the Libr of the Univ of Cambridge, Cambridge 1858, 3.551 (MS 8); 4(1861).499 (MS 8a).

Hackman A, Catalogi Codicum Manuscriptorum Bibliothecae Bodleianae, Oxford 1860, 4.637 (MS 6).

Catalogue of Additions to the MSS in the British Museum in the Years MDCCCLIV–MDCCCLX, London 1875, p 623 (MS 13).

Catalogue of Additions to the MSS in the British Museum in the Years MDCCCLIV–MDCCCLXXV, London 1877, p 334 (MS 14).

Coxe H O, Catalogi Codicum Manuscriptorum Bibliothecae Bodleianae, Oxford 1878, 2.181 (MS 2), 378 (MS 1), 502 (MS 3).

James M R, A Descriptive Catalogue of the MSS in the Libr of Sidney Sussex Coll Cambridge, Cambridge 1895, p 52 (MS 8a); The Western MSS in the Libr of Trinity Coll Cambridge A Descriptive Catalogue, Cambridge 1901, 2.83 (MS 9).

Summary Cat, 2.291 (MS 4).

Borland C R, A Descriptive Catalogue of the Western Mediaeval MSS in Edinb Univ Libr, Edinburgh 1906, p 149 (MS 17).

Warner G F and J P Gilson, Catalogue of Western MSS in the Old Royal and King's Collections, London 1921, 2.220 (MS 12).

Cumming W P, A ME MS in the Bibliothèque Ste Geneviève, Paris, PMLA 42(1927).862 (MS 18).

de Ricci Census, 1.74 (MS 20), 894 (MS 19).

Humphreys K W and J Lightbown, Two MSS of the Pricke of Conscience in the Brotherton Collection, Leeds SE 7–8(1952).30 (MS 21).

Aarts F G A M, ed, The Pater Noster of Richard Ermyte, The Hague 1967, p xi (MS 15).

Wakelin M F, The MSS of John Mirk's Festial, Leeds SE 1(1967).107 (MS 5).

Ker Manuscripts, 1.314 (MS 16), 422 (MS 15); 3.67 (MS 21).

Doyle A I, Univ Coll Oxford MS 97 and Its Relationship to the Simeon MS (BL Add 22283), in M Benskin and M L Samuels, edd, So meny people longages and tonges, Philological Essays in Scots and Mediaeval Eng Presented to Angus McIntosh, Edinburgh 1981, p 265 (MSS 7, 13).

Hanna R III, Leeds Univ Libr MS Brotherton 501: A Redescription, Manuscripta 26(1982).38 (MS 21).

Pyper R, An Abridgement of Wyclif's De Mandatis Divinis, MÆ 52(1983).306 (description of MS 1).

Hanna R III, The Index of ME Prose, Handlist I, A Handlist of Manuscripts containing ME Prose in the Henry E Huntington Library, Woodbridge 1984, p 33.

Editions. Francis W N, The Book of Vices and Virtues, EETS 217, London 1942, p 317 (MS 13).

Martin C A, Edinb Univ Libr 93: An Annotated Edn of Selected Devotional Treatises, diss Univ of Edinburgh 1978 (MS 17).

Textual, Cultural, and Literary Relations. Kellogg A L and E W Talbert, The Wycliffe Pater Noster and Ten Commandments, with Special Reference to Eng MSS 85 and 90 in the John Rylands Libr, JRLB 42(1960).363.

Cawley A C, ME Metrical Versions of the Decalogue with Reference to the Eng Corpus Christi Cycles, Leeds SE 8(1975).133.

Martin A, The ME Versions of the Ten Commandments, with Special Reference to Rylands MS 85, JRLB 64(1981).191.

[44] JOHN LACY'S TREATISE ON
THE TEN COMMANDMENTS.

MS. St John's Oxford 94, ff 119ᵃ–126ᵃ (1420–34).

MS Commentary. Coxe H O, Catalogi Codicum MSS
qui in Collegiis Aulisque Oxoniensibus Hodie Adservantur, Oxford 1852, 2.26.

Edition. Royster J F, A ME Treatise on the Ten Commandments, SP 6(1910).5.

Author. Pepler C, John Lacy: a Dominican Contemplative, Life of the Spirit 5(1951).397.

Clay R M, Further Studies of Medieval Recluses,
Journ of the British Archaeological Assoc 3s
16(1953).74; Some Northern Anchorites, Archaeologia Aeliana 33(1955).202.

General References. Owst G R, Literature and Pulpit
in Medieval England, Cambridge 1933, p 439.

Wenzel, p 121.

[45] DIVES AND PAUPER.

MSS. 1, Bodl 6951 (Ashmole 750), ff 42ᵇ–48ᵃ
(1475–1500; fragment); 2, Bodl 21869 (Douce
295), ff 1ᵃ–221ᵇ (1450–1500); 3, Bodl 30521 (Eng
theol e.1), ff 1ᵃ–2ᵇ (1450–1500; fragment); 4,
Bodl Eng theol d.36, ff 10ᵃ–213ᵃ (1400–50); 5,
BL Addit 10053, ff 94ᵇ–98ᵇ (1400–25; fragment);
6, BL Harley 149, ff 1ᵃ–182ᵇ (ca 1450); 7, BL
Royal 17.C.xx, ff 3ᵇ–269ᵇ (1400–50); 8, BL Royal
17.C.xxi, ff 1ᵃ–245ᵃ (1400–50); 9, Lichfield Cath
35 (olim 5), ff 1ᵃ–214ᵇ (ca 1450); 10, Glasgow
Univ Hunter 270, ff 11ᵃ–270ᵃ (ca 1450); 11, Oscott Coll Birmingham Pastedown in R Persons, A
Christian Directorie, 1585; 12, Yale Univ 228, ff
1ᵃ–220ᵇ (ca 1450). PRINTS: 13, R Pynson, Lon-
don 1493 (STC, no 19212); 14, Wynkyn de
Worde, Westminster 1496 (STC, no 19213); 15,
T Berthelet, London 1536 (STC, no 19214).

MSS Commentary. A Catalogue of the Harleian MSS
in the British Museum, London 1808, 1.44 (MS
6).

List of Additions to the MSS in the British Museum
in the Years MDCCCXXXVI–MDCCCXL, Lon-
don 1843, p 7 (MS 5).

Black W H, A Descriptive, Analytical, and Critical
Catalogue of the MSS Bequeathed unto the Univ
of Oxford by Elias Ashmole, Oxford 1845, p 358
(MS 1).

Cox J C, Catalogue of the Muniments and MS Books
Pertaining to the Dean and Chapter of Lichfield,
William Salt Archaeological Soc 6(1886).204
(MS 9).

Summary Cat, 2.1115 (MS 1); 4.583 (MS 2); 5.824
(MS 3).

Young J and P H Aitken, A Catalogue of the MSS
in the Hunterian Museum in the Univ of Glasgow,
Glasgow 1908, p 217 (MS 10).

Warner G F and J P Gilson, Catalogue of Western
MSS in the Old Royal and King's Collections, London 1921, 2.246 (MS 7), 247 (MS 8).

de Ricci Census, 3.43 (MS 12).

Ker N R, Fragments of Medieval MSS and Pastedowns in Oxford Bindings, Oxford Bibliographical Soc Publications ns 5(1951–52).174, no 1954
(MS 11).

Pullen G F, Recusant Books of St. Mary's Oscott,
New Oscott 1964, p 60 (MS 11).

Ker Manuscripts, 3.124 (MS 9).

Editions. Sheeran F J, An Edn of Wynkyn de Worde's
Dives and Pauper, diss Univ of Nebraska 1970;
Ten Verse Fragments in Dives and Pauper, NM
76(1975).257.

Barnum P H, Dives and Pauper, EETS 275, 280,
London 1976, 1980 (base text: MS 10), in progress (crit J M Cowen, N&Q ns 25.170).

Selection. Clark F, Eucharistic Sacrifice and the Reformation, London 1952, p 558 (excerpt from
1536 edition).

Textual Matters. Morgan M, Pynson's MS of Dives et
Pauper, Libr 5s 8(1953).217 (based on MS 4).

Barnum P H, A Preliminary Edn of the Table, Prologue on Holy Poverty, and Commandment I of
Dives et Pauper, diss Syracuse Univ 1967; A Note
on Bodleian MS Eng. th.e.1, Thoth 10(1969).36.

Bühler C F, Further Notes on Pynson's 1493 Dives
and Pauper, PBSA 65(1971).393.

Sheeran F J, Printing Errors in the Texts of Dives
and Pauper, PBSA 65(1971).150.

Linström B, Two Notes on Dives et Pauper, SN
46(1974).331; Four ME Passages, SN 46
(1974).156.

Date and Authorship. Bale J, Scriptorum Illustrium
Majoris Britanniae Catalogus, Basle 1559, p 609.

DNB, 15.237 (sv Parker, Henry).

Richardson H G, Dives et Pauper, N&Q 11s
4(1911).321.

Pfander H G, Dives et Pauper, Libr 4s 14(1933).299.

Richardson, Dives et Pauper, Libr 15(1934).31.

Sources and Literary Relations. Deanesly M, The Lollard Bible and Other Medieval Biblical Versions,
Cambridge 1920, pp 326, 342.

Owst G R, Preaching in Medieval England, Cambridge 1926, pp 38, 58, 88, 93, 207, 322; The
People's Sunday Amusements in the Preaching of
Mediaeval England, Holborn Rev ns 17(1926).36;
Literature and Pulpit in Medieval England, Cambridge 1933, pp 483, 485, 543 (relation to medieval stage; regards it as a cross between the
sermon dialogues and the moralities).

Dickison R B, Dives and Pauper, a Study of a 15-Cent Homiletic Tract, diss Univ of Florida 1950.

Kolve V A, The Play Called Corpus Christi, Palo Alto 1966, p 131 (relation to medieval stage).

Slater A, Dives and Pauper: Orthodoxy and Liberalism, Journ of the Rutgers Univ Libr 31(1967).1.

Linström B, Two descriptions of the Signs before the Last Judgement, SN 48(1976).307 (an interpolation into the Glasgow text).

Aston M, Lollardy and Literacy, History 62 (1977).365.

General References. Gasquet F A, The Eve of the Reformation, London 1900, pp 284, 298, 353, 354; Parish Life in Mediaeval England, London 1906, pp 140, 160, 174, 179.

Rock D, The Church of Our Fathers, London 1905, 1.364, 365, 392; 2.232; 3.164, 171, 175, 200, 201, 285, 286; 4.162, 168, 202.

CHEL, 2.365.

Manning B L, People's Faith in the Time of Wyclif, Cambridge 1919, p 84 and passim.

Deanesly M, Vernacular Books in England in the 14 and 15 Cents, MLR 15(1920).358.

Gasquet, How Our Fathers Were Taught in Catholic Days, in Monastic Life in the Middle Ages, London 1922, p 67.

Owst, Literature and Pulpit, pp 148, 483, 485, 543.

Smith H M, Pre-Reformation England, London 1938, p 91.

Coulton G G, Medieval Panorama, Cambridge 1940, p 96 and passim.

Workman S K, 15-Cent Translation as an Influence on Eng Prose, Princeton 1940, p 63.

Rodgers E C, Discussion of Holidays in the Later Middle Ages, Columbia Univ Stud in History, Economics, and Public Law 48, N Y 1940, pp 27, 31 n20, 32 n32, 33 n38, 35 n48, 38 notes 73 and 83, 42 n111, 43 n111, 45 n136, 49, 63 n2, 65, 78, 84 notes 25 and 44.

Bennett OHEL, p 305.

Baugh LHE, p 289.

Fry T, A Medieval Defense of Women, American Benedictine Rev 3(1952).122.

Pantin, p 189.

Dickison R B, Superstitions and Some Common Sense Refutations in 15-Cent England, Southern Folklore Quart 24(1960).164.

Woolf, pp 39 n2, 48.

Bibliography. Gasquet, The Biblio of Some Devotional Books Printed by the Earliest Eng Printers, Trans of the Bibliographical Soc of London 7(1902–04).184.

Duff E G, 15-Cent Eng Books, Oxford 1917, nos 339, 340.

Doyle Survey, 1.93.

New CBEL, 1.690.

Hodnett E, Eng Woodcuts 1480–1535, Oxford 1973, p 77, no 464 (PRINT 14).

[46] THE FLOURE OF THE COMMAUNDEMENTES OF GOD.

MSS. No MS extant. PRINT: Wynkyn de Worde, London 1505 (STC, no 23875.1); 1510 (STC, no 23876); 1521 (STC, no 23877).

Robbins-Cutler, nos 2702.5, 3481.5, 3689.5, 4155.3.

Selection. Bühler C F, At thy golg first ent of the hous vlysse the saynge thus, SR 6(1959).229 (prints verses on the Ten Commandments).

General References. Pfander H G, Dives et Pauper, Libr 4s 14(1933).299 n1.

Bühler C F, The Apostles and the Creed, Spec 28(1953).338.

Bennett H S, Eng Books and Readers 1475–1557, 2nd edn, Cambridge 1969, p 250.

Bibliography. Gasquet F A, The Biblio of Some Devotional Books Printed by the Earliest Eng Printers, Trans of the Bibliographical Soc of London 7(1902–04).186.

[47] A TRACT ON THE TEN COMMANDMENTS.

MSS. 1, Bodl 655 (Laud Misc 23), ff 3ᵃ–23ᵃ (1400–25); 2, BL Cotton Titus D.xix, ff 120ᵃ–147ᵃ (1400–50); 3, St Alban's Cath, ff 5ᵃ–44ᵇ (1400–25).

MS. Related version: 4, BL Harley 211, ff 47ᵃ–65ᵃ (1400–50).

MSS. Independent Versions: Version A: 5, BL Harley 4172, ff 53ᵃ–63ᵃ (1426); 6, Bodl 1292 (Laud Misc 210), ff 147ᵇ–156ᵇ (1400–25); *Version B:* 7, Bodl 15432 (Rawl Poet 145), ff 8ᵃ–9ᵇ (1300–50); *Version C:* 8, Trinity Camb 337 (B.14.54), ff 17ᵇ–93ᵇ (15 cent); 9, Norwich Castle Mus 158.926/4.g.3, ff 82ᵇ–105ᵃ (ca 1450).

MSS Commentary. A Catalogue of the MSS in the Cottonian Libr Deposited in the British Museum, London 1802, p 565 (MS 2).

A Catalogue of the Harleian MSS in the British Museum, London 1808, 1.66 (MS 4); 3.121 (MS 5).

Coxe H O, Catalogi Codicum Manuscriptorum Bibliothecae Bodleianae, Oxford 1858, 2.65 (MS 1), 181 (MS 6).

Summary Cat, 3.426 (MS 7).

James M R, The Western MSS in the Libr of Trinity Coll Cambridge A Descriptive Catalogue, Cambridge 1900, 1.463 (MS 8).

Owst G R, A 15th-Cent MS in St Alban's Abbey, St Alban's and Hertfordshire Architectural and Archaeological Soc Trans (1924), p 43 (MS 3).

Ker Manuscripts, 3.521 (MS 9).

Edition. Lloyd D J, An Edn of the Prose and Verse in the Bodleian MS Laud Miscellaneous 23, diss Yale Univ 1943.

General Reference. Deanesly M, The Lollard Bible and Other Medieval Biblical Versions, Cambridge 1920, p 345.

Owst G R, Preaching in Medieval England, Cambridge 1926, p 292.

[48] TEN VENGEAUNCES OF GOD.

MSS. 1, BL Harley 2343, ff 78ᵇ–80ᵃ (1400–50); 2, Pierpont Morgan 861, ff 3ᵇ–4ᵇ (ca 1450); 3, ?Hopton Hall (Chandos-Pole-Gell) (1400–25).

MSS Commentary. A Catalogue of the Harleian MSS in the British Museum, London 1808, 2.660.

Historical MSS Commission, 9th Report of the Royal Commission on Historical MSS, pt 2, London 1883, appendix, p 384 (MS 3).

de Ricci Census, 3.365 (MS 2).

Edition. Bühler C F, The ME Texts of Morgan MS 861, PMLA 69(1954).692.

[49] SUNDAY OBSERVANCE.

MSS. 1, BL Harley 2339, ff 104ᵇ–116ᵃ (1400–50); 2, Durham Univ Cosin V.iv.2, ff 122ᵇ–124ᵇ (1477).

MSS Commentary. A Catalogue of the Harleian MSS in the British Museum, London 1808, 2.658 (MS 1).

Raine J, Catalogues of The Libr of Durham Cathedral, Surtees Soc 7(1838).174 (MS 2).

Doyle A I, A Treatise of the Three Estates, DomS 3(1950).351.

Cultural Background. Rodgers E C, Discussion of Holidays in the Later Middle Ages, Columbia Univ Stud in History, Economics, and Public Law 48, N Y 1940, p 28 (theory and practice of Sunday observance).

v. Works of Mercy

[50] THE SEVEN WORKS OF BODILY MERCY and [51] THE SEVEN WORKS OF SPIRITUAL MERCY.

MSS. Prose: 1, Bodl 8714 (Bodley 841), f 1ᵇ (1475–1500); 2, Bodl Lyell 29, ff 102ᵇ–104ᵃ (ca 1400); 3, Univ of Leeds Brotherton 501, f 81ᵃ (ca 1450); 4, St Cuthbert's Coll Ushaw 28, ff 50ᵇ–55ᵃ (ca 1450).

Verse: Version A: 5, Bodl 3938 (Eng poet a.1), f

115ᵇ (1380–1400); 6, BL Addit 22283, f 158ᵃ (1380–1400); 7, BL Addit 37787, f 158ᵃ (1400–25); *Version B*: 8, Salisbury Cath 126, f 5ᵇ (1400–25); *Version C*: 9, Henry E Huntington HM 127, f 62ᵇ (1400–25); *Version D*: 10, Bodl 8174 (Ashmole 1286), f iᵇ (ca 1400). PRINT: 11, Floure of the Commaundementes of God, Wynkyn de Worde, London 1510 (STC, no 23876).

Brown-Robbins, nos 645, 1959, 3263, 3459; Robbins-Cutler, nos 825.3, 1959, 4155.3.

MSS Commentary. Black W H, A Descriptive, Analytical, and Critical Catalogue of the MSS Bequeathed unto the Univ of Oxford by Elias Ashmole, Oxford 1845, p 1051 (MS 10).

Catalogue of Additions to the MSS in the British Museum in the Years MDCCCLIV–MDCCCLX, London 1875, p 623 (MS 6).

A Catalogue of the Libr of the Cathedral Church of Salisbury, London 1880, p 24 (MS 8).

Summary Cat, 2.789 (MS 5), 1216 (MS 1).

Catalogue of Additions to the MSS in the British Museum in the Years MDCCCCVI–MDCCCCX, London 1912, p 140 (MS 7).

de Ricci Census, 1.53 (MS 7).

Serjeantson Index, p 250.

Humphreys K W and J Lightbown, Two MSS of the Pricke of Conscience in the Brotherton Collection, Leeds SE 7–8(1952).30 (MS 2).

De la Mare A, Catalogue of the Collection of Medieval MSS Bequeathed to the Bodleian Libr Oxford by James R P Lyell, Oxford 1971, p 59 (MS 1).

Hanna R III, Leeds Univ Libr, MS Brotherton 501: A Redescription, Manuscripta 26(1982).38 (MS 3).

Hanna R III, The Index of ME Prose, Handlist I, A Handlist of Manuscripts containing ME Prose in the Henry E Huntington Library, Woodbridge 1984, p 12.

Editions. Horstmann C, The Minor Poems of the Vernon MS, Pt I, EETS 98, London 1892, p 34 (MS 3).

Schofield B, Muchelney Memoranda, Publs of the Somerset Record Soc 42(1927).99.

Baugh N S, A Worcestershire Miscellany, Phila 1956, p 146 (MS 5).

vi. Virtues

[52] SEVEN PRINCIPAL VIRTUES.

MSS. No MS extant. PRINT: BL single sheet, printed on one side, ca 1500 (STC, no 17037).

Robbins-Cutler, no 272.5.

Ringler BEV, no 97.
Edition. Schreiber W L, Handbuch der Holz- und Metallschnitte des XV Jahrhunderts, Leipzig 1928, 6.51.
Textual Matters. Mabbott T O, The Text of the Eng Xylographic Poem on the Seven Virtues, MLN 65(1950).545 (emendations to Schreiber's text).

[53] THRE GOOD VERTUES.

MSS. 1, New Oxford 95, ff 124ᵃ–127ᵇ (1400–25); 2, BL Royal 17.A.xxvi, ff 27ᵇ–28ᵇ (1400–25); 3, York Minster XVI L.12, ff 27ᵃ–32ᵇ (1400–25); 4, Glasgow Univ Gen 223, ff 221ᵃ–222ᵇ (1400–25); 5, Glasgow Univ Hunter 512, ff 22ᵇ–25ᵃ (1400–25); 6, Bibliothèque Ste Geneviève Paris 3390, ff 30ᵃ–37ᵃ (1400–25); 7, Trinity Dublin 245, ff 27ᵃ–30ᵇ (1400–25).
Jolliffe, p 87, no G.11.
MSS Commentary. Coxe H O, Catalogi Codicum MSS qui in Collegiis Aulisque Oxoniensibus Hodie Adservantur, Oxford 1852, 1.34 (MS 1).
Abbott T K, Catalogue of the MSS in the Libr of Trinity Coll Dublin, Dublin 1900, p 36 (MS 7).
Young J and P H Aitken, A Catalogue of the MSS in the Hunterian Museum in the Univ of Glasgow, Glasgow 1908, p 419 (MS 5).
Warner G F and J P Gilson, Catalogue of Western MSS in the Old Royal and King's Collections, London 1921, 2.220 (MS 2).
Cumming W P, A ME MS in the Bibliothèque Ste Geneviève, Paris, PMLA 42(1927).862.
Kellogg A L and E W Talbot, The Wycliffite Pater Noster and Ten Commandments, with Special Reference to Eng MSS 85 and 90 in the John Rylands Libr, JRLB 42(1960).353 (MS 6).
Ker Manuscripts, 2.904 (MS 4).
Editions and Related Versions. Manual, 2.525 [22].

[54] FAITH HOPE AND CHARITY.

MSS. 1, Bodl 21896 (Douce 322), f 19ᵃ⁻ᵇ (1425–50); 2, BL Harley 1706, f 19ᵃ⁻ᵇ (1450–1500).
Jolliffe, p 87, no G.9.
MSS Commentary. Summary Cat, 4.593 (MS 1).
A Catalogue of the Harleian MSS in the British Museum, London 1808, 2.178 (MS 2).

[55] FAITH (or A SHORT DECLARATION OF BELIEF).

MSS. 1, Bodl 655 (Laud Misc 23), ff 60ᵃ–62ᵇ (1400–25); 2, Trinity Camb 601 (R.3.21), ff 9ᵇ–10ᵃ (1475–1500); 3, Trinity Camb 1099 (O.1.74), ff 27ᵃ–50ᵇ (1450–1500); 4, Magdalene Camb Pepys 2125, ff 124ᵇ–125ᵃ (ca 1450); 5, BL Addit 10053,

ff 99ᵃ–114ᵃ (1400–25); 6, John Rylands Manchester Eng 85, f 24ᵇ (1400–25); 7, Durham Cath A.iv.22, p 103 (1400–25).
MS. Related Text: A Comfortable Tretys: 7, Corpus Christi Camb 268, ff 2ᵃ–9ᵇ (1425–50).
Jolliffe, pp 85, no G.2; 122, no K.13.
MSS Commentary. List of Additions to the MSS in the British Museum in the Years MDCCCXXXVI–MDCCCXL, London 1843, p 7 (MS 5).
Coxe H O, Catalogi Codicum Manuscriptorum Bibliothecae Bodleianae, Oxford 1858, 2.65 (MS 1).
James M R, The Western MSS in the Libr of Trinity Coll Cambridge A Descriptive Catalogue, Cambridge 1901, 2.83 (MS 2); 3(1902).74 (MS 3); A Descriptive Catalogue of the MSS in the Libr of Corpus Christi Coll Cambridge, Cambridge 1912, 2.24 (MS 7); A Descriptive Catalogue of the Libr of Samuel Pepys, Pt III, Medieval MSS, London 1923, p 72 (MS 4).
Ker Manuscripts, 3.409 (MS 6).
Edition. Lloyd D J, An Edn of the Prose and Verse in the Bodleian MS Laud Misc 23, diss Yale Univ 1943 (MS 1).

[56] ON FAITH AND REASON.

MS. Victoria and Albert Mus Dyce 45, ff 25ᵇ–27ᵇ (1475–1550).
Robbins-Cutler, no 4162.5.

[57] CHARITY I.

MSS. Version A: 1, Corpus Christi Camb 385, pp 221–222 (ca 1400); 2, Trinity Camb 601 (R.3.21), ff 12ᵇ–16ᵇ (1475–1500); 3, Durham Cath A.iv.22, pp 105–116 (1400–25); 4, John Rylands Manchester Eng 85, ff 24ᵇ–37ᵃ (1400–25); *Version B:* 5, St John's Camb 95, ff 168ᵇ–170ᵇ (15 cent).
Jolliffe, p 85, no G.3.
MSS Commentary. James M R, The Western MSS in the Libr of Trinity Coll Cambridge A Descriptive Catalogue, Cambridge 1901, 2.83 (MS 2); A Descriptive Catalogue of the MSS in the Libr of Corpus Christi Coll Cambridge, Cambridge 1912, 2.232 (MS 1); A Descriptive Catalogue of the MSS in the Libr of St John's Coll Cambridge, Cambridge 1912, p 125 (MS 5).
Ker Manuscripts, 3.409 (MS 4).
Source. Yksh Wr, 2.72.

[58] THE SIXTENE CONDICIOUNS OF CHARITE.

MSS. Prose: Version A: 1, BL Addit 28026, f 188ᵃ (1400–50); 2, Longleat (Marquis of Bath) 32, f

85^{a-b} (1400–50); *Version B*: 3, BL Cotton Titus D.xix, ff 164^a–165^a (1400–50); 4, BL Addit 60577, ff 137^a–138^a (1475–1550); 5, Trinity Dublin 70, ff 187^a–188^a (15 cent); 6, Columbia Univ Plimpton 258, f 5^{a-b} (ca 1400); *Version C*: 7, Trinity Dublin 155, p 90 (1475–1500); *Version D*: 8, BL Royal 8.C.i, ff 159^a–161^a (1400–50); 9, St Cuthbert's Coll Ushaw 28, ff 29^b–34^b (ca 1450); 10, Trinity Dublin 155, pp 127–135 (1475–1500); *Version E*: 11, Bodl 1292 (Laud misc 210), ff 134^b–136^b (1400–25); 12, Bodl 3054 (Bodley 938), ff 56^a–58^a (1450–1500); 13, Bodl 12071 (Rawl C.209), ff 16^b–20^a (1400–25); 14, New Oxford 67, f 1^{a-b} (ca 1400); 15, Trinity Oxford E.86, ff 35^a–36^a (1475–1500); 16, Camb Univ Ii.6.43, ff 14^b–15^a (1400–25); 17, Trinity Camb 1053 (O.1.29), ff 75^a–76^b (1400–50); 18, BL Harley 2343, ff 87^b–89^b (1400–50); 19, St Alban's Cath, ff 3^b–4^a (1400–25); *Version F*: 20, Bodl 12071 (Rawl C.209), ff 16^a–19^b (1400–25); 21, Emmanuel Camb 246, ff 66^a–67^a (1375–1400); 22, Trinity Camb 337 (B.14.54), pp 186–197 (15 cent); 23, BL Addit 27592, ff 52^b–54^a (ca 1400); 24, Edinburgh Univ 93, ff 36^b–38^a (1430–50); 25, Glasgow Univ Hunter 472, ff 85^b–87^a (1382); *Version G*: 26, BL Lansdowne 388, f 368^{a-b} (1475–1500). *Verse: Version A*: 27, National Libr of Scotland Advocates 18.7.21, f 33^b (1372); *Version B*: 28, Camb Univ Ii.6.39, f 157^a (1400–50); 29, Lambeth Palace 853, pp 42–47 (1400–50).

Jolliffe, p 85, no G.4.

Brown-Robbins, nos 593, 2040.

MSS Commentary. A Catalogue of the MSS in the Cottonian Library Deposited in the British Museum, London 1802, p 565 (MS 3).

A Catalogue of the Harleian MSS in the British Museum, London 1808, 2.660 (MS 18).

A Catalogue of the Lansdowne MSS in the British Museum, London 1819, p 112 (MS 26).

Coxe H O, Catalogi Codicum MSS qui in Collegiis Aulisque Oxoniensibus Hodie Adservantur, Oxford 1852, 1.19 (MS 14); 2.35 (MS 15); Catalogi Codicum Manuscriptorum Bibliothecae Bodleianae, Oxford 1858, 2.181 (MS 11).

A Catalogue of the MSS Preserved in the Libr of the Univ of Cambridge, Cambridge 1858, 3.535 (MS 28), 540 (MS 16).

Historical MSS Commission, Third Report of the Royal Commission on Historical MSS, London 1872, p 183 (MS 2).

Catalogue of Additions to the MSS in the British Museum in the Years MDCCCLIV–MDCCCLXXV, London 1877, pp 334 (MS 23), 399 (MS 1).

Macray W D, Catalogi Codicum Manuscriptorum Bibliothecae Bodleianae, Oxford 1878, 5(2).96 (MSS 13, 20; both in Bodl 12071).

Summary Cat, 2.578 (MS 12).

Abbott T K, Catalogue of the MSS in the Libr of Trinity Coll Dublin, Dublin 1900, pp 9 (MS 5), 20 (MSS 7, 10; both in Trinity Dublin 155).

James M R, The Western MSS in the Libr of Trinity Coll Cambridge A Descriptive Catalogue, Cambridge 1900, 1.463 (MS 22); 3(1902).33 (MS 17); The Western MSS in the Libr of Emmanuel Coll A Descriptive Catalogue, Cambridge 1904, p 144 (MS 21).

Young J and P H Aitken, A Catalogue of the MSS in the Hunterian Museum in the Univ of Glasgow, Glasgow 1908, p 392 (MS 25).

Borland C R, A Descriptive Catalogue of the Western Mediaeval MSS in Edinb Univ Libr, Edinburgh 1916, p 149 (MS 24).

Warner G F and J P Gilson, Catalogue of Western MSS in the Old Royal and King's Collections, London 1921, 1.228 (MS 8).

Owst G R, A 15-Cent MS in St Alban's Abbey, St Alban's and Hertfordshire Architectural and Archaeological Soc Trans (1924), p 43 (MS 19).

James M R and C Jenkins, A Descriptive Catalogue of the MSS in the Libr of Lambeth Palace, Cambridge 1932, p 809 (MS 29).

Guddat-Figge G, Catalogue of MSS Containing ME Romances, Munich 1976, p 209 (MS 26).

Editions. Furnivall F J, Hymns to the Virgin and Christ, EETS 24, London 1867, p 114 (MS 29).

Arnold T, Select Eng Works of John Wyclif, Oxford 1871, 3.266 (Wycliffite version).

Wilson E, A Descriptive Index of the Eng Lyrics in John of Grimestone's Preaching Book, Oxford 1973, p 10.

Facsimiles. Plimpton G A, The Education of Chaucer, London and N Y 1935 (MS 6).

The Winchester Anthology with an Introd by E Wilson and I Fenlon, Woodbridge 1981 (MS 4).

[59] XV DEGREES OF CHARITE.

MS. St John's Oxford 173, f 129^a (1500–25).

Brown-Robbins, Robbins-Cutler, no 3558.

MS Commentary. Coxe H O, Catalogi Codicum MSS qui in Collegiis Aulisque Oxoniensibus Hodie Adservantur, Oxford 1852, 2.56.

[60] A TRETIS OF PERFIT LOVE.

MS. Camb Univ Ii.6.40, ff 75^a–76^b (1450–1500). Jolliffe, p 87, no G.8.

MS Commentary. A Catalogue of the MSS Preserved in the Libr of the Univ of Cambridge, Cambridge 1858, 3.538.

[61] SIXTENE TOKENES OF LOVE.

MSS. 1, Edinburgh Univ 93, f 83ᵃ⁻ᵇ (1430–50); 2, Glasgow Univ Hunter 512, ff 29ᵃ–30ᵃ (1400–25). Jolliffe, p 88, no G.14.
MSS Commentary. Young J and P H Aitken, A Catalogue of the MSS in the Hunterian Museum in the Univ of Glasgow, Glasgow 1908, p 419 (MS 2).
Borland C R, A Descriptive Catalogue of the Western Mediaeval MSS in Edinb Univ Libr, Edinburgh 1916, p 149 (MS 1).
Edition. Martin C A, Edinb Univ Libr MS 93: An Annotated Edn of Selected Devotional Treatises, diss Univ of Edinburgh 1978 (MS 1).

[62] CHARITY II.

MS. Bodl 3054 (Bodley 938), ff 58ᵃ–59ᵇ (1450–1500).
Jolliffe, p 90, no G.25.
MS Commentary. Summary Cat, 2.578.

[63] THOU SCHALT LOVE THI LORD.

MSS. 1, Bodl 1292 (Laud misc 210), ff 94ᵃ–97ᵇ (1400–25); 2, Bodl 21820 (Douce 246), ff 103ᵇ–106ᵃ (1400–50); 3, Univ Oxford 97, ff 97ᵃ–98ᵃ (1400–25); 4, BL Harley 2385, ff 5ᵇ–6ᵇ (1400–25); 5, Westminster School London 3, ff 119ᵇ–121ᵃ (1400–50).
Jolliffe, p 90, no G.26.
MSS Commentary. A Catalogue of the Harleian MSS in the British Museum, London 1808, 2.676 (MS 4).
Coxe H O, Catalogi Codicum Manuscriptorum Bibliothecae Bodleianae, Oxford 1858, 2.181 (MS 1).
Summary Cat, 4.566 (MS 2).
Aarts F G A M, ed, The Pater Noster of Richard Ermyte, The Hague 1967, p xi (MS 5).
Ker Manuscripts, 1.422 (MS 5).
Doyle A I, Univ Coll Oxford MS 97 and Its Relationship to the Simeon MS (BL Add 22283), in M Benskin and M L Samuels, edd, So meny people longages and tonges, Philological Essays in Scots and Mediaeval Eng Presented to Angus McIntosh, Edinburgh 1981, p 265 (MS 3).
Edition. Yksh Wr, 2.454.

[64] FOWRE TOKENS OF LOVE.

MS. BL Royal 18.A.x, f 15ᵃ (1400–25).
Jolliffe, p 90, no G.30.

Revell, p 46.
MS Commentary. Warner G F and J P Gilson, Catalogue of Western MSS in the Old Royal and King's Collections, London 1921, 2.265.

[65] VERSES ON CHARITY, PURITY, AND HOPE.

MS. Bodl 15432 (Rawl poet 145), ff 9ᵇ–10ᵇ (1400–25).
Brown-Robbins, no 1093.
MS Commentary. Summary Cat, 3.426.

[66] DEUS CARITAS.

MSS. 1, Bodl 3938 (Eng poet a.1), f 407ᵇ (1380–1400); 2, BL Addit 22283, f 129ᵃ (1380–1400).
Brown-Robbins, no 678.
MSS Commentary. Catalogue of Additions to the MSS in the British Museum in the Years MDCCCLIV–MDCCCLX, London 1875, p 623 (MS 2).
Summary Cat, 2.789.
Serjeantson Index, p 251.
Editions. Varnhagen H, Kleinere Gedichte der Vernon- und Simeon-Handschrift, Angl 7(1884).291 (MS 1).
Furnivall F J, The Minor Poems of the Vernon MS, Pt II, EETS 117, London 1901, p 668 (MS 1).
Guddat-Figge G, Catalogue of MSS Containing ME Romances, Munich 1976, pp 145 (MS 2), 269 (MS 1).
Furnivall, Early Eng Poems and Lives of Saints, Berlin 1862, p 127 (MS 2).
Brown RLxivC, p 136 (MS1).

[67] PATIENCE I.

MS. Trinity Camb 601 (R.3.21), f 18ᵃ (1475–1500).
Jolliffe, p 86, no G.5.
MS Commentary. James M R, The Western MSS in the Libr of Trinity Coll Cambridge A Descriptive Catalogue, Cambridge 1901, 2.83.
Sources and Background of Literature on Patience. Hanna R III, Some Commonplaces of Late Medieval Patience Discussions: An Introd, in The Triumph of Patience, ed G J Schiffhorst, Orlando 1978, p 65.

[68] PATIENCE II.

MS. Magdalene Camb Pepys 2125, f 83ᵇ (ca 1450).
Jolliffe, p 87, no G.7.

MS Commentary. James M R, A Descriptive Catalogue of the Libr of Samuel Pepys, Pt III, Medieval MSS, London 1923, p 72.

Bazire J and E Colledge, edd, The Chastising of God's Children, Oxford 1957, p 7.

[69] PATIENCE III.

MS. BL Arundel 158, ff 8ª–9ª (ca 1400).

Jolliffe, p 89, no G.24.

MS Commentary. Catalogue of MSS in The British Museum ns I, Pt I: The Arundel MSS, London 1840, p 44.

[70] HOW MEN SHULDE BE MEKE AND PACIENT.

MS. Trinity Camb 601 (R.3.21), ff 17ᵇ–18ª (1475–1500).

Jolliffe, p 87, no G.6.

MS Commentary. James M R, The Western MSS in the Libr of Trinity Coll Cambridge A Descriptive Catalogue, Cambridge 1902, 2.83.

[71] THE BOOK OF TRIBULATION.

MSS. 1, Bodl 2322 (Bodley 423), ff 205ª–226ª (ca 1450); 2, BL Arundel 286, ff 100ª–115ª (1400–50); 3, BL Harley 1197, ff 61ª–74ᵇ (1425–50).

Jolliffe, p 116, nos J.3(a), 3(e).

MSS Commentary. A Catalogue of the Harleian MSS in the British Museum, London 1808, 1.595 (MS 3).

Catalogue of MSS in the British Museum, Vol I, pt 1: The Arundel MSS, London 1840, p 84 (MS 2).

Summary Cat, 2.308 (MS 1).

Edition. Barratt A, The Book of Tribulation, Heidelberg 1983, pp 38 (base text: MS 1), 134 (MS 2 abridgment); Introd, pp 7 (the text and its MSS), 18 (French source), 22 (Latin versions), 29 (other ME versions), 32 (language).

[72] VII DEGREES OF PATIENCE.

MS. St John's Oxford 173, f 136ª (1500–25).

MS Commentary. Coxe H O, Catalogi Codicum MSS qui in Collegiis Aulisque Oxoniensibus Hodie Adservantur, Oxford 1852, 2.56.

[73] OF PACIENCE IN SICKNESS.

MS. Bodl 1291 (Laud misc 517), ff 182ª–184ª (ca 1450).

MS Commentary. Coxe H O, Catalogi Codicum Manuscriptorum Bibliothecae Bodleianae, Oxford 1858, 2.374.

[74] VERSES ON PATIENCE.

MSS. 1, Bodl 29746 (Lat theol d.1), f 175ª (1430–36); 2, Bodl 29179 (Add B.60), ff 125ᵇ–126ª (1475–1500); 3, Durham Univ Cosin V.iii.9, f 83ª (ca 1500).

Brown-Robbins, nos 478, 1706, 2740; Robbins-Cutler, nos 95.8, 3492.3.

MSS Commentary. Raine J, Catalogues of the Libr of Durham Cathedral, Surtees Soc 7(1840).165 (MS 3).

Summary Cat, 5.578 (MS 2), 685 (MS 1).

Editions. Furnivall F J and I Gollancz, Hoccleve's Works: The Minor Poems, Pt I, EETS 61, London 1892, p 224 (MS 3).

Robbins R H, Popular Prayers in ME Verse, MP 36(1939).337 (a quatrain from MS 2).

Bühler C, Patience in Adversity, Angl 78(1960).418 (MS 2).

[75] VII DEGREES OF HUMILITY.

MS. St John's Oxford 173, f 136ª (1500–25).

MS Commentary. Coxe H O, Catalogi Codicum MSS qui in Collegiis Aulisque Oxoniensibus Hodie Adservantur, Oxford 1852, 2.56.

[76] VII DEGREES OF HUMYLYTE.

MSS. 1, Bodl 11263 (Rawl A.381), f 6ª (ca 1450); 2, BL Harley 1706, f 94ᵇ (1450–1500).

Jolliffe, p 87, no G.10.

Revell, p 46.

MSS Commentary. A Catalogue of the Harleian MSS in the British Museum, London 1808, 2.178 (MS 2).

Macray W D, Catalogi Codicum Manuscriptorum Bibliothecae Bodleianae, Oxford 1862, 5(1).380 (MS 1).

General Reference. Doyle A I, Books Connected with the Vere Family and Barking Abbey, Trans of the Essex Archaeological Soc 25(1958).227.

Source. Migne PL, 159.666.

[77] XII DEGREES OF HUMILITY.

MSS. 1, Bodl 1291 (Laud misc 517), ff 175ᵇ–181ª (ca 1450); 2, Bodl 2103 (Bodley 220), ff 101ª–103ª (1400–50); 3, Bodl 3657 (e Mus 232), ff 18ª–23ᵇ (1400–25); 4, Bodl 12728 (Rawl C.894), ff 65ª–67ᵇ (1475–1500); 5, Bodl Lat theol e.26, ff 139ª–142ᵇ (1400–50); 6, BL Harley 4011, ff 16ª–

18^b (1475–1500); 7, BL Harley 4012, ff 79^a–83^a (1475–1500); 8, BL Royal 17.C.xviii, ff 77^b–81^a (1475–1500); 9, BL Addit 60577, ff 184^a–189^b (1475–1550); 10, Worcester Cath F.172, ff 44^a–46^b (1450–1500); 11, Coughton Court (Throckmorton), ff 5^b–8^a (1450–75).

Jolliffe, p 89, no G.19.

Revell, pp 45, 46.

MSS Commentary. A Catalogue of the Harleian MSS in the British Museum, London 1808, 3.103 (MSS 6, 7).

Coxe H O, Catalogi Codicum Manuscriptorum Bibliothecae Bodleianae, Oxford 1858, 2.374 (MS 1).

Macray W D, Catalogi Codicum Manuscriptorum Bibliothecae Bodleianae, Oxford 1878, 5(2).465 (MS 4).

Summary Cat, 2.213 (MS 2), 722 (MS 3).

Floyer J K and S G Hamilton, Catalogue of MSS Preserved in the Chapter Libr of Worcester Cathedral, Oxford 1906, p 96 (MS 10).

Warner G F and J P Gilson, Catalogue of Western MSS in the Old Royal and King's Collections, London 1921, 2.245 (MS 8).

Allen WAR, p 279 (MS 3).

Doyle A I, An Unrecognized Piece of Piers the Ploughman's Creed and Other Work by Its Scribe, Spec 34(1959).431 (MS 10).

Wilson E, A ME MS at Coughton Court, Worcestershire, and British Libr MS Harley 4012, N&Q ns 24(1977).295 (MSS 7, 11).

Edition. Angiello D M, An Edn of the Twelve Degrees of Meekness, diss Fordham Univ 1971.

Facsimile. The Winchester Anthology with an Introd by E Wilson and I Fenlon, Woodbridge 1981 (MS 9).

Sources and Literary Relations. Doyle A I, A Text Attributed to Ruusbroec Circulating in England, in A Ampe, ed, Dr L Reypens-Album, Antwerp 1964, p 153.

General Reference. Milosh J, The Scale of Perfection and the Eng Mystical Tradition, Madison 1966, p 140.

[78] HUMILITY.

MSS. 1, Bodl 21896 (Douce 322), f 19^b (1450–60); 2, BL Harley 1706, f 94^b (1450–1500).

Jolliffe, p 90, no G.29.

MSS Commentary. A Catalogue of the Harleian MSS in the British Museum, London 1808, 2.178 (MS 2).

Summary Cat, 4.593 (MS 1).

[79] THE VII TOKENES OF MEKENES.

MSS. 1, Bodl 12071 (Rawl C.209), ff 15^a–16^b (1400–25); 2, Camb Univ Ff.2.38, f 35^a–b (ca 1450); 3, BL Addit 60577, ff 145^a–146^b (1475–1500); 4, Edinburgh Univ 93, ff 81^b–82^b (1430–50); 5, Trinity Dublin 70, ff 193^a–194^a (15 cent); 6, Pierpont Morgan 861, f 6^a–b (ca 1450).

Jolliffe, p 87, no G.12.

MSS Commentary. A Catalogue of the MSS Preserved in the Libr of the Univ of Cambridge, Cambridge 1857, 2.404 (MS 2).

Macray W D, Catalogi Codicum Manuscriptorum Bibliothecae Bodleianae, Oxford 1878, 5(2).96 (MS 1).

Abbott T K, Catalogue of the MSS in the Libr of Trinity Coll Dublin, Dublin 1900, p 9 (MS 5).

Borland C R, A Descriptive Catalogue of the Western Mediaeval MSS in Edinb Univ Libr, Edinburgh 1916, p 149 (MS 4).

Bühler C F, The ME Texts of Morgan MS 861, PMLA 69(1954).686 (MS 6).

Guddat-Figge G, Catalogue of MSS Containing ME Romances, Munich 1976, p 94 (MS 2).

Edition. Martin C A, Edinb Univ MS 93: an Annotated Edn of Selected Devotional Treatises, diss Univ of Edinburgh 1978, 2.469 (MS 4).

Facsimiles. Cambridge Univ Libr MS Ff.2.38, with an Introd by F McSparran and P R Robinson, London 1979 (MS 2).

The Winchester Anthology, with an Introd by E Wilson and I Fenlon, Woodbridge 1981 (MS 3).

[80] VERSES ON HUMILITY.

MSS. 1, BL Harley 7322, f 141^b (1400–50); 2, Nat Libr of Scotland Advocates 18.7.21, f 58^a (1372).

Brown-Robbins, Robbins-Cutler, nos 101, 480.

MSS Commentary. A Catalogue of the Harleian MSS in the British Museum, London 1808, 3.525 (MS 1).

Editions. Furnivall F J, Political, Religious and Love Poems, EETS 15, rvsd edn London 1903, p 260 (MS 1).

Wilson E, A Descriptive Index of the Eng Lyrics in John of Grimestone's Preaching Book, Oxford 1973, p 17.

[81] THRE THOUT3.

MS. BL Harley 1022, f 81^a (1400–25).

Jolliffe, p 90, no G.28.

MS Commentary. A Catalogue of the Harleian MSS in the British Museum, London 1808, 1.510.

[82] VII DEGREES OF OBEDIENCE.

MS. St John's Oxford 173, ff 135ᵇ–136ᵇ (1500–25).
Jolliffe, p 89, no G.21.
MS Commentary. Coxe H O, Catalogus Codicum MSS
qui in Collegiis Aulisque Oxoniensibus Hodie Adservantur, Oxford 1852, 2.56.

vii. Sacraments

[83] DEFENSES AND EXPOSITIONS
OF THE SEVEN SACRAMENTS.

MSS. 1, Bodl 3054 (Bodley 938), ff 267ᵇ–270ᵇ
(1450–1500); 2, Univ Oxford 123, ff 76ᵃ–77ᵇ
(1475–1500); 3, Trinity Camb 374 (B.5.43), ff 1ᵃ–
2ᵃ (1450–1500; a fragmentary version of MS 4
text); 4, BL Royal 17.A.xxv, ff 1ᵃ–13ᵃ (1400–25;
the tract on purgatory occurs on ff 11ᵃ–13ᵃ).
Jolliffe, p 133, no N.18 (MS 2).
MSS Commentary. Coxe H O, Catalogus Codicum
MSS qui in Collegiis Aulisque Oxoniensibus
Hodie Adservantur, Oxford 1852, 1.123 (MS 2).
Summary Cat, 2.578 (MS 1).
James M R, The Western MSS in the Libr of Trinity
Coll Cambridge A Descriptive Catalogue, Cam-
bridge 1900, 1.510 (MS 3).
Warner G F and J P Gilson, Catalogue of Western
MSS in the Old Royal and King's Collections, Lon-
don 1921, 2.219 (MS 4).

[84] THE CLENSYNG OF MANNES SOWLE.

MSS. 1, Bodl 27701 (Bodley 923), ff 1ᵃ–153ᵇ (ca
1400); 2, Camb Univ Ii.1.2, ff 1ᵃ–112ᵃ (ca 1450);
3, Magdalene Camb Pepys 2125, ff 56ᵇ–60ᵇ
(1400–50); 4, BL Harley 4012, ff 1ᵃ–68ᵇ (ca
1460); 5, BL Sloane 774, ff 1ᵃ–136ᵇ (1475–1500);
6, Durham Cath Hunter 15, ff 44ᵇ–48ᵇ (1400–
25); 7, Coughton Court (Throckmorton), ff 24ᵇ–
52ᵇ (1450–75).
Jolliffe, pp 67, no C.2; 68, no C.5; 77, no E.14.
Revell, pp 116, 117, 119, 120.
MSS Commentary. A Catalogue of the Harleian MSS
in the British Museum, London 1808, 3.103 (MS
4).
A Catalogue of the MSS Preserved in the Libr of
the Univ of Cambridge, Cambridge 1858, 3.314
(MS 2).
Summary Cat, 5.342 (MS 1).
Liddell M H, A New Source of the Parson's Tale, in
an Eng Miscellany Presented to Dr Furnivall in
Honour of His 75th Birthday, Oxford 1901, p 258
(MS 1).

James M R, A Descriptive Catalogue of the Libr of
Samuel Pepys, Pt III, Medieval MSS, London
1923, p 72 (MS 3).
Bazire J and E Colledge, edd, The Chastising of
God's Children, Oxford 1957, pp 36, 43 (MS 1).
Ker Manuscripts, 2.493 (MS 6).
Wilson E, A ME MS at Coughton Court, Warwick-
shire, and British Library MS Harley 4012, N&Q
ns 24(1977).295 (MSS 4, 7).
Editions. Regan C L, The Cleansing of Man's Soul
Edited from MS Bodley 923, diss Harvard 1963
(Introd: pp viii, description of MSS; xv, language;
lxvii, relation to contemporary church literature;
xcix, sources; cxxxiii, circumstances of composi-
tion).
Everett W K, A Critical Edn of the Confession Sec-
tion of The Clensyng of Mannes Soule, diss Univ
of North Carolina 1974 (base text: MS 2).
Selections. Kirchberger C, The Coasts of the Coun-
try, London n d, p 146; The Cleansing of Man's
Soul, Life of the Spirit 4(1949–50).290.
Sources, Date, Literary Relations. Liddell M H. A New
Source of the Parson's Tale, p 254.
Allen H E, Some 14-Cent Borrowings from Ancren
Riwle, MLR 18(1923).1.
Pfander Manuals, p 251.
Dwyer J B, The Tradition of Medieval Manuals in
the Poems of John Gower, diss Univ of N Carolina
1950, p 119.
Everett, The Clensyng of Mannes Soule: An Introd
Study, Southern Quart 13(1975).265.
Patterson L W, The Parson's Tale and the Quitting
of the Canterbury Tales, Trad 34(1978).339, 340,
345.
General References. Deanesly M, The Lollard Bible
and Other Medieval Biblical Versions, Cambridge
1920, p 397 (Clensyng written for a nun of Bark-
ing); Vernacular Books in England in the 14 and
15 Cents, MLR 15(1920).358.
Pfander H G, Some Medieval Manuals of Religious
Instruction in England and Observations on
Chaucer's Parson's Tale, JEGP 35(1936).251, 255
n32.
Bloomfield SDS, p 185.
Bazire and Colledge, p 43 (structure of The Chastising of God's Children and [83]).
Doyle A I, Books Connected with the Vere Family
and Barking Abbey, Trans of the Essex Archaeological Soc 25(1958).234 n4, 240 n4.
Wenzel, pp 84, 229, 232, 247.
Wenzel S, Sloth in ME Devotional Lit, Angl
79(1961).290 n2, 317, 318.
Oiji T, Chusei Bungaku ni okeru Kokkai no Hi-
seki—14 Seiki no Eishi no Baai, Sophia: Studies
in Western Civilization and the Cultural Interac-

tion of East and West (Tokyo) 23(1974).36 (Sacrament of Penance in ME Lit).

Braswell M F, The Medieval Sinner, Rutherford 1983, pp 29, 41, 75, 76, 82, 84, 133 n24.

Bibliography. Ives D V, The Seven Deadly Sins in Eng Lit, London Univ MA thesis 1931, p 50.

[85] WEY TO PARADISE.

MS. BL Harley 1671, ff 2ᵃ–85ᵇ (1390–1410).
Jolliffe, p 78, no E.15.
Revell, p 47.
MS Commentary. A Catalogue of the Harleian MSS in the British Museum, London 1808, 2.170.
Sources. Robert de Sorbon, De Consciencia et De Tribus Dietis, ed F Chambon, Paris 1902, p 35.
Keith G H, A Study of an Anonymous Prose Voie de Paradis: A Partial Edn with Prologomena, diss Univ of California Berkeley 1965.
General References. Owst G R, Literature and Pulpit in Medieval England, Cambridge 1933, p 104.
Bloomfield SDS, p 395 n85.
Keith, p 63.
Patterson L W, The Parson's Tale and the Quitting of the Canterbury Tales, Trad 34(1978).339, 340, 345.

[86] TELL THI SYNS.

MS. Bodl 1999 (Bodley 131), f 140ᵃ (1425–75).
Jolliffe, p 79, no E.18.
MS Commentary. Summary Cat, 2.152.

[87] EXHORTATIONS TO CONFESSION AND EXAMINATION OF CONSCIENCE.

MSS. 1, Camb Univ Gg.6.26, ff 22ᵇ–23ᵃ (15 cent); 2, Trinity Hall Camb 16, f 92ᵇ (1450–1500).
MSS Commentary. A Catalogue of the MSS Preserved in the Libr of the Univ of Cambridge, Cambridge 1858, 3.229 (MS 1).
James M R, A Descriptive Catalogue of the MSS in the Libr of Trinity Hall, Cambridge 1907, p 33 (MS 2).

[88] CONFESSIONAL MANUALS.

MSS. 1, Bodl 13679 (Rawl D.913), ff 16ᵇ–17ᵃ (1400–50); 2, St John's Camb 257, ff 1ᵃ–89ᵇ (15 cent); 3, BL Cotton Vespasian A.xxv, ff 46ᵃ–55ᵇ, 55ᵇ–65ᵃ (1450–1500); 4, BL Harley 4172, ff 116ᵃ–122ᵇ (1426); 5, BL Sloane 1584, ff 7ᵃ–10ᵃ, 19ᵃ–21ᵇ, 63ᵃ–79ᵃ (1500–25).
Jolliffe, pp 76, no E.2; 77, nos E.7, E.10, E.11, E.12; 79, no E.17.

MS Commentary. A Catalogue of the MSS in the Cottonian Libr Deposited in the British Museum, London 1802, p 438 (MS 3).
A Catalogue of the Harleian MSS in the British Museum, London 1808, 3.121 (MS 4).
Macray W D, Catalogi Codicum Manuscriptorum Bibliothecae Bodleianae, Oxford 1898, 5(4).136 (MS 1).
James M R, A Descriptive Catalogue of the MSS in the Libr of St John's Coll Cambridge, Cambridge 1913, p 293 (MS 2).

[89] A GUIDE TO CONFESSION.

MSS. *Version A*: 1, BL Royal 8.F.vii, ff 41ᵇ–45ᵃ (1450–1500); *Version B*: 2, St John's Oxford 173, ff 134ᵇ–135ᵇ (1500–25).
Jolliffe, pp 76, no E.4; 78, no E.16.
MS Commentary. Coxe H O, Catalogus Codicum MSS qui in Collegiis Aulisque Oxoniensibus Hodie Adservantur, Oxford 1852, 2.56 (MS 2).
Warner G F and J P Gilson, Catalogue of Western MSS in the Old Royal and King's Collections, London 1921, 1.165 (MS 1).

[90] ON DAYLY OR FREQUENT CONFESSION.

MSS. 1, BL Harley 494, ff 94ᵃ–96ᵃ (ca 1500); 2, BL Cotton Nero A.iii, f 137ᵃ⁻ᵇ (1475–1500).
Jolliffe, p 76, no E.1.
MS Commentary. A Catalogue of the MSS in the Cottonian Libr Deposited in the British Museum, London 1802, p 200 (MS 2).
A Catalogue of the Harleian MSS in the British Museum, London 1808, 1.329 (MS 1).

[91] HOW THOU SCHALT RYSE FRO SYNNE.

MS. BL Addit 28026, f 189ᵃ (1400–25).
Jolliffe, p 76, no E.3.
MS Commentary. Catalogue of Additions to the MSS in the British Museum in the Years MDCCCLIV–MDCCCLXXV, London 1877, p 399.

[92] HOU MANY MANERS WEYES SYNNE IS FORYEVE.

MSS. 1, BL Harley 2406, ff 7ᵇ–8ᵇ (1475–1500); 2, Trinity Camb 601 (R.3.21), ff 7ᵇ–8ᵃ (1475–1500).
Jolliffe, p 77, no E.6.
MSS Commentary. A Catalogue of the Harleian MSS in the British Museum, London 1808, 2.688 (MS 1).

James M R, The Western MSS in the Libr of Trinity Coll Cambridge A Descriptive Catalogue, Cambridge 1901, 2.83 (MS 2).

[93] THE FOUR MANER OF WASSHINGIS.

MS. BL Harley 4012, f 104a–b (ca 1460).
Jolliffe, p 77, no E.8.
MS Commentary. Wilson E, A ME MS at Coughton Court, Warwickshire, and British Library MS Harley 4012, N&Q ns 24(1977).295.

[94] SEVEN WASHINGS OF SIN.

MS. St John's Oxford 94, f 126b (1420–34).
MS Commentary. Coxe H O, Catalogus Codicum MSS qui in Collegiis Aulisque Oxoniensibus Hodie Adservantur, Oxford 1852, 2.26.

[95] SEVEN THINGS NECESSARY
FOR PARDON.

MSS. 1, Corpus Christi Oxford 237, ff 235a–b (1475–1500); 2, Henry E Huntington HM 140, f 169a (1475–1500).
MSS Commentary. Coxe H O, Catalogus Codicum MSS qui in Collegiis Aulisque Oxoniensibus Hodie Adservantur, Oxford 1852, 2.98 (MS 1).

[96] SEVEN THINGS THAT PREVENT
MEN FROM READING THE BOOK OF
THEIR CONSCIENCE.

MSS. 1, Trinity Oxford E.86, ff 37b–38a (1475–1500); 2, BL Lansdowne 388, f 369a–b (1475–1500).
MSS Commentary. A Catalogue of the Lansdowne MSS in the British Museum, London 1819, p 112 (MS 2).
Coxe H O, Catalogus Codicum MSS qui in Collegiis Aulisque Oxoniensibus Hodie Adservantur, Oxford 1852, 2.35 (MS 1).
Guddat-Figge G, Catalogue of MSS Containing ME Romances, Munich 1976, p 200.

[97] VERSES ON THE INDIVIDUAL
SACRAMENTS.

MSS. Verses on the Seven Sacraments: 1, BL Addit 24660, f 39a (ca 1400).
Verses on Confession and Penance: Version A: 2, St John's Oxford 94, ff 149a–151a (1420–34; John Lacy's Hou that a Man sall knowen the Perelles that longeth to Schrifte); Version B: 3, Camb Univ Dd.1.1, ff 296b–298b (1400–25; on the necessity of Lenten confession); Version C: 4, Trinity Camb

323 (B.14.39), f 27b (13 cent; ten lines on Penance); Version D: 5, Sion Coll L.40.2/E.25, ff 1a–12b (ca 1400; prose version in Jacob's Well).
Verses on the Eucharist: Version A: 6, Bodl 1703 (Digby 102), ff 123b–124b (1400–25; Sacrament of the Altere); Version B: 7, Hereford Cath 0.4.14, f 225a (15 cent; four monoriming lines on the Host); Version C: 8, Durham Univ Cosin V.v.19, f 72a (1475–1500; three couplets on the Sacrament); Version D: 9, Durham Univ Cosin V.v.19, f 73a (1475–1500; six-line stanza on the Host); Version E: 10, BL Royal 17.A.xvi, f 27b (1475–1500); 11, Durham Univ Cosin V.i.12, f 65a (1425–50); 12, Royal Libr Copenhagen ?29264, f 163a (15 cent; not seen; four lines on the Host).
Brown-Robbins, no 1389; Brown-Robbins, Robbins-Cutler, nos 542, 1640, 1860, 2372, 2746; Robbins-Cutler, nos 557.3, 1561.5, 3318.
MSS Commentary. Raine J, Catalogues of the Libr of Durham Cathedral, Surtees Soc 7(1840).141 (MSS 8, 9, 11).
Coxe H O, Catalogus Codicum MSS qui in Collegiis Aulisque Oxoniensibus Hodie Adservantur, Oxford 1852, 2.26 (MS 2).
A Catalogue of the MSS Preserved in the Libr of the Univ of Cambridge, Cambridge 1856, 1.1 (MS 3).
Catalogue of Additions to the MSS in the British Museum in the Years MDCCCLIV–MDCCCLXXV, London 1877, p 94 (MS 1).
Macray W D, Catalogi Codicum Manuscriptorum Bibliothecae Bodleianae, Oxford 1883, 9.116 (MS 6).
James M R, The Western MSS in the Libr of Trinity Coll Cambridge, A Descriptive Catalogue, Cambridge 1900, 1.438 (MS 4).
Warner G F and J P Gilson, Catalogue of Western MSS in the Old Royal and King's Collections, London 1921, 2.217 (MS 10).
Bannister A T, A Descriptive Catalogue of the MSS in the Hereford Cathedral Libr, Hereford 1927, p 48 (MS 7).
Doyle A I, A Prayer Attributed to St Thomas Aquinas, DomS 1(1948).230 (MS 2).
Ker Manuscripts, 1.289 (MS 5).
Editions. Kail J, Twenty-Six Political and Other Poems from the Bodleian MSS Digby 102 and Douce 322, Pt I, EETS 124, London 1904, p 103 (Sacrament of the Altere).
Brown Reg, 1.444 (MS 11); 446 (MS 7).
Robbins R H, Popular Prayers in ME Verse, MP 36(1939).344 (four lines on Host in MSS 10, 11, 12).
Person H A, Cambridge ME Lyrics, rvsd edn, N Y 1962, p 26 (MS 4).

Davies R T, Medieval Eng Lyrics, Evanston 1964, p 196 (MS 10).

Heffernan T J A, On the Importance of Schrifte a ME Poem on Penance, NM 82(1981).362 (MS 3).

Authorship. Pepler C, John Lacy: A Dominican Contemplative, Life of the Spirit 5(1951).397 (MS 2).

Clay R M, Further Studies on Medieval Recluses, Journ of the British Archaeological Assoc 3s 16(1953).74 (Lacy); Some Northern Anchorites, Archaeologica Aeliana 33 (1955).202 (Lacy).

viii. Sins

[98] THE XII ABUSIONS (or MYSUSES).

MSS. 1, All Souls Oxford 24, ff 38^b–59^a (1400–25); 2, Camb Univ Ii.6.55, ff 66^a–78^a (1400–50); 3, BL Egerton 2877, ff 97^b–98^a (17 cent); 4, BL Harley 2330, ff 100^b–119^b (1400–50).

Jolliffe, p 80, no F.5.

MSS Commentary. A Catalogue of the Harleian MSS in the British Museum, London 1808, 2.655 (MS 4).

Coxe H O, Catalogus Codicum MSS qui in Collegiis Aulisque Oxoniensibus Hodie Adservantur, Oxford 1852, 2.6 (MS 1).

A Catalogue of the MSS Preserved in the Libr of the Univ of Cambridge, Cambridge 1858, 3.545 (MS 2).

Catalogue of Additions to the MSS in the British Museum in the Years MDCCCCVI–MDCCCCX, London 1912, p 250 (MS 3).

Source. Migne PL, 40.1079.

Literary Relations. Woolf, p 103.

General Reference. Fristedt S L, The Wycliffite Bible, pt 1, Stockholm Stud in Eng 4(1953).43 (MSS 2 and 4 written by Lollards).

Bibliography. Manual, 2.530 [65]; corrected by A Hudson, Contributions to a Biblio of Wycliffite Writings, N&Q ns 20(1973).452.

[99] HOW THOU SHALT NOT SET LYTLI BY SYNNE.

MS. Westminster Cath Diocesan Archives H38, f 149^b (ca 1400).

Jolliffe, p 79, no F.1.

MS Commentary. Ker Manuscripts, 1.419.

[100] SIX MANER CONSENTIS TO SYNNE.

MSS. 1, Bodl 21820 (Douce 246), f 106^b (1400–50); 2, BL Royal 17.A.xxvi, ff 28^b–29^a (1400–50); 3,

Edinburgh Univ 93, f 22^a–b (1430–50); 4, Glasgow Univ Hunter 512, f 26^a (1400–25).

Jolliffe, p 82, no F.11.

MSS Commentary. Summary Cat, 4.566 (MS 1).

Young J and P H Aitken, A Catalogue of the MSS in the Hunterian Museum in the Univ of Glasgow, Glasgow 1908, p 419 (MS 4).

Borland C R, A Descriptive Catalogue of the Western Mediaeval MSS in Edinb Univ Libr, Edinburgh 1916, p 149 (MS 3).

Warner G F and J P Gilson, Catalogue of Western MSS in the Old Royal and King's Collections, London 1921, 2.220 (MS 2).

Edition. Martin C A, Edinb Univ MS 93: An Annotated Edn of Selected Devotional Treatises, diss Univ of Edinburgh 1978 (MS 3).

[101] THE THREE SPEECHES IN THE HEART.

MSS. 1, Trinity Camb 305 (B.14.19), ff 149^a–150^a (1400–25); 2, Downside Abbey 26542 (Dartford), ff 90^b–92^b (1450–1500).

Jolliffe, p 82, no F.12.

MSS Commentary. James M R, The Western MSS in the Libr of Trinity Coll Cambridge, A Descriptive Catalogue, Cambridge 1900, 1.418 (MS 1).

Watkin A, Some MSS in the Downside Abbey Libr, Downside Rev 59(1941).75 (MS 2).

Ker Manuscripts, 2.442 (MS 2).

Modernization. Kirchberger C, The Coasts of the Country, London nd, p 75.

[102] FOURE ERROURS.

MSS. 1, Camb Univ Ff.6.31(2), ff 98^b–99^b (1425–50); 2, Camb Univ Ff.6.55, ff 168^b–170^b (ca 1400); 3, Trinity Camb 601 (R.3.21), f 17^a (1475–1500); 4, BL Harley 2398, f 36^a–b (ca 1450); 5, Soc of Antiquaries 300, ff 99^b–100^a (ca 1400); 6, Edinburgh Univ 93, ff 83^b–85^a (1430–50); 7, Glasgow Univ Hunter 512, ff 220^a–221^b (1400–25); 8, Glasgow Univ Hunter 520, pp 295–297 (1450–1500); 9, Durham Cath A.iv.22, pp 149–150 (1425–50).

Jolliffe, p 82, no F.13.

MSS Commentary. A Catalogue of the Harleian MSS in the British Museum, London 1808, 2.684 (MS 4).

A Catalogue of the MSS Preserved in the Libr of the Univ of Cambridge, Cambridge 1857, 2.533 (MS 1), 547 (MS 2).

James M R, The Western MSS in the Libr of Trinity Coll Cambridge, A Descriptive Catalogue, Cambridge 1901, 2.83 (MS 3).

Young J and P H Aitken, A Catalogue of the MSS in the Hunterian Museum in the Univ of Glasgow, Glasgow 1908, pp 419, 422 (MSS 7, 8).

Borland C R, A Descriptive Catalogue of the Western Medieval MSS in Edinb Univ Libr, Edinburgh 1916, p 149 (MS 6).

Ker Manuscripts, 1.310 (MS 5); 2.493 (MS Hunter 15).

Edition. Martin C A, Edinb Univ MS 93: An Annotated Edn of Selected Devotional Treatises, diss Univ of Edinburgh 1978, p 194 (MS 6).

General Reference. Doyle Survey, 1.168.

[103] VII THINGS TO BEAR IN MIND.

MS. St John's Oxford 173, f 129ᵃ (1500–25).

Jolliffe, p 84, no F.26.

MS Commentary. Coxe H O, Catalogus Codicum MSS qui in Collegiis Aulisque Oxoniensibus Hodie Adservantur, Oxford 1852, 2.56.

[104] THE FORM OF LIVING.

MS. BL Cotton Tiberius E.vii, ff 85ᵇ–90ᵃ (1350–1400).

Brown-Robbins, Robbins-Cutler, no 1442.

MS Commentary. A Catalogue of the MSS in the Cottonian Libr Deposited in the British Museum, London 1802, p 40.

Edition. Yksh Wr, 2.283.

Discussion. Blake N F, The Form of Living in Prose and Poetry, Arch 211(1974).300.

[105] ON DEADLY AND VENIAL SIN.

MSS. 1, Camb Univ Dd.5.55, f 100ᵃ⁻ᵇ (ca 1400); 2, Camb Univ Ff.5.40, ff 96ᵇ–97ᵇ (1400–50).

Jolliffe, p 80, no F.3.

MSS Commentary. A Catalogue of the MSS Preserved in the Libr of the Univ of Cambridge, Cambridge 1856, 1.275 (MS 1); 2(1857).498 (MS 2).

Edition. Yksh Wr, 1.182 (MS 1).

[106] A LITIL TRETYS ON THE
SEVEN DEADLY SINS.

MSS. 1, Bodl 655 (Laud misc 23), ff 23ᵃ–39ᵇ (1400–25); 2, Bodl 6951 (Ashmole 750), ff 89ᵃ–96ᵃ (1475–1500); 3, Bodl 12146 (Rawl C.288), ff 1ᵃ–13ᵇ (1400–50); 4, Bodl 21634 (Douce 60), ff 193ᵃ–213ᵃ (1450–1500); 5, Camb Univ Ff.6.31, ff 11ᵃ–60ᵃ (1425–50); 6, Trinity Camb 305 (B. 14.19), ff 243ᵃ–258ᵃ (1400–25); 7, BL Harley 211, ff 35ᵃ–46ᵇ (1400–25); 8, BL Harley 1197, ff 9ᵃ–28ᵇ (1425–50); 9, BL Harley 1288, ff 64ᵃ–75ᵃ (1450–1500); 10, BL Harley 2383, ff 65ᵃ–75ᵇ

(1425–50); 11, BL Royal 8.C.i, ff 144ᵃ–156ᵇ (1400–50); 12, BL Sloane, ff 4ᵃ–23ᵃ (1450–1500); 13, Dr William's Libr London Anc 3, ff 133ᵇ–145ᵇ (1450–1500); 14, Soc of Antiquaries London 687, ff 383ᵇ–411ᵇ (ca 1400); 15, Univ of Leeds Brotherton 501, ff 68ᵃ–74ᵃ (ca 1450); 16, St Peter Hungate Mus Norwich 48.158.926, ff 31ᵃ–58ᵇ (1400–50).

Jolliffe, p 79, no F.2.

Robbins-Cutler, nos 621.5, 879.5, 4110.5 (verse tags).

MSS Commentary. A Catalogue of the Harleian MSS in the British Museum, London 1808, 1.66 (MS 7), 595 (MS 8), 648 (MS 9); 2.675 (MS 10).

Black W H, A Descriptive, Analytical, and Critical Catalogue of the MSS Bequeathed unto the Univ of Oxford by Elias Ashmole, Oxford 1845, p 357 (MS 2).

A Catalogue of the MSS Preserved in the Libr of the Univ of Cambridge, Cambridge 1857, 2.533 (MS 5).

Coxe H O, Catalogi Codicum Manuscriptorum Bibliothecae Bodleianae, Oxford 1858, 2(1).65 (MS 1).

Macray W D, Catalogi Codicum Manuscriptorum Bibliothecae Bodleianae, Oxford 1878, 5(2).125 (MS 3).

James M R, The Western MSS in the Libr of Trinity Coll Cambridge, A Descriptive Catalogue, Cambridge 1900, 1.418 (MS 6).

Wakelin M F, The MSS of John Mirk's Festial, Leeds SE 1(1967).98 (MS 9), 104 (MS 4).

Summary Cat, 4.508 (MS 4).

Herbert, 3.100, 681 (MS 9).

Warner G F and J P Gilson, Catalogue of Western MSS in the Old Royal and King's Collections, London 1921, 1.228 (MS 11).

Humphreys K W and J Lightbown, Two MSS of the Pricke of Conscience in the Brotherton Collection, Leeds SE 7–8(1952).30 (MS 15).

Bazire J and E Colledge, edd, The Chastising of God's Children, Oxford 1957, p 5 and note 3 (MS 9).

Ker Manuscripts, 1.314 (MS 14), 426 (MS 13); 3.67 (MS 15), 523 (MS 16).

Editions. Lloyd D J, An Edn of the Prose and Verse in the Bodleian MS Laud Miscellaneous 23, diss Yale Univ 1943 (MS 1).

Zutphen J P W M van, A Litil Tretys on the Seven Deadly Sins by Richard Lavynham, Rome 1956, p 1 (base text: MS 7; Introd: pp vii, literary background; xii, content and sources; xxviii, authorship; xxxiii, description of MSS [except MS 13]; l, relationship of MSS; lix, language) (crit B Sundby, ESts 41.267; E Zeeman, MLR 52.581;

K Brunner, Angl 75.441; E Colledge RES 9.58; J F Vanderheyden, LB [1958].51).

Selection. Matthews W, ed, Later Medieval Eng Prose, N Y 1963, p 118.

Authorship. DNB, 11.652 (sv Lavenham or Lavyngham, Richard).

Xiberta B, De Scriptoribus Scholasticis Saeculi XIV ex Ordine Carmelitarum, Louvain 1931, pp 42, 49, 117, 188, 334.

Emden A B, A Biographical Register of the Univ of Oxford to AD 1500, Oxford 1958, 2.1109.

Literary Relations. Deanesly M, The Lollard Bible and Other Medieval Biblical Versions, Cambridge 1920, pp 297, 379.

Owst G R, Literature and Pulpit in Medieval England, Cambridge 1933, p 443.

Pfander H G, Some Medieval Manuals of Religious Instruction in England and Observations on Chaucer's Parson's Tale, JEGP 35(1936).256.

Bloomfield SDS, pp 167, 216, 410.

Wenzel, pp 232, 233, 293.

Wenzel S, Sloth in ME Devotional Lit, Angl 79(1961).293.

Fischer N, Handlist of Animal References in ME Lit, Leeds SE 4(1970).58, 68, 101, 105.

Bibliography. New CBEL, 1.504.

Barratt A, Works of Religious Instruction, in A S G Edwards, ME Prose, New Brunswick 1984, p 42.

[107] A TRACT ON THE DEADLY SINS.

MS. BL Addit 30944, ff 3ᵃ–154ᵇ (1475–1500).
Jolliffe, p 81, no F.9.

MS Commentary. Catalogue of Additions to the MSS in the British Museum in the Years MDCCCLXXVI–MDCCCLXXXI, London 1882, p 133.

General Reference. Francis W N, ed, The Book of Vices and Virtues, EETS 217, London 1942 (rptd 1968), p xl.

[108] A TRACT ON THE SEVEN DEADLY SINS.

MSS. 1, BL Royal 17.A.xxvi, ff 22ᵃ–26ᵇ (1400–50); 2, Glasgow Univ Gen 223, ff 217ᵃ–221ᵃ (1400–25); 3, Glasgow Univ Hunter 512, ff 12ᵇ–21ᵃ (1400–25). *Related tract*: 4, ?Hopton Hall (Chandos-Pole-Gell) (1400–25).

MSS Commentary. Historical MSS Commission, 9th Report of the Royal Commission on Historical MSS, pt 2, London 1883, appendix, p 384 (MS 4).

Young J and P H Aitken, A Catalogue of the MSS in the Hunterian Museum in the Univ of Glasgow, Glasgow 1908, p 419 (MS 3).

Warner G F and J P Gilson, Catalogue of Western MSS in the Old Royal and King's Collections, London 1921, 2.220 (MS 1).

Ker Manuscripts, 2.904 (MS 2).

Literary Relations. Kellogg A L and E W Talbert, The Wyclifite Pater Noster and Ten Commandments, with Special Reference to Eng MSS 85 and 90 in the John Rylands Libr, JRLB 42(1960).350 (relationship to Wycliffite exposition).

[109] PRIDE, ENVY, AND WRATH.

MSS. 1, Camb Univ Ii.6.43, ff 9ᵇ–11ᵃ (1400–25); 2, Soc of Antiquaries London 300, ff 106ᵇ–107ᵃ (ca 1400); 3, Trinity Dublin 70, ff 183ᵃ–185ᵃ (15 cent).

Jolliffe, p 83, no F.19.

MSS Commentary. A Catalogue of the MSS Preserved in the Libr of the Univ of Cambridge, Cambridge 1858, 3.540 (MS 1).

Abbott T K, Catalogue of the MSS in the Libr of Trinity Coll Dublin, Dublin 1900, p 9 (MS 3).

Ker Manuscripts, 1.310 (MS 2).

[110] DEVILS AND DEADLY SINS.

MS. Trinity Oxford E.86, f 31ᵃ⁻ᵇ (1475–1500).

MS Commentary. Coxe H O, Catalogus Codicum MSS qui in Collegiis Aulisque Oxoniensibus Hodie Adservantur, Oxford 1852, 2.35.

[111] NOTES ON THE DEADLY SINS.

MS. Salisbury Cath 126, f 198ᵇ (1400–25).

MS Commentary. A Catalogue of the Libr of the Cathedral Church of Salisbury, London 1880, p 24.

Authorship. Emden A B, A Biographical Register of the Univ of Oxford to 1500, Oxford 1957, 1.531.

[112] FIVE SINS AGAINST THE HOLY GHOST.

MSS. 1, Trinity Oxford E.86, f 35ᵃ (1475–1500); 2, BL Lansdowne 388, f 368ᵃ (1475–1500).

MSS Commentary. Catalogue of the Lansdowne MSS in the British Museum, London 1819, p 12 (MS 2).

Coxe H O, Catalogus Codicum MSS qui in Collegiis Aulisque Oxoniensibus Hodie Adservantur, Oxford 1852, 2.34 (MS 1).

Guddat-Figge G, Catalogue of MSS Containing ME Romances, Munich 1976, p 209 (MS 2).

[113] THE TEMPTACIONS OF THE DEVILLE.

MS. BL Addit 10106, ff 47ᵃ–49ᵃ (1475–1500).
Jolliffe, p 120, no K.6.

MS Commentary. List of Additions to the MSS in the British Museum in the Years MDCCCXXXVI–MDCCCXL, London 1843, p 12.

[114] MAN'S ENEMIES.

MS. BL Cotton Titus D.xix, ff 165ª–168ª (1400–50). Jolliffe, p 84, no F.24.

MS Commentary. A Catalogue of the MSS in the Cottonian Libr Deposited in the British Museum, London 1802, p 565.

[115] PRIDE, WRATH, AND ENVIE SYNNES OF THE FEND.

MSS. 1, Bodl 2289 (Bodley 85), ff 115ᵇ–116ᵇ (1375–1400); 2, Bodl 10027 (Tanner 201), f 2ᵃ⁻ᵇ (1400–25); 3, Bodl Lyell 29, ff 99ᵇ–102ᵇ (1400–50); 3a, Trinity Oxford E.86, ff 30ᵇ–31ª (1475–1500); 4, Camb Univ Nn.4.12, ff 7ᵇ–9ª (1400–25); 5, Emmanuel Camb 246, ff 58ᵇ–59ᵇ (1350–1400); 6, BL Royal 18.A.x, ff 85ᵇ–86ᵇ (1400–25); 7, BL Harley 2343, ff 80ª–81ᵇ (1400–50); 8, BL Addit 27592, ff 45ᵇ–46ᵇ (ca 1400); 9, John Rylands Eng 85, ff 9ª–13ª (1400–25); 10, Edinburgh Univ 93, ff 11ª–15ª (1430–50); 11, Glasgow Univ Hunter 472, ff 76ᵇ–78ª (1382); 12, Pierpont Morgan 861, f 4ᵃ⁻ᵇ (ca 1450); 13, Henry E Huntington HM.502, ff 87ª–90ᵇ (1450–1500). Jolliffe, p 83, no F.21.

MSS Commentary. A Catalogue of the Harleian MSS in the British Museum, London 1808, 2.660 (MS 7).

Coxe H O, Catalogus Codicum MSS qui in Collegiis Aulisque Oxoniensibus Hodie Adservantur, Oxford 1852, 2.34 (MS 3a).

Hackman A, Catalogi Codicum Manuscriptorum Bibliothecae Bodleianae, Oxford 1860, 4.637 (MS 2).

A Catalogue of the MSS Preserved in the Libr of the Univ of Cambridge, Cambridge 1860, 4.499 (MS 4).

Catalogue of Additions to the MSS in the British Museum in the Years MDCCCLIV–MDCCCLXXV, London 1877, p 334 (MS 8).

Summary Cat, 2.291 (MS 1).

James M R, The Western MSS in the Libr of Emmanuel Coll, a Descriptive Catalogue, Cambridge 1904, p 144 (MS 5).

Young J and P H Aitken, A Catalogue of the MSS in the Hunterian Museum in the Univ of Glasgow, Glasgow 1908, p 392 (MS 11).

Borland C R, A Descriptive Catalogue of the Western Mediaeval MSS in Edinb Univ Libr, Edinburgh 1916, p 149 (MS 10).

Warner G F and J P Gilson, Catalogue of Western MSS in the Old Royal and King's Collections, London 1921, 2.265 (MS 6).

Bühler C F, The ME Texts of Morgan MS 861, PMLA 69(1954).686 (MS 12).

De La Mare A, Catalogue of the Collection of Medieval MSS Bequeathed to the Bodleian Libr Oxford by James P R Lyell, Oxford 1971, p 59 (MS 3).

Ker Manuscripts, 3.409 (MS 9).

Hanna R III, The Index of ME Prose, Handlist I, A Handlist of Manuscripts containing ME Prose in the Henry E Huntington Library, Woodbridge 1984, p 30.

Edition. Martin C A, Edinb Univ MS 93: an Annotated Edn of Selected Devotional Treatises, diss Univ of Edinburgh 1978 (MS 10).

General Reference. Fisher J H, review of Bloomfield SDS, in Spec 28(1953).864.

[116] GIVE ME LICENSE TO LIVE IN EASE.

MSS. 1, Camb Univ Ff.1.6, ff 56ᵇ–58ᵇ (1450–1500); 2, BL Sloane 747, ff 95ª–96ª (1500–25); 3, BL Addit 11307, f 121ª (19-cent transcript of MS 4); 4, Henry E Huntington HM 183, f 5ª (1450–1500).

Brown-Robbins, no 373.

MSS Commentary. List of Additions to the MSS in the British Museum in the Years MDCCCXXXVI–MDCCCXL, London 1843, p 2 (MS 3).

A Catalogue of the MSS Preserved in the Libr of the Univ of Cambridge, Cambridge 1857, 2.286 (MS 1).

de Ricci Census, 1.63 (MS 4).

Robbins R H, The Findern Anthology, PMLA 69(1954).610 (MS 1).

Guddat-Figge G, Catalogue of MSS Containing ME Romances, Munich 1976, p 90 (MS 1).

Editions. Brydges S E, Censura Literaria, 2nd edn, London 1815, 10.150 (MS 4).

Halliwell-Phillipps J O, Nugae Poeticae, London 1844, p 64 (MS 1).

Furnivall F J, Political, Religious and Love Poems, EETS 15, rvsd edn, London 1903, p 244 (MS 1).

Brown RLxvC, p 273 (MS 4).

Facsimile. The Findern MS. Cambridge Univ Libr MS Ff.1.6, with an introd by R Beadle and A E B Owen, London 1977.

General Reference. Bloomfield SDS, p 205.

[117] AUGUSTINUS DE PECCATIS VENIALIBUS.

MS. Trinity Camb 1144 (0.2.40), f 103ᵃ⁻ᵇ (1475–1500).

Brown-Robbins, Robbins-Cutler, no 806.
MS Commentary. James M R, The Western MSS in the Libr of Trinity Coll Cambridge, A Descriptive Catalogue, Cambridge 1932, 3.142.
Edition. Person H A, Cambridge ME Lyrics, rvsd edn, N Y 1962, p 22.

[118] ON THE REMISSION OF VENIAL SINS.

MSS. No MS extant. PRINT: W Caxton, Ars Moriendi, Westminster 1491 (STC, no 786).
Edition. Morgan G R, A Critical Edn of Caxton's The Art & Craft to Know Well to Die and Ars Moriendi Together with the Antecedent MS Material, diss Oxford Univ 1972, p 229.

[119] DECEM REMEDIA CONTRA PECCATA VENIALIA.

MS. Trinity Camb 1144 (0.2.40), f 104^a (1475–1500).
Brown-Robbins, Robbins-Cutler, no 3866.
MS Commentary. James M R, The Western MSS in the Libr of Trinity Coll Cambridge, A Descriptive Catalogue, Cambridge 1932, 3.142.
Edition. Person H A, Cambridge ME Lyrics, rvsd edn, N Y 1962, p 23.

[120] VII DEGREES OF PRYDE.

MSS. 1, Bodl 11263 (Rawl A.381), f 6^{a-b} (ca 1450); 2, BL Harley 1706, f 94^b (1450–1500).
Jolliffe, p 80, no F.6.
Revell, p 48.
MSS Commentary. A Catalogue of the Harleian MSS in the British Museum, London 1808, 2.178 (MS 2).
Macray W D, Catalogi Codicum Manuscriptorum Bibliothecae Bodleianae, Oxford 1862, 5(1).380 (MS 1).
General Reference. Doyle A I, Books Connected with the Vere Family and Barking Abbey, Trans of the Essex Archaeological Soc 25(1958).227.

[121] AYENST THE EXCUSACION OF LECHERY AND OTHIR DEDLY SYNNES.

MS. Bodl 2322 (Bodley 423), ff 166^a–167^a (ca 1450).
Jolliffe, p 84, no F.23.
MS Commentary. Summary Cat, 2.308.

[122] POLLUCION.

MS. BL Harley 1288, ff 86^b–87^b (1450–1500).
Jolliffe, p 83, no F.18.

MS Commentary. A Catalogue of the Harleian MSS in the British Museum, London 1808, 1.648.
Zutphen J P W M van, ed, A Lityl Tretys on the Seven Deadly Sins by Richard Lavynham, Rome 1956, p xxxvii.
Bazire J and E Colledge, edd, The Chastising of God's Children, Oxford 1957, p 5.

[123] AGAINST SWEARING AND FLATTERY.

MS. Bodl lat misc c.66, f 128^{a-b} (1475–1500).
Jolliffe, pp 83, no F.15; 84, no F.27.
MS Commentary. Historical MSS Commission, 2nd Report of the Royal Commission on Historical MSS, London 1871, appendix, p 80.

[124] LOKE AFTIRWARD THAT THOU BE WEL OCUPIED.

MS. Westminster Cath Diocesan Archives H38, f 149^b (ca 1400).
Jolliffe, p 79, no F.1.
MS Commentary. Ker Manuscripts, 1.419.

[125] PUNISHMENTS FOR ADULTERY.

MS. St John's Camb 37, f 55^b (15 cent).
MS Commentary. James M R, A Descriptive Catalogue of the MSS in the Libr of St John's Coll Cambridge, Cambridge 1913, p 48.

[126] MISCELLANEOUS VERSES ON SIN.

MSS. 1, BL Egerton 2810, ff 180^b–181^a (ca 1450); 2, BL Addit 17013, f 5^a (1400–25); 3, BL Harley 957, f 27^b (14 cent); 4, BL Harley 7322, ff 140^b, 143^b, 148^b, 158^a (1400–50); 5, BL Royal 18.A.x, ff 125^a–126^a (1400–25); 6, BL Sloane 2275, f 245^a (1350–1400); 7, Lambeth Palace 78, f 67^a (1400–50); 8, Lambeth Palace 180, f 224^b (1375–1400); 9, Nat Libr of Scotland Advocates 18.7.21, f 16^b (1372).
Brown-Robbins, nos 174, 1217, 1431, 1466, 2671, 2772, 2773, 2864, 3506; Robbins-Cutler, nos 174, 1217, 1466, 2602.4, 2671, 2773, 2864, 3084.3, 3506.
MSS Commentary. A Catalogue of the Harleian MSS in the British Museum, London 1808, 1.484 (MS 3); 3.525 (MS 4).
Catalogue of Additions to the MSS in the British Museum in the Years MDCCCXLVI–MDCCCXLVII, London 1864, p 347 (MS 2).
Catalogue of Additions to the MSS in the British Museum in the Years 1894–1899, London 1901, p 557 (MS 1).

Warner G F and J P Gilson, Catalogue of Western MSS in the Old Royal and King's Collections, London 1921, 2.265 (MS 5).

James and Jenkins, edn, pp 128 (MS 7), 283 (MS 8).

Editions. Rel Ant, 1.260 (MS 1).

Furnivall F J, Political, Religious, and Love Poems, EETS 15, rvsd edn, London 1903, pp 257, 258, 260, 263 (MS 4).

Brown Reg, 1.354 (MS 4, f 158ª).

James M R and C Jenkins, A Descriptive Catalogue of the MSS in the Libr of Lambeth Palace, Cambridge 1930, pp 133 (MS 7; six verses only), 284 (MS 8).

Francis W N, The Book of Vices and Virtues, EETS 217, London 1942, p 340 (MS 2).

Bloomfield SDS, pp 166 (MS 4), 168 (MS 8).

Bowers R H, A ME Diatribe against Backbiting, MLN 69(1954).160 (MS 5).

Bowers R H, A ME Mnemonic Poem on Usury, MS 17(1955).230.

Wilson E, A Descriptive Index of the Eng Lyrics in John of Grimestone's Preaching Book, Oxford 1973, p 4 (MS 9).

Sources and Literary Relations. Bloomfield SDS, pp 160, 165, 166, 167, 168, 203, 209.

Woolf, pp 119, 218, 220, 222, 224, 233, 322, 361, 375, 377.

ix. Gifts of the Holy Ghost

[127] THE GIFTS OF THE HOLY GHOST.

MSS. Verse: 1, Camb Univ Ii.4.9, ff 188ᵇ–190ª (ca 1450).

Prose: 2, Bodl 4061 (Hatton 26), f 211ª (1200–50); 3, Bodl Lat liturg e.17, f 105ᵇ (1450–1500); 4, Emmanuel Camb 246, f 61ᵇ (1350–1400); 5, BL Lansdowne 388, f 368ª (1475–1500); 6, Soc of Antiquaries London 300, f 106ª⁻ᵇ (ca 1400).

Brown-Robbins, Robbins-Cutler, no 215.

MSS Commentary. A Catalogue of the MSS Preserved in the Libr of the Univ of Cambridge, Cambridge 1858, 3.448 (MS 1).

Summary Cat, 2.819 (MS 2).

James M R, The Western MSS in the Libr of Emmanuel Coll, A Descriptive Catalogue, Cambridge 1904, p 144 (MS 4).

Ker Manuscripts, 1.310 (MS 6).

Guddat-Figge G, Catalogue of MSS Containing ME Romances, Munich 1976, p 209.

Edition. Bowers R H, A ME Poem on the Seven Gifts of the Holy Ghost, MLN 70(1955).249 (MS 1).

x. Beatitudes

[128] BEATITUDES.

MSS. Verse: 1, Nat Libr of Scotland Advocates 18.7.21, f 25ª (1372; two versions); 2, Bodl 1703 (Digby 102), ff 121ᵇ–123ª (1400–25).

Prose: 3, Bodl 2628 (Bodley 788), f 246ª (ca 1400); 4, Bodl 12716 (Rawl C.882), f 74ª (1400–25); 5, Trinity Oxford E.86, ff 36ᵇ–37ª (1475–1500); 6, BL Harley 2343, f 90ª⁻ᵇ (1400–50); 7, BL Lansdowne 388, ff 368ᵇ–369ª (1475–1500); 8, Camb Univ Ii.6.43, ff 15ª–16ª (1400–25); 9, BL Addit 30897, ff 65ᵇ–66ª (1400–50); 10, BL Addit 60577, ff 156ª–157ª (1475–1550); 11, Columbia Univ Plimpton 258, f 6ª (ca 1400).

Brown-Robbins, nos 526, 2762, 2763.

MSS Commentary. A Catalogue of the Harleian MSS in the British Museum, London 1808, 2.660 (MS 6).

A Catalogue of the MSS Preserved in the Libr of the Univ of Cambridge, Cambridge 1858, 3.540 (MS 8).

Catalogue of Additions to the MSS in the British Museum in the Years MDCCCLXXVI–MDCCCLXXXI, London 1882, p 126 (MSS 9, 10).

Macray W D, Catalogi Codicum Manuscriptorum Bibliothecae Bodleianae, Oxford 1878, 5(2).460 (MS 4); Oxford 1883, 9.116 (MS 2).

Summary Cat, 2.457 (MS 3).

de Ricci Census, 2.1800 (MS 11).

Guddat-Figge G, Catalogue of MSS Containing ME Romances, Munich 1976, p 209 (MS 7).

Editions. Kail J, 26 Political and Other Poems, EETS 124, London 1904, p 96 (MS 2).

Wilson E, A Descriptive Index of the Eng Lyrics in John of Grimestone's Preaching Book, Oxford 1973, p 8 (MS 1).

Facsimiles. Plimpton G A, The Education of Chaucer, N Y 1935, plate IX.11–12.

The Winchester Anthology with an Introd by E Wilson and I Fenlon, Woodbridge 1981 (MS 10).

III. Guides to the Christian Life

[129] NO MAN MAY SERVE TWO LORDIS.

MS. Camb Univ Ff.6.31 (2), ff 80ᵃ–92ᵃ (1425–75).
Jolliffe, p 101, no H.24.
MS Commentary. A Catalogue of the MSS Preserved in the Libr of the Univ of Cambridge, Cambridge 1857, 2.533.

[130] TWO WEYES CONTRARIOUS.

MSS. 1, Magdalene Camb Pepys 2125, ff 125ᵇ–126ᵃ (1425–75; copy of MS 2); 2, BL Harley 2398, ff 174ᵇ–175ᵇ (1400–25).
Jolliffe, p 104, no I.2.
MSS Commentary. A Catalogue of the Harleian MSS in the British Museum, London 1808, 2.684.
James M R, A Descriptive Catalogue of the Libr of Samuel Pepys, pt 3, Mediaeval MSS, London 1923, p 72 (MS 1).

[131] THE WORLD IS CONTRARIE TO GOD.

MSS. 1, BL Harley 2339, ff 16ᵃ–17ᵃ (1400–50); 2, Soc of Antiquaries London 300, f 99ᵃ⁻ᵇ (ca 1400). It is also incorporated in a Wycliffite commentary on the Seven Deadly Sins in: 3, Camb Univ Nn.4.12, ff 7ᵃ–11ᵃ (1400–25).
Jolliffe, pp 83, no F.17; 112, no I.28.
MSS Commentary. A Catalogue of the Harleian MSS in the British Museum, London 1808, 2.658 (MS 1).
Doyle A I, A Treatise of the Three Estates, DomS 3(1950).351 (MS 1).
Ker Manuscripts, 1.310 (MS 2).

[132] HOW LORDIS AND HOUSBONDEMEN SCHULDE TECHE GODDIS COMAUNDEMENTIS AND THE GOSPEL TO SUGGETTIS AND ANSWERE FOR HEM TO GOD ON DOMESDAY.

MSS. 1, Camb Univ Hh.1.3, f 2ᵃ (ca 1400; a fragment); 2, Edinb Univ 93, ff 87ᵇ–90ᵃ (1430–50); 3, Westminster School London 3, ff 117ᵇ–119ᵇ (1400–50).
Jolliffe, p 104, no I.1.
MSS Commentary. A Catalogue of MSS Preserved in the Libr of the Univ of Cambridge, Cambridge 1858, 3.236 (MS 1).
Borland C R, A Descriptive Catalogue of the Western Mediaeval MSS in Edinb Univ Libr, Edinburgh 1916, p 149 (MS 2).

Ker Manuscripts, 1.422 (MS 3).
Edition. Martin C A, Edinb Univ Libr 93. An Annotated Edn of Selected Devotional Treatises with a Survey of Parallel Versions, diss Univ of Edinb 1978, 1.229.

[133] SIR JOHN CLANVOWE'S THE TWO WAYS.

MSS. 1, Univ Oxf 97, ff 114ᵃ–123ᵇ (1390–1400); 2, BL Addit 22283, f 116ᵃ (1380–1400).
MSS Commentary. Coxe H O, Catalogus Codicum MSS qui in Collegiis Aulisque Oxoniensibus Hodie Adservantur, Oxford 1857, 1.28 (MS 1).
Catalogue of the Additions to the MSS in the British Museum in the Years MDCCCLIV–MDCCCLX, London 1875, p 623 (MS 2).
Guddat-Figge G, Catalogue of MSS Containing ME Romances, Munich 1976, p 145 (MS 2).
Editions. Scattergood V J, The Two Ways—An Unpublished Religious Treatise by Sir John Clanvowe, Eng Philological Stud 10(1967).33.
Scattergood, The Works of Sir John Clanvowe, Ipswich and Totowa 1975, p 57 (Introd: Religious Context, p 18; Description of MSS, p 21; Clanvowe's Life and Writings, p 22; crit N F Blake, N&Q ns 23.116; C Sisam, RES 28.199).
Authorship. Waugh W T, The Lollard Knights, SHR 11(1914).75 (Clanvowe's career; no evidence of Lollardry).
McFarlane K B, Lancastrian Kings and Lollard Knights, Oxford 1972, p 148 (disputes Waugh).
Scattergood, The Authorship of The Book of Cupide, Angl 82(1964).37.
Jacobs N, Clanvowe, N&Q ns 25(1978).292 (name derives from Llanfocha, the Welsh name of St Maughans, Monmouthshire).
Textual Matters. Wilson E, A Supplementary Note to an Edn of Sir John Clanvowe's Treatise The Two Ways, Eng Philological Stud 11(1968).55 (variants from MS 2).
General References. Renwick-Orton, p 278.
Cottle B, The Triumph of English 1350–1400, London 1969, p 248 (religious views).
Middleton A, The Idea of Public Poetry in the Reign of Richard II, Spec 53(1978).94.
Green R F, Poets and Princepleasers, Toronto 1980, pp 3, 65, 110, 130, 196.
Scattergood V J and J W Sherborne, edd, Eng Court Culture in the Later Middle Ages, N Y 1983, pp 40, 168.
Bibliography. New CBEL, 1.504.

[134] VOR TO SSEAWY THE LOKINGE
OF MAN WYTH INNE.

MS. BL Arundel 57, ff 94^b–96^b (1340).
Jolliffe, p 106, no I.11.
Editions. Brandl A and O Zippel, Me Sprach- und
Literaturproben, 2nd edn, Berlin 1927, p 227.
Wilson R M, Sawles Warde, Leeds 1938, p 3.
Gradon P, Dan Michel's Ayenbite of Inwyt or Re-
morse of Conscience, EETS 23, London 1965,
1.263 (revision of R Morris's edn of 1866); 2.1
(description of MS), 14 (language).
Latin Source. Southern R W and F S Schmitt, Me-
morials of St Anselm, Auctores Britannici Medii
Aevi 1, London 1969, 1.355.
Becker W, The Source Text of Sawles Warde, Man-
uscripta 24(1980).44.
General References. Vollhardt W, Einfluss der latei-
nischen geistlichen Literatur auf einige kleinere
Schöpfungen der engl Übergangsperiode, Leipzig 1888, p 26.
Konrath M, Die lateinische Quelle zu Ayenbite, ed
Morris ... und zu Sawles Warde, EStn 12
(1889).459.
Cornelius R D, The Figurative Castle, Bryn Mawr
1930, pp 27, 29.

[135] A GOOD TRETYS TO GODE LEVYNG
TO ALL MANER ASTATES OF THE PEOPLE.

MS. BL Addit 10106, ff 44^a–47^a (1475–1500).
MS Commentary. List of Additions to the MSS in the
British Museum in the Years MDCCCXXXVI–
MDCCCXL, London 1893, p 12.

[136] HOW ECH MAN AND WOMAN MAY
LERNE TO LOVE AND SERVE GOD ECH
IN HIS DEGREE.

MS. BL Harley 2339, ff 72^a–78^a (1400–50).
Jolliffe, p 104, no I.5.
MS Commentary. A Catalogue of the Harleian MSS
in the British Museum, London 1808, 2.658.
Edition. Doyle A I, A Treatise of the Three Estates,
DomS 3(1950).351.

[137] IFF THOU HAVE GODIS OF GRACE.

MSS. 1, Bodl 655 (Laud misc 23), f 43^{a–b} (1400–25);
2, Corpus Christi Camb 385, ff 220^b–221^a (ca
1400); 3, Trinity Camb 601 (R.3.21), f 12^{a–b}
(1475–1500); 4, Trinity Camb 1099 (O.1.74), ff
24^a–26^b (1450–1500); 5, Edinb Univ 93, ff 25^b–
27^a (1430–50).
Jolliffe, p 109, no I.19.

MSS Commentary. Coxe H O, Catalogi Codicum
Manuscriptorum Bibliothecae Bodleianae, Oxford 1858, 2(1).65 (MS 1).
James M R, The Western MSS in the Libr of Trinity
Coll Cambridge, A Descriptive Catalogue, Cambridge 1901, 2.83 (MS 3); 3(1902).74 (MS 4); A
Descriptive Catalogue of the MSS in the Libr of
Corpus Christi Coll Cambridge, Cambridge 1912,
2.232 (MS 2).
Borland C R, A Descriptive Catalogue of the Western Mediaeval MSS in Edinb Univ Libr, Edinburgh 1916, p 149 (MS 5).
Edition. Martin C A, Edinb Univ Libr 93. An Annotated Edn of Selected Devotional Treatises with
a Survey of Parallel Versions, diss Univ of Edinb
1978, 1.172.

[138] IX POYNTYS.

MSS. 1, Trinity Camb 181 (B.15.39), ff 170^b–171^b
(1400–25); 2, BL Harley 1706, ff 151^a–154^b
(1450–1500).
Jolliffe, p 111, no I.26.
MSS Commentary. A Catalogue of the Harleian MSS
in the British Museum, London 1808, 2.178 (MS
2).
James M R, The Western MSS in the Libr of Trinity
Coll Cambridge, A Descriptive Catalogue, Cam-
bridge 1900, 1.232 (MS 1).
Edition. Yksh Wr, 2.375 (MS 2).
General References. Doyle Survey, 1.172.
Bloomfield SDS, p 178.

[139] CLENNESSE OF SOWLE.

MSS. Version A: 1, BL Sloane 982, f 60^b (1400–25);
Version B: 2, Bodl 12143 (Rawl C.285), f 61^{a–b}
(1400–50); 3, Camb Univ Ff.5.40, f 117^b (1400–
50); *Version C:* 4, Bodl 1999 (Bodley 131), f 131^a
(1425–75); 5, Trinity Camb 336 (B.14.53), ff
140^b–141^a (1400–50); 6, BL Arundel 197, f 10^a
(ca 1400); 7, BL Royal 18.A.x, f 10^{a–b} (1400–25);
8, Chetham's Hospital Manchester acc.6690, f
130^{a–b} (ca 1450). The passage also appears in: 9,
BL Harley 2409, ff 71^a–72^a (1400–50).
Jolliffe, p 105, no I.7.
Revell, p 1.
MSS Commentary. A Catalogue of the Harleian MSS
in the British Museum, London 1808, p 690 (MS
9).
Catalogue of MSS in the British Museum, ns, vol 1,
London 1840, pt 1: The Arundel MSS, p 51 (MS
6).
A Catalogue of the MSS Preserved in the Libr of
the Univ of Cambridge, Cambridge 1857, 2.498
(MS 3).

Macray W D, Catalogi Codicum Manuscriptorum Bibliothecae Bodleianae, Oxford 1878, 5(2).125 (MS 2).

Summary Cat, 2.152 (MS 4).

James M R, The Western MSS in the Libr of Trinity Coll Cambridge, A Descriptive Catalogue, Cambridge 1906, 1.462 (MS 5).

Warner G F and J P Gilson, Catalogue of Western MSS in the Old Royal and King's Collections, London 1921, 2.265 (MS 7).

Ker Manuscripts, 3.343 (MS 8).

Edition. Yksh Wr, 1.108 (MS 2).

Selection. Brewer D, Chaucer in His Time, London 1963, p 226.

Language. McIntosh A, A New Approach to ME Dialectology, ESts 44(1963).9 (MS 9).

General Reference. Allen WAR, p 318.

[140] GOSTLY RICHESSES AND VERTUES OF SOLE.

MSS. 1, Trinity Hall Camb 16, f 88^b (1450–1500); 2, BL Royal 5.A.vi, f 77^b (1475–1500); 3, John Rylands Manchester Lat 341, f 82^a (ca 1400).

Jolliffe, p 114, no I.38.

MSS Commentary. James M R, A Descriptive Catalogue of the MSS in the Libr of Trinity Hall, Cambridge 1907, p 33 (MS 1).

Warner G F, and J P Gilson, Catalogue of the Western MSS in the Old Royal and King's Collections, London 1921, 1.96 (MS 2).

[141] VI THYNGES THAT WILLE BRYNG A MANNYS SOULE TO HEVYN.

MS. BL Sloane 1009, ff 27^a–28^a (1475–1500).

Jolliffe, p 114, no I.36.

[142] GOD'S WORDS TO SAINT MOLL (or MAWDE).

MSS. Version A: 1, Camb Univ Dd.14.26 (3), ff 45^a–46^a (ca 1450); *Version B:* 2, BL Harley 4012, ff 77^b–78^a (1460); 3, Coughton Court (Throckmorton), f 5^{a-b} (1450–75).

Jolliffe, p 113, no I.31.

Revell, p 41.

MSS Commentary. A Catalogue of the MSS Preserved in the Libr of the Univ of Cambridge, Cambridge 1856, 1.530 (MS 1).

Wilson E, A ME MS at Coughton Court, Warwickshire, and British Libr MS Harley 4012, N&Q ns 24(1977).295 (MS 2).

General Reference. Halligan T A, ed, The Book of Gostlye Grace of Mechtild of Hackeborn, Toronto 1979, pp 47, 48.

[143] TWELF POYNTES.

MSS. Version A: 1, BL Arundel 197, ff 46^a–47^b (ca 1400); 2, BL Addit 37790, f 236^b (1425–75; ends imperfectly); *Version B:* 3, Taunton Mus Horae, ff i–ii (15 cent); *Version C:* 4, Bodl 1999 (Bodley 131), f 131^{a-b} (1425–75).

Jolliffe, p 108, no I.13.

Revell, p 33.

MSS Commentary. Catalogue of MSS in the British Museum, vol 1, London 1840, pt 1: The Arundel MSS, p 51 (MS 1).

Summary Cat, 2.152.

Catalogue of Additions to the MSS in the British Museum in the Years MDCCCCVI–MDCCCCX, London 1912, p 153 (MS 2).

General Reference. Bazire J and E Colledge, edd, The Chastising of God's Children and The Treatise of Perfection of the Sons of God, Oxford 1957, p 10.

[144] FOURE THINGIS THAT MAKEN GOD OURE FREEND.

MS. Bodl 2643 (Bodley 789), f 156^{a-b} (1400–50).

Jolliffe, p 109, no I.17.

MS Commentary. Summary Cat, 2.467.

[145] HAVE IN MYNDE.

MS. Bodl 2322 (Bodl 423), ff 241^b–242^b (1425–75).

Jolliffe, p 108, no I.14.

MS Commentary. Summary Cat, 2.308.

[146] FOUR TOKENS OF SALVATION.

MSS. 1, Bodl 2628 (Bodley 788), f 246^a (ca 1400); 2, Bodl 12071 (Rawl C.209), ff 20^b–22^a (1475–1500); 3, Trinity Oxford E.86, f 37^{a-b} (1475–1500); 4, BL Harley 2343, ff 89^b–90^a (1400–25); 5, BL Lansdowne 388, f 369^a (1475–1500); 6, BL Addit 60577, f 155^{a-b} (1475–1500); 7, Westminster Cath Diocesan Archives H38, f 114^b (ca 1400); 8, Glasgow Univ Hunter 512, f 218^b (1400–25); 9, Columbia Univ Plimpton 258, f 7^b (ca 1400).

Jolliffe, p 106, nos I.10, 37.

MSS Commentary. A Catalogue of the Harleian MSS in the British Museum, London 1808, 2.600 (MS 4).

A Catalogue of the Lansdowne MSS in the British Museum, London 1819, p 12 (MS 5).

Coxe H O, Catalogus Codicum MSS qui in Collegiis Aulisque Oxoniensibus Hodie Adservantur, Oxford 1857, 2.34 (MS 3).

Macray W D, Catalogi Codicum Manuscriptorum Bibliothecae Bodleianae, Oxford 1878, 5(2).209 (MS 2).

Summary Cat, 2.457 (MS 1).

Young J and P H Aitken, A Catalogue of the MSS in the Hunterian Museum in the Univ of Glasgow, Glasgow 1908, p 419 (MS 8).

de Ricci Census, 2.1800 (MS 9).

Ker Manuscripts, 1.419 (MS 7).

Guddat-Figge G, Catalogue of MSS Containing ME Romances, Munich 1976, p 209 (MS 5).

Facsimiles. Plimpton G A, The Education of Chaucer, London and N Y 1935, appendix, p 34 (MS 9).

The Winchester Anthology, with an introd by E Wilson and I Fenlon, Woodbridge 1981 (MS 6).

[147] FOURE THINGIS BE NEDEFUL.

MSS. 1, Bodl 3054 (Bodley 938), f 10^{a-b} (1450–1500); 2, Trinity Oxford E.86, f 38^{a-b} (1475–1500); 3, BL Harley 4012, f 73^{a} (1460); 4, BL Harley 2343, ff 94^{a}–95^{b} (1400–50); 5, BL Lansdowne 388, f 369^{b} (1475–1500); 6, BL Royal 17.A.xxvi, ff 29^{a}–30^{a} (1400–50); 7, Edinburgh Univ 93, ff 27^{b}–28^{a} (1430–50); 8, Glasgow Univ Gen 223, f 223^{a} (1400–25); 9, Coughton Court (Throckmorton), f 2^{a-b} (1450–75); 10, Columbia Univ Plimpton 258, ff 7^{b}–8^{a} (ca 1400).

Jolliffe, p 105, no I.9.

MSS Commentary. A Catalogue of the Harleian MSS in the British Museum, London 1801, 3.103 (MS 3); London 1808, 2.660 (MS 4).

A Catalogue of the Lansdowne MSS in the British Museum, London 1819, p 12 (MS 5).

Coxe H O, Catalogus Codicum MSS qui in Collegiis Aulisque Hodie Adservantur, Oxford 1852, 2.34 (MS 2).

Summary Cat, 2.578 (MS 1).

Borland C R, A Descriptive Catalogue of the Western Mediaeval MSS in Edinb Univ Libr, Edinburgh 1916, p 149 (MS 7).

Warner G F and J P Gilson, Catalogue of Western MSS in the Old Royal and King's Collections, London 1921, 2.220 (MS 6).

de Ricci Census, 2.1800 (MS 10).

Ker Manuscripts, 2.904 (MS 8).

Guddat-Figge G, Catalogue of MSS Containing ME Romances, Munich 1976, p 209 (MS 5).

Wilson E, A ME MS at Coughton Court, Warwickshire, and British Libr MS Harley 4012, N&Q ns 24(1977).295 (MSS 3, 9).

Edition. Martin C A, Edinburgh Univ Libr 93. An Annotated Edn of Selected Devotional Treatises, diss Univ of Edinburgh 1978 (MS 7).

Facsimile. Plimpton G A, The Education of Chaucer, London and N Y 1935, appendix, p 34 (MS 10).

[148] IX PERFECCIONS.

MSS. 1, BL Cotton Faustina D.iv, ff 51^{a}–56^{a} (1475–1500); 2, Hereford Cath P.i.9, f 151^{a-b} (1475–1500).

Jolliffe, p 109, no I.16.

MSS Commentary. A Catalogue of the MSS in the Cottonian Libr Deposited in the British Museum, London 1802, p 611 (MS 1).

Bannister A T, A Descriptive Catalogue of the MSS in the Hereford Cathedral Libr, Hereford 1927, p 105 (MS 2).

Allen WAR, p 261.

[149] V POYNTES.

MS. St John's Oxford 173, ff 33^{b}–34^{b} (1500–25).

Jolliffe, p 105, no I.6.

MS Commentary. Coxe H O, Catalogus Codicum MSS qui in Collegiis Aulisque Oxoniensibus Hodie Adservantur, Oxford 1852, 2.56.

Modernization. Kirchberger C, The Coasts of the Country: An Anthology of Prayer Drawn from the Early Eng Spiritual Writers, London n d, p 31.

[150] ON THE SOUL.

MS. BL Sloane 1009, ff 17^{a}–25^{b} (1475–1500).

Jolliffe, p 114, no I.41.

Revell, p 61.

[151] OF WIDOWHOOD.

MS. Bodl 3054 (Bodley 938), ff 265^{a}–267^{b} (1450–1500).

MS Commentary. Summary Cat, 2.578.

[152] A MIRROUR FOR MAYDENES.

MS. BL Harley 2388, ff 4^{a}–7^{b} (ca 1450).

Jolliffe, p 113, no I.34.

MS Commentary. A Catalogue of the Harleian MSS in the British Museum, London 1808, 2.678.

[153] A NOBLE TRETYS OF MAYDENHODE.

MSS. 1, BL Arundel 286, ff 134^{b}–148^{a} (1400–25); 2, Westminster School London 3, ff 137^{a}–153^{a} (1400–50).

Jolliffe, p 88, no G.16.

MSS Commentary. Catalogue of MSS in the British Museum, vol 1, London 1840, pt 1: The Arundel MSS, p 84 (MS 1).

Ker Manuscripts, 1.422 (MS 2).

Source. Migne PL, 183.1012.

[154] A TRETIS OF MAYDENHOD.

MSS. 1, Camb Univ Ii.6.39, ff 71ᵇ–74ᵇ (1400–25); 2, Camb Univ Ii.6.55, ff 24ᵇ–28ᵇ (1400–50).

Jolliffe, p 102, no H.29.

MSS Commentary. A Catalogue of the MSS Preserved in the Libr of the Univ of Cambridge, Cambridge 1858, 3.535, 545.

General Reference. Doyle A I, A Prayer Attributed to St Thomas Aquinas, DomS 1(1948).232.

[155] THE COUNSELS OF SAINT ISIDORE.

MSS. Version A: 1, BL Harley 2388, ff 59ᵃ–64ᵇ (ca 1450); *Version B*: 2, Bodl 6943 (Ashmole 59), ff 78ᵃ–82ᵇ (1450–1500); *Version C*: 3, Bodl 2103 (Bodley 220), ff 103ᵃ–106ᵃ (1400–50); 4, Bodl 655 (Laud misc 23), ff 102ᵇ–110ᵇ (1400–25); 5, Bodl 11263 (Rawl A.381), ff 3ᵃ–5ᵇ (ca 1450); 6, Bodl 12728 (Rawl C.894), ff 86ᵇ–91ᵃ (1475–1500); 7, Trinity Camb 181 (B.15.39), ff 165ᵃ–169ᵇ (ca 1450); 8, Trinity Camb 1099 (0.1.74), ff 1ᵃ–16ᵇ (1450–1500); 9, BL Addit 14408, ff 66ᵇ–72ᵇ (1473); 10, BL Addit 37788, ff 64ᵃ–80ᵇ (ca 1450); 11, BL Harley 1706, ff 90ᵃ–92ᵇ (1450–1500); 12, BL Harley 2371, ff 142ᵃ–148ᵇ (ca 1450); 13, BL Harley 4011, ff 18ᵇ–20ᵇ (1475–1500); 14, BL Royal 17.C.xviii, ff 104ᵇ–110ᵇ (1475–1500); 15, BL Cotton Titus C.xix, ff 128ᵃ–143ᵃ (1475–1525); 16, Henry E Huntington HM 744, ff 4ᵃ–10ᵃ (1400–25); *Version D*: 17, Trinity Dublin 516, ff 26ᵃ–27ᵃ (15 cent).

Jolliffe, p 110, no I.22.

MSS Commentary. A Catalogue of the MSS in the Cottonian Libr Deposited in the British Museum, London 1802, p 563 (MS 15).

A Catalogue of the Harleian MSS in the British Museum, London 1808, 2.678 (MS 1), 178 (MS 11), 671 (MS 12); 3.103 (MS 13).

Black W H, A Descriptive, Analytical, and Critical Catalogue of the MSS Bequeathed unto the Univ of Oxford by Elias Ashmole, Oxford 1845, p 95 (MS 2).

Catalogue of Additions to the MSS in the British Museum in the Years MDCCCXLI–MDCCCXLV, London 1850, p 64 (MS 9).

Macray W D, Catalogi Codicum Manuscriptorum Bibliothecae Bodleianae, Oxford 1862, 5(1).380 (MS 5); 5(2)(1878).465 (MS 6).

Coxe H O, Catalogi Codicum Manuscriptorum Bibliothecae Bodleianae, Oxford 1858, 2.65 (MS 4).

Summary Cat, 2.213 (MS 3).

Abbot T K, Catalogue of MSS in the Libr of Trinity Coll Dublin, Dublin 1900, pp 78 (MS 17).

James M R, The Western MSS in the Libr of Trinity Coll Cambridge, Cambridge 1900, 1.232 (MS 7); 3(1902).74 (MS 8).

Catalogue of Additions to the MSS in the British Museum in the Years MDCCCCVI–MDCCCCX, London 1912, p 151 (MS 10).

Warner G F and J P Gilson, Catalogue of the Western MSS in the Old Royal and King's Collections, London 1921, 2.245 (MS 14).

de Ricci Census, 1.74 (MS 16).

Hanna R III, The Index of ME Prose, Handlist I, A Handlist of Manuscripts containing ME Prose in the Henry E Huntington Library, Woodbridge 1984, p 33.

Editions. Yksh Wr, 2.367 (MSS 6, 11, 14).

Lloyd D J, An Edn of the Prose and Verse in the Bodleian MS, Laud Miscellaneous 23, diss Yale Univ 1943.

Source. Monita de verbis beati Ysidori extracta ad instruendum hominem qualiter vicia valeant evitare et in bonis se debeat infirmare (printed with [15] by William de Machlinia, London ?1486; STC, no 26012).

Migne PL 83.845.

General References. Doyle Survey 1.171.

Duff E G, 15-Cent Eng Books, Oxford 1917, p 116, no 415 (Machlinia).

Doyle A I, Books Connected with the Vere Family and Barking Abbey, Trans of the Essex Archaeological Soc 25(1958).222.

[156] THE FIVE WITS.

MSS. The Outer Wits only: Prose: 1, BL Royal 8.C.i, ff 122ᵇ–143ᵇ (ca 1450); 2, BL Harley 2398, ff 106ᵇ–127ᵇ (ca 1450); 3, Glasgow Univ Hunter 520, pp 337–342 (1400–25); 4, Princeton Univ Garrett 143, ff 26ᵇ–29ᵇ (1400–25); *Verse:* 5, Bodl 2298 (Bodley 549), f 77ᵇ (ca 1400).

The Inner and Outer Wits combined: Prose: 6, Bodl Lyell 29, ff 102ᵇ–104ᵃ (1400–50); 7, Trinity Camb 337 (B.14.54), f 198ᵃ (15 cent); *Verse:* 8, Camb Univ Ff.2.38, f 32ᵃ (ca 1450); 9, Magdalene Camb Pepys 1584, f 107ᵃ (1475–1500); 10, BL Harley 1706, f 207ᵃ (1450–1500); 11, BL Harley 2339, f 121ᵃ (1400–50); 12, Lambeth Palace 491, f 295ᵃ (15 cent); 13, St Cuthbert's Coll Ushaw 28 (1450–75).

Jolliffe, pp 74, nos D.2, D.6; 75, no D.9.

Brown-Robbins, nos 1126, 1815, 1816; Robbins-Cutler, nos 1126, 1815.

MSS Commentary. A Catalogue of the Harleian MSS in the British Museum, London 1808, 2.178 (MS 10), 658 (MS 11), 684 (MS 2).

A Catalogue of the MSS Preserved in the Libr of the Univ of Cambridge, Cambridge 1877, 2.404 (MS 8).

Summary Cat, 2.295 (MS 5).

James M R, The Western MSS in the Libr of Trinity Coll Cambridge A Descriptive Catalogue, Cambridge 1900, 1.463 (MS 7).

Young J and P H Aitken, A Catalogue of the MSS in the Libr of the Hunterian Museum in the Univ of Glasgow, Glasgow 1908, p 422 (MS 3).

Warner G F and J P Gilson, Catalogue of Western MSS in the Old Royal and King's Collections, London 1921, 1.228 (MS 1).

James M R, A Descriptive Catalogue of the Libr of Samuel Pepys, pt 3, Mediaeval MSS, London 1923, p 19 (MS 9).

James M R and C Jenkins, A Descriptive Catalogue of the MSS in the Libr of Lambeth Palace, Cambridge 1930, p 681.

de Ricci Census, 1.894 (MS 4).

De La Mare A, Catalogue of the Collection of Medieval MSS Bequeathed to the Bodleian Libr Oxford by James P R Lyell, Oxford 1971, p 59.

Editions. Bülbring K D, Über die Handschrift NR 491 der Lambeth-Bibliothek, Archiv 86 (1891).388 (MS 12).

Baugh A C, The Eng Text of the Ancrene Riwle Edited from British Museum MS Royal 8.C.i, EETS 232, London 1956 (MS 1).

Person H A, Cambridge ME Lyrics, rvsd edn, Seattle 1962; rptd N Y 1969, p 24 (MS 8).

Krochalis J E, Contemplations of the Dread and Love of God: Two Newly Identified Pennsylvania MSS, LC 42(1977).13 (prints meditation on five wits from MS Univ of Pennsylvania 8, ff 145b–146b).

[157] NINE VIRTUES.

MSS. Verse: Version A: 1, Camb Univ Dd.1.1, ff 298b–300b (1400–50); *Version B:* 2, Bodl 14528 (Rawl poet 34), ff 9b–10a (1475–1500); 3, Camb Univ Ff.1.14, ff 5a–7a (1450–1500); 4, Camb Univ Ii.4.9, ff 63b–65a (ca 1450); 5, BL Harley 2409, ff 75b–77b (1400–50); *Version C:* 6, Bodl 21876 (Douce 302), f 8a (1425–50).

Prose: Version A: 7, Lambeth Palace 432, ff 75a–76a (1450–1500); *Version B:* 8, BL Arundel 197, ff 6b–7a (ca 1450); 9, Longleat 29, ff 17a–18a (1400–50); *Version C:* 10, BL Royal 17.A.xxvi, ff 2a–3a (1400–50); *Version D:* 11, Camb Univ Dd.14.26 (3), ff 46b–50a (ca 1450); *Version E:* 12, Camb Univ Dd.11.89, ff 1a–2a (ca 1400); 13, Trinity Camb 1157 (0.2.53), f 23b (1475–1500); 14, Bodl 21715 (Douce 141), f 138a–b (1400–50); 15, Bodl 3938 (Eng poet a.1), f 333b (1380–1400); 16, BL Harley

1704, ff 48b–49a (ca 1465); 17, BL Addit 22283, ff 146b–147a (1380–1400); 18, BL Royal 8.F.vii, f 45a–b (1450–1500); *Version F:* 19, Leeds Univ Brotherton 501, f 90b (ca 1450); *Version G:* 20, BL Lansdowne 762, f 9a–b (16 cent); *Version H:* 21, Trinity Dublin 245, ff 218b–219a (1400–25); *Version I:* 22, Columbia Univ Plimpton 259, f 47b (15 cent); *Version J:* 23, Camb Univ Ff.6.33, ff 37b–38b (1475–1525); 24, Sotheby's Sale, July 6, 1964, lot 237; *Version K:* 25, Bodl Lat Liturg e.17, ff 54a–55a (1450–1500); *Version L:* 26, Longleat 32, ff 1a–2a, and possibly 85b (1400–50); *Version M:* PRINT. 27, Wynkyn de Worde, Tretys of Love, 1493 (STC, no 24234).

Brown-Robbins, nos 212, 1188, *71; Robbins-Cutler, nos 1188, 3780.5.

Jolliffe, p 106, no I.12, and possibly no G.20.

MSS Commentary. A Catalogue of the Harleian MSS in the British Museum, London 1808, 2.177 (MS 16), 690 (MS 5).

A Catalogue of the Lansdowne MSS in the British Museum, London 1819, p 168 (MS 20).

A Catalogue of the MSS Preserved in the Libr of the Univ of Cambridge, Cambridge 1856, 1.1 (MS 1), 481 (MS 12), 530 (MS 11); 2(1857).295 (MS 3), 534 (MS 23); 3(1858).448 (MS 4).

Catalogue of the Additions to the MSS in the British Museum in the Years MDCCCLIV–MDCCCLX, London 1875, p 623 (MS 17).

Catalogue of MSS in the British Museum, ns, vol 1, London 1890, pt 1: The Arundel MSS, p 51 (MS 8).

Summary Cat, 2.789 (MS 15); 3.291 (MS 2); 4.535 (MS 14), 585 (MS 6).

Abbot T K, Catalogue of the MSS in the Libr of Trinity Coll Dublin, Dublin 1900, p 36 (MS 21).

James M R, The Western MSS in the Libr of Trinity Coll Cambridge, A Descriptive Catalogue, Cambridge 1902, 3.169 (MS 13).

Warner G F and J P Gilson, Catalogue of Western MSS in the Old Royal and King's Collections, London 1921, 1.165 (MS 18); 2.220 (MS 10).

James M R and C Jenkins, A Descriptive Catalogue of the MSS in the Libr of Lambeth Palace, Cambridge 1930, p 599 (MS 7).

de Ricci Census, 2.1800 (MS 22).

Serjeantson Index, p 258.

Manly & Rickert, 1.343 (MS 9).

Ker Manuscripts, 3.67 (MS 19).

Guddat-Figge G, Catalogue of MSS Containing ME Romances, Munich 1976, pp 100 (MS 4), 145 (MS 17), 267 (MS 2), 269 (MS 15).

Hanna R III, Leeds Univ Libr, MS Brotherton 501: A Redescription, Manuscripta 26(1982).38 (MS 19).

Editions. Whiting E K, The Poems of John Audelay, Percy Soc 14, London 1844, p 51.

Rel Ant, 1.245 (MSS 20, 23).

Yksh Wr, 1.110 (MSS 15, 16); 2.455 (MS 5).

Fisher J H, The Tretys of Love, EETS 225, London 1951, p 126.

Bowers R H, A ME Poem on the Nine Virtues, Southern Folklore Quart 31(1967).37 (MS 1).

General References. Allen WAR, p 317 n3.

Bloomfield SDS, p 177.

Bibliography. Booker J M, A ME Biblio, Heidelberg 1912, p 33.

[158] THE POWERS OF MAN'S SOUL.

MSS. 1, Bodl 3054 (Bodley 938), ff 243ᵇ–246ᵃ (1450–1500); 2, Camb Univ Kk.6.26, ff 28ᵃ–31ᵃ (1450–1500).

Jolliffe, p 74, no D.1.

MSS Commentary. A Catalogue of MSS Preserved in the Libr of the Univ of Cambridge, Cambridge 1858, 3.722 (MS 2).

Summary Cat, 2.578.

[159] HOW MAN IS MADE TO THE IMAGE OF GOD.

MSS. 1, All Souls Oxford 24, ff 35ᵃ–38ᵇ (1400–25); 2, Camb Univ Ii.6.39, ff 120ᵇ–122ᵇ (1400–25); 3, Camb Univ Ii.6.55, ff 63ᵇ–66ᵃ (1400–50); 4, BL Harley 2330, ff 98ᵃ–100ᵇ (1400–50). For a similar text see: 5, Camb Univ Kk.6.26, ff 26ᵇ–28ᵃ (1450–1500). *De Anima Pulchra*: 6, Camb Univ Dd. 14.26(3), ff 1ᵇ–2ᵃ (ca 1450); 7, Trinity Hall Camb 16, f 92ᵇ (1450–1500).

Jolliffe, p 74, nos D.3, D.7.

MSS Commentary. A Catalogue of the Harleian MSS in the British Museum, London 1808, 2.655 (MS 4).

Coxe H O, Catalogus Codicum MSS qui in Collegiis Aulisque Oxoniensibus Hodie Adservantur, Oxford 1852, 2.6 (MS 1).

A Catalogue of the MSS Preserved in the Univ of Cambridge, London 1856, 1.530 (MS 6); 3 (1858).535 (MS 2), 545 (MS 3), 722 (MS 5).

James M R, A Descriptive Catalogue of the MSS in the Libr of Trinity Hall, Cambridge 1907, p 33 (MS 7).

Fristedt S L, The Wycliffe Bible, Pt I, The Principal Problems Connected with Forshall and Madden's Edn, Stockholm Stud in Eng 4(1953).43 (MS 3).

Edition. McCann J, The Cloud of Unknowing, London 1924, p 243 (MS 5).

Latin Source. Migne PL, 100.563.

General References. Doyle A I, A Prayer Attributed to St Thomas Aquinas, DomS 1(1948).232.

Fristedt S L, The Wycliffite Bible, pt 1, Stockholm Stud in Eng 4(1953).43 (MSS 3 and 4 written by Lollards).

[160] CHARITE ALLE THING LEEVETH.

MS. BL Addit 24202, ff 25ᵃ–26ᵃ (1400–25).

Jolliffe, p 74, no D.4.

MS Commentary. .Catalogue of Additions to the MSS in the British Museum in the Years MDCCCLIV–MDCCCLXX, London 1877, p 22.

[161] ICHE CRYSTEN SOWLE HATH THREE MYGHTES.

MS. Bodl 6921 (Ashmole 41), f 135ᵃ⁻ᵇ (1400–25).

Jolliffe, p 74, no D.5.

MS Commentary. A Descriptive Analytical and Critical Catalogue of the MSS Bequeathed unto the Univ of Oxford by Elias Ashmole, Oxford 1845, p 62.

[162] THE NATURE OF MAN.

MSS. 1, BL Harley 2398, ff 128ᵃ–130ᵃ (1400–25); 2, Glasgow Univ Hunter 520 (V.8.23), pp 352–356 (1450–1500); 3, Princeton Univ Garrett 143, ff 36ᵃ–38ᵃ (1400–25).

Jolliffe, p 75, nos D.8, D.13.

MSS Commentary. A Catalogue of the Harleian MSS in the British Museum, London 1808, 2.684 (MS 1).

Young J and P H Aitken, A Catalogue of the MSS in the Libr of the Hunterian Museum in the Univ of Glasgow, Glasgow 1908, p 422 (MS 2).

de Ricci Census, 1.894.

Editions. Fleming J V, A ME Treatise on the Nature of Man, N&Q ns 14(1967).243 (MS 3, ff 36ᵇ–38ᵃ).

[163] HOW RESON SCHAL BE KEPER OF THE SOULE.

MSS. 1, BL Arundel 286, ff 15ᵇ–19ᵇ (1400–25); 2, BL Harley 6615, ff 104ᵃ–109ᵇ (1450–1500).

Jolliffe, p 75, no D.10.

MSS Commentary. A Catalogue of the Harleian MSS in the British Museum, London 1808, 3.380 (MS 2).

Catalogue of MSS in the British Museum, ns, vol 1, London 1890, pt 1: The Arundel MSS, p 84 (MS 1).

Bazire J and E Colledge, edd, The Chastising of God's Children, Oxford 1957, p 4 (description of MS 2).

Ellis R, Flores ad fabricandum . . . coronam: an Investigation into the Use of Revelations of St Bridget in 15-cent England, MÆ 51(1982).163.

[164] NAMMORE NE IS BE TUENE ANE MANNE AND ANE BESTE BOTE INE ONDERSTONDYNGE.

MS. BL Arundel 57, f 96ᵇ (1340).
Jolliffe, p 75, no D.11.
Edition. Gradon P, ed, Dan Michel's Ayenbite of Inwyt or Remorse of Conscience, EETS 23, London 1965, 1.270 (revision of R Morris edn of 1866); 2.1 (description of MS).

[165] HOW A MAN SHULDE KNOWE HIMSELF.

MS. BL Harley 2388, ff 36ᵇ–37ᵃ (1450–1500).
Jolliffe, p 75, no D.12.
MS Commentary. A Catalogue of the Harleian MSS in the British Museum, London 1808, 2.678.

[166] VERSE TRACTS ON SELF-KNOWLEDGE.

MSS. Love God and Drede: 1, Bodl 1703 (Digby 102), ff 98ᵃ–99ᵇ (1400–25); *Each Man ought Himself to know*: 2, Bodl 3938 (Eng poet a.1), f 407ᵇ (1380–1400); 3, BL Addit 22283, f 129ᵇ (1380–1400); *Man, know thy self and lerne to dye*: 4, Bodl 1703 (Digby 102), ff 104ᵇ–105ᵇ (1400–25); *Know thyself*: 5, Balliol Oxford 354, f 156ᵇ (1500–25).
Brown-Robbins, nos 697, 1455, 2088, *64; Robbins-Cutler, no 3553.5.
MSS Commentary. Catalogue of Additions to the MSS in the British Museum in the Years MDCCCLIV–MDCCCLX, London 1875, p 623 (MS 3).
Macray W D, Catalogi Codicum Manuscriptorum Bibliothecae Bodleianae, Oxford 1883, 9.116 (MSS 1, 4; both from Bodl 1703).
Summary Cat, 2.789.
Serjeantson Index, p 260.
Mynors R A B, Catalogue of the MSS of Balliol Coll Oxford, Oxford 1963, p 352 (MS 5).
Editions. Furnivall F J, Early Eng Poems and Lives of Saints, Berlin 1862, p 130 (MS 3).
Varnhagen H, Die kleineren Gedichte der Vernon- und Simeon-Handschrift, Angl 7(1884).294 (Each Man ought Himself to know).
Furnivall F J, The Minor Poems of the Vernon MS, pt 2, EETS 117, London 1901, p 672 (Each Man ought Himself to know).
Flügel E, Liedersammlungen des XVI Jahrhunderts besonders aus der Zeit Heinrichs VIII.III, Angl 26(1903).170 (MS 5).

Kail J, 26 Political and Other Poems from the Oxford MSS Digby 102 and Douce 322, pt 1, EETS 124, London 1904, pp 1 (Love God and Drede), 27 (Man, know thy self and lerne to dye).
Dyboski R, Songs, Carols and Other Miscellaneous Poems from the Balliol MS 354, Richard Hill's Commonplace Book, EETSES 101, London 1907, p 82 (Know thyself).
Brown RLxivC, p 139 (Each Man ought Himself to know).
Guddat-Figge G, Catalogue of MSS Containing ME Romances, Munich 1976, pp 145 (MS 3), 269 (MS 2).

[167] TROUTHE HOPE LOVE.

MS. BL Royal 17.B.xvii, ff 100ᵃ–101ᵃ (1375–1400).
Jolliffe, p 114, no I.39.
MS Commentary. Warner G F and J P Gilson, Catalogue of Western MSS in the Old Royal and King's Collections, London 1921, 2.228.
Edition. Yksh Wr, 1.66.

[168] THE ABSEY OF SEYNT BONAVENTURE (or THE LYFE OF A RELIGIOUS PERSONE).

MS. BL Cotton Faustina D.IV, ff 65ᵃ–71ᵃ (1475–1500).
Jolliffe, p 104, no I.3.
MS Commentary. A Catalogue of the MSS in the Cottonian Libr Deposited in the British Museum, London 1802, p 611.

[169] THE SEVEN COMMANDMENTS OF THE NEW TESTAMENT.

MS. Univ Oxford 97, f 93ᵇ (1400–25).
MS Commentary. Doyle A I, Univ Coll Oxford MS 97 and Its Relationship to the Simeon MS (BL Add 22283), in M Benskin and M L Samuels, edd, So meny people longages and tonges, Philological Essays in Scots and Mediaeval Eng Presented to Angus McIntosh, Edinburgh 1981, p 265.
Coxe, H O, Catalogus Codicum MSS qui in Collegiis Aulisque Oxoniensibus Hodie Adservantur, Oxford 1852, 1.28.

[170] FIVE POINTS ON GOOD LIVING.

MS. St John's Oxford 173, ff 33ᵇ–34ᵇ (1500–25).
MS Commentary. Coxe H O, Catalogus Codicum MSS qui in Collegiis Aulisque Oxoniensibus Hodie Adservantur, Oxford 1858, 2.56.

Edition. Kirchberger C, Coasts of the Country, London n d, p 31.

[171] SEVEN TOKENS OF CHRIST'S LOVE.

MS. Glasgow Univ Hunter 512, ff 218^b–220^a (1400–25).

MS Commentary. Young J and P H Aitken, A Catalogue of the MSS in the Hunterian Museum in the Univ of Glasgow, Glasgow 1908, p 419.

[172] THE FIVE COMMANDMENTS OF THE CHURCH.

MSS. No MS extant. PRINT: Wynkyn de Worde, The Ordynarye of Crysten Men, London 1502 (STC, no 5198); 1506 (STC, no 5199).
Robbins-Cutler, no 3481.5.

Edition. Dibdin T F, Typographical Antiquities, London 1812, 2.103 (rev by J Ames and W Herbert).

IV. Allegorical Works

1. Works Based on Allegorical Devices

[173] A TRETYSE OF GOSTLY BATAYLE.

MSS. 1, Bodl 12728 (Rawl C.894), ff 33^a–48^a (1450–1500); 2, Bodl 21896 (Douce 322), ff 39^a–52^b (1450–1500); 3, Corpus Christi Oxf E.220, ff 42^a–59^b (1450–1500); 4, Corpus Christi Camb 142, ff 111^a–121^a (1450–1500); 5, BL Harley 1706, ff 36^b–47^b (1450–1500); 6, BL Royal 17.C.xviii, ff 39^a–57^a (1450–1500); 7, John Rylands Eng 94, ff 137^b–152^b (1425–1450).
Jolliffe, p 96, no H.13.

MSS Commentary. A Catalogue of the Harleian MSS in the British Museum, London 1808, 2.178 (MS 5).

Coxe H O, Catalogus Codicum MSS qui in Collegiis Aulisque Oxoniensibus Hodie Adservantur, Oxford 1852, 2.87 (MS 3).

Macray W D, Catalogi Codicum Manuscriptorum Bibliothecae Bodleianae, Oxford 1878, 5(2).465 (MS 1).

Summary Cat, 4.593 (MS 2).

James M R, A Descriptive Catalogue of the MSS in the Libr of Corpus Christi Coll Cambridge, Cambridge 1912, 1.327 (MSS 3, 4).

Warner G F and J P Gilson, Catalogue of Western MSS in the Old Royal and King's Collections, London 1921, 2.245 (MS 6).

Tyson M, Handlist of the Collection of Eng MSS in the John Rylands Libr, 1928, Manchester 1929, p 21 (MS 7).

Editions. Yksh Wr, 2.420 (MS 5).

Murray V, An Edn of a Tretyse of Gostly Batayle and Milicia Christi, diss Oxford 1970 (MS 2, with variants from the other MSS).

MS Relationships. Morgan G R, A Critical Edn of Caxton's Art and Craft to Know Well to Die and Ars Moriendi together with the Antecedent MS Material, diss Oxford Univ 1972, 1.193 (corrects Murray's stemma).

Literary Relations and Analysis. LeMay M de L, The Allegory of the Christ-Knight in Eng Lit, Washington D C 1932, p 34 (analysis in historical perspective).

Vogel M V, Some Aspects of the Horse and Rider Analogy in the Debate between the Body and the Soul, Washington D C 1948, p 31 (history of horse and rider image).

Brook S, Religious Allegory in ME, diss Manchester Univ 1955, chap 2.

Style. Blake N F, Varieties of ME Religious Prose, in B Rowland, ed, Chaucer and ME Stud in Honour of Rossell Hope Robbins, Kent 1974, p 351.

General References. Ives D V, The Seven Deadly Sins in Eng Lit, Univ of London MA thesis 1931, p 23.
Bloomfield SDS, p 220.

Schlauch M, Eng Medieval Lit and Its Social Foundations, Warsaw 1956, p 194.

Doyle A I, Books Connected with the Vere Family and Barking Abbey, Trans of the Essex Archaelogical Soc 25(1958).226.
Wenzel, p 237.
Woolf, p 225, n 3.

[174] MILICIA CHRISTI.

MSS. 1, BL Arundel 286, ff 20^a–81^b (1425–75); 2, BL Egerton 842, ff 247^a–256^b (1400–10; incomplete, approximately one-third of text).
Jolliffe, p 103, no H.33.
Revell, p 45.

MSS Commentary. List of Additions to the MSS in the British Museum in the Years MDCCCXXXVI–MDCCCXL, London 1843, p 18.

Catalogue of MSS in the British Museum, ns, vol I, Pt I: The Arundel MSS, London 1840, p 84 (MS 1).

Hodgson P, ed, Deonise Hid Divinite, EETS 231, London 1958, p xii (MS 1).

Edition. Murray V, An Edn of a Tretyse of Ghostly Batayle and Milicia Christi, diss Oxford Univ 1970.

Source. Southern R W and F S Schmidt, edd, Memorials of St Anselm, Auctores Britannici Medii Aevi I, London 1969, p 97 (Liber de Humanis Moribus per Similitudines).

Literary Relations. LeMay M de L, The Allegory of the Christ-Knight in Eng Lit, Washington D C 1932.

Vogel M V, Some Aspects of the Horse and Rider Analogy in The Debate between the Body and the Soul, Washington D C 1948, p 31 (history of the horse and rider image).

Woolf R, The Theme of Christ the Lover-Knight in Medieval Eng Lit, RES 13(1962).1.

[175] DESERT OF RELIGION.

MSS. 1, BL Cotton Faustina B.vi, pars II, ff 3^a–23^b (1400–50); 2, BL Stowe 39, ff 10^b–31^b (1400–50); 3, BL Addit 37049, ff 46^a–67^a (1400–50).

Brown-Robbins, no 672; Robbins-Cutler, nos 91.8, 1367.3 (verses surrounding the pictures of Rolle in MSS 1 and 2 and several saints in MS 3).

MSS Commentary. A Catalogue of the MSS in the Cottonian Libr Deposited in the British Museum, London 1802, p 606 (MS 1).

Catalogue of the Stowe MSS in the British Museum, London 1895, p 23 (MS 2).

Catalogue of Additions to the MSS in the British Museum in the Years MDCCCC–MDCCCCV, London 1907, p 324 (MS 3).

Rickert M, Painting in Britain The Middle Ages, Baltimore 1954, p 183 (miniatures in MS 1; plate 183^b reproduces portrait of Rolle).

Hogg J, Unpublished Texts in the Carthusian Northern ME Religious Miscellany British Libr MS Add 37049, in Essays in Honor of Erwin Stürzl on his 60th Birthday, ed J Hogg, no 1, Salzburger Studien zur Anglistik und Amerikanistik, Salzburg 1980, p 241 (detailed description of MS 3).

Editions. Hubner W, The Desert of Religion, Arch 126(1911).58. (MS 3 collated with MSS 1, 2).

Doty B L, An Edn of British Museum MS: Additional 37049: A Religious Miscellany, diss Michigan State 1963, p 289 (MS 3).

Text, Language, and Versification. Hubner W and K Schreiner, The Desert of Religion. II. Handschriften kritik. Reim und Sprache. Zu Quellenkunde, Arch 126(1911). 360.

Sources. Allen H E, The Desert of Religion: Addendum, Arch 126(1911).388.

Literary Relations and Analysis. Brook S, Religious Allegory in ME, diss Manchester Univ 1955, chap 2.

General References. Allen WAR, pp 54, 309, 526.

Messenger R E, Ethical Teachings in the Latin Hymns of Medieval England, N Y 1930, p 178.

Patch H R, The Other World According to Descriptions in Medieval Lit, Cambridge 1950, p 191.

Anderson G K, Old and ME Lit from the Beginnings to 1485, in A Hist of Eng Lit, ed H Craig, N Y 1950, p 110.

Bloomfield SDS, p 179.

Doyle Survey, 1.85; 2.191.

Wenzel, pp 80, 115, 117, 231.

Wenzel S, Sloth in ME Devotional Lit, Angl 79(1961).299.

Pantin, p 234.

Ackerman R W, Backgrounds to Medieval Eng Lit, N Y 1966, pp 89, 95.

Möske B, Caritas: Ihre figurative Darstellung in der engl Literatur des 14 bis 16 Jahrhunderts, Bonn 1977, p 34.

[176] THE QUATREFOIL OF LOVE.

MSS. 1, Bodl 29003 (Bodley Addit A.106), ff 6^a–15^b (1450–1500); 2, BL Addit 31042, ff 98^a–101^b (ca 1440). PRINT: 3, Wynkyn de Worde, The iiii leves of the truelove, ca 1510 (STC, no 15345).

Brown-Robbins, no 1453.

MSS Commentary. Catalogue of Additions to the MSS in the British Museum in the Years MDCCCLXXVI–MDCCCLXXXI, London 1882, p 148.

Summary Cat, 5.540.

Guddat-Figge G, Catalogue of MSS Containing ME Romances, Munich 1976, p 159 (MS 2).

Stern K, The London Thornton Miscellany: A New Description of British Museum Additional MS 31042, Scriptorum 30(1976).26, 201.

Horrall S M, The London Thornton MS, A New Collation, Manuscripta 23(1979).99.

Editions. Gollancz I, The Quatrefoil of Love, in An Eng Miscellany Presented to Dr Furnivall, Oxford 1901, p 112 (basis of text: MS 2).

Gollancz I and M M Weale, The Quatrefoil of Love, EETS 195, London 1935; rptd 1971, p 1 (basis of text: MS 2; crit K Brunner, AnglB 46.260; D Everett, YWES 15.118; J P Oakden, MLR 31.209; C L Wrenn, RES 13.374; TLS November 23, 1935, p 774; N&Q 169.18; G V Smithers, MÆ 6.51).

Date, Language, Versification. Oakden J P, Alliterative Poetry in ME, Manchester 1935, 1.114, 217; 2.79.

McIntosh A, A New Approach to ME Dialectology, ESts 44(1963).9 (MS 2).

Literary Relations. Sandison H E, The Chanson d'Aventure in ME, BrynMawrMon 12.142.

Blake N F, Wynkyn de Worde and the Quatrefoil of Love, Arch 206(1969).189 (analysis of Wynkyn de Worde's handling of Northern text).

General References. Sandison, BrynMawrMon 12.142.

Bennett OHEL, p 119.

Bennett H S, Eng Books and Readers 1475 to 1557, Cambridge 1952, p 256.

Schlauch M, Eng Medieval Lit and Its Social Backgrounds, Warsaw 1956, p 194.

Turville-Petre T, Summer Sunday, De Tribus Regibus Mortuis, and The Awntyrs Off Arthure: Three Poems in the 13-Line Stanza, RES 25 (1974).13.

Blake N, The Eng Lang in Medieval Lit, London 1977, p 20.

Pearsall D, OE and ME Poetry, London 1977, p 185.

Turville-Petre, The Alliterative Revival, Cambridge 1977, pp 35, 44, 62.

Wenzel S, Verses in Sermons, Cambridge 1978, p 159.

Bibliography. New CBEL, 1.507.

[177] AN HONEST BEDE
(or LECTUM BONUM).

MSS. Version A: 1, Univ Oxford 123, ff 74ᵇ–75ᵇ (1475–1500); *Version B:* 2, Bodl 493 (Laud Misc 19), ff 22ᵇ–30ᵇ (ca 1500); 3, Bodl 1123 (Laud Misc 99), ff 223ᵃ–234ᵃ (ca 1500; incorporated in version of [11]); 4, Bodl 21876 (Douce 302), ff 32ᵇ–33ᵇ (1425–50); 5, Bodl Eng theol c.57, ff 131ᵇ–132ᵇ (1475–1500; incorporated in version of [12]); 6, Jesus Oxford 39, pp 560–562 (1425–50; incorporated in version of [11]); 7, St John's Camb 176, ff 49ᵇ–52ᵃ (15 cent).

Jolliffe, p 113, no I.35.

MSS Commentary. Coxe H O, Catalogus Codicum MSS qui in Collegiis Aulisque Oxoniensibus Hodie Adservantur, Oxford 1852, 1.123 (MS 1); 2.14 (MS 6); Catalogi Codicum Manuscriptorum Bibliothecae Bodleianae, Oxford 1878, 2.63 (MS 2), 104 (MS 3).

Summary Cat, 4.585 (MS 4).

James M R, A Descriptive Catalogue of the MSS in the Libr of St John's College Cambridge, Cambridge 1913, p 210 (MS 7).

General Reference. Wulfing J E, Der Dichter John Audelay und sein Werk, Angl 18(1896).212.

[178] THE CASTLE OF THE SOUL.

MS. Bodl 1963 (Bodley 110), f 154ᵃ⁻ᵇ (ca 1450).

MS Commentary. Summary Cat, 2.135.

Doyle Survey, 2.272.

Background. Cornelius R D, The Figurative Castle, Bryn Mawr 1930, p 20 (The Castle and The Wardens of the Soul).

[179] A MORALIZATION ON ARTICLES OF CLOTHING.

MS. Camb Univ Hh.1.11, ff 130ᵇ–132ᵇ (ca 1450).

MS Commentary. A Catalogue of the MSS Preserved in the Libr of the Univ of Cambridge, Cambridge 1858, p 262.

Colledge E and N Chadwick, Remedies against Temptation. The Third Eng Version of William Flete, Archivio italiano per la storia della pietà, 5(1967).206.

[180] OF THE FLODE OF THE WORLD.

MSS. 1, BL Royal 17.B.xvii, ff 101ᵃ–104ᵇ (1375–1400); 2, BL Addit 25013, ff 15ᵇ–18ᵇ (1400–50).

Brown-Robbins, no 1014.

MSS Commentary. Catalogue of Additions to the MSS of the British Museum in the Years MDCCCLIV–MDCCCLXXV, London 1877, p 140 (MS 2).

Warner G F and J P Gilson, Catalogue of Western MSS in the Old Royal and King's Collections, London 1921, 2.228 (MS 1).

Edition. Yksh Wr, 2.67.

Literary Relations and Analysis. Owst G R, Lit and Pulpit in Medieval England, Cambridge 1933, p 69 (use of symbolic ship in sermons).

Brooke S, Religious Allegory in ME, diss Manchester Univ 1955, chap 2.

[181] THE LADDRE OF HEVYNE.

MS. Longleat (Marquis of Bath) 29, ff 4ᵇ–10ᵃ (1400–50).

MS Commentary. Historical MSS Commission, Third Report of the Royal Commission on Historical MSS, London 1872, appendix, p 181.

Manly & Rickert, 1.343.

Doyle Survey, 2.81.

Edition. Ogilvie-Thomson S, An Edn of the Eng Works in MS Longleat 29 Excluding the Parson's Tale, diss Oxford Univ 1981, p 124.

[182] VERSIONS OF GROSSETESTE'S CHATEAU D'AMOUR.

MSS. Version A: Castle of Love: 1, Bodl 3938 (Eng poet a.1), ff 293ᵃ–296ᵇ (1380–1400); 2, Bodl 29560 (Addit B.107), ff 1ᵃ–45ᵇ (1425–50); 3, BL Addit 22283, ff 84ᵇ–87ᵇ (1380–1400); *Version B: Myrour of Lewed Men:* 4, BL Egerton 927, ff 1ᵃ–28ᵃ (1400–50); *Version C: King and Four Daughters:* 5,

Bodl 6922 (Ashmole 61), ff 78ᵇ–83ᵃ (1475–1500); *Version D: Foure Daughters*: 6, BL Cotton Appendix VII, ff 1ᵃ–2ᵇ (1400–50).

Brown-Robbins, nos 1677, 1879, 3270, 4145; Robbins-Cutler, nos 1879, 4145.

MSS Commentary. Black W H, A Descriptive, Analytical, and Critical Catalogue of the MSS Bequeathed unto the Univ of Oxford by Elias Ashmole, Oxford 1845, p 106 (MS 5).

Catalogue of Additions to the MSS in the British Museum in the Years MDCCCXLI–MDCCCXLV, London 1850, p 70.

Catalogue of Additions to the MSS in the British Museum in the Years MDCCCLIV–MDCCCLX, London 1875, p 623.

Summary Cat, 2.789 (MS 1); 5.642 (MS 2).

Serjeantson Index, p 245.

Bliss A J, ed, Sir Orfeo, Oxford 1961, pp xi, xxv (MS 5).

Sajavaara K, The Relationship of the Vernon and Simeon MSS, NM 68(1967).428.

Guddat-Figge G, Catalogue of MSS Containing ME Romances, Munich 1976, pp 145 (MS 3), 249 (MS 5), 269 (MS 1).

Editions of ME Versions. Halliwell J O, The Castle of Love, Brixton Hill 1849, p 1 (MS 2).

Cooke M, Grosseteste's Chasteau d'Amour: To Which Are added La Vie de Sainte Marie Egyptienne and an Eng Version of the Chasteau d'Amour. R Grosseteste Carmina Anglo-Normannica, Publications of the Caxton Soc 15, London 1852, p 133 (Myrour).

Weymouth R F, Castel off Love by Robert Grosseteste, Philological Society's Early Eng Volume, Pt 3, London 1865, p 1.

AELeg 1881, p 349 (King and Four Daughters).

Horstmann C, The Minor Poems of the Vernon MS, EETS 98, London 1892, pp 355 (Castle of Love), 407 (Myrour), 394 (variants of MS 3 from Vernon).

Hupe H, Robert Grosseteste's Chasteau d'Amour (Castle of Love): MS Egerton Collection 927, Angl 14(1892).415.

Furnivall C, The Minor Poems of the Vernon MS, pt 2, EETS 117, London 1901, p 751 (Castle of Love with variants of MS 3 from Vernon).

Brunner K, Der Streit der vier Himmelstochter, EStn 68(1934).188 (Foure Daughters).

Sajavaara K, The ME Trans of Robert Grosseteste's Chateau d'Amour, Mémoires de la Société Néophilologique de Helsinki 32, Helsinki 1967, pp 260 (Castle of Love), 320 (Myrour), 354 (King and Four Daughters), 366 (Foure Daughters); see also Introd, pp 25 (Robert Grosseteste, bishop and scholar), 36 (MSS, edns, date, authorship, and themes of Chateau d'Amour), 101 (Castle of

Love: MSS, relationship of MSS, dialect, date, authorship, versification), 165 (Myrour: MS, dialect, date, authorship, versification), 185 (King and Four Daughters: MS, dialect, date, authorship, versification), 198 (Foure Daughters: MS, dialect, date, authorship, versification), 208 (interrelationship of the Eng and French versions; techniques and qualities of the translations) (crit V J Scattergood, MLR 65.367).

Editions of Chateau d'Amour. Cooke edn, p 1.

Michel F, Libri Psalmorum, versio antiqua gallica, Oxford 1860, p xxii (extract only).

Murray J, Le Château d'Amour de Robert Grosseteste évêque de Lincoln, Paris 1918, p 89 (crit M Hamilton, MLN 37.49; S de Grave, Neophil 5.278).

Selection. Kaiser R, Middle English, 3rd edn, Berlin 1958, p 243 (Castle of Love, lines 1–308).

Modernizations. Watts N H, Love Songs of Sion: A Selection of Devotional Verse from Old Eng Sources, London 1924, p 17.

Os A B van, Religious Visions, Amsterdam 1931, pp 145, 163.

Textual Matters and Relationship of MSS. Weymouth R F, Bishop Grosseteste's Castle of Love, TPSL 1862–63, p 48.

Weymouth edn, p 111 (Castle of Love).

Haase F K, Die ae Bearbeitungen von Grosseteste's Chasteau d'Amour, Halle a S 1889, p 3; Die ae Bearbeitungen von Grosseteste's Chasteau d'Amour verglichen mit der Quelle, Angl 12(1889–90).311 (MS 2).

Holthausen F, Zu Alt- und me Dicthungen. III. Die nordengl Übersetzung von Robert Grosseteste's Chasteau d'Amour, Angl 14(1892).393 (emends Cooke's edn).

Sajavaara K, The Relationship of the Vernon and Simeon MSS, NM 68(1967).438.

Language. Hupe edn, Angl 14.418 (Castle of Love, NE Midlands).

Jordon R, Handbuch des me Grammatik, 2nd edn, Heidelberg 1934, p 7 (Castle of Love, Worcestershire dialect).

Moore Meech and Whitehall, p 56 (MS 4 dialect).

Kaiser R, Zur Geographie des me Wortschatzes, Palaes 205, Leipzig 1937, pp 107, 113 (Castle of Love, SE Midlands; Myrour, Northern).

Date of Chateau d'Amour. Gröber, p 691 (ca 1250).

Murray edn, p 62 (ca 1230).

Thomson S H, The Writings of Robert Grosseteste, Cambridge 1940, p 152 (1215–30).

Creek M I, The Sources and Influence of the Chasteau d'Amour, diss Yale Univ 1941, p 15 (1200–30).

Russell J C, Phases of Grosseteste's Intellectual Life, Harvard Theological Rev 48(1950).110 (before 1199), 119.

Legge M D, Anglo-Norman in the Cloisters, Edinburgh 1950, p 100 (ca 1250); Anglo-Norman Lit and Its Background, Oxford 1963, p 223 (ca 1250).

Bloomfield SDS, p 400, n 149 (much later than ca 1230).

Sajavaara edn, p 43 (1230–53; possibly toward the end of the 1240s).

Authorship of Chateau d'Amour. Warton T, Hist of Eng Poetry, I, London 1840, p 72 (doubts Grosseteste's authorship).

Felten J, Robert Grosseteste, Bischof von Lincoln, Freiburg im Breisgau 1887, p 88 (denies authorship).

Paris G, La Littérature française du Moyen Age, Paris 1905, p 201 (leaves question open).

Thomson, Writings, p 152 (refutes Felten and establishes work as Grosseteste's).

Sajavaara edn, p 40.

Authorship of English Versions. Warton, History, p 72 (suggests Mannyng).

Horstmann edn, EETS 98.335 (ascribes Castle of Love to author of Harrowing of Hell and Marina).

Creek, diss Yale, p 171 (denies attribution).

Sources and Literary Relations. Migne PL, 94.505 (Rex et Famulus; included among Bede's spurious works).

Scherer W, Die vier Tochter Gottes, ZfDA 21 (1877).414.

Haureau B, Notices et extraits de quelques manuscrits latins de la Bibliotèque Nationale, Paris 1891, 3.260 (Rex et Famulus).

Muret E, Le Château d'Amour, Lausanne 1908.

Traver H, Four Daughters of God, BrynMawrMon 6.29; The Four Daughters of God: A Mirror of Changing Doctrine, PMLA 40(1925).44.

Murray edn, p 66.

Cornelius R, Figurative Castle, Bryn Mawr 1930, p 44.

Os A B van, Religious Visions, Amsterdam 1932, pp 145 and 164 (Castle of Love), 146 and 165 (Myrour).

Owst G R, Literature and Pulpit in Medieval England, Cambridge 1933, pp 77, 90, 95.

Langfors A, Notice des manuscrits 535 de la Bibliotèque municipale de Metz et 10047 des nouvelles acquisitions du fonds français de la Bibliothèque Nationale, Notices et extraits des manuscrits de la Bibliothèque Nationale et autres bibliotèques 42(1933).189 (theme and texts of Four Daughters of God).

Rivière J, Le Dogme de la rédemption au debut du moyen âge, Paris 1934, p 306.

McGarry L, The Holy Eucharist in ME Homiletic and Devotional Verse, Washington D C 1936, pp 131, 258 (analysis of the Sacrament of Altar included in Myrour).

Creek, diss Yale, p 18.

Chew S C, The Virtues Reconciled, Toronto 1947, pp 35, 38.

Patch H R, The Other World, Cambridge 1950, p 181.

Bloomfield SDS, p 141 (Psychomachia tradition).

Katzenellenbogen A, Allegory of the Virtues and Vices in Mediaeval Art, N Y 1964, p 40 (Four Daughters of God).

Sajavaara edn, p 48.

Hunt T, The Four Daughters of God: A Textual Contribution, Archives d'histoire doctrinale et littérature du Moyen Age 48(1981).287 (critical text of Rex et Famulus).

Other Scholarly Problems. Powell C L, The Castle of the Body, SP 16(1919).198.

Amos F R, Early Theories of Translation, N Y 1920, pp 9, 13.

Legge, A-N Lit, p 223 (suggests that Chateau incorporates Grosseteste's optical theories; denied in Sajavaara edn, p 98).

Influence. Loomis R S, The Allegorical Siege in the Art of the Middle Ages, AJA 2s 23(1919).268.

Hoopes T T, An Ivory Casket in the Metropolitan Museum of Art, Art Bull 8(1926).127 (siege of the Castle of Love motif carved on lid).

Owst G R, Preaching in Medieval England, Cambridge 1926, pp 227, 277, 288, 325 n4.

Cornelius, Figurative Castle, p 63 (possible influence on Castle of Perseverance).

LeMay M de L, The Allegory of the Christ-Knight in Eng Lit, Washington D C 1932, p 3.

Bühler C F, The Sources of the Court of Sapience, Beiträge zur engl Philologie 23, Leipzig 1932, p 21.

Owst, Lit and Pulpit, p 83.

Creek M I, The Four Daughters of God in the Gesta Romanorum and the Court of Sapience, PMLA 57(1942).951.

Pecheux M C, Aspects of the Treatment of Death in ME Poetry, Washington D C 1957, pp 62, 129.

Sajavaara edn, p 98; The Use of Robert Grosseteste's Chateau D'Amour As a Source of Cursor Mundi: Additional Evidence, NM 68(1967).184.

Wimsatt J I, Allegory and Mirror, N Y 1970, pp 95, 114, 124.

Harvey E R, ed, The Court of Sapience, Toronto 1984, p xxvii.

General References. Brandl, pp 639, § 40; 696 § 55.

Courthope, p 342.

Jusserand J J, A Lit Hist of the Eng People, London 1895, 1.213.

Schofield, pp 133, 386.

Mosher J A, The Exemplum in the Early Religious and Didactic Lit of England, N Y 1911, pp 84, 85.

Owst, Preaching, pp 227, 277, 288.

Renwick-Orton, p 280.

Baugh LHE, pp 139, 201, 206.

Bloomfield SDS, p 140.

Schlauch M, Eng Medieval Lit and Its Social Foundations, Warsaw 1956, pp 165, 194.

Wenzel, p 167.

Wenzel S, Verses in Sermons, Cambridge 1978, p 114 n29.

Möske B, Caritas: Ihre figurative Darstellung in der engl Literatur des 14 bis 16 Jahrhunderts, Bonn 1977, p 46.

Bibliography. Booker J M, A ME Biblio, Heidelberg 1912, p 5.

Vising J, Anglo-Norman Lang and Lit, London 1923, pp 17, 56, 66, 69.

Thomson, Writings, p 152.

Bossuat MBLF, p 332.

New CBEL, 1.506.

[183] TEMPLUM DOMINI.

MS. BL Addit 32578, ff 105ᵃ–116ᵃ (1405).

Brown-Robbins, no 967.

Brown Reg, 1.410.

MS Commentary. Catalogue of Additions to the MSS in the British Museum in the Years MDCCCLXXXII–MDCCCLXXXVII, London 1889, p 157.

Edition. Cornelius R D, The Figurative Castle, Bryn Mawr 1930, pp 90 (discussion), 91 (text).

Sources and Literary Relations. Thomson S H, The Writings of Robert Grosseteste, Cambridge 1940, p 138 (MS and analysis).

Bauer G, Claustrum Animae: Untersuchungen zur Geschichte der Metapher von Herzen als Kloster I, Munich 1873, p 282 (In Claustro Animae Deus debet esse Abbas).

Goering J and F A C Mantello, edd, Robert Grosseteste Templum Domini, Toronto 1984.

General References. Bloomfield SDS, pp 140, 233.

Pantin, p 193.

Möske B, Caritas: Ihre figurative Darstellung in der engl Literatur des 14 bis 16 Jahrhunderts, Bonn 1977, p 46.

Boyle L E, Robert Grosseteste and the Pastoral Care, Medieval and Renaissance Stud 8(1979).9.

Gillespie V, Doctrina and Predicacio: The Design and Function of Some Pastoral Manuals, Leeds SE 11(1980).38.

Bibliography. Bloomfield M W, B-G Guyot, D R Howard and T B Kabealo, Incipits of Latin Works on the Virtues and Vices 1100–1500 A D, Cambridge Mass 1979, pp 222, no 2526; 516, no 5982.

[184] THE ABBEY OF THE HOLY GHOST.

MSS. 1, Bodl 1292 (Laud misc 210), ff 180ᵃ–186ᵇ (1400–25); 2, Bodl 3938 (Eng poet a.1), ff 359ᵃ–360ᵇ (1380–1400); 3, Bodl 21715 (Douce 141), ff 139ᵃ–145ᵃ (1400–25); 4, Bodl 21897 (Douce 323), ff 154ᵇ–159ᵇ (1475–1500); 5, Corpus Christi Oxford 155, ff 260ᵃ–268ᵇ (ca 1450); 6, Camb Univ Dd.11.89, ff 2ᵃ–8ᵇ (ca 1400); 7, Camb Univ Ii.4.9, ff 69ᵇ–74ᵃ (ca 1450); 8, Camb Univ Ll.5.18, ff 1ᵃ–9ᵇ (1475–1500); 9, Jesus Camb 46, ff 146ᵃ–154ᵇ (15 cent); 10, Trinity Camb 1053 (0.1.29), ff 77ᵃ–84ᵃ (1400–50); 11, BL Cotton Vespasian D.xiii, f 181ᵃ (1400–50; missing folio of MS 5); 12, BL Egerton 3245, ff 156ᵇ–166ᵇ (ca 1400); 13, BL Harley 1704, ff 32ᵇ–37ᵇ (ca 1465); 14, BL Harley 2406, ff 61ᵃ–68ᵃ (1475–1500); 15, BL Harley 5272, ff 105ᵃ–115ᵇ (1450–1500); 16, BL Addit 22283, f 165ᵃ–ᵇ (1380–1400); 17, BL Addit 36983, ff 281ᵃ–285ᵇ (ca 1442); 18, Lambeth Palace 432, ff 37ᵇ–46ᵇ (1450–1500); 19, Nat Libr of Wales Aberystwyth Peniarth 334A, pp 77–92 (1400–1425); 20, Lincoln Cath 91, ff 271ᵃ–276ᵃ (1440); 21, Stonyhurst Coll B.xxiii, ff 45ᵇ–60ᵃ (1400–25); 22, Winchester Coll 33, ff 94ᵃ–98ᵇ (1450–75); 23, Hopton Hall (Chandos-Pole-Gell), pp 43–56 (1400–25); 24, Bradfer-Lawrence 8 (olim Greg), ff 1ᵃ–7ᵃ (1400–50). PRINTS: 25, Wynkyn de Worde, Westminster 1496 (Morgan Libr); 26, Wynkyn de Worde, Westminster 1496/1497 (STC, no 13609); 27, Wynkyn de Worde, Westminster 1500 (STC, no 13610).

Jolliffe, p 98, no H.16.

MSS Commentary. A Catalogue of the Harleian MSS in the British Museum, London 1808, 2.177 (MS 13), 688 (MS 14); 3.257 (MS 15).

Coxe H O, Catalogus Codicum MSS qui in Collegiis Aulisque Oxoniensibus Hodie Adservantur, Oxford 1852, 2.63 (MS 5); Catalogi Codicum Manuscriptorum Bibliothecae Bodleianae, Pt II, Oxford 1858, p 181 (MS 1).

A Catalogue of the Manuscripts Preserved in the Libr of the Univ of Cambridge, Cambridge 1856, 1.481 (MS 6); 3(1858).448 (MS 7); 4(1861).100 (MS 8).

Historical MSS Commission, 2nd Report of the Royal Commission on Historical MSS, London 1871, pp 106 (MS 19), 144 (MS 21); 9th Report of the Royal Commission on Historical MSS, pt 2, London 1883, appendix, p 384 (MS 23).

Catalogue of Additions to the MSS in the British Museum in the Years MDCCCLIV–MDCCCLX, London 1875, p 623 (MS 16).

Summary Cat, 2.789 (MS 2); 4.535 (MS 3), 595 (MS 4).

James M R, A Descriptive Catalogue of the MSS in the Libr of Jesus Coll Cambridge, London 1895, p 70 (MS 9); The Western MSS in the Libr of Trinity Coll Cambridge, A Descriptive Catalogue, Cambridge 1902, 3.33 (MS 10).

Catalogue of Additions to the MSS in the British Museum in the Years MDCCCC–MDCCCCV, London 1907, p 265 (MS 17).

Wooley R M, Catalogue of the MSS of Lincoln Cathedral Chapter Libr, London 1927, p 51 (MS 20).

Allen WAR, p 336 (MS 24).

James M R and C Jenkins, A Descriptive Catalogue of the MSS in the Libr of Lambeth Palace, Cambridge 1930, p 599 (MS 18).

Serjeantson Index, p 250.

Robbins R H, The Gurney Series of Religious Lyrics, PMLA 54(1939).369.

Collins A J, ME Devotional Pieces, British Museum Quart 14(1940).87 (MS 12).

Manly & Rickert, 1.238 (MS 13), 519 (MS 21).

Handlist of MSS in the National Libr of Wales, Aberystwyth 1943, p 2 (MS 19).

The British Museum Catalogue of Additions to the MSS 1936–1945, London 1970, p 358 (MS 12).

Giles P M, A Handlist of the Bradfer-Lawrence MSS Deposited on Loan at the Fitzwilliam Museum, Trans of the Cambridge Biblio Soc 6(1972).88 (MS 24).

Owen A E B, The Collation and Descent of the Thornton MS, Trans of the Cambridge Biblio Soc 6(1975).218 (MS 20).

Guddat-Figge G, Catalogue of MSS Containing ME Romances, Munich 1976, pp 100 (MS 7), 135 (MS 20), 145 (MS 16), 166 (MS 17), 269 (MS 2).

Davis N, Non-Cycle Plays and the Winchester Dialogues, Leeds 1979, p 135 (MS 22).

Editions. Perry G G, Religious Pieces in Prose and Verse from R Thornton's MS, EETS 26(London 1867; rptd 1973).51 (MS 20).

Yksh Wr, 1.321 (MS 20, with variants from MSS 1, 2, 13, 14).

Consacro D P, A Critical Edn of The Abbey of the Holy Ghost from All Known Extant Eng MSS with Introd, Notes, and Glossary, diss Fordham Univ 1971, p 1 (base text: MS 2); see also Introd, pp iii (description of MSS), cxii (relationship of MSS), cxvii (base text), cxxi (early prints), cxxiv (relationship of French and Eng texts), cxxx (authorship), cxxxiii (language of MS 2), clxix (style).

Blake N F, ME Religious Prose, Evanston 1972, p 88 (base text: MS 1).

Facsimiles. The Abbaye of the Holy Ghost, Printed at Westminster by Wynkyn de Worde about the Year 1496, Cambridge 1907 (with a prefatory note by F Jenkinson).

The Thornton MS (Lincoln Cathedral MS 91) with introds by D S Brewer and A E B Owen, London 1975 (MS 20).

Selections. Kirchberger C, ed, The Coasts of the Country: an Anthology of Prayer Drawn from the Early Eng Spiritual Writers, London n d, p 40 (MS 20).

Matthews W, ed, Later Medieval Eng Prose, N Y 1963, p 244 (excerpt from Yksh Wr, 1.321).

Authorship. Allen WAR, p 337.

Scott St M, The Eng Sermons of John Alcock, with an Account of His Life, diss Fordham Univ 1947, p 42.

Consacro P, The Author of the Abbey of the Holy Ghost: a Popularizer of the Mixed Life, FCEMN 2(1976).15.

Language and Style. Moore Meech and Whitehall, p 54.

Workman S K, 15-cent Translation as an Influence on Eng Prose, Princeton 1940, pp 63, 69.

Consacro edn, p 17.

Blake N F, Varieties of ME Prose, in B Rowland, ed, Chaucer and ME Stud in Honour of Rossell Hope Robbins, London 1974, p 351.

Sources and Literary Relationships. Chew S C, The Virtues Reconciled: an Iconographic Study, Toronto 1907.

Traver H, The Four Daughters of God: a Study of the Versions of This Allegory with Special Reference to Those in Latin, French and Eng, Bryn Mawr 1907, p 126.

Allen WAR, p 315.

Cornelius R D, The Figurative Castle, Bryn Mawr 1930, pp 6, 50.

Allen H E, Wynkyn de Worde and a Second French Compilation from the Ancrene Riwle with a Description of the First (Trinity Coll Camb MS 883), Essays and Studies in Honor of Carleton Brown, N Y 1940, p 188 (Douce MS 365).

Chesney K, Notes on Some Treatises of Devotion Intended for Margaret of York (MS Douai 365), MÆ 20(1951).11.

Brook S, Religious Allegory in ME, diss Manchester Univ 1955, chaps 2, 11; The Charter of the Abbey of the Holy Ghost, MLR 54(1959).481 (differences between Abbey and Charter).

Conlee J W, The Abbey of the Holy Ghost and the Eight Ghostly Dwelling Places of Huntington Libr HM.744, MÆ 44(1975).137.

General References. Mosher J A, The Exemplum in the Early Religious and Didactic Lit of England, N Y 1911, pp 118, 126.

Deanesly M, The Lollard Bible and Other Medieval Biblical Versions, Cambridge 1920, pp 199, 217; Vernacular Books in England in the 14 and 15 Cents, MLR 15(1920).358.

Owst G R, Preaching in Medieval England, Cambridge 1926, p 288; Literature and Pulpit in Medieval England, Cambridge 1933, pp 78 n5, 80 n5, 86, 107.

Workman S K, 15-Cent Translation as an Influence on Eng Prose, Princeton 1940, p 61 n7.

Bloomfield SDS, p 141.

Doyle Survey, 2.6.

Schlauch M, Eng Medieval Lit and Its Social Foundations, Warsaw 1956, p 194.

Seaton E, Sir Richard Roos: c 1400–83 Lancastrian Poet, London 1961, p 301.

Pantin, p 253.

Möske B, Caritas: Ihre figurative Darstellung in der engl Literatur des 14 bis 16 Jahrhunderts, Bonn 1977, p 49.

Riehle W, The ME Mystics, London 1981, pp 16, 19, 20.

Bibliography. Booker J M, A ME Biblio, Heidelberg 1912, p 3.

Duff E G, 15-Cent Eng Books, London 1917, p 1, nos 1, 2.

Bühler C F, The First Edn of The Abbey of the Holy Ghost, SB 6(1954).100; The ME Texts of Morgan MS 861, PMLA 69(1954).686 nl.

Bennett H S, Notes on Two Incunables: The Abbey of the Holy Ghost and A Ryght Profytable Treatyse, Libr 5s 10(1955).120; Eng Books and Readers, 1475–1557, 2nd edn, Cambridge 1969, p 253.

New CBEL, 1.505.

[185] EIGHT GHOSTLY DWELLING PLACES.

MS. Henry E Huntington HM 744, ff 12ᵇ–13ᵃ (1400–25).

MS Commentary. Schulz H C, Thomas Hoccleve, Scribe, Spec 12(1927).71.

de Ricci Census, 1.74.

Hanna R III, The Index of ME Prose, Handlist I, A Handlist of Manuscripts containing ME Prose in the Henry E Huntington Library, Woodbridge 1984, p 33.

Edition. Conlee J W, The Abbey of the Holy Ghost and the Eight Ghostly Dwelling Places of Huntington Libr HM.744, MÆ 44(1975).142.

[186] THE CHARTER OF THE ABBEY OF THE HOLY GHOST.

MSS. 1, Bodl 1292 (Laud misc 210), ff 136ᵃ–146ᵃ (1400–25); 2, Bodl 3938 (Eng poet a.1), ff 360ᵇ–

363ᵃ (1380–1400); 3, Bodl 21897 (Douce 323), ff 140ᵇ–154ᵇ (1475–1500); 4, Camb Univ Ii.4.9, ff 74ᵃ–87ᵃ (ca 1450); 5, Camb Univ Ll.5.18, ff 9ᵇ–24ᵇ (1475–1500); 6, Magdalene Camb Pepys 2125, ff 89ᵃ–96ᵇ (ca 1450); 7, Trinity Camb 1053 (0.1.29), ff 84ᵃ–101ᵇ (1400–50); 8, Jesus Camb 46, ff 154ᵇ–172ᵃ (15 cent); 9, BL Egerton 3245, ff 166ᵇ–183ᵃ (ca 1400); 10, BL Harley 1704, ff 37ᵇ–48ᵃ (ca 1465); 11, BL Harley 2406, ff 68ᵃ–83ᵃ (1475–1500); 12, BL Harley 5272, ff 115ᵇ–137ᵇ (1450–1500); 13, BL Addit 22283, ff 165ᵇ–168ᵃ (1380–1400); 14, BL Addit 36983, ff 285ᵇ–297ᵇ (ca 1442); 15, Lambeth Palace 432, ff 47ᵃ–68ᵃ (1450–1500); 16, Nat Libr of Wales Aberystwyth Peniarth 334A, pp 92–123 (1400–25); 17, Maidstone Mus 6, ff 41ᵃ–58ᵇ (1400–25); 18, Stonyhurst Coll B.xxiii, ff 45ᵇ–60ᵃ (1400–25); 19, Stonyhurst Coll B.liii, f 99ᵃ⁻ᵇ (15 cent); 20, Winchester Coll 33, ff 99ᵃ–108ᵇ (1450–75); 21, Hopton Hall (Chandos-Pole-Gell), pp 43–56 (1400–25); 22, Longleat 4, last item, no foliation (1400–25); 23, Columbia Univ Plimpton 263, ff 379ᵃ–386ᵃ (ca 1450); 24, Bradfer-Lawrence Libr 8 (olim Greg), ff 1ᵃ–7ᵃ (1400–50). PRINTS: 25, Wynkyn de Worde, Westminster 1496 (Morgan copy); 26, Westminster 1497 (STC, no 13609); 27, Wynkyn de Worde, Westminster 1500 (STC, no 13610).

Jolliffe, p 94, no H.9.

MSS Commentary. A Catalogue of the Harleian MSS in the British Museum, London 1808, 2.177 (MS 10), 688 (MS 11); 3.257 (MS 12).

Coxe H O, Catalogi Codicum Manuscriptorum Bibliothecae Bodleianae, Pt II, Oxford 1858, p 181 (MS 1).

A Catalogue of the MSS Preserved in the Libr of the Univ of Cambridge, Cambridge 1858, 3.448 (MS 4); 4(1861).100 (MS 5).

Historical MSS Commission, 2nd Report of the Royal Commission on Historical MSS, London 1871, appendix, pp 144, 145 (MSS 18, 19); 3rd Report, London 1872, p 180 (MS 22); 9th Report, pt 2, London 1883, appendix, p 384 (MS 21).

Catalogue of Additions to the MSS in the British Museum in the Years MDCCCLIV–MDCCCLX, London 1875, p 623 (MS 13); Catalogue . . . in the Years MDCCCC–MDCCCCV, London 1907, p 265 (MS 14).

James M R, A Descriptive Catalogue of the MSS in the Libr of Jesus Coll Cambridge, London 1895, p 70 (MS 8); The Western MSS in the Libr of Trinity Coll Cambridge A Descriptive Catalogue, Cambridge 1902, 3.33 (MS 7); A Descriptive Catalogue of the Libr of Samuel Pepys, Pt III, Medieval MSS, Cambridge 1923, p 72 (MS 6).

Summary Cat, 2.789 (MS 2); 4.595 (MS 3).

Allen WAR, p 336.

James M R and C Jenkins, A Descriptive Catalogue of the MSS in the Libr of Lambeth Palace, Cambridge 1930, p 899 (MS 15).

de Ricci Census, 1.1801 (MS 23).

Serjeantson Index, p 250.

Collins A J, ME Devotional Pieces, British Museum Quart 14(1940).87 (MS 9).

Manly & Rickert, 1.238 (MS 10), 519 (MS 18).

Ives S A, Corrigenda and Addenda, Spec 17 (1942).45 (MS 23).

Handlist of MSS in the National Libr of Wales, Aberystwyth 1943, p 2.

Kane G, ed, Piers Plowman: The A Version, London 1960, p 3 (MS 3).

Ker Manuscripts, 3.330 (MS 17).

The British Museum Catalogue of Additions to the MSS 1936–45, London 1970, p 358 (MS 9).

Giles P M, A Handlist of the Bradfer-Lawrence MSS Deposited on Loan at the Fitzwilliam Museum, Trans of the Cambridge Biblio Soc 6(1972).88 (MS 24).

Guddat-Figge G, Catalogue of MSS Containing ME Romances, Munich 1976, pp 166 (MS 14), 269 (MS 2).

Davis N, ed, Non-Cycle Plays and the Winchester Dialogue, Leeds 1979, p 135 (MS 20).

Editions. Yksh Wr, 1.337 (base texts: MSS 1, 2).

Fanning C E, The Charter of the Abbey of the Holy Ghost: A Critical Edn from All Known Extant MSS, diss Fordham Univ 1975, p 1 (base text: MS 2); see also Introd, pp iv (description of MSS), xciii (relationship of MSS), cii (early editions), cv (authorship), cviii (language of MS 2), clix (traditions, sources, and style).

Facsimiles. The Abbaye of the Holy Ghost. Printed at Westminster by Wynkyn de Worde about the Year 1496, Cambridge 1907 (with a prefatory note by F Jenkinson).

The Thornton MS (Lincoln Cathedral MS 91) with Introds by D S Brewer and A E B Owen, Lincoln 1975.

Sources and Literary Relations. Traver H, The Four Daughters of God: A Study of the Versions of this Allegory with Special Reference to Those in Latin, French, and Eng, Bryn Mawr 1907, p 125 (Charter follows general tradition of Pseudo-Bonaventuran Meditations; shows affinities with versions in Castle of Perseverance (XII [27]) and Ludus Coventriae (XII [12]); crit R L Ramsey, MLN 24.91).

Spalding M C, The ME Charters of Christ, BrynMawrMon 15.xxxviii.

Allen WAR, p 336.

Cornelius R D, The Figurative Castle, Bryn Mawr 1930, p 55.

Chew S C, The Virtues Reconciled: an Iconographic Study, Toronto 1947.

Klinefelter R A, The Four Daughters of God: a New Version, JEGP 52(1953).90 (a version from Trinity Coll Dublin MS 423 which, according to Brook, p 484 below, derives either from the Charter or from a common source).

Literary Criticism and Analysis. McQuillan P A, Critical Edn of the Life of the Virgin Mary and the Christ, MA thesis Duquesne Univ 1951 (Trinity Coll Dublin MS 423).

Brook S, Religious Allegory in ME, diss Manchester Univ 1955, appendix D; The Charter of the Abbey of the Holy Ghost, MLR 54(1959).481.

General References. Workman S K, 15-Cent Translation as an Influence on Eng Prose, Princeton 1940, p 61 n7.

Bloomfield SDS, p 141.

Katzenellenbogen A, Allegories of the Virtues and Vices in Mediaeval Art, N Y 1964, p 40 (representations of Four Daughters in art).

Woolf, p 212.

Riehle W, The ME Mystics, London 1981, p 155 (Charter said to be the only Eng tract in which the term synderesis is found).

Bibliography. Booker J M, A ME Biblio, Heidelberg 1912, p 6.

Duff E G, 15-Cent Eng Books, Oxford 1917, p 1, nos 1, 2.

Bühler C F, The ME Texts of Morgan MS 861, PMLA 69(1954).686 n1.

Bennett H S, Notes on Two Incunables: The Abbey of the Holy Ghost and A Ryght Profytable Treatyse, Libr 5s 10(1955).120; Eng Books and Readers 1475–1557, 2nd edn, Cambridge 1969, p 253.

New CBEL, 1.505.

[187] THE CHARTER OF CHRIST
(or CARTA CHRISTI or CARTA DEI
or TESTAMENTUM CHRISTI or MAGNA
CARTA DE LIBERTATIBUS MUNDI
or CARTA REDEMPCIONIS HUMANE
or TESTAMENTUM DOMINI
or FEOFFEMENT IHESU or BONA CARTA
GLORIOSE PASSIONIS DOMINI
NOSTRI IHESU CHRISTI).

MSS Version A: Carta Dei: 1, Bodl Kent Charter 233 (dorso) (1400–25); *Version B: Short Charter:* 2, Bodl 5088 (Dodsworth 147), f 79b (17 cent; probably a copy of MS 22 below); 3, Bodl 6777 (Ashmole 189), f 109a–b (1475–1500); 4, Bodl 6922 (Ashmole 61), f 106a (1475–1500); 5, Camb Univ Ee.2.15, ff 107a–111a (1475–1500); 6, Camb Univ Ii.6.44, ff 1a–2b (1450–1500); 7, Camb Univ Addit 6686 (olim Ashburnham 140), p 270 (1400–50);

8, Gonville and Caius Camb 230, p 58 (15 cent); 9, St John's Camb 37, f 53ᵃ (15 cent); 10, Magdalene Camb Pepys 1236, ff 7ᵇ–8ᵃ (1637); 11, BL Harley 116, f 97ᵇ (1450–1500); 12, BL Harley 237, f 100ᵃ⁻ᵇ (1475–1500); 13, BL Harley 3775, f 138ᵃ⁻ᵇ (1475–1500); 14, BL Harley 6848, ff 239ᵇ–240ᵃ (18 cent; perhaps a copy of MS 22 below); 15, BL Stowe 620, f 11ᵇ (1550–1600); 16, BL Stowe 1055, pp 40–42 (18 cent; copy of MS 2 above); 17, BL Sloane 3292, f 2ᵃ (16 cent); 18, BL Addit 5465, ff 119ᵃ–124ᵃ (1500–25); 19, BL Addit 24343, ff 6ᵇ–7ᵃ (1475–1500); 20, BL Addit 37049, f 23ᵇ (1400–50); 21, BL Addit 60577, ff 114ᵇ–115ᵃ (1475–1550); 22, BL Addit Charter 5960 (ca 1500); 23, John Rylands Latin 176, f 202ᵇ (1475–1500); 24, Harvard Univ Richardson 22, ff 71ᵇ–72ᵃ (1400–25); 25, olim J W Dod (present location unknown); *Version C: Long Charter A-Text:* 26, Bodl 1886 (Bodley 89), ff 45ᵃ–49ᵃ (ca 1400); 27, Bodl 3938 (Eng poet a.1), f 317ᵃ⁻ᵇ (1380–1400); 28, Bodl 14667 (Rawl poet 175), ff 94ᵇ–95ᵃ (ca 1350); 29, Bodl 29572 (Add C.280), ff 124ᵃ–125ᵃ (1400–50); 30, Magdalen Oxford St Peter in the East 18, e (dorso) (1400–25); 31, Camb Univ Addit 6686 (olim Ashburnham 140), pp 270–271 (1400–50); 32, BL Harley 2346, ff 51ᵃ–55ᵃ (1400–50); 33, BL Harley 5396, ff 301ᵃ–305ᵇ (1475–1500); 34, BL Addit 11307, ff 89ᵃ–97ᵃ (1400–50); *B-Text:* 35, Camb Univ Ee.2.15, ff 90ᵃ–94ᵃ (1475–1500); 36, Camb Univ Ff.2.38, ff 47ᵇ–50ᵇ (ca 1450); 37, Camb Univ Ii.3.26, ff 235ᵃ–237ᵃ (1430–50); 38, Camb Univ Ii.4.9, ff 42ᵇ–47ᵃ (ca 1450); 39, BL Cotton Caligula A.ii, ff 77ᵃ–79ᵃ (1475–1500); 40, BL Harley 2382, ff 111ᵇ–118ᵃ (1470–1500); 41, olim Phillipps 8820, art 3 (present location unknown); 42, Harvard Univ Deposit: W K Richardson 22, ff 82ᵇ–90ᵇ (ca 1400); 43, Corning Mus of Glass 6, ff 123ᵇ–130ᵇ (1475–1500); *C-Text:* 44, BL Royal 17.C.xvii, ff 112ᵇ–116ᵇ (1400–25).

Brown-Robbins, nos 1174, 1718, 1740, 1828, 4154, 4184; Robbins-Cutler, nos 1740, 4154, 4182.5, 4184.

Revell, pp 7, 8.

MSS Commentary. A Catalogue of the MSS in the Cottonian Libr Deposited in the British Museum, London 1802, p 42 (MS 39).

A Catalogue of the Harleian MSS in the British Museum, London 1808, 1.35 (MS 11), 73 (MS 12); 2.662 (MS 32), 675 (MS 40); 3.60 (MS 33), 435 (MS 14).

List of Additions to the MSS in the British Museum in the Years MDCCCXXXVI–MDCCCXL, London 1843, p 2 (MS 34).

Black W H, A Descriptive Analytical and Critical Catalogue of the MSS Bequeathed unto the Univ of Oxford by Elias Ashmole, Oxford 1845, pp 106 (MS 4), 150 (MS 3).

Catalogue of Additions to the MSS in the British Museum in the Years MDCCCXLI–MDCCCXLV, London 1850, p 64 (MS 22).

A Catalogue of the MSS Preserved in the Libr of the Univ of Cambridge, Cambridge 1857, 2.31 (MSS 5, 35; both from Camb Univ Ee.2.15), 404 (MS 36); 3(1858).429 (MS 37), 448 (MS 38), 542 (MS 6).

Catalogue of Additions to the MSS in the British Museum in the Years MDCCCLIV–MDCCCLXXV, London 1877, p 57 (MS 19).

Summary Cat, 2.98 (MS 26), 789 (MS 27), 954 (MS 2); 3.321 (MS 28); 5.646 (MS 29).

Catalogue of the Stowe MSS in the British Museum, London 1895, 1.482 (MS 15), 678 (MS 16).

Catalogue of Additions to the MSS in the British Museum for the Years MDCCCC–MDCCCCV, London 1907, p 324 (MS 20).

James M R, A Descriptive Catalogue of the MSS in the Libr of Gonville and Caius College, Cambridge 1907, 1.268 (MS 8); A Descriptive Catalogue of the MSS in the Libr of St John's Coll Cambridge, Cambridge 1913, p 48 (MS 9); A Descriptive Catalogue of the Latin MSS in the John Rylands Libr at Manchester, Manchester 1921, 1.299 (MS 23); A Descriptive Catalogue of the Libr of Samuel Pepys, Pt III, Mediaeval MSS, London 1923, p 8 (MS 10).

Warner G F and J P Gilson, Catalogue of Western MSS in the Old Royal and King's Collections, London 1921, 2.243 (MS 44).

de Ricci Census, 1.961 (MS 24; both from Richardson 22); 3.317 (MS 43).

Serjeantson Index, p 247.

Manly & Rickert, 1.126 (MSS 5, 35; both from Camb Univ Ee.2.15), 245 (MS 40), 295 (MS 37).

Stevens J, Music and Poetry in the Early Tudor Court, London 1961, p 351 (MS 18); Early Tudor Songs and Carols, Musica Britannica 36, London 1975, p xv (MS 18).

Doyle A I, The Shaping of the Vernon and Simeon MSS, in B Rowland, ed, Chaucer and ME Stud in Honour of R H Robbins, London 1974, p 328 (MS 27).

Seymour M C, The MSS of Hoccleve's Regiment of Princes, Edinburgh Biblio Soc Trans 4(1974).265 (MS 11).

Guddat-Figge G, Catalogue of MSS Containing ME Romances, Munich 1976, pp 94 (MS 36), 110 (MS 38), 169 (MS 39), 249 (MS 4), 269 (MS 27).

Hogg J, Unpublished Texts in the Carthusian Northern ME Religious Miscellany British Libr MS Add 37049, in Essays in Honor of Erwin Stürzl on His Sixtieth Brithday, ed J Hogg, I,

Salzburger Studien zur Anglistik und Amerikanistik, Salzburg 1980, p 241 (detailed description of MS 20).

The Winchester Anthology, with an Introd by E Wilson and I Fenlon, Woodbridge 1981, p 1 (MS 21).

Editions. Astle T, An Ancient Poem, in the Antiquarian Repertory, ed F Grose and T Astle, London 1807, 1.21 (MS 2).

Ancient Eng Poems: from a MS Belonging to J W Dod, Esq MP, The Gentlemen's Magazine, June 1848, p 612 (MS 25).

Riley H T, Annales Monasterii S Albani, Amundesham, Rolls Series 28, Pt 5, London 1870, 1.457 (MS 13).

Horstmann C, Nachträge zu den Legenden, Arch 79(1887).424 (MSS 27, 40).

Macray W D, 15-Cent Religious Verses, N&Q 9s 8(1901).240 (MS 1).

Furnivall F J, The Minor Poems of the Vernon MS, Pt II, EETS 117, London 1901, p 637 (MSS 27, 40, 44).

Fehr B, Die Lieder des Fairfax MS (Add 5465, Brit Mus), Arch 106(1901).69 (MS 18).

Forster M, Kleinere me Texte, Angl 42(1918).192 (MS 4, with variants from MS 3).

Spalding M C, The ME Charters of Christ, BrynMawrMon 15.1 (all Short Charters except MSS 2, 6, 7, 10, 13, 17, 21, 24), 18 (all Long A-Text Charters except MSS 27, 31), 46 (all Long B-Text Charters except MSS 40–43), 97 (MS 1); see also Introd, pp xix (description of MSS), xxxvi (history and sources), lxiii (relationship of MSS of Short Charter), xciii (relationship of MSS of Long Charter), appendix 83 (language of Charters); (crit K Brunner, EStn 49.287; B Fehr AnglB 26.24; G Binz, LfGRP 38.23).

James M R, Descriptive Catalogue of the Latin MSS in the John Rylands Libr at Manchester, Manchester 1921, 1.300 (MS 23).

Stevens J, Music and Poetry in the Early Tudor Court, London 1961, p 383 (MS 18); Early Tudor Songs and Carols, Musica Britannica 36, London 1975, p 146, no 68 (MS 18).

Doty B L, An Edn of British Museum MS Additional 37049: A Religious Miscellany, diss Michigan State 1963, p 143 (MS 20).

Facsimile. The Winchester Anthology, with an Introd by E Wilson and I Fenlon, Woodbridge 1981 (MS 21).

Modernization. Adamson M R, Treasury of ME Verse, London 1930, p 91 (MS 4).

Sources and Literary Relations. Migne PL, 15.1895 (Ambrose's Expos Ev sec Luc X).

Thien H, Über die engl Marienklagen, Kiel 1906, p 82.

Perrow E C, The Last Will and Testament as a Form of Lit, Trans of the Wisconsin Acad of Sciences Arts and Letters 17(1913).687, 701.

Rice W H, The European Ancestry of Villon's Satirical Testaments, N Y 1941, p 85.

Literary Criticism. Brook S, Religious Allegory in ME, diss Manchester Univ 1955, chap 2.

Woolf, p 210.

Influence. Taylor G C, The Relation of the Eng Corpus Christi Play to the ME Religious Lyric, MP 5(1907–08).8.

General References. Pearsall D, Old Eng and ME Poetry, London 1877, p 141.

Cook A S, ed, The Christ of Cynewulf, Boston 1900, p 208.

Forster M, Zu den kleineren me Texten, Angl 43(1919).194.

Bloomfield SDS, p 199.

Gray D, Themes and Images in Medieval Eng Religious Lyric, London 1972, p 130 (facsimile of MS 20 opp p 86).

Bibliography. New CBEL, 1.505.

[188] THE BRANCHES OF THE APPLE TREE.

MS. No MS extant. PRINT: Wynkyn de Worde, The Tretyse of Love, Westminster 1493–94 (STC, no 24234).

2. Works Based on Personification

[189] THE REBELLION OF PRIDE AND HER DAUGHTER ENVY.

MS. Olim Sir Fergus Graham (Cumberland), ff 120b–122b (1375–1400; Sotheby Sale Cat, Dec 12, 1966, item 215; present location unknown).

Brown-Robbins, no 3705.

Edition. Historical MSS Commission, 6th Report of the Royal Commission on Historical MSS, Pt I, Report and Appendix, London 1877, p 319.

[190] SPECULUM MISERICORDIE.

MSS. 1, Penrose 6 (olim Delamere), ff 14b–19b (ca 1450); 2, BL Addit 38181, ff 33a–34b (18-cent transcript of lines 1–136).

Brown-Robbins, Robbins-Cutler, no 1451.

MSS Commentary. Catalogue of Additions to the MSS in the British Museum in the Years MDCCCCXI–MDCCCCXV, London 1925, p 88 (MS 2).

de Ricci Census, 2.1996 (MS 1 listed as Penrose 10).

Manly & Rickert, 1.108 (MS 1 listed as Delamere).

Guddat-Figge G, Catalogue of MSS Containing ME Romances, Munich 1976, p 112.

Edition. Robbins R H, The Speculum Misericordie, PMLA 54(1939).935.

Literary Relations and Analysis. Brook S, Religious Allegory in ME, diss Manchester Univ 1955, chap 3.

General Reference. Knowlton M A, The Influence of Richard Rolle and of Julian of Norwich on the ME Lyrics, The Hague 1973, p 168 (influence of Rolle's Song of Mercy).

[191] THE TESTAMENT OF LOVE.

MSS. No MS extant. PRINT: Thynne W, ed, The Workes of Geffray Chaucer Newly Printed, with Dyvers Workes Which Were Never in Print Before, as in the Table More Playnly Dothe Appere, London 1532, L11 1ᵃ–Rrr 2ᵃ (STC, no 5068; rpts STC, nos 5069–76).

Robbins-Cutler, no 945.8 (concluding couplet).

Editions. Skeat W W, The Complete Works of Geoffrey Chaucer, Oxford 1897, 7.1 (Thynne's text with extensive emendations, particularly of the orthography).

Jellech V B, The Testament of Love by Thomas Usk: A New Edn, diss Washington Univ 1970, p 127 (diplomatic transcription of Thynne); see also Introd, pp 1 (textual problem), 17 (Usk's political career and autobiographical sources), 53 (literary sources), 119 (style and meaning).

Facsimiles. Chaucer G, The Works of Geoffrey Chaucer and Others Being a Reprod in Facsimile of the First Collected Edn of 1532 from the Copy in the British Museum, with an Introd by W W Skeat, London 1905; The Works 1532 with Supplementary Material from the Edns of 1542, 1561, 1598 and 1602, Ilkley 1969.

Selections. Matthews W, Late ME Prose, N Y 1963, p 247.

Brewer D, ed, Chaucer: The Critical Heritage, London 1978, 1.42 (Usk's tribute to Chaucer).

Textual Matters. Bradley H, Thomas Usk and The Testament of Love, EStn 23(1897).438 (acrostic); The Testament of Love, Athen Feb 6 1897, p 184 (rptd as Thomas Usk, The Testament of Love in the Collected Papers of Henry Bradley, Oxford 1928, p 229).

Skeat W W, The Testament of Love, Athen Feb 13 1897, p 215 (acknowledges Bradley's rearrangement of the text).

Schaar C, Notes on Thomas Usk's Testament of Love, Lund 1950 (crit J S [wart], Neophil 35.182; D S Bland, ESts 35.24).

Heyworth P L, The Punctuation of ME Texts, in Medieval Studies for J A W Bennett, ed P L Heyworth, Oxford 1981, p 141.

Language. Prins A A, French Influence in Eng Phrasing, Leiden 1952, p 299.

Conley J, Scholastic Neologisms in Usk's Testament of Love, N&Q ns 11(1964).209.

Date. Bressie R, The Date of Thomas Usk's Testament of Love, MP 26(1928).17.

Authorship. Godwin W, Life of Geoffrey Chaucer, 2nd edn, London 1804, 4.32 (Testament ascribed to Chaucer).

Hertzberg W, Geoffrey Chaucer's Canterbury-Geschichten, Hildburghausen 1866, 1.34 (rejects attribution to Chaucer).

Nicolas H, Life of Chaucer, in The Poetical Works of Geoffrey Chaucer, ed R Morris, London 1891, 1.32 (accepts attribution to Chaucer).

Lounsbury T R, Stud in Chaucer, His Life and Writings, N Y 1892, 1.180 (on misattribution to Chaucer).

Skeat W W, The Author of The Testament of Love, Acad Mar 11 1893, p 222 (discovery of acrostic).

Bradley, Athen Feb 6 1897, p 184 (correction of acrostic).

Skeat, Thomas Usk and Ralph Higden, N&Q 10s 1(1904).245.

Bradley H, DNB, 20.60 (Usk, Thomas).

Bressie R, A Study of Thomas Usk's Testament of Love as Autobiography, diss Univ of Chicago 1928.

Tout T F, Lit and Learning in the Eng Civil Service in the 14 Cent, Spec 4(1929).386 (Usk's career).

Usk T, The Appeal of Thomas Usk against John Northampton, in A Book of London Eng 1384–1425, ed R W Chambers and M Daunt, Oxford 1931, p 22.

Sources and Literary Relations. Tatlock J S P, The Development and Chronology of Chaucer's Work, ChS 2s 37, London 1907, p 20 (Usk's borrowing from Legend of Good Women).

Root R K, Chaucer's Legend of Medea, PMLA 24(1909).138 (denies Usk's use of Legend of Good Women).

Perrow E C, The Last Will and Testament as a Form of Lit. Wisconsin Acad of Sciences Arts and Letters 17(1911–13).687, 712.

Devlin M A, The Date of the C Version of Piers the Plowman, diss Univ of Chicago 1926, chap 6 (Usk's use of tree image from Piers Plowman).

Schmitt F S, ed, S Anselmi Opera Omnia, Rome 1940, 2.243 (De concordia praescientiae et praedestinationis et gratiae dei cum libero arbitrio).

Sanderlin G, Usk's Testament of Love and St Anselm, Spec 17(1942).69.

Patch H R, The Other World, Cambridge 1950, p 190.

Stokes M and J Scattergood, Travelling in November: Sir Gawain, Thomas Usk, Charles of Orléans, and De Re Militari, MÆ 53(1954).78 (possible use of Vegetius).

Schaar C, Usk's knot in the hert, ESts 37(1956).20 (Usk's use of Alanus de Insulis).

Norton-Smith J, Lydgate's Metaphors, ESts 42 (1961).91 (criticism of Schaar), 232 (Schaar's response), 234 (Norton-Smith's rejoinder).

Leyerle J, The Heart and the Chain, in The Learned and the Lewed, Stud in Chaucer and Medieval Lit, ed L D Benson, Cambridge 1974, p 118.

Minnis A J, The Influence of Academic Prologues in the Prologues and Literary Attitudes of Late Medieval Eng Writers, MS 48(1981).358.

Interpretation and Analysis. Lewis C S, The Allegory of Love, Oxford 1936, p 222.

Heninger S K Jr, The Margarite-Pearl Allegory in Thomas Usk's Testament of Love, Spec 32 (1951).92.

Hallmundsson M N, The Community of Law and Letters; Some Notes on Thomas Usk's Audience, Viator 9(1978).357 (The Testament appealing to members of the chancery as a court of law).

Reiss E, The Idea of Love in Usk's Testament of Love, Mediaevalia 6(1980).261.

Strohm P, Chaucer's 15-Cent Audience and the Narrowing of the Chaucer Tradition, Stud in the Age of Chaucer 4(1982).14 (Usk as a member of Chaucer's circle).

Style. Schlauch M, The Art of Chaucer's Prose, in Chaucer and Chaucerians, ed D S Brewer, Univ Alabama 1966, p 161 (Usk's and Chaucer's styles contrasted); The Two Styles of Thomas Usk, Brno Stud in Eng 8(1969).167; Usk as Translator, in Medieval Lit and Folklore Stud: Essays in Honor of F L Utley, ed J Mandel and B A Rosenberg, New Brunswick 1971, p 97.

General References. Morley, 5.261.

Saintsbury G, A Short Hist of Eng Lit, N Y 1907, p 145 n1.

Hammond, p 458.

Krapp G P, The Rise of Eng Literary Prose, N Y 1915, p 29.

Jusserand J J, A Literary Hist of the Eng People, 3rd edn, London 1925, p 411 n1.

Spurgeon C F E, 500 Years of Chaucer Criticism and Allusion 1357–1900, Cambridge 1925, 1.8.

Garnett R, Eng Lit: an Illustrated Record, N Y 1931, 1.203.

Tuve R, Seasons and Months, Paris 1933, p 173.

Anderson G K, Old and ME Lit from the Beginnings to 1485, in A Hist of Eng Lit, ed H Craig, N Y 1940, p 110.

Steel A, Richard II, Cambridge 1941, p 157.

Bennett OHEL, p 178.

Baugh LHE, p 268.

Clark C, A Mediaeval Proverb, ESts 35(1954).13.

Schlauch M, Eng Medieval Lit and Its Social Foundations, Warsaw 1956, p 299.

McKisack M, The 14 Cent, Oxford 1968, p 54.

Stevens J, Music and Poetry in the Early Tudor Court, Lincoln 1961, p 209.

Brewer D S, Images of Chaucer 1386–1900, in Chaucer and Chaucerians, ed D S Brewer, Univ Alabama 1966, pp 243, 249; Chaucer in His Time, London 1963, p 60.

Koonce B G, Chaucer and the Tradition of Fame, Princeton 1966, pp 32 n42, 85 n83.

Ackerman R W, Backgrounds to Medieval Eng Lit, N Y 1966, p 75.

Mathew G, The Court of Richard II, London 1968, p 54.

Robertson D W Jr, Chaucer's London, N Y 1968, pp 156, 167.

Conley J, The Lord's Day as the 8th Day: A Passage in Thomas Usk's The Testament of Love, N&Q ns 17(1970).367.

Kelly H A, Love and Marriage in the Age of Chaucer, Ithaca 1975, pp 67, 209, 310 n35, 327.

Blake N, The Eng Language in Medieval Lit, London 1977, p 106.

Middleton A, The Idea of Public Poetry in the Reign of Richard II, Spec 53(1978).97.

Green R F, Poets and Princepleasers, Toronto 1980, pp 3, 129, 148, 166, 211.

Coleman J, Eng Lit in History 1350–1400, London 1981, pp 21, 46, 55, 130, 161.

Scattergood V J, Literary Culture at the Court of Richard II, in Eng Court Culture in the Later Middle Ages, ed V J Scattergood and J W Sherborne, N Y 1983, p 39.

Bibliography. New CBEL, 1.506.

3. Works Based on Allegorical Action

[192] VERSIONS OF GUILLAUME DE GUILLEVILLE'S PÈLERINAGE DE LA VIE HUMAINE (THE PILGRIMAGE OF THE LYFE OF THE MANHODE).

MSS. 1, Bodl 1239 (Laud misc 740), ff 1ᵃ–128ᵇ (1450–1500); 2, Camb Univ Ff.5.30, ff 5ᵃ–140ᵇ (1425–50); 3, St John's Camb 189, ff 1ᵃ–136ᵇ

(1450–1500); 4, Sion Coll Arc L.40.2/E.44, ff 1ᵃ–
93ᵇ (ca 1450); 5, Glasgow Univ Hunter 239, ff 1ᵃ–
102ᵃ (1400–25); 6, State Libr of Victoria Melbourne 217, ff 1ᵃ–95ᵇ (1450–1500).

Robbins-Cutler, no 2271.4 (concluding couplet).

MSS Commentary. A Catalogue of the MSS Preserved
in the Libr of the Univ of Cambridge, Cambridge
1857, 2.492 (MS 2).

Coxe H O, Catalogi Codicum Manuscriptorum Bibliothecae Bodleianae, Oxford 1858, 2.525 (MS 1).

Hammond, pp 333, 515 (MS 4 and other Shirley
MSS).

Young J and P G Aitken, A Catalogue of the MSS
in the Libr of the Hunterian Museum in the Univ
of Glasgow, Glasgow 1908, p 190 (MS 5).

James M R, A Descriptive Catalogue of the MSS in
the Libr of St John's Coll Cambridge, Cambridge
1913, p 225 (MS 3).

Allen WAR, p 241 (MS 5).

Ker Manuscripts, 1.290 (MS 4).

Sinclair K V, Descriptive Catalogue of Medieval and
Renaissance Western MSS in Australia, Sydney
1969, p 364 (MS 6).

Pächt O and J J G Alexander, Illuminated MSS in
the Bodleian Libr Oxford, Oxford 1973, 3.81, no
925 (MS 1).

Editions. Wright W A, The Pilgrimage of the Lyf of
the Manhode, Roxb Club 91, London 1869, p 1
(base text: MS 2).

Henry A K, A Critical Edn of Bk I of The Pilgrimage of the Lyf of the Manhode, diss Oxford Univ
1976 (base text: MS 2 with variants from other
MSS).

Selection. Matthews W, ed, Later Medieval Eng
Prose, N Y 1963, p 252.

French Text. Guillaume de Guileville, Le Pèlerinage
de Vie Humaine, ed J J Sturzinger, Roxb Club
124, London 1893, p 1.

Sources and Literary Relations. Perrow E C, The Last
Will and Testament as a Form of Lit, Wisconsin
Acad of Sciences Arts and Letters 17(1911–
13).687.

Rice W H, The European Ancestry of Villon's Satirical Testaments, N Y 1941, p 86.

Chew S C, The Virtues Reconciled, Toronto 1947,
p 39.

Bloomfield SDS, pp 229, 245.

Wenzel, pp 116, 123, 135.

Wimsatt J I, Allegory and Mirror, N Y 1970, pp 108,
138 (regards Vie as a reaction to Romance of the
Rose).

Wenzel S, The Pilgrimage of Life as a Late Medieval
Genre, MS 35(1973).370 (general background).

Blythe J H, The Influence of Latin Manuals on Medieval Allegory: Deguileville's Presentation of
Wrath, Rom 95(1974).256.

Keenan J M, The Cistercian Pilgrimage to Jerusalem in Guillaume de Guilleville's Pèlerinage de la
Vie Humaine, in Stud in Medieval Cistercian Hist
II, ed J R Sommerfeldt, Kalamazoo 1976, p 166
(influence of Cistercian ideas and literary forms).

Möske B, Caritas: Ihre figurative Darstellung in der
engl Literatur des 14 bis 16 Jahrhunderts, Bonn
1977, pp 95, 97, 100.

Literary Criticism and Analysis. Lewis C S, The Allegory of Love, London 1933, p 264.

Tuve R, Allegorical Imagery, Princeton 1966, p 149
and passim.

Walls K M, The Pilgrimage of the Lyf of the Manhode: The Prose Translation from Guillaume de
Guilleville, diss Toronto Univ 1976.

Russell J S, Allegorical Monstrosity: The Case of
Deguileville, Allegorica 5(1980).95 (analysis of
"eyes-into-ears" sequence).

Influence. Wharey J B, A Study of the Sources of
Bunyan's Allegories, Baltimore 1904, p 9.

Owst G R, Lit and Pulpit in Medieval England, Cambridge 1933, pp 57, 84, 97, 102, 104, 107.

General References. Ten Brink, 3.5.

Courthope, p 342.

Deanesly M, The Lollard Bible and Other Medieval
Versions, Cambridge 1920, pp 153, 154, 322n.

Legouis HEL, p 157.

Baugh LHE, p 288.

Pecheux M C, Aspects of the Treatment of Death in
ME Poetry, Washington D C 1951, pp 57, 64, 68.

Schlauch M, Eng Medieval Lit and Its Social Foundations, Warsaw 1956, p 165.

Legge M D, Anglo-Norman Lit and Its Background,
Oxford 1963, p 16.

Pearsall D and E Salter, Landscape and Seasons of
the Medieval World, London 1973, p 172.

Pearsall D, OE and ME Poetry, London 1977,
pp 199, 201, 224, 232, 296.

Bibliography. Workman S K, 15-Cent Translation as
an Influence on Eng Prose, Princeton 1940,
p 180.

Bennett OHEL, p 308.

Manual, 6.2143 (biblio of Lydgate's trans of Vie).

[193] VERSIONS OF GUILLAUME DE
GUILLEVILLE'S PÈLERINAGE DE L'AME
(THE PILGRIMAGE OF THE SOUL or GRACE
DIEU or GRACE DE DIEU).

MSS. 1, Bodl 2552 (Bodley 770), ff 1ᵃ–99ᵇ (1425–
50); 2, Corpus Christi Oxford 237, ff 16ᵃ–133ᵃ
(1475–1500); 3, Univ Oxford 181, ff 1ᵃ–153ᵇ
(1400–25); 4, Cambridge Univ Kk.1.7 (D), ff 1ᵃ–
124ᵇ (1400–25); 5, Gonville and Caius Camb 124,
pp 1–258 (15 cent); 6, BL Addit 34193, ff 5ᵃ–98ᵇ
(1400–25); 7, BL Addit 37049, ff 69ᵇ–71ᵇ, 73ᵇ–

77ᵃ (1400–50); 8, BL Egerton 615. ff 4ᵃ–106ᵃ (1400–50); 9, BL Harley 7333, f 148ᵃ (1450–1500); 10, Hatfield House (Cecil), ff 1ᵃ–75ᵇ (1400–50); 11, New York Public Libr Spencer 19, ff 4ᵃ–106ᵃ (ca 1430); 12, Henry E Huntington HM 111, ff 3ᵃ–7ᵇ (1400–30); 13, State Libr of Victoria Melbourne 27, ff 96ᵃ–215ᵇ (1450–1500). PRINT: 14, W Caxton, Westminster 1483 (STC, no 6473).

For the fourteen poems in the Pilgrimage of the Soul ascribed to Hoccleve and their Brown-Robbins, and Robbins-Cutler numbers, see Manual, 3.907.

MSS Commentary. List of Additions to the MSS in the British Museum in the Years MDCCCXXXVI–MDCCCXL, London 1843, p 43 (MS 8).

Coxe H O, Catalogus Codicum MSS qui in Collegiis Aulisque Oxoniensibus Hodie Adservantur, Oxford 1852, 1.49 (MS 3); 2.98 (MS 2).

A Catalogue of the MSS Preserved in the Libr of the Univ of Cambridge, Cambridge 1858, 3.565 (MS 4).

Ward, 2.584 (MS 6).

Catalogue of Additions to the MSS in the British Museum in the Years MDCCCLXXXVIII–MDCCCXCIII, London 1894, p 225 (MS 6).

Summary Cat, 1.423 (MS 1).

Catalogue of Additions to the MSS in the British Museum in the Years MDCCCC–MDCCCCV, London 1907, p 324 (MS 7).

James M R, A Descriptive Catalogue of the MSS in the Libr of Gonville and Caius College, Cambridge 1907, 1.133 (MS 5).

Hammond, p 176 (MS 9).

Paltsits V H, The Petworth MS of Grace Dieu or The Pilgrimage of the Soul, BNYPL 32(1928).715 (MS 11).

de Ricci Census, 1.50 (MS 12); 2.1339 (MS 11).

Manly & Rickert, 1.207 (MS 9).

Sinclair K V, Descriptive Catalogue of Medieval and Renaissance Western MSS in Australia, Sydney 1969, p 217 (MS 13).

Pächt O and J J G Alexander, Illuminated MSS in the Bodleian Libr Oxf, Oxford 1971, 3.81, no 924.

Seymour M C, The MSS of Hoccleve's Regiment of Princes, Edinb Biblio Soc Trans 4(1974).269 (MS 9).

Hogg edn, p 241 (detailed description of MS 7).

Editions. Cust K L, The Boke of the Pylgremage of the Sowle Printed by Caxton, London 1859 (PRINT 14 reduced by a third).

Furnivall F J and I Gollancz, Hoccleve's Works The Minor Poems, EETSES 61 (1892); 73 (1925 for 1897); rvsd by J Mitchell and A I Doyle and rptd in one vol, London 1970, p 1 (Complaint of the Virgin from MS 12).

Furnivall F J, Hoccleve's Works, III. The Regiment of Princes and 14 of Hoccleve's Minor Poems, EETSES 72, London 1897, p xxiii.

Barry M D, The Pilgrimage of the Soul, a 15-cent Eng Prose Version of Le pèlerinage de l'âme by Guillaume de Guilleville, diss Toronto Univ 1931 (MS 11).

Clubb M D Jr, The ME Pilgrimage of the Soul, an Edn of MS Egerton 615, diss Univ of Michigan 1954, p 1 (description of MS 8 on p xl).

Doty B L, An Edn of British Museum MS Addit 37049: A Religious Miscellany, diss Michigan State 1963, p 376 (MS 7).

Zehner H V Jr, An Edn of the Apple of Solace, diss Fordham Univ 1971, p 1 (base text: PRINT 14).

Flynn J S, Pilgrimage of the Soul: an Edn of the Caxton Imprint, diss Auburn Univ 1973, p 76.

Roberts P D, Some Unpublished ME Lyrics and Stanzas in a Victoria Pub Libr MS, ESts 54 (1973).105 (MS 13).

Hogg J, Unpublished Texts in the Carthusian Northern ME Religious Miscellany British Libr MS Add 37049, in Essays in Honor of Erwin Stürzl on His 60th Birthday, ed J Hogg, I, Salzburger Studien zur Angl und Amerikanistik, Salzburg 1980, p 268 (Apple of Solace; MS 7).

Seymour M C, Selections from Hoccleve, Oxford 1981, p 1 (Complaint of the Virgin).

Gray D, ed, The Oxford Book of Late Medieval Verse and Prose, Oxford 1985, p 97.

Selection. Blake N F, ed, Caxton's Own Prose, London 1973, p 128 (Caxton's Incipit and Explicit).

French Text. Guillaume de Guileville, Le Pèlerinage de l'Ame, ed J J Sturzinger, Roxb Club 127, London 1895, p 1.

Authorship. Kern J H, Een en ander over Thomas Hoccleve en zijn werken, VMKVA 1915, p 382 (argues that only Complaint of the Green Tree is by Hoccleve).

Schulz H C, Thomas Hoccleve, Scribe, Spec 12 (1937).71 (ascribes Complaint of the Green Tree to Hoccleve).

Seymour edn, p xiv n12 (suggests Hoccleve wrote all 14 poems and translated the Ame).

Sources and Literary Relations. Migne PL, 2.1113 (De Pascha, probably the source of Apple of Solace).

Gröber, 2.749.

Hultman J E, Guillaume de Deguileville En Studie i Fransk Litteraturhistoria, Uppsala 1902, p 65.

Galpen S L, On the Sources of Guillaume De Guileville's Pèlerinage de l'Ame, PMLA 25(1910).275.

Peebles R J, The Dry Tree: Symbol of Death, Vassar Mediaeval Stud, ed C F Fiske, New Haven 1923, p 59.

Chew S C, The Virtues Reconciled, Toronto 1947, p 39 (Four Daughters of God motif).

Hench A L, The Allegorical Motif of Conscience and Reason, Counsellors in Eng Stud in Honor of James Southall Wilson, ed F Bowers, Univ of Virginia Stud 4(1951).193.

Greenhill E S, The Child in the Tree: a Study of the Cosmological Tree in Christian Tradition, Trad 10(1954).354 (The Green Tree and The Dry Tree).

Quinn E C, The Quest of Seth for the Oil of Life, Chicago 1962, p 102 (The Green Tree and The Dry Tree).

Katzenellenbogen A, Allegories of the Virtues and Vices in Mediaeval Art, N Y 1964, p 63 (artistic conventions of contrasting trees).

Woolf, pp 211 (Charter of Christ), 328, 330, 405 (dialogue of body and soul).

Brandon S G F, The Weighing of the Soul, in Myths and Symbolic Stud in Honor of Mircea Eliade, ed J M Kitagawa and C H Long, Chicago 1969, p 91.

Owen D D R, The Vision of Hell, Edinburgh 1970, p 165.

Wenzel S, The Pilgrimage of Life as a Late Medieval Genre, MS 35(1973).370.

Literary Criticism and Analysis. Gray D, Themes and Images in the Medieval Eng Religious Lyric, London 1872, p 218.

Smalley J, The Poems of the ME Pilgrimage of the Soul, MA thesis Liverpool Univ 1954.

Woolf, p 254 (transformation of theme of Virgin and Cross).

Mitchell J, Thomas Hoccleve, Urbana 1968, p 38.

Other Literary Problems. Panofsky E, Early Netherlandish Painting, Cambridge 1966, 1.113, 213, 262 (MSS illustrations).

Tuve R, Allegorical Imagery, Princeton 1966, pp 146 n1, 148, 150, 150 n7, 193 (MSS, illustrations, sources, popularity in England).

Influence. Wharey J B, A Study of the Sources of Bunyan's Allegories, Baltimore 1904, p 14.

Chew S C, The Pilgrimage of Life, New Haven 1962, pp 174, 235 (possible influence on Bunyan).

General References. Deanesly M, The Lollard Bible and Other Medieval Versions, Cambridge 1920, pp 154, 342, 392; Vernacular Books in England in the 14 and 15 Cents, MLR 15(1920).351, 356.

Bennett OHEL, p 308.

Baugh LHE, p 288.

Patch H R, The Other World, Cambridge 1950, p 188.

Bloomfield SDS, p 245.

Ackerman R W, Backgrounds to Medieval Eng Lit, N Y 1966, p 117.

Wilson R M, The Lost Lit of Medieval England, 2nd edn, London 1970, pp 147, 149, 155.

Gray D, Themes and Images in the Medieval Eng Religious Lyric, London 1972, p 158.

Blake N F, Caxton: England's First Publisher, London 1975, pp 69, 163, 183, 194 (mistakenly ascribes trans of Ame to Lydgate).

Bibliography. Gasquet F A, The Biblio of Some Devotional Books Printed by the Earliest Eng Printers, Trans of the Biblio Soc of London 7(1902–04).182.

de Ricci S, A Census of Caxtons, Oxford 1909, p 78.

Duff E G, 15-Cent Eng Books, Oxford 1917, no 267, p 75.

Hare W L, A Newly Discovered Vol Printed by William Caxton, Pilgrimage of the Sowle, Appollo 7(1931).205.

Workman S K, 15-Cent Translation as an Influence on Eng Prose, Princeton 1940, p 180.

Bossuat MBLF, nos 4904–25.

Manual, 3.907 (additional biblio of 14 poems ascribed to Hoccleve).

V. Service and Service-Related Works

1. The Mass

[194] ARA DEI.

MS. Bodl 30252 (Add C.87), ff 1ᵃ–220ᵇ (1475–1500; folios 221–225 are separately bound in Add C.87*).

Jolliffe, p 113, no I.32 (independent treatise against despair incorporated into Ara Dei).

MS Commentary. Summary Cat, 5.768.

Edition. Yksh Wr, 2.377 (treatise against despair).

Selection. Kirchberger C, ed, The Coasts of the Country, London nd, p 59.

General References. Doyle Survey, 1.170 n5.

Doyle A I, Books Connected with the Vere Family and Barking Abbey, Trans of the Essex Archaeological Soc 25(1958).227 n1.

[195] LAY FOLKS' MASS BOOK.

MSS. 1, Corpus Christi Oxf 155, ff 252ᵇ–260ᵇ (1425–50); 2, Camb Univ Gg.5.31, ff 1ᵃ–5ᵇ (1450–1500); 3, Camb Univ Ii.4.9, ff 55ᵃ–60ᵃ (ca 1450); 4, Gonville and Caius Camb 84, ff 173ᵃ–179ᵃ (ca 1450); 5, Newnham Camb, ff 104ᵇ–109ᵇ (ca 1450); 6, BL Royal 17.B.xvii, ff 3ᵃ–13ᵃ (ca

1400); 7, BL Addit 36523, ff 88ᵃ–93ᵃ (1425–1500); 8, Nat Libr Scotland Advocates 19.3.1, ff 57ᵃ–58ᵇ (1450–1500); 9, Liverpool Univ 23 (f.4.9), ff 203ᵇ–207ᵇ (1400–25).

Brown-Robbins, nos 1323, 3507; Robbins-Cutler, no 3507 (for a similar version of the Levation Prayer in MS 5, see Brown-Robbins, Robbins-Cutler, no 3882).

MSS Commentary. Coxe H O, Catalogus Codicum MSS qui in Collegiis Aulisque Oxoniensibus Hodie Adservantur, Oxford 1852, 2.63 (MS 1).

A Catalogue of the MSS Preserved in the Libr of the Univ of Cambridge, Cambridge 1859, 3.199 (MS 2), 448 (MS 3).

James M R, A Descriptive Catalogue of the MSS in the Libr of Gonville and Caius Coll, Cambridge 1907, 1.79 (MS 4).

Catalogue of the Additions to the MSS in the British Museum in the Years MDCCCC–MDCCCCV, London 1907, p 124 (MS 7).

Warner G F and J P Gilson, Catalogue of Western MSS in the Old Royal and King's Collections, London 1921, 2.228 (MS 6).

A Guide to the MSS Collections in Liverpool Univ Libr, Liverpool 1962, no 23 (MS 9).

Ker Manuscripts, 3.308 (MS 9).

Guddat-Figge G, Catalogue of MSS Containing ME Romances, Munich 1976, pp 100 (MS 3), 127 (MS 8), 165 (MS 7).

Editions. Turnbull W D D, The Visions of Tundale Together with Metrical Moralizations and Other Fragments of Early Poetry, Hitherto Unedited, Edinburgh 1843, p 147 (MS 8).

Simmons T F, The Lay Folks Mass Book, EETS 71, London 1879 (rptd 1968), p 2 (parallel texts of MSS 1, 4, 5, 6); introd, pp xl (identification of author), xlix (trans into Eng), liv (dialect), lxv (description of MSS 1, 2, 4, 5, 6, 8).

Yksh Wr, 2.1 (MS 6).

Gerould G G, The Lay-Folks' Mass-Book from MS Gg.V.31, Cambridge Univ Libr, EStn 33(1904).1.

Bulbring K D, Das Lay-Folks' Mass Book in der Handschrift der Advocates Libr in Edinburgh, EStn 35(1905).28.

Selections. Patterson, pp 47, 70.

Clark F, Eucharistic Sacrifice and the Reformation, Oxford 1967, p 543.

Modernization. Watts N H, Love Songs of Sion: A Selection of Devotional Verse from Old Eng Sources, London 1924, p 24.

Language. Serjeantson M S, The Language of the West Midlands in ME, RES 3(1927).326 (MS 4).

Moore Meech and Whitehall, pp 52, 54.

Prins A A, French Influence in Eng Phrasing, Leiden 1952, pp 298, 300.

Authorship. Yksh Wr, 2.xlii (ascription to Rolle).

Deanesly M, The Lollard Bible, Cambridge 1920, p 212 (ascription to Jeremy of Rouen).

Allen WAR, p 258 (denies Rolle's authorship).

Comper F R, The Life of Richard Rolle, London and Toronto 1928, p 219 (denies Rolle's authorship).

Clay C, Notes on the Early Archdeacons in the Church of York, Yorkshire Archaeological Journ 36(1944–47).412 (Jeremy's Career).

Sources and Literary Relations. Wordsworth C and H Littlehales, The Old Service-Books of the Eng Church, London 1904, p 284.

McGarry L, The Holy Eucharist in ME Homiletic and Devotional Verse, Washington D C 1936, pp 173 (analysis), 233 (levation prayer).

Bussard P, The Vernacular Missal in Religious Education, Washington D C 1937, p 2.

Robbins R H, The Gurney Series of Religious Lyrics, PMLA 54(1939).373; Private Prayers in ME Verse, SP 36(1939).466.

Ong W J, A Liturgical Movement in the Middle Ages, American Ecclesiastical Rev 114(1946).104.

Pecheux M C, Aspects of the Treatment of Death in ME Poetry, Washington D C 1951, p 26.

Taylor J, Notes on the Rise of Written Eng in the Late Middle Ages, Proc of the Leeds Philosophical and Literary Soc 8(1956).130.

Priscandaro M T, ME Eucharistic Verse: Its Imagery, Symbolism, and Typology, diss St John's Univ 1975, p 34.

Aston M, Lollardy and Literacy, History 62 (1977).350.

General References. Brandl, §60, p 650.

Cutts E L, Parish Priests and Their People in the Middle Ages in England, London 1898, p 243.

Gasquet F A, Parish Life in Medieval England, London 1906, p 1145.

Krapp G P, The Rise of Eng Literary Prose, N Y 1915, p 257.

Manning B L, The People's Faith in the Time of Wyclif, Cambridge 1919, passim.

Browe P, Die Verehrung der Eucharistie im Mittelalter, Munich 1933, rptd 1967, p 26 (on elevation of Host).

Bennett H S, The Author and His Public in the 14 and 15 Cents, E&S 23(1938).21.

Smith H M, Pre-Reformation England, London 1938, p 99.

Moorman J R H, Church Life in England in the 13 Cent, Cambridge 1945, pp 70, 127n.

Morison S, Eng Prayer Books, Cambridge 1945, p 44.

Bennett OHEL, p 119.

Thurston H, Familiar Prayers, London 1952, pp 16, 18.

Dugmore C W, The Mass and the Eng Reformers, London 1958, p 74.

Dickens A G, The Eng Reformation, London 1964, p 12.

Ackerman R W, Backgrounds to Medieval Eng Lit, N Y 1966, p 97.

Clark F, Eucharistic Sacrifice and the Reformation, Oxford 1967, p 62n.

Woolf, p 380.

Cuming G J, A Hist of Anglican Liturgy, London 1969, p 18.

Brooke C, Medieval Church and Society, N Y 1971, p 163.

Gray D, Themes and Images in the Medieval Eng Religious Lyrics, London 1972, p 159.

Bibliography. Booker J M, A ME Biblio, Heidelberg 1912, p 22.

New CBEL, 1.496.

[196] THE MANNER AND MEDE
OF THE MASS.

MS. Bodl 3938 (Eng poet a.1), ff 302^b–303^b (1380–1400). For a similar treatise see Bodl 29387 (Add A.268), ff 139^a–145^b (1400–25) and BL Royal 17.C.xvii, ff 155^b–162^b (1400–25).

Brown-Robbins, nos 3268, 4276.

MS Commentary. Summary Cat, 2.789 (Eng poet a.1); 5.610 (Add A.268).

Warner G F and J P Gilson, Catalogue of Western MSS in the Old Royal and King's Collections, London 1921, 2.243.

Serjeantson Index, p 258.

Guddat-Figge G, Catalogue of MSS Containing ME Romances, Munich 1976, p 269 (Eng poet a.1).

Editions. Simmons T F, The Lay Folks Mass Book, EETS 71, London 1879 (rptd 1968), pp 128 (text), 360 (commentary).

Furnivall F J, The Minor Poems of the Vernon MS, EETS 117, pt 2, London 1901, p 493.

Selections. Rel Ant, 1.59.

Patterson, p 47.

Sources and Literary Relations. Patterson, p 159 (relation to [195]).

Deanesly M, The Lollard Bible, Cambridge 1920, p 213 (relation to manual literature).

McGarry L, The Holy Eucharist in ME Homiletic and Devotional Verse, Washington D C 1936, p 121 (analysis of [196] and [197] together).

Priscandaro M T, ME Eucharistic Verse: Its Imagery, Symbolism, and Typology, diss St John's Univ 1975, p 32.

General References. Brandl, §55, p 646.

Schofield, p 389.

Manning B L, The People's Faith in the Time of Wyclif, Cambridge 1919, passim.

Smith H M, Pre-Reformation England, London 1938, p 95.

Ong W J, A Liturgical Movement in the Middle Ages, American Ecclesiastical Rev 114(1946).109.

Clark F, Eucharistic Sacrifice and the Reformation, Oxford 1967, pp 60, 62 n22.

[197] DE MERITIS MISSE.

MSS. 1, Bodl 21876 (Douce 302), ff 10^b–12^a (1425–50); 2, BL Harley 3954, ff 74^a–76^a (1400–50).

Brown-Robbins, no 1986.

MSS Commentary. Summary Cat, 4.585.

A Catalogue of the Harleian MSS in the British Museum, London 1808, 3.98.

Editions. Whiting E K, The Poems of John Audelay, EETS 184, London 1931, p 65 (MS 1).

Halliwell J O, Audelay's Poems, PS 14(1844).66 (MS 1).

Selection. Rel Ant, 1.59 (MS 2).

Literary Relations. McGarry L, The Holy Eucharist in ME Homiletic and Devotional Verse, Washington D C 1936, p 121 (analysis of [197] and [196] together).

Priscandaro M T, ME Eucharistic Verse: Its Imagery, Symbolism, and Typology, diss St John's Univ 1975, p 32.

[198] MERITA MISSE.

MS. BL Cotton Titus A.xxvi, ff 154^a–157^a (1475–1500).

Brown-Robbins, no 957.

MS Commentary. A Catalogue of the MSS in the Cottonian Libr Deposited in the British Museum, London 1902, p 515.

Seymour M C, The Eng MSS of Mandeville's Travels, Edinb Biblio Soc Trans 4(1966).187 (MS 2).

Edition. Simmons T F, The Lay Folks Mass Book, EETS 71, London 1879; rptd 1968, p 148.

Authorship. Schirmer W F, John Lydgate, London 1961, p 269 (accepts Simmons' ascription to Lydgate).

Literary Relations. McGarry L, The Holy Eucharist in ME Homiletic and Devotional Verse, Washington D C 1936, p 132 (analysis).

General References. Brandl, §129, p 710.

Owst G R, Preaching in Medieval England, Cambridge 1927, pp 52 (a sermon), 277.

Bennett OHEL, p 119.

Dugmore C W, The Mass and the Eng Reformers, London 1958, p 70.

[199] HOW TO SING MASS.

MS. BL Harley 3810, f 86^b (1450–1500).

Brown-Robbins, no 3198.

MS Commentary. A Catalogue of the Harleian MSS in the British Museum, London 1808, 3.83.

Edition. Jordan R, Das Trentalle Gregorii in der Handschrift Harley 3810, EStn 40(1909).366.

[200] THE SACRIFICE OF THE MASS.

MS. Balliol Oxford 354, f 205ᵃ⁻ᵇ (1500–25).
Brown-Robbins, Robbins-Cutler, no 1941.
MS Commentary. Mynors R A B, Catalogue of the MSS of Balliol Coll Oxford, Oxford 1963, p 352.
Editions. Flugel E, Liedersammlungen des XVI Jahrhunderts besonders aus der Zeit Heinrichs VIII, III, Angl 26(1903).204.
Dyboski R, Songs, Carols, and Other Miscellaneous Poems from the Balliol MS 354, EETSES 101, London 1907, p 68.
Modernization. Watts N H, Love Songs of Sion: A Selection of Devotional Verse from Old Eng Sources, London 1924, p 7.

[201] PARTS OF THE MASS.

MS. Camb Univ Gg.4.32, f 81ᵃ (16 cent).
Brown-Robbins, no 381.
MS Commentary. A Catalogue of the MSS Preserved in the Libr of the Univ of Cambridge, Cambridge 1858, 3.177.

[202] VIRTUES OF THE MASS
(or VIRTUTES MISSARUM).

MSS. *Verse: Version A*: 1, BL Harley 3954, ff 76ᵃ–78ᵃ (1400–50); *Version B*: 2, Bodl 14530 (Rawl poet 36), ff 6ᵃ–9ᵇ (1450–1500); *Version C*: 3, Camb Univ Ii.6.2, f 2ᵃ (1400–25); 4, Henry E Huntington EL.26.A.13, f iii (ca 1450); *Version D*: 5, Bodl 14526 (Rawl poet 32), ff 35ᵇ–37ᵇ (1450–1500); *Version E*: 6, Camb Univ Hh.3.13, ff 113ᵇ–115ᵃ (1425–50); *Version F*: 7, Bodl 14611 (Rawl poet 118), f 118ᵇ (1450–75); 8, Trinity Camb 601 (R.3.21), f 214ᵇ (1475–1500); *Version G*: 9, Bodl 6943 (Ashmole 59), f 67ᵃ⁻ᵇ (1450–1500).
Prose: 10, Magdalene Camb 1047, f 23ᵇ (1475–1500); 11, Camb Univ Kk.1.5, ff 53ᵃ–54ᵃ (ca 1500); 12, Bibliothèque Mazarine 514, f 71ᵃ⁻ᵇ (15 cent).
Brown-Robbins, nos 1988, 2323, 2373, 3573; Brown-Robbins, Robbins-Cutler, nos 333, 3427, 4244; Brown-Robbins, no 4244 lists [202] and [235] as one poem.
MSS Commentary. A Catalogue of the Harleian MSS in the British Museum, London 1808, 3.98 (MS 1).
Black W H, A Descriptive, Analytical, and Critical Catalogue of the MSS Bequeathed unto the Univ

of Oxford by Elias Ashmole, Oxford 1845, p 95 (MS 9).
A Catalogue of the MSS Preserved in the Libr of the Univ of Cambridge, Cambridge 1858, 3.280 (MS 6), 497 (MS 3), 558 (MS 11).
Catalogue des manuscrits de la Bibliothèque Mazarine, Paris 1885, p 201 (MS 12).
Summary Cat, 3.290 (MS 5), 292 (MS 2), 307 (MS 7).
James M R, The Western MSS in the Libr of Trinity Coll Cambridge, Descriptive Catalogue, Cambridge 1901, 2.83 (MS 8); A Descriptive Catalogue of the Libr of Samuel Pepys, Pt III, Mediaeval MSS, London 1923, p 5 (MS 10).
Hammond E P, Ashmole 59 and Other Shirley MSS, Angl 30(1907).330 (MS 9).
de Ricci Census, 1.131 (MS 4).
Seymour M C, The Eng MSS of Mandeville's Travels, Edinburgh Biblio Soc Transactions, 4 (1966).167 (MS 1).
Guddat-Figge G, Catalogue of MSS Containing ME Romances, Munich 1976, p 103 (MS 11).
Barratt A, Two ME Lyrics in the Bibliothèque Mazarine, N&Q ns 31(1984).25 (MS 12).
Editions. Rel Ant, 1.61 (MS 1; extract only).
Lumby J R, Ratis Raving and Other Moral and Religious Pieces in Prose and Verse, EETS 43, London 1870, p 113 (MS 11).
Simmons T F, The Lay Folks Mass Book, EETS 71, London 1879 (rptd 1968), pp 367 (MS 1; extracts only), 368 (MS 2; extracts only).
MacCracken H N, The Minor Poems of John Lydgate, EETSES 107, London 1916, p 115 (MS 8).
Lucan P L, The Versions by John Shirley, William Gybbe and Another of the Poem On the Virtues of the Mass: A Collation, N&Q ns 28(1981).394 (texts of MSS 7 and 9).
Selections. Bennett H S, England from Chaucer to Caxton, London 1928, p 185 (reprint of Rel Ant).
General References. McGarry L, The Holy Eucharist in ME Homiletic and Devotional Verse, Washington D C 1936, p 121.
Smith H M, Pre-Reformation England, London 1938, p 94 n4.
Dugmore C W, The Mass and the Eng Reformers, London 1958, p 70.
Clark F, Eucharistic Sacrifice and the Reformation, Oxford 1967, p 70.

[203] BIDDING PRAYERS
(or THE BIDDING OF THE BEDES).

MSS. *Verse*: 1, BL Cotton Cleop B.vi, f 204ᵇ (ca 1250).
Prose: 2, Bodl 1963 (Bodley 110), ff 166ᵇ–167ᵇ (ca 1450); 3, Bodl 2298 (Bodley 549), f 79ᵇ (ca 1400);

4, Bodl 21820 (Douce 246), f 57ᵃ (added in the margin in a 16-cent hand); 5, Bodl 6417 (Barlow 5), ff 2ᵇ–3ᵇ (1400–50); 6, Bodl 12019 (Rawl C.155), pp 460–465 (18 cent); 7, Camb Univ Ee.4.19, ff 89ᵃ–91ᵇ (1350–1400); 8, Pembroke Camb 285, ff 62ᵇ–65ᵃ (1400–25); 9, Sidney Sussex Camb 55, ff 52ᵃ–54ᵇ (ca 1450); 10, BL Burney 356, ff 54ᵇ–55ᵃ (1400–25); 11, BL Harley 335, ff 19ᵇ–20ᵇ (1400–50); 12, BL Addit 60577, ff 81ᵇ–85ᵇ (1475–1550); 13, Lambeth Palace 216, f 111ᵃ–ᵇ (1400–25); 14, Lambeth Palace 559, ff 43ᵃ–45ᵃ (1400–50; begins as a versified form of confession; Brown-Robbins, no 1324); 15, Durham Univ Cosin V.iv.2, ff 140ᵇ–142ᵃ (1477); 16, Salisbury Cath 148, ff 11ᵇ–12ᵃ (ca 1450); 17, York Minster XVI.M.4, pp 172–177, 178 (ca 1450); 18, Shrewsbury School 3 (1484); 19, Harvard Univ Widener 1 (olim Lawson), ff 105ᵃ–107ᵃ (1400–25). PRINTS: 19, William Caxton, Quattuor Sermones, 1483 (STC, no 14394); 20, Wynkyn de Worde, Manuale secundum usum matris ecclesie Eboracensis, 1509 (STC, no 16160).

Brown-Robbins, no 519.

MSS Commentary. A Catalogue of the MSS in the Cottonian Libr Deposited in the British Museum, London 1802, p 578 (MS 1).

A Catalogue of the Harleian MSS in the British Museum, London 1808, 1.201 (MS 11).

Catalogue of MSS in the British Museum, ns, vol 1, pt 2: The Burney MSS, London 1840, p 95 (MS 10).

A Catalogue of the MSS Preserved in the Libr of the Univ of Cambridge, Cambridge 1857, 2.126 (MS 7).

Macray W D, Catalogi Codicum Manuscriptorum Bibliothecae Bodleianae, London 1878, 5(2).64 (MS 6).

James M R, A Descriptive Catalogue of the MSS in the Libr of Sidney Sussex Coll Cambridge, Cambridge 1895, p 39 (MS 9); A Descriptive Catalogue of the MSS in the Libr of Pembroke Coll Cambridge, Cambridge 1905, p 258 (MS 8); A Descriptive Catalogue of the MSS in the Libr of Lambeth Palace, Cambridge 1932, pp 347 (MS 13), 765 (MS 14).

Summary Cat, 2.135 (MS 2), 295 (MS 3), 1045 (MS 5); 4.566 (MS 4).

Editions. L'Estrange H, The Alliance of Divine Offices Exhibiting All the Liturgies of the Church of England, London 1659, p 180 (MS 6 and Post-Medieval Forms).

Burnet G, Hist of the Reformation of the Church of England, London 1681, 2.104 (MS 6).

Hearne T, Robert of Gloucester's Chronicle, Oxford 1724, 2.682 (MS unidentified).

Coxe H O, Forms of Bidding Prayer, Oxford 1840, pp 11 (MS 6), 27 (MS 4), 29 (PRINT 19), 40 (York Manual, 1509).

Rel Ant, 1.22 (MS 1).

Collier J, An Ecclesiastical Hist of Great Britain, London 1846, 9.234 (Worcester Manual).

Henderson W G, Manuale et processionale ad usum insignis Ecclesiae Eboracensis, Surtees Soc 63 (1875).123 (MS 7), 220* (MS 5), 223* (MS 11), 225* (MS 16).

Simmons T F, The Lay Folks Mass Book, London 1879 (rptd 1968), pp 64, 68, 74 (York Manual), 75 (York Manual, 1509), 315 (commentary).

Maskell, 3.401 (MS 16).

Calvert E, Extracts from a 15-Cent MS, Shropshire Archaeological and Natural Hist Soc Trans 2s 6(1894).104 (MS 18).

Wordsworth C, Ceremonies and Processions of the Cathedral Church of Salisbury, Cambridge 1901, p 22 (MS 16).

Brightman F E, The Eng Rite, London 1921, 2.1050 (MS 5), 1020 (history of practice).

Brown RLxiiiC, p 126 (MS 1).

Sisam C and K, The Oxford Book of Medieval Eng Verse, Oxford 1970, p 16 (MS 1).

Facsimile. The Winchester Anthology with an Introd by E Wilson and I Fenlon, Woodbridge 1981 (MS 12).

General References. Chambers J D, Divine Worship in England in the 13 and 14 Cents, London 1877, p 186.

Gasquet F A, Parish Life in Medieval England, London 1906, p 222.

Deanesly M, The Lollard Bible, Cambridge 1920, pp 139, 212.

Owst G R, Preaching in Medieval England, Cambridge 1926, pp 213, 262, 263, 317.

Smith H M, Pre-Reformation England, London 1938, p 127.

Thurston H, Familiar Prayers, Their Origin and Hist, London 1953, p 23.

[204] LEVATION PRAYERS.

MSS. Prose: Version A: 1, Bodl 15799 (Rawl liturg e.3), ff 125ᵇ–126ᵃ (1400–50); *Version B*: 2, Univ Oxf 123, f 74ᵃ (1475–1500); *Version C*: 3, Camb Univ Ii.4.9, f 95ᵃ–ᵇ (ca 1450); *Version D*: 4, Trinity Camb 600 (R.3.20), f 372ᵃ (1425–50); *Version E*: 5, BL Addit 39574, f 88ᵃ–ᵇ (1400–25); *Version F*: 6, BL Arundel 197, f 47ᵇ (1450–1500); *Version G*: 7, BL Royal 17.C.xvii, f 98ᵇ (1400–25); *Version H*: 8, Lambeth Palace 546, f 57ᵃ (1450–1500).

Verse: Version A: 9, BL Royal 17.C.xvii, f 98ᵇ (1400–25); *Version B*: 10, Hereford Cath O.iv.14, pt 2, inside back cover (1400–25); *Version C*: 11,

BL Egerton 3245 (olim Gurney), f 182ª (1400–25); *Version D*: 12, Bodl 3938 (Eng poet a.1), f 115ª (1380–1400); 13, Balliol Oxf 316A, f 110ᵇ (15 cent); 14, Christ Church Oxf 151, f 126ᵇ (1400–50); 15, BL Addit 37787, f 12ª⁻ᵇ (1400–25); 16, Lambeth Palace 559, f 32ª⁻ᵇ (1400–50); 17, Univ of Pennsylvania 2, f 135ª⁻ᵇ (1400–50); *Version E*: 18, Camb Univ Ii.6.2, f 98ᵇ (1400–25); 19, BL Addit 29724, f 231ª⁻ᵇ (1400–50); 20, BL Egerton 3245 (olim Gurney), f 189ᵇ (1400–25); 21, Bodl Lyell 30, f 300ᵇ (1441); 22, Bibl Nat Paris f. fr. 1830, f 137ª (15 cent); *Version F*: 23, York Minster Addit 2, ff 206ª–207ª (1450–1500); *Version G*: 24, Lambeth Palace 559, ff 24ᵇ–25ª (1400–50); *Version H*: 25, BL Egerton 3245 (olim Gurney), f 185ª (1400–25); 26, Camb Univ Gg.5.31, f 4ª (1400–50); *Version I*: 27, Bodl 3938 (Eng poet a.1), f 115ª (1380–1400); 28, Bodl 6922 (Ashmole 61), f 26ª⁻ᵇ (1450–1500); 29, BL Harley 5396, f 273ª⁻ᵇ (1456); 30, BL Addit 37787, f 160ª⁻ᵇ (1400–50); 31, Lambeth Palace 559, ff 25ª–26ª (1400–50); *Version J*: 32, Emmanuel Camb 27, f 162ª⁻ᵇ (13 cent); *Version K*: 33, Bodl 21876 (Douce 302), f 10ª⁻ᵇ (1400–25).

Brown-Robbins, nos 1052, 1071, 2512, 4052; Brown-Robbins, Robbins-Cutler, nos 1368, 1372, 1729, 1734, 3882, 3883, 3884.

MSS Commentary. Catalogue of the MSS in the British Museum, ns, vol I, London 1840, pt 1; The Arundel MSS, p 197 (MS 6).

Black W H, A Descriptive, Analytical, and Critical Catalogue of the MSS Bequeathed unto the Univ of Oxf by Elias Ashmole, Oxford 1845, p 106 (MS 28).

Coxe H O, Catalogus Codicum MSS qui in Collegiis Aulisque Oxoniensibus Hodie Adservantur, Oxford 1852, 1.36 (MS 2).

A Catalogue of the MSS Preserved in the Libr of the Univ of Cambridge, Cambridge 1858, 3.497 (MS 18).

Kitchin G W, Catalogus Codicum MSS qui in Bibliotheca Aedis Christi Apud Oxonienses Adservantur, Oxford 1867, p 52.

Catalogue of Additions to the MSS in the British Museum in the Years MDCCCLIV–MDCCCLXXV, London 1877, p 376 (MS 19).

Summary Cat, 3.499 (MS 1); 2.789 (MSS 12, 27; both from Eng poet a.1); 4.585 (MS 33).

James M R, The Western MSS in the Libr of Trinity Coll Cambridge, A Descriptive Catalogue, Cambridge 1901, 2.275 (MS 4); The Western MSS in the Libr of Emmanuel Coll, A Descriptive Catalogue, Cambridge 1904, p 22 (MS 32); A Descriptive Catalogue of the MSS in the Libr of Lambeth Palace, Cambridge 1932, pp 433, 750 (MS 8), 765 (MSS 16, 24, 31; all from Lambeth 559).

Catalogue of Additions to the MSS in the British Museum in the Years MDCCCCVI–MDCCCCX, London 1912, p 141 (MSS 15, 30; both from Addit 37787).

Warner G F and J P Gilson, Catalogue of Western MSS in the Old Royal and King's Collections, London 1921, 2.243 (MSS 7, 9; both from BL Royal 17.C.xvii).

Catalogue of Additions to the MSS in the British Museum, 1916–20, London 1933, p 46 (MS 5).

Serjeantson Index, p 254.

Collins A J, ME Devotional Pieces, Brit Mus Quart 14(1940).87 (MSS 11, 20, 25; all from Egerton 3245).

Mynors R A B, Catalogue of the MSS of Balliol College Oxford, Oxford 1963, p 333 (MS 13).

The British Museum Catalogue of Additions to the MSS 1936–45, London 1970, p 255 (MSS 11, 20, 25; all from Egerton 3245).

De La Mare A, Catalogue of the Collection of Medieval MSS Bequeathed to the Bodleian Libr Oxford by James P R Lyell, Oxford 1971, p 61 (MS 21).

Guddat-Figge G, Catalogue of MSS Containing ME Romances, Munich 1976, p 269 (MSS 12, 27; both from Eng poet a.1).

Krochalis J E, Contemplations of the Dread and Love of God: Two Newly Identified Pennsylvania MSS, LC 42(1977).16 (MS 17).

Editions. Horstmann C, The Minor Poems of the Vernon MS, Part I, EETS 98, London 1892, pp 24 (Verse version D), 25 (Verse version I).

Patterson, p 70 (MSS 12 and 27, both from Bodl 3938; MSS 7 and 9, both from Royal 17.B.xvii).

Day M, The Wheatley MS, EETS 155, London 1921, p 100 (MS 5).

Whiting E K, The Poems of John Audelay, EETS 184, London 1931, p 62 (MS 33).

Kirchberger C, The Coasts of the Country, London nd, p 62 (MS 1).

McGarry L, The Holy Eucharist in ME Homiletic and Devotional Verse, Washington D C 1936, pp 224 (MS 32), 235 (rubric only).

Brown RLxvC, p 181 (MS 23).

Robbins R H, The Gurney Series of Religious Lyrics, PMLA 54(1939).369 (MSS 11, 20, 25; all from Egerton 3245); Private Prayers in ME Verse, SP 36(1939).472 (MS 13); Levation Prayers in ME Verse, MP 40(1942).131 (MSS 7, 9; both from Royal 17.C.xvii; MSS 10, 15, 18, 19, 24, 26).

Gray D, A Selection of Religious Lyrics, Oxford 1955, p 54 (MS 18).

Baugh N S, A Worcestershire Miscellany, Phila 1956, pp 97, 149 (MSS 15, 30; both from BL Addit 37787).

Person H A, Cambridge ME Lyrics, rvsd edn, N Y 1962, p 28 (MS 32).

Davies R T, Medieval Eng Lyrics, Evanston 1964, p 115 (MS 19).

Barratt A, A ME Lyric in an Old French MS, MÆ 52(1983).228.

Selections and Modernizations. Watts N H, Love Songs of Sion: A Selection of Devotional Verse from Old Eng Sources, London 1924, pp 19, 22 (from Mirk, [233]).

Comper F M, Spiritual Songs from Eng MSS, London and N Y 1936, p 242.

Literary Relations and Analysis. Knowlton M A, The Influence of Richard Rolle and of Juliana of Norwich on the ME Lyrics, The Hague 1973, p 166 (influence of Rolle's Song of Mercy).

Priscandaro M T, ME Eucharistic Verse: Its Imagery, Symbolism, and Typology, diss St John's Univ 1975, p 34.

Harris-Matthews J M, Lay Devotions in Late Medieval Eng MS, MLitt diss Cambridge Univ 1980, p 144.

Gray, Themes and Images in the Medieval Eng Religious Lyric, London 1972, p 158.

[205] MEDITATIONS FOR GOOSTELY EXERCISE IN THE TYME OF THE MASSE.

MSS. 1, Bodl 8605 (Wood empt 17), ff 1ᵃ–25ᵇ (1450–1500); 2, BL Harley 494, ff 63ᵃ–75ᵃ (ca 1500). *Related Text:* 3, Columbia Univ Plimpton 263, ff 386ᵃ–388ᵇ (1475–1500).

MSS Commentary. A Catalogue of the Harleian MSS in the British Museum, London 1808, 1.329 (MS 2).

Summary Cat, 2.1202 (MS 1).

de Ricci Census, 1.1801 (MS 3).

Edition. Legge J W, Tracts on the Mass, Henry Bradshaw Soc 27, London 1904, p 19.

Selection. Simmons T F, ed, Lay Folks Mass Book, EETS 71, London 1879 (rptd 1968), p 168.

General References. Stone D, A History of the Doctrine of the Holy Eucharist, London 1909, 1.384.

Dix G, The Shape of the Liturgy, London 1945, p 605.

Ong W, A Liturgical Movement in the Middle Ages, American Ecclesiastical Rev 114(1946).112.

Dugmore C W, The Mass and the Eng Reformers, London 1958, p 78.

Clark F, Eucharistic Sacrifice and the Reformation, Oxford 1967, pp 228 (Langford's emphasis on the relation of the Mass to the Passion), 548 (excerpts).

Cuming G J, A Hist of the Anglican Liturgy, London 1969, p 19.

[206] A GOOD CONTEMPLACION FOR A PRESTE OR HE GO TO MASSE.

MSS. 1, Bodl 12728 (Rawl C.894), f 58ᵃ–59ᵇ (1475–1500); 2, BL Royal 17.C.xviii, ff 69ᵃ–71ᵃ (1475–1500).

Jolliffe, p 133, no N.17.

MSS Commentary. Macray W D, Catalogi Codicum Manuscriptorum Bibliothecae Bodleianae, Oxford 1878, 5(2).465 (MS 1).

Warner G F and J P Gilson, Catalogue of Western MSS in the Old Royal and King's Collections, London 1921, 2.245 (MS 2).

[207] PRAEPARATIO EUCHARISTIAE.

MS. Bodl 8174 (Ashmole 1286), ff 223ᵇ–226ᵃ (1400–25).

MS Commentary. Black W H, A Descriptive, Analytical and Critical Catalogue of the MSS Bequeathed unto the Univ of Oxford by Elias Ashmole, Esq, Oxford 1845, p 1051.

Edition. Simmons T F, The Lay Folks Mass Book, EETS 71, London 1879 (rptd 1968), pp 122 (text), 360 (commentary).

2. Festivals

[208] THE FEASTS OF THE CHURCH.

MS. BL Royal 18.A.x, ff 130ᵇ–134ᵇ (1400–50).

Brown-Robbins, no 3415.

MS Commentary. Warner G F and J P Gilson, Catalogue of Western MSS in the Old Royal and King's Collection, London 1921, 2.265.

Edition. Morris R, Legends of the Holy Rood, EETS 46, London 1871, p 210.

Literary Relations. Priscandaro M T, ME Eucharistic Verse: Its Imagery, Symbolism, and Typology, diss St John's Univ 1975, p 150.

Authorship. Pickering O S, A ME Poem on the Eucharist and Other Poems, Arch 215(1978).280.

General Reference. Brandl, §46, p 642.

[209] OF THE SACRAMENT OF THE ALTAR.

MS. Bodl 1703 (Digby 102), ff 123ᵇ–124ᵇ (1400–25).

Brown-Robbins, no 1389.

MS Commentary. Macray W D, Catalogi Codicum Manuscriptorum Bibliothecae Bodleianae, Oxford 1883, 9.116.

Edition. Kail J, Twenty-Six Political and Other Poems from the Bodleian MSS Digby 102 and Douce 322, Pt I, EETS 124, London 1904, p 103.

Literary Relations. McGarry L, The Holy Eucharist in ME Homiletic and Devotional Verse, Washington D C 1936, p 258 (analysis).

Bloomfield SDS, p 161.

Priscandaro M T, ME Eucharistic Verse: Its Imagery, Symbolism, and Typology, diss St John's Univ 1975, p 146.

3. The Ceremonies of the Ritual

i. Baptism

[210] THE SERVICE FOR BAPTISM.

MSS. 1, BL Addit 30506, ff 23ᵃ–24ᵃ (15 cent); 2, BL Stowe 13, f 22ᵃ (1400–50); 3, Durham Univ Cosin V.iv.2, ff 136ᵃ, 143ᵃ (1477). PRINTS: 4, Manuale ad usum Matris Ecclesie Eboracensis, ?Paris 1509 (STC, no 16160); 5, Manuale ad usum Percelebris Ecclesie Sarisburiensis, Rouen 1523 (STC, no 16150).

MSS Commentary. Catalogue of Additions to the MSS in the British Museum in the Years MDCCCLXXVI–MDCCCLXXXI, London 1882, p 84.

Editions. Henderson W G, Manuale et processionale ad usum insignis Ecclesie Eboracensis, Surtees Soc 63(1875).18 (York Manual).

Maskell, 1.ccli (York Manual), 31 (Sarum Manual).

Littlehales H, Eng Fragments from Latin Medieval Service-Books, EETSES 90, London 1903, p 5 (MS 1).

Wordsworth C and H Littlehales, The Old Service-Books of the Eng Church, London 1904, p 52 (MS 1).

Collins A G, Manuale ad usum Percelebris Ecclesie Sarisburiensis, Henry Bradshaw Soc 91(1960).38 (Sarum Manual).

ii. Confession

[211] FORMS OF CONFESSION.

MSS. Prose: Version A: 1, Durham Univ Cosin V.iv.2, ff 159ᵃ–160ᵇ (1477); *Version B*: 2, BL Sloane 1584, ff 46ᵃ–54ᵇ (1500–25); *Version C*: 3, St. John's Oxford 94, ff 142ᵇ–148ᵇ (1425–50); *Version D*: 4, Trinity Oxford E.86, ff 1ᵃ–21ᵃ, 48ᵃ⁻ᵇ, 56ᵇ–69ᵃ (1475–1500); *Version E*: 5, BL Harley 6041, ff

97ᵃ–102ᵇ (1425–50); *Version F*: 6, BL Royal 18.A.x, ff 60ᵇ–61ᵇ (1400–25); *Version G*: 7, Camb Univ Addit 3042, ff 79ᵃ–80ᵇ (1400–50); *Version H*: 8, BL Harley 2383, ff 60ᵇ–61ᵃ (1425–50); *Version I*: 9, Hopton Hall (Chandos-Pole-Gell), pp 22–25 (1400–25); *Version J*: 10, Hopton Hall (Chandos-Pole-Gell), pp 1–2 (1400–25); *Version K*: 11, Bodl 6943 (Ashmole 59), f 130ᵇ (1450); *Version L*: 12, BL Harley 1288, ff 76ᵃ–81ᵇ (1450–1500); *Version M*: 13, BL Sloane 1584, ff 55ᵇ–62ᵃ (1500–25); *Version N*: 14, Bodl 21634 (Douce 60), ff 213ᵃ–222ᵇ (exclusive of ff 215ᵇ–216ᵃ) (1450–1500); 15, Soc of Antiquaries London 687, pp 359–381 (ca 1400); *Version O*: 16, BL Cotton Caligula A.ii, ff 69ᵇ–70ᵃ (1475–1500); *Version P*: 17, Trinity Oxford E.86, ff 69ᵃ–71ᵇ (1475–1500); *Version Q*: 18, Bodl 1292 (Laud misc 210), ff 157ᵃ–165ᵃ (1400–25); 19, Bodl 8174 (Ashmole 1286), ff 252ᵃ–260ᵇ (1400–25); 20, Longleat (Marquis of Bath) 29, ff 24ᵇ–29ᵇ, 31ᵃ (1400–50); *Version R*: 21, Bodl 2376 (Bodley 596), ff 31ᵇ–34ᵃ (1400–25); 22, Addit 22283, f 170ᵇ (1380–1400); 23, BL Addit 37787, ff 3ᵃ–11ᵇ (1400–25); 24, BL Harley 1706, ff 17ᵇ–18ᵃ (1450–1500); 25, Bodl 21896 (Douce 322), f 17ᵃ⁻ᵇ (1425–50); 26, Bodl 3938 (Eng poet a.1), ff 366ᵃ–367ᵃ (1380–1400); 27, Bristol Central Ref 6, ff 134ᵃ–137ᵇ (1502); *Version S*: 28, Bristol Central Ref 14, f 2ᵃ (15 cent); *Version T*: 29, BL Harley 172, ff 11ᵃ–19ᵃ (1400–25); *Version U*: 30, BL Addit 37075, ff 39ᵇ–40ᵇ (1475–1500); *Version V*: 31, BL Harley 494, ff 91ᵃ–94ᵃ (ca 1500); *Version W*: 32, Bodl 2643 (Bodley 789), ff 105ᵃ–107ᵃ (1400–50); *Version X*: 33, BL Harley 2383, ff 57ᵃ–60ᵃ (1425–50); 34, Camb Univ Ee.1.18, ff 175ᵇ–176ᵇ (ca 1450); 35, Lincoln Cath 210, ff 85ᵇ–87ᵇ (15 cent); *Version Y*: 36, Trinity Camb 1099 (0.1.74), ff 60ᵇ–70ᵃ (1450–1500); *Version Z*: 37, Trinity Oxford E.86, ff 1ᵃ–19ᵇ (1475–1500); *Version AA*: 38, Corpus Christi Camb 142, ff 107ᵇ–110ᵇ (15 cent); *Version BB*: 39, Bodl 12543 (Rawl C.699), ff 86ᵃ–88ᵃ, 162ᵇ–179ᵇ (after 1460); 40, Bodl 21896 (Douce 322), ff 98ᵃ–100ᵃ, 101ᵃ⁻ᵇ (1450–60); 41, Queen's Oxford 210, ff 1ᵃ–11ᵇ (15 cent); 42, Camb Univ Hh.1.12, ff 52ᵃ–59ᵇ (ca 1450); 43, BL Harley 1706, ff 84ᵃ–88ᵃ (1450–1500); 44, Lambeth Palace 541, ff 150ᵇ–165ᵃ (ca 1450); 45, Bibl Nat Paris Ang 41, ff 162ᵇ–179ᵃ (ca 1450); *Version CC*: 46, York Minster Addit 2, ff 1ᵃ–4ᵃ, 209ᵃ–210ᵇ (ca 1450); *Version DD*: 47, Bodl 1999 (Bodley 131), ff 136ᵇ–139ᵃ (ca 1450); *Version EE*: 48, BL Sloane 1584, ff 10ᵃ–12ᵃ (1500–25); *Version FF*: 49, St John's Camb 102, f 49ᵃ (ca 1400); *Version GG*: 50, Bodl 10027 (Tanner 201), f 1ᵃ (1400–25); *Version HH*: 51, Trinity Camb 1099 (0.1.74), f 1ᵃ (1450–1500); *Version II*: 52, Emmanuel Camb 229, a roll (16 cent); *Version JJ*: 53, Leeds Univ Brotherton

501, ff 82ᵃ–86ᵃ (ca 1450); *Version KK*: 54, Gonville and Caius Camb 803/807, fragment 53 (15 cent); *Version LL*: 55, Trinity Oxford E.86, f 48ᵃ⁻ᵇ (1475–1500); *Version MM*: 56, BL Cotton Nero A.iii, ff 135ᵇ–137ᵃ (1475–1500); *Version NN*: 57, BL Royal 18.A.x, ff 55ᵇ–60ᵃ (1400–25); *Version OO*: 58, BL Harley 7578, f 1ᵃ⁻ᵇ (1450–1500); *Version PP*: 59, BL Harley 2391, f 238ᵇ (1400–25); *Version QQ*: 60, Bodl 8176 (Ashmole 1288), ff 112ᵃ–130ᵃ (1375–1400); *Version RR*: 61, Magdalene Camb 13, ff 123ᵇ–135ᵃ (1516); *Version SS*: 62, Ipswich Public Libr 7, f 82ᵇ (1500–25); *Version TT*: 63, Lambeth Palace 559, ff 45ᵃ–47ᵇ (1400–50); *Version UU*: 64, Bodl 21820 (Douce 246), f 58ᵇ (1400–50); *Version VV*: 65, Yale Univ 163 (olim Petworth 8), ff 179ᵃ–183ᵇ (1475–1500); *Version WW*: 66, Bodl 12143 (Rawl C.285), ff 60ᵇ–61ᵃ (1400–25); *Version XX*: 67, Bodl 21820 (Douce 246), ff 4ᵃ–10ᵇ (1400–50); *Version YY*: 68, Camb Univ Ii.6.2, f 3ᵃ (1400–25); *Version ZZ*: 69, BL Addit 60577, ff 160ᵃ–180ᵇ (1475–1550); *Version AAA*: 70, BL Harley 2391, ff 134ᵃ–138ᵃ (1400–50).

Verse: Version A: 71, BL Egerton 3245 (olim Gurney), ff 183ᵇ–185ᵃ (1400–25); *Version B*: 72, BL Addit 37049, ff 87ᵇ–88ᵃ (1400–50); *Version C*: 73, BL Arundel 285, ff 1ᵃ–4ᵇ (1500–25); *Version D*: 74, Bodl 11755 (Rawl B.408), ff 4ᵇ–5ᵃ (1400–50). For a prayer of confession, see Brown-Robbins, no 3231.

Jolliffe, p 67 ff, nos C.1–5, C.7–45 (Prose Versions A–PP).

Revell, pp 116, 117, 118, 119, 120.

Brown-Robbins, nos 10 (A Prayer to Christ in 4 couplets preceding Prose Version VV), 271, 804, 3231; Robbins-Cutler, nos 271, 2551.5.

MSS Commentary. A Catalogue of the MSS in the Cottonian Libr Deposited in the British Museum, London 1802, pp 42 (MS 16), 200 (MS 56).

A Catalogue of the Harleian MSS in the British Museum, London 1808, 1.60 (MS 29), 329 (MS 31), 648 (MS 12); 2.178 (MSS 24, 43; both from BL Harley 1706), 675 (MSS 8, 33; both from BL Harley 2383), 680 (MS 59); 3.313 (MS 5), 538 (MS 58).

Black W H, A Descriptive, Analytical, and Critical Catalogue of the MSS Bequeathed unto the Univ of Oxford by Elias Ashmole, Oxford 1845, pp 95 (MS 11), 1051 (MS 19), 1053 (MS 60).

Coxe H O, Catalogus Codicum MSS qui in Collegiis Aulisque Oxoniensibus Hodie Adservantur, Oxford 1852, 2.26 (MS 3), 35 (MSS 4, 17, 37, 55; all from Trinity Coll Oxf E.86); Catalogi Codicum Manuscriptorum Bibliothecae Bodleianae, Oxford 1858, 2.181 (MS 18).

Hackman A, Catalogi Codicum Manuscriptorum Bibliothecae Bodleianae, Oxford 1860, 4.637 (MS 50).

Catalogue of Additions to the MSS in the British Museum in the Years MDCCCLIV–MDCCCLX, London 1875, p 623 (MS 22).

Macray W D, Catalogi Codicum Manuscriptorum Bibliothecae Bodleianae, Oxford 1862, 5(1).666 (MS 74); 5(2)(1878).123 (MS 66), 352 (MS 39).

Historical MSS Commission, 3rd Report of the Royal Commission on Historical MSS, London 1872, appendix, p 181 (MS 20); 9th Report of the Royal Commission on Historical MSS, pt 2, London 1883, appendix, p 384 (MSS 9, 10).

Catalogue of MSS in the British Museum ns vol 1, London 1890, pt 1: The Arundel MSS, p 82 (MS 73).

Summary Cat, 2.152 (MS 47), 335 (MS 21), 467 (MS 32), 789 (MS 26); 4.508 (MS 14), 566 (MSS 64, 67; both from Douce 246), 593 (MSS 25, 40; both from Douce 322).

James M R, The Western MSS in the Libr of Trinity Coll Cambridge, A Descriptive Catalogue, Cambridge 1902, 3.74 (MSS 36, 51; both from Trinity Camb 1099); The Western MSS in the Libr of Emmanuel Coll, A Descriptive Catalogue, Cambridge 1903, p 135 (MS 52).

Legge J W, ed, Tracts on the Mass, Henry Bradshaw Soc 27(1904).xxiv (MS 56).

Catalogue of Additions to the MSS in the British Museum in the Years MDCCCC–MDCCCCV, London 1907, pp 324 (MS 72), 344 (MS 30).

Hammond E P, Ashmole 59 and Other Shirley MSS, Angl 30(1907).320 (MS 11).

James M R, A Descriptive Catalogue of the MSS in the Coll Libr of Magdalene Coll Cambridge, Cambridge 1909, p 24 (MS 61); A Descriptive Catalogue of the MSS in the Libr of Corpus Christi Coll Cambridge, Cambridge 1912, 1.327 (MS 38); Supplement to the Catalogue of MSS in the Libr of Gonville and Caius Coll, Cambridge 1914, p 43 (MS 54).

Catalogue of Additions to the MSS in the British Museum in the Years MDCCCCVI–MDCCCCX, London 1912, p 140 (MS 23).

Warner G F and J P Gilson, Catalogue of Western MSS in the Old Royal and King's Collections, London 1921, 2.265 (MSS 6, 57; both from Royal 18.A.x).

Wooley R M, Catalogue of the MSS of Lincoln Cathedral Chapter Libr, Oxford 1927, p 149 (MS 35).

Serjeantson, Index, p 250.

James M R, A Descriptive Catalogue of the MSS in the Libr of Lambeth Palace, The Medieval MSS, Cambridge 1932, pp 743 (MS 44), 765 (MS 63).

de Ricci Census, 2.1902 (MS 65).

Manly & Rickert, 1.343 (MS 20).

The Friends of York Minster, 16th Annual Report, 1944, p 14, and 17th Annual Report, 1945, p 27 (MS 46).

Doyle Survey, 2.81 (MS 20).

Kane G, ed, Piers Plowman: The A Version, London 1960, pp 6 (MS 5), 11 (MS 15).

Kuriyagawa F, ed, Walter Hilton's Eight Chapters on Perfection, Tokyo 1967, p xiii (MS 45).

Ker Manuscripts, 1.314 (MS 15); 2.20 (MS 28), 203 (MS 27); 3.67 (MS 53).

Wakelin M F, The MSS of John Mirk's Festial, Leeds SE 1(1967).98 (MS 12), 100 (MS 70), 104 (MS 14).

Guddat-Figge G, Catalogue of MSS Containing ME Romances, Munich 1976, pp 169 (MS 16), 269 (MS 26).

The Winchester Anthology, with an Introd by E Wilson and I Fenlon, Woodbridge 1981, p 1 (MS 69).

Hanna R III, Leeds Univ Libr, MS Brotherton 501: A Redescription, Manuscripta 26(1982).38 (MS 53).

Editions. Maskell, 3.301 (MS 56), 304 (Douce 246: MSS 64, 67), 417 (from Harley 2383 copy of De Visitacione Infirmorum: MSS 8, 33).

Horstmann C, The Minor Poems of the Vernon MS, Pt 1, EETS 98, London 1892, p 19 (MS 26).

Yksh Wr, 2.340 (MS 26).

Patterson, p 50.

Bowers R H, The ME St Brendan's Confession, Arch 175(1939).40 (Prose Version DD: MS 42 base text, with variants from MSS 41 and 43).

Robbins R L, The Gurney Series of Religious Lyrics, PMLA 54(1939).372 (MS 71).

Baugh N S, A Worcestershire Miscellany, Phila 1956, p 87 (MS 23).

Doty B L, An Edn of British Museum MS Addit 37049: A Religious Miscellany, diss Michigan State Univ 1963 (MS 72).

Kuriyagawa F, The ME St Brendan's Confession, Tokyo 1968 (Prose Version BB: MS 44 base text, with variants from MSS 39, 41, 42, 43, and 45).

Manual, 4.1266 (for editions of Dunbar's version, X [104], in MS 73).

Facsimile. The Winchester Anthology, with an Introd by E Wilson and I Fenlon, Woodbridge 1981 (MS 69).

Modernization. Sagar M G, A Mediaeval Anthology, London 1915, p 38 (MS 26).

Authorship. Doyle A I, A Prayer Attributed to St Thomas Aquinas, DomS 1(1948).229 (John Lacy).

Pepler C, John Lacy: A Dominican Contemplative, Life of the Spirit 5(1951).397 (John Lacy as author of Prose Version C).

Clay R M, Further Studies of Medieval Recluses, Journ of British Archaeological Assoc 3s 16 (1953).74 (John Lacy); Some Northern Anchorites, Archaeologia Aeliana 33(1955).202 (John Lacy).

General References. Ives D V, The Seven Deadly Sins in Eng Lit, MA thesis London Univ 1931, p 50.

Owst G R, Literature and Pulpit in Medieval England, Cambridge 1933, p 383 n1.

Arnould, p 49 n1.

Bloomfield SDS, pp 170, 171.

Doyle A I, Books Connected with the Vere Family and Barking Abbey, Trans of the Essex Archaeological Soc 25(1958).225, 227 n4.

Wenzel, pp 229, 233.

Wenzel S, Sloth in ME Devotional Lit, Angl 79(1961).290, 303.

Southern R W and F S Schmitt, edd, Memorials of St Anselm, Auctores Britannici Medii Aevi I, London 1969, p 353 (MS 66 and other versions as part of the office for the visitation of the sick).

Bibliography. Booker J M, A ME Biblio, Heidelberg 1912, p 13.

[212] TRACTATUS DE MODO CONFITENDI.

MS. Camb Univ Addit 2830, ff 80ᵃ–83ᵇ (1425–50).

Jolliffe, p 76, no E.13.

Edition and Discussion. Meech S B, John Drury and His Eng Writings, Spec 9(1934).70.

Language. Moore Meech and Whitehall, p 51.

General Reference. Orme N, Schoolmasters, 1307–1509, in C H Clough, ed, Profession, Vocation and Culture in Later Medieval England, Liverpool 1982, p 233.

iii. Marriage

[213] THE MARRIAGE SERVICE.

MSS. 1, Bodl 15840 (Rawl liturg e.41), f 113ᵃ (1400–25); 2, Bodl 15841 (Rawl liturg e.44), ff 19ᵃ–20ᵃ (15 cent); 3, Bodl 15847 (Rawl liturg d.5), f 12ᵃ⁻ᵇ (14 cent); 4, Keble Oxford 58, ff 235ᵃ–240ᵇ (ca 1400); 5, Trinity Oxford E.86, ff 42ᵇ–43ᵃ (1475–1500); 6, Univ Oxford 78A, ff 220ᵇ–221ᵃ (1400–25); 7, Camb Univ Ee.4.19, ff 21ᵃ–24ᵃ (1350–1400); 8, Camb Univ Mm.1.15, ff 13ᵇ–14ᵃ (15 cent); 9, Camb Univ Mm.3.21, f 218ᵇ (15 cent); 10, Peterhouse Camb 222, f 2ᵃ (15 cent); 11, BL Addit 30506, ff 25ᵃ–27ᵇ (15 cent); 12, BL Harley 4172, f 10ᵃ⁻ᵇ (1426); 13, Durham Univ Cosin V.iv.2, ff 137ᵃ, 150ᵃ–152ᵇ (1477); 14, Exeter Cath 3513, f 94ᵃ⁻ᵇ (ca 1400); 15, Hereford Cath P.3.iv, ff 12ᵇ–18ᵇ (15 cent); 16, York Minster XVI.M.4, ff 37ᵃ–39ᵃ (ca 1450); 17, ? Buckland House (Throckmorton); 18, Harvard Univ Widener 1 (olim Lawson), f 62ᵃ⁻ᵇ (1400–25); 19, Henry E Huntington HM 30986, ff 12ᵇ–13ᵃ (ca 1400). PRINTS: 20, Manuale ad usum Matris Ecclesie Eboracensis, ? Paris 1509 (STC, no 16160); 21, Manuale ad usum Percelebris Ecclesie Sarisburiensis, Rouen 1543 (STC, no 16150).

Brown-Robbins, no 4204.

MSS Commentary. A Catalogue of the Harleian MSS in the British Museum, London 1808, 3.121 (MS 12).

Coxe H O, Catalogus Codicum MSS qui in Collegiis Aulisque Oxoniensibus Hodie Adservantur, Oxford 1852, 1.23 (MS 6); 2.34 (MS 5).

A Catalogue of the MSS Preserved in the Libr of the Univ of Cambridge, Cambridge 1857, 2.126 (MS 7); 4(1861).107 (MS 8), 200 (MS 9).

Parkes M B, The Medieval MSS of Keble Coll Oxford, London 1879, p 265 (MS 4).

James M R, A Descriptive Catalogue of the MSS in the Libr of Peterhouse, Cambridge 1899, p 271 (MS 10).

Summary Cat, 3.515 (MSS 1, 2), 517 (MS 3).

Bannister A T, A Descriptive Catalogue of the MSS in the Hereford Cathedral Libr, Hereford 1927, p 131 (MS 15).

Ker Manuscripts, 2.821 (MS 14).

Catalogue of Additions to the MSS in the British Museum in the Years MDCCCLXXVI–MDCCCLXXXI, London 1882, p 84 (MS 11).

Editions. Maskell W, The Ancient Liturgy of England, 2nd edn, London 1846, p cliv (Salisbury, York, Bangor, Hereford uses).

Barnes R, Liber Pontificalis of Edmund Lacy, Bishop of Exeter, Exeter 1847, p 257.

Henderson W G, Manuale et Processionale ad usum Insignis Ecclesiae Eboracensis, Surtees Soc 63 (1875).24 (York), 19* (Sarum Manual), 117* (Hereford Manual), 167* (Hereford Manual).

Maskell, 1.42 (Sarum and York Manuals).

James M R, A Descriptive Catalogue of the MSS in the Libr of Peterhouse, Cambridge 1899, p 271 (MS 10).

Littlehales H, Eng Fragments from Latin Medieval Service-Books, EETSES 90, London 1903, p 5 (MS 11).

Wordsworth C and H Littlehales, The Old Service-Books of the Eng Church, London 1904, p 53 (MS 11).

Collins A J, Manuale ad usum Percelebris Ecclesie Sarisburiensis, Henry Bradshaw Soc 91(1960).47 (PRINT 21).

Facsimile. Wordsworth C and H Littlehales, The Old Service-Books of the Eng Church, London 1904, opp p 213 (MS 11).

General Reference. Gasquet F A, Parish Life in Medieval England, London 1906, p 207.

Owst G R, Preaching in Medieval England, Cambridge 1926, pp 268, 297, 306.

Tavormina M T, A Ful Greet Sacrement: Liturgical Backgrounds of Nuptial Themes in ME Lit, diss Yale Univ 1978, p 23.

Bibliography. Stevenson K, Nuptial Blessing: A Study of Christian Marriage Rites, Alcuin Club Collections 64, London 1982, p 76.

[214] BENEDICTA SIT SANCTA TRINITAS.

MS. Balliol Oxford 354, f 146ᵃ⁻ᵇ (1500–25).

Brown-Robbins, no 506.

MS Commentary. Mynors R A B, Catalogue of the MSS of Balliol Coll Oxf, Oxford 1963, p 352.

Editions. Flugel E, Liedersammlungen des XVI Jahrhunderts besonders aus der Zeit Heinrichs VIII. III, Angl 26(1903).162.

Dyboski R, Songs, Carols and Other Miscellaneous Poems from the Balliol MS 354, Richard Hill's Commonplace-Book, EETSES 101, London 1907, p 66.

iv. Visitation of the Sick

[215] DE VISITACIONE INFIRMORUM.

MSS. Version A: 1, St John's Oxford 47, ff 125ᵇ–126ᵇ (1400–25); 2, Bodl 6951 (Ashmole 750), ff 11ᵇ–14ᵃ (1475–1500); 3, Gonville and Caius Camb 209, ff 149ᵇ–156ᵃ (15 cent); 4, BL Harley 237, ff 93ᵃ–94ᵇ (ca 1450); 5, Camb Univ Ee.5.13, ff 13ᵇ–15ᵇ (1375–1400); *Version B*: 6, Bodl 1963 (Bodley 110), f 162ᵃ (1400–25); 7, Bodl 12143 (Rawl C.285), ff 60ᵇ–61ᵃ (1400–25); 8, Trinity Oxford E.86, f 42ᵃ⁻ᵇ (1475–1500); 9, Camb Univ Ff.5.40, f 117ᵃ⁻ᵇ (1400–50); 10, Camb Univ Ff.6.21, ff 20ᵇ–21ᵇ (ca 1400); 11, BL Stowe 13, f 48ᵃ⁻ᵇ (1400–50; same text as MS 7); *Version C*: 12, BL Harley 2383, ff 24ᵇ–25ᵇ (1425–50); *Version D*: 13, Bodl 2643 (Bodley 789), ff 156ᵃ–160ᵃ (1400–50); 14, Camb Univ Ii.6.55, ff 23ᵃ–24ᵇ (1400–50); *Version E*: 15, Bodl 3054 (Bodley 938), ff 236ᵇ–243ᵇ (1450–1500); 16, Bodl 1292 (Laud misc 210), ff 98ᵃ–99ᵃ (1400–25); 17, Univ Oxford 4, ff 16ᵇ–23ᵃ (1400–50); 18, Univ Oxford 97, ff 93ᵇ–97ᵃ (1400–25); 19, Camb Univ Dd.1.17, ff 31ᵃ–32ᵃ (1375–1400); 20, Camb Univ Nn.4.12, ff 29ᵇ–37ᵇ (1400–25); 21, BL Addit 32320, ff 13ᵇ–19ᵇ (15 cent); 22, BL Harley 211, ff 65ᵃ–69ᵃ (1400–25); 23, BL Harley 2398, ff 156ᵃ–160ᵇ (1400–25); 24, BL Royal 17.A.xxvi, ff 30ᵃ–37ᵃ (1400–50); 25, Lambeth Palace 432, ff 68ᵇ–75ᵃ (1450–1500); 26, Westminster School 3, ff 105ᵇ–112ᵃ (ca 1450); 27, Trinity Dublin 432, ff 88ᵃ–89ᵃ (1450–1500); *Version F*: 28, BL Lansdowne 762, ff 21ᵇ–22ᵇ (1475–1525). Related Text: 29, BL Addit 30506, ff 50ᵇ–52ᵃ (15 cent).

Jolliffe, pp 123, no L.2; 124f, nos L.5–7.

MSS Commentary. A Catalogue of the Harleian MSS in the British Museum, London 1908, 1.66 (MS 22), 73 (MS 4); 2.675 (MS 12), 684 (MS 23). A Catalogue of the Lansdowne MSS in the British Museum, London 1819, p 168 (MS 28).

Black W H, A Descriptive, Analytical, and Critical Catalogue of the MSS Bequeathed unto the Univ of Oxford by Elias Ashmole, Oxford 1845, p 357 (MS 2).

Coxe H O, Catalogus Codicum MSS qui in Collegiis Aulisque Oxoniensibus Hodie Adservantur, Oxford 1852, 1.1 (MS 17), 28 (MS 18); 2.14 (MS 1), 34 (MS 8); Catalogi Codicum Manuscriptorum Bibliothecae Bodleianae, Oxford 1858, 2.181 (MS 16).

A Catalogue of the MSS Preserved in the Libr of the Univ of Cambridge, Cambridge 1856, 1.15 (MS 19); 2(1857).175 (MS 5), 498 (MS 9), 527 (MS 10); 3(1859).545 (MS 14); 4(1861).499 (MS 20).

Macray W D, Catalogus Codicum Manuscriptorum Bibliothecae Bodleianae, Oxford 1878, 5(2).123 (MS 7).

Catalogue of Additions to the MSS in the British Museum in the Years MDCCCLXXXII–MDCCCLXXXVII, London 1889, p 102 (MS 21).

Summary Cat, 2.135 (MS 6), 467 (MS 13), 578 (MS 15).

Abbott T K, Catalogue of the MSS in the Libr of Trinity Coll Dublin, Dublin 1900, p 67 (MS 27).

Legge J W, ed, Tracts on the Mass, Henry Bradshaw Soc 27(1904).xxxi (MS 29).

James M R, A Descriptive Catalogue of the MSS in the Libr of Gonville and Caius College, Cambridge 1907, 1.244 (MS 3).

Warner G F and J P Gilson, Catalogue of Western MSS in the Old Royal and King's Collections, London 1921, 2.220 (MS 24).

James M R and C Jenkins, A Descriptive Catalogue of the MSS in the Libr of Lambeth Palace, Cambridge 1932, p 599 (MS 25).

Aarts F G A M, ed, The Pater Noster of Richard Ermyte, The Hague 1967, p xi (MS 26).

Ker Manuscripts, 1.422 (MS 26).

Doyle A I, Univ Coll Oxf MS 97 and Its Relationship to the Simeon MS (BL Addit 22283), in M Benskin and M L Samuels, edd, So meny people longages

and tonges, Philological Essays in Scots and Medieval Eng Presented to A McIntosh, Edinburgh 1981, p 265.

Editions. Hearne T, Robert of Gloucester's Chronicle, in S Bagster, ed, The Works of Thomas Hearne, London 1810, 3.683 (prints confessional portion of text identical with MS 1).

Peacock E, Instructions for Parish Priests by John Myrc, EETS 31, London 1868 (rvsd by Furnivall, 1903), p 63 (MS 28).

Henderson W G, Manuale et processionale ad usum insignis Ecclesiae Eboracensis, Surtees Soc 63 (1874).110* (MS 1).

Maskell, 3.410 (MS 12), 413 (MS 1).

Yksh Wr, 1.107 (MS 7); 2.449 (MS 18).

Littlehales H, Eng Fragments from Latin Medieval Service-Books, EETSES 90, London 1903, p 6 (MS 21).

Kinpointer R J, An Edn of De Visitacione Infirmorum, diss Fordham Univ 1974, pp 1 (Version A, collating all MSS except MS 5; base text: MS 1), 20 (MS 20), 32 (MS 12), 35 (MS 9), 37 (MS 13); introd, pp ix (MSS), xxii (language), l (relationship of MSS), lxxiii (tradition and content).

Sources and Literary Relations. Migne PL, 40.1147 (De Visitacione infirmorum); 158.685 (Admonitio morienti).

Maskell, 1.cclxix (origin and development of service).

Schmitt F S, Eine neue unvollendete Werk des Hl Anselm von Canterbury, Beiträge zur Geschichte der Philosophie und Theologie des Mittelalters, 33(1936).5.

O'Connor M C, The Art of Dying Well: The Development of the Ars Moriendi, N Y 1942, pp 23, 24 n74, 26, 33, 34, 38 n176, 43 n206.

Beaty N E, The Craft of Dying: The Literary Tradition of the Ars Moriendi, New Haven and London 1970, pp 2, 237, 239.

Style. Blake N F, Varieties of ME Prose, in B Rowland, ed, Chaucer and ME Stud in Honour of R H Robbins, London 1974, p 353.

General References. Swete F A, Parish Life in Mediæval England, London 1906, p 201.

Bloomfield SDS, p 222.

Doyle Survey, 1.219.

Porter H B, The Origin of the Medieval Rite for Anointing the Sick or Dying, Journ of Theological Stud ns 7(1956).221.

Priscandaro M T, ME Eucharistic Verse: Its Imagery, Symbolism, and Typology, diss St John's Univ 1975, p 27.

[216] BOKE OF CRAFT OF DYING.

MSS. 1, Bodl 12728 (Rawl C.894), ff 18ᵇ–33ᵃ (1475–
1500); 2, Bodl 2322 (Bodley 423), ff 228ᵃ–241ᵇ
(ca 1450); 3, Bodl 21896 (Douce 322), ff 26ᵇ–39ᵃ
(1450–75); 4, Corpus Christi Oxf E.220, ff 24ᵇ–
42ᵃ (ca 1500); 5, Camb Univ Ff.5.45, ff 24ᵇ–46ᵇ
(1475–1500); 6, Camb Univ Kk.1.5 (6), ff 1ᵃ–4ᵃ
(ca 1500); 7, Trinity Camb 601 (R.3.21), ff 18ᵇ–
32ᵇ (1475–1500); 8, BL Addit 10596, ff 1ᵃ–24ᵇ
(1450–75); 9, BL Harley 1706, ff 25ᵇ–36ᵇ (1475–
1500); 10, BL Harley 4011, ff 3ᵃ–16ᵃ (1475–
1500); 11, BL Lansdowne 762, ff 21ᵇ–22ᵇ (1475–
1525; an extract from the second series of interrogations in chap 3); 12, BL Royal 17.C.xviii, ff
21ᵃ–39ᵃ (1475–1500); 13, John Rylands Manchester Eng 94, ff 125ᵃ–137ᵇ (1425–50); 14, Beeleigh (olim Foyle, present location unknown), ff
109ᵇ–126ᵃ (1450–1500); 15, Univ of Illinois 80,
ff 6ᵃ–8ᵃ (15 cent).

Jolliffe, p 123, nos L.2, 4.

Revell, p 52.

MSS Commentary. A Catalogue of the Harleian MSS
in the British Museum, London 1808, 2.178 (MS
9); 3.103 (MS 10).

A Catalogue of the Lansdowne MSS in the British
Museum, London 1819, p 168 (MS 11).

Coxe H O, Catalogus Codicum MSS qui in Collegiis
Aulisque Oxoniensibus Hodie Adservantur, Oxford 1852, 2.87 (MS 4).

A Catalogue of the MSS Preserved in the Libr of
the Univ of Cambridge, Cambridge 1857, 2.501
(MS 5); 3(1858).558 (MS 6).

Macray W D, Catalogi Codicum Manuscriptorum
Bibliothecae Bodleianae, Oxford 1878, 5(2).465
(MS 1).

Summary Cat, 2.308 (MS 2); 4.593 (MS 3).

James M R, The Western MSS in the Libr of Trinity
Coll Cambridge, A Descriptive Catalogue, Cambridge 1901, 2.63 (MS 7).

Warner G F and J P Gilson, Catalogue of Western
MSS in the Old Royal and King's Collections, London 1921, 2.245 (MS 12).

Tyson M, Handlist of the Collection of Eng MSS in
the John Rylands Libr 1928, Manchester 1929,
p 21 (MS 13).

Editions. Peacock E, Instructions for Parish Priests
by John Myrc, EETS 31, London 1868 (rvsd by
Furnivall, 1903), p 63.

Lumby J R, Ratis Raving and Other Moral and Religious Pieces in Prose and Verse, EETS 43, London 1870, p 1 (MS 6).

Yksh Wr, 2.406 (MS 1).

Girvan R, Ratis Raving and Other Early Scots Poems
on Morals, PSTS 3s 11, Edinburgh and London
1939, p 166 (MS 6).

Morgan G R, A Critical Edn of Caxton's The Art
and Craft to Know Well to Die and Ars Moriendi
with the Antecedent MS Material, diss Oxford
Univ 1972, p 1 (collates all MSS except MS 14;
MS 2 is basis of text).

Scott M E, Go, Crysten Soul: A Critical Edn of The
Craft of Dying, diss Miami Univ (Oxford, Ohio)
1975 (MS 3 is basis of text; also provides text of
MS 6 in Appendix, p 340).

Modernization. Comper F M, ed, The Book of the
Craft of Dying and Other Early Eng Tracts Concerning Death, London 1917, p 1.

Literary Relations and Sources. O'Connor M C, The
Art of Dying Well, N Y 1942 (comprehensive
study of origin, sources, MSS and printed edns of
ars moriendi tradition).

Duclow D F, Everyman and the Ars Moriendi: 15-
cent Ceremonies of Dying, 15-Cent Stud 6
(1983).59.

General References. Deanesly M, Vernacular Books in
England in the 14 and 15 Cents, MLR 15
(1920).358.

Owst G R, Preaching in Medieval England, Cambridge 1926, p 342.

Workman S K, 15-Cent Translation as an Influence
on Eng Prose, Princeton 1940, p 169.

Bennett OHEL, p 302.

Pecheux M C, Aspects of the Treatment of Death in
ME Poetry, Washington D C 1951, pp 29, 31, 77
n149.

Doyle Survey, 1.219.

Schlauch M, Eng Medieval Lit and Its Social Foundations, Warsaw 1956, p 300.

Doyle A I, Books Connected with the Vere Family
and Barking Abbey, Trans of the Essex Archaeological Soc 25(1958).226 n3, 233, 241.

Woolf, p 375.

Chené-Williams A, Vivre sa mort et mourir sa vie:
L'Art de mourir au XVe siècle, in Le Sentiment
de la Mort, ed C Sutto, Montreal 1979, p 172.

Beaty N L, The Craft of Dying, New Haven and
London 1979, p 5.

Bibliography. New CBEL, 1.504.

[217] THE ART AND CRAFT
TO KNOW WELL TO DIE.

Edition. Morgan G R, A Critical Edn of Caxton's The
Art and Craft to Know Well to Die and Ars Moriendi Together with the Antecedent MS Material,
diss Oxford Univ 1972, p 221.

For fuller bibliographical treatment, see Manual,
3.944 (IX [43]).

[218] ARS MORIENDI.

Edition. Morgan G R, A Critical Edn of Caxton's The Art and Craft to Know Well to Die and Ars Moriendi Together with the Antecedent MS Material, diss Oxford Univ 1972, p 229.

Facsimile. Nicholson E W B, facsimile edn, rptd London 1969.

For fuller bibliographic treatment, see Manual, 3.943 (IX [42]).

[219] DE VISITACIONE INFIRMORUM ET CONSOLACIONE MISERORUM.

MS. Bodl 21876 (Douce 302), ff 12^b–14^b (1425–50).
Brown-Robbins, no 2853.
MS Commentary. Summary Cat, 4.585.
Edition. Whiting E K, The Poems of John Audelay, EETS 184, London 1931, p 82.
General Reference. Pecheux M C, Aspects of the Treatment of Death in ME Poetry, Washington D C 1951, pp 33, 78.

[220] SEX OBSERVANDA OMNI CHRISTIANO IN EXTREMIS.

MSS. 1, Bodl 21896 (Douce 322), ff 18^a–19^a (ca 1450); 2, BL Harley 1706, ff 18^b–19^a (1450–1500).
Brown-Robbins, no 741.
MSS Commentary. A Catalogue of the Harleian MSS in the British Museum, London 1808, 2.178 (MS 2).
Summary Cat, 4.593.

[221] TO KUNNE TO DI3E (or SCIRE MORI).

MSS. Version A: 1, Lichfield Cath 16 (olim 6), ff 17^a–34^b (1375–1400); *Version B*: 2, Bodl 21896 (Douce 322), ff 20^a–25^b (1450–60); 3, BL Addit 37049, ff 39^a–43^b (1400–50); 4, BL Harley 1706, ff 20^a–24^b (1450–1500); 5, Camb Univ Ff.5.45, ff 14^a–22^b (1400–25); *Version C*: 6, Bodl 2643 (Bodley 789), ff 123^a–139^b (1400–50); 7, Glasgow Univ Hunter 496, ff 164^a–178^b (1375–1400).
Jolliffe, p 125, no L.8.
Revell, p 43.
MSS Commentary. A Catalogue of the Harleian MSS in the British Museum, London 1808, 2.178 (MS 4).
A Catalogue of the MSS Preserved in the Libr of the Univ of Cambridge, Cambridge 1857, 2.501 (MS 5).
Benedikz B S, Lichfield Cathedral Libr A Catalogue of the Cathedral Libr MSS, rvsd version, Birmingham 1878, p 9 (MS 1).

Summary Cat, 2.467 (MS 6); 4.593 (MS 2).
Catalogue of Additions to the MSS in the British Museum in the Years MDCCCC–MDCCCV, London 1907, p 324 (MS 3).
Young J and P H Aitken, A Catalogue of the MSS in the Libr of the Hunterian Museum in the Univ of Glasgow, Glasgow 1908, p 408 (MS 7).
Ker Manuscripts, 3.116 (MS 1).
Edition. Armstrong E P, Heinrich Suso in England: an Edn of the Ars Moriendi from the Seven Points of True Love, diss Indiana Univ 1966.
Modernization. Comper F M, ed, The Book of the Craft of Dying and Other Early Eng Tracts Concerning Death, London 1917, pp 105 (MS 2), 123 (discussion).
Source. Horstmann C, Orologium Sapientiae or The Seven Poyntes of True Wisdom aus MS Douce 114, Angl 10(1888).323.
General References. Ten Brink, 3.7.
Wichgraf W, Susos Horologium Sapientiae in England, nach Handschriften des 15 Jahrhunderts, Angl 53(1929).124.
O'Connor M C, The Art of Dying Well; The Development of the Ars Moriendi, N Y 1942, p 108 n269.
Doyle Survey, 1.212.
Doyle A I, Books Connected with the Vere Family and Barking Abbey, Trans of the Essex Archaeological Soc 25(1959).226 n1.
Woolf, p 331.

[222] THE V WYLES OF PHARAO.

MSS. 1, Bodl 21589 (Douce 15), ff 78^a–141^a (1400–50); 2, Bodl 21947 (Douce 372), ff 160^b–163^b (1425–50); 3, Camb Univ Ff.6.33, ff 67^b–88^a (ca 1450); 4, Camb Univ Gg.6.26, ff 104^a–105^a (ca 1500); 5, BL Addit 35298, ff 165^a–167^a (1450–1500); 6, BL Harley 1197, ff 75^a–76^b (1425–50); 7, BL Harley 2388, ff 7^b–20^a (1450–1500); 8, BL Harley 4775, f 262^a–b (ca 1450); 9, Lambeth Palace 72, ff 431^a–437^a (1450–1500).
Jolliffe, p 120, no K.7.
MSS Commentary. A Catalogue of the Harleian MSS in the British Museum, London 1808, 1.595 (MS 6); 2.678 (MS 7); 3.203 (MS 8).
A Catalogue of the MSS Preserved in the Libr of the Univ of Cambridge, Cambridge 1857, 2.534 (MS 3); 3(1858).229 (MS 4).
Catalogue of Additions to the MSS in the British Museum in the Years 1894–1899, London 1901, p 244 (MS 5).
Summary Cat, 4.493 (MS 1), 610 (MS 2).
James M R, A Descriptive Catalogue of the MSS in the Libr of Lambeth Palace: The Mediaeval MSS, Cambridge 1932, 1.116 (MS 9).

Kurvinen A, Caxton's Golden Legend and the MSS of the Gilte Legende, NM 60(1959).353 (detailed description of contents of MS 5).

Hamer R, ed, Three Lives from the Gilte Legende, Heidelberg 1978, p 26 (description of MSS 2, 5, 8, 9).

Sources and Literary Relations. Butler P, Legenda Aurea—Légende Dorée—Golden Legende, Baltimore 1899, p 50.

Görlach M, The South Eng Legendary, Gilte Legende and Golden Legend, Braunschweig 1972.

[223] THE DIRECCION OF A MANNYS LYFE.

MSS. 1, Camb Univ Ff.6.33, ff 98ᵇ–114ᵃ (ca 1450); 2, Trinity Camb 1375 (0.7.47), ff 87ᵃ–95ᵇ (1400–25).

Jolliffe, p 120, no K.4.

MSS Commentary. A Catalogue of the MSS Preserved in the Libr of the Univ of Cambridge, Cambridge 1857, 2.533 (MS 1).

James M R, The Western MSS in the Libr of Trinity Coll Cambridge: a Descriptive Catalogue, Cambridge 1920, 3.386 (MS 2).

[224] THE THRE ARGUMENTIS THAT THE DEVEL WILL PUTTE TO MAN IN HIS DIINGE.

MS. BL Harley 2339, ff 100ᵇ–104ᵇ (1400–50).

Jolliffe, p 120, no K.5.

MS Commentary. A Catalogue of the Harleian MSS in the British Museum, London 1808, 2.658.

Doyle A I, A Treatise of the Three Estates, DomS 3(1950).351.

4. Non-liturgical and Occasional Services and Devotions

[225] PRIMER (or LAY FOLKS' PRAYER BOOK).

MSS. 1, Bodl 2289 (Bodley 85), ff 7ᵃ–109ᵃ (after 1410); 2, Bodl 8176 (Ashmole 1288), ff 9ᵃ–130ᵃ (1400–20); 3, Bodl 12543 (Rawl C.699), ff 7ᵃ–92ᵃ (after 1460); 4, Bodl 21820 (Douce 246), ff 11ᵃ–100ᵃ (1400–50); 5, Bodl 21849 (Douce 275), ff 1ᵃ–77ᵇ (ca 1400); 6, Queen's Oxford 324, ff 1ᵃ–77ᵃ (1400–25); 7, Univ Oxford 179, ff 9ᵃ–97ᵃ (1400–50); 8, Camb Univ Dd.11.82, ff 1ᵃ–98ᵇ (1425–50); 9, Emmanuel Camb 246, ff 7ᵃ–52ᵇ (ca 1400); 10, St John's Camb 192, ff 9ᵃ–95ᵇ (ca 1400); 11, BL Addit 17010, ff 1ᵃ–77ᵃ (1400–25); 12, BL Addit 17011, ff 1ᵃ–108ᵇ (ca 1400); 13, BL Addit 27592, ff 12ᵃ–41ᵃ (1400–25); 14, BL Addit 36683, ff 1ᵃ–175ᵇ (1400–25); 15, London Univ Fragment 57 (15 cent; bound as two flyleaves in John Welles, The Art of Stenographie, London 1623); 16, Glasgow Univ Hunter 472, ff 6ᵃ–71ᵃ (ca 1400); 17, Glasgow Univ Hunter 512, ff 37ᵃ–217ᵇ (ca 1400). For a versified version of the Hours of the Cross, interspersed in the English Primer, see [227] below.

MSS Commentary. Black W H, A Descriptive, Analytical, and Critical Catalogue of the MSS Bequeathed unto the Univ of Oxford by Elias Ashmole, Oxford 1845, p 1053 (MS 2).

A Catalogue of the MSS Preserved in the Libr of the Univ of Cambridge, Cambridge 1856, p 477 (MS 8).

Catalogue of Additions to the MSS in the British Museum in the Years MDCCCXLVI–MDCCCXLVII, London 1864, p 346 (MSS 11, 12).

Catalogue of Additions to the MSS in the British Museum in the Years MDCCCLXIV–MDCCCLXXV, London 1877, p 324 (MS 13).

Macray W D, Catalogi Codicum Manuscriptorum Bibliothecae Bodleianae, Oxford 1878, 5(2).352 (MS 3).

Summary Cat, 1.291 (MS 1); 4.366 (MS 4), 577 (MS 5).

James M R, The Western MSS in the Libr of Emmanuel Coll: a Descriptive Catalogue, Cambridge 1904, p 144 (MS 9); A Descriptive Catalogue of the MSS in the Libr of St John's Coll Cambridge, Cambridge 1913, p 227 (MS 10).

Catalogue of Additions to the MSS in the British Museum in the Years MDCCCC–MDCCCCV, London 1907, p 189 (MS 14).

Young J and P H Aitken, A Catalogue of the MSS in the Libr of the Hunterian Museum in the Univ of Glasgow, Glasgow 1908, pp 392 (MS 16), 419 (MS 17).

Editions. Maskell, 3.3 (MS 11).

Littlehales H, The Prymer, 2 pts, London 1891–92 (pt 1, text of MS 10; pt 2, collation of all MSS except 7, 14, 17).

Littlehales, The Prymer or Lay Folks' Prayer Book, EETS 105, 109, London 1895–97 (pt 1, text of MS 8; pt 2, commentary).

Facsimile. Littlehales H, Pages in Facsimile from A Layman's Prayer Book in Eng about 1400 AD, London 1890 (MS 13).

Selections. Kirchberger C, The Coasts of the Country, London nd, pp 60, 61, 62, 63.

Textual Matters. Harris-Matthews J M, Lay Devotions in Late Medieval Eng MSS, diss Cambridge Univ 1980, p 82 (relationship of MSS).

Krieg M F, A Computer-Assisted Edn of the Eng Primer, Fifteenth-Cent Stud 4(1981).105.

Language. Samuels M L, Some Applications of ME Dialectology, ESts 44(1963).85.

Sources and Literary Relations. Maskell, 3.i (origin and early development of primer).

Bishop E, On the Origin of the Prymer, in Littlehales edn, The Prymer, pt 2, p 1.

Brown C, A Study of the Miracle of Our Lady Told by Chaucer's Prioress, ChS 2s 45(1910).126 (detailed discussion of Eng primer).

Krapp G P, The Rise of Eng Literary Prose, N Y 1915, p 257.

Thurston H, ed, The Prymer, London 1923, p i (introd: sources and content).

Hargreaves H, The ME Primers and the Wycliffite Bible, MLR 51(1956).215 (psalms and readings connected with text of the later version of the Wycliffite Bible).

Other Problems. Deanesly M, The Lollard Bible, Cambridge 1920, pp 357, 368 (ecclesiastical suspicion of primer as a Lollard document).

Later Development and Influence. Tupper F, Chaucer's Bed's Head, MLN 30(1915).9 (Chaucer's use of the primer in his Hymn to Mary).

Birchenough E, Parallel Translation of the Sarum Prymer, BQR 7(1932).457; The Prymer in English, Libr 4s 18(1938).177 (primarily history of printed primer).

Hennig J, Primer-Versions of Liturgical Prayers, MLR 39(1944).325 (Cranmer's use of primers; problems of classifications); Primer-Versions of Liturgical Prayers: A Correction, MLR 40 (1945).131.

White H C, The Tudor Books of Private Devotion, Madison Wisc 1951, p 67.

Butterworth C C, The Eng Primers (1529–45), Phila 1953, p 1.

Wormald F and C E Wright, The Eng Library before 1700, London 1958, p 165 (on the destruction of illustrated service books and books of hours in accordance with the 1550 Act against Superstitious Books and Images).

Barrett A, The Prymer and Its Influence on 15-Cent Passion Lyrics, MÆ 44(1975).264.

General References. Gasquet F A, The Eve of the Reformation, London 1900, pp 223, 286.

Wordsworth C and H Littlehales, The Old Service Books of the Eng Church, London 1904, pp 13, 25, 32, 36, 60, 248.

Watson F, The Eng Grammar School to 1660, Cambridge 1908, p 28.

Deanesly M, The Lollard Bible, Cambridge 1920, pp 320, 337, 342, 394.

Hughes A, Horae, Laudate 3(1925).227 (analysis of content).

Swete H B, Church Services and Service-Books before the Reformation, rvsd by A J Maclean, London 1930, p 163.

Messenger R E, Ethical Teachings in the Latin Hymns of Medieval England, N Y 1930, p 59.

McGarry L, The Holy Eucharist in ME Homiletic and Devotional Verse, Washington D C 1936, p 179 n24.

Smith H M, Pre-Reformation England, London 1938, p 101.

Morison S, Eng Prayer Books, Cambridge 1945, p 33.

Ackerman G K, Old and ME Lit from the Beginnings to 1485, in A Hist of Eng Lit, ed H Craig, N Y 1950, p 98.

Pecheux M C, Aspects of the Treatment of Death in ME Poetry, Washington D C 1951, p 131.

Thurston H, Familiar Prayers, Their Origin and History, London 1953, pp 24, 33, 35 (on the Primer forms of the Pater Noster).

Dugmore C W, The Mass and the Eng Reformers, London 1958, p 73.

Dickens A G, The Eng Reformation, London 1964, p 12.

Cuming G J, A Hist of the Anglican Liturgy, London 1969, p 24.

Orme N, Eng Schools in the Middle Ages, London 1973, p 63.

Pearsall D, OE and ME Poetry, London 1977, p 135.

Bibliography. Hoskins E, Horae Beatae Mariae Virginis or Sarum and York Primers, London 1901, p xiv.

New CBEL, 1.497.

[226] LITANY.

MSS. Version A: 1, Balliol Oxford 354, f 209^{a–b} (1500–25); 2, BL Cotton Tib B.iii, ff 143^a–149^b (1400–25); 3, BL Sloane 1584, ff 16^b–18^a (1500–25); 4, Steeple Ashton Vicarage, last two flyleaves (1475–1500); 5, olim Ashburnham 49, present location unknown; 6, Longleat House (Marquis of Bath) 30, f 17^a (ca 1450); 7, Fitzwilliam Mus Camb 40–1950, ff 81^a–82^a (ca 1425); 8, Fitzwilliam Mus Camb 40–1951, ff 54^a–58^b (ca 1425); 9, Henry E Huntington HM.142, f 15^{a–b} (ca 1460); 10, Blairs 1, ff 96^a–98^b (1450–1500); *Version B:* 11, Bodl 29734 (Eng poet e.1), ff 49^a–50^a (1460–80); *Version C:* 12, Longleat House (Marquis of Bath) 30, f 40^a (ca 1450); 13, Henry E Huntington HM.142, ff 41^b–44^b (ca 1460); *Version D:* 14, Bodl 27691 (Bodley 939), ff 117^b–118^a (1475–1500);

Version E: 15, Bodl 3938 (Eng poet a.1), f 114ᵇ (1380–1400); 16, Camb Univ Dd.14.26, ff 42ᵇ–45ᵃ (ca 1400); 17, BL Harley 210, f 36ᵃ (1400–25); 18, BL Addit 37787, ff 15ᵇ–16ᵃ (1400–25); 19, Edinburgh Univ 114, f 1ᵇ (ca 1450); 20, Quaritch Sales Cat, 1931, Illuminated Manuscripts, item 82, and Cat 609, 1943, item 500. For the Hours of St George, a litany in MS Bodl 3615 (e Mus 35), ff ix–x (1475–1500), see Brown-Robbins, no 2902. PRINTS: *Version A*: 21, Wynkyn de Worde, Matyns of Our Lady, 1513, ff 126ᵇ–128ᵇ (STC, no 15914, A Devoute Orison); 22, Wynkyn de Worde, Horae beatissimae virginis marie, 1510 (STC, no 15908.5); 23, Wynkyn de Worde, Horae beatissimae virginis marie ad legitimum Sarisburiensis ecclesie ritum, 1519 (STC, no 15922); 24, Wynkyn de Worde, Horae beatissimae virginis marie ad consuetudinem ecclesie Sarisburiensis, 1526 (STC, no 15948); 25, Horae beatae marie virginis secundum usum Eboracensem, Rouen ca 1516, ff 170ᵃ–172ᵃ (York Minster MS XI.O.28; STC, no 16103, A Glorious Oryson).

Brown-Robbins, nos 1704, 1831, 2115; Brown-Robbins, Robbins-Cutler, nos 914, 3027.

MSS Commentary. A Catalogue of the MSS in the Cottonian Libr Deposited in the British Museum, London 1802, p 35 (MS 2).

A Catalogue of the Harleian MSS in the British Museum, London 1808, 1.66 (MS 17).

A Catalogue of the MSS Preserved in the Libr of the Univ of Cambridge, Cambridge 1856, 1.530 (MS 16).

Historical MSS Commission, 3rd Report of the Royal Commission on Historical MSS, London 1872, appendix, p 181 (MSS 6, 12; both in Longleat House 30).

Summary Cat, 2.789 (MS 15); 5.337 (MS 14), 679 (MS 11).

James M R, A Descriptive Catalogue of the Second Series of 50 MSS in the Collection of Henry Yates Thompson, Cambridge 1902, p 218 (MSS 7, 8).

Catalogue of Additions to the MSS in the British Museum in the Years MDCCCCVI–MDCCCCX, London 1912, p 140 (MS 18).

Borland C R, A Descriptive Catalogue of the Western Mediaeval MSS in Edinburgh Univ Libr, Edinburgh 1916, p 183 (MS 19).

de Ricci Census, 1.47 (MSS 9, 13; both from Huntington HM.142).

Serjeantson Index, p.255.

Schulz H C, ME Texts from the "Bement" MS, HLQ 3(1940).443 (MSS 9, 13; both from Huntington HM.142).

Mynors R A B, Catalogue of the MSS of Balliol Coll Oxf, Oxford 1963, p 352 (MS 1).

Ker Manuscripts, 2.113 (MS 10).

Guddat-Figge G, Catalogue of MSS Containing ME Romances, Munich 1976, p 269 (MS 15).

Editions. Simmons T F, The Lay Folks Mass Book, EETS 71, London 1879 (rptd 1968), p 200 (one stanza from PRINT 25).

Horstmann C, The Minor Poems of the Vernon MS, pt I, EETS 98, London 1892, p 21 (MS 15).

Flugel E, Liedersammlungen des XVI Jahrhunderts, besonders aus der Zeit Heinrichs VIII. III, Angl 26(1903).220 (MS 1).

Dyboski R, Songs, Carols and Other Miscellaneous Poems from the Balliol MS 354, Richard Hill's Commonplace-Book, EETSES 101, London 1907, p 62 (MS 1).

Patterson, pp 67 (reprint of Simmons edn), 68 (MS 11).

Wright T, Songs and Carols, PPS 23.76 (MS 11).

Borland C R, A Descriptive Catalogue of the Western Mediaeval MSS in Edinburgh Univ Libr, Edinburgh 1916, p 334 (MS 19).

Wordsworth C, Horae Eboracenses, Surtees Soc 132(1920).161 (MS 4).

Greene E E, Carols, p 212; 2nd edn, p 187 (MS 11).

Brown RLxvC, p 190 (MS 14).

Robbins R H, Private Prayers in ME Verse, SP 36(1939).471 (MS 3; stanza 6 only).

Schulz H C, ME Texts from the "Bement" MS, HLQ 3 (1940).460 (MS 13).

Baugh N S, A Worcestershire Miscellany, Phila 1956, p 102 (MS 18).

Gray D, A ME Illustrated Poem, in Medieval Stud for J A W Bennett, ed P L Heyworth, Oxford 1981, p 185 (MS 7, with variants from all MSS except MSS 9, 13).

General References. Wordsworth C and H Littlehales, The Old Service-Books of the Eng Church, London 1904, p 54.

Manning S, Wisdom and Number, Lincoln 1962, p 64.

Bibliography. Hoskins E, Horae Beatae Mariae Virginis, London 1901, nos 36, 41, 51, 73, 74.

[227] HOURS OF THE CROSS.

MSS. Verse: Version A: 1, National Libr of Scotland Advocates 18.7.21, ff 2ᵇ–3ᵃ (1372); *Version B*: 2, Bodl 21876 (Douce 302), ff 15ᵇ–16ᵃ (1425–50); *Version C*: 3, Bodl 3938 (Eng poet a.1), ff 115ᵇ–116ᵃ (1380–1400); 4, Gonville and Caius Camb 175, ff 118ᵇ–120ᵇ (15 cent); 5, BL Royal 19.B.v, f 103ᵃ–ᵇ (16 cent); 6, BL Addit 37787, ff 12ᵇ–13ᵇ (1400–25); *Version D*: 7, Camb Univ Addit 4120, ff 50ᵃ–55ᵃ (ca 1470); *Version E*: 8, Camb Univ Ee.1.12, ff 1ᵇ–2ᵇ (1475–1500); *Version F*: 9, St John's Camb 237, p 35 (1441); *Version G*: 10, BL Royal 2.B.x, f 1ᵃ (ca 1500); *Version H*: 11, Bodl

3894 (Fairfax 14), f 110ᵃ⁻ᵇ (1375–1400); 12, BL Cotton Vesp A.iii, ff 141ᵇ–142ᵇ (1400–25); 13, Göttingen Univ theol 107, ff 168ᵃ–169ᵃ (1350–1400); *Version I*: 14, York Minster XVI.K.6, ff 1ᵃ–2ᵇ (ca 1450); *Version J*: 15, BL Addit 37049, f 68ᵃ (1400–50); *Version K*: 16, Bodl 30605 (Misc Liturg 104), ff 49ᵃ–50ᵃ (ca 1340); *Version L*: 17, Bodl 2289 (Bodley 85), f 26ᵃ, etc (after 1410); 18, Bodl 12543 (Rawl C.699), f 24ᵃ, etc (after 1460); 19, Bodl 21820 (Douce 246), f 26ᵃ, etc (1400–25); 20, Bodl 21849 (Douce 275), f 15ᵃ, etc (ca 1400); 21, Queen's Coll Oxford 324, f 14ᵇ, etc (ca 1400–25); 22, Camb Univ Dd.11.82, f 16ᵇ, etc (ca 1400); 23, Emmanuel Camb 246, f 15ᵃ, etc (ca 1400); 24, St John's Camb 192, f 14ᵃ, etc (ca 1400); 25, BL Addit 36683, f 18ᵇ, etc (ca 1425); 26, Glasgow Univ Hunter 472, f 25ᵃ, etc (ca 1400); 27, Glasgow Univ Hunter 512, f 66ᵃ, etc (ca 1400); *Version M*: 28, BL Addit 17376, ff 182ᵃ–185ᵃ (1325–50).
Prose Version: 29, Taunton Castle Mus, ff i–ii (15 cent).

Brown-Robbins, nos 623, 1155, 1318, 1664, 1775, 2075, 3230, 3681; Brown-Robbins, Robbins-Cutler, nos 441, 701, 1770, 1963, 3499.

MSS Commentary. A Catalogue of the MSS in the Cottonian Libr Deposited in the British Museum, London 1802, 2.433 (MS 12).

Coxe H O, Catalogus Codicum MSS qui in Collegiis Aulisque Oxoniensibus Hodie Adservantur, Oxford 1852, 1.77 (MS 21).

A Catalogue of the MSS Preserved in the Libr of the Univ of Cambridge, Cambridge 1856, 1.477 (MS 22); Cambridge 1857, 2.11 (MS 8).

Catalogue of Additions to the MSS in the British Museum in the Years MDCCCXLVIII–MDCCCLIII, London 1868, p 11 (MS 28).

Macray W D, Catalogi Codicum Manuscriptorum Bibliothecae Bodleianae, Oxford 1878, 5(2).352 (MS 18).

Summary Cat, 2.291 (MS 17), 789 (MS 3); 4.566 (MS 19), 577 (MS 20), 584 (MS 2); 5.848 (MS 16).

James M R, The Western MSS in the Libr of Emmanuel Coll: A Descriptive Catalogue, Cambridge 1904, p 144 (MS 23); A Descriptive Catalogue of the MSS in the Libr of Gonville and Caius Coll, Cambridge 1907, p 199 (MS 4); A Descriptive Catalogue of the MSS in the Libr of St John's Coll Cambridge, Cambridge 1913, pp 227 (MS 24), 275 (MS 9).

Catalogue of Additions to the MSS in the British Museum in the Years MDCCCC–MDCCCCV, London 1907, pp 189 (MS 25), 324 (MS 15).

Young J and P H Aitken, A Catalogue of the MSS in the Libr of the Hunterian Museum in the Univ of Glasgow, Glasgow 1908, pp 392 (MS 26), 419 (MS 27).

Catalogue of Additions to the MSS in the British Museum in the Years MDCCCCVI–MDCCCCX, London 1912, p 140 (MS 6).

Warner G F and J P Gilson, Catalogue of the Western MSS in the Old Royal and King's Collections, London 1921, 1.48 (MS 10); 2.324 (MS 5).

Guddat-Figge G, Catalogue of MSS Containing ME Romances, Munich 1976, p 269 (MS 3).

Editions. Wright T, The Religious Poems of William de Shoreham, PPS 28, London 1849, p 82 (MS 28).

Morris R, Legends of the Holy Rood, EETS 46, London 1871, p 222 (MS 16).

Simmons T F, The Lay Folks Mass Book, EETS 71, London 1879 (rptd 1968), p 84 (MS 14).

Horstmann C, The Minor Poems of the Vernon MS, Pt I, EETS 98, London 1892, p 37 (MSS 3, 16).

Littlehales H, The Prymer or Lay Folks' Prayer Book, Pt I, EETS 105, London 1895, pp 15, 19, 22, 25, 28, 30, 34 (MS 22).

Konrath M, The Poems of William of Shoreham, Pt I, EETSES 86, London 1902, p 79 (MS 28).

Hauser W, With an O and an I, Angl 27(1904).312 (MS 3).

Patterson, p 66 (MS 14; 10 lines only).

Brown RLxivC, pp 50 (MS 16), 69 (MS 1).

Whiting E K, The Poems of John Audelay, EETS 184, London 1931, p 101 (MS 2).

Brown RLxvC, p 136 (MS 8).

Bowers R H, Palden's ME Prayer, N&Q 196 (1951).134 (MS 10; conflates Brown-Robbins, nos 1750 and 1770).

Baugh N S, A Worcestershire Miscellany, Phila 1956, p 98.

Doty B L, An Edn of Brit Mus MS Addit 37049; A Religious Miscellany, diss Michigan State Univ 1963 (MS 15).

Modernization. Watts N H, Love Songs of Sion: A Selection of Devotional Verse from Old Eng Sources, London 1924, p 111 (York Hours).

Source. Dreves G M and C Blume, edd, Analecta Hymnica, Leipzig 1898, 30.35 (Patris sapientia).

Wordsworth C, ed, Horae Eboracenses, Surtees Soc 122, Durham 1920, p xxiv (liturgical development and usage).

Literary Problems. Jacoby M, Vier ME geistliche Gedichte, Berlin 1890, p 29 (relation of Shoreham's version, MS 28, to other Hours).

Hardiment A, Liturgical and Other Influences on the Carols of James Ryman, diss Univ of London 1971, p 453 (argues that MS 8 version is a carol by Ryman).

General References. Manning S, Wisdom and Number, Lincoln 1962, p 73.

Woolf, pp 223, 232, 234, 242, 268, 362, 390.

Barrett A, The Prymer and Its Influences on 15-Cent Passion Lyrics, MÆ 44(1975).272.

Bibliography. Wilson E, A Descriptive Index of the Eng Lyrics in John of Grimestone's Preaching Book, Oxford 1973, p 1.

[228] STATIONS OF THE CROSS.

MS. Lambeth Palace 546, ff 1ᵃ–7ᵃ (1475–1500).

MS Commentary. James M R and C Jenkins, A Descriptive Catalogue of the MSS in the Libr of Lambeth Palace, Cambridge 1932, p 750.

[229] THE SENTENCE OF CURSING
(also THE GREAT SENTENCE and
THE GENERAL SENTENCE
OF EXCOMMUNICATION).

MSS. 1, Bodl 1963 (Bodley 110), ff 162ᵇ–166ᵇ (ca 1450); 2, Bodl 1986 (Bodley 123), ff 2ᵃ–6ᵇ (1480–90); 3, Bodl 2508 (Bodley 692), f 31ᵃ (1442–50); 4, Bodl 2727 (Bodley 736), ff 191ᵇ–193ᵃ (15 cent); 5, Bodl 3656 (e Mus 212), ff 1ᵃ–16ᵃ (15 cent); 6, Bodl 6951 (Ashmole 750), ff 15ᵃ–22ᵇ (1475–1500); 7, Bodl 11263 (Rawl A.381), ff 1ᵇ–2ᵇ (ca 1450); 8, Bodl 11755 (Rawl B.408), f 1ᵃ–ᵇ (1400–50); 9, Bodl 21634 (Douce 60), ff 161ᵃ–163ᵇ (1450–1500); 10, Bodl 21677 (Douce 103), ff 134ᵇ–136ᵇ (ca 1450); 11, Trinity Oxford E.86, ff 44ᵃ–47ᵃ (1475–1500); 12, Trinity Oxford F.7, ff 172ᵃ–176ᵇ (15 cent); 13, Camb Univ Ee.4.19, ff 85ᵇ–89ᵃ (14 cent); 14, Corpus Christi Camb 142, ff 121ᵃ–126ᵃ (15 cent); 15, Emmanuel Camb 248, ff 41ᵇ–45ᵇ (15 cent); 16, Pembroke Camb 285, ff 57ᵇ–60ᵃ (1400–25); 17, Sidney Sussex Camb 55, ff 52ᵇ–53ᵇ (ca 1450); 18, BL Arundel 130, f 118ᵃ (ca 1450); 19, BL Burney 356, ff 50ᵇ–53ᵃ, 53ᵃ–54ᵇ (1400–50); 20, BL Cotton Claudius A.ii, ff 123ᵇ–126ᵇ (1425–50); 21, BL Harley 335, ff 21ᵃ–24ᵇ (1400–50); 22, BL Harley 665, f 301ᵇ (1475–1500); 23, BL Harley 2383, ff 43ᵃ–45ᵃ, 46ᵃ–54ᵃ (1450–1475); 24, BL Harley 2399, ff 65ᵃ–68ᵇ (ca 1450); 25, BL Harley 4172, ff 10ᵇ–15ᵇ (1426); 26, BL Royal 8.B.xv, ff 186ᵇ–187ᵃ (14 cent); 27, BL Addit 11579, ff 141ᵃ–143ᵃ (ca 1350); 28, BL Addit 33784, ff 162ᵃ–170ᵃ (1400–25); 29, Lambeth Palace 172, ff 172ᵃ–173ᵇ (ca 1400); 30, Lambeth Palace, Register of Archbishop Henry Chichele, II, f 100ᵇ (1454); 31, Soc of Antiquaries London 285, ff 5ᵇ–8ᵇ (ca 1400); 32, Soc of Antiquaries London 687, pp 552–558 (ca 1400); 33, Dulwich Coll 22, f 28ᵃ–ᵇ (1475–1500); 34, Lincoln Cath 66, ff 24ᵇ–26ᵇ (ca 1450); 35, Lincoln Cath 229, ff 124ᵇ–126ᵇ (ca 1400); 36, Salisbury Cath 103, ff 9ᵇ–12ᵃ, 20ᵃ–22ᵇ (ca 1445); 37, Salisbury Cath 148, ff 19ᵇ–20ᵇ (ca 1450); 38, Worcester Cath F.172, ff 150ᵃ–154ᵃ

(1450–60); 39, York Minster XVI.M.4, pp 166–172 (1440–50); 40, Durham Univ Cosin V.iv.2, ff 128ᵇ–131ᵃ, 131ᵇ, 131ᵇ–133ᵇ (1477); 41, Eton Coll 98, ff 331ᵇ–332ᵃ (1400–50); 42, National Libr of Scotland Advocates 18.3.6, ff 7ᵇ–8ᵃ (14 cent); 43, Harvard Univ Widener 1 (olim Lawson), ff 101ᵇ–105ᵃ (1400–25); 44, Sotheby's Sale Cat, April 4, 1939, item 295; 45, Sotheby's Sale Cat, July 4–5, 1955, item 877. Two Middle Scots versions are extant: one in the Liber Sancti Terrenani Ecclesie de Arbuthnot (1491–92) and the other, promulgated by Archbishop Gavin Dunbar in 1525, in St Andrews Formulare and MS BL Cotton Caligula B.ii. PRINTS: 46, William Caxton, Quattuor Sermones, 1483–84 (STC, no 17957); 47, Manuale ad usum insignis ecclesie Sarum, Rouen 1510 (STC, 2nd edn, no 16140.7); Antwerp 1523 (STC, no 16145); Paris 1529 (STC, no 16148), 1530 (STC, no 16148.2).

Brown-Robbins, Robbins-Cutler, no 3372 (riming lines prefacing and concluding the text in MS 20).

MSS Commentary. A Catalogue of the MSS in the Cottonian Libr Deposited in the British Museum, London 1802, p 188 (MS 20).

A Catalogue of Harleian MSS in the British Museum, London 1808, 1.201 (MS 21), 400 (MS 22); 2.675 (MS 23), 685 (MS 24); 3.121 (MS 25).

Black W H, A Descriptive, Analytical, and Critical Catalogue of the MSS Bequeathed unto the Univ of Oxford by Elias Ashmole, Oxford 1845, p 357 (MS 6).

Coxe H O, Catalogus Codicum MSS qui in Collegiis Aulisque Hodie Adservantur, Oxford 1852, 2.3 (MS 12), 34 (MS 11).

A Catalogue of the MSS Preserved in the Libr of the Univ of Cambridge, Cambridge 1857, 2.126 (MS 13).

Macray W D, Catalogi Codicum Manuscriptorum Bibliothecae Bodleianae, Oxford 1862, 5(1).380 (MS 7).

Royal MSS Commission. 5th Report of Royal Commission on Historical MSS, London 1876, appendix, p 305 (MS 43).

A Catalogue of the Libr of the Cathedral Church of Salisbury, London 1880, pp 21 (MS 36), 27 (MS 37).

Catalogue of MSS in the British Museum, ns, vol I, London 1890, Pt I: Arundel MSS, p 30 (MS 18); Pt II: Burney MSS, p 95 (MS 19).

Catalogue of Additions to the MSS in the British Museum in the Years MDCCCLXXXVIII–MDCCCXCIII, London 1894, p 109.

James M R, A Descriptive Catalogue of the MSS in the Libr of Sidney Sussex Coll Cambridge, Cambridge 1895, p 39 (MS 17); The Western MSS in the Libr of Emmanuel Coll: A Descriptive Catalogue, Cambridge 1904, p 146 (MS 15); A Descriptive Catalogue of the MSS in the Libr of Pembroke Coll Cambridge, Cambridge 1905, p 258 (MS 16); A Descriptive Catalogue of the MSS in the Libr of Corpus Christi Coll Cambridge, Cambridge 1912, 1.327 (MS 14).

Summary Cat, 2.135 (MS 1), 147 (MS 2), 402 (MS 3), 516 (MS 4), 722 (MS 5); 4.508 (MS 9), 522 (MS 10).

Floyer J K, Catalogue of MSS Preserved in the Chapter Libr of Worcester Cathedral, Oxford 1906, p 96 (MS 38).

Warner G F and J P Gilson, Catalogue of Western MSS in the Old Royal and King's Collections, London 1921, 1.225 (MS 26).

Wooley R M, Catalogue of the MSS of Lincoln Cathedral Chapter Libr, Oxford 1927, pp 35 (MS 34), 164 (MS 35).

James M R and C Jenkins, A Descriptive Catalogue of the MSS in the Libr of Lambeth Palace, Cambridge 1931, p 270 (MS 29).

Pantin W A, The Eng Church in the 14 Cent, Cambridge 1955, p 277 (MS 19).

Wakelin M F, The MSS of John Mirk's Festial, Leeds SE 1(1967).107 (MS 7).

Ker Manuscripts, 1.42 (MS 33), 309 (MS 31), 314 (MS 32); 2.711 (MS 41).

Watson A G, Catalogue of Dated and Datable MSS, ca 700–1600, in the Dept of MSS, the British Libr, London 1979, 1.142 (MS 25).

Editions. Lyndwood W, Provinciale, seu Constitutiones Angliae, Oxford 1679, app, p 73 (MS 41).

State Papers of Henry VIII, London 1836, 4(4).417 (Middle Scots version: St Andrews Formulare).

Forbes A P, Liber Ecclesie beati Terrenani de Arbuthnott: Missale secundum Usum Ecclesiae Sancti Andreae in Scotia, Burntisland 1864, p lxx.

Peacock E, Instructions for Parish Priests by John Myrc, EETS 31, London 1868, p 21 (MS 9); rvsd F J Furnivall, 1902, p 65 (MS 20).

Henderson W G, Manuale et processionale ad usum insignis Ecclesiae Eboracensis, Surtees Soc 63 (1875).86* (PRINT 47, Rouen 1510 edn), 119 (MS 13).

Royal Commission on Historical MSS, 5th Report, London 1876, app, p 305 (MS 43).

Maskell, 3.309 (PRINT 47, Paris 1530; STC, no 16148.2).

Brandeis A, Jacob's Well, EETS 115, pt 1, London 1900, pp 13, 55.

Wordsworth C, Ceremonies and Processions of the Cathedral Church of Salisbury, Cambridge 1901, pp 44 (MS 37), 245 (PRINT 47, Antwerp 1523 edn).

Clark A, The Eng Register of Godstow Nunnery, near Oxford, Pt 1, EETS 129, London 1905, p 1 (MS 8).

Patrick D, Statutes of the Scottish Church, 1225–1559, Publs of the Scottish Hist Soc 54(1907).5 (Middle Scots version: Liber Ecclesie beati Terrenani).

Pothmann A, Zur Textkritik von John Mirk's Pars Oculi, Bonn 1914, p 49 (MS 19).

Owst G R, Preaching in Medieval England, Cambridge 1926, p 359 (excerpts from MSS 7, 19, 42).

Donaldson G and C Macrae, St Andrews Formulare, Stair Soc 7(1942).268 (Middle Scots version).

Jacob E F, The Register of Henry Chichele, Archbishop of Canterbury 1414–43, vol 3, Canterbury and York Soc 46, Oxford 1945, p 257.

Collins A J, Manuale ad Usum Percelebris Ecclesie Sarisburiensis, Henry Bradshaw Soc 91, London 1960, pp xv (influence of Oculus Sacerdotis on the Sarum Manual), xvii, xxi (printed editions).

Kristensson G, John Mirk's Instructions for Parish Priests, Lund SE 49(1974).104 (MS 9).

Blake N F, Quattuor Sermones, ME Texts 2, Heidelberg 1975, p 81 (PRINT 46).

Textual Matters. Pothmann edn, p 20.

Pickering O S, Notes on the Sentence of Cursing in ME; or, A Case for the Index of ME Prose, Leeds SE 12(1981).229 (interrelations of texts and sources).

Sources and Background. Wilkins D, ed, Concilia Magnae Britanniae et Hiberniae AD 466–1717, London 1737, 2.696 (Constitutions of John Stratford), 413 (Oculus Sacerdotis).

Hyland F E, Excommunication Its Nature, Historical Development and Effects, Washington D C 1928.

Cheney C R, Eng Synodalia of the 13 Cent, London 1941, pp 112, 115, 147.

Boyle L E, The Oculus Sacerdotis and Some Other Works of William of Pagula, Trans of the Royal Historical Soc 5s 5(1955).87.

Powicke F M and C R Cheney, Councils and Synods, with Other Documents Relating to the Eng Church, II, AD 1205–1313, Oxford 1964, 1.106 (Constitutions of Stephan Langton); 2.792 (Constitutions of Boniface), 848, 905 (Constitutions of John Peckham).

General References. Wordsworth C and H Littlehales, The Old Service-Books of the Eng Church, London 1904, pp 21, 216, 270.

Owst edn, pp 265, 296.

Smith H M, Pre-Reformation England, London 1938, p 129.

Jacob E F, Archbishop Henry Chichele, London 1967, p 66 n3.

Bibliography. Duff E G, 15-Cent Eng Books, Oxford 1917, no 299, p 84.

STC, no 2.82 (Manuals), 85 (Processionals).

[230] HAVE MERCY UPON ME O LORD.

MSS. 1, BL Addit 32427, f 141ᵃ (ca 1470); 2, Salisbury Cath 152, f 159ᵇ (ca 1460).

Robbins-Cutler, no 1123.8.

MSS Commentary. A Catalogue of the Libr of the Cathedral Church of Salisbury, London 1880, p 29.

Catalogue of Additions to the MSS in the British Museum in the Years MDCCCLXXXII–MDCCCLXXXVII, London 1889, p 116 (MS 1).

Editions. Kingdon H T, An Early Vernacular Service, Wiltshire Archaeological and Natural Hist Magazine 18(1879).65 (facsimile opp p 66).

Wordsworth C and H Littlehales, The Old Service-Books of the Eng Church, London 1904, p 51.

[231] THE ROSARY.

MS. Exeter Oxford 47, f 127ᵇ (1475–1525).

MS Commentary. Coxe H O, Catalogus Codicum MSS qui in Collegiis Aulisque Oxoniensibus Hodie Adservantur, Oxford 1852, 1.17.

5. General Directions

[232] DIRECTIONS FOR DEACONS AND SUBDEACONS AT CHURCH SERVICES.

MS. BL Sloane 1584, ff 2ᵃ–4ᵃ, 4ᵇ–5ᵃ, 5ᵃ–6ᵃ (1500–25).

Authorship. Dickens A G, The Eng Reformation, London 1964, p 4.

VI. Tracts on the Duties of the Clergy

[233] INSTRUCTIONS FOR PARISH PRIESTS.

MSS. 1, Bodl 3829 (Greaves 57), ff 1ᵃ–33ᵇ (1475–1500); 2, Bodl 10022 (Tanner 196), ff 241ᵃ–243ᵇ (ca 1500; lines 1765–1934 only); 3, Bodl 21634 (Douce 60), ff 147ᵃ–188ᵇ (ca 1450; in same hand as MS 4); 4, Bodl 21677 (Douce 103), ff 119ᵃ–164ᵇ (ca 1450; in same hand as MS 3); 5, Camb Univ Ff.5.48, ff 2ᵃ–8ᵃ (1475–1500; lines 57–185, 274–301, 643–848 only); 6, BL Cotton Cladius A. ii, ff 127ᵃ–154ᵇ (1425–50); 7, BL Royal 17.C.xvii, ff 67ᵃ–80ᵃ (1400–25); 8, Trinity Dublin 211, f 226ᵃ⁻ᵇ (1450–1500; abstract corresponding to lines 410–525). The poem on freemasonry is in: 9, BL Royal 17.A.i, ff 1ᵃ–32ᵇ (1400–25).

Brown-Robbins, nos 961, 1062; Robbins-Cutler, nos 1326.5, 2708.5, and 3305.6 (Instructions); Brown-Robbins, Robbins-Cutler, no 4149 (poem on freemasonry).

MSS Commentary. Catalogi Codicum Manuscriptorum Bibliothecae Bodleianae Pars Quarta, Oxford 1855, p 634 (MS 2).

A Catalogue of the MSS Preserved in the Libr of the Univ of Cambridge, Cambridge 1857, 2.505 (MS 5).

AELeg 1881, p cxiii (MS 6), cxix (MS 3).

Summary Cat, nos 2.749 (MS 1); 4.508 (MS 3), 522 (MS 4).

Warner G F and J P Gilson, Catalogue of Western MSS in the Old Royal and King's Collections in the British Museum, London 1921, 2.213 (MS 9), 243 (MS 7).

Zutphen J P W M van, ed, A Litil Tretys on the Seven Deadly Sins by Richard Lavynham, O Carm, Rome 1956, p xliii (MS 3).

Wakelin M F, The MSS of John Mirk's Festial, Leeds SE ns 1(1967).94 (MS 6), 104 (MS 3).

Kristensson edn, p 13 (all MSS except MSS 8 and 9).

Editions. Halliwell-Phillipps J O, The Early Hist of Freemasonry in England, London 1840, p 10 (MS 9).

Peacock E, Instructions for Parish Priests by John Myrc, EETS 31, London 1868; rvsd F J Furnivall, 1902.

Speth W G, Quattuor Coronatorum Antigrapha, Margate 1889, 1, pt I (facsimile of ff 127ᵃ, 180ᵃ, and transcription of lines 1–4, 264–329, of MS 6).

Whymper H J, Constituciones Artis Gemetriae Secundum Euclydem, London and Boston 1889 (transcript and facsimile of MS 9 with corrections of Halliwell-Phillipps).

Jones G P and D Hamer, The Medieval Mason, Manchester 1933, p 261 (MS 9); The Two Earliest Masonic MSS, Manchester 1938, pp 104 (MS 9), 139 (parallel passages from Mirk).

Downing J, A Critical Edn of Cambridge Univ MS Ff.5.48, diss Univ of Washington 1969 (MS 5).

Kristensson G, John Mirk's Instructions for Parish Priests, Lund SE 49(1974).67 (MS 6), 177 (MS 7); introd, pp 9 (previous works, author, sources, present edn), 10 (MSS), 23 (relationship of MSS), 27 (language), 55 (meter), 57 (dialects of MSS; crit P Heath, EHR 91.636; B Wallner, ESts 58.452; M F Wakelin, RES 28.199; B Lindstrom, SN

50.146; K Bitterling, Angl 96.225; A Hudson, Yearbook of Eng Stud 7.202).

Bitterling K, An Abstract of John Mirk's Instructions for Parish Priests, N&Q ns 24(1977).146 (MS 8).

Selections. Emerson O F, A ME Reader, N Y 1905, p 119.

Cook A S, A Literary ME Reader, Boston 1915, p 287.

Poole H, ed, Gould's Hist of Freemasonry, London 1951, 1.255 (excerpt from MS 9).

Kaiser R, Medieval Eng, 3rd edn, Berlin 1958, p 453.

Modernizations. Watts N H, Love Songs of Sion; A Selection of Devotional Verse from Old Eng Sources, London 1924, p 22.

Corrigan F X, ME Readings in Translation, Boston 1963, p 138.

Textual Matters. Pothmann A, Zur Textkritik von John Mirk's Pars Oculi, Bonn 1914 (affiliations of all MSS except MS 1).

Pickering O S, Notes on the Sentence of Cursing in ME; or, A Case for the Index of ME Prose, Leeds SE 12(1981).229.

Language. Rynall A, The Rivalry of Scandinavian and Native Synonyms in ME Especially Taken and Nimen, Lund SE 13(1948).201.

Authorship. DNB, 13.497 (sv Mirk, John).

Source. Boyle L E, The Oculus Sacerdotis and Some Other Works of William of Pagula, Trans of the Royal Historical Soc 5s 5(1955).86.

General References. Ten Brink, 3.4; Brandl, §72, p 660; Schofield, p 395.

Gasquet F A, Parish Life in Medieval England, London 1906, pp 148, 153, 164, 199.

Mosher J A, The Exemplum in the Early Religious and Didactic Lit of England, N Y 1911, pp 107, 113, 138.

Manning B L, People's Faith in the Age of Wycliff, Cambridge 1919, pp 33, 34, 37, and passim.

Deanesly M, The Lollard Bible, Cambridge 1920, p 343.

Owst G R, Preaching in Medieval England, Cambridge 1926, pp 32, 35, 46, 55, 165, 167, 172, 175, and passim; The People's Sunday Amusements in the Preaching of Mediaeval England, Holborn Rev ns 17(1926).43; Literature and Pulpit in Medieval England, Cambridge 1933, p 416.

McGarry L, The Holy Eucharist in ME Homiletic and Devotional Verse, Washington D C 1936, pp 10 n32, 22 n71, 83 n90, 130 n105, 182 n27, 196 n61.

Pfander Manuals, p 252.

Smith H M, Pre-Reformation England, London 1938, p 98.

Robbins R H, Popular Prayers in ME Verse, MP 36(1939).343 n25.

Bennett OHEL, pp 19, 119.

Baugh LHE, p 205.

Coulton G G, Five Centuries of Religion, Cambridge 1950, 4.130.

McNeill J T, A Hist of the Cure of Souls, N Y 1951, p 156.

Pecheux M C, Aspects of the Treatment of Death in ME Poetry, Washington D C 1951, p 26.

Bloomfield SDS, p 210.

Douie D L, Archbishop Pecham, Oxford 1952, p 140.

Pantin, p 214.

Schlauch M, Eng Medieval Lit and Its Social Foundations, Warsaw 1956, p 173.

Hussey M, Petitions of the Pater Noster in Mediaeval Eng Lit, MÆ 27(1958).10.

Dugmore C W, The Mass and the Eng Reformers, London 1958, pp 70, 73.

Ackerman R W, Backgrounds to Medieval Eng Lit, N Y 1966, p 90.

Aarts F G A M, ed, The Pater Noster of Richard Ermyte, The Hague 1967, pp cvii, cix n5; The Pater Noster in Medieval Eng Lit, Papers in Lang and Lit 5(1969).9.

Priscandaro M T, ME Eucharistic Verse: Its Imagery, Symbolism, and Typology, diss St John's Univ 1975, p 25.

Pearsall D, Old Eng and ME Poetry, London 1977, p 243.

Aston M, Lollardy and Literacy, History 62 (1977).350.

Dickinson J C, The Later Middle Ages, London 1979, p 275.

Coleman J, Eng Lit in Hist 1350–1400; Medieval Readers and Writers, London 1981, p 184.

Bibliography. New CBEL, 1.488, 497, 687, 692.

[234] THE OFFICE OF A BISHOP OR PRIEST.

MS. Worcester Cath F.172, f 33ᵃ (1450–1500).

Jolliffe, p 131, no N.8.

MS Commentary. Floyer J F and J G Hamilton, Catalogue of MSS Preserved in the Chapter Libr of Worcester Cathedral, Oxford 1906, p 96.

Doyle A I, An Unrecognized Piece of Pierce the Ploughman's Creed and Other Work by Its Scribe, Spec 34(1959).430 (scribe of Worcester MS).

[235] THE ORDER OF MELCHISEDECH.

MS. Camb Univ Hh.3.13, ff 112^b–113^a (1475–1500).

Brown-Robbins, no 4244 (lists [235] and [202] as one poem).
MS Commentary. A Catalogue of the MSS Preserved in the Libr of the Univ of Cambridge, Cambridge 1868, 3.280.

2. Works of Philosophical Instruction

I. Translations of Cicero

[236] CICERO'S OF OLD AGE and OF FRIENDSHIP.

(Note: For supplementary bibliography, see VII [44] in Manual, 3.873.)

MS. Bodl 3774 (Ashmole 861), f 78^a–b (17 cent; modernized extracts from Caxton's Of Old Age and Of Friendship). PRINT: William Rastell, ca 1530 (STC, no 5275).
MS Commentary. Black W H, A Descriptive, Analytical, and Critical Catalogue of MSS Bequeathed unto the Univ of Oxford by E Ashmole, Oxford 1845, p 687.
Facsimile Edition. Of Old Age, Of Friendship by Marcus Tulius Cicero. William Caxton 1481, The Eng Experience, no 861, Amsterdam and Norwood N J 1977.
Selections. Blake N F, Caxton's Own Prose, London 1873, p 120 (Prologues and Epilogues of Old Age, Of Friendship, and Declamation of Noblesse).
Literary Criticism. Fahrenbach W J, Vernacular Translations of Classical Lit in Late-Medieval Britain: Eight Translations Made Directly from Latin between 1400 and 1525, diss Univ of Toronto 1976, chap 4.
Authorship. Clark C, Caxton's Tullius of Old Age, TLS August 22 1952, p 549 (ascription of authorship to Worcester).
McFarlane K B, William Worcester, A Preliminary Survey, in Studies Presented to Sir Hilary Jenkinson, ed J Conway Davies, London 1957, p 196.
Emden A B, Biographical Register of the Univ of Oxford to A D 1500, Oxford 1959, 3.1877 (Tiptoft), 2086 (Worcester).
Davis N, The Epistolary Usages of William Worcester, in Medieval Lit and Civilization Studies in Memory of G N Garmonsway, ed D A Pearsall and R A Waldron, London 1969, p 249.

Orme N, The Education of a Courtier, in Eng Court Culture in the Later Middle Ages, ed V J Scattergood and J W Sherburne, N Y 1983, pp 71 (Tiptoft), 72 (Worcester), 77, 81, 179 (all Tiptoft).
Textual Matters. Duff E G, Caxton's Tully of Old Age and Friendship, London 1912 (textual variants).
General References. Dibdin T F, Typographical Antiquities, London 1810, 1.119; 3(1816).370.
Gasquet F A, The Old Eng Bible and Other Essays, London 1897, p 286 (on Worcester).
de Ricci S, A Census of Caxtons, Oxford 1909, no 31.
Lathrop H B, The Translations of John Tiptoft, MLN 41(1926).496.
Weiss R, The Libr of John Tiptoft, Earl of Worcester, BQR 8(1936).157, 234; 8(1937).343.
Bennett H S, The Production and Dissemination of Vernacular MSS in the 15 Cent, Libr 5s 1(1946–47).176.
Kendrick T D, British Antiquity, London 1950, p 29 (on Worcester).
Bolgar R R, The Classical Heritage and Its Beneficiaries, Cambridge 1954, p 498.
Mitchell R J, John Free: from Bristol to Rome in the 15 Cent, London 1955, p 102.
Schirmer W F, Der engl Frühhumanismus, Tübingen 1963, p 106.
Weiss, Humanism in England during the 15 Cent, Oxford 1967, p 112.
McFarlane K B, The Nobility of Later Medieval England, Oxford 1973, pp 233, 242.
Hay D, England and the Humanities in the 15 Cent, in Itinerarium Italicum: the Profile of the Italian Renaissance in the Mirror of Its European Transformation (dedicated to P O Kristeller), ed H A Oberman with T A Brady, Stud in Medieval and Renaissance Thought 14(1975).330, 337.
Blake N F, Caxton: England's First Publisher, N Y 1976, pp 82, 112, 119, 170, 175, 193.

William Caxton: an Exhibition to Commemorate the Quincentary of the Introd of Printing into England, London 1976, p 50, no 43.

Green R F, Poets and Princepleasers, Toronto 1980,

pp 8, 109, 153, 157 (Tiptoft); 19, 27, 29, 205 (Worcester).

Bibliography. New CBEL, 1.693, 806 (Worcester). Manual, 3.873 (VII [44]).

II. The Tradition of Boethius

1. Translation of the
Consolation of Philosophy

[237] JOHN WALTON'S
BOETHIUS TRANSLATION.

MSS. 1, Bodl 3588 (e Mus 53), ff 1ᵃ–112ᵇ (1425–50); 2, Bodl 14643 (Rawl poet 151), ff 1ᵃ–108ᵇ (1450–1500); 3, Bodl 21674 (Douce 100), ff 1ᵃ–105ᵇ (1450–1500); 4, Balliol 316A, ff 2ᵃ–109ᵇ (1400–25); 5, Balliol 316B, ff 2ᵃ–113ᵇ (1400–25); 6, Christ Church Oxford 151, ff 1ᵃ–126ᵃ (1400–50); 7, New Oxford 319, ff 1ᵃ–104ᵇ (1400–50); 8, Trinity Oxford 21, ff 4ᵃ–107ᵇ (1400–25); 9, Camb Univ Gg.iv.18, ff 1ᵃ–112ᵇ (1400–50); 10, Camb Univ Addit 3573, ff 1ᵃ–92ᵇ (ca 1440); 11, St John's Camb 196, ff 1ᵃ–80ᵇ (1475–1500); 12, Fitzwilliam Mus McClean 184, ff 1ᵃ–119ᵃ (1475–1500); 13, BL Harley 43, ff 4ᵃ–86ᵇ (1500–10); 14, BL Harley 44, ff 2ᵃ–102ᵃ (1475–1500); 15, BL Royal 18. A.xiii, ff 1ᵃ–113ᵇ (1400–50); 16, BL Sloane 554, ff 1ᵃ–52ᵇ (1450–1500); 17, Soc of Antiquaries London 134, ff 283ᵇ–297ᵇ (1400–50); 18, Durham Univ Cosin V.ii.15, ff 2ᵃ–112ᵇ (1400–50); 19, Lincoln Cath 103, ff 3ᵃ–100ᵇ (1400–50); 20, Royal Libr Copenhagen Thottske Saml.304, 2°, ff 1ᵃ–75ᵇ (1400–50); 21, Newberry Chicago Gen Add 8, f 36ᵃ (1480); 22, Rosenbach Foundation Phila 1083/30 (olim Phillipps 1099), art 2, ff 78ᵃ–175ᵇ (1475–1525).

With lines 83–90 of the Prologue only: 23, Bodl 3354 (Arch Selden B.24), f 119ᵃ (1475–1500); 24, BL Harley 2251, f 152ᵇ (1450–1500); 25, BL Royal 20.B.xv, f 1ᵇ (1400–25); 26, BL Addit 29729, f 288ᵇ (16 cent); 27, National Libr of Scotland Advocates 1.1.6, f 75ᵇ (1568); 28, John Rylands Manchester Latin 201, f 227ᵃ (1450–1500); 29, Yale Univ 163 (olim Wagstaff 9, Petworth 8), f 29ᵃ (15 cent).

Other brief extracts: 30, Buhler 17, flyleaf 5ᵇ (15 cent); 31, BL Royal 9.C.ii, f 119ᵇ (1475–1525); PRINT: 32, Rychard T, The Boke of Comfort, Tavistock 1525 (STC, no 3200; four 8-line stanzas appear as an envoy at the end).

Brown-Robbins, Robbins-Cutler, nos 736, 1254, 1597, 2820; Robbins-Cutler, no 856.5.

MSS Commentary. A Catalogue of the Harleian MSS in the British Museum, London 1808, 1.12 (MSS 13, 14); 2.578 (MS 24).

Coxe H O, Catalogus Codicum qui in Collegiis Aulisque Oxoniensibus Hodie Adservantur, Oxford 1852, pt 1, p 114 (MS 7); pt 2, p 10 (MS 8).

A Catalogue of the MSS Preserved in the Libr of the Univ of Cambridge, Cambridge 1858, 3.164 (MS 9).

Kitchin G W, Catalogus Codicum MSS qui in Bibliotheca Aedis Christi Apud Oxonienses Adservantur, Oxford 1867, p 52 (MS 6).

Catalogue of Additions to the MSS in the British Museum in the Year 1864–1875, London 1877, 2.696 (MS 26).

Wylie J H, Walton's Version of Boethius, Athen May 7, 1892, p 600 (notice of MS 20).

Summary Cat, 2.614 (MS 23), 693 (MS 1); 3.335 (MS 2); 4.521 (MS 3).

Hammond, p 342 (MS 23).

James M R, A Descriptive Catalogue of the MSS in the Libr of St John's Coll Cambridge, Cambridge 1913, p 231 (MS 11); A Descriptive Catalogue of the McClean Collection of MSS in the Fitzwilliam Museum, Cambridge 1912, p 354 (MS 12).

Warner G F and J P Gilson, British Museum Catalogue of Western MSS in the Old Royal and King's Collections, London 1921, 1.267 (MS 15), 291 (MS 31); 2.367 (MS 25).

Wooley R M, Catalogue of the MSS of Lincoln Cathedral Chapter Libr, Oxford 1927, p 66 (MS 19).

de Ricci Census, 2.1902 (MS 29).

An Exhibition of 15-Cent MSS and Books in Honor of the Birth of Chaucer, Rosenbach Company, Phila 1940, p 15 (MS 22).

Bühler C F, The Newberry Libr MS of the Dictes and Sayings of the Philosophers, Angl 74 (1957).281 (MS 21).

Faye C U and W H Bond, Supplement to the Census of Medieval and Renaissance MSS in the U S and Canada, N Y 1962, p 148 (MS 21).

Mynors R A B, Catalogue of the MSS of Balliol Coll Oxford, Oxford 1963, p 333 (MSS 4, 5).

Bolton D K, MSS and Commentaries on Boethius, De Consolatione Philosophiae, in England in the Middle Ages, thesis Oxford Univ 1965, p 310.

Ker Manuscripts, 1.306 (MS 17).

Norton-Smith J, ed, James I of Scotland The Kingis Quair, Oxford 1971, p xxxi (MS 23).

Dwyer R A, The Newberry's Unknown Revision of Walton's Boethius, Manuscripta 17(1973).27 (MS 21).

Seymour M C, The MSS of Hoccleve's Regiment of Princes, Edinburgh Biblio Soc Trans 4(1974).292 (MS 22).

Blayney M S, ed, 15-Cent Eng Translations of Alain Chartier's Le Traité de L'espérance and Le Quadrilogue Invectif, EETS 281, Oxford 1980, 2.9 (MS 21).

Editions. Schuemmer L, John Waltons metrische Übersetzung der Consolatio Philosophiae, BSEP 6, Bonn 1914 (MS 15 basis of text; 346 stanzas only).

Science M, Boethius: De Consolatione Philosophiae translated by John Walton, EETS 170, London 1927, p 1 (MS 19 basis of text); introd, pp vii (description of MSS and PRINT 32), xxi (relationship of MSS), xlii (date and authorship), l (method of translation), lxii (language), lxvi (versification) (crit N&Q 154.467; H Buckhurst, RES 5.341; TLS Oct 10 1929, p 780; H Flasdieck, LfGRP 50.18; A Ekwall, AnglB 40.228; A Kirkman, MLR 25.197; J R Hulbert, MLN 45.334).

Selections. Todd H J, Illustrations of the Lives and Writings of Gower and Chaucer, London 1810, p xxxii.

[Pickering's] Aldine Edn of the British Poets, London 1845 (rvsd edn 1866), 6.296 (MS 23).

Blades W, The Life and Typography of William Caxton, England's First Printer, London 1863, 2.68.

Wülker R P, Ae Lesebuch, Halle a/S 1880, 2.56.

Stewart H F, Boethius, London 1891 (rptd N Y 1974), p 229.

Flugel E, Neuenglisches Lesebuch, Halle a/S 1895, p 99 (excerpt from PRINT 32).

Murdoch J B, ed, The Bannatyne MS, Glasgow 1896, 2.204 (MS 27).

Skeat W W, ed, The Complete Works of Geoffrey Chaucer, Oxford 1899, 1.47 (MS 23); 2.xvi (MS 15).

Brown Reg, 1.363 (MS 31).

Fawtier E C and R, From Merlin to Shakespeare, JRLB 5(1919).389 (MS 28).

Brusendorff A, The Chaucer Tradition, Copenhagen 1925 (rptd Oxford 1967), p 436 (MS 25).

Hammond E P, Eng Verse between Chaucer and Surrey, Durham 1927, p 39.

Science edn, p xliii (Rychard's Envoy, PRINT 32).

Ritchie W T, ed, The Bannatyne MS Written in Tyme of Pest, PSTS 22, Edinburgh 1928, p 186 (MS 27).

Brown RLxvC, p 259 (MS 31).

Greene R L, The Port of Peace: Not Death But God, MLN 69(1954).307 (MS 31).

Bühler C F, A ME Stanza on The Commonwealth and the Need for Wisdom, Eng Lang Notes 2(1964).4 (MS 30).

Brewer D, The Critical Heritage, London 1978, p 61 (introd, lines 33–64).

Gray D, ed, The Oxford Book of Late Medieval Verse and Prose, Oxford 1985, p 266.

Language. Hittmair R, Das Zeitwort Do in Chaucers Prosa, WBEP 51(1923).112.

Aldridge M V, An Annotated Glossary, with Introd, to John Walton's Translation of Boethius, De Consolatione Philosophiae (1410), thesis Oxford Univ 1967.

Authorship. DNB, 20.735 (sv Walton, John).

Emden A B, A Biographical Register of the Univ of Oxford to A D 1500, Oxford 1959, 3.484 (Rychard), 1975 (Walton).

Sources and Literary Relations. Cossack A, Über die ae metrische Bearbeitung von Boethius De Consolatione Philosophiae, Leipzig 1889 (Walton's use of Chaucer).

Fehlauer F, Die engl Übersetzungen von Boethius De Consolatione Philosophiae, Berlin 1909, p 48.

Dolson G B, The Consolation of Philosophy of Boethius in Eng Lit, diss Cornell Univ 1926; published abstract, Ithaca nd.

Minnis A, Aspects of the Medieval French and Eng Traditions of the De Consolatione Philosophiae, in Boethius, His Life, Thought, and Influence, ed M Gibson, Oxford 1981, p 312 (Walton's sources).

Kaylor N H, John Walton's 1410 Verse Trans of the De Consolatione Philosophiae in the Context of Its Medieval Tradition, 15-Cent Stud 6(1983).121.

Literary Criticism. Pearsall D, The Eng Chaucerians, in Chaucer and Chaucerians, ed D S Brewer, Univ Alabama 1966, p 225.

Hertzig M J, The Early Eng Recension and Continuity of Certain ME Texts in the 16 Cent, diss Univ of Penn 1973, p 332 (Rychard's modernization of Walton and use of Chaucer).

Fahrenbach W J, Vernacular Translations of Classical Lit in Late-Medieval Britain: Eight Translations Made Directly from Latin between 1400 and 1525, diss Univ of Toronto 1976, chap 1 (Walton's method as a translator).

Copeland R, Translation and Literary Style in Medieval Eng Religious Texts, diss Univ of California (Berkeley) 1983.

General References. Warton T, Hist of Eng Poetry, ed W C Hazlitt, London 1871, 3.39.

Ten Brink, 2.220.

Wülcker, p 188.

Hammond E P, Boethius: Chaucer: Walton: Lydgate, MLN 41(1926).534 (different interpretations of Book 2, Meter 5).

Lathrop H B, Translations from the Classics into Eng from Caxton to Chapman 1477–1620, Univ of Wisc Stud in Lang and Lit 35, Madison 1933 (rptd N Y 1967), pp 53, 255.

Patch H R, The Tradition of Boethius, N Y 1935, p 73.

Bennett OHEL, pp 109, 126, 127, 153, 154, 300.

Baugh LHE, p 301.

Schlauch M, Eng Medieval Lit and Its Social Foundations, Warsaw 1956, p 299.

Pearsall D, Old Eng and ME Poetry, London 1977, pp 224, 238, 298.

Green R F, Poets and Princepleasers, Toronto 1980, pp 4, 89, 144, 145, 146, 154.

Bibliography. New CBEL, 1.688.

2. Commentary on the *Consolation of Philosophy*

[238] BOETHIUS — COMMENTARY.

MS. Bodl 2684 (Auct.F.3.5), ff 198ᵃ–220ᵇ (ca 1450).

MS Commentary. Summary Cat, 2.494.

General Reference. Liddell M, Chaucer's Boethius Commentary, Acad 49(1896).199.

3. Works Partially Modelled on the *Consolation of Philosophy*

[239] GEORGE ASHBY'S
A PRISONER'S REFLECTIONS.

MS. Trinity Camb 599 (R.3.19), ff 41ᵃ–45ᵇ (1475–1500).

Brown-Robbins, no 437.

MS Commentary. James M R, MSS in the Libr of Trinity Coll Cambridge A Descriptive Catalogue, Cambridge 1901, 2.69.

Editions. Forster M, George Ashby's Trost in Gefangenschaft, Angl 20(1898).139.

Bateson M, George Ashby's Poems, EETSES 76, London 1899, 1.

Holthausen F, Ashby-Studien II, Angl 45(1921).77.

Authorship. DNB, 1.636 (sv Ashby, George).

General References. Ferguson A B, The Articulate Citizen and the Eng Renaissance, Durham 1965, p 107 (Ashby's political philosophy).

Pearsall D, The Eng Chaucerians, in Chaucer and Chaucerians, ed D S Brewer, Univ Alabama 1966, pp 205 (verse pattern), 237.

Holzknecht K J, Literary Patronage in the Middle Ages, N Y 1966, p 190.

Scattergood V J, Politics and Poetry in the 15 Cent, N Y 1972, p 17.

Pearsall D, Old Eng and ME Poetry, London 1977, pp 229, 239.

Baugh LHE, p 298.

Green R F, Poets and Princepleasers, Toronto 1980, p 147.

Bibliography. New CBEL, 1.648.

[240] DE LIBERO ARBITRIO.

MS. Stevens Cox J (Guernsey), ff 1ᵃ–48ᵃ (1475–1525).

Facsimile. St Anselm's Treatise on Free Will, The Booke of Seynt Anselme which treatith of Free Wylle translated in to Englysche, With an introd by G Stevens Cox, St Peter Port (Guernsey) 1977.

Source. Schmitt F S, ed, S Anselmi Opera Omnia, Seckau 1938 (rptd Edinburgh 1946), 1.205 (De libertate arbitrii).

[241] DIALOGUE ON TRUE NOBILITY.

(Note: For supplementary bibliography, see VII [43] in Manual, 3.873.)

Edition. Mitchell R J, John Tiptoft, London 1938, pp 175 (sources and quality of translation), 213 (text).

Selection. Matthews W, Later Medieval Eng Prose, N Y 1963, p 173.

Gray D, ed, The Oxford Book of Late Medieval Verse and Prose, Oxford 1985, p 271.

General References. Ten Brink, 2.322.

Mitchell R J, Italian Nobilità and the Idea of the Eng Gentleman in the 15 Cent, Eng Miscellany 9(1958).23.

Willard C, The Concept of True Nobility at the Burgundian Court, Stud in the Renaissance 14 (1967).33.

Schlauch M, The Doctrine of Vera Nobilitas as Developed after Chaucer, Kwartalnik Neofilologiczny (Warsaw) 17(1970).119.

McFarlane K B, The Nobility of Later Medieval England, Oxford 1973, pp 233, 242.

Hay D, England and the Humanities in the 15 Cent, in Itinerarium Italicum: the Profile of the Italian

Renaissance in the Mirror of Its European Transformation (dedicated to P O Kristeller), ed M A Oberman with T A Brady, Stud in Medieval and

Renaissance Thought 14(1975).330.
Trinkaus C, Adversity's Noblemen, N Y 1940.
Greaves M, The Blazon of Honour, London 1964.

III. Translations of Petrarch

[242] PETRARCH'S SECRETUM.

MS. BL Addit 60577, ff 8ª–22ª (1475–1550).
Facsimile. The Winchester Anthology (with an introd and list of contents by E Wilson and an account of the music by I Fenlon), Woodbridge 1981.

MS Commentary. Fenlon I, Instrumental Music, Songs and Verse from 16-Cent Winchester: British Libr Addit MS 60577, in Music in Medieval and Early Modern Europe, Patronage, Sources and Texts, ed I Fenlon, Cambridge 1981, p 93.
Selection. Gray D, ed, The Oxford Book of Late Medieval Verse and Prose, Oxford 1985, p 269.

3. Undistributed Works

I. The Joys of Paradise

[243] DE QUATTUORDECIM
PARTIBUS BEATUDINIS.

MS. Lichfield Cath 16 (olim 6), ff 206ª–232ª (1375–1400).
MS Commentary. A Catalogue of the Printed Books and MSS in the Libr of the Cathedral Church of Lichfield, London 1888, p 119.
Ker Manuscripts, 3.116.
Benedikz B S, Lichfield Cathedral Libr A Catalogue of the Cathedral Libr MSS, rvsd version, Birmingham 1978, p 9.
Source. Southern R W and R S Schmitt, edd, Memorials of St Anselm, Auctores Britannici Medii Aevi I, London 1969, p 127.

[244] THE DOWERS OF THE BODY
AND THE SOUL.

MSS. Prose: Dowers: 1, Magdalene Camb Pepys 1584, ff 109ᵇ–111ª (1475–1500); *Verse: Joys of Paradise*: 2, BL Harley 2383, ff 25ᵇ–29ª (1450–75).
Brown-Robbins, Robbins-Cutler, no 2063.
MSS Commentary. A Catalogue of the Harleian MSS in the British Museum, London 1808, 2.675 (MS 2).
James M R, A Descriptive Catalogue of the Libr of Samuel Pepys, Pt 3, Mediaeval MSS, London 1923, p 19 (MS 1).
Edition. Bowers R H, ME Poems by Mydwynter, MLN 64(1949).454.

II. The Pains of Hell

[245] FOUR MANERS OF HELLE.

MSS. Prose: Four Maners: 1, BL Addit 37677, ff 106ᵇ–107ª (1400–50); *Verse: Pains of Purgatory*: 2, BL Harley 2383, ff 29ª–30ª (1450–75).
Brown-Robbins, Robbins-Cutler, no 2079.
MSS Commentary. A Catalogue of the Harleian MSS in the British Museum, London 1808, 2.675 (MS 2).
Catalogue of Additions to the MSS in the British

Museum in the Years MDCCCCVI–MDCCCCX, London 1912, p 102 (MS 1).
Edition. Bowers R H, ME Poems by Mydwynter, MLN 64(1949).459.
Sources and Literary Relations. Wicki N, Die Lehr von der himmlischen Seligfreit im der mittelalterlichen Scholastik von Petrus Lombardus bis Thomas von Aquini, Freiburg 1954, pp 40, 202.
Goering J, The De Dotibus of Robert Grosseteste, MS 44(1982).83.

[246] XIV MANERIS OF HELLE.

MS. Bodl 655 (Laud misc 23), ff 53ᵇ–55ᵃ (1400–25).
MS Commentary. Coxe H O, Catalogi Codicum Manuscriptorum Bibliothecae Bodleianae, Oxford 1858, 2.65.
Edition. Lloyd D J, An Edn of the Prose and Verse in the Bodleian MS Laud Misc 23, diss Yale Univ 1943.

Sources. Silverstein T, ed, Visio Sancti Pauli. The Hist of the Apocalypse in Latin together with Nine Texts, Studies and Documents, ed K and S Lake, IV, London 1935.
Southern R W and F S Schmitt, edd, Memorials of St Anselm, Auctores Britannici Medii Aevi I, London 1969, p 57 (De Moribus).
Relihan R L Jr, A Critical Edn of the Anglo-Norman and Latin Versions of Les Peines de Purgatorie, diss Univ of Iowa 1978.

III. Prayer

[247] THE VERTUE OF HOLY PRAYERE.

MS. Camb Univ Ff.5.40, ff 21ᵇ–26ᵇ (1400–50).
Jolliffe, p 128, no M.6.
MS Commentary. A Catalogue of the MSS Preserved in the Libr of the Univ of Cambridge, Cambridge 1857, 2.498.

[248] THE XII LETTYNGIS OF PREYERE.

MSS. 1, Bodl 655 (Laud misc 23), ff 44ᵇ–46ᵇ (1400–25); 2, Trinity Camb 601 (R.3.21), ff 10ᵃ–12ᵃ (1475–1500); 3, Trinity Camb 1099 (O.1.74), ff 50ᵇ–60ᵃ (1450–1500); 4, BL Cotton Titus D.xix, ff 158ᵃ–161ᵇ (1400–50); 5, Durham Cath A.iv.22, pp 98–103 (1400–25); 6, John Rylands Manchester Eng 85, ff 19ᵃ–24ᵇ (1400–25).
Jolliffe, p 127, no M.4.

MSS Commentary. A Catalogue of the MSS in the Cottonian Libr Deposited in the British Museum, London 1802, p 565 (MS 4).
Rud T, Codicum Manuscriptorum Ecclesiae Cathedralis Dunelmensis Catalogus Classicus, ed J Raine, Durham 1825, p 72 (MS 5).
Coxe H O, Catalogi Codicum Manuscriptorum Bibliothecae Bodleianae. Pars Secunda Codices Latinos et Miscellaneos Laudianos Complectens, Oxford 1858, 1, pt 2, p 65 (MS 1).
James M R, The Western MSS in the Libr of Trinity Coll Cambridge, A Descriptive Catalogue, Cambridge 1901, 2.83 (MS 2); Cambridge 1902, 3.74 (MS 3).
Tyson M, Hand-List of the Collection of Eng MSS in the John Rylands Libr 1928, Manchester 1929, p 19 (MS 6).
Lloyd D J, An Edn of the Prose and Verse in the Bodleian MS Laud Misc 23, diss Yale Univ 1943.
Aarts F G A M, ed, The Pater Noster of Richard Ermyte, The Hague 1967, p xviii (MS 5).

IV. Fasting

[249] SEVEN FRIDAYS WHEN IT IS GOOD TO FAST.

MS. BL Lansdowne 762, f 7ᵃ (1475–1525).
MS Commentary. A Catalogue of the Lansdowne MSS in the British Museum, London 1819, p 168.

[250] A LYTEL TREATYSE TO FASTE ON THE WEDNESDAY.

MSS. No MS extant. PRINT: Wynkyn de Worde,

1500 (STC, no 24224); 1532 (STC, no 24225); rptd Fugitive Tracts Written in Verse, 1s, London 1875, no 4 (selected by W C Hazlitt with a pref by H Huth).
Robbins-Cutler, no 3496.6.
Ringler BEV, no 70.
General References. Duff E G, 15-Cent Eng Books, Oxford 1917, no 413, p 115.
Bennett H S, English Books & Readers 1475 to 1557, 2nd edn Cambridge 1969, p 268.

Index

A boldface number indicates the main reference in the Commentary; a number preceded by B indicates the reference in the Bibliography. Titles are indexed under the first word following an article. Indexed are all literary works and their authors, names of early printers, and main subdivisions. No attempt has been made to index the names of characters and places in the literary works nor the names of scholars.